Choices Writers Make

A Guide

Susan L. DeRosa
Stephen A. Ferruci
Eastern Connecticut State University

Longman

Boston   Columbus   Indianapolis   New York   San Francisco   Upper Saddle River
Amsterdam   Cape Town   Dubai   London   Madrid   Milan   Munich   Paris Montreal   Toronto
Delhi   Mexico City   Sao Paulo   Sydney   Hong Kong   Seoul Singapore   Taipei   Tokyo

Senior Acquisitions Editor: Lauren A. Finn	Cover Designer/Manager: Wendy Ann Fredericks
Senior Development Editor: Marion Castellucci	Cover Illustration/Photo: © Robynmac/
Senior Marketing Manager: Sandra McGuire	istockphoto.com
Senior Supplements Editor: Donna Campion	Photo Researcher: Rebecca Karamehmedovic
Production Coordinator: Scarlett Lindsay	Senior Manufacturing Buyer: Dennis J. Para
Project Coordination, Text Design, and Electronic Page	Printer and Binder: Edwards Brothers
Makeup: Electronic Publishing Services, Inc., NYC	Cover Printer: Lehigh-Phoenix Color – Hagerstown

For permission to use copyrighted material, grateful acknowledgment is made to the copyright holders on pp. 591, which are hereby made part of this copyright page.

"President Obama: Healthcare, you promised" by Anne Lamott, originally published in the Los Angeles Times. Copyright © 2009 by Anne Lamott, used with permission of The Wylie Agency, LLC.

"Real Food" by chimamanda Adichie, originally published in The new Yorker, Copyright © 2007 by chimamanda Adichie, used with permission of the Wylie Agency, LLC.

Photo Credits

page 33: Courtesy Save the Children
page 90: Courtesy Parasaildestin.com
page 93: Courtesy Ad Council
page 94: (both images): Jim Cole/AP
page 97: Courtesy Save the Children
page 102: Courtesy US Coast Guard
page 103: Yossi Lemel
page 104: Todd Davidson/Getty
page 105: Courtesy the Iron Horse

page 107: Courtesy Ad Council
page 260: Michael Coles
page 265: Anthony Russo
page 319: Danny Wilcox Frazier/Redux
page 322: (both images): Danny Wilcox Frazier/Redux
page 323: (both images): Danny Wilcox Frazier/Redux
page 359: Courtesy Simply Smiles
page 360: Courtesy Simply Smiles
page 479: Courtesy Matt Snyder

Library of Congress Cataloging-in-Publication Data

DeRosa, Susan L.
    Choices writers make : a guide / Susan DeRosa & Stephen Ferruci.
       p. cm.
    Includes bibliographical references and index.
    ISBN 978-0-205-61705-0
  1.   English language—Rhetoric—Problems, exercises, etc. 2.   Report writing—Problems, exercises,
etc. I.   Ferruci, Stephen A. II.   Title.
    PE1408.D462 2010
    808'.0420711—dc22

                                                                                      2010045742

Copyright © 2011 by Pearson Education, Inc.

Longman
is an imprint of

www.pearsonhighered.com

1 2 3 4 5 6 7 8 9 10—EB—13 12 11 10

ISBN-13: 978-0-205-61705-0
ISBN-10: 0-205-61705-0

Detailed Contents

Thematic Contents   xi
Preface   xv

PART ONE: READING GENRES, ANALYZING ARGUMENTS   1

CHAPTER 1: Introduction to Genre   3

What Is Genre?   3
The Social Settings of Genres   3
The Characteristics of Genres   4
The Functions of Genres   4
Audience Expectations and Genre   5
The Writer and Genre   5

Choices Writers Make: Rhetorical Situation and Genre   6
The Rhetorical Situation   7
Academic Genres   8
Civic Genres   9

Transformations: The Flexibility of Genres   10
Genre Blurring: What Is It? Why Do It?   10
An Example of Genre Blurring: The Travel Memoir   11
Sara Schneider (student), Just Another Beautiful Thunderstorm: A Travel Memoir   12
Genre Crossing: What Is It? Why Do It?   18
An Example of Genre Crossing: From Open Letter to Research Report   18
Gloria Ramos (student), Same-Sex Marriage: An Open Letter to Social Conservatives   19
Transforming the Open Letter to a Research Report   21
Gloria Ramos (student), A Report on Same-Sex Marriage in America: A Human Right, a Family Right (APA Format Paper)   22

CHAPTER 2: Critical Reading and Analysis Strategies   31

What Is Critical Reading?   31
Why Read Critically?   32

Reading a Text for What It Means   32
Previewing   32
Save the Children, Katrina Response: Protecting the Children of the Storm   33
Annotating   34
Terry Starkey Williston, A View to the Contrary   35
Outlining   36
Summary   37
Response   38
Ray French, Taking Back Our Tuition: Students Need to Push to Keep College Affordable   40

Reading a Text for How It Works   41
Jay Weiner, Sports Centered   42
Analyzing the Contexts of a Text   45
Analyzing Parts of a Text   48
Mary Frances Berry, Gay but Equal?   53

Providing Comments for Revision: Practicing Peer Review   55
Why Writers and Readers Benefit from Peer Review   55
Providing Comments to Help Writers Revise: Specific v. Vague   56

CHAPTER 3: Analyzing and Writing Arguments   61

Arguments and Persuasion: It's Not About Fighting   61

Argument and Rhetoric   62
  Creating Convincing Arguments   62

Analyzing Arguments   63

Speech Analysis Example   63
  *Barack Obama, Speech Against
    the Iraq War*   63
  WebLinks: The World of Rhetoric   66

The Structure of Argument: Claims,
Evidence, and Assumptions   67
  Claims: Claims of Fact, Value, and Policy   67
  Kinds of Evidence   72
  Assumptions   74

The Hard and Soft Sell of Argument:
Rhetorical Appeals and Language
Choices   77
  Ethos, Logos, and Pathos: The Rhetorical
    Appeals   77
  "Humorous" Rhetorical Devices   81
  *Anne Lamott, Sign me up for Barack Obama's
    Death Panel!*   81
  *The Onion Staff, Homeless People
    Shouldn't Make You Feel Sad Like That*   83

Words that Resound: Lexicon, Ultimate
Terms, and Repetition   84

Rhetorical Analysis   85

Writing Assignment: Rhetorical Analysis
and Evaluation of an Argument   85
  *Joseph Kellard, An Open Letter to
    Dan Marino*   86

CHAPTER 4: Analyzing Visual
Rhetoric   89

Reading Visual Arguments Critically   89
  *Rhetorical Analysis: "Just Chute Me"
    Advertising Brochure*   89

Writing Assignment: Rhetorical
Analysis of a Visual Message   91

Elements of Visual Rhetoric   91
  What Readers Consider When They
    Analyze Visual Messages   91
  Texts and Images in Visual Messages   92
  *US Department of Agriculture,
    School Supplies*   93
  Considering the Context for the Image   95
  Images and Graphics that Support Text   96
  The Rhetorical Appeals in Visual Arguments   101
  U.S. Coast Guard, Fishing Tips from Bill Dance   102
  Yossi Lemel, Blood Bath, 2002   103
  Claims and Evidence in Visual Arguments   104
  Todd Davidson, Man Controlling Globe   104
  Iron Horse Hotel Advertisements   105
  WebLinks: Exploring Visual Messages   106
  Visual Design: Fonts, Color, and Arrangement   106
  *U.S. Department of Justice, Think
    Before You Post*   107

Theory into Practice: Constructing
Your Own Visual Messages   109
  What Writers Consider When Constructing
    Visual Messages   109

Writing Assignment Options: Visual
Messages   109

PART TWO: EXPLORING GENRES   111

CHAPTER 5: Public Letters   113

What Is a Public Letter?   113
  The Purpose of Public Letters   114

Reading Public Letters Critically   114
  Genre Analysis: *Walidah Imarisha and
    Not4Prophet, Dearest Hip Hop
    (open letter)*   115
  *Michael Stinebrink and Tommy
    Balestracci (student), An Exchange
    of Letters on College Football
    Championships*   119
  *Anne Lamott, President Obama:
    Healthcare; You Promised*   122
  Christian De Graff, Science in Defense   124

Writing Assignment Options:
Public Letters   126

Writing Public Letters   127
What Writers Consider When They
Write Public Letters   127
Generating Ideas for Public Letters   127
Thinking about Audience, Purpose,
and Situation   130
Researching Public Letters   130
Drafting Public Letters   132
Revising Public Letters   136
Peer Review Guidelines: Public Letters   137
Reflecting on the Process   138

ONE WRITER'S JOURNEY: Katie Hicks's
Open Letter   139
Generating Ideas for the Open Letter   139
Thinking about Audience, Purpose,
and Situation   139
Drafting the Open Letter   140
Revising the Open Letter: Peer Review   142
*Katie Hicks (student), "Dear Uninvolved
    Parents" (final draft)*   144
Reflecting on the Process   148

TRANSFORMATIONS: Genre Crossing:
From Public Letter to Research Report   149

Genre Crossing Writing Assignment:
From Public Letter to
Research Report   149
*Katie Hicks (student), After School
    Programs: Benefits for Adolescents,
    Benefits for Communities*   150

CHAPTER 6: Reviews   159
What Is a Review?   159
The Purpose of Reviews   159

Reading Reviews Critically   161
Genre Analysis: *Peter Meehan, Will
    Pigs' Feet Fly?*   161

*Timothy Rutten, Review of 'The Anatomist:
    A True Story of Gray's Anatomy.*   164
*John Phillips, 2008 Maserati GranTurismo -
    Road Test*   167
*Peter Kvetko, Noora: A Golden Voice; Wah
    Rangiya: Passionate Punjab; Bol Ni
    Chakkiye: The Singing Wheel of Life*   170
Writing Assignment Options:
Reviews   174

Writing Reviews   175
What Writers Consider When They
Write Reviews   175
Generating Ideas for Reviews   176
WebLinks: The World of Film Reviews   176
Thinking about Audience, Purpose, and
Situation   176
Researching Reviews   177
Drafting Reviews   179
Revising Reviews   183
Peer Review Guidelines: Reviews   185
Reflecting on the Process   186

ONE WRITER'S JOURNEY: Patrick
Merrigan's Film Review   187
Thinking about Audience, Purpose, and
Situation: Developing Criteria   187
Drafting: Integrating Background Research   187
Drafting: Using Evaluative Language
and Tone   188
Revising: Balancing Detail with Audience
Needs   190
*Patrick Merrigan (student), Superbad:
    Super Movie or Just Bad? (final draft)*   194
Reflecting on the Process   197

TRANSFORMATIONS: Genre Blurring:
Rhetorical Analysis of a Documentary   198

Genre Blurring Writing Assignment:
Rhetorical Analysis of a Documentary   198
*Kim Thomassen Strand (student), There
    Is Nothing Called Hope in My Future:
    A Rhetorical Analysis of Born Into
    Brothels*   199

CHAPTER 7: Essays   **205**

What Is an Essay?   **205**
The Purposes of Essays   206

Reading Essays Critically   **206**
Genre Analysis: *Jo Ann Beard, Out There*   207
Jim Kuerschner (student), Big Brother Is on the Facebook   212
Jennifer Moses, Stepping Out   221
James A. Banks, Remembering Brown: Silence, Loss, Rage, and Hope   227

Writing Assignment Options: Essays   **235**

Writing Essays   **235**
What Writers Consider When They Write Essays   236
Generating Ideas for Essays   236
Thinking about Audience, Purpose, and Situation   237
Researching Essays   238
Incorporating Research   240
Drafting Essays   240
Organizing Essays   243
Revising Essays   245
Peer Review Guidelines: Essays   246
Reflecting on the Process   247

ONE WRITER'S JOURNEY: Colin Keane's Personal Essay   **248**
Generating Ideas for the Personal Essay: Starting with What You Know   248
Thinking about Audience, Purpose, and Situation   249
Drafting: Researching Experiences and Connecting to the Larger Issue   249
Revising: Focusing on the Subject, Emphasizing Commentary   252
Colin Keane (student): Big Change in a Small Town: A Personal Essay (Final Draft)   254
Reflecting on the Process   257

TRANSFORMATIONS: Genre Blurring: The Photographic Essay   **258**
WebLinks: Photo Essays on the Web   258

Genre Blurring Writing Assignment: The Photographic Essay   **258**
Michael Coles: Smash Palace – Model Four Hundred   259

CHAPTER 8: Memoirs   **263**

What Is a Memoir?   **263**
The Purposes of Memoirs   264

Reading Memoirs Critically   **264**
Genre Analysis: *Chimamanda Ngozi Adichie, Real Food*   265
Adam King (student), These Stories   267
David Sedaris, Let It Snow   276
Chitrita Banerji, A Shared Plate   278
WebLinks: Creative Nonfiction and Fourth Genre: Explorations in Nonfiction   282

Writing Assignment Options: Memoirs   **283**

Writing Memoirs   **283**
What Writers Consider When They Write Memoirs   283
Generating Ideas for Memoirs   284
Thinking About Audience, Purpose, and Situation   286
Researching Memoirs   286
Drafting Memoirs   287
Developing Sensory Descriptions and Concrete Details   287
Organizing Memoirs   288
Revising Memoirs   290
Peer Review Guidelines: Memoirs   292
Reflecting on the Process   293

ONE WRITER'S JOURNEY: Eliza Poulos's Memoir   **294**
Generating Ideas for the Memoir: Recalling Past Experiences   294
Thinking about Audience, Purpose, and Situation   294
Drafting the Memoir: Choosing Details and Specifics   295
Revising: Developing Reflection in the Memoir   297
Eliza Poulos (student), Lucky? (final draft)   299
Reflecting on the Process   303

TRANSFORMATIONS: Genre Blurring:
The Travel Memoir   305

Genre Blurring Writing Assignment:
The Travel Memoir   305
  Ted Conover, On The Trail of Poppa's
  Alaska   305

CHAPTER 9: Profiles   313
What Is a Profile?   313
  The Purposes of Profiles   314

Reading Profiles Critically   314
  Genre Analysis: *Larry Rohter, Part of*
  the Carnival Show: The Man Behind
  the Masks   315
  Charlie LeDuff, End of the Line   318
  Elaine Miller, Being Rosie the Riveter   324
  Marie O. Parker, Bingo!   326

Writing Assignment Options:
Profiles   329

Writing Profiles   330
  What Writers Consider When They
  Write Profiles   330
  WebLinks: The Genre of Profiles   330
  Generating Ideas for Profiles   330
  Thinking about Audience, Purpose, and
  Situation   331
  Researching Profiles   332
  Drafting Profiles   334
  Revising Profiles   338
  Visual Rhetoric and Profiles   340
  Peer Review Guidelines: Profiles   341
  Reflecting on the Process   341

ONE WRITER'S JOURNEY: Brynna
Williams's Profile   343
  Generating Ideas for the Profile   343
  Thinking about Audience, Purpose, and
  Situation   343
  Drafting: Gathering Research, Organizing
  Ideas, and Discovering the Angle   344
  Revising: Framing the Angle, Emphasizing the
  Writer's Perspective   346

Brynna Williams (student), Simply Smiles
  (final draft)   349
  Reflecting on the Process   356

TRANSFORMATIONS: Genre Crossing:
From Profile to Brochure   357

Genre Crossing Writing Assignment:
From Profile to Brochure   357
  Brynna Williams (student), Simply Smiles:
  Transforming Lives of Impoverished
  Peoples (brochure)   358

CHAPTER 10: Research Reports   363
What Is a Research Report?   363
  The Purposes of Research Reports   364

Reading Research Reports Critically   364
  Genre Analysis: *RI-PIRG, Rhode Island's*
  Food Safety Net : Ensuring Safe Food from
  Production to Consumption   365
  Rich Morin, Black-White Conflict Isn't
  Society's Largest: The Public Assesses
  Social Divisions   371
  Steven Clark, M.D., Alicia Mangram,
  M.D., Ernest Dunn, M.D, Car Surfing:
  Case Studies of a Growing Dangerous
  Phenomenon   379
  Colonel Elspeth Cameron Ritchie,
  MC USA, and Robert Andrew Cardona,
  MD, U.S. Military Enlisted Accession
  Mental Health Screening: History and
  Current Practice   383
  WebLinks: Exploring the World of
  Research Reports   394

Writing Assignment Options:
Research Reports   394

Writing Research Reports   395
  What Writers Consider When They Write
  Research Reports   395
  Generating Ideas for Research Reports   395
  Thinking about Audience, Purpose, and
  Situation   398

Researching Research Reports   399
Drafting Research Reports   400
Colin Keane, The Aftermath of September 11
(executive summary)   403
Revising Research Reports   405

**ONE WRITER'S JOURNEY: Patrick Merrigan's
Research Report   410**
Generating Ideas for the Research Report 410
Thinking about Audience, Purpose, and
Situation: Writing a Research Proposal   411
Researching the Research Report: Writing
the Annotated Bibliography   412
Drafting: Writing the Introductory Material 413
Revising the Research Report: Working
with Sources   414
Patrick Merrigan (student), Civic
Duties and Young Adults
(MLA Format Paper)   415
Reflecting on the Process   421

**TRANSFORMATIONS: Genre
Crossing: From Report to Proposal   423**

**Genre Crossing Writing Assignment:
From Report to Proposal   423**
Patrick Merrigan, Civic Duties:
Fixing the Problem of Civic Engagement
in Two Easy Steps   424

CHAPTER 11: Proposals   431

What Is a Proposal?   431
The Purposes of Proposals   432
The Rhetorical Situation of Proposals   433

Reading Proposals Critically   433
Genre Analysis: *Women's Committee of*
100, An Immodest Proposal: Rewarding
Women's Work to End Poverty   434
Brian Halweil, A Community Farm
for Stanford   438
James Jay Carafano, Ph.D., Fighting
Terrorism, Addressing Liability:
A Global Proposal   442

Patricia J. Sulak, MD, Adolescent
Sexual Health   449

Writing Assignment Options: Proposals 453

Writing Proposals   453
What Writers Consider When Writing
Proposals   454
Generating Ideas for Proposals   454
Thinking about Audience, Purpose,
and Situation   456
Researching Proposals   459
Drafting Proposals   460
Revising Proposals   465
Peer Review Guidelines: Proposals   466
Reflecting on the Process   467

**ONE WRITER'S JOURNEY: Christina
Schirone's Proposal   468**
Generating Claims for the Proposal   468
Drafting: Developing Differing Views   469
Revising: Addressing the Audience's
Concerns   470
Christina Schirone (student), Union
University Needs Our Help
(final draft)   471
Reflecting on the Process   476

**TRANSFORMATIONS: Genre Crossing:
From Proposal to Public Service
Announcement   478**

**Genre Crossing Writing Assignment:
From Proposal to Public Service
Announcement   478**
Christina Schirone (student), Make
a Difference   478

CHAPTER 12: Portfolios   481

What Is a Writing Portfolio?   481
The Purposes of a Writing Portfolio   481
The Rhetorical Situation of a Writing
Portfolio   482

Constructing Writing Portfolios   483

What Writers Consider When Preparing
Portfolios   483
Writing a Reflective Letter   483
*Christina Schirone (student), Reflective
    Portfolio Letter*   484

Writing Assignment Option: Reflective Portfolio Letter   487

Writing an Introductory Paragraph for
Each Item   487
*Lisa Warford (student), Introductory
    Paragraph for a Portfolio Selection*   488
Preparing a Case Study   488
*Lisa Warford (student), Portfolio Case
    Study with Revisions*   490
*Christina Schirone (student), Portfolio
    Case Study with Peer Review*   492
Arranging a Writing Portfolio   493
*Jenna Clark (student), Arrangement of
    Portfolio Items*   494
*Christina Schirone (student), Portfolio
    Table of Contents*   495

Preparing an Electronic Portfolio   496
WebLinks: E-portfolios   497

PART THREE: RESEARCH METHODS AND SOURCES   499

CHAPTER 13: Research and the Rhetorical Situation   501

Why Writers Do Research   501
Research and the Rhetorical Situation   501
Making Research Meaningful   503

Thinking about Research   504
Assessing the Topic   504
Considering Your Purpose, Audience,
and Genre   505
Asking Questions   509
Developing Key Word Search Terms   510
Creating a Research Plan   511

Gathering Information: Where to Go and Why   513

Types of Sources Primary and
Secondary Sources   513
WebLinks: The Internet Archive   515
Searching Library Catalogs   516
Searching Databases   518
Searching the Archives   520
Researching on the World Wide Web   521
Conducting Field Research   523
WebLinks: Designing and Using Surveys
and Questionnaires   532

Evaluating Sources   533
Evaluating Print Sources   534
Evaluating Web Sources   536
WebLinks: Duke University Research Guide   538

Writing an Annotated Bibliography   538

Writing Assignment: Creating an Annotated Bibliography   539

CHAPTER 14: Using and Citing Sources   541

Using Sources   541
Using Research for Rhetorical Effects   541
Why Writers Use Sources   542
Genre and Using Sources   543

Using Quotations, Paraphrases, and Summaries   544
Direct Quotation   544
Paraphrase   547
Summary   548

Integrating and Introducing Sources   550
Integrating Sources   550
Introducing Sources   552

Synthesizing Your Research   555
Constructing a Research Chart and
Synthesis   557

Avoiding Plagiarism   561
Procrastination and Intentional Plagiarism   563
WebLinks: Avoiding Plagiarism   564

Documenting Sources   **565**
  Making Note of Bibliographic Information   565
  MLA and APA Documentation Formats   568
  MLA In-Text Citations   570
  WebLinks: MLA and APA Citation Guides   573
  MLA Works Cited Entries   574

  APA In-Text Citations   580
  APA References Entries   584
  MLA and APA Sample Papers   589

Credits   **591**
Index   **594**

Thematic Contents

Choices Writers Make: A Guide provides a broad and thoughtful selection of 60 texts, many of them written by students. Each thematic cluster contains a variety of genres, enabling students to see how writers and artists communicate similar ideas differently depending on the genre.

Ethics and Values

Gloria Ramos (student), Same-Sex Marriage: An Open Letter to Social Conservatives 19

Gloria Ramos (student), A Report on Same-Sex Marriage in America: A Human Right, a Family Right 22

Jay Weiner, Sports Centered (editorial) 42

Mary Frances Berry, Gay But Equal? (opinion piece) 53

Anne Lamott, Sign Me Up for Barack Obama's Death Panel (excerpt) (open letter) 81

Onion Staff, Homeless People Shouldn't Make You Feel Sad Like That (commentary) 83

Blood Bath 2002 (poster) 103

Think Before You Post (public service announcement) 107

Katie Hicks (student), Dear Uninvolved Parents (open letter) 144

Colin Keane (student), Big Change in a Small Town: A Personal Essay 254

Brynna Williams (student), Simply Smiles (profile) 349

Brynna Williams (student), Simply Smiles: Transforming Lives of Impoverished Peoples (brochure) 358

Patrick Merrigan (student), Civic Duties and Young Adults (research report) 415

Patrick Merrigan (student), Civic Duties: Fixing the Problem of Civic Engagement in Two Easy Steps (proposal) 424

Women's Committee of 100, An Immodest Proposal: Rewarding Women's Work to End Poverty (proposal) 434

Patricia J. Sulak, M.D., Adolescent Sexual Health (proposal) 449

Christina Schirone (student), Union University Needs Our Help (proposal) 471

Christina Schirone (student), Make a Difference (public service announcement) 478

Family

Gloria Ramos (student), Same-Sex Marriage: An Open Letter to Social Conservatives (open letter) 19

Gloria Ramos (student), A Report on Same-Sex Marriage in America: A Human Right, a Family Right (research report) 22

Katie Hicks (student), Dear Uninvolved Parents (open letter) 144

Katie Hicks (student), After-School Programs: Benefits for Adolescents, Benefits for Communities (research report) 150

Women's Committee of 100, An Immodest Proposal: Rewarding Women's Work to End Poverty (proposal) 434

Identity

Walidah Imarisha and Not4Prophet, Dearest Hip Hop (open letter) 115

Chimamanda Ngozi Adichie, Real Food (memoir) 265

Chitrita Banerji, A Shared Plate (memoir) 278

Larry Rohter, Part of the Carnival Show: The Man Behind the Masks (profile) 315

Elaine Miller, Being Rosie the Riveter (profile) 324

Adam King (student), These Stories (memoir) 267

Marie O. Parker, Bingo! (profile) 326

Gender and Sexuality

Gloria Ramos (student), Same-Sex Marriage: An Open Letter to Social Conservatives (open letter) 19

Gloria Ramos (student), A Report on Same-Sex Marriage in America: A Human Right, a Family Right (research report) 22

Mary Frances Berry, Gay But Equal? (opinion piece) 53

The Iron Horse Hotels (advertisement) 105

Kim Thomassen Strand (student), There Is Nothing Called Hope in My Future: A Rhetorical Analysis of Born Into Brothels 199

Elaine Miller, Being Rosie the Riveter (profile) 324

Women's Committee of 100, An Immodest Proposal: Rewarding Women's Work to End Poverty (proposal) 434

Patricia J. Sulak, M.D., Adolescent Sexual Health (proposal) 449

Race and Ethnicity

Chimamanda Ngozi Adichie, Real Food (memoir) 265

Chitrita Banerji, A Shared Plate (memoir) 278

Rich Morin, Black-White Conflict Isn't Society's Largest: The Public Assesses Social Divisions (research report) 371

Women's Committee of 100, An Immodest Proposal: Rewarding Women's Work to End Poverty (proposal) 434

Youth and Popular Culture

AdCouncil, Think Before You Post (public service announcement) 107

Walidah Imarisha and Not4Prophet, Dearest Hip Hop (open letter) 115

Michael Stinebrink and Tommy Balestracci (student), An Exchange of Letters on College Football Championships (letters to the editor) 119

Katie Hicks (student), After-School Programs: Benefits for Adolescents, Benefits for Communities 150

Patrick Merrigan (student), Superbad: Super Movie or Just Bad? (review) 194

Jim Kuerschner (student), Big Brother Is on the Facebook (essay) 212

Eliza Poulos (student), Lucky? (memoir) 299

Brynna Williams (student), Simply Smiles (profile) 349

Steven Clark, M.D., Alicia Mangram, M.D., Ernest Dunn, M.D., Car Surfing: Case Studies of a Growing Dangerous Phenomenon (research report) 379

Patrick Merrigan (student), Civic Duties and Young Adults (research report) 415

Patrick Merrigan, Civic Duties: Fixing the Problem of Civic Engagement in Two Easy Steps (proposal) 424

Patricia J. Sulak, M.D., Adolescent Sexual Health (proposal) 449

Christina Schirone (student), Union University Needs Our Help (proposal) 471

Christina Schirone (student), Make a Difference (public service announcement) 478

Music and the Arts

Walidah Imarisha and Not4Prophet, Dearest Hip Hop (open letter) 115

Timothy Rutten, Review of "The Anatomist: A True Story of Gray's Anatomy" (review) 164

Peter Kvetko, Noora: A Golden Voice; Wah Rangiya: Passionate Punjab; Bol Ni Chakkiye: The Singing Wheel of Life (review) 170

Patrick Merrigan (student), Superbad: Super Movie or Just Bad? (review) 194

Kim Thomassen Strand (student), There Is Nothing Called Hope in My Future: A Rhetorical Analysis of Born Into Brothels 199

Jennifer Moses, Stepping Out (essay) 221

Larry Rohter, Part of the Carnival Show: The Man Behind the Masks (profile) 315

Sports

Jay Weiner, Sports Centered (editorial) 42

Joseph Kellard, An Open Letter to Dan Marino (open letter) 86

Fishing Tips from Bill Dance (public service announcement) 102

Steven Clark, M.D., Alicia Mangram, M.D., Ernest Dunn, M.D., Car Surfing: Case Studies of a Growing Dangerous Phenomenon (research report) 379

Michael Stinebrink and Tommy Balestracci (student), An Exchange of Letters on College Football Championships 119

Food and Culture

U.S. Department of Agriculture, School Supplies (public service announcement) 93

Peter Meehan, Will Pigs' Feet Fly? (review) 161

Jennifer Moses, Stepping Out (essay) 221

Chimamanda Ngozi Adichie, Real Food (memoir) 265

Chitrita Banerji, A Shared Plate (memoir) 278

RIPIRG Education Fund, Rhode Island's Food Safety Net: Ensuring Safe Food from Production to Consumption (research report) 365

Brian Halweil, A Community Farm for Stanford (proposal) 438

Medical and Health Issues

Anne Lamott, President Obama: Healthcare; You Promised (letter to the editor) 122

Timothy Rutten, Review of "The Anatomist: A True Story of Gray's Anatomy" 164

Steven Clark, M.D., Alicia Mangram, M.D., Ernest Dunn, M.D., Car Surfing: Case Studies of a Growing Dangerous Phenomenon (research report) 379

Colonel Elspeth Cameron Ritchie, MC USA, and Robert Andrew Cardona, M.D., U.S. Military Enlisted Accession Mental Health Screening: History and Current Practice (research report) 383

Patricia J. Sulak, M.D., Adolescent Sexual Health (proposal) 449

Place and the Environment

Sara Schneider (student), Just Another Beautiful Thunderstorm: A Travel Memoir 12

Terry Starkey Williston, A View to the Contrary (letter to the editor) 35

Parasail Destin, Just Chute Me (advertising brochure) 89

Jennifer Moses, Stepping Out (essay) 221

Colin Keane (student): Big Change in a Small Town: A Personal Essay 254

Ted Conover, On the Trail of Poppa's Alaska (memoir) 305

Charlie LeDuff, End of the Line (profile) 318

Brian Halweil, A Community Farm for Stanford (proposal) 438

Science and Technology

Terry Starkey Williston, A View to the Contrary (letter to the editor) 35

AdCouncil, Think Before You Post (public service announcement) 107

Christian De Graff, Science in Defense (letter to the editor) 124

John Phillips, 2008 Maserati GranTurismo—Road Test (review) 167

Jim Kuerschner (student), Big Brother Is on the Facebook (essay) 212

Michael Coles, Smash Palace—Model Four Hundred (essay) 259

RIPIRG Education Fund, Rhode Island's Food Safety Net: Ensuring Safe Food from Production to Consumption (research report) 365

Colonel Elspeth Cameron Ritchie, MC USA, and Robert Andrew Cardona, M.D., U.S. Military Enlisted Accession Mental Health Screening: History and Current Practice (research report) 383

Patricia J. Sulak, M.D., Adolescent Sexual Health (proposal) 449

War and Military

Barack Obama, Speech Against the Iraq War (speech) 63

Yossi Lemel, Blood Bath 2002 (poster) 103

Christian De Graff, Science in Defense (letter to the editor) 124

Adam King (student), These Stories (memoir) 267

Colonel Elspeth Cameron Ritchie, MC USA, and Robert Andrew Cardona, M.D., U.S. Military Enlisted Accession Mental Health Screening: History and Current Practice (research report) 383

James Jay Carafano, Ph.D., Fighting Terrorism, Addressing Liability: A Global Proposal (proposal) 442

Work

Larry Rohter, Part of the Carnival Show: The Man Behind the Masks (profile) 315

Charlie LeDuff, End of the Line (profile) 318

Women's Committee of 100, An Immodest Proposal: Rewarding Women's Work to End Poverty (proposal) 434

Brian Halweil, A Community Farm for Stanford (proposal) 438

Global Issues

Terry Starkey Williston, A View to the Contrary (letter to the editor) 35

Barack Obama, Speech Against the Iraq War (speech) 63

Yossi Lemel, Blood Bath 2002 (poster) 103

Adam King (student), These Stories (memoir) 267

Brynna Williams (student), Simply Smiles (profile) 349

Brynna Williams (student), Simply Smiles: Transforming Lives of Impoverished Peoples (brochure) 358

James Jay Carafano, Ph.D., Fighting Terrorism, Addressing Liability: A Global Proposal (proposal) 442

Humor

Anne Lamott, Sign Me Up for Barack Obama's Death Panel (excerpt) (open letter) 81

Onion Staff, Homeless People Shouldn't Make You Feel Sad Like That (commentary) 83

Anne Lamott, President Obama: Healthcare; You Promised (letter to the editor) 122

Patrick Merrigan (student), Superbad: Super Movie or Just Bad? (review) 194

David Sedaris, Let It Snow (memoir) 276

Preface

Choices Writers Make: A Guide evolved from two concerns we had about teaching a genre approach to writing: theoretically, the need to understand genre as dynamic and flexible; and pedagogically, the disconnection between the sample texts from which we taught and the ones which students produced. We saw the need for a textbook that illustrates the *whys* and *hows* of writing: why writers make particular rhetorical choices and then how they enact those choices in their writing.

All writers negotiate complex rhetorical situations by making careful choices about what to say, to whom to say it, how to say it, and how to present themselves. *Choices Writers Make* allows writers to see that these choices are dynamic, *how* they can alter and shape their writing to address a particular rhetorical situation, and most importantly, *why* they might want to.

Writing often blurs the boundaries among genres to meet the specific expectations of rhetorical contexts. (For instance, travel writing often blends the genres of memoir, essay, and reportage.) Writers often repurpose writing and research from one genre into another to meet a different audience's needs and new writing purposes. *Choices Writers Make* foregrounds flexibility and responsiveness, helping students explore a variety of genres, transform ideas and information from one genre to another, and practice blurring the boundaries among genres to create rhetorically effective writing.

Students are also encouraged to see that there are many ways to complete a piece of writing. Because writing processes vary by rhetorical situation and by writer, each chapter emphasizes and reinforces that writing involves *processes,* and *not a single process.* Much of the sample writing presented in *Choices* is student written. From prewriting notes to final drafts, writing samples show students how other student writers work through, question, and address the challenges they face in a given writing situation. These writing samples demystify some of the ways in which writers negotiate their ideas and offer students an opportunity to consider other possible choices the writer did not make—but could have—and why.

The Features of *Choices Writers Make*

Because *Choices Writers Make* came out of our own teaching and conversations we had with other instructors from different writing programs, our goal was to make this text easy and flexible to use and as reflective as possible of how writers actually work. The following key features support this goal:

A Variety of Academic and Civic Genres. Part Two includes examples of academic genres (such as academic essays or reports) and civic genres (such as letters to the editor or reviews). In addition to the eight featured genres in Part Two, each chapter offers variations to illustrate the dynamic nature of genres and the choices writers make dependent on their particular rhetorical situations. For example, in Chapter 5, students can read open letters, and letters to the editor.

Transformations. *Choices Writers Make* presents a practical and realistic way of working with genres that reinforces how writers work: writers often "recycle" ideas and research for different purposes and audiences, and they often blur the features of the genres in subtle ways to create a "hybrid" genre that addresses their particular writing situation. In the **Transformations** feature in each chapter in Part Two, students experience firsthand how genres are dynamic and rhetorically shaped.

In **Transformations: Genre Crossing,** students work on a single issue or subject but repurpose their ideas and research into a different genre and for a different audience and purpose. For example, a research report about the impact of over-fishing on the local economy can be transformed into a proposal offering solutions to fishery problems, and possibly reworked again as a letter to the editor of a regional newspaper on the same issue. Genre crossing illustrates how ideas, arguments, and research can be reworked to serve a new rhetorical situation and use a new genre to do so.

In **Transformations: Genre Blurring,** writers blur the boundaries of genres in ways that closely mirror the often messy writing done in civic life. For example, a travel memoir, a genre that combines some of the features of travel reportage and memoir, may include historical, geographic, and field research about a particular place as well as the personal, subjective perspective or commentary of the writer's experience of that place. Thus genre blurring illustrates how two (or more, sometimes) genres may work together to create a new genre that meets and expands the expectations of readers and the rhetorical situation at hand.

One Writer's Journey. Each chapter in Part Two showcases the work of a student writer in *One Writer's Journey* in order to demystify the process of working with genres that first-year writers may have no experience with. This feature provides examples of the choices these writers have made as they generate and develop ideas, consider the audience and purpose for a writing situation, make revisions and work with peer review comments, use sources, and reflect on their choices along the way to final drafts. Seeing concrete examples of the choices student writers *can* make and understanding the ones they ultimately *do* make is critical to helping writers learn how writing is a dynamic activity.

A Genre and Rhetorical Approach. Each chapter in Part Two investigates a genre of writing by guiding students through their writing processes. Students don't need to flip around to other parts of the book as they complete their assignment because relevant instruction and student-written examples of thinking rhetorically, prewriting, drafting, developing and organizing, revising, and reflecting are covered in each genre chapter. This approach emphasizes the writers' processes as they work through genres—stops and starts, negotiations, and reasoning—rather than the final polished piece a writer may produce. Students benefit from the concrete examples of another *writer's movements through a genre* (rather than simply having that process described to them), as they witness the rhetorical choices writers make.

Research as Rhetorically Influenced. While chapters in Part Three cover fundamental research writing skills of locating and evaluating source material, integrating that source material into original writing through paraphrase, summary, and quotation, and avoiding plagiarism by using accurate and appropriate citation, each chapter in Part Two includes a section on research that encourages students to think rhetorically about their audience and context and identify the kinds of research that makes sense for different genres. For example, Chapter 9 on Profiles offers suggestions for interviews and observation techniques.

Genre Analysis. *Choices Writers Make* emphasizes that understanding how genres work can assist writers in the development and refinement of their ideas. Writers, beginning or otherwise, sometimes approach a new writing situation with some trepidation: How do I begin? What kinds of things can I or can't I say? In such situations, understanding the *characteristics* of a genre can be of enormous help. Thus *Choices Writers Make* provides students with the tools for analyzing genres and then using what they find to help them in the development of their own writing. In Chapter 1, students are introduced to both academic and civic genres; in Chapters 2 – 4, they are shown how to analyze them from a variety of perspectives in order to understand both how genres work to persuade audiences and how students can work with genres as they consider different rhetorical strategies. Then, at the start of each genre chapter in Part Two, students are invited to further analyze the genres they will be writing in, and to develop a list of characteristics that they can then use to guide them through the writing processes.

Writing Assignments. *Choices Writers Make* provides multiple major Writing Assignments in each chapter in Part Two. With multiple-assignment options per chapter, *Choices* often provides assignments for both academic and civic uses of a genre as well as informative, analytic, and persuasive purposes. (For example, assignments in Chapter 6 include an evaluative restaurant or performance review, a critical academic article review, an academic literature review, and an analytic review, among others.) One assignment option is always a Community-based Writing Assignment in order to facilitate service-learning approaches. The primary writing assignment for each genre chapter is illustrated in a student sample, *One Writer's Journey*. Finally, the feature Transformations offers instructors an additional Writing Assignment Option that is either a genre crossing or a genre blurring assignment, which may ask students to cross-reference another chapter to create a new, hybrid genre or transform material from one genre they have written to a new genre entirely.

Writing Activities. Each chapter also offers several individual and group Writing Activities for different stages of the writing process in which students analyze genres, revise parts of drafts, conduct peer review, or discuss rhetorical choices writers make and their impacts on audience. Instructors can choose from an array of low-stakes exercises to use as is or adapt as needed, and students gain additional practice as they work on their full-length project.

Post-Reading Questions for Comprehension and Analysis. In Part One, *Choices Writers Make* provides students with the tools to read a variety texts, academic and civic, print and visual, in order to understand the text (what it is about) and to analyze the text rhetorically (how it works). This work is reinforced in each genre chapter where students are provided with post-reading questions for all the readings. The first set of questions, called Reading for Comprehension, asks students to articulate their understanding of a reading by considering a part of the text (e.g., opening); the second set of questions, called Analyzing the Genre, asks students to analyze the text rhetorically by asking students to examine features like the audience of and purpose for the text.

What Writers Consider. Each writing process section in Part Two begins with a brief list of the general features or characteristics of a particular genre that writers should consider as they draft. This list serves as a quick orientation for students, and the features listed are the same ones that the chapter covers in detail.

Guidelines. *Choices Writers Make* provides students with specific guidelines for writing activities and approaches they may need to consider as they write; some of these activities are genre specific, thus emphasizing the need for writers to make choices as they write in a variety of situations. The guidelines serve as another useful orientation device for students, and at the same time allow for flexibility in their approach to writing.

How This Book Is Organized

Choices Writers Make is organized to provide coherence and flexibility. Part One introduces fundamental rhetorical ideas and strategies about genre, critical reading, argument, and visuals so that students can work with genres in creative and persuasive ways. Part Two features eight genres chosen to reflect the kinds of writing students will be asked to do in and out of the classroom. For example, instructors emphasizing academic writing can choose to teach the research report or essay while teachers emphasizing civic genres and writing for social change might teach the proposal or public letters. Part Three guides students through research processes and the skills of integrating that research into their writing.

Chapter 1: Introduction to Genre introduces students to the fundamental idea that genres are generative and dynamic. Students explore genres they are already familiar with (such as email messages or action films) and consider how genre and the larger rhetorical situation affect one another. Through an exploration of how one student transformed, or reworked, a piece of writing from one genre into another, students will come to understand how different genres serve different purposes. Both *genre crossing* and *genre blurring* are discussed, and the chapter concludes with student-written examples of each.

Chapter 2: Critical Reading and Analysis Strategies prepares students to read genres critically and analytically. The first part of the chapter develops students' abilities to read for meaning with sample texts and guided exercises; students learn how to preview, annotate, and outline, among other reading strategies, in order to hone their comprehension skills. In the second part of the chapter, students develop an understanding of *how* a text actually *works*. Students examine texts in terms of the larger rhetorical situation and the genre. Both approaches are reinforced in the chapter's concluding discussion of and instruction in effective peer review.

Chapter 3: Analyzing and Writing Arguments focuses on written and spoken arguments and prepares students to analyze rhetorical texts and make use of argumentative strategies in their own writing. Students gain practice analyzing and developing claims, evidence, and assumptions; they develop an understanding of the rhetorical appeals and the ways in which rhetors make choices about language in order to develop, support, and defend their arguments. This chapter concludes with an assignment that asks students to write a rhetorical analysis and evaluation of an argument.

Chapter 4: Analyzing Visual Rhetoric teaches writers to apply the skills developed in Chapter 3 to visual arguments and design. Chapter 4 helps students read visual elements critically and rhetorically, focusing both on visual messages (such as the public service announcement) and on genres that make use of images, graphics, or the visual elements of design (such as might be used in a research report). There are two major assignments in Chapter 4: One asks students to conduct a rhetorical analysis of a visual text and the other asks students to create their own visual message (e.g., a brochure or public service announcement).

Part Two: Exploring Genres consists of eight genre-specific chapters: **Public Letters, Reviews, Essays, Memoirs, Profiles, Research Reports, Proposals, and Portfolios.** Chapters 5 through 11 provide:

- An overview of a specific genre and a basic rhetorical analysis of it
- Student and professional readings with questions for comprehension and analysis
- A detailed analysis of one sample reading
- Writing Assignment Options for each genre to provide ample choices
- Writing process instruction, examples, writing activities, and peer review strategies
- One Writer's Journey showcasing a student's notes, drafts, revisions, and analyses of their writing—the "messy work" writers do
- A Transformations section with instruction and a Writing Assignment to either *cross* or *blur* the genre to illustrate the dynamic nature of genres

Part Two concludes with **Chapter 12: Portfolios,** which focuses on the choices writers make to put together a writing portfolio. As with the other genre chapters, the focus here is on student writing, and aspects of a writing portfolio are illustrated with excerpts from student portfolios. Included are sections on writing a reflective narrative for the portfolio, introductions for sections of a portfolio, conducting a case study of one particular assignment, and developing an e-portfolio.

Chapter 13: Research and the Rhetorical Situation, found in Part Three: Research Methods and Sources, focuses on research processes. Students learn why research is important regardless of genre, and they learn how to analyze their rhetorical situation in order to identify the types of research that would make their writing most effective. Students are shown how to develop research questions and come up with key terms to locate sources in libraries, online databases, and the Internet and other web-based resources. Since some genres lead writers to work with primary source materials from field research, we include a section on how to conduct interviews, draw conclusions from observations, and work with survey information. The chapter concludes with instruction on how to evaluate sources given the assignment, genre, and rhetorical situation and offers assignments for constructing an annotated bibliography.

Finally, in **Chapter 14: Using and Citing Sources,** students learn how to choose research material, how to see its connection to their ideas, how to synthesize research from multiple sources, and how to introduce and integrate it into their texts through quotation, paraphrase, and summary. Ways to recognize and avoid plagiarism are explained. The chapter concludes with instruction and examples of documenting sources, in-text and on a references page, in both MLA and APA styles.

Supplements

Instructors Manual. *Choices Writers Make* includes an instructor's manual written by the authors that offers guidance in teaching genre and rhetorical analysis, as well as discussions of how to incorporate the Transformations feature into the classroom, sample syllabi, and further instruction in teaching peer review and research, with a particular focus on helping teachers show their students the importance of research to the rhetorical situation.

MyCompLab. The only online application to integrate a writing environment with proven resources for grammar, writing, and research, MyCompLab gives students help at their fingertips as they draft and revise. Instructors have access to a variety of assessment tools including commenting capabilities, diagnostics and study plans, and an e-portfolio. Created after years of extensive research and in partnership with faculty and students across the country, MyCompLab offers a seamless and flexible teaching and learning environment built specifically for writers.

CourseSmart. Students can subscribe to *Choices Writers Make* as a CourseSmart eText (at CourseSmart.com). The site includes all of the book's content in a format that enables students to search the text, bookmark passages, save their own notes, and print reading assignments that incorporate lecture notes.

Acknowledgments

As we celebrate writing as a collaborative endeavor in this book, we also recognize that though writing can often be isolating, it is rarely done in isolation. And we have many people to thank for helping and guiding us along the way.

First, we want to thank Lauren Finn, the editor of *Choices Writers Make,* for seeing in our initial proposal the seeds of what turned into *Choices.* We are thankful for her support, patience, and sense of humor as we worked through this book together.

We would still be writing were it not for the excellent assistance from Marion Castellucci, our development editor. Her thoughtful and coherent guidance helped us see our way to the end of the book, and her humor and willingness to work with our sometimes only partially formed ideas made the writing process less arduous. In this regard, too, we would like to thank Erin Reilly, associate development editor, for her close and careful reading of our drafts.

Thanks as well to Melinda Durham, our EPS Project Editor, and Pearson production manager Scarlett Lindsay, for seeing *Choices* through to its final, published version and for keeping us very busy during the final month of work.

Of course, this book would not exist at all were it not for our students, whose willingness to work on their writing was the genesis and driving force behind *Choices.* So we thank not only the students in our classes who generously gave us permission to use their writing in this textbook but also the hundreds of students over the past four years who helped us develop and refine our approach to teaching writing and who were willing test subjects for various chapter drafts.

We would like to thank our colleagues at Eastern Connecticut State University. ECSU is a small, public liberal arts institution that puts a premium on good teaching, and so we have benefited enormously from conversations about teaching with our colleagues among the faculty and administration. We have also benefited directly through grants of time and money to work on this project as well as sabbatic leave. Thanks, too, to our English department colleagues who asked about the project and then had to listen to us complain (or rejoice) poetically for hours.

And thanks to the many instructors across the country who reviewed versions—sometimes rather rough versions—of *Choices Writers Make*. Your feedback and suggestions helped us shape and reshape the text, transforming it from a book about our teaching to a textbook that serves the needs of students: Diann Ainsworth, Weatherford College; Shazia Ali, Eastfield College; Nancy Benson, University of Massachusetts Dartmouth; Lisa Bickmore, Salt Lake Community College; Shane Borrowman, University of Nevada, Reno; Kristi S. Brock, Northern Kentucky University; Kevin Brooks, North Dakota State University; Kimberly Burwick, Washington State University; Farrah M. Cato, University of Central Florida; Ron Christiansen, Salt Lake Community College; Deborah Coulter-Harris, University of Toledo; Jay Ann Cox, Richland College; T. Allen Culpepper, State College of Florida, Manatee-Sarasota; Dominic DelliCarpini, York College of Pennsylvania; Sarah Duerden, Arizona State University; Erika Lynn Dyquisto, San Francisco State University; Samantha Earley, Indiana University Southeast; Anthony Edgington, University of Toledo; Stacy Esch, West Chester University of Pennsylvania; Patrice Fleck, Northern Virginia Community College; Susanmarie Harrington, University of Vermont; Matthew Hartman, Ball State University; Dave Higginbotham, University of Nevada, Reno; Kerry L. Johnson, Merrimack College; T. R. Johnson, Tulane University; Sally Lahmon, Sinclair Community College; Jennifer Lawrence, Virginia Tech; Mary Pat McQueeney, Johnson County Community College; Susan Miller, University of Utah; Rhonda Morris, Sante Fe Community College; Shelley Palmer, Rowan-Cabarrus Community College; Amy Patrick, Western Illinois University; Katrina M. Powell, Virginia Tech; Charlotte Teresa Reynolds, Indiana University Southeast; Beth Sherman, San Diego State University; Brittany Stephenson, Salt Lake Community College; William Sweigart, Indiana University Southeast; Michael Verderber, Texas A&M University–Kingsville; Elaine White, University of Southern Mississippi Gulf Coast; and Anne Wilson Twite, Eastern New Mexico University–Ruidoso.

Ultimately, we could never have completed this project without the unquestioning support of our families.

Thanks to my husband, Jeff Cahoon, for his love and support always, but especially while *Choices* was being written and revised over the years. A special thanks to my daughter, Sophia, whose charm and humor always keeps me focused on the important things in my life, and to my newborn son, Noah, who is an inspiration. And finally, thanks to my dear friend, collaborator, and colleague, Steve Ferruci, whose focus and determination made this book possible, and whose friendship I will always treasure.

Thanks to my wife, Jennifer Beck, for her unwavering love, support and patience, especially during the summers when all I could do (it seemed) was complain about how hard writing was; and thanks to Elsabet, my daughter, for calling me down out of my office to play and reminding me that all things can bring joy. Of course, none of this would have happened had not Susan said to me one day, "You know, we should write a book." And so all thanks go to Susan for her vision, her hard work, and most especially her friendship.

To our families, then, we promise no more big projects for a while. . .we think.

Susan L. DeRosa
Stephen A. Ferruci

PART ONE

Reading Genres, Analyzing Arguments

CHAPTER 1   Introduction to Genre   3

CHAPTER 2   Critical Reading and Analysis
Strategies   31

CHAPTER 3   Analyzing and Writing
Arguments   61

CHAPTER 4   Analyzing Visual Rhetoric   89

Introduction to Genre

You already know what a genre is, although you might not be aware of it. You like to read mystery novels, see romance films, and listen to country-western music. You see advertisements on billboards, read flyers in the doctor's office, and posters in the university dining hall. Genres surround us.

What Is Genre?

In simple terms, a *genre* is a kind of text—whether a type of literature, a kind of artwork, or a category of music—that share certain loose characteristics. For example, country music is a genre identifiable by a strong story line, traditionally about rural life; the use of guitars, banjos, fiddles, and similar instruments; a simple chord progression; and other characteristics.

We experience genres when we listen to rock music on the radio, turn on a television sitcom, or go see an animated film. As we drive, we are immersed in genres when we see visual messages on road signs and advertisements on billboards. We encounter genres when we open our mailboxes and find thank-you cards, personal letters, or letters requesting donations, and more genres—blogs or message board posts—when we go online. Not only do we know these genres but we also make personal choices about them on a daily basis.

For instance, when you decide to watch one of Shia LaBeouf's *Transformers* films, you are responding not just to LaBeouf's acting abilities but to the genre of the sci-fi film as well. In fact, you may have really enjoyed him in *I, Robot*, but not in *New York, I Love You*, which suggests you have an affinity toward the sci-fi rather than the romance film genre.

The Social Settings of Genres

Deciding to see a *Transformers* movie was a genre decision made largely in isolation. But most decisions you make about genres of writing are determined by the situation in which you find yourself. Simply, we encounter social situations every day that involve communicating ideas or thoughts with other people. When you email a friend, talk to coworkers, discuss ideas in class, or participate in a town meeting, you are communicating in a social setting. Some of this communication requires a written genre. For instance, when your boss asks you for a project update, you must choose a genre, perhaps a progress report or a memo, to provide the information. Or when you volunteer to work on the campaign of a town council member, you may design posters, answer voter emails, or send thank-you notes on behalf of the candidate.

As writers, we choose genres that seem appropriate to the social situation, the context (work, school, personal life, etc.), and the purpose for our communication. These elements, as well as others, make up what is called the rhetorical situation.

WRITING ACTIVITY   The Genres You Know

Think for a minute about the kinds of genres you are familiar with in your everyday life. Make a list of as many as you can think of. What social situations do you find yourself in as you encounter these genres?

■ ■ ■

The Characteristics of Genres

You probably came up with a sizeable list of familiar genres; still, you may be surprised by how many items you might not have thought of as genres: the shopping list, the text message, and so on. Even more surprising than the number of genres you know is *what* you actually know about each one of them. Most of us can quickly and easily establish the *characteristics* of genres we are familiar with. Take, for example, the action movie genre. Because we are familiar with the action film, just a moment's reflection would allow us to articulate some of its characteristics:

Characteristics of the Action Movie Genre

1. A muscular, tough (often handsome) leading man as the hero, more rarely a woman
2. A beautiful, seductive love interest
3. An arch villain, often with the fatal flaw of hubris
4. The arch villain's "love" interest, who might become the hero's by the end (or was in the past) and who might be same character as in item 2 above
5. A dire threat to the United States, the world, the universe
6. A lot of car, plane, or train crashes with explosions
7. Multiple, highly choreographed fight scenes
8. Car or other vehicular chase scenes
9. Music with throbbing bass and fast tempo

These action film characteristics are pretty well established and expected by viewers. We could write, with some ease, a basic script for an action film that everyone would recognize *as* an action film.

The Functions of Genres

Knowing the characteristics and audience expectations of the action film genre tells us what we can and cannot accomplish with it. For example, with the action film, we can thrill the audience, maybe even get them to consider a social, political or personal problem, but we probably cannot make them feel romantically connected with their partner. If we wanted to get them to rekindle a romance, we would probably have to make a drama or romantic comedy instead.

And just as with film genres, written genres serve different purposes as well – some are useful for explaining complex problems (the research report) while others are better at calling attention to a particular problem (the letter to the editor). Trying to use the letter to the editor to explain or even explore a complex problem would likely fail, in part because letters to the editor are brief and in part because readers do not expect to have complex issues explained in them. So understanding the characteristics and functions of the genre also allows you to understand what purposes that genre might potentially serve. Such knowledge allows you to *choose* genres when you want to communicate your ideas.

GROUP WRITING ACTIVITY   Identifying the Characteristics and Functions of a Genre

Choose a genre that all members of the group are familiar with. You might start with the list of genres you made above.

1. Discuss the characteristics of the genre and list them all. Keep listing even if there is some disagreement. Be sure to provide some examples of that genre.
2. When you have exhausted all possible characteristics, consider the following questions: What does this genre allow you to accomplish? How does it do so? In other words, why choose this genre to communicate? Are there certain "messages" this genre would work better for than others? Are there certain social situations in which you might choose this genre to communicate your message?

■   ■   ■

Audience Expectations and Genre

Returning to our earlier action film example, we can distinguish an action film from a romantic comedy because of the particular characteristics we can identify in it. We expect an action film to have loud, heart-stopping music, heavy on the bass. We expect the heroes and heroines to be attractive and physically fit and to triumph over any villains in the film. We expect there to be car chases and the like. These characteristics help us recognize the genre.

To put it another way, an action film is an action film because it conforms to a loose set of characteristics. When we are familiar with a genre, its characteristics help guide our expectations—we know and can predict what might happen (in the action film, the hero gets shot but of course doesn't die) or what might be said ("I'll be back") or portrayed (evil fiend rubbing his hands together in euphoric anticipation of victory over our hero)—and when our expectations are fulfilled, this becomes part of our enjoyment of the genre.

The Writer and Genre

Similarly, generic characteristics can also guide *writers,* helping them create a text that accomplishes goals appropriate to that genre. Think about the horror film. Its goal is to frighten the audience, and that helps a screenwriter think about what needs to be included in such a film: helpless characters and a villain who is odd, strange looking, or freaky. In certain versions of the genre, there is a group of young men and women who can't figure out that they need to leave the house/hotel/camp in the woods *right away*. The screenwriter hopes, of course, that audiences will be scared by these horror film elements. If the audience is entertained and scared, the genre has fulfilled its purpose—and the writer has accomplished her purpose as well.

Of course, genres can sometimes surprise us. They can push the boundaries of generic characteristics and defy our expectations, for example, the action film in which the good guy fails or dies or the country song about urban ghettos. Knowing the characteristics of a particular genre allows you as a writer both to meet an audience's expectations and, if it's your purpose, to subvert those expectations as well.

So genres have characteristics but **those characteristics are not static**. They are in fact malleable, that is, changeable and flexible; characteristics of a genre are *loosely* connected to it. A genre is not set in stone.

This malleability is part of the power of genres: *genres are flexible*. The characteristics of a genre may serve as guidelines, to be sure, but they can also be stretched, pushed, and reshaped to meet the specific needs of the *rhetorical situation*.

Choices Writers Make: Rhetorical Situation and Genre

Audience, purpose, the social situation, and the writer are all components of what is called the *rhetorical situation*. *Rhetoric* simply means the ways ideas are used to influence others. In Chapter Three we go into more detail about rhetoric, but for now, let's think about genres in terms of the factors that are part of the rhetorical situation. What determines the genre choices we might make as writers?

Our choices for genres are socially and culturally influenced given the situations or events in which we find ourselves. So writing a personal letter may be the appropriate form of communicating your thoughts and feelings in a situation where you are familiar with the person—a family member, a friend, an individual with whom you have a relationship. But in other social situations you may not be able to use a personal letter. When you want to share with your coworkers ideas about a new project you've started, a memo might be the appropriate genre given the social situation. The workplace "culture" warrants more formal expectations for writing situations.

We decide what genre works best for our purposes as writers and the rhetorical situations in which we find ourselves.

Say, for instance, you find yourself feeling remorseful after an argument on the phone with a good friend who lives far away. You want to make amends. There's the social situation: friendship, argument, remorse, and the need to make amends. Well, you have some choices to make on how you want to convey this remorse or sadness. Do you send an email? That would be quick. But given what you know about email, you decide email is too impersonal a genre since tone often gets lost in such messages. It's good for sending good news, short messages, sometimes formal messages too, but not so good when you want to make sure your audience understands exactly how you feel. You know your friend likes greeting cards, a genre that suggests connection, caring, and so you send a card that conveys your sentiments about the situation.

Thus the *rhetorical situation* demanded a genre that allowed the writer to meet the expectations of the larger social situation—a genre that would effectively and appropriately influence his friend to forgive him.

As writers, we choose genres because of the rhetorical situation in which we find ourselves: who we write for (**audience**), why we write (**purpose**), and when and where we find ourselves writing (**context**).

The Rhetorical Situation

When we talk about writers choosing appropriate genres, what we are really talking about is writers understanding how they want to present themselves, who they are writing to, and the context that motivates the writing: Writer, Audience, Context. These three factors influence a fourth choice: the *purpose* of the writing—why the writer has decided to write anything at all and why she chose a particular genre for that situation.

Choices writers make about genre and its relevance to a writing situation do not get made linearly. Instead, purpose, audience, context, and the writer's role become clearer as the writer works through choices and begins to make some decisions about how best to respond in a given situation.

The Situation: You are a new university student, and have discovered some surprises on your first day in the dorm: your furniture is held together by duct tape, the air-conditioning doesn't work, and the neighbors party until all hours of the morning—during the week.

Purpose 1: You're really annoyed and need to vent to someone.	**Purpose 2**: You want to alert someone in charge of the problem with the furniture and the lack of cool air in your room. You want someone to make some changes—and soon—since the usual September heat wave is about to happen.
Audience 1: You decide to vent to your best friend back home about the poor living conditions in your dorm.	**Audience 2**: You decide to inform your residential director and send a copy to the president of the university.
Genre 1: Your friend is never without her cell phone—she has it hooked to her hip. You choose to send a series of text messages detailing all of the annoyances you've come across in the dorm because texting is fast, inexpensive, and may get you a response right away.	**Genre 2:** The RD and president are both professionals, people who have the authority and power to make changes. You choose to write a formal letter to the RD and president to be sure there is documentation of the problems, and so someone in charge who cares about students' safety and academic success may make some changes soon.
Your Message: In a series of messages, you tell your friend about all the problems—the stuffy room is making your skin dry and your roommate's dirty laundry stinks. The small, rickety furniture makes wrinkles in your jeans as you stuff them in the drawers. The loud neighbors, who never even invite you to their parties, cramp your social life when you try to have your own parties.	**Your Message:** You write in your letter about how you are trying to be a good student and study, but the air quality in your room is preventing you from focusing. You share your concerns about the loud neighbors and their parties, noting how you and other students find it hard to focus on academics with little sleep. And you mention that the furniture is falling apart and could prove to be a safety hazard to you and other students, which of course, the university would want to avoid.

As you can see, writers choose genres that make sense given the situation, the audience they hope to influence, and the purpose for their writing. In this way, too, those choices are flexible and malleable: they can (and often do) change as you develop your ideas. But genres are flexible enough to accommodate changes in the rhetorical situation.

Issue ⟷ You ⟷ Audience ⟷ Purpose ⟷ Genre

Understanding the rhetorical situations you find yourself in—whether in the work you do for your courses, or on the job, or in your volunteer or civic work—can help you make informed and critical choices about genre and content.

Academic Genres

Although we've been talking a lot about genres that you find in your everyday life—music, movies, and personal writing, like letters—we are concerned in this book, in part, with some genres you might be expected to write in your academic life. That is, we focus on *academic* genres: writing done to influence and inform other people in the academic community.

Understanding academic writing in this way might seem like a stretch when you consider the kinds of writing you have been asked to do so far in your career as a student. Your research papers may be written for only one person—your instructor. Thus the purpose of those papers is to show your instructor that you can conduct research, work with sources, and write intelligently about what you have learned. But one key aspect of genre is that *writers imagine a real and varied audience: no writer writes to "everyone" or "anyone."* Thus *academic genres* are those that your professors, other scholars, or professionals might write and read themselves: a research report, a proposal, a book review, or a rhetorical analysis.

These genres exist outside of the classroom and are used for particular purposes by specific academic and professional writers and readers. For instance, the lab report is used by scientists because it is a structured method of presenting research data and drawing conclusions which in turn allows for the experiment or study to be replicated by others (a key component of the work of scientific research).

The audiences for these genres are real. Those who read a lab report read it to understand the latest research: they have a vested interest in the material; they have background knowledge that might lead them to disagree with or refute the findings. However, not every scientist will be interested in or be able to understand the contents of all lab reports. So the audience is not "all scientists," but those who share similar research backgrounds.

Such readers are interested in the findings, of course, but they may also want to see where the writer got the information used or referred to in the report. Thus academic genres may require a certain way of presenting and working with source material because of audience expectations.

Academic genres also, very often, require a particular persona for the writer: a formal, objective or disinterested voice, or no discernable authorial voice at all.

Civic Genres

Civic genres, like academic genres, also imagine *very real audiences*. The difference here is that you would not expect to find an academician (a professor, researcher, or teacher) reporting results of her study to her colleagues in the form of a letter to the editor, for instance. Instead, *civic genres,* as the name suggests, are the kinds of writing that we do as citizens concerned with world events and issues. For example, we might write a letter to the editor which celebrates the activities of our local town officials; we might write a profile of our grandmother for a local or state magazine; or we might write a memoir about a time in our lives for a national publication because we feel that our experiences will resonate with others. (For a comparison of academic and civic genres, see Table 1.1.)

Here, then, is another key facet of genre: *the choice of genre and purpose are intimately linked.* If your purpose is to explore the larger significance of the consequences of an event in your youth, the research report is not going to serve you. Instead, you might turn to the personal essay or the memoir, two kinds of civic genres.

Since civic genres can be written by anyone—not just trained scholars or experts—they do not always require that the writer do much research or know much about the issue being addressed. You are sure to have read some editorials by people who are simply ranting; they clearly have not spent much time thinking about the issue.

Of course, the opposite is often true as well: some civic genres are well researched and written by experts with lots of knowledge on the issues. But that's not the point. The fact

Table 1.1   A Comparison of Academic and Civic Genres

	Academic Genres	*Civic Genres*
What are they like?	–concerned with discipline-specific issues –research documented in formal ways –formal in language and tone and often discipline-specific	–concerned with public issues –research sometimes documented informally –language and tone ranging from informal to formal and often audience-specific
Why are they written? (purposes)	–to disseminate information or provide background –to join an ongoing academic or professional discussion –to analyze an existing assertion	–to influence others –to sway public opinion –to change people's ideas –to move readers to action
Who writes them? (writers)	–academics and other professionals –scholars and experts	–ordinary citizens –journalists –experts and researchers –bloggers
Who reads them? (audiences)	–academics and other professionals –scholars and experts	–ordinary people interested in issues –politicians and government officials
What are typical genres?	–research report –lab report –academic essay –literary analysis	–letter to the editor –commentary –profile –blog

that it is "civic discourse" does not distinguish between knowledge and ignorance. The audience decides whether or not the writer has established his credibility.

Civic genres, then, also require that the writer conducts research to understand more fully his or her subject. But unlike academic genres, the way in which source material (research) gets used and incorporated is different. One obvious difference is that while you would expect to see a list of sources attached to a research report, you would find it odd if one were included with a letter to the editor. This may seem a minor difference, and it certainly is not the only one, but it does reflect a difference in purpose: the academic genre seeks to disseminate information in some form (through reportage, critique, analysis) and to provide the background that allows the writer to make assertions. Civic genres, as the name suggests, are interested in influencing the public, and those genres often are concerned with issues that need attention or discussion (e.g. health care) and are accompanied by a call that some action be taken.

Finally, civic genres offer a range of *styles and tone.* Many use very casual, colloquial language (the profile "End of the Line" in Chapter 9 is a good example), while others allow both first person narrative and direct address (e.g. "I ask you to consider voting for me in November"). And many civic genres are equally appropriate to formal tone and purpose as informal: a letter to the editor can be either colloquial or formal.

Transformations: The Flexibility of Genres

You may have gathered that genre is more than a container, more than a form into which you might pour your ideas. Genres are more interesting and much more useful than that. They are in fact *generative:* they help you understand what you can say, not just how you can say it. But this is not the only way that genres are flexible. The lines of genres, the characteristics that define them, blur very easily, and that's partly what makes them so powerful. Genres are *loosely defined by their characteristics,* not absolutely defined by them.

Genres offer writers creative ways to approach many different situations that call for writing. We've called this section (and others throughout the book) *Transformations* because of the ways we see boundaries being blurred between genres and the ways genres often cross over into each other. As writers explore the blurring and crossing of genres, they may see how genre is dynamic in the ways it generates new ideas and offers different ways of looking at rhetorical situations.

Genre Blurring: What Is It? Why Do It?

Sometimes the type of writing you want to do and the ways you imagine presenting your writing and its purpose to your audience don't seem to fit within just one genre. In this instance, you may find that *genre blurring, blending two or more genres and their particular characteristics,* works for you given the social situation (and your rhetorical tasks). Blurring often creates a "hybrid" genre: one that borrows characteristics of multiple genres for the purpose of fulfilling the writer's goals.

Examples of genre blurring are all around us: hip-hop is a blurring of rapping (speaking poetically and in rhyme) and the percussive breaks in disco and funk. Sometimes blurring happens when artists (musicians, writers, etc.) think that the situation calls for a creative spin on a traditional genre that's been used before; out of that creativity comes a new version, a hybrid, one that combines familiar characteristics of two or more genres.

In written texts, you may be familiar with genre blurring in the forms of graphic novels (e.g. *Sin City,* a combination of comic book and novella) or the food memoir/travel/exposé (e.g. Travel Channel personality Anthony Bourdain's *Kitchen Confidential,* a humorous memoir of his travels and life as a professional chef mixed with cultural criticism and exposé of the "underside" of the restaurant world).

Blurring genres of writing must, of course, serve particular purposes; so we will concern ourselves with situations that might call for genre blurring.

An Example of Genre Blurring: The Travel Memoir

Sara Schneider, a student in a writing class, was given a writing assignment that asked her to recall a place to which she had traveled or lived, one she had strong memories of and which had defined who she was in some way. Schneider was to interpret the place in order to capture its larger significance for readers—those who have never visited Hutchinson Island, Florida—and immerse them in that location. To do so, she had to provide reflection and commentary on her experiences and personal memories of the place, for better or worse.

Her first idea was to use memoir to focus on her past personal experiences on Hutchinson Island. Schneider was aware that the genre of memoir requires a writer to make her experiences *resonate* with readers and tap into some larger significance in readers' lives. So, some critical reflection was important to the writing. Yet memoir didn't quite capture all she wanted to do, since the place, Hutchinson Island, was just as important as her memories of being there. To capture the essence of this place, she needed to do what some travel writers do: carefully observe the place (its people, their actions, and so on) and interpret the place and its unique culture for readers.

Schneider chose to blur genres by creating a travel memoir. She chose travel memoir rather than a travel report or essay because she wanted the readers to understand how Hutchinson Island had changed *her,* and think about how other places significant to readers' lives change them as well. She also chose travel memoir because her purpose was to provide social commentary on Hutchinson Island and the contradictions inherent in its "landscape"—both the beautiful and *unbeautiful* aspects of the island.

Schneider knew that readers might never have been to Hutchinson Island or even heard of it, so she provided lots of sensory descriptions to help them imagine the place—the smells of the island's fishing spots, the oppressive heat, and the habits and attitudes of its people. These sensory details immersed readers in the location.

While Schneider used personal experiences, anecdotes, and observations to develop her travel memoir, a travel memoir may also call for geographical, archival, or historical information that one might find in local archives. The information from research a writer chooses to include in her travel piece reflects her purpose for writing about the place and her subjective experiences in it.

As Schneider's travel memoir illustrates, when writers blur genres, they create a hybrid, one that blends characteristics of two or more genres to fulfill their purposes and to resonate with their readers. Let's take a look at how she works with the characteristics of both memoir and travel writing to create a *travel memoir* that serves her purposes and audience expectations.

Sara Schneider

Professor DeRosa

English 100

15 April 2010

Just Another Beautiful Thunderstorm: A Travel Memoir

On cool days in March in Florida, you can tell the tourists from the locals by how their legs reflect the sunlight instead of absorbing it. My aunts are still wearing their long sleeves and closed toe shoes, while I, visiting from Connecticut, am wearing a skirt and a shirt with no sleeves and the brightest sandals I can find. Since I've been going to college in New England, even my mother who lives in South Carolina finds my weather senses are skewed; she doesn't understand that fifty-five degrees and sunny *is* beautiful to me.

On nice days, there is no better place to be than the beaches of Hutchinson Island, a Florida barrier island they have tried to nail down and build up. It's worked fairly well so far; my mom, however, told me stories that when she was a kid in the sixties, the beach was farther east and you could see the pilings of old buildings out in the ocean. During World War II, the current Route A1A was not the easternmost road on the coast as it is now. But barrier islands move and erode; that's just what happens.

Hutchinson Island is home to some of the best things in Fort Pierce, including hotels that are just now coming back into business after hurricanes Frances, Jeanne, and Wilma. There are metaphorical blue tarps and peeling paint all over the South, but Florida is covered with the real thing, even today. The mobile home park that used to be by the water treatment plant just on the island side of the South Bridge is *completely gone,* and the land has been bought by a condo development company. Two years after Hurricane Wilma, you still see blue rooftops and closed hotels and condemned property signs. And construction is the biggest industry in Florida, still.

* * *

The summer I turned 19, I visited with my aunts for two weeks in early August while my mother stayed in South Carolina. But I remember the first time I stayed with my aunt Beverly, whom I liked a lot more when her husband Rad was still alive, and I was still eight years old and he and I went snook fishing in the canals at 4:30 in the morning and had Ho-Hos and

---

An important reflection here: how development has begun to encroach on the natural landscape, but also on how the landscape undergoes natural changes itself.

The writer describes this place as a character, one who has survived adversity and came through changed. She uses details here to help readers visualize an island.

She segments the memoir to separate the particulars she recollects and her general commentary from a later perspective.

There's a time shift here, but readers follow it easily because she situates: "the summer I was 19..." and "since Rad passed away...."

The anecdotes and details provide readers with insights about the writer's experiences; it serves as a lead-in to some later memories of her times on the island.

Obviously, the writer's relationship with Rad informs the vivid details of his office, her fishing trips with him, and so on.

Yoo-Hoo for breakfast. The canals in Florida are all surrounded by steep muddy banks, and he hoisted me up by my back pockets more than once to get me over the top. My mother tells me I did anything he asked or told me to. One time at the dock where the *Abaco Treasure,* a freighter from the Bahamas, stayed, Rad saw a pelican and sent me off to feed it with a piece of bread—this proved to be a mistake because the pelican had some problems differentiating between its food and my finger.

Since Rad passed away in 2000 from a brain tumor, Beverly has aged. She was 50 when he died and she has gotten much older than she should. She lives with Doug, a friend's brother, who seems older by a decade. They go to bed no later than 8 p.m. and Doug is on a first name basis with the newspaper boy, who comes around before 4 a.m.

I only stayed with them for a week.

At night, I spent a lot of time online on Rad's old computer in the office, surrounded by pictures and memorabilia from the 32 years he was married to Beverly—fishing poles, campaign stickers, drawings, old wine bottles, hats, guns, police reports from the 80s, comic strips.

And I was feeling guilty that I had eventually hit puberty and was more interested in being a *girl* than fishing with Rad and then all of a sudden . . . all of a sudden he had a brain tumor, and nothing was ever going to be the same, ever. And for some reason *My Immortal* was on the radio—telling me that *there's just too much that time cannot erase*—constantly playing at me while I sat in this office trying not to blame myself for the random happenings of nature; and I couldn't get it out of my head, not for two weeks.

I stayed the second week with aunt Susan and Rodney. Although they went to bed only slightly later than Beverly and Doug (and had reasons, like having to go to work), they at least had my cousins Michael and Matthew, identical twins one year my junior, desperate for human interaction.

The writer captures a sense of the place by describing the island's businesses, locals, foods, and so on. This contrasts nicely with the newer develop-ments she mentioned earlier that dot the island's landscape.

During the two-week visit, I decided I needed something to do, because skin starts to cook when it's left too long in the sun. I talked to Rodney, and he got me a job at Archie's for the remaining week and a half that I'd be in town.

My uncle Rodney's favorite bar is a place called Archie's Seabreeze, on Seaway Drive (A1A) on Hutchinson Island. This place, whose motto is "No

Shirt, No Shoes, No Problem," has been open since 1947, serving bikers and beach bums despite the new ownership. As Rodney said, "Oh, it'll never be *respectable.*" It was opened by one of the Summerlins, a prominent family in Fort Pierce; the same family who had fish fries, the best in town, but also served swamp cabbage (which is to say, the hearts of sable palms, which is also to say, illegal). They didn't care, and apparently neither did anyone else; the Summerlin family has produced some of the best cooks in the county, always manning the kitchen at Archie's, and serving nothing but the best smoked fish and seafood around.

The writer uses her descriptions to immerse readers in the scene and local flavor of the island.

Archie's is nothing but a bar: It smells of cigarettes and the salty sea air that sweeps it out the oversized doorways. They serve food, of course, but their main attraction is the old wizened fishermen sitting at the bar, as often as not shoeless, flirting with the bartender Amy, who probably rides a bike better than half the guys there, a woman who lost part of her foot in a bike accident, a woman who wears blue eye-shadow and makes it look good because she just doesn't give a shit what you think. . . . And there I was, in a biker bar, asking Amy if I could work for a few days because Rodney thought it would be a good experience for me. She said yes and went to get the owner, and I stood on the slate and sand floor, looked at the pool tables, and pirate signs about rum, and the license plates that lined the ceiling and beams, and at the men at the bar.

Here the writer only glosses over the dark side of life on the island; probably, she could have gone further with this description to emphasize the contrast between the easygoing nature at Archie's and the daily struggle that both make up peoples' lives on the island.

The owner agreed to pay me $7 an hour to stand between the kitchen and the waitresses and make sure fish had lemon, bread had butter, hamburgers had ketchup and mustard and mayonnaise, that sort of thing.

I stood in the bar and watched the Weather Channel, saw Charley come to land on the west coast of Florida in Charlotte Harbor, while someone who had lived there and escaped to the east coast, wandered from barfly to pool-shark to barfly begging for an extra trailer or generator. The night before, I had helped Beverly weigh down her aluminum ladders outside and take all the plants inside just in case we got hit. We got nothing—just another beautiful Florida thunderstorm that made me nervous as I drove home in a truck from the 1980s.

During my shifts at Archie's, I flirted with one of the cooks, who was my age and lived down the road on the beach, and the customers. One day, after mentioning that my legs were tired from a run, I got an offer from a bald and goateed, 6'5", 350-lb biker (whose name had to have been Tiny).

"You can come sit on my hand," he said gruffly, but not without humor. I didn't laugh alone, which was good because that way no one could hear my nervous laughter. On a different day, they were teasing me that since I was behind a screen, I should be pole dancing—and, having learned some, but not enough, from my interaction with Tiny, I said, "Well, you find me a pole, and I'll see what I can do," aiming mostly for witty. Someone found a length of PVC pipe in the storage shed and handed it to me. They are the only ones that have called my bluff and forced me to back down.

What am I doing here? I thought. I spent most of my life in a city, albeit a southern city, but a city nonetheless, and at 19, I had gone to school in Rhode Island and Connecticut, and now suddenly I was surrounded by beach bums and barflies and bikers, and people were asking me to pole dance at 3 p.m. like it wasn't a big deal or anything. I handled it fine, while it was happening. And I loved it.

But *why* did I go back to Connecticut and pretend none of it ever happened, only leaking choicer stories to my closest friends, like it was something I was embarrassed of?

On 4th of July, while my mother, her boyfriend Stanley, and I were on vacation on the island, it finally stopped raining. The downpour hadn't been constant, but every day was unbearably humid. I remember thinking, it's the 4th of July, dammit—I want to be *hot,* sweating at 9:30 p.m. when the light show takes off and slapping so many bugs that I sound like a one-woman step team. That's what I like; that's what I miss about Florida. I am a beach baby, born a fifteen-minute drive from the sandy shores of the Atlantic Ocean. We moved away from that paradise four years later and have been working our way steadily away from the pull of the tides ever since. We've been living for the last 12 years about 5 hours away from any ocean, which is, frankly, 4½ too many.

The 4th itself was a long and beautiful day: it started at about 4:45 a.m. We went on my uncle Rodney and aunt Susan's boat for some early-morning ocean fishing—the best type. The sunrise on the Atlantic was partially blocked

The writer includes the anecdote to put readers in the scene and give them a sense of the attitude of some locals who frequent Archie's.

This reflection serves as a commentary for her ambivalence about the place and her own sense of belonging to it versus her college life up north.

The writer again uses segmentation to organize the stories about her experiences. Here she uses another time marker to situate readers in her narration.

Here the writer inserts a digression, some analysis about why the island, and the water, has such an influence on her. She seems conflicted here: the heat is unbearable and it draws her to the place, the beach.

Her descriptions sound idyllic—the beauty she sees in the place.

by pale columnar clouds, but enough light got through for us to need sunglasses: such is the Florida sun. We were surrounded by baitfish, blue runners, but they weren't hungry—or they were too smart for us. I caught a couple, and Stanley caught one too, but they were all too large for bait and too small for us, so we threw them back.

After many hours of fishing, seeing a few schools of dolphins, and even a sea turtle, we headed over to the cove, a calm and cool section of the Indian River shore. Sitting in the crystal green water, you could feel little fish nibbling at your fingers and toes if you stayed still too long. A couple of boys in a nearby boat caught a sea turtle after he swam harmlessly past us. Everything was cool and blue-green and perfect.

The rest of the afternoon passed languidly with Beverly and Doug. We spoke briefly and lazily about politics; I carefully stuck with general topics, after our hostile debate the night before over immigration, a popular topic on the island. Then we gradually drifted off into the crossword puzzle, the three of us batting words around like a Little League practice; I half-read while Doug put lotion on Beverly's feet and legs, and Beverly worked on the puzzle.

Finally my mother called; Doug answered the phone. "Can you be ready in 45 minutes? Your mom wants to know," he asked in his jaunty Kentucky accent.

"Hell yes," I said, "I've *been* ready for an hour." Doug laughed ("ah-he-hee!") and relayed the message. The puzzle had, by that time, nearly been abandoned, and Doug was just watching golf with the sound almost off.

Earlier that week, we decided we were going to this little Cuban restaurant, Don Ramon, a few towns south of Fort Pierce in Stuart. Before dinner, however, Stanley, my mother, and I picked up my grandmother and headed out to Clara Oliver's house, an old friend of my grandmother's and president of the Fort Pierce chapter of the United Daughters of the Confederacy. Clara was about 82, the same age as my grandmother, but living by herself in a spacious hardwood-floored condo, as opposed to my grandmother's assisted-living dorm-like setting on Southwest 25th Street.

So we sat and we talked; or rather, we sat and they talked. The conversation drifted from how long it had been since Clara had seen me or my sister (about 8 years) to how much weight my mother had lost (about 30 pounds) to the size of the condo and Clara's allergies/asthma, and naturally

---

The writer continues to provide clear details about the beauty of the river that puts readers in the scene.

Note the ways the writer alternates scenes in this section: the beautiful landscape of Hutchinson Island, and the ugliness of the racism she recalls from some of the residents.

came to rest on the influx of immigrants in the area—the same topic Doug and Beverly and I had been arguing about.

If I had to hear one more time how "the neighborhood was a nice place to live before the Cubans/Haitians/Jamaicans/blacks/Mexicans/Orientals took over," I would feel no qualms about ripping out Clara's bitter, brittle old trachea and using it as a cigarette holder, or perhaps someplace to store my pencils.

"It was a nice place until, you know, now, I'm not prejudiced or anything" ("oh no, no, of course not" chimed the chorus) "but it was nice until the blacks and Asians moved in," Clara said. I clenched my teeth. "But," she continued, "they all improved the house or the yard"—she sounded slightly surprised. "But, you know, it's just not a nice place to live anymore."

"Sounds like," I was saying before I could stop myself, "they actually made the neighborhood *better,* then." I expected a glare from my mother; it never came.

But Clara looked at me like I had transformed from what she remembered—loving, adorably polite child—to what she undoubtedly saw now—a *goddamn hippie,* some young insurgent, probably an atheist, an alcoholic, and a sex addict, and very definitely a *liberal.*

"Yes," she said in her dry Southern voice, "but there are children in the street all the time," she warbled, "impossible to drive through."

I held my tongue because I didn't want an argument, even one I knew I was right about. Besides, she was probably right: I *was* a goddamn hippie, an insurgent, at least agnostic, working on alcoholic, and probably inherently some vague and harmless form of sex addict.

Don Ramon's was closed—of course. It was, after all, the 4th of July. Closed, no Cuban food—but the trip down US-1, over the bridge crossing the Intercoastal Waterway, made the whole ride worthwhile—like so many Jimmy Buffett album covers, full of palm trees and sailboats and bright blue seawater.

We ended up eating at Mulligan's, a seafood grill and raw bar in Jensen Beach. When we had finished, the sun had already gone down, and as we were right on the water, we crossed the street to a seawall and watched the fireworks. From there, we could see nine sets of fireworks, all over the water. It wasn't too hot, and there weren't too many bugs, even so close to the water, but that was the spot I wanted to be in. Hands down. Forever.

Although the writer's purpose is to provide a subjective view of place, does she need to define herself outright here? Or is it obvious she holds positions opposite to Clara?

She ends with visual details about the "beautiful" aspects of the island's natural landscape—and her recollections about her deep connections to it, despite its "unbeautiful" aspects.

Questions for Analysis

1. To capture her ambivalence about Hutchison Island, Schneider sets up many contrasts that describe both its beautiful and unbeautiful parts. How does she get readers thinking about her ambivalence?
2. How does Schneider immerse readers in this place and her memories of it? Is she successful in fulfilling her purpose?
3. How does Schneider want readers to feel about this place? Give examples that make you have strong reactions to the island, its people, and so on.

Genre Crossing: What Is It? Why Do It?

While blurring genres lends itself to meeting complicated and often novel situations, *crossing genres* lends itself more to meeting the needs of separate and varied audiences and purposes. Writers, thus, may find themselves *crossing genres* when the rhetorical situation changes, or when they come to understand that situation differently.

For instance, a letter to the editor on a local homeless shelter and its impact on the community may be *transformed* into a research report on how local government is addressing the issue of homelessness through policymaking and legislative processes when the writer realizes how little citizens know about homelessness. The purpose of the letter is to praise the efforts of the shelter while urging readers to think about what they can do to help solve the local problem of homelessness. In contrast, the purpose of the research report might be to inform readers of how effectively various local governments deal with homelessness and to argue for changes in the state's policies to help solve the problem.

Crossing genres, clearly, is more than simply rewriting a text in a new genre; a new understanding of the rhetorical situation is needed, and further research may be necessary. A writer of the report on homelessness would need to know what the state's current policies are regarding homelessness, and how various agencies carry out those policies—effectively or not. And the audience's knowledge and attitudes about homelessness would determine which arguments or ideas the writer would include and just how that information would be used—to advocate for a local shelter in the letter or to critique government policies and actions and suggest alternatives in the research report. The writer's purpose, thus, also helps decide which arguments are made.

An Example of Genre Crossing: From Open Letter to Research Report

In her writing course, Gloria Ramos was asked to write an open letter on a current issue that was important to her. She began not by thinking about topics or even issues, but of recent conversations she had had with friends and family. She finally settled on the issue of gay marriage, because she had recently had a "discussion" with friends about it and found herself upset by their opposition to gay marriage. Thus, her first step in thinking about the subject of her letter was to focus on an audience: those who disagreed with her position. She also had a purpose: to convince them that they were wrong, or, at least, to encourage them to think more carefully about their positions and why they held them.

Because it is a civic genre, the open letter is a good genre for generating discussion and argument, and open letters in particular are often used to call attention to serious problems and concerns; because they are "open," writers address them to particular groups, though they may sometimes address them to individuals. As she started thinking about her audience, Ramos began to name them—they were social conservatives, people who would generally hold more traditional values and would be opposed to gay marriage.

Because her purpose was to convince them, Ramos had to figure out what they already believed and then conduct some background research to help her make her claims, and refute theirs. Working within this civic genre, Ramos learned how to use her research and *frame arguments* for a public and broad audience—one that did not need or want to know everything about the subject, but one which would critically examine the claims she made and evidence she provided.

Ramos begins by finding common ground—"we all know"—even though it might not actually be true.

And here she hits the audience with the point of her letter; rhetorically, she has set them up to agree with her, because she is claiming that "if you believe X, you must also believe Y." Does her reasoning (logos) work here?

Here, again, she maintains a civil tone, acknowledging that they have a right to their beliefs, as does she.

Notice her shift in tone here—she brings in some sarcasm in order to point out the unreasonableness of their beliefs.

Same-Sex Marriage: An Open Letter to Social Conservatives

Dear Social Conservatives,

We all know that society is ever-changing, and along with it our morals and values. What we believed in the past is no longer important or even true. For instance, we used to think the world was flat; we know better now. We no longer see African Americans as slaves to sell. We no longer see women as baby-making machines or men as sole bread-winners. Men can stay home; women can make six figures. Clearly, traditional assumptions about men and women have evolved. And so the traditional view of the family doesn't have to be "a man and wife" anymore. Americans are starting to see that a man and a man or a woman and woman can have a successful *marriage,* too. Times are changing. It may seem like a crazy concept to you, but sooner or later you're going to have to accept it. Same-sex marriage is going to happen. The institution of marriage is evolving whether you like it or not.

Now I understand that you have your beliefs that don't quite agree with the idea of same-sex marriage. I don't expect you to all of a sudden change your beliefs; that would be unrealistic of me, and it would mean you didn't really believe what you said you believed. You grew up with your beliefs, and I with mine. But just because you grew up with them doesn't mean they are right.

You call same-sex marriage an abomination, an act against God. Okay, I guess I can see that: two people who love one another, yep, that's an abomination. I mean, straight marriages are so great . . . except that 50% end

Here Ramos calls
attention to the
absurdity of their
beliefs by using an
example that is truly
abominable.

in divorce. Did you know that Darren Spedale of Stanford University found
that gay married men in Denmark had only a 17% divorce rate? Hmmm. Okay,
so maybe you are thinking, but straight marriages are loving and wonderful,
and gays are promiscuous, so their marriages must be bad. Two words:
spousal abuse. A man beating his wife in front of his children? Or beating his
children? Now that's an abomination. Why aren't you so up in arms about
that issue? Why no ballot initiatives about that?

Ramos again makes
use of sarcasm and
humor—open letters
can be informal, they
can address readers
directly, and Ramos
makes good use of
those characteristics.

Calling same-sex marriage an abomination and a violation to nature is
hurtful, and I thought *that* was unchristian. Love thy brother? Imagine if you
were prevented from marrying the person you loved, the one you have been in
a relationship with for ten years or more? Seventy-one percent of Americans
agree with the statement that "God's plan for marriage is one man, one
woman for life." So the Bible tells you so. Okay, I know it defines marriage as
between a man and a woman . . . or is it between one man and many women?
I forget. The Bible is a good reference for how to act, sometimes, that's for
sure. "Thou shalt not kill" and "Thou shalt not steal." Those are good ones. But
they don't interfere with the rights of others—no one has the right to kill,
after all. But everyone has the right to love.

Notice the lack of cita-
tion for the research.
This genre does not
require formal, aca-
demic citation.

Even Disney, that family-oriented corporation, has decided to accept the
legalization of same-sex unions by allowing homosexuals to use their
Fairytale Wedding Packages. The company already allowed same-sex couples
to tie the knot on the premises, but now same-sex unions are being given the
formal sanction of an official Disney wedding planner. Disney, seller of family
values, is joining in on what Massachusetts helped start in May 2004 when it
first started letting same-sex couples legally marry. The President should not
feel like he has to protect the sanctity of marriage if Disney doesn't!

She provides some
specific instances that
show her audience
that acceptance of gay
marriage is on the rise.

Same-sex marriage should not be banned simply because it makes people
uncomfortable. Sometimes it seems like people are forgetting that homosexuals
are people. They have the same needs and desires as everyone else. "Men and
women of full age, without any limitation due to race, nationality, or religion,
have the right to marry and to found a family. They are entitled to equal rights
as to marriage, during marriage, and at its dissolution," says the Universal

She concludes with an
appeal to not only our
emotions (pathos) but
also to our reason
(logos).

Declaration of Human Rights. Sexual preference is not an issue when it comes to creating a loving family, and recognizing same-sex marriage would not "undermine families," as President Bush suggests. It's time you realized that.

Yours truly,
A Concerned Citizen

Transforming the Open Letter to a Research Report

The open letter is a good genre for stirring up discussion and controversy, for getting people to think about an issue or topic that they may never have considered before. Writers use it to point out problems, suggest solutions, call for change, and so on. But as wonderful a genre as it is, there are some things a writer cannot do with it. The open letter is not good for informing people about an issue; it's generally not meant to give readers a deep understanding of an issue or topic. For that, writers turn to more formal genres such as the research report.

Writers choose to cross genres—to move from one to another drawing on the same material—to meet the changing needs of the rhetorical situation. A writer's purpose may change, or they may want to appeal to a different audience, or they themselves might come to understand the issue deeply. Any or all of these can lead a writer to rework material in a new genre.

For Ramos, the research report was a good choice for crossing genres; while she enjoyed writing the open letter *because* it created conversation and controversy, she really does believe in the importance of this issue and she felt that a lot of people do not know much about the issue. So the research report was a logical choice for her, but it did mean she had to conduct much more extensive research, and she had to use it formally—which meant in part, she had to synthesize it and cite it (look at Chapter 13: Research and the Rhetorical Situation for further discussion of how to use research in your writing).

Ramos formats her
paper in APA style.

A Report on Same-Sex Marriage in America

A Human Right, a Family Right

Gloria Ramos

English 100P

Professor Ferruci

March 18, 2008

SAME-SEX MARRIAGE   2

Overview

The issue of legalizing same-sex marriage in America has become a heated issue recently; it was even the main topic of discussion at the Democratic Forum in Los Angeles in August, 2007, a forum that all nine Republican candidates declined to attend. Clearly, same-sex marriage will be an important issue in the upcoming election, and understanding the facts about gay marriage has never been more important.

- Religion is an important factor in the opposition to gay marriage: "Overall, nearly six-in-ten Americans (59%) oppose gay marriage, up from 53% in July. But those with a high level of religious commitment now oppose gay marriage by more than six-to-one (80%–12%)." (Pew Forum, 2003, para. 3)
- The Bush Administration is making persistent efforts to pass a constitutional amendment defining marriage as between a man and woman.
- Yet, the American population is becoming more accepting of same-sex marriage. The Pew Forum (2006) found that opposition to same-sex marriage dropped from 65% in 1996 to 51% in 2006.

The banning and opposition to same-sex marriage is not an issue of the "sanctity of marriage," but an issue of *limiting the civil and human rights of some Americans.*

- According to the Universal Declaration of Human Rights, "men and women of full age, without any limitation due to race, nationality or religion, have the right to marry and to found a family. They are entitled to equal rights, as to marriage, during marriage, and at its dissolution" (United Nations, 1948).

Laws banning same-sex marriages restrict the rights of states and of the people themselves, limiting the choice they have about legalizing same-sex marriage.

Introduction

The legalization of same-sex marriage has become a very important topic in America today.

Here she provides the thesis of her report, then supports it with a quotation. Notice how she has revised the sarcastic and strident tone of her open letter, though she is essentially making the same argument.

Ramos taps into one of the characteristics of research reports: the **repetition of key ideas**—this is similar to the Overview, but she knows that some readers skip the Overview and that others need the repetition.

The Bush administration is restricting the rights of people that are rightfully theirs. Gay couples should have the right to marry if they choose. The religious beliefs and social beliefs of those who oppose gay marriage are nothing more than the suppression of the constitutional and human rights of homosexuals. Opposition based on myths about gay couples—that they are more promiscuous, less stable—are equally invalid and harmful and in denial of the facts about marriages between men and women.

The issue of gay marriage is one that affects us all, as it is an issue of human rights and dignity.

Opposition to Gay Marriage:
The Defense of Marriage Act and the Federal Marriage Amendment

Her section headings communicate the focus of the section.

Currently, there is one federal law restricting same-sex marriages. The Defense of Marriage Act (DOMA) was signed into law in 1996 by President Clinton after receiving overwhelming support in both houses of Congress. Pressure to pass DOMA came as a result of a court ruling in Hawaii that conservatives feared would result in that state granting marriage rights to homosexuals.

She provides her own overview of the act, and then quotes it directly, since she assumes that most people have not read it. Doing so establishes her *ethos*: she has read it, thought about it, and so what she says about it is valid.

DOMA is split into two sections. The first redefines the powers of states in regard to the issue of gay marriage. DOMA limited the definition of marriage to that between a man and woman, and the first section explains that states have a right to "make their own decisions of marriage" (DOMA Watch, n.d.):

> In determining the meaning of any Act of Congress, or of any ruling, regulation, or interpretation of the various administrative bureaus and agencies of the United States, the word 'marriage' means only a legal union between one man and one woman as husband and wife, and the word 'spouse' refers only to a person of the opposite sex who is a husband or a wife. (*Defense*, 1996)

The second part of DOMA was given over to defining marriage as a union between a man and a woman:

> In determining the meaning of any Act of Congress, or of any ruling, regulation, or interpretation of the various administrative bureaus and

agencies of the United States, the word 'marriage' means only a legal union between one man and one woman as husband and wife, and the word 'spouse' refers only to a person of the opposite sex who is a husband or a wife. (*Defense,* 1996)

DOMA does not change the constitution—it is not an amendment, and it only applies to Federal law, so states can still permit gay marriage. So to back up DOMA, President Bush and his administration, with the support of some members of Congress, and conservative groups across the country, is trying to push forward the Federal Marriage Amendment (FMA), also referred to as the Marriage Protection Amendment. President Bush's support for this amendment stems from his fundamental belief that "the institution of marriage is between a man and a woman" (Baker, 2006, p. A04). The amendment reads: "Marriage in the United States shall consist solely of the union of a man and a woman. Neither this Constitution, nor the constitution of any State, shall be construed to require that marriage or the legal incidents thereof be conferred upon any union other than the union of a man and a woman" (H.R. 3313, 2004).

The Bush Administration's views on same-sex marriage have been repeatedly expressed in public statements. But their position should raise concerns about states' rights and human rights, since the Federal Marriage Amendment goes one step further than DOMA by proposing to banish the rights of states to decide what laws governing marriage should include.

Religious Opposition to Gay Marriage

An important factor in public opposition to gay marriage is religion— many people claim that gay marriage goes against the teachings of the Bible.

In October 2003, the Pew Forum conducted a survey of more than 1500 people over the age of 18 to determine the importance of religion in their opposition to gay marriage. The survey finds that:

A 55% majority believes it is a sin to engage in homosexual behavior, and that view is much more prevalent among those who have a high level of religious commitment (76%). About half of all Americans have an unfavorable opinion of gay men (50%) and lesbians (48%), but

Here, too, we can see how Ramos has reimagined the material from her open letter, while at the same time giving us much-needed context for the opposition to gay marriage.

Most reports do not cite their research in this way—this is an artifact of Ramos' situation: she is writing it for a class.

highly religious people are much more likely to hold negative views. (Pew Forum, 2003, para. 2)

Clearly, opposition to gay marriage is tied up in both fears and distrust of homosexuals and biblical understandings of "sin."

Family Rights and Civil Rights

Research reports often make use of "call out" boxes to highlight items of importance—here Ramos uses one to show readers how complicated the issue really is. Her section heading also suggests that.

> Hundreds of statutes relate to marriage and its benefits, many concerning property rights, such as tax laws, probate laws, protection from creditors, insurance provisions, and many more. Other areas of statutory rights include marital privilege, bereavement, child custody, and a panoply of other non-property related rights. The children of married couples enjoy legal, social, and economic protections. . . . Without the right to marry—or more properly, the right to choose to marry—one is excluded from the full range of human experience and denied full protection of the laws for one's "avowed commitment to an intimate and lasting human relationship." (Cunningham, 2005, p. 20)

Here she counters the procreation argument against gay marriages—an argument not present in her open letter.

Opposition to gay marriage ignores those very facts—it is a human right to be able to choose whom you want to love and whom you want to marry, and with whom you want to start a family.

In the *Journal of Church and State,* Cunningham (2005) notes that the Massachusetts Supreme Court has defined the institution of marriage as a "civil right" (p.20). He points out that the court, arguing against the Department of Health's position that procreation was the reason for marriage, "found that it is commitment to each other, not procreation, that is the essence of marriage" (p.20).

Notice how differently from the open letter she handles the question of religion and homosexuality.

Arguments that gay marriage is wrong because homosexuals cannot start and raise families ignores the truth: there are many ways to start a family, many of them not "natural." Couples unable to conceive naturally can turn to fertility drugs, artificial insemination, sperm donors, and even surrogate mothers. They may also adopt. And they do so in order to start a family. Gay couples have the same options, and for lesbian partners, that includes carrying "their own" child to term and giving birth.

SAME SEX MARRIAGE   6

And gay couples are already "making families," to no ill effect. A study done by the Williams Institute of the University of California, Los Angeles found that "almost 2% of the nation's 3 million same-sex households include adopted children" (Padgett, 2007, n.p.).

Case Study: Familial Rights—The Price of DOMA and FMA

In 2006, Carla Underwood, an active woman and a homosexual, had an epileptic seizure. It is standard procedure for nurses or caretakers to ask for a contact number of a close family member who could be reached and called upon to make critical health decisions in an emergency situation. When Carla was asked, her immediate thought was her "spouse," Bridgette Joyner.

I began to cry, because I knew that even though Bridgette and I were three years, two children, and new home into our lives together, she could not give a single order for my care. Did I want to be resuscitated if I went into cardiac arrest? Did I want to be an organ donor if I died? Bridgette knows the answers to these questions, but she'd have no say-so, because she's my woman, not my man" (as cited in "Family Values," 2006, p.144).

Carla Underwood had two children from a previous marriage to a man. According to current laws, if Carla dies, her partner, Bridgette, "would have no right to continue caring for our kids" (as cited in "Family Values," 2006, p. 144).

"Our lives are ordinary: household chores, chaperoning school field trips, homework, lullabies, and prayers before bed at night. Since Bridgette and I can't marry, we've taken what few options are available. We have living wills and dual powers of attorney . . . I think back to that day in March when I was in the ambulance. I knew that Bridgette intended to stick by me every step of the way. I know that even if I had died, I wouldn't have been alone" (As cited in "Family Values", 2006, p. 144).

Carla Underwood's experiences and concerns are common. Very few states give the same benefits of marriage or civil unions to same-sex couples. Vermont issues licenses that "give homosexual couples exactly the same

Case studies—the focus on one particular group or person to illustrate a larger point—are common in research reports and other genres.

Ramos uses this case study to put a human face on the issue.

Note that Underwood's voice predominates – Ramos does not inter-ject much.

SAME SEX MARRIAGE   7

"Concluding" with this case study allows Ramos to leave readers with more than a lot of information—they have that, but now they have someone to tie that information to.

benefits and opportunities as they give heterosexual couples—except for the name 'marriage' on the licenses issued to secure the rights and benefits. The licenses for gay and lesbian couples instead have 'civil union' written on them" (Mohr, 2004, p. 34). It's a good start, but according to a study done by the *Advocate,* less than 25% of same-sex partners reside in a state that gives "marriage or marriage like rights" ("20%," 2007, p. 14).

Conclusion

As is typical of the genre, Ramos' conclusion is a short reiteration of her primary points.

The legalization of marriage for homosexuals has become a fight for the human rights of the gay community. Civil unions for homosexuals, an option in only a few states, are only a very small step. The struggle for gay marriage has become not only a fight for the right to marry but, as Carla Underwood states, a fight "for family" ("Family Values," 2006, p.144). DOMA and FMA, pushed by the Bush administration and conservatives across the country, seek to limit the right to a family and unfairly and unethically segregate one part of our society.

SAME SEX MARRIAGE   8

Ramos' sources are formatted in the American Psychological Association style. Please see Chapter 14: Using and Citing Sources for further discussion.

References

20%. (2007, March 27). *Advocate, 982,* 14.

Baker, P. (2007, June 3). Bush re-enters gay marriage fight. *The Washington Post.* Retrieved from http://www.washingtonpost.com

Cunningham, M. T. (2005). Catholics and the concon: The church's response to the Massachusetts gay marriage decision. *Journal of Church & State, 47*(1), 19–42.

Defense of Marriage Act of 1996, *Pub. Law No. 104-199, 110 Stat. 2419 (1996).*

DOMA watch. (n.d.). Federal defense of marriage act (DOMA). Retrieved March 1, 2008, from http://www.domawatch.org/about/federaldoma.html

Family values. (2006, December). *Essence, 37*(8), 144.

Marriage Protection Act of 2004, H.R. 3313, 108th Cong. (2004). Retrieved from http://www.govtrack.us/congress/bill.xpd?bill=h108-3313

Mohr, R. D. (2004) Equal dignity under the law. *Gay & Lesbian Review Worldwide, 11*(5), 30–35.

Padgett, T. (2007). Gay family values. *Time, 170*(3), 51–52.

Pew Forum on Religion and Public Life. (2003). Religious beliefs underpin opposition to homosexuality. Retrieved from http://pewforum.org/docs/?DocID=37

Pew Forum on Religion and Public Life. (2006). Pragmatic Americans liberal and conservative on social issues. Retrieved from http://pewforum.org/docs/?DocID=150

United Nations. (1948). Universal declaration of human rights. Retrieved from http://www.un.org/Overview/rights.html

Questions for Analysis

1. Having read both Ramos' open letter and her research report, how successfully do you think she crossed genres? What might you have done differently?

2. Ramos addressed some concerns in her open letter that were not present in her research report. Why do you think she made this choice? Do you think she could have effectively dealt with those same concerns in the report?

CHAPTER 2

Critical Reading and Analysis Strategies

You may not think of yourself as a careful and critical reader, especially if you don't do a lot of reading. This, however, is not necessarily the case. Critical reading is something you practice daily as you look at the world around you. Because when we talk about reading, we are talking about more than what you do when you look at words on a page. When we use the term read, we mean something more like "decode," and when we use the term text, we mean any message—written, visual, spoken—that can be decoded.

What Is Critical Reading?

During a normal day, we read a lot of different kinds of texts—often without even realizing that we are doing so. When we get up in the morning, we might look over the newspaper or check our email, making decisions or drawing conclusions about what we read. If we turn on the television to watch the last night's sports highlights on ESPN, we immediately go into critical reading mode as we ask questions to ourselves: How can they make such claims about the Cubs? Haven't they looked at the statistics? Or we might start talking to our spouse or roommate and realize that they are a bit surlier this morning than usual, so we read them: What's going on?

So, to read something critically is to first read in order to understand the content. We read our spouse or the sports highlights and we understand the content: Our spouse is grumpy and the Cubs are behind in the standings. But reading critically goes beyond comprehension. When we read critically we try to understand at least three things: 1) why something is so; 2) how it came to be so; and 3) whether and how it is valid. When we read a text critically to understand it, we are asking: What and how does this text mean?

You are already a critical reader—someone who observes, analyzes, questions, and comments on the texts around you. This chapter aims to simply help you discover and build on these skills and give you the language to describe what you already do.

Why Read Critically?

In fundamental terms, being critical about something means to be both skeptical and open-minded. In a sense we are saying, "Okay, I'm going to assume you are telling me the truth, but I'm also going to make sure that you are." Critical readers are not cynics who believe that everyone is out to take advantage of them. Instead, critical readers assume that all individuals have a vested interest in their own biases and needs. After all, we all want to believe that our view is correct, reasonable, and unbiased, but if we are honest, we realize that often it is not—at least not entirely. Reading critically helps us to identify the logical flaws, irrational assumptions, and biases in the messages we encounter.

The rest of the chapter focuses on two approaches to reading: reading for comprehension and reading analytically—that is, reading to understand what a text means and reading to understand how a text works.

For both approaches, though, we suggest beginning in the same place: with the genre. Understanding what genre you are reading gives you valuable insight into the content and purpose of the text. Knowing that you are about to read a research report, for instance, tells you a lot before you read it: You know it will be formal, will draw heavily on research, and will help you to better understand the issue or topic, and so on. Similarly, knowing that you are about to read a memoir tells you not to expect a formal tone, but instead to expect to learn something about the author's past experiences.

Reading a Text for What It Means

Before we can really understand how a text is working, we have to first understand what it is saying. In other words, we have to read first for comprehension, to understand the message of a particular text.

You may already be familiar with some strategies for how to read a text for comprehension, such as previewing, annotating, summarizing, outlining, and responding. These are tools to help you engage with the text in order to both understand and evaluate it.

Remember that these strategies do not necessarily have to happen in this particular order, nor must they all be followed in order to successfully read and understand a text. In fact, as you become more practiced at critical reading, these strategies may become less discrete; thus you'll be annotating as you outline, for instance.

Previewing

A movie preview gives you the gist of the film without all the details. When you preview a text, you perform a similar act; you preview the text to try to get a quick, general sense of what it is about in order to anticipate and predict what the author will say.

■ For instance, when you are first given the syllabus for a course, you preview its contents. That is, you skim over it and look at the way it is laid out on the page. You know that when something is in bold or bulleted or has a subheading, it means the instructor wants to draw your attention to that part of the text. You read the syllabus and other genres looking for something in particular. Knowing that a syllabus gives you information about the work you'll be doing in the course, you might find yourself quickly scanning the "assignments" section to find out just how much work you'll be asked to do. Similarly, when you receive an email from your boss, because you know something about the writer, you scan looking for what she wants from you.

There are many reasons why we preview a text:

- To establish whether we are already familiar with the subject or other texts like it.
- To be able to evaluate the text's effectiveness.
- To find out whether we want to read it at all.
- To find out the major points.

Perhaps most importantly, previewing helps you better understand the material because skimming a text helps you get a sense of what it is about.

Of course, why you actually read a text will depend on the context in which you find yourself reading it. If you have been assigned a text for a course, you don't really have the choice of previewing it in order to figure out if you want to read it at all. However, if you preview an assigned text and you really don't think you're going to enjoy it, this gives you a good starting point for later evaluation: Did you actually end up enjoying it after you finished, or were your initial assumptions correct?

NUMBER TWO   SEPTEMBER 2006

Is this the organization? If so, all the issues, including this one, will be focused on children, I would think.

Katrina Response: *Protecting the Children of the Storm*

Issue Brief tells me at least two things: this text will be brief and it will focus on one issue.

Two titles: so is the first an ongoing subject and the second the specific content of this "issue brief"?

In August 2005, Hurricane Katrina wreaked havoc along the U.S. Gulf Coast, leaving more than 1,300 people dead, forcing 1 million people from their homes, and inflicting unprecedented property damage. It also left 372,000 children without schools.

The brunt of the storm fell hardest on the region's poorest and neediest children and adults, who fled their homes and took shelter in hastily improvised facilities in convention centers, churches and even cruise ships. Assistance for displaced families came from all quarters: Federal, state and local agencies joined forces with nongovernmental organizations, churches and community groups to provide shelter, food and medical care.

This looks like a report, so I'm going to expect lots of research?

This paragraph summarizes the problems children in the region faced post-Katrina and explains the urgency and purpose for the report.

However, as in most large-scale crises, the unique needs of children were not a priority in disaster relief or recovery plans. Children struggled to cope with the aftermath of the storm, often in overcrowded, noisy, poorly equipped shelters without safe places to play and surrounded by strangers. Many had experienced the devastating loss of family members, neighbors or friends. Virtually all had lost their homes, schools and neighborhoods. The routines that defined their daily lives—studies, school activities and play—were swept away overnight.

Now, a year after the storm, children still face enormous challenges. Many still live in temporary and often unwelcoming situations. They have lost their communities and schools, disrupting social networks and learning. And studies have found high rates of depression, anxiety and behavioral problems among many children trying to make their way in a post-Katrina world.

"One key lesson learned from Hurricane Katrina is that the unique needs of children in crisis situations must be addressed in future national emergency response plans. Save the Children's goal is to ensure that children are a top priority at every phase of a U.S. humanitarian response."

Mark Shriver, Vice President and Managing Director of U.S. Programs, Save the Children

Sample Preview

Notice as you look at the example below that the reader's response to this text is rather casual; that is, she has responded to it based on her own personal reaction while at the same time she has taken note of what seems to be important. As you look over her response, measure it against your own. What would you have commented on? Why?

> In just looking at this first page of the report, I already know that I'm going to be given a lot of information about the response to Katrina and how it has affected the children. I also know that this is an ongoing concern—at least the concern for children, since the "author" is a group called Save the Children. I don't know much, yet, about the content or what they are going to recommend, though I can probably predict that they'll argue the need for better protection of children and the need to address some of the problems children faced as a result of Hurricane Katrina as the last paragraph suggests.

GUIDELINES: PREVIEWING

1. Identify the genre. What do you know about it?
2. Read the title. What does it tell you about the subject and the writer's position on it?
3. Make note of where the text was published. What does the type of publication tell you about the text?
4. Does it reveal anything about the likely focus of the text in front of you?
5. Scan the pages looking for subtitles or other distinctive textual features. Do they tell anything about how the writer is developing his or her point? Sometimes subheadings serve as a kind of outline.
6. Examine if the text is heavily researched. Are there in-text citations? Is there a bibliography and how extensive is it?
7. When you are done previewing, take a minute and jot down some notes on what you learned about the text and what you think the writer is going to say in it.

Annotating

You might notice that the reader's preview of the *Save the Children* Issue Brief is expressed as notes to herself in the margins of the text. Her strategy of marginal and interlinear notes is called annotation. Annotation, the simple act of making notes on the page in order to make sense of the text, is the single most important step in critically reading a text because it forces you to pay attention to what is being said. We all have a tendency to doze off as we read or get distracted by what's around us. Annotating keeps us focused on the text.

In the text that follows, we provide a sample annotation of a common civic genre—the op-ed. An op-ed (so-called because it appears opposite the newspaper's editorials) is a genre used to comment on current issues and concerns, to open up a dialogue between writers and readers. In the past, this dialogue was more metaphorical than real, but now online newspapers routinely provide a "reader's forum" or a comment feature where readers can respond directly to articles.

As you read this op-ed, notice what the reader has chosen to comment on, but consider too what you might have reacted to differently.

A View to the Contrary

Terry Starkey Williston
Bismarck Tribune February 4th, 2008

This is an op-ed, so I know it will be opinionated. The title tells me he's going to argue another side of something.

What bothers me is there is virtually no debate on whether or not warming is good or bad. Environmentalists believe it's bad, and greenhouse gas emissions are the culprit, but some reputable climate scientists argue that warming could be the result of solar activity.

Whoa, jumps right into it here. So he doesn't buy what the media is saying.

Are certain groups genuinely concerned about the environment, or is there a political agenda?

Not about the media, after all. Whose political agenda?

Al Gore is flitting about the world trashing the United States, claiming we are the world's biggest polluter, ignoring that China and India are at least as bad as we are.

Are we? Can't really picture Gore flitting around.

He and the United Nations International Panel for Climate Change received a Nobel Peace Prize "for their efforts to build up and disseminate greater knowledge about man-made climate change, and to lay the foundations for the measures that are needed to counteract such change."

Disseminate: to share.

A British High Court justice ruled that Gore's movie, "An Inconvenient Truth," had a minimum of nine seriously incorrect assertions and couldn't be shown to school children without a warning. The justice ruled the video could still be shown in school, but only if it is accompanied by guidance notes warning of its inaccuracies and one-sidedness. He also stated there was "a view to the contrary."

Why is the British court mentioned?

Must be where he got his title from?

Many European nations signing on to the Kyoto Accord have soaring rates of greenhouse emissions after having agreed to caps. The U.S. has the best emissions record in the industrialized world for the past decade.

According to whom? What is our record? How does it compare to other "industrialized nations"?

I don't know what Gore's agenda is, but I am uncomfortable with how he presents the United States and scary scenarios to the rest of the world.

I also am uncomfortable with the thought of the United Nations dictating environmental policy for the U.S.

Isn't the point of the U.N. to find ways to get countries to work together?

Global warming may be bad or it may be good. My feeling is that it is a little of both, and we have to be wary of those who claim to know what is best for the planet.

Well, I kind of get what this guy's writing about—he certainly raises a good point about the need for a conversation about global warming. He seems really to have a problem with Gore and those like him. Wonder why? He's also not a big fan of the U.N., but I'm not sure how it connects. I'm not entirely convinced, because he doesn't provide much evidence. I think if I wrote him back, I'd begin there, with what I felt was missing from the letter.

GUIDELINES: ANNOTATING

1. Read with pen in hand. Do not use a highlighter because it's easy to lose focus, and before you know it you've turned the whole page bright yellow. Reserve the highlighter for the most important parts of the text after you've read the whole thing.
2. Underline or circle key terms and phrases. In the margins, note why you underlined or circled them (you're likely to forget by the time you come back to them later).
3. Circle words you don't know, then look them up and write the definitions in the margins. After all, if you don't understand the language, you won't understand the text. This step is particularly important when reading texts that are written by and for specialists, as they often use a particular vocabulary (or jargon) that non-specialists are unfamiliar with.
4. Make notes in the margins about ideas or statements that engage you and why.
5. Make notes in the margins about ideas or statements that confuse you. Say why it confuses you.: Is the language difficult? Is the example unclear? It might be the writer's explanation is unclear, the audience is not on target, or the example is unfamiliar to you. In these cases, the writer may need to do some revising.
6. Make notes in the margins about how the material is arranged. Do you notice how the writer has moved logically from one idea to the next? Is the writer making use of any obvious arrangement strategies (e.g. subheadings)? Why might the writer have done so?
7. Reflect on your comments. What is your understanding of the text now? How did the actual content compare with what you thought it was about as you previewed it? What's your reaction to the text? Are you confused, clear, or a little of both?

Outlining

We tend to think of outlining as a writing strategy, but it is also a good reading strategy. Outlining is simply the process of writing down the subjects or main ideas that a text addresses. So when we outline a text, we are really looking to see how it fits together on a larger scale—what each paragraph is about and how each paragraph connects to the ones around it.

When we outline, then, we are really just getting a sense of topics and arrangement. And since at this point we are only interested in a rough sense of how the text fits together, the simplest approach is to make a scratch outline. With a scratch outline, you don't need to use formal outlining notation (no Roman numerals, no A- and B-heads); instead, you simply note in the margins or on a separate sheet of paper what each paragraph is about and how it connects to the one before it.

A scratch outline of the op-ed piece "A View to the Contrary" by Terry Starkey (p. 34) might look something like this:

Paragraph 1:   Established the problem that the jury is still out on global warming
Paragraph 2:   Because the author doesn't believe what he has read, he suggests that there is another agenda
Paragraph 3:   Introduces Gore as the person with another agenda—says he ignores the true polluters
Paragraph 4:   Tells us that Gore and the U.N. won the Nobel Peace Prize
Paragraph 5:   Calls into question the Nobel by quoting British High Court saying there was another view on the matter
Paragraph 6:   Says that Europe has signed onto the Kyoto accord, and the U.S. has the best emissions record. (Is he saying that we have not signed on to it, because of this?)
Paragraph 7:   Returns to Gore, and he's upset by Gore's accusations about the U.S.
Paragraph 8:   Returns to the U.N., and he is worried that the U.N. might tell the U.S. what to do
Paragraph 9:   Concludes by saying global warming may or may not be bad, but that we should be wary of people saying they know what to do

What you'll probably notice here is that the outline begins to suggest some of the reasons why the writer might have written what he did. So in this case, the outline also serves as a valuable tool for understanding the purpose of a text, as well as how the argument is put together.

GUIDELINES: OUTLINING

1. Preview the text to see if there are section headings, sub-headings, or other such devices that might reveal an organizational pattern or specific content.
2. Skim the text, looking for major points – Each paragraph may or may not have a single claim.
3. Make note of how one point builds on the previous – If it is unclear to you how the arguments build on each other, indicate that lack of connectivity among the arguments.
4. Write out a brief outline in which you list all of the major points. Use your own words to do so, perhaps quoting key phrases or words used by the writer.

Summary

A summary is essentially an overview of what the text is about: the writer's argument and purpose, major points, and evidence. Sometimes, in a critical summary, you might also evaluate the text—but that kind of summary requires closer reading than the kind we address here. All the information you just noted in your annotation and outline will help you to write a summary.

The basic premise behind the use of summarizing as a critical strategy is simple: If you are unable to state clearly and succinctly what a text is about (or what the writer's argument is), then you have not read it closely enough and you cannot respond to it in any meaningful way.

A basic summary for the op-ed "A View to the Contrary" (p. 35) would look something like this:

Summary of "A View to the Contrary"

Identifies the writer and title, and then articulates what the main point of the article is.
States the main points and the evidence provided by the author.

Points out that the author returns to his main point in the conclusion of the article.

In his op-ed called "A View to the Contrary," Terry Starkey claims that we are moving too fast in our assumption that global warming is the threat we are told it is. He suggests that there may be another agenda at work, and further suggests that this agenda comes from Al Gore and the U.N. International Panel for Climate Change. His claim that this agenda is not completely accurate is supported by a statement from the British High Court. He also supports this by mentioning that the U.S. has the best emissions record. He concludes by expressing concern about Al Gore's comments about the U.S. and the U.N.'s possible involvement with U.S. policy. In his conclusion, he returns to his initial point that we should be wary of anyone who claims to have the answer, because global warming is still not proven.

GUIDELINES: SUMMARIZING

1. Preview, annotate, and outline the text (see Guidelines, pp. 33, 35, and 36).
2. Look over your notes.
3. Begin your summary by telling the reader the name of the text and author (and sometimes where it was published) and identify the primary argument or point.
4. Identify the main points the author used to develop the argument and note briefly the evidence or support she uses to develop them, ending with the author's own conclusions.

Response

You respond to texts in any number of ways, from "this is great" to "I can't believe she'd write this!" In this chapter, "response" also means something more than just saying "I like it" or "I don't like it," although such a reaction is often where we start when we respond critically to a text. Critical response prompts the readers of a text to dig deeper—to make sense of that initial gut reaction to a text and to ask why we may or may not like something, or why it confuses us, or why the text makes us think about something else.

A critical response to Starkey's letter (p. 34) might look something like this:

Quotes from the text in order to support claims about the text.

Offers a counterargument to the author's point.

Starkey seems to jump right into the issue about global warming in paragraph one, "What bothers me is there is virtually no debate on whether or not global warming is good or bad," but the rest of his letter isn't really talking about that. Starkey's questioning the political agendas of Gore and the U.N., suggesting that the Nobel prize perhaps was what Gore had his eyes on, while offering criticisms from various groups (who is the British High Court?) on

Suggests how the author could have better developed his ideas.

Tries to figure out what the author might really be worried about.

Points out flaws in the author's argument.

Gore's film. It would be a more persuasive argument if he had included one or two examples of the supposed "errors" in the film as "evidence" to support his claims. But what Starkey really seems worried about is that the U.N. will have a hand in designing U.S. environmental policies. Why? Who is this author and what is his agenda? He keeps mentioning he doesn't know if global warming is good or bad, repeating again in the last paragraph the opening statement. That makes no sense, argumentatively—would anyone say global warming is "good?"

How you respond to a text depends a lot on why you are reading it in the first place. For instance, your boss might want your reaction to the latest report on sales or your friend might want to know what you think about the claim a writer is making about the best movie of all time.

The guidelines below should help you read to respond to a text. When readers practice responding critically, they are also working on decoding a text or taking it apart. We call that kind of reading *critical analysis*.

GUIDELINES: RESPONDING

1. Preview the text. What is your initial reaction to it?
2. Read and annotate the text, perhaps writing a scratch outline in the margins.
3. Write a response. When you have finished, consider the following for your response writing questions:
   - Did your initial reaction change as you read the text more carefully?
   - What is the writer's argument, and do you agree or disagree with it?
   - What do you think about the quality of the writer's evidence?
   - Did the writer leave important ideas out? Do you think the writer developed her ideas fully?
   - What influences your response? Previous experiences? Familiarity with the topic? Other things?

WRITING ACTIVITY   Practice Reading a Text for What It Means

Apply the skills you just learned to the following letter to the editor written by Ray French called "Taking Back Our Tuition," published in the University of Wisconsin student newspaper, the *Spectator*.

First preview the text to get a sense of what it's about, then read it closely, annotating it as you read. Construct a scratch outline, and then conclude with a brief summary. When you have finished, compare your response to those of your classmates. How were the responses similar? How were they different? What do you think accounts for the differences, especially in constructing the scratch outline and the summary?

■ ■ ■

Taking Back Our Tuition:
Students Need to Push to Keep College Affordable

Ray French **Posted: 2/7/08**

With the current state of higher education funding in Wisconsin and the country, how can tuition rise any more? Well I'm writing to tell you that it will continue to rise, with a significant jump occurring in the next two years, if we let it happen. OK, I'm getting ahead of myself.

Before initiating this revolution, I need to address how I know that tuition is going to keep increasing. First, all signs are pointing toward this end. According the 07–08 UW System Fact Book, students and the state are contributing nearly identical amounts of money to fund this system. In the last ten years alone, the percentage of the total cost of instruction—how much it costs for us to attend classes—what students are paying has increased from 35.8 percent to 55.8 percent. In those same ten years, the state contribution to the whole UW System has decreased from 33.75 percent to 24.21 percent. There is a plethora of information out there to show the state is failing to provide for the UW System and that students are picking up the slack.

Another indication that tuition is going to significantly increase very soon is through a draft report released over Winterim by the UW System Tuition and Financial Aid Workgroup. This committee's goal was to determine how to raise tuition and get the most out of it in the least controversial manner. Throughout the entire report there is negligible regard for the amount students are currently paying. Their main argument is because the UW System is about $1,000 below the median of our peer institutions, we should at the very least raise tuition $1,000. And if we look closely to the Advantage Wisconsin efforts of the UW System, we will see that they are trying to figure out how to do the most with the money we keep losing. Remember when the 2-year colleges received a tuition freeze for this academic year? If I were a betting man, I would bet that the main reason it happened was so we could stay competitive with the Wisconsin Technical College System that has lower tuition than our 2-year colleges, and not out of concern for students. The Tuition and Financial Aid Workgroup report nearly lets that cat out of the bag.

Another interesting fact is that since its conception in 1972, the UW System has been losing money from the state. Every year, the UW System is cut. Every year, the UW System raises tuition. But these tuition increases do not match the money we are losing. In 1972, the state provided $272.3 million to the UW System. In 2006, the state provided $218.2 million, in 1972 dollars adjusted for inflation. Slowly but surely, the UW System is going from a state supported public higher education system to a user and donor supported private education system.

As you know, we are the debt generation. Many of us have credit card debt. Many of us also have significant federal loans to pay back after graduation. In the latest UW System report, the average student will graduate with more than $20,000 worth of loan debt, not accounting for credit card debt. This is outrageous. We currently have administration and a few select student leaders telling us to be realistic about this budget cycle and not fret about tuition.

It's not going to be that easy.

It is time that we, as students, organize and tell our administration, regents and legislators that we are not going to stand for any more tuition abuse. We chose the UW System because it is one of the greatest public higher education systems in the country. It didn't get that way through the unrelenting taxing of students. We are who we are because of the foresight of past administrators, regents and legislators. What amazes me is that the data is there. We know and can prove what a significant investment in higher education can do for this state. Instead we focus on how to raise tuition without upsetting students and how to do the most with the money that we're losing.

Students, this is our time. Our involvement in the 2006 midterm elections changed the tide of politics in Wisconsin. Our involvement in the primaries around the country has already had significant effects on the candidates. We need to organize, get upset and demand that our administrations, regents and legislators prioritize higher education in Wisconsin the way they did in the past. This is the beginning of a movement. We want lower tuition. We want the money stolen from the UW System to be returned. Our education, for Wisconsin's sake and ours, is too fragile for politics. We're losing the tuition battle but we can't afford to lose the education war.

French is the student body president and guest columnist for The Spectator.

Reading a Text for How It Works

As suggested at the start of this chapter, we read critically in order to understand not only *what* a text says but also *how* it says it. We recognize, as readers, that messages are created for various reasons: the advertisement to sell, the love letter to woo, the essay to explore. Understanding how a text works requires that we understand what it is about; once we understand the text, we can then begin to analyze it.

As critical readers, once we see how a text is constructed, we can begin to *evaluate* the choices a writer made when putting the text together: What is his purpose? What is his position on the subject? What kinds of arguments does he make? How does he use evidence to support his arguments, and what kinds did he choose? How is the text organized? How does the text appeal to us, the readers? Thus, we can determine if the text does effectively what the writer intends it to do.

Analyzing a text in part means decoding, or breaking it down into parts to see how it is put together to create meaning. Think of it this way: A film critic may look at a film and analyze the parts (acting, camera angles, setting, lighting, musical score, etc.) to understand its composition. Then the critic evaluates how well the film is put together to do what the director intended it to do. Similarly, when we read written texts analytically, we examine the parts that make up the whole text.

Throughout the remainder of this chapter, we will use the editorial "Sports Centered" by Jay Weiner to explore some of the specific elements that you should consider when analyzing a text—including genre, the writer, the publication, introductions and conclusions, the writer's position, arguments, and evidence. "Sports Centered" by Jay Weiner was originally written for the *Minneapolis Star Tribune* and reprinted in the *Utne Reader*, a publication which compiles articles from a variety of newspaper and magazine sources.

Sports Centered

Jay Weiner, Utne Reader

The writer begins with questions to introduce the issue and pique our interest.

How far back must we go to remember that sports matter? How deeply into our personal and national pasts must we travel to recall that we once cared?

Do we have to return to 1936? Adolf Hitler tried to make the Olympics into a propaganda machine for anti-Semitism and racism. In that case, American track star Jesse Owens, demonstrating that the master race could be mastered at racing, stole Hitler's ideological show. Were not sports a vehicle of significant political substance then?

Notice the references to and examples of sports figures who made significant social contributions—who made sports matter in American culture. He must have done his research.

Or should we return to 1947 and Jackie Robinson? A baseball player integrated our "national pastime" a year before the U.S. Army considered African Americans equal. Robinson's barrier-break may have been largely based on ticket-selling economics for the Brooklyn Dodgers' owners, but didn't sports do something good?

Their fists raised, their dignity palpable, track stars Tommie Smith and John Carlos spread the American black power and student protest movements to the world when they stood on the victory stand at the 1968 Olympics in Mexico City. Politics and sports mixed beautifully then.

Weiner's getting at his argument . . . why he wants to write about sports—how things seem to have changed in the sports world today.

Remember when tennis feminist Billie Jean King took on an old fart named Bobby Riggs in 1973, boldly bringing the women's movement to the playing fields? That moment of sports theater stirred up sexual politics as much as any Betty Friedan essay or Miss America bra burning could ever do.

Sports had meaning. And sports were accessible.

He uses language that is sensory, making us think about when we were kids going to sports events with family and friends—he really wants us to tap our memories and emotions about sports' meaning for us.

Remember when your grandfather or your uncle—maybe your mother—took you to a game when you were a little kid? The hot dog was the best. The crowd was mesmerizing. The colors were bright. The crack of the bat under the summer sun, or the autumn chill wrapped around that touchdown run, was unforgettable. Back then, some nobody became your favorite player, somebody named Johnny Callison or Hal Greer or Clarence Peaks or Vic Hadfield, someone who sold cars in the off-season and once signed autographs for your father's men's club for a $50 appearance fee. Those "heroes" were working-class stiffs, just like us.

More colorful language here.

Now you read the sports pages—or, more exactly, the business and crime pages—and you realize you've disconnected from the institution and it from you. Sports is distant. It reeks of greed. Its politics glorify not the majestic drama of pure competition, but a drunken, gambling masculinity epitomized by sports-talk radio, a venue for obnoxious boys on car phones.

Aha, here's the problem, clearly identified as Weiner sees it. . . .

How can we reconcile our detachment from corporatized pro sports, professionalized college sports—even out-of-control kids' sports—with our appreciation for athleticism, with our memories? And how, after we sort it all out, can we take sports back?

Here's one of his major claims—we are part of the problem.

Part of the problem is that we want sports to be mythological when, in our hearts, we know they aren't. So reclaiming sports requires that we come to grips with our own role in the myth-making. Owens, Robinson, Smith, Carlos, and King played to our highest ideals and so have been enshrined in our sports pantheon. But we've also made heroes of some whose legacies are much less clear-cut. Take Joe Namath, the 1960s quarterback who represented sexual freedom, or Bill Walton, the 1970s basketball hippie who symbolized the alienated white suburban Grateful Dead sports antihero. Neither deserves the reverence accorded Owens or Robinson or even King, but both captured the essence of their era. Or how about relief pitcher Steve Howe, who symbolized the evils of drug addiction in the '80s, or Mike Tyson, who currently plays the archetypal angry black male? No less than Tommie Smith and John Carlos, these anti-icons were emblematic of their age.

We, sports fans, have contributed to the problem—look at these examples, obviously he's done research.

He reiterates the claim, here—the genre allows for this.

It may be discomfiting, but it's true: The power of sports and sports heroes to mirror our own aspirations have also contributed to the sorry state of the institution today. The women's sports movement Billie Jean King helped create proved a great leap forward for female athletes, but it also created a generation of fitness consumers, whose appetite for Nikes and Reeboks created a new generation of Asian sweatshops.

Here he uses colorful language to imply the problem.

Fans applauded the courage of renegade Curt Flood, the St. Louis Cardinals outfielder who in 1969 refused to be traded, arguing that baseball players should be free to play where they want to play. We cheered—all the way to the Supreme Court—his challenge to the cigar-smoking owners' hold on their pinstripe-knickered chattel. Now players can sell their services to the highest bidder, but their astronomical salaries—deserved or not—alienate us from the games as much as the owners' greed.

The language used in this section moves readers to become angry—angry at how fans have been lied to, how players, owners have become focused on love of money v. love of game. . . .

The greed isn't new, of course. The corporate betrayal of the fan is as traditional as the seventh-inning stretch. The Boston Braves moved to Milwaukee in 1953, and the Dodgers and New York Giants fled to California in 1958, for money, subsidized facilities, and better TV contracts. But what has always been a regrettable by-product of sports has suddenly become its dominant ethos. Our worship of sports and our worship of the buck have now become one and the same. So it shouldn't surprise us that we get the heroes we expect—and maybe deserve.

Weiner signals that he's about to offer some suggestions to fix the problem.

So how do we as a society reclaim sports from the corporate entertainment behemoth that now controls it? Some modest proposals:

- **Deprofessionalize college and high school sports.**
  Let's ban college athletic scholarships in favor of financial aid based on need, as for any other student. And let's keep high school athletics in perspective. Why should local news coverage of high school sports exceed coverage given to the band, debating society, or science fair? Sports stars are introduced to the culture of athletic privilege at a very young age.

Notice that he does not say "we should do this first" or "this is the most important step"—he seems to allow the reader to choose which are most important.

- **Allow some form of public ownership of professional sports teams.**
  Leagues and owners ask us to pay for the depreciating asset of a stadium but give us no share of the appreciating asset of a franchise. Lease agreements between teams and publicly financed stadiums should also include enforceable community-involvement clauses.

- **Make sports affordable again.**
  Sports owners call their games "family entertainment." For whose family? Bill Gates'? Owners whose teams get corporate subsidies should set aside 20 percent of their tickets at prices no higher than a movie admission. And, like any other business feeding at the public trough, they should be required to pay livable wages even to the average schmoes who sell hot dogs.

- **Be conscious of the messages sports is sending.**
  Alcohol-related advertising should be banned from sports broadcasting. Any male athlete convicted of assaulting a woman should be banned from college and pro sports. Fighting in a sports event should be at least a misdemeanor and maybe a felony, rather than a five-minute stay in the penalty box.

These examples of how we view sports appeal to fans' values—sports bring us together, unifies us, we have heroes to admire . . .

Let's take the sports establishment by its lapels and shake it back toward us. Because even with all the maddening messages of male dominance, black servility, homophobia, corporate power, commercialism, and brawn over brains, sports still play an important role in many lives. When we watch a game, we are surrounded by friends and family. There are snacks and beverages. We sit in awe of the players' remarkable skills. We can't do what they do. They extend our youth. The tension of the competition is legitimate. The drama is high.

Again, he repeats his major claim.

And therein lies the essence of modern American sport. It's a good show, albeit bread and circuses. And we just can't give it up. So why not take it back for ourselves as best we can, looking for ways to humanize an institution that mirrors our culture, understanding that those who own sport won't give it up without a fight, knowing that we like it too much to ever just walk away.

Some information on the author for readers to think about his credibility

Jay Weiner is a sportswriter for the Minneapolis-based Star Tribune *and author of the forthcoming book* Stadium Games: Fifty Years of Big League Greed and Bush League Boondoggles, *to be published this spring by University of Minnesota Press.*

Analyzing the Contexts of a Text

When we read analytically, we look for information that might identify the writer, his perspective, where and when the text was published, how the writer connects with his audience, the kinds of language he uses, the genre, and the situation a writer finds himself in that makes him choose that genre.

Looking at the Genre

When you read critically, begin with what you know or can find out about the genre. Not only will this information tell you how to approach the text, but it will also allow you to critically evaluate it. Additionally, it will enable you to figure out quickly what characteristics of the genre you should look for. For example, if you're reading a research report, you know you're going to be reading a research heavy document. If you don't find that research or if it seems a little "light," that tells you something important right away—and you are less likely to trust the writer's conclusions because she has not backed up her claims or reflect the characteristics of the genre.

In Weiner's example, he chose to write an editorial, a genre that enables a writer to express his opinion on a subject freely without having to formally use sources. Editorials also allow writers to use colloquial and colorful expressions, which in Weiner's case is important because of his subject and his audience. Editorials are also concise and persuasive, so Weiner establishes the problem and proposes solutions in a limited space—he does not have to be overly detailed about his solutions or in defining the problem.

GUIDELINES: LOOKING AT THE GENRE

1. Identify the genre. Sometimes the title will give it away: "The Ozarks: A Memoir" or "A Report on the Increased Use of Oxycontin in Rural Maine." Where it is published may reveal something about the genre: On the op-ed page, it's probably a letter to the editor.
   - Is the genre clear in the first few paragraphs? If you can't tell what the genre is just by glancing at the text, read a few lines or paragraphs. For example, the use of informal language, lots of very colorful expressions, and no cited research suggests a civic genre.
2. What are some of the characteristics of this genre?

Looking at the Writer

Examining the writer may help you better understand his position and why he is making the arguments he makes. When we examine the writer, we want to know about the writer's expertise, organizational or group affiliations, professional status, or educational background—all information that may help us determine credibility.

So, if for instance our global warming letter writer (p. 34) is a staff science columnist for the *Boston Globe,* we'd want to know that in order to better understand the writer's credibility to speak on the issue at hand. The key word here is credibility. We want to know what gives the writer the expertise to comment on or establish a position on a topic, and we are more inclined to listen, even if we don't agree, knowing that the writer has a credible reputation—or to read even more carefully if the writer does not.

We may also want to know if the writer belongs to any political groups, advocacy organizations, or community groups that can reveal something about his perspective to us. If our global warming letter writer is the CEO of a major automobile manufacturing corporation which is under scrutiny for contributing to global warming, this would certainly tell us something about why the writer has such a hard time with Gore's film and the U.N.'s potentially setting U.S. environmental policy.

Often, we can find out about the writer's expertise, organizational or group affiliations, professional status, or educational background simply from reading the biographical note that appears either at the beginning or the end of articles in many magazines and newspapers.

However, many times an author note is not provided. How then do we get information about the author that can help us understand why he felt compelled to write what he did or what gives the writer authority to speak on the issue? All the information you probably need about an author is right there in front of you, in the text he has written. We can use our critical reading and analyzing skills to sift through the text and glean from it information that will reveal to us some things about the writer.

Like what, you may ask? Well, one place to look at is the writer's use of research and the sources from which he draws his evidence. For example, if our global warming writer uses references from environmental science journals or includes expert opinions on legislation passed recently on global warming, we can probably understand that he has done some research or knows his subject well enough to draw from these sources. We look at the kinds of evidence the writer provides to say "yes, this is convincing or persuasive" or "no, I'm still not sure how this writer drew his conclusions; the evidence is a little fuzzy." Similarly, some genres, like the research report or academic proposal, include a works cited or reference list that establishes what sources the writer has drawn upon. We may examine such references for their relevance and credibility, which in turn lets us evaluate the writer's credibility.

If you are still unsure about the writer's credibility, you can then do some background research on the author. Again, while your first instinct is probably to do a Google search, you might want to try one of your library's online databases first. It is actually much easier to find what you want in databases since they contain popular *and* scholarly texts. (See Chapter 13: Research and the Rhetorical Situation for further discussion.)

For example, if we wanted to find out more about Jay Weiner, the author of "Sports Centered," we would begin by evaluating the short blurb about him found at the end of the article. Because he has written a book on sports, we can assume that he is an expert on his subject, and that he is employed full time as a writer also tells us something important— his work is good enough that a major publisher pays him for it. So initially, anyway, we can consider him credible.

But if we felt that this wasn't enough, we could search in a database to find out just how much he has written, and on what. Using LexisNexis, because it covers articles and news items published in major newspapers and other sources, we found out the following about Jay Weiner. (Remember, this was not an in-depth study, just enough to get a sense of the writer.)

- He's published numerous articles, many for the *Star Tribune,* including those picked up by other publications like the *New York Times* and *Business Week Online.*
- He's also published scholarly essays in journals like the *Journal of Exercise and Sports Psychology.* This fact gives us a sense of his credibility, because academic journals often

have high standards for the quality of the essays they publish, and they have a rigorous peer review process (where others in the field read and evaluate potential articles for the journal).

Given the kinds of material he has published and where, we can be confident that he has the authority and credibility to make the kinds of claims he does.

GUIDELINES: LOOKING AT THE WRITER

1. Analyze the writer's use of research.
   - Does the writer seem like an authority on his subject? What kinds of research does the writer draw from to build his credibility?
   - Does the writer provide appropriate support for his claims?
2. Analyze the writer's credentials.
   - What are the writer's credentials? Is the writer an expert or professional on the subject?
   - What else has the writer written on the subject?
   - Does the writer belong to any political, advocacy, or community organization groups that tell us something about his biases?
   - Is there a headnote, author note, or can I check a library database to find out more about this author?

Examining the Publication

When we examine the publication, we should look at both the publication type (newspaper, a blog, a magazine, a book, etc.) and the publisher, which is the company or organization that paid for it to be published. You know that certain publications cater to certain kinds of interests—readers read *People* magazine to find out about Hollywood stars; readers read *Timber Homes Illustrated* to get ideas about remodeling or building their log home. When we analyze the publication, then, we are asking a number of questions: What kinds of texts does this publisher print? Have they published other texts on similar topics? Who tends to read this publication?

Finding out about a publication is pretty straightforward. Since most publications have a website, we need to simply find it and go to the "about" section. There we can get most of what we need such as how long it has been in existence, the history of the publication, the political agenda or "slant" of the publication; this information is useful to readers so they can read critically with this background on the publication in mind. While you are on the website, you might also want to skim the site to get a better sense of what is published and who might be reading it. In this way, you can understand who the audience is and their values or biases.

Jay Weiner had his article published in the *Star Tribune*. A quick perusal of the newspaper's website reveals the following narrative:

> It's 1867. St. Paul is home to 14,000 people and Minneapolis 7,000. Minneapolis doesn't have a fire department, sewage system or even a water supply, but it does have a daily morning newspaper—the *Minneapolis Tribune.*
>
> From these roots we have grown with the community we serve, maintaining our tradition as Minnesota's preferred source of news and information. As the leading newspaper in Minnesota, we are read by 1.8 million people each week.

Throughout our rich history, we have been a trusted, dependable source of reliable news coverage, extensive consumer information and independent editorial commentary. We play a key role ensuring access to information that is essential for informed citizens to make decisions.

While it's true that there is a bit of self-celebration going on here, no publication is going to say, "Oh, well, we publish some pretty mediocre stuff we don't really care about." So you need to look beyond the celebration to the parts that matter for being a critical reader. In this case, we know that it's the major newspaper in this area, and has been for a while. Furthermore, it claims independence, so supposedly the publication is not biased due to large corporate ownership, and for your present purposes, you would want to take them at their word. In Chapter 3 we will examine how to evaluate such claims of independence, but for now we can be content with what the publication tells us because we are most concerned with the text in front of us.

GUIDELINES: EXAMINING THE PUBLICATION

1. Determine the publication type (magazine, newspaper, discipline-specific journal, etc.).
2. Analyze the publication.
   - How long has the publication been in business?
   - What kinds of material does it tend to publish? Does it have a specific focus or does it tend to publish anything?
   - Is the publication affiliated with any other organizations?
3. Look at the kinds of articles in the publication. Does that tell you anything about the biases of the publication? Do the types of articles tell you anything about the readers?

Analyzing Parts of a Text

Looking at the context of a text, as we have done with Weiner's editorial, gives you a broad overview of the author and her purposes in writing: We come to understand the appropriateness of the genre, the credibility of the writer, and the focus and purpose of the publication. Once we understand those "big picture components" we can turn our attention back to the text and examine specific parts of it as we continue to read it critically.

There are any number of areas we could focus on, but here we look at four parts of a writer's text: introductions and conclusions, the writer's position, the writer's argument, and the writer's use of evidence to support the argument. In Chapter 3: Analyzing and Writing Arguments, we will delve more deeply into these areas and others (such as tone, humor, and other language choices).

Looking at Openings and Closings

Because they are the first and last words the author writes, openings and closings are the logical place to start when we look at the text analytically. And depending on the genre, it may be where the author states her argument or purpose and where she sums it up or repeats it. Of course there are other ways of beginning and ending a text, but no matter the genre, the writer is working to engage you. And how the writer engages you (or how she doesn't) reveals something important about her purpose and agenda for writing the text in the first place.

Take a look at Weiner's opening (the first two paragraphs):

> How far back must we go to remember that sports matter? How deeply into our personal and national pasts must we travel to recall that we once cared?
>
> Do we have to return to 1936—Adolf Hitler tried to make the Olympics into a propaganda machine for anti-Semitism and racism. In that case, American track star Jesse Owens, demonstrating that the master race could be mastered at racing, stole Hitler's ideological show. Were not sports a vehicle of significant political substance then?

What we learn about Weiner from these two paragraphs might seem obvious, especially since we know already that he is a sports writer: he cares about sports. But we also learn that this text is going to come from the position that we, the audience, think that sports no longer matter, that we no longer care about sports in any real or profound way— that something has changed in Americans' attitudes and values about sports, and for very specific reasons. He offers us valuable insight into the text; we can be pretty sure that he doesn't see the same value in sports that there once was.

If we turn, then, to look at the closing, we can see that he never strays too far from that opening idea:

> And therein lies the essence of modern American sport. It's a good show, albeit bread and circuses. And we just can't give it up. So why not take it back for ourselves as best we can, looking for ways to humanize an institution that mirrors our culture, understanding that those who own sport won't give it up without a fight, knowing that we like it too much to ever just walk away.

Here, as in the opening, he asks us to consider the importance of sports, and he acknowledges, as his introduction suggests, that sports today are less important than they were in the past—the reference to "bread and circuses" is telling in this regard. It refers to giving the "people" what they think they want. For example, the Roman rulers gave citizens food and entertainment in order to distract them from their otherwise rather desperate lives. Weiner is echoing his opening to suggest that the condition of sports in some ways reflects American culture—and the reflection he sees is grim.

Closings rarely simply summarize what has already been said. What they do instead is keep readers thinking about the subject or extend an idea suggested in the text earlier. Closings may offer conclusions that have been built up to in the rest of the text. Of course, closings function in different ways for different genres, but in general, if a text is worth reading, the closing will offer readers food for thought.

GUIDELINES: LOOKING AT OPENINGS AND CLOSINGS

1. Look at the introduction.
   - How does the writer use the opening to engage and hold readers' attention? Ask a question? Make a bold statement? Use an anecdote? Other?
   - How does the writer suggest the subject of the text in the opening paragraphs? Does it signal what's to come?
   - What does the opening reveal about the writer and his position on the subject?

(continued)

2. Look at the closing.
   - How does the closing leave readers thinking about the subject?
   - Does the closing make sense based on what the writer has said in the rest of the text?

Identifying the Writer's Position

When we look for a writer's position, we are asking what their biases, values, likes or dislikes might be. We are examining who they are and why they might hold true to their beliefs. Often, we start out by wondering "are they for it or against it?" While this can be a good place to begin, usually the positions writers take are more complicated than simple either/or situations. So when we are identifying the writer's position, we need to look for nuance and subtleties in the writer's arguments.

Sometimes writers will "telegraph" their position by coming right out and stating what it is. Other times, and for various reasons, writers might withhold such a statement, opting instead for a less direct approach. By taking a less direct route, writers can avoid unnecessarily alienating their readers and give themselves a better chance of convincing an audience that might otherwise disagree with them.

Looking again at Weiner's introduction, we can see the limitations of the "for or against" outlook:

> How far back must we go to remember that sports matter? How deeply into our personal and national pasts must we travel to recall that we once cared?

Based on these two sentences, it seems that the writer is saying sports once mattered to us and that something has happened to change Americans' attitudes about sports. One way to identify his position is a matter of reading carefully his language: "We once cared" implies that we should care again. He suggests here that we must go back to some other time to remind ourselves about how sports were important once in our lives.

So when we allow ourselves to accept a bit of gray in the positions writers take, we often get a better understanding of what they are trying to argue. In Weiner's case, he is committed to sports as a part of American culture, but he's for a particular way of understanding the relationship between sports and the public. Locating Weiner's arguments is a matter of understanding that most well-constructed arguments are not black or white, for or against, but settle in the gray areas; that is the writer's position is more complicated.

GUIDELINES: IDENTIFYING THE WRITER'S POSITION

1. Look for a thesis. Does the writer come right out and take a position on the topic?
2. Analyze examples. Does the writer use examples or anecdotes that suggest a particular position? Does the writer ask questions that suggest a particular answer is the preferred one?

Identifying the Arguments

When we read most texts, we expect that their writers will make identifiable arguments and give reasons for why they hold the position on the issue that they do. Often, but not always, a writer's argument is articulated in a thesis statement—a statement that signals the primary point the writer wants to make. The reasons used to develop the writer's position or *thesis* are called *claims*. *Claims* are arguable statements that warrant support in the form of evidence—a statement is an arguable claim when someone can reasonably disagree with it. The writer uses claims to develop a line of reasoning or reasons to support his position throughout a persuasive or argumentative text. Claims are different from statements that cannot be argued, or facts.

For instance, during the 2008 primaries, we could have made a claim that either Hillary Clinton or Barak Obama could successfully challenge John McCain, the Republican Party presidential candidate, in the general election, or that John McCain could successfully challenge and beat either Democratic candidate. A *fact* would be that Clinton, Obama, and McCain were all senators. Fact is information that is known and unchangeable, while claims are statements that are often supported by facts and other kinds of evidence.

> **GUIDELINES:** IDENTIFYING THE WRITER'S ARGUMENT
>
> 1. Examine the thesis.
>   - Does the writer express his or her argument in the form of a thesis statement? Or is the writer's argument implied throughout the writing?
> 2. Examine the claims.
>   - Does the writer develop his or her argument with claims that move us through his reasoning?
>   - How do the claims build on each other to logically develop the argument?
>   - Are the writer's claims supported and developed with relevant and sufficient evidence—formal research or some other kind of supporting material?

There are different kinds of claims or reasons a writer provides to develop and support an argument in a text. We'll go into depth about claims in Chapter 3: Analyzing and Writing Arguments, but for now it's important that you are able to recognize the claims, or arguable statements, that the writer uses to develop his argument. And that you see that claims require evidence to support them. Without evidence, the argument falls apart and the reader is not persuaded.

Examining the Evidence

Claims need support in the form of evidence, which comes from the writer doing research. Although in many civic genres writers do not include citations like you might see in a research report (e.g. footnotes), research is still blended into a text in ways that signal to readers that the writer has in fact researched his topic and drawn from sources to back up his points.

For instance, in "Taking Back Our Tuition" (p. 39), author Ray French cites university documents that show how tuition increases are factored: "According the 07–08 UW System Fact Book . . ." is a phrase that signals to readers that French is about to include research to support his claims of unfair tuition hikes that rely on equal contributions from the state and the student.

When we read critically, we want to examine whether or not the writer is using relevant, credible, and sufficient evidence, and, of course, we check for how the evidence is being used so we may judge the value of the writer's arguments.

There are many kinds of evidence that a writer can draw from, but here are some common kinds and a brief overview of how they might be used by writers and evaluated by readers. Chapter 3: Analyzing and Writing Arguments discusses in more detail how writers use evidence as well as the types of evidence, and Chapter 13: Research and the Rhetorical Situation covers how to evaluate sources.

Expert Opinions/Testimony— The opinions of individuals who have the credentials to speak on the issue (researchers, professionals, people with firsthand knowledge and experience, etc.) and have established themselves as experts are often used as supporting evidence. Writers often draw from this knowledge because it adds credibility to the writer's own position on the issue. Writers may also use expert opinions to offer viewpoints that differ from their own and then respond to those differences or refute them with additional evidence. Responding to differing views is discussed further in Chapter 3.

Research Studies— All sorts of institutions and organizations do research: from colleges and universities to nonprofit organizations, to state and federal governments and private research groups. Writers might use information from research studies or conclusions drawn by the researchers as supporting evidence for their claims, including data analysis results and case studies.

Statistics— Statistics are a type of factual evidence that are based on research generated by surveys, opinion polls, or research studies of particular populations, groups, and other demographic features. Statistics come out of a research context in which an individual or group conducts the research, chooses the parameters for it, and has a question(s) in mind at the start they'd like to answer. Knowing the research context (the who, what, where, and why for the research) from which the statistics emerge can help readers understand how the numbers were derived—and whether they can be considered valid evidence to back a writer's claim.

Examples— Examples can be based on the writer's own personal experiences, or come from observations, case studies, or comparative examples from other peoples' research. They serve to illustrate the writer's claim or point.

GUIDELINES: EXAMINING EVIDENCE

1. Examine the evidence's appropriateness.
   - Does the writer use sufficient evidence to back up and develop her claims?
   - Is the evidence relevant to her argument and larger concern? How so?
   - Does she use appropriate evidence for each claim, given the genre?
2. Examine the evidence's reliability.
   - Is the evidence reliable? Does it come from reputable sources (academic journals, government research, etc.)?
   - Is the evidence recent and up-to-date?

Apply the skills you just learned on reading a text for how it works to the following editorial by Mary Frances Berry, "Gay But Equal?" which appeared in the *New York Times*.

First, analyze the contexts by focusing your analysis writing on the genre, background of the writer, and publication information. Next, when you have finished, turn to the parts of the text by looking at the parts of the writer's text: introductions and conclusions, the writer's position, arguments, and the evidence used to support and develop those arguments.

Finally, after you complete your writing, compare your responses with your classmates'. How were the responses similar? How were they different? What do you think accounts for the differences, especially in how you evaluate the arguments and evidence the writer used?

Op-Contributor

Gay But Equal?

MARY FRANCES BERRY
Published: January 15, 2009 Philadelphia

As the country prepares to enter the Obama era, anxiety over the legal status and rights of gays and lesbians is growing. Barack Obama's invitation to the Rev. Rick Warren, an evangelical pastor who opposes same-sex marriage, to give the invocation at his inauguration comes just as the hit movie "Milk" reminds us of the gay rights activism of the 1970s. Supporters of gay rights wonder if the California Supreme Court might soon confirm the legitimacy of Proposition 8, passed by state voters in November, which declares same-sex marriage illegal—leaving them no alternative but to take to the streets.

To help resolve the issue of gay rights, President-elect Obama should abolish the now moribund Commission on Civil Rights and replace it with a new commission that would address the rights of many groups, including gays.

The fault lines beneath the debate over gay rights are jagged and deep. Federal Social Security and tax benefits from marriage that straight people take for granted are denied to most gays in committed relationships. And because Congress has failed to enact a federal employment nondiscrimination act, bias against gays in the workplace remains a constant threat.

Gays are at risk under the military's "don't ask, don't tell" policy. And people who are only assumed to be homosexual have been subject to hate crimes. José and Romel Sucuzhañay, two brothers, were attacked in New York City last month by men yelling anti-gay and anti-Latino epithets. José Sucuzhañay died from being beaten with a bottle and a baseball bat. Yet the effort in Congress to enact a law that would increase the punishment for hate crimes against gays and lesbians is going nowhere.

Only two states, Massachusetts and Connecticut, permit gay marriage. New York acknowledges marriages from those states and from other countries, despite the federal Defense of Marriage Act of 1996, which was meant to allow other states not to recognize gay marriages performed elsewhere. Vermont, New Jersey and New Hampshire permit civil unions, which provide gay partners the rights, protections and responsibilities of marriage. On the other hand, a referendum that just passed in Arkansas goes beyond banning gay marriage to prohibit the adoption of children by unmarried couples. Mississippi, Florida and Utah have similar bans. And many Americans believe their religion forbids gay marriage or even civil unions.

In the 1950s, race relations in America generated escalating tension and strife. As Secretary of State John Foster Dulles told President Dwight Eisenhower, other nations vilified us for our treatment of "negroes" as less-than-first-class citizens. It was in this context that Congress, in 1957, granted Eisenhower's request for an independent civil rights commission to "put the facts on top of the table."

The commission conducted interviews and public hearings, prepared detailed reports and recommended new protections that would ultimately be passed in the form of the Civil Rights Act of 1964 and the Voting Rights Act of 1965. These laws embodied the goals of the protestors who marched, went to jail and died to end racial discrimination.

The commission became what the Rev. Theodore Hesburgh, who was the chairman from 1969 to 1972, called the "conscience of the government" on civil rights issues. There is no need to analogize the battle for the rights of gay and lesbian people to the struggle of African Americans to overcome slavery, Jim Crow and continued discrimination. But as Coretta Scott King said to me as she tried to imagine what position the Rev. Dr. Martin Luther King Jr. would take on "don't ask, don't tell": "What's the yardstick by which we should decide that gay rights are less important than other human rights we care about?"

The Commission on Civil Rights has been crippled since the Reagan years by the appointments of commissioners who see themselves as agents of the presidential administration rather than as independent watchdogs. The creation of a new, independent human and civil rights commission could help us determine our next steps in the pursuit of freedom and justice in our society. A number of explosive issues like immigration reform await such a commission, but recommendations for resolving the controversies over the rights of gays, lesbians and transgendered people should be its first order of business.

Mary Frances Berry, the chairwoman of the Commission on Civil Rights from 1993 to 2004, is the author of "And Justice for All: The United States Commission on Civil Rights and the Continuing Struggle for Freedom in America."

Providing Comments for Revision: Practicing Peer Review

Every writer needs readers.

Writers benefit from having careful and critical readers give them feedback during the writing process. Chances are pretty good that you have had experience both giving and receiving feedback, and you may have worked collaboratively with other writers on a group project or on your own individual projects. One particular type of collaboration is called *peer review* (sometimes called peer commentary or peer feedback).

Peer review, simply, is having other interested writers read and respond to your work. No special skills are required—just a willingness to engage with someone else's writing and to respond honestly and helpfully to what you read.

Why Writers and Readers Benefit from Peer Review

Peer Review and the Writer

As with other kinds of collaborative work, peer review does not have to happen at a certain point in the writing process—there is nothing that says you must get feedback only on the first draft.

Feedback is useful at any point in writers' processes because it helps them think about the rhetorical situation. Even feedback on unformed ideas about what the writer might say can provide an early sense of what might work and what might not. So writers might seek peer feedback on messy first drafts, ideas they've generated, or final versions of their work. It depends on the writers' thoughts on what will help them the most.

Another benefit of peer review you may be unaware of is that peer review allows writers to reflect on their writing in progress. Often writers are able to talk to their peer reviewers about what they've written and why they've made certain choices for content, style, organization, and so on. Conversing with readers engages writers in a kind of critical reflection as they explain and work out some parts of their drafts. In turn, such critical reflection can help with idea generating for their writing, and later it can help them understand why and how their writing worked or didn't.

And as the writer you can always choose to accept, ignore, or modify the feedback you are given by a peer reviewer—it is your paper, after all, your ideas, your purpose. Ask yourself first: Should I revise based on readers' comments? What comments seem important to my purpose, goals, and so on? So don't avoid peer review because you don't want to have to take the advice you are given—you never have to, so long as you are clear about why you are ignoring the advice.

Peer Review and the Reader

You might be reluctant to be a peer reviewer and feel like you have nothing to say to another writer. You might truthfully feel that, since you don't really understand an assignment or perhaps are struggling with your own paper, you aren't in a position to offer anything useful to another writer. Sort of the blind leading the blind, right?

Not necessarily so. In fact, as a reader, you have lots to say about a text: Your reactions to it may help the writer clarify, expand, delete, or change the order of what they write. You may not consider yourself an "expert" (whatever that means), but you do know what makes sense to you, where you get confused, where you are engaged, and so on as you read something. These are all important abilities for being a good critical reader, and thus, a good peer reviewer.

It seems obvious that peer review can help the writer—they are getting the feedback after all. But peer review benefits the reader as well: Doing peer review helps readers see how others have approached a particular assignment or worked in a genre that may be new to them. Readers can actually get some good ideas and strategies for their own writing by reading other writers' texts.

And that's not the same as plagiarizing; you are not copying what the writer has said or how they have said it. Instead you might adapt a style or organization pattern, or play around with voice, because you get a good idea from reading how another writer has done so.

On the other hand, you might learn what to avoid as a writer from reading another person's text, what not to do, or what doesn't work well. Either way, peer review helps writers develop critical reading and writing strategies.

Providing Comments to Help Writers Revise: Specific v. Vague

One of the difficulties in peer review is actually figuring out what you want to say and how to say it. Often when we are asked to do peer review our response is something like "What? I don't know what I want to say or how to say it," or "How am I going to tell another writer what to do when I don't even understand what I need to do?"

Luckily, it is not your job to tell another writer what to do. Your role is simply to respond to the text and give the reader your honest feedback. You don't need specialized knowledge; you don't need to know exactly what the instructor wants or what the instructor would consider a good paper.

What you do need to do is be a careful reader and learn how to provide writers with useful and specific comments to help them move to the next version of their drafts.

Just as there is no one right time to get feedback from your peers, there is no one right way to conduct peer review. There are, however, some general "rules of thumb."

GUIDELINES: PEER REVIEW

1. Understand what the assignment is and what it entails. This includes understanding the writer's particular rhetorical situation: If it isn't clear, ask.
2. Understand the writer's purpose for writing and the kinds of response she might be expecting of her audience.
3. Read from your own perspective. Don't try to read as an instructor; instead, read as an informed and interested reader who understands the rhetorical situation.
4. Attend to areas of the text that demand *your* attention as a reader. These will be areas that you think are solid and those that you think need work by the writer. Use your expertise as a reader: you know what interests you, you know what you need for a piece of writing to make sense.

(continued)

5. Phrase your responses to be helpful to and understandable by the writer. For example: vague comments like "Good," "I like this," or "Huh?" are not all that helpful. But specific comments might include saying, "This is good because you have used an example here that appeals to my sense of fairness, and as reader, I really respond to your situation. Try to do this more often, maybe in the previous paragraph where you. . . ." Or, "This part confuses me because I don't know if you mean that the use of stem cells is always wrong or just when there is no medical necessity. Clarify which it is."

These general ideas for giving good feedback to other writers are a good baseline to start. Of course, your instructor may give you other guidelines, but even then, the ones listed above may still apply.

Peer Readers: Writing Effective Peer Review Commentary

Even if you have taken the advice above and have accepted that you do not need to be an expert, it is sometimes hard to know what exactly you can say and how you can say it. You're not alone in this concern; even writing instructors are sometimes at a loss for how to respond to a text. But the more you do it, the better you get at it, and as long as you are trying to be helpful, there really is no such thing as a wrong response to another person's text (but see 5 above).

It all boils down to two simple questions: What do I want to say? And how do I want to say it?

Generally, there are four broad categories of comments that you can give to another writer, and ideally any feedback you give to a writer offers some or all of these kinds of comments.

Outlining Comments: Sometimes writers respond by "echoing back" what the writer is doing in a particular part of the draft by providing comments that outline the content. Such comments are useful for the reader because it helps her stay focused on what the writer is saying and how the text is organized. And such comments are helpful for the writer because he can see where he is being clear and where he is not.

For example: "Here you seem to be saying that we simply need to accept that steroids are part of professional sports and move on. Is that right?"

Affective Comments: Very often when we read something, we have an emotional (or affective) response to the text—we react positively or negatively given what is being said, how it is being said, and what we already think and feel about the topic. Such comments are useful for the reader because they keep him engaged and they can later be used to help him make sense of why he reacted as he did.

Affective comments are useful to a writer because they show the writer how a reader reacted to the text. If that was not the reaction desired, the writer knows she needs to rework what she says and how she says it.

For example: "It really bothers me that you say Attention Deficit Disorder is not a real disease, that it's just a parent's way of not dealing with the fact that their kid is lazy. My brother has it, and I have friends who have it, and I know it's real."

Editorial Comments: When we read we are often paying attention to not only what is being said but how it is being said, and so it is natural to point out sentences, phrases, or words that catch our eyes for whatever reason. Sometimes we are correcting a mistake, other times commenting on the use of a particular word, and so on. Such comments are useful for the reader because they keep her focused on the how, not just the what of the text. And for the writer, such feedback is useful in crafting a more precise and articulate text.

> For example: "I don't really understand this sentence—I think because it is too long, by the time I get to the end, I've forgotten where you started."

Substantive Comments: Often the most useful comments a writer can receive are those we call substantive. These are the comments that not only point out what is or is not working but also offer suggestions for how to address the concern or do more with what is working well. These kinds of comments are useful for the reader because they allow him to comment not just on what is in front of him—a paragraph, for instance—but also to show and make connections to other parts of the text.

For the writer, these comments are particularly important because they address content and so often ask the writer to rethink ideas, synthesize more carefully, make ideas or concepts less complicated, and so on. In short, these comments ask the writer to revise deeply and thoughtfully.

> For example: "I like this example because it helps me understand the effects of the recession on real people, but I wonder if you provide this too late in your essay? Maybe you could move to an earlier section? It could work, I think, on the second page where you first start talking about the effects of the recession."

> For example: "I'm really confused here because you seem to be saying the exact opposite to what you claimed in your introduction—I think you need to be clearer about why you think softball should be reinstated as an Olympic sport."

Writer: Revising from Peer Feedback

While it might seem obvious, there are two parts to effective and useful peer review: the quality of the comments readers give, and what the writer actually does with the feedback.

The second part, what writers do with the feedback, can often be a difficult process. You may have been given two or more sets of responses from readers with very different backgrounds, expectations, and skill levels. The comments they have given you may sometimes send you in opposite or at least competing directions. How do you begin to negotiate and make sense of those comments?

It takes practice to sort through readers' comments, and you'll get better at it as you work more and more with the feedback you are given, but it always begins with your own sense of your text.

WRITING ACTIVITY   What to Do with Peer Feedback

Consider the rhetorical situation. Write down the subject, audience, and purpose of your paper on one of the drafts your readers have read. Having the rhetorical situation in mind will help you to evaluate how the comments you've been given address that situation.

Read with an open mind. As you read through the comments, keep in mind that your readers are trying to help you, to the best of their abilities with good intentions, revise the next version of your draft. Read their comments with an open mind, even when you think they are not useful.

Read through the comments critically. As you work through each of your peer readers' comments, keep the following questions in mind. Be clear about why you are accepting or rejecting the comments, and keep your audience and purpose and the writing assignment in mind.

- Do the comments make sense to you given your own understanding of the purpose, audience, and subject? Mark those that seem to accurately reflect your purpose, audience, and so on.
- Do the comments reflect your understanding of the assignment? Is what your reader asking you to do in line with what the assignment actually calls for? If you are unsure, check with your instructor.
- Do the comments accurately reflect the genre you are writing in? For example, if your reader asks you to include personal experience, ask yourself if that is appropriate for the genre.
- Do the comments make sense given what you actually say in that section of the paper? In other words, has the reader read your text accurately? Be especially careful here; don't automatically assume that the reader has misunderstood.
- Do the comments provide you with suggestions appropriate to the arguments or points you are making? In other words, has the reader read correctly or misread your line of reasoning?

Assess the kinds of comments provided. Depending on your skill with working with peer comments, it might be a good idea initially to get a sense of which kinds of comments your readers have given you: outlining, affective, editorial, or substantive. So for the first few times you work with peer review comments, spend some time categorizing the comments you have received. This analysis will help you figure out not only what to do with them but also which ones to respond to first.

For each comment, categorize it as outlining, affective, editorial, or substantive. If a comment fits more than one category, label it as both.

Compare the comments provided. When you have read over all the responses you received, it's time to start comparing them.

- Have your readers made similar comments about your paper? For instance, have they all commented on the need for more detail? As a general rule of thumb, if more than one reader makes the same suggestion, you should attend to the concern.
- Have your readers made different comments or suggestions about the same sections? (For instance, one reader suggests you delete paragraph two while another suggests you move it to support another argument in your paper.) Which suggestion makes the most sense?
- A lot of writers tend to take the advice that is easiest to address. So be aware of that tendency and look at your paper with a critical eye.
- Look at the suggestions and ask yourself which make the most sense given the genre and, again, your purpose and audience.

Revise your writing. You might choose to make revisions on the print copies of the drafts your readers read, or you might open the most recent version on your computer and revise directly. Either way is fine. And keep in mind that you can always ask readers for clarification of their comments Also, you can ask readers to reread sections they commented on to see if your revisions addressed their concerns.

Please see the One Writer's Journey sections in Chapters 5 through 12 for examples of students working with peer comments.

▪ ▪ ▪

3

Analyzing and Writing Arguments

Whether you know it or not, you are good at making arguments in order to persuade others. From our first attempts at persuasion—screaming from our cribs in order to let our parents know that they need to come get us—to our equally important but more subtle arguments to get our parents to lend us the car for the night ("You won't have to come get me," or, "If I don't drive, Jeremy might, and you know what a bad driver he is"), we have learned how to convince others that we are right, or at least worth listening to.

Argument and Persuasion: It's Not about Fighting

When we talk about argument and persuasion, we are not talking about the kind of arguments you might hear on morning talk radio or reality TV: shouting matches by individuals who "win" arguments through sheer volume; or on the more extreme shows, through screaming, hair pulling, obscenities, and flying chairs. Instead, when we talk about *argument* here and in other chapters, we mean the ways in which individuals make, support, and refute claims. When we talk about *persuasion,* we mean the devices and techniques that we use to "win our audience over" and "bring them around" to our way of thinking; we mean the ways we negotiate with others and their ideas, values, and beliefs in order to get them to listen to us, to get them to recognize our point of view as one worth considering, and maybe to change their minds or behaviors.

WRITING ACTIVITY   How You Argue

Think of a recent argument that you "won" and write down a few of the details: What was it about? Why were you having that argument and who with? Where were you when you had it? Look over what you wrote, consider how you argued:

1. Was the subject of the argument something you knew a lot about? Or not? Did the other person (or people) know that you either knew a lot or did not?

2. What were your main points?
3. How did you support them?
4. Did you use your knowledge of the other person (or people) in your argument?
5. Did you make use of your surroundings to help you make the argument?

■ ■ ■

Argument and Rhetoric

When we talk about argument we are also talking about *rhetoric*. We will use this broader term throughout this book. Rhetoric is the art of persuasion, though it has been given other varying definitions by rhetoricians and philosophers: "It is the art of winning the soul by discourse," says Plato, writing during the fourth and third centuries BCE, while Cicero (writing in the first century BCE) claims that it is "speech designed to persuade." Cicero's definition seems a little spare, while Plato's seems a little grandiose, but both are accurate in that we use rhetoric to convince others to do, think, or feel something they might not otherwise.

Rhetoric is all around us—from ads on television that persuade us to buy a shampoo to make our hair shiny and "sexy," to campaign speeches by presidential nominees, to highway billboards telling us to stop at Dairy Queen for a Blizzard. *Rhetoric,* the art of using language and ideas to persuade or move others, is part of our everyday lives. And we experience social situations that call for various types of rhetoric to be used given the circumstances, audience, and the *rhetor* (a term used to describe the speaker or writer in a rhetorical situation).

Creating Convincing Arguments

Just as you are familiar with argument, you are familiar with rhetoric and the art of persuasion. You know, for instance, how to use emotional appeals to get what you want (we call this *pathos*). You know when to draw on ethical and moral arguments to persuade your audience (we call this *ethos*) as well as how to use your own expertise and experience to convince others to listen to you (this, too, we call *ethos*). And you know that the manner in which you structure your argument is important (we call this *logos*).

You also know that certain kinds of *claims* or arguments work best for certain situations and that you need particular kinds of evidence to support these claims. For example, when trying to convince your boss that you deserve a raise, you would probably begin your argument by making claims about your worth to the company: You're a hard worker, whose evidence in support of this claim is the multimillion-dollar project you just completed. If you make the claim that you are dedicated to the company's success, you could support that claim by citing your long hours of overtime as evidence to prove your commitment. *Evidence,* then, supports the arguments or claims you make while taking into consideration the rhetorical situation.

Finally, you know that the way you "package" your argument—for instance, the *tone* you use, the word choices you make—plays an important role. When asking for a raise, you know that sarcasm will not be the best approach; instead you should speak or write in a formal, matter-of-fact way. You know that there are certain terms you *should* use, as they resonate with this particular audience (your boss). Phrases such as "increase productivity," "team builder," "leadership," and "dedicated" will carry a lot of weight with this audience.

To put it another way: you and your boss share *assumptions,* underlying values and beliefs, about what kinds of activity warrant a raise. If this seems complicated, it might only be because we are analyzing what we all tend to do without thinking. Think of what would happen if you tried to analyze *how* you were wind-surfing while you were actually doing it; you'd very quickly fall off the board. So it might help to look at what we just discussed graphically, using the rhetorical triangle we introduced in Chapter 2.

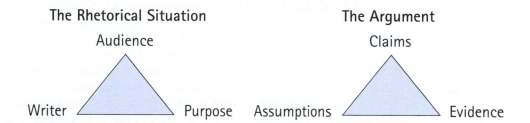

The rhetorical situation helps the rhetor understand how the different parts of the situation influence the others. For example, knowing who your audience is helps you understand and refine your purpose, and it also helps you understand how you will present yourself. Recall the example above where you were asking for a raise from your boss. Your understanding of the audience allowed you to make choices about how to present yourself and your claims. The second triangle shows the parts of an argument and how each part influences the other. Once you understand the components of the rhetorical situation, you can begin to generate claims that help you meet your purpose; those claims and your understanding of the audience will help you figure out what kinds of evidence you need.

Analyzing Arguments

It is important to consider the rhetorical situation to better understand how arguments are made and how people persuade us so that we might be effective critical thinkers and make good judgments or decisions. These skills carry over into everyday life and help us become conscientious public citizens.

Speech Analysis Example

The example that follows is a speech given by then Senator Barack Obama in the Federal Plaza in Chicago in October 2002.

Speech Against the Iraq War

Barack Obama

Speaker refers to a value he believes the people hold for the country—unity.

Good afternoon. Let me begin by saying that although this has been billed as an anti-war rally, I stand before you as someone who is not opposed to war in all circumstances. The Civil War was one of the bloodiest in history, and yet

Language that appeals
to audience's values.

Obama establishes his
credibility to speak by
connecting himself
with a veteran.

Pathos appeal: Obama
appeals to the audi-
ence's emotions—
fighting the evils of
Nazism.

The claim "I don't
oppose all wars" sup-
ported by previous
examples and the next;
the repetition of the
phrase is a focusing
device for the audience.

Speaker defines what
he means by a "dumb
war."

These names function
rhetorically as foils to
Obama—they are all
that he is not.

Speaker knows that he
has to be careful not to
be seen as "soft" on
Hussein.

Speaker qualifies his
position on Hussein.

In this paragraph he
makes his claims about
why the war would be
a dumb and rash one.

The speaker uses an
appeal to emotion
(pathos): Who would
not want to protect
children?

it was only through the crucible of the sword, **the sacrifice of multitudes,** that we could begin to perfect this union, and drive the **scourge of slavery from our soil**. I don't oppose all wars.

My grandfather signed up for a war the day after Pearl Harbor was bombed, fought in Patton's army. He saw the dead and dying across the fields of Europe; he heard the stories of fellow troops who first entered **Auschwitz and Treblinka**. He fought in the **name of a larger freedom,** part of that arsenal of democracy that triumphed over evil, and he did not fight in vain. **I don't oppose all wars**.

After September 11th, after witnessing the carnage and destruction, the dust and the tears, I supported this administration's pledge to hunt down and root out those who would slaughter innocents in the name of intolerance, and I would willingly take up arms myself to prevent such tragedy from happening again. I don't oppose all wars. And **I know that in this crowd today, there is no shortage of patriots, or of patriotism**.

What I am opposed to is a dumb war. **What I am opposed to is a rash war.** What I am opposed to is the cynical attempt by **Richard Perle** and **Paul Wolfowitz** and other armchair, weekend warriors in this administration to shove their own ideological agendas down our throats, irrespective of the costs in lives lost and in hardships borne.

What I am opposed to is the attempt by political hacks like Karl Rove to distract us from a rise in the uninsured, a rise in the poverty rate, a drop in the median income—to distract us from corporate scandals and a stock market that has just gone through the worst month since the Great Depression. That's what I'm opposed to. A dumb war. A rash war. A war based not on reason but on passion, not on principle but on politics. Now let me be clear—I suffer no illusions about **Saddam Hussein. He is a brutal man. A ruthless man**. A man who butchers his own people to secure his own power. He has repeatedly defied UN resolutions, thwarted UN inspection teams, developed chemical and biological weapons, and coveted nuclear capacity. He's a bad guy. The world, and the Iraqi people, would be better off without him.

But I also know that Saddam poses no imminent and direct threat to the United States, or to his neighbors, that the Iraqi economy is in shambles, that the Iraqi military a fraction of its former strength, and that in concert with the international community he can be contained until, in the way of all petty dictators, he falls away into the dustbin of history. I know that even a successful war against Iraq will require a US occupation of undetermined length, at undetermined cost, with undetermined consequences. I know that an invasion of Iraq without a clear rationale and without strong international support will only fan the flames of the Middle East, and encourage the worst, rather than best, impulses of the Arab world, and strengthen the recruitment arm of Al Qaeda. **I am not opposed to all wars. I'm opposed to dumb wars.**

So for those of us who seek a more just and **secure world for our children,** let us send a clear message to the President today. **You want a fight,**

This phrase functions as a "lead-in" for the next four paragraphs, followed by examples.

The speaker also uses logos here: What is unreasonable to fight for and what is reasonable to fight for are contrasted.

President Bush? Let's finish the fight with Bin Laden and Al Qaeda, through effective, coordinated intelligence, and a shutting down of the financial networks that support terrorism, and a homeland security program that involves more than color-coded warnings. You want a fight, President Bush?

Let's fight to make sure that the UN inspectors can do their work, and that we vigorously enforce a non-proliferation treaty, and that former enemies and current allies like Russia safeguard and ultimately eliminate their stores of nuclear material, and that nations like Pakistan and India never use the terrible weapons already in their possession, and that the arms merchants in our own country stop feeding the countless wars that rage across the globe. You want a fight, President Bush?

Let's fight to make sure our so-called allies in the Middle East, the Saudis and the Egyptians, stop oppressing their own people, and suppressing dissent, and tolerating corruption and inequality, and mismanaging their economies so that their youth grow up without education, without prospects, without hope, the ready recruits of terrorist cells. You want a fight, President Bush? **Let's fight to wean ourselves off Middle East oil, through an energy policy that doesn't simply serve the interests of Exxon and Mobil**. Those are the battles that we need to fight. Those are the battles that we willingly join. The battles against ignorance and intolerance. Corruption and greed. **Poverty and despair.**

Ethos appeal: Obama presents himself as a reasonable, not rash, person by offering solutions other than war.

Pathos appeals: Who would not be willing to fight to eliminate these problems?

The consequences of war are dire, the sacrifices immeasurable. We may have occasion in our lifetime to once again rise up in defense of our freedom, and pay the wages of war. But we ought not—we will not—travel down that hellish path blindly. Nor should we allow those who would march off and pay the ultimate sacrifice, who would prove the full measure of devotion with their blood, to make such an awful sacrifice in vain.

Rhetorical Analysis of Senator Obama's Speech

A **rhetorical analysis** is an academic genre in which writers analyze and address the use of rhetorical appeals, claims, and evidence to evaluate how the rhetor created his argument and how effective the argument was. The rhetorical analysis that follows illustrates how a rhetor (Obama) persuades an audience using claims, evidence, and rhetorical appeals, and how the rhetor considers his choices of those elements based on the rhetorical situation at hand. In this chapter, we explore the many elements of argument and provide you with the tools necessary to conduct your own rhetorical analyses.

Knowing the rhetorical situation prompting this speech and the location in which it takes place helps readers understand the ways that Obama argues. For instance, the speech was given in 2002, during a time when the Bush administration was shifting the focus of the "war on terrorism" from Afghanistan to Iraq. The speech is on the cusp of the crucial decision being debated in the Senate of which Obama is a part. Since he knows it is critical that he position himself clearly as a rhetor here, he begins by making ethos appeals: "... I stand before you as someone who is not opposed to war in all circumstances." And in the next paragraph, he aligns himself with his grandfather, a WWII veteran who served in what he calls a "justifiable war." The whole speech aims to set Obama apart from those who would encourage what he calls a "dumb war" and he continues to remind the audience, Americans who might be potentially anti-war themselves and who may be part of the military or from military families, that he believes there are times when war is necessary. He continues with what Richard Weaver would call an ultimate term, Sept. 11, which is a reference that has profound resonance with American audiences: "I would willingly take up arms myself to prevent such tragedy from happening again," establishing himself as a patriot and as a reasonable person, while at the same time tapping into the audience's emotions about the tragic events.

In the first three paragraphs, Obama repeats a sentence that is a major claim of his speech: "I don't oppose all wars." This repetition lets the audience know that Obama is not unequivocally against war in situations where it may be justified; he provides examples of the Civil War as evidence to support his claim: "... yet it was only through the crucible of the sword, the sacrifice of multitudes, that we could begin to perfect this union, and drive the scourge of slavery from our soil," and calls upon the example of his grandfather serving in "Patton's army" as "he fought in the name of a larger freedom, part of that arsenal of democracy that triumphed over evil...." These examples set up Obama's next claim: "What I am opposed to is a dumb war. What I am opposed to is a rash war," which are repeated throughout the paragraphs that follow with examples of rash, dumb, and self-serving behaviors on the part of the Bush administration. Obama states that such irresponsible behavior is shown by "weekend warriors" whose goal is "to shove their own ideological agendas down our throats, irrespective of the costs in lives lost and in hardships borne." And later he clarifies his point that a "dumb" or "rash" war would have other dire consequences: "I know that an invasion of Iraq without a clear rationale and without strong international support will only fan the flames of the Middle East, and encourage the worst, rather than best, impulses of the Arab world, and strengthen the recruitment arm of Al Qaeda."

The logos is clear in his argument. If we continue to pursue war in Iraq in the ways the Bush administration has done, we will certainly be participating in a dumb, rash war. He has defined what he means by those terms, and makes it difficult for readers to disagree with his definitions by providing concrete examples. The reasoning here is simple: The war thus far is a dumb war based on political agendas, not justifiable actions, and therefore, we need to stop U.S. participation in the war.

What makes Obama's claims effective are the alternatives to war he offers to end the Al Qaeda threat "through effective,

---

WebLinks

The World of Rhetoric

For examples of speeches, many of them made by famous American rhetoricians, go to the website of the organization, American Rhetoric.

coordinated intelligence, and a shutting down of the financial networks that support terrorism," and in the three paragraphs that follow, changing our lifestyle to use alternate energy programs thereby ending our dependence on Middle East oil, and finally, checking the threat of nuclear war if "we vigorously enforce a non-proliferation treaty." This makes Obama seem like a reasonable and political savvy individual who has thought through his proposals for addressing U.S. problems but without going to war in Iraq. Notice again here as he shifts into proposing alternatives that his claims are emphasized by repetition of a key phrase, "You want a fight, President Bush?" followed by examples of things he deems worth fighting for ("Let's fight for ...") and that he knows his audience will value as well.

The Structure of Argument: Claims, Evidence, and Assumptions

The basic structure of any argument includes the claims (the statements or points that writers make), the evidence provided (the material that supports and develops those claims), and the assumptions that connect a claim and its evidence. If, for example, a writer claims that video games lead to real-world violence because students who play violent video games get into more fights than students who don't, then this writer is making the assumption that students transfer their experiences in gaming worlds into the real world.

OVERVIEW OF RHETORICAL ELEMENTS

- **Claims** are the arguable points or propositions a rhetor makes that require support.

- A **major claim** is the actual argument a rhetor makes.

- **Evidence** is anything material a rhetor uses to back up, support, and develop the claims.

- **Assumptions** are the ideas or beliefs that link a specific piece of evidence to a claim; a bridge between claims and evidence.

Claims: Claims of Fact, Value, and Policy

Claims are the points or statements that you make as you argue your position. For example: "We should eat at Smittie's tonight"; "Ronald Reagan was the most effective president of the last 50 years"; or "Raphael Nadal is the best men's tennis player in the world." Claims are *arguable* statements writers make that usually require support or evidence to be convincing. Thus, a claim that Ronald Reagan was the most effective president of the last 50 years would require some evidence to develop and support that point: accomplishments Reagan made during his presidency, for example, in comparison to what other presidents in similar circumstances have done. Claims are *disputable;* people will and do have varying positions on an issue: Was Reagan a more effective president than Bill Clinton? What about

Lyndon Johnson? Because claims often require evidence, they help us develop rational, reasonable arguments about an issue. There are distinct kinds of claims that writers make and choose given the particular rhetorical situation they find themselves in.

Claims of Fact

The definition of *claims of fact* might seem pretty obvious: *Claims of fact assert that something is, was, or will be.* For example, "Jimmy Carter was the thirty-ninth president" or "The Moon orbits the Earth every 27.3 days" are both claims of fact. Not all claims of fact, however, are so immediately obvious. For instance, a factual claim such as "Students who live on campus have higher grade point averages than those who commute" would require the rhetor to prove this point, perhaps by citing studies that compare the two groups. Similarly, claims of fact can argue the *causes and effects* of something happening: For example, "Increased use of fossil fuels is a significant cause of global warming trends" would require evidence from research studies to show the effects of fossil fuel usage and its connection to global warming.

Other kinds of factual claims rely on evidence that is not yet available; such claims make *predictions about the future*: "The Lakers will be national champions this year," "This bridge will crumble in a year if not repaired now," and so on. Finally, another claim of fact is one that *provides or disputes a definition*. For instance, if you are asked to conduct an evaluation of an employee, you might say "Janie is committed to her work." That word, "committed," is something that is disputable: One person's definition of what it means to be committed is not necessarily another person's. So if you were to write such an evaluation, you'd need to provide evidence of what you think being "committed" entails and particularly, how the employee exhibits such behavior.

Claims of Value

Claims of value are those that we articulate from a sense of what is right or wrong, pleasurable or unpleasant, and so on. In other words, they are *judgments* about a thing or condition: "*Rocky V* was the best in the series" is a claim of value because it makes or implies a judgment.

Sometimes claims of value are *personal opinion* and thus are not subject to critical analysis. How would you defend your assertion that pasta fagioli is the soup you like the best? More importantly, why would you need to defend it? Such claims require no more evidence than "because that's what I think." But other claims of value—those dealing with questions of good or bad, right and wrong (moral or ethical issues), questions of beauty and ugliness (aesthetics), or effectiveness or ineffectiveness (utility)—do require evidence precisely because they, too, stem from our beliefs, and such claims need to be supported and *proven* to those whose beliefs differ from ours. So, for instance, if we make the claim of value that "homosexuality is wrong," we will be asked to defend it. *Upon what basis is that claim made? What authority?* It is up to the rhetor to convince the audience that not only the claim is valid but that the support and underlying assumptions are as well. As listeners or readers, then, we ask those questions to ascertain the validity of the claim. But as critical readers or listeners, we also want to be sure that we are objective in our criticism: Are we invalidating the speaker's claim because the logic is faulty, because the evidence is lacking, or because we, personally, don't share the same set of assumptions?

Claims of Policy

Claims of policy are claims that suggest certain actions should be taken or plans must be implemented. Writers use claims of policy when they are responding to a situation that has gone awry and needs addressing. For example, because of budget cuts your town's public parks have not been maintained. You propose that the town should hold a "clean up the parks" festival and provide food and drink for those who volunteer. This claim, your proposition, is a claim of policy. Claims of policy, unlike most claims of value or fact, require that the speaker or writer first establish that there is a problem (and provide evidence to support it), for without that agreement between rhetor and audience, claims of policy will make no sense to the audience.

Differing Views: Refutation, Concession, and Finding Common Ground

Sometimes writers make particular kinds of claims that are meant to specifically address possible counterarguments to the one the writer is making. These counterarguments are referred to collectively as **differing views,** and there are three common ways which writers address them: *refutation, concession,* and *finding common ground.*

When you refute a differing view, you disavow it entirely; you are saying, essentially, that the differing view is wrong, or inaccurate, or shortsighted, and so on. **Refutation** works best when the differing view is clearly opposite to your own. You run the risk, however, of alienating readers who may not be inclined to listen to your ideas if you say that they are wrong—so be wary not to simply dismiss ideas unless you can point out a clear logical flaw or inaccuracy.

Often, though, differing views are not completely inaccurate, but instead have pieces that are useful, applicable, and even worth considering. So when you approach a differing view from a standpoint of **concession,** you are acknowledging that the author has some good points to make, but those points are too narrow or limited or shortsighted or that their reasons are not entirely applicable to your situation.

If you are entering into a discussion about an issue that you know is contentious, your best approach might be one of seeking **common ground**—that is, finding the areas you and those who disagree with you can agree on in order to move the discussion forward. This might sound like **concession,** but the difference is one of audience, as in this case, you are actively seeking to bring the opposing group into your camp.

Writers don't always need to address differing views; that depends on the audience the writer is addressing and the subject itself. For example, a writer writing a commentary on the need for increased embryonic stem cell research to an audience of religious conservatives would certainly need to deal directly with those differing views. Such a writer would do so in order to build some trust with that audience by acknowledging the validity of their concerns. Thus, addressing differing views enables the writer to develop his or her own *ethos,* or credibility.

How Claims Work

Now that we understand the different types of claims, let's examine how they work in practice. Below is an excerpt from an academic essay by Jim Kuerschner, a former student at New York University. In his essay, "Big Brother Is on the Facebook," he argues that Facebook is a tool for both voyeurism and surveillance. As you read this short excerpt, notice how he uses the various kinds of claims we discuss above (we have highlighted many but not all of them). You can read Kuerschner's entire essay in Chapter 7.

Claim of Fact

Claim of Fact

Claim of Value

Claim of Value

Claim of Value

Claim of Fact

Claim of Fact

Claim of Fact

Claim of Value

Claim of Fact

Claim of Value

Claim of Policy

Claim of Fact

Whatever stance you take, Facebook usage is here to stay. Over 10.5 million unique visitors explored the Facebook in February of 2006 alone, making it one of the most popular sites on the web (Yuan). College newspapers, as well as student sentiment and interest groups on the Facebook itself, curse its hypnotic, addicting powers, yet students are still unable to free themselves from checking the Facebook countless times a day. Even with the knowledge of Facebook access by administrators and prospective employers, students fearlessly post incriminating pictures of themselves—some nearly softcore pornography, others more akin to Smirnoff advertisements. Clearly, college students have many better things to do with their lives than sit for hours on end examining the Facebook profiles of their friends and coming up with witty comments to post on their pages (or "walls," in Facebook lingo), yet for some reason the majority of the college populous is enamored with the Harvard-created site. Why then, when we have the ability to speak face-to-face with a vast number of college students simply by walking through our campuses, do we feel the need to use such a profile service?

The Facebook embodies the Big Brother spirit of our generation. While some post purely for viewing by their own friends (and indeed there are privacy controls that allow very limited visibility), many update their pages constantly, knowing that someone will probably see their new silly or sexy picture, perhaps inducing a message or a "poke"—one of the more strange features of the page, which allows users to send any member of the Facebook, even if you have no idea who they are, a message reading, "You have been poked by [insert real name of Creepy McCreepster here]." In a generation when Internet chat rooms and online dating services have been around for most of our lives, we are much more comfortable sending messages to those we don't know than people have been in the past. Facebook allows us to put every moment of our personal lives up for public display, if we wish. And many do.

Yet while we are okay with everyone knowing our personal affairs via Facebook, we hotly protest (and rightfully so) the ever-increasing surveillance that has been imposed on our society post-September 11th. Is there a difference? Perhaps we fall into a false sense of security, refusing to believe that anyone other than our college buddies and other university students can view what we make publicly available. Facebook's privacy policy, made available to every member, however, states that the site has the right to share information with a third-party when it is "reasonably necessary to offer the service"—a quite vague description ("Privacy"). But if I'm not doing anything wrong, why do I care that someone knows what I'm doing? The problem is that added surveillance can turn into added control, especially when we are not aware of how we are being monitored. When do we draw the line between harmless monitoring of Internet profiles and constant Orwellian watch?

Surveillance and voyeurism, binaries evoked by the Facebook, have caused riffs in society for hundreds of years. "The philosopher Jeremy Bentham," writes Ellen Goodman of the *Boston Globe*, "once described the perfect

Claim of Fact

Claim of Fact

Claim of Value

prison as a 'panopticon' where prisoners were under complete surveillance and yet could not see the watcher." Would modern society feel the same way? As hundreds of thousands of people over the years have applied and auditioned for television programs such as MTV's *The Real World* or *Big Brother* on CBS, it appears as if Bentham's penitentiary would be far less frightening. On these TV shows, participants have every moment of their lives recorded and broadcast to millions of viewers across the country and the world. By freely giving away their rights to privacy, these individuals seem to illustrate a growing acceptance in today's culture of constant surveillance.

In this excerpt, Kuerschner relies heavily on *claims of fact*. Kuerschner's audience is likely those who use Facebook, and probably enjoy doing so; in short, they want to be on Facebook and like connecting with their friends. So Kuerschner needs to assert, strongly, that there is a problem, and making claims of fact gives his essay a tone of authority. When he makes *claims of value*, he does so in rather cautious ways, since he does not want to alienate his audience (who might be uncritically pro-Facebook) by saying or implying that what they are going is somehow wrong. For example, he poses questions to get the readers thinking about their actions: "Why then, when we have the ability to speak face-to-face with a vast number of college students simply by walking through our campuses, do we feel the need to use such a profile service?" Kuerschner is trying to get his audience to think critically by inserting questions like this one throughout his essay.

Finally, note that there is only one claim of policy—this, too, makes sense because in the excerpt he is not advocating a particular change or course of action; he is making us aware of the problem and wondering about its implications. The one claim of policy, in fact, simply suggests that "the effects of the FB's privacy policy could be read as Orwellian surveillance." This part seems like a warning to the unwary FB consumer: you could be duped by this policy into thinking that "privacy" is actually guaranteed.

GROUP ACTIVITY Constructing Claims

1. Identify some problems you have noticed in a community you are connected to (hometown, employment, school, civic group, etc.). Examine the rhetorical situation and use that information to generate a series of claims to defend and support your positions on the problems. Based on the lists your group members have generated, choose one problem that all members can relate to and write it down. For example, "There are not enough entry-level summer jobs in our town for students."

2. Identify your purpose. Why are you writing about this problem? To solve it? To make people aware of it?

3. Identify your audience. If you are writing to solve the problem, who can do so? Who would care and why? If you want people to be aware of the problem, who is it that you think is not aware of it?

4. Describe your connection to the problem. Who are you and how are you involved?

5. State your position on the issue—your thesis or major claim. What position are you taking in this situation based on your role as a writer?

6. Given your audience, purpose, and position, generate a list of claims to develop your argument. Come up with three possible claims of each type (i.e. fact, value, and policy).

7. Present your group's problem, audience, purpose, position, and claims to the rest of the class. Which claims do the other groups think are the most effective? What other claims can the class suggest to your group?

■ ■ ■

Kinds of Evidence

No matter what the argument is that you are making, you will need some kind of support for the claims and for the argument. Even in casual conversations you will often find yourself using some sort of support for the claims that you make:

Claim "We should watch *CSI Miami*."
Evidence "Because it's the most realistic crime drama on TV."

Generally, when we talk about support or evidence, we break it down into three broad categories: factual evidence, opinion, and appeals (ethos, pathos, logos). These are not absolute categories, as there is some blending of the three; for instance, you could very well draw on expert testimony (a kind of opinion) which makes use of factual evidence. This statement shows blending: "According to the Pew Research Center's recent survey of 2000 adults in the U.S., 'Some 50% of college graduates have high levels of social trust, compared with 28% of those with a high school education or less.'" This bit of evidence contains both expert testimony (the Pew Research Center is a respected source of polling information on various social issues) and statistics. So, as you think about the evidence you might use for any particular claim you make, keep in mind that it is never an either-or situation, and in fact the most persuasive support is that which draws on different kinds of evidence.

Factual Evidence

While the obvious definition of factual evidence is anything that is a fact, that definition quickly becomes unhelpful because even fact is disputable. Some "facts" we take for granted may for others be less set in stone. For example, you might take as fact the idea that the United States and Western nations (Europe, etc.) were primarily responsible for the fall of the former Soviet Union. However, from the perspective of the former U.S.S.R. and Soviet bloc nations, the fall of the Soviet Union was the consequence of internal reform which turned into revolution. So when we talk about factual evidence, we mean evidence that a majority of people accept as fact.

Claim of Policy We should develop a volunteer program to serve the elderly living in their own homes.

Factual Evidence The president of AARP, Ron Smith, reports that "in-home accidents tend to increase with age."

Claim of Fact Americans are increasingly opposed to stem-cell research being conducted.

Factual Evidence Those opposed to the destruction of stem-cells for research rose from 35% in 2002 to 38% in 2007.

Claim of Value *Gone with the Wind* is the best film ever made.

Factual Evidence It is the highest-grossing film of all time.

Even after we agree that a piece of evidence is factual, we do not always agree about what that fact means. An easy example is the current debate on global climate change. Nearly everyone agrees that on average the Earth is warmer now than it was a century ago; nearly everyone agrees that the ice sheets are melting. So far so good, but not everyone agrees about what these facts *mean*. Is the Earth in a normal warming cycle? Are warmer temperatures caused by greenhouse gasses? Will global climate change really be a problem for humans? And so on. There are many kinds of factual evidence that a writer can draw from, but here are some common kinds and a brief overview of how they might be used by writers and evaluated by readers.

Types of Factual Evidence

Definition	Use	Source	Evaluation
Research Studies offer in-depth coverage of an issue or topic. They may offer some historical or contextual background as well.	Writers use conclusions from research studies because they provide depth to the writer's argument.	Government agencies, research universities and institutions, and corporations and foundations.	• Who are the researchers conducting the study? • What motivates their research? • What questions have they asked? • How was their research conducted?
Statistical Data provide numbers, percentages, or comparisons that indicate a trend or show a change that has been concluded from research.	Writers use statistics to persuade us of a particular claim based on how researchers have examined the subject.	Research studies are the source for statistics—that is, someone or group takes a poll, does a survey, or conducts a study.	• Who was studied, surveyed or polled? • How was the research conducted? • What was being researched? • How were the data collected?
Examples offer writers evidence that comes from their own or other's personal experience.	Writers often use examples to put a "human face" on a topic or subject, to illustrate how a policy or idea might affect a particular group, or to explain a complex or controversial idea.	Anecdotes, case studies and field research (interviews, surveys, etc...)	• Are they relevant to the point being illustrated? • Does the writer use enough examples to illustrate an idea?

Even though the factual evidence may come from a reputable source, careful critical readers need to ask questions about how it was gathered. The table above contains important questions to ask when evaluating factual evidence. Knowing something about the study a writer uses as evidence will allow readers to analyze the writer's argument.

Opinion

When we talk about opinion as evidence, we mean a range of things: expert opinion (a scholar's argument in a journal article); expert testimony (an interview with a noted automobile industry insider); opinions of everyday folks (the pedestrian who saw what happened at the corner of Fourth and Main when the tractor-trailer flipped over, or the "woman on the street" who is asked what she thinks about the current administration). We all have opinions, and it's a truism that "we are all entitled to our own opinions," but when we talk about opinion in terms of evidence, not everyone's opinion is equal, or at least, not every audience will respect every opinion. So when we think about opinion as evidence, we have to be very clear about our audience and what *they* would find acceptable. For example, if you are making the argument that the laws prohibiting smoking near the entrances to public buildings are an infringement of your rights, you would want to think carefully about the claims you make in relation to whom you are speaking. If you are speaking to a group of like-minded smokers, you might be able to simply draw on your own experiences and those of smokers like you. If on the other hand you are making a case to the New Mexico state legislature, you would need to present more than your own opinion. You would need the testimonials of many people like you who have a similar concern (perhaps accompanied by a signed letter), the expert opinion of a civil rights lawyer, the expert opinion of a medical professional discounting the health-related claims of such a ban, and other evidence.

Let's look at examples of how opinions can be used to support different kind of claims.

Claim of Policy The town needs to hire and maintain its own resident state trooper.

Evidence of Opinion The National Association of Mayors reported that towns with its own state trooper are safer.

Claim of Fact A resident state police officer will help lower crime.

Evidence of Opinion According to the National Association of State Police, a police officer living in the community in which he or she patrols has an immediate and tangible effect on public morale and, consequently, the decrease in crime.

Claim of Value Lowering crime rates is the most important goal we have.

Evidence of Opinion Cindy Hudson, a life-long resident and active member on the town council, remembers when the town used to have its own state police officer, and she clearly remembers there being less crime.

Assumptions

Assumptions are the ideas or beliefs that enable us to say that this claim is supported by this piece of evidence. In other words, assumptions allow us to connect evidence to a claim. We use the word assumption here deliberately because we want to underscore the idea that arguments are not written in stone; they are human discourse, and thus exist in the fuzzy world of human thought and emotion. The assumptions we make in our arguments are not necessarily truths, and they are not necessarily accurate. Assumptions are based on our perceptions of the world around us and our values. Assumptions reveal to readers how the rhetor is able to make the claims that she makes based on her beliefs.

Here are some examples:

Claim This town needs a state police officer.

Evidence In the two years we have been without a state police officer, town crime has risen.

Assumption Consistent and constant police presence is a deterrent to crime.

Claim We should develop a volunteer program to serve the elderly living in their own homes.

Evidence In-home accidents increase with age.

Assumption Elderly who are served by a volunteer program will have fewer accidents.

Claim Roger Clemens is the best pitcher ever.

Evidence He has had fewer losses than any other pitcher.

Assumption A great pitcher rarely loses.

Let's take a close look at that last one to understand how *fuzzy* assumptions are, that is, how inexact and sometimes nonfactual they can be. One need only look briefly at the assumption "A great pitcher rarely loses" in order to understand that assumptions are useful primarily for understanding the mindset and belief system of the rhetor. For someone to assume this statement is fact, she has to believe that pitchers are the determining factor in whether a baseball team wins or loses. But anyone who has ever watched or played a game knows that it is much more complicated than that. Assumptions are often broader and more general than the argument being made. An assumption can support claims other than the ones being made by a particular writer or speaker. For example, the assumption that video games are analogous to real life could be used to make the claim that playing video games leads to violence *and* that playing video games helps develop important skills (problem-solving, hand-eye coordination, etc.).

Finally, assumptions are not always stated directly by a speaker or writer. If the writer believes that his audience shares his basic assumptions, he may not explicitly state them. But if he feels that his audience is skeptical or hostile, he may be more direct about them. So assumptions may be implied or explicitly stated depending on the audience the writer is intending to reach.

It's important to understand the assumptions you and other rhetors might make: once an audience sees the assumptions, they can contest the claims the assumptions are justifying. In other words, by articulating a rhetor's assumptions, you can dismantle their argument—showing it to be faulty; conversely, when you are aware of your own assumptions, you can be sure that others will have a hard time critiquing your argument, because you will make sure your assumptions are sound as well as your claims and evidence.

WRITING ACTIVITY   Claims, Evidence, and Assumptions at Work

In the following excerpt from the Scientology website, the Scientology religion is explained. Yet even though its primary purpose is to inform, it is also making an argument and thus makes rhetorical use of claims and evidence; because of that, it is ripe for rhetorical analysis.

1. Underline the claims being made about Scientology. Are they claims of fact, policy, or value?
2. Annotate the evidence used to support those claims. What kinds of evidence are used and why are they used to support the claims? Note, too, where no evidence is given.
3. Finally, identify the assumptions that connect the evidence to the claims. Remember, assumptions may be implicit or explicit. What do those assumptions reveal about followers of Scientology? What do they reveal about the site's intended audience? Explain.

The Scientology Religion

Thanks to scientific and technical advances over the last hundred years, most people are today materially wealthier than their forefathers. Yet, by their own accounts, the improvement in the quality of their lives has not matched their material gains. In fact, it may be argued that people once were happier and more fulfilled. For some, material affluence breeds anxiety, a gnawing fear that if someone doesn't take away their hard-earned acquisitions, the end of their days will prematurely arrive to finish the job. Others find death easier to face than a lifetime of assembly-line slavery, while most, in a less dramatic fashion, simply buckle down to lives of quiet desperation.

As the twenty-first century dawns, most individuals have no real grasp of the factors governing their existence. And yet, simply stated, if they had a greater understanding of themselves and their fellows they would be able to improve conditions and thus live happier lives. This, then, is the purpose of Scientology: to enable man to improve his lot through understanding. Before Scientology, the tremendous scientific advances of this era were not matched by similar advances in the humanities. Man's knowledge of the physical universe had far outdistanced his knowledge of himself. The resulting pressures from such an imbalance account for much that has unsettled society and threatens our future. What Scientology represented to many when it appeared in the early 1950s was a restoration of the balance. Despite its many successes, science has not provided answers to questions man has been asking himself since time immemorial: Who are we? What do we consist of? Where do we come from? Where are we going? What are we doing? These questions have always been the province of philosophy and religion, but traditional answers became inadequate in the face of the H-bomb. Scientology, drawing on the same advances in knowledge that led to the understanding of nuclear physics, provides modern answers to these questions. And it supplied workable methods of application which made it possible for man to reach the ancient goal he has been striving toward for thousands of years: to know himself and, in knowing himself, to know and understand other people and, ultimately, life itself. Scientology is a religion. It holds in common many of the beliefs of other religions and philosophies. Scientology considers man to be a spiritual being, with more to him than flesh and blood. This, of course, is a very different view to that espoused by prevailing scientific thought which views man as only a material object, a complex combination of chemical compounds and stimulus-response mechanisms. Scientology believes man to be basically good, not evil. It is man's experiences that have led him to commit evil deeds, not his nature. Often, he mistakenly seeks to solve his problems by considering only his own interests, which then causes trouble for both himself and others. Scientology believes that man advances to the degree he preserves his spiritual integrity and values, and remains honest and decent. Indeed, he deteriorates to the degree he abandons these qualities. But because man is basically good he is capable of spiritual betterment, and it is the goal of Scientology to bring him to a point where he is capable of sorting out the factors in his own life and solving his own problems. Other efforts to help man have tried to solve his problems for him and in this respect Scientology is different. Scientology believes that an individual placed in a position where he can increase his abilities, where he can confront life better, where he can identify the factors in his life more easily, is also in a position to solve his own problems and so better his own life.

■ ■ ■

The Hard and Soft Sell of Argument: Rhetorical Appeals and Language Choices

While the claims you make, the evidence you use to support those claims, and the assumptions that underlie your argument are the workhorses of your argument, they will not always, by themselves, carry the day. Why? Because your audience might see a problem from a completely different perspective than you; that is, their assumptions might be very different from yours. When they are, an audience is likely to resist being convinced or moved by even the best claims and evidence. In those cases, you'll need to turn to other persuasive devices, other strategies, to further develop and support your claims.

Ethos, Logos, and Pathos: The Rhetorical Appeals

While these rhetorical terms might appear foreign, you're likely familiar with their application. You have, without a doubt, made informal use of them in your discussions with family or friends, and you may also have made more formal use of them, say, in a debate or paper for a class or your job.

Rhetorical appeals are often categorized under evidence because their function is to support your claims, but we have listed them separately from the section on evidence to emphasize their importance to rhetors.

Ethos

When we talk about ethos, we are really talking about two kinds of appeals to authority: those appeals that tap into an ethical or moral set of assumptions (e.g. "You should do this because it is the right thing to do") and those appeals that rely on or establish the character of the rhetor or some other figure (e.g. "She's trustworthy, so let's buy the product she is endorsing"). We'll deal with each separately.

Ethos as Appeal to Values. When we use ethos to persuade, we are essentially tying our argument and claims to a set of moral or ethical beliefs. Ethos appeals come down to a rhetor asserting that "we need to do this because it is the *right* thing to do." It's important to keep in mind that in the world of argument, ethos (and values and morality) is not universal; just as a claim of fact is not necessarily factual or true, an appeal to values or morality are appeals to an audience's beliefs about what is good and right. This is not to say that morality is relative; if you say that we should save the children, no one is likely to say, oh, let them die. But, someone might disagree that they need saving in the first place, and so in that way, appeals to morality and ethics reflects the rhetor's and audience's shared beliefs. For example:

> Abortion should be made illegal because it is murder.
> Abortion should be kept legal because women have the right to decide what happens to their bodies.

In both cases, a claim is being made about abortion and ethical evidence is being used to support it. Of course, the ethical systems being used differ radically: In the first case, abortion is seen as a crime against the fetus, which is seen as an unborn child—a person; in the second, abortion is seen as a medical procedure a woman may choose to have.

Ethos as Appeal to Character. While sometimes rhetors use ethos to appeal to values, other times they will use it to establish their own credibility, either by directly calling attention to themselves or by connecting themselves to someone else whom the audience will value. Rhetors make use of this aspect of ethos when they feel their audience might not know or fully appreciate who they are and what they have done:

> When I was a girl growing up in rural Mississippi, I saw a lot of poverty—I saw a lot of it, because I lived it. So when I say I know how to address the problems of poverty, I know through hard-scrabble experience.

This excerpt is an obvious example of the impact of ethos as appeal to character: We trust the person who has experienced hardship because we assume that hard times build character.

Sometimes rhetors use appeals to character because they need to establish rapport or trust with a skeptical or hostile audience:

> I know you don't know me. But your long-time mayor, Samantha Jones, knows me.
>   And when she asked me to come here to Centerville, to help you develop a plan for the riverfront that would help this community grow, I couldn't say no. You know as well as I do that it's hard to say no to Sam. She's too smart, too nice, too committed to this town to refuse. So here I am, ready to work for you.

Here, too, you can see the way the comparison works: Samantha Jones loves Centerville, is popular, and has the town's best interests at heart. By showing the audience that he, too, has a relationship with Jones, the rhetor is asking the audience to associate those same good qualities they see in Jones with himself, the outsider.

Appeals to character or to values have a risk, of course. If the audience thinks you are trying too hard to establish your character, you may be seen as lacking character, as someone maybe with something to hide. A notable example comes from John Kerry's opening line at the Democratic National Convention in 2004 when he accepted the nomination to be the Democratic presidential candidate. Knowing that Democrats were seen as soft on terrorism, he began his speech by saluting and saying "I'm John Kerry and I'm reporting for duty." This ethos appeal was a misstep because it was too obvious an attempt to assert military experience. His need to remind the audience of his military experience served only to underscore the opposite: that Democrats were not prepared to be strong on homeland security. One thing to heed in ethos appeals: People who occupy prestigious or powerful positions, or are deemed experts, may tend to get listened to simply because of their status (e.g. the president, a doctor, a celebrity). As you read arguments, remind yourself to read critically (or listen critically) to what the rhetor is saying and the arguments she is making, and not simply accept her arguments as "truth" based on her title or presumed expertise.

Pathos

When we talk about pathos we are talking about appeals to our emotions. Rhetors make references or use examples to elicit a particular emotional reaction. Sometimes that emotional appeal can be as blunt as using a cute puppy, an adorable baby, an American flag waving in the background, or a picture of devastated downtown New Orleans. Pathos works and it works well—even on those who consider themselves sophisticated critics. It's hard for an audience to discount the plight of the poor when we are shown the effects of poverty on children. The logic is obvious, if not, well, logical: We care about children. When we see them suffering, we want to help. If we're unmoved by the sight of them suffering, there is something fundamentally wrong with us. Let's look again at the example of the woman from Mississippi. In the example, we saw her use of ethos to establish her credibility. In this case, we can see that while she appeals to ethos, she also appeals to pathos:

> When I was a girl growing up in rural Mississippi, I saw a lot of poverty—I saw a lot of it, because I lived it. So when I say I know how to address the problems of poverty, I know through hard-scrabble experience.

It works both ways because while we see struggle as character building, we see poverty as something terrible, something that simply should not be in our wealthy country. So when we hear people are experiencing profound poverty, we are moved: moved because we *imagine them suffering*, we imagine ourselves in their situation, and we perhaps feel a tad guilty because we never have suffered in that way or in that extreme. Pathos is strong stuff. It can be overdone, and when it is too obvious an appeal to our emotional selves, it backfires easily. When President Bush landed a Lockheed S-3 Viking on the aircraft carrier the U.S.S. Abraham Lincoln in order to declare "mission accomplished," his message backfired because the powerful emotional appeal to military and American strength rang false with much of his audience.

Logos

Of the three appeals, logos is the hardest to see and to use, in part because it is a *structural* appeal. That is, logos is the logic of the argument itself; it is the arrangement of the material (claims and evidence) that make up the argument. Writers often make use of two broad structures in argument: *induction* and *deduction*. *Inductive reasoning* involves movement from the specific to the general while *deductive reasoning* moves from the general to the specific. "For example, fewer violent criminals have been incarcerated since the state reinstituted capital punishment, so capital punishment is a deterrent to violent crime" is an example of *inductive* reasoning because it begins with a specific case and concludes with a general theory. *Deductive reasoning* treats the same subject this way: "Capital punishment deters violent crime; in states that have recently reinstituted it, violent crime has dropped markedly."

Appeals to logos are often framed in relationships, for example, cause and effect: "If consumers make an effort to purchase hybrid vehicles, then the greenhouse gas emissions may decrease." Comparison and contrast statements also employ logos: "Hybrid vehicles are similar to electric vehicles in this way, and different in this way." Appeals to logos also make use of expert testimony and statistics: "According to the Pew Forum on Religious and Public Life, nearly two-thirds of Americans support the death penalty for murderers." Logos, then, is an appeal to reason, logic, and rationality. But by logos we mean *how* writers use appeals to logic to make an argument *sound* reasonable. Logos appeals sometimes use facts, definitions, and examples to present an argument, but that does not guarantee that those facts, definitions, and examples are accurate or truthful.

There is a distinction here that is important enough to repeat: Logos does not mean the argument is *actually* reasonable, logical, or even truthful. What matters is whether it *sounds* reasonable, logical, or true to the intended audience. Logos is concerned with reasonableness, not truthfulness. For instance, the argument that the death penalty is a deterrent to violent crime sounds reasonable because, as rational beings, we naturally believe that if we see the negative consequences of our actions that we will change our behavior. We believe, then, that the argument about the death penalty is sound because we assume that a reasonable person would choose not to do something that may result in harm to themselves. Whether or not the argument is truthful has not been determined. For those reasons, logos is a powerful strategy for persuasion. We can see logos at work in the Human Rights Watch report "A Dose of Reality: Women's Rights in the Fight against HIV/AIDS":

> HIV risk is fundamentally linked to abuses of women's and girls' rights, yet prevention policies and programs often ignore this link. A prime example of misguided HIV prevention programs are those that emphasize an "ABC" approach ("A" for abstinence, "B" for be faithful, and "C" for condom use) over programs promoting women's and girls' rights. ABC programs advocate behavioral changes that do not address the social realities limiting women's and girls' sexual autonomy and putting them at risk of HIV. Many women and girls cannot "abstain" from being brutally raped, cannot stop their husband's infidelity, and lack the negotiating power within their abusive relationship to insist on condom use. Sules Kiliesa, a Ugandan widow, told Human Rights Watch that her husband "would beat me to the point that he was too ashamed to take me to the doctor. He forced me to have sex with him and beat me if I refused. . . . Even when he was HIV-positive he still wanted sex. He refused to use a condom. He said he cannot eat sweets with the paper [wrapper] on."

Why does this passage sound logical? Partly, because we are familiar and comfortable with the overall structure, a form of *deductive reasoning*: The writer moves from a claim to the evidence. Reasonable people proceed methodically through an argument. The writer also argues through *refutation*: The writer objects to the premise that "ABC" approaches to HIV prevention work and proceeds to point out *how* that premise is incorrect. Finally, the writer has made use of *testimony*: The writer uses the case of a woman who has been abused by her husband to illustrate and put a human face on the problem. Because it is hard for us to argue against this kind of firsthand experience, we accept her, and by extension the writer's, argument that women who have no real rights cannot make their husbands or abusers change their behaviors. Of course, this passage also works because it relies heavily on an emotional appeal: *pathos*. We cannot help but be moved by the plight of the women the report highlights.

The Human Rights Watch passage is an example of deductive reasoning, but inductive reasoning is just as persuasive, perhaps more so because it is the method employed in scientific analysis and reasoning: Scientists observe the natural world and formulate theories based on those observations (specific to general). In the editorial "Sports Centered," which appears in Chapter 2, Jay Weiner uses inductive reasoning by providing examples that will resonate with his audience who do not know, yet, what his claims will be. Note too his use of pathos appeals in the piece. He concludes the following excerpt with his major claim, and by that point readers are ready to agree with him because they accept the examples he has already given us:

> Their fists raised, their dignity palpable, track stars Tommie Smith and John Carlos spread the American black power and student protest movements to the world when they stood on the victory stand at the 1968 Olympics in Mexico City. Politics and sports mixed beautifully then. Remember when tennis feminist Billie Jean King took on an old fart named Bobby Riggs in 1973, boldly bringing the women's movement to the playing fields? That moment of sports theater stirred up sexual politics as much as any Betty Friedan essay or Miss America bra burning could ever do. Sports had meaning. And sports were accessible.

"Humorous" Rhetorical Devices

Often people who are trying to persuade use rhetorical strategies that fall under the larger category called "humor". Irony, sarcasm, and satire are just a few of the rhetorical strategies writers use to create humor. Writers need to consider the rhetorical situation, of course, as they use humor in their writing.

Irony

Irony is used when what a writer *states* and what she *means* are incongruous—not in line with each other. The writer knows (hopefully) the audience well enough to believe that they will pick up on the intentional twisting of her meaning, that she really means the contrary to what she is saying or writing.

In this excerpt from her humorous open letter, "Sign me up for Barack Obama's death panel," which appeared on the web site Salon.com, acclaimed essayist Anne Lamott uses irony to discuss how the Obama administration's health care reform proposals have been met with some resistance from those who reject these reforms. Lamott's title by itself clues readers in to the irony of the situation while the opening paragraph extends her use of irony.

Sign Me Up for Barack Obama's Death Panel!

Anne Lamott, Salon.com.

Deciding the fate of all those helpless Americans won't be an easy task. But I'm ready for the job.

Dear Mr. Obama,

Like many Americans, I was initially shocked upon hearing of your proposed death panels. But after a short cooling-off period, I have come around.

Lamott signals her use of irony immediately—it's unlikely that a rational person could ever "come around" to the idea of death panels.

It troubled me at first to hear that your followers would be deciding the fate our grandparents—i.e., who would be rescued, and who would be thrown on the death pile. Then I began to wonder if there might be some sort of rebate program for those of us whose grandparents are all dead. Since no one in my family from this generation will need to be processed, I wonder if the government might be willing to pay $100 in savings per grandparent—sort of a variation on the "Cash for Clunkers." You and your people would make it worthwhile for us not to have random old people lying around. It goes without saying that this would only include American grandparents. My mother's father, John Wyles, died in Liverpool in 1933, and would therefore not qualify. I think we could all agree on this.

The irony is further communicated by Lamott's use of the "Cash for Clunkers" program as a model for who should be rescued—this program gave car buyers a rebate if they traded in their old car for a more fuel efficient one.

Self Deprecation

Self deprecation is another form of humor in which writers put themselves under a critical lens—to point out their own flaws—sometimes in an attempt to make a larger point about human nature in general.

For example, in his essay "Turbulence," which appeared in the magazine, *The New Yorker*, essayist David Sedaris puts himself under scrutiny to point out his self-consciousness and insecurities—leading readers to put themselves in situations when they've thought or done the same.

It's pathetic how much significance I attach to the *[New York] Times* puzzle, which is easy on Monday and gets progressively harder as the week advances. I'll spend fourteen hours finishing the Friday, and then I'll wave it in someone's face and demand that they acknowledge my superior intelligence. I think it means that I'm smarter than the next guy, but all it really means is that I don't have a life.

Humorous Rhetorical Devices at Work: Exaggeration, Sarcasm, and Satire

Exaggeration is another form of humor in which a writer goes to an extreme to make her point. But in doing so, the makes it clear to a reader that her intentions should not to be taken too seriously.

Sarcasm is a form of irony that is often more biting. It involves rhetors launching criticisms at a person or a group, namely, their thoughts, actions, or values. This kind of humor works only if the audience is familiar with the situation and persons or group who are being criticized so they can "get" the underlying message intended by the rhetor.

Satire works in similar ways to sarcasm—a rhetor holds a critical lens up to a particular group (vegetarians, politicians, rock stars, accountants, English professors, college students, etc.) in order to reveal the flaws or vices of that group. The end purpose is often to bring about change in the readers' ways of thinking.

In the satirical essay below, which appeared in the "fake" newspaper, *The Onion*, the writer uses a few humorous rhetorical devices—exaggeration, sarcasm, and satire—to comment on a serious subject: the condition of the homeless. The commentary makes readers pause to consider the absurdity of how some readers may view the homeless: as an "annoyance" to be tolerated.

Homeless People Shouldn't Make You Feel Sad Like That

The Onion Staff

The writer uses satire to ridicule the sensibilities of the wealthy with these examples—those who might take "offense" to the way the homeless act. At the same time, the writer is commenting on how the rest of her readers might react to situations that make them feel uncomfortable.

I realize not everybody can make mid-six figures like my husband. But just because you're not as fortunate as others, that doesn't give you the right to go around depressing people. That's my problem with the homeless: They spend all their time shuffling around in their tattered, smelly clothes, making you feel awful about having a nice home and job. Well, I don't think they should make you feel sad like that.

Whether you're stopped at a light in your Mercedes 450 SLC Coupe, shopping for a new pair of Manolo Blahniks, or strolling through the park, the homeless always show up to beg for change. Or they push around their rusty shopping carts full of empty cans and filthy plastic bags. How depressing! Of course, the homeless should be afforded a certain minimal level of human dignity, but they shouldn't get to lord their poverty over people.

If the homeless want to be treated better, they should understand that people like me want to be able to enjoy a meal at an outdoor cafe without having to look at some scabby man digging through the trash. If they must hang around restaurants, why not go to fast-food places like McDonald's or Burger King, where people more like them tend to eat? They shouldn't hang around nice places. Decent people want to enjoy their mesclun salad without having to see a vagrant passed out on a bench, reeking of his own urine. Nothing kills an appetite faster.

And why sleep on benches, anyway? Can't the homeless at least put the effort into finding a room at a city shelter? How can I head home on a frosty evening to enjoy a cup of cocoa and a warm bed when, along the way, I have to trip over a man sleeping on a grate? It's especially galling in light of the fact that my husband pays hundreds of thousands of dollars in taxes to buy places for these homeless people to sleep, and they aren't even using them. Instead they're sleeping outside, wasting our dollars, and making me feel bad, to boot.

The writer makes use of sarcasm here to get her message to her real audience: those people who may actually think this way about the homeless; those readers are the targets of her criticism.

Though the homeless should be allowed to go almost anywhere they want without harassment, they should at least have the decency to go where people aren't trying to enjoy themselves. Stay away from the art museums and movie theaters. Do your loitering and panhandling outside places where people aren't having fun, like the DMV or dry cleaners.

And, if I may make a request to any homeless person reading this, please don't ask for money from people with children. Trying to explain your miserable plight to a child is one of the hardest things a parent can do. They're

The writer uses exaggeration and goes to extremes in her "claims" about the "responsibilities" of the homeless, and in doing so, shows the obvious absurdity of such beliefs.

too young to understand what makes certain people fall through the cracks of society, and it's not fair of you to force parents' hands with your presence.

<u>The homeless need to understand that other people have feelings, too, and that it's really pretty selfish of them to display their suffering out in the open like that. If they must be someplace where everyone can see them, can't they at least fake a smile? A smile is free, after all. Even a homeless person can afford that.</u>

Words That Resound: Lexicon, Ultimate Terms, and Repetition

Whether you are persuading an audience who holds similar beliefs to your own, an audience who is "on the fence," or one who holds completely opposite ideas to your own, your job as a rhetor is to at least get people engaged enough to listen to what you are saying. To do so, you need to determine if the audience speaks the "same language" as you. By this we don't mean the actual language (English, Spanish, Scottish, or Japanese). Instead we mean the terminology, vocabulary, slang, or vernacular language of a particular audience—words and phrases that they will respond to; their particular *lexicon*. In this short excerpt from Obama's speech on page 63–64, we can see some of the lexicon of the political left at work:

> What I am opposed to is the attempt by **political hacks** like Karl Rove to distract us from a rise in the **uninsured,** a rise in the **poverty rate,** a drop in the median income—to distract us from **corporate scandals** and a stock market that has just gone through the worst month since the **Great Depression**. . . . Now let me be clear—I suffer no illusions about **Saddam Hussein**. He is a brutal man. A ruthless man. A man who **butchers his own people** to secure his own power.

The language Obama makes use of here resonates with his specific audience: Democrats. Phrases like "political hack" and words such as "uninsured" are a kind of liberal shorthand and suggest what the Republican Party has done wrong. At the same time, he uses names of people and historical events to evoke particular emotional responses: Hussein is a terrible person (which he uses to suggest that Democrats are against him) and the Great Depression was bad for everyone (suggesting the Republicans have made a worse one). "Hussein" and the "Great Depression" are examples of a particular kind of lexicon: "ultimate terms."

Ultimate Terms

In those cases where a speaker or writer needs to really move an audience or to overcome a serious obstacle, they can make use of what noted scholar Richard Weaver calls "ultimate terms" (also called "god" or "devil terms"). These terms are words or phrases that evoke a deep reaction from the audience, and they tap into the core values and beliefs of that group. Ultimate terms evoke a group's fears, desires, cultural beliefs because they resonate with the experiences of that group at a particular time and place in history or in the moment. God and devil terms change with the times, of course. The devil term "communism," for instance, does not have the same resonance as it did during the 1950s and into the 1980s. Similarly "9/11" would have had no cultural resonance prior to the attacks on the World Trade Center, nor would "Osama bin Laden." Ultimate terms are especially effective because they tend to function below thought. When a writer uses such a term, we unconsciously associate his argument with it. For example, when most of us hear the devil term "terrorism" and we automatically think "evil," and, most likely, protection from terrorism.

Repetition

Many rhetors use repetition of words and phrases to emphasize the ideas they want their audience to remember. Repetition is a particularly powerful tool when used in speeches. In a speech, there is no instant replay button. A rhetor only has one chance to drive home his message to the audience, and he must make sure it is clearly and correctly received. Repetition of key phrases focuses the audience's attention on the message. It's similar to music lyrics. Usually songs have a refrain that is repeated throughout for listeners to focus on, and one that captures the feeling and message in the song. Look at the example of Obama's speech again where he repeats "I don't oppose all wars" throughout. In nearly every passage in which the phrase is repeated, it appears at the end of a paragraph, a pause in the speech the audience hears. The repetition also creates a rhythm for the speech—a tool of emphasis like one we might hear in a sermon. The repetition mostly comes after a poignant claim and example to end a paragraph, and thus, makes a lasting impression. This rhythm continually reminds us of Obama's major claim: He's not opposed to all wars, only to wars that he believes are unjustified. Of course, repetition is not only used in speeches; it's a common rhetorical strategy in many genres, from research reports to memoirs.

Rhetorical Analysis

Analyzing an argument in part means decoding it, or breaking it down into parts, to see how it is put together to create meaning. Now that we have explored the specific elements you should consider when creating or analyzing an argument, let's "put it all together" in a rhetorical analysis. A rhetorical analysis examines the writer's use of the rhetorical appeals, claims, and evidence to evaluate the effectiveness of the argument. For a sample rhetorical analysis, see the analysis of Barack Obama's speech on pages 65–66.

WRITING ASSIGNMENT   Rhetorical Analysis and Evaluation of an Argument

Use the following open letter by Joseph Kellard or choose another public letter (an open letter, a letter to the editor, an editorial) that you've found in a recent newspaper or magazine and write a rhetorical analysis.

A *rhetorical analysis* is an academic genre, and as such your rhetorical analysis should contain **your thesis** (a claim of evaluation) about how well the writer makes his/her argument.

> **GUIDELINES:** FOR RHETORICAL ANALYSIS AND EVALUATION
>
> Focus on the rhetorical strategies used by the writer and discussed in this chapter. As you read the letter you've chosen closely, annotate the argument and as you do so, consider all or some of the following: the writer's claims, use of evidence, and the assumptions connecting them; the writer's use of ethos, pathos, and logos; the ways in which the writer establishes a relationship with this audience, including the use of differing views; the specific language the writer uses; and, if applicable, the writer's use of humor.
>
> When you have finished, write your rhetorical analysis and evaluation of the public letter. Consider beginning with your evaluation claim about the overall persuasiveness of the text. You might qualify your claim by stating what was done well, and what seemed to fall short. Discuss the rhetorical elements at work, and be sure to provide evidence from the letter to develop your analysis. In your conclusion, consider making suggestions for how this letter writer could have made the argument more persuasive.

■ ■ ■

The following open letter appeared in the online publication *Capitalism Magazine,* "an online magazine providing articles from a pro-capitalist, laissez-faire, pro-individual rights perspective."

Dan Marino

Joseph Kellard

Dan Marino, who retired as the most productive quarterback in National Football League history, was inducted into the Pro Football Hall of Fame in Canton, Ohio, in 2005. I wrote the following letter to the football legend prior to the August 2 induction ceremony.

"[T]he sight of an achievement [is] the greatest gift a human being could offer to others." ~ Ayn Rand, *Atlas Shrugged*

The events that prompted the writer to write an open letter.

Readers know this is a tribute to the athlete and an argument for more role models who embody these qualities.

Dear Dan Marino,
Congratulations on your induction into the Pro Football Hall of Fame. I thought this momentous occasion was the best time to tell you that you are among a select few people who have had a particularly positive influence on me. These few include my mother, who sparked in me a love for knowledge, Leonardo da Vinci, the Renaissance man devoted to an impassioned pursuit to know the world, and novelist Ayn Rand, a philosopher who discovered the knowledge necessary to achieve success and happiness in life.

Unlike most professions, professional sports put a spotlight on their participants for everyone to see, and athletics (particularly football, my favorite sport) illustrate, in a condensed, intensely exciting fashion, the virtues and values necessary for success in any field. Further, sport is one of the few fields left in our society in which achievement, excellence and even perfection are widely pursued and celebrated. Sports fans can routinely observe all of these qualities displayed in concrete action and be inspired to apply them to their own lives and work.

So I dismiss the detractors who deride sport as "just a game," and who say "it contributes nothing to society." Instead, I liken the careers of some athletes to works of art, such as novels or movies that project what men should and can be. At a certain level, an elite athlete stands as a real-life fictional hero, like a Roy Hobbes in *The Natural*. This is what your Hall of Fame career means to me. By faithfully following your play with the Miami Dolphins (my favorite team), I was offered the sight of a man who projected, game in and game out for 17 years, a host of exemplary virtues and values.

Your top value was to win every game and, ultimately, a championship. That this singleness of purpose was never subordinated to any other goal was made clear by your disappointed demeanor after you had tied or broken NFL career quarterback records in games the Dolphins nevertheless lost. Your brash confidence was an outgrowth of your ability to throw a football with unprecedented laser speed and pinpoint accuracy. This competence fueled your unshakable belief that at any point in a game you could put your team on your shoulders and singlehandedly command a victory. Some of the most memorable games in which these qualities shinned were your defeat of the undefeated Bears in 1985, your five touchdown passes against the Patriots on your return from a season-ending Achilles injury in 1994, and the come-from-behind victory on your fake-spike play against the Jets later that year.

And it was the hope that you gave to your fans—the hope that even with mere seconds left on the clock you could still stage a comeback (something you did in a near record number of games)—that was the most inspirational part of your career. Even in games the Dolphins were almost certain to lose, you still continued to play your heart out. You knew no other way to play. And you would undoubtedly have won many such games if your teammates had suddenly exhibited just half of your exemplary confidence, competence and will to win.

That is why it is myopic and unjust that some people highlight that you never won a Super Bowl. In actually, it was primarily the Dolphins teams around you that never won. When the greatest pure passer, the most productive quarterback, and one of the fiercest competitors in NFL history is the leader of a team, the fault for never having won a championship must lie elsewhere.

Claim: Marino's expertise makes him an exceptional athlete and role model.

Add to all the above your study of the game, particularly of the opposing defenses that you famously picked apart, and the thought with which you approached your craft. Your intelligence—along with your considerable mental and physical toughness that allowed you to play in an outstanding 145 consecutive games for 17 seasons—are the keys to why you are the quarterback with the second most victories ever.

Considering all that you had to endure around you, it's no wonder you became a fiery leader. Your leadership was captured best by that trademark piercing stare you darted at your teammates who failed to give their all as you always did. That stare said everything about your approach to football: take your work intensely seriously and expect the same in others. And I learned from an interview with your son, Dan Jr., on Inside the NFL, that your leadership on he field carried over into your everyday life. He stressed that instead of telling him what the right things to do are, you mainly taught by example. And Dan Jr., an aspiring actor, also said something that reveals that you taught him a crucial lesson. "I don't play a lot of sports," he said. "But my father doesn't really care about that. What he cares about is that you work really hard at what you love to do. And I really learned that from him."

Evidence to support Kellard's claim that Marino's leadership makes him inspirational to fans—and to his son.

This reminds me of a scene from Ayn Rand's novel *The Fountainhead*, when Howard Roark, a heroic, innovative architect, sits on a boulder overlooking a valley dotted with summer resort homes that he created. A boy on a bike comes across this view and is awed by Roark's achievement. The scene ends with this inspiring passage: "Roark looked after [the young man who headed down a path toward the houses below]. He had never seen that boy before and he would never see him again. He did not know that he had given someone the courage to face a lifetime."

I'm writing this letter because I want you to know that by offering me the sight of an outstanding athlete over his long career, you have played an important part in giving me the inspiration to pursue a lifetime of values. A poor student in school who in early adulthood had one foot on a road to self-destruction, I was able to turn my life around to the point where I have both feet firmly planted on a path to self-fulfillment. Today, I'm pursuing my passion, a writing career, with the seriousness, singleness of purpose and love of work that, in part, your career illustrated is desirable and possible and can bring success and happiness to a person's life.

Ethos appeal, the writer positions himself as someone who, through seeing examples like Marino, turned around his life.

In closing, Dan Marino, I simply want to say to you what the boy on the bike told Roark before he headed toward his valley of homes: "Thank you."

Joseph Kellard*

The letter printed here was moderately edited from its original version.
Joseph Kellard is a journalist and freelance writer. To read more of Mr. Kellard's work, visit his commentary blog The American Individualist at theamericanindividualist.blogspot.com, and his journalism blog at josephkellard.blogspot.com

CHAPTER 4

Analyzing Visual Rhetoric

One of the challenges of reading visual messages is overcoming the assumption that anything so short and so clearly informative can't be rhetorically complex or difficult to read critically. After all, anyone born within the last 40 years has grown up in a visual culture and so assumes they are savvy consumers and critics of visual messages. But remember that the creators of those visual messages have also grown up in the same visual culture, and they are just as savvy about how images move us. Visual messages often are in fact powerfully persuasive in ways that we may not notice at first glance.

Reading Visual Arguments Critically

Like written arguments, visual arguments can be analyzed for *how* they work. As we critically look at the wide variety of visual messages in various media, we should ask:

- *What* message does this image send?
- *Where* is our attention directed? Where is our attention not directed?
- *How* are we being persuaded?

Rhetorical Analysis: "Just Chute Me" Advertising Brochure

The first step in understanding how visual images work on us (and by extension how we can use them in our own writing) is simply to look closely at a familiar example: the advertising brochure. In the following example, we have analyzed the brochure using the approaches for analyzing visual messages discussed throughout this chapter and following the rhetorical analysis assignment provided on page 91.

The "Just Chute Me!" brochure is distributed by the Just Chute Me Parasail Company of Destin, Florida. The company has been in business since 1992. As you look over the brochure, notice the ways in which the company has presented information—how it has combined text and images to persuade you to make use of their services on your next trip to southern Florida. Next to the brochure is an analysis of what is going on rhetorically in the text.

Overall this is an effective brochure, though it does not stand out in any particular way. But the use of color is good (blue sky, blue-green water), and makes sense given its location on the water. The designers go out of their way to make claims that appeal to vacationing families more so than spring breakers. For instance, safety is mentioned twice, and hinted at in almost every line, and they tell us they have 16 years of experience. We are also told we will be "gently winched" from the boat. That all makes sense since the idea of parasailing suggests it is dangerous, and they would want to reassure families that it is a safe and fun activity. This reassurance is reinforced by the design elements—all the photos, even the perspective on the back page, suggest "calmness" and fun.

The audience is pretty clearly families, since most of the pictures show families, or at least they look more like family photos than "wild" spring break photos. The photo on the back is especially effective, because it makes the reader feel like they are sitting on the beach. The boat is in the center of the picture drawing our attention, maybe to the idea that the parachute is attached to a boat, and so suggesting, again, that parasailing is safe. Everything else seems to frame the boat: the pictures, the sail itself, and the person on the sail. The picture on the front, of the two women, doesn't work as well—I wonder why they chose two women? Are they assuming that women are less likely to want to do this and so they show them having fun? Or are they trying to appeal to men by showing two attractive women? It's not really clear from that picture but everything else (the focus on safety, the view from the beach, etc.) points to families, so maybe they assume that the women will be making the travel plans, not the men?

Finally, the photographs at the bottom of the second page seem like ones we would take ourselves—and their staggered arrangement makes it all look so casual, almost like a photo album from a trip. Again, the photo album design idea seems to target families—like a family photo album they might put together after their own trip. We are meant to make that association and thus to think seriously about taking such a trip ourselves.

As you can see, rhetorical analyses of visual messages do a couple of things. First, they examine closely *how* writers are putting together the message using visuals, text, graphics, and so on. Second, they evaluate whether or not the rhetorical strategies the writer uses is effective and *why* it is—or is not.

WRITING ASSIGNMENT   Rhetorical Analysis of a Visual Message

Choose a visual message (advertisement, brochure, poster, public service announcement, flyer, etc.) of interest to you and analyze the message rhetorically. As you analyze the visual message, consider whether or not you think the message is effective, but do so in the context of *how* it tries to persuade you.

Consider these questions as you write your rhetorical analysis:

1. What is the overall message or point? How is that message communicated—primarily through visuals or through text (or a combination)?
2. What claims are being made? How are those claims communicated? What evidence or support is given to develop them?
3. What are the visual elements (color, images, etc.) of the text? How are these elements working together and on readers?
4. What is the "resonance" of the visual elements? How is the material arranged? Is there a movement from left-right, up-down, etc.? What makes that movement obvious to you?
5. If there are textual and visual elements, what is the connection between them? Are they saying the same thing? Is one complementing or supporting the other? Do they contradict, and for what purpose? What is the "tone" of the text?
6. What are the emotional (pathos), ethical (ethos), and logical (logos) appeals of the image and text?

■ ■ ■

Elements of Visual Rhetoric

WHAT READERS CONSIDER WHEN THEY ANALYZE VISUAL MESSAGES
In general, when readers analyze visual messages, they . . .

- Identify the creators of the message and any allegiances, biases, or affiliations to understand their purpose.
- Understand the message or purpose of the visual images and how it intends to influence viewers.
- Examine how the message is constructed: combinations of text, visuals, color, font, and how they are arranged to convey its purpose.
- Locate any claims and evidence that support the message.
- Consider how the visuals might resonate or "ring true" with the intended audience(s).
- Identify the emotional (pathos), ethical (ethos), and logical (logos) appeals of the images and text.

Just as with written texts, there are tools and strategies that people use when constructing visual messages. In many cases, the strategies used in visual persuasion are similar to those you analyzed in Chapter 3—rhetorical appeals, claims and evidence, assumptions, and so on. These same elements may be used in visual arguments but may function differently. These and some additional key elements used specifically in visual persuasion are important to understand as you learn not only to read visual images critically but to use them in your own writing as well.

Texts and Images in Visual Messages

Texts and images usually work together in visual arguments—though images rarely exist on their own. Often images are accompanied by text that defines or suggests what a viewer *should see* or explains what they *are seeing*. This text can be limited to a word or phrase or may be much more involved. For example, think about a billboard you've seen as you drive by on the interstate—limited text (you can't read much as you zoom by) with images that try to persuade us of the advertiser's message. But a more complicated visual message might be a public service announcement (PSA) in a magazine, where visuals rely on text for evidence to support the claims being made. In both cases, the relationship between text and image is important and should be examined critically.

Straightforward Use of Text and Images

To understand how texts and images can work together, let's look at a PSA. A PSA is a visual message intended to inform and often persuade readers or viewers to take a certain course of action. You're probably familiar with the PSAs from the Ad Council concerning drug use ("This is your brain on drugs"); or drunk driving ("Buzzed driving is drunk driving"); or preventing forest fires ("Only you can prevent forest fires"). PSAs are usually produced by government agencies like the Department of Education or nonprofit organizations like the American Red Cross. PSAs differ from commercial advertisements in that they serve the public interest; the PSA does not "sell" a product to viewers, but instead "sends a message" to evoke a public action or change. Thus, PSAs are civic genres that encourage public discourse and actions on issues of the day.

This PSA, "School Supplies," is produced by the U.S. Department of Agriculture and advocates the commonly known food pyramid nutrition guidelines. Obviously, the core of this PSA's argument aims at helping parents and other caregivers make sure children eat healthy food according to the five food groups of the pyramid.

Notice the images of smiling, healthy-looking children—of various ethnic backgrounds and eating different fruits—suggesting that the ability to eat healthily, and thus to succeed in school, should be accessible to all children. The message of the relationship between good nutrition and school success is reinforced by the images of children with vegetables sticking out of their shirt pockets like pens or protractors and milk containers situated side by side with pencils and notebooks and calculators—all *necessary* "school supplies."

The text and graphics work with the images to reinforce the message. The colors in the original are bold and bright and the boxed headings coordinate with the pyramid image below. The layout draws the audience's attention to the graphic and to text giving the MyPyramid.com website address for more information.

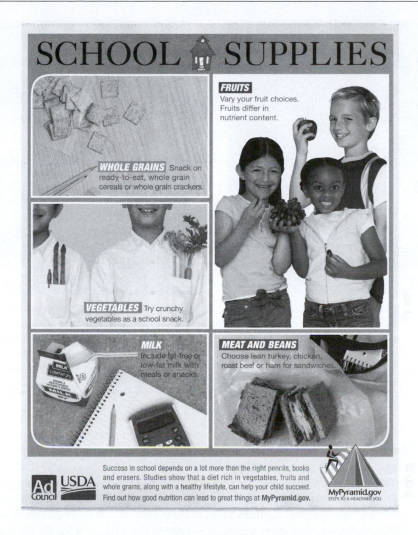

Clearly, the PSA argues that when children are "supplied" with the nutritional essentials they need, they are more likely to succeed in school.

The Complex Relationship Between Text and Images

The PSA about healthy eating is fairly straightforward, but sometimes the relationship between text and image is harder to define. While text is often used to help contextualize an image, the text can also be used to misdirect and mislead audiences, as can the images themselves.

For example, captions are often used to help readers understand a photograph. Sometimes the caption is a title, other times it is a description of content. Regardless of its purpose, the relationship between a photograph and its caption is rarely simple. Consider the following two nearly identical photographs:

Democratic presidential hopeful Sen. Hillary
Clinton of New York reacts to seeing an old
friend during a campaign stop at the National
Education Association New Hampshire,
in Concord, N.H., Friday, March 30, 2007.
(AP Photo/Jim Cole)

Democratic presidential hopeful Sen. Hillary
Clinton of New York yells at a volunteer
during a campaign stop at the National
Education Association New Hampshire,
in Concord, N.H., Friday, March 30, 2007.
(AP Photo/Jim Cole)

In the photograph on the left, we see former presidential candidate Hillary Clinton caught in an unscripted moment; we all have candid photographs like this. They are not staged, and thus we believe that such shots reflect "true moments" that reveal the "real person." After all, the subjects of candid photos are not aware that they are being photographed at that particular moment and so they do not have time to "put on an act" or pose in a way they feel captures them at their best. When we print out or display candid photographs, we often apply a caption to remind ourselves of what the photograph is actually showing us: "Jimmy being Jimmy" or "Maria when she won her first award for Best Science Project."

The same is done in the media; since photographs do not speak for themselves, photographers, writers, and publishers apply descriptive captions to them. And even though they are descriptive, the captions encourage us to see what is happening in the photo in a particular way. That is, captions become *prescriptive*.

In the case of the photograph on the left, we are asked to see then Senator Clinton showing surprise and pleasure in seeing an old friend. Yet in the second version, we are asked to see a very different exchange and a different Clinton because the caption in that one implies Clinton's expression is one of anger or annoyance.

Depending on our view of the former presidential candidate, of female politicians in particular and politicians in general, either one of the captioned photos reveals the *true* exchange depicted in the photo and thus the "true" Hillary Clinton.

Without knowing that we captioned the second photograph and that the one on the left is the original, it would be hard for a casual viewer to know for sure if one or the other really happened; which is why we so often simply either accept or reject what photographs tell us based on what we already believe.

A photograph, although we often assume otherwise, can be "read" in many ways—it does not show one message. Captions, context, even other photographs and visual design can alter or suggest different meanings.

Considering the Context for the Image

We need to consider both what is actually in front of us (in this case, the photo) and the context—what we know about Hillary Clinton and the political climate during the 2008 presidential primaries. Context is particularly important when viewing photographs because they capture a brief moment in time—a moment, to point out the obvious, that does not include what happened before and after the millisecond that is accounted for in the photograph. In the particular millisecond accounted for in the photograph of Clinton, we see an expression that does not look like excitement or pleasure, but actually does more resemble anger or frustration. Furthermore, in evaluating this photograph of Clinton, we may recall the negative portrayals of her throughout the campaign and as far back as when she was First Lady. Amanda Fortini described reactions to Clinton in an article for the *New York Magazine* in November 2008: "She was likened to Tracy Flick for her irritating entitlement, to Lady Macbeth for her boundless ambition. She was a grind, scold, harpy, shrew, priss, teacher's pet, killjoy—you get the idea. . . . Tucker Carlson deemed her 'castrating, overbearing, and scary' and said, memorably, 'Every time I hear Hillary Clinton speak, I involuntarily cross my legs.'" The knowledge—or assumptions—we have about a subject inform the way we view a photograph of them (and it works the same way for photographs of places, events, and so on).

Text and images work together in complex ways to deliver a message, but those aspects can be analyzed to figure out *how* we are actually being persuaded to see, think, or feel.

GROUP ACTIVITY   Analyzing Texts and Images

Texts and images work together in dynamic and complex ways. Choose a visual message (PSA, advertisement, captioned photograph, etc.) and analyze the relationship between the text and image. Consider the following questions to guide your analysis:

1. What is the genre of the visual message? How does the genre chosen to convey the message influence the way it persuades viewers? Was the genre chosen for a particular purpose?
2. Consider the source. Who produced the visual and what is the person or organization's mission statement or philosophy? Where does the visual image appear? Publication location may tell you a lot about who the intended audience is and how they are expected to read the image.
3. How does the image resonate with viewers? Are there particular values or beliefs it taps into? Does the image complicate or challenge or contradict the underlying values it evokes in viewers? That is, does the text say one thing and the image show another?

4. What is the larger context in which viewers will read the text and image? How do the social, political, or cultural values of the time influence the ways viewers might read the image and its message? How does the message change depending on the context it's read in?

■ ■ ■

Images and Graphics That Support Text

We've been talking primarily about visual messages that are supported by text, but often images and graphics are there to *support* and *augment* the text. Just as in visual messages, these images and graphics have a rhetorical purpose, and they are not (usually) just there as window dressing. Thus, they too need to be critically analyzed.

Because images and graphics are rhetorical, we can learn a lot about the argument being made if we analyze them. Colors, for instance, have certain effects on readers: Red makes us anxious, blue is soothing, and so on. Similarly, borders, lines, and other graphic devices can help orient readers to important information by highlighting it or, literally, drawing a line to it. They can also distract us.

Let's look at an example—the Save the Children Issue Brief on the next page. In Chapter 2, we analyzed an excerpt from it, looking at it in terms of genre. Here, we want to examine the ways in which it makes use of images and graphics.

You might notice that this is a simple design—it's meant to help focus our attention and to provide us with reasons to keep reading. The colors blue and red work in two ways: blue is calming, reassuring—we should be reassured that this organization is working for the children. The color blue is used in three places on this page and red in only two. The blue is used to call attention to the quotation on the right-hand side; again, we should be reassured by what the quotation says, and the color helps to reinforce this. But, because it is an organization that needs money (it's a charity), it has to maintain a sense of urgency. The color red for the text "Protecting the Children of the Storm" helps serve this purpose.

The use of images and graphics can be straightforward, as in the case above, or fairly complex—it depends a lot on the genre and the rhetorical situation.

Photographs

Photographs can be a powerful means of persuasion and writers often make use of them because they can communicate so much in such a small space. Photographs are particularly useful because they can be ambiguous—that is, a photograph often gets defined by what is around it, not necessarily solely by what it depicts. So, photographs must be "read" in the context of the text and graphics that accompany it. The examples on page 94 shows the power of captioned photographs.

But even when photographs are not captioned, their meaning can be suggested by the surrounding text. We can see this at page 98, in the excerpt from the research report *The State of Nutrition and Physical Activity in Our Schools,* by Environment and Human Health, Inc. Environment and Human Health, Inc. is non-profit organization focused on the dangers to the health and welfare of all U.S. citizens.

The authors of this report have used two photographs in this section of the report, entitled "What are the factors involved in childhood obesity?"

The text is about "the growing obesity crisis," and the photographs serve to reinforce the message—which is that poor eating and large portions, suggested by the photo of fast

NUMBER TWO   SEPTEMBER 2006

Katrina Response: *Protecting the Children of the Storm*

In August 2005, Hurricane Katrina wreaked havoc along the U.S. Gulf Coast, leaving more than 1,300 people dead, forcing 1 million people from their homes, and inflicting unprecedented property damage. It also left 372,000 children without schools.

The brunt of the storm fell hardest on the region's poorest and neediest children and adults, who fled their homes and took shelter in hastily improvised facilities in convention centers, churches and even cruise ships. Assistance for displaced families came from all quarters: Federal, state and local agencies joined forces with nongovernmental organizations, churches and community groups to provide shelter, food and medical care.

However, as in most large-scale crises, the unique needs of children were not a priority in disaster relief or recovery plans. Children struggled to cope with the aftermath of the storm, often in overcrowded, noisy, poorly equipped shelters without safe places to play and surrounded by strangers. Many had experienced the devastating loss of family members, neighbors or friends. Virtually all had lost their homes, schools and neighborhoods. The routines that defined their daily lives—studies, school activities and play—were swept away overnight.

Now, a year after the storm, children still face enormous challenges. Many still live in temporary and often unwelcoming situations. They have lost their communities and schools, disrupting social networks and learning. And studies have found high rates of depression, anxiety and behavioral problems among many children trying to make their way in a post-Katrina world.

"One key lesson learned from Hurricane Katrina is that the unique needs of children in crisis situations must be addressed in future national emergency response plans. Save the Children's goal is to ensure that children are a top priority at every phase of a U.S. humanitarian response."

Mark Shriver, Vice President and Managing Director of U.S. Programs, Save the Children

---

food, and sedentary lifestyles, suggested by the girl on the counter, leads to obesity. This is further described as toxic by the text in the left-hand side border, and repeated in the first paragraph under the subheading.

Borders, Shading, and Other Design Elements

Photographs are not the only design element at work in this report—the authors have simply, and effectively, used color and borders to focus the reader's attention, and, of course, to communicate the importance of their message. The color choices here—echoed throughout the report—for the left-hand border, which frames the photographs, is red, which suggests concern or danger; the color is also used to border the top and bottom of each page, and is repeated in the subheading.

The repetition of these design elements aid the reader in a number of ways: since the pattern is repeated throughout, it has the effect of keeping the reader on track as they read.

THE STATE OF NUTRITION AND PHYSICAL ACTIVITY IN OUR SCHOOLS

to become overweight or obese adults, and morbidity from obesity in adults may be as great as from poverty, smoking, or problem drinking.[30] Obesity is estimated to contribute to more than 280,000 deaths every year in the U.S.,[31] and the total cost of obesity was estimated to be $117 billion in the year 2000 alone.[32]

What are the factors involved in childhood obesity?

The growing obesity crisis is due to a changing environment, one that researchers have described as "toxic."[33] For the vast majority of individuals, obesity results from excess caloric intake paired with inadequate physical activity.[34]

An overabundance of food, much of which is high in fat and sugar, coupled with sedentary lifestyles, is driving these rising obesity rates. In 1997, American children obtained 50 percent of their calories from added fat and sugar, and only 1 percent regularly ate diets that resembled the USDA's dietary guidelines.[35]

A study by the Centers for Disease Control and Prevention (CDC) found that 64 percent of young people ages 6 to 17 eat too much total fat, and 68 percent eat too much saturated fat.[36] According to another national survey, less than 50 percent of children participate in any physical activity that would promote long-term health benefits.[37]

The growing obesity crisis is due to a changing environment, one that researchers have described as "toxic."

10

The repetition offers consistency, guiding the reader through the material which is quite long—the report from which this page is excerpted is 117 pages long. Because of its length, the writers needed a way to break it into easily read and digested "chunks." They have done so be marking off each section with a subheading in red (the repetition of color helps . . .) and by providing the top and bottom page borders. While it might not seem important, such borders make readers feel as though what they are seeing on the page is all there is—even though they know that the report goes on (and on).

Charts and Graphs

When writers include information in the form of charts or graphs, they do so often because that information is too complex to communicate in a single sentence or two; charts and graphs are methods of presenting and simplifying complex or comprehensive data. Graphic portrayals of information help us to understand an issue in statistical ways without having to understand the math or science behind it. Sometimes writers use graphs to make claims or draw conclusions based on large amount of data that's been collected, like surveys or polls or the results of questionnaires.

But it is important to remember that graphs and charts do not show *all* the data a writer might have—instead, writers choose the most important data they have. Research report writers often use charts and graphs to present the range of data or information from a study, but then only discuss certain parts of it in the text. So, a critical reader will examine carefully the conclusions or claims made by the writer about the information presented in graphs, and ask questions about the sources of the information.

Of course, sometimes writers will choose the data that best suits their purpose. But serious researchers and writers understand the ethics of portraying information in graphs and charts—the information has to actually reflect what the data shows, even if that data is not what the writer wanted or expected. To do otherwise is to lie. Thus, writers may talk about the results of graphs and charts by revealing how the data was gathered, who was polled, and so on, all of which gives readers some insights into their research process, builds their credibility, and thus, makes the message more persuasive. Examining carefully *the context* in which the data was gathered and the situation it is referring to provides readers with a deeper understanding of how the message was constructed.

GUIDELINES: FOR READING GRAPHS AND CHARTS CRITICALLY

■ How was the data gathered?

■ Who was surveyed, polled or interviewed, and how many responded? What are the demographics of those involved in the research?

■ How representative are the findings? How large was the population being surveyed, polled, or interviewed?

■ What is the context in which the graph, chart, or data collection was created?

■ Are the conclusions drawn in the graph or chart (or in the accompanying text) reflective of the actual data?

In the following excerpt from the report *Pest Control Practices in Connecticut Public Schools,* by Environment and Human Health, Inc., we learn a lot about what the chart is telling us by reading the accompanying text. The information shown and discussed in this report came from a survey of 147 school districts in Connecticut. That number, 147, is important as we'll see when we look at one of the findings of the report.

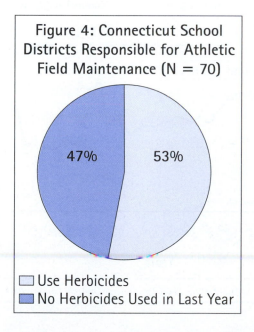

Figure 4: Connecticut School Districts Responsible for Athletic Field Maintenance (N = 70)

47%   53%

☐ Use Herbicides
☐ No Herbicides Used in Last Year

In this example, we are given the notation (N=70), and that simply tells us the total number that makes up the 100% being shown here. Thus, the 53% indicated here refers to 37 of the school districts out of the 70.

That number is important because it helps us understand how much weight we should give to these percentages. We are told that 77 surveys were returned, out of a total of 147, that's just over 50%, which means almost half of the districts are not represented by this data. Does that mean the data is not accurate? No, a 50% return is good for surveys, but it does mean that this data does not give us the complete picture.

Furthermore, only 70 out of the 77 are actually reflected in this chart, because those 70 indicated that the district was responsible for athletic field maintenance.

By understanding how the data was gathered, we can see more clearly what we are actually being shown in a particular graph. But sometimes, we also need to understand something about the subject before we can really evaluate the information in a graph. For example, the two graphs on page 100, both from the brochure called *A Primer on Gasoline*

Figure 2. Average Annual U.S. Motor Gasoline Prices, 1994 to 2007, By Grade.

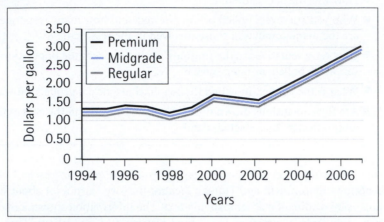

Source: Energy Information Administration.

Figure 4. Historical Average Annual Gasoline Prices—Nominal and Real (Regular Grade).

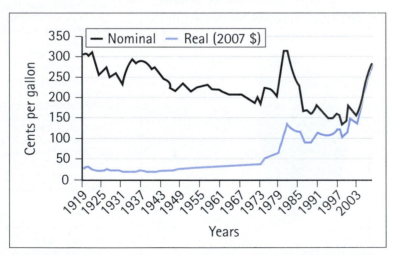

Source: Energy Information Administration, *Short Term Energy Outlook, January 2007.*

Prices, produced by the Energy Information Administration, a statistical agency created by Congress in 1977, show the average *annual cost* of gasoline: figure 2 shows prices for all three grades of gasoline from 1994 to 2007, and figure 4 shows prices from 1919 to 2003.

If we were to only see figure 2, we might reasonably draw the conclusion that we are currently paying more for gas than any time in the last decade. The problem with the graph—and what it shows us—is that it *only* shows us that the price has gone up; it does not tell us how much gas *actually* costs in real terms. Because a 2009 dollar is not worth the same as a 1994 dollar (that is, it cannot buy as much), knowing that gas costs $3 a gallon now and $1.50 then does not tell us as much as we think it does.

So to understand what we are actually being show in that graph, we have to understand something about the way our economy works, and in particular, we have to understand inflation (inflation is the decreased buying power of the dollar, or the increased cost of things we buy). So if we look at figure 4, we get a much better understanding about the cost of gasoline—this figure shows us actual prices (the nominal price)—just as figure 2 did—but it also shows us the cost as *adjusted* for inflation (the "real" price).

If we just look at the nominal cost of a gallon of gas, which is what figure 2 shows us, then we would think that prices have always gone up; but looking at the "real" price, shows us a much different picture. Gasoline is actually cheaper now than it was in 1919 and cheaper than it was in the mid-1980s.

Understanding the context, as in this example, is crucial to evaluating the information we are given; it's not that figure 2 misleads us intentionally, but that it gives us only a small piece of the larger picture. To put it another way, someone could look at the information in figure 2 and demand that the government do something about it—indeed, if you watched the news during the summer and fall of 2008, you heard a lot about the high gas prices and calls to do something about it. Few media outlets talked about what is shown in figure 4: the real price of gas. In that figure, gas prices are still on the rise, but the increase is not as sensational, and thus not as easily used to get people riled up.

WRITING ACTIVITY   Analyzing Images and Graphics That Support Text

Working with a text of your choosing (perhaps one from this chapter or one you find on your own), analyze the role of images and graphics following the directions below.

1. How do the colors, subheadings, and graphics work to reinforce the writer's message? How do these elements aim to persuade readers of the text's message?
2. How do the photographs and text convey the writer's position or arguments? How does the writer use photos or images to move readers?
3. What arguments or conclusions do the charts or graphs serve to support in the text? Why does the writer choose them to present the data? How does the writer build his own credibility using charts and graphs?
4. What is the context of the information presented in charts or graphs? Analyze what you know about the subject, data and the way it was gathered, the writer's background, the organization and so on to determine the context of the graphic or chart.

■ ■ ■

The Rhetorical Appeals in Visual Arguments

In speeches or print texts, the rhetorical appeals—*ethos* (appeals to ethics and character), *pathos* (appeals to emotion), and *logos* (appeals to logic and rationality)—are powerful persuasive devices. Rhetorical appeals work just as effectively visually as they do textually or verbally; thus, for the composer of a visual message, they offer a powerful means of persuasion.

Ethos in Visual Arguments

Consider the public service announcement put out by the U.S. Coast Guard shown here.

As a PSA, it's pretty standard: It communicates a message meant to encourage readers to change a behavior or to act or do something differently. In this case, readers are being urged to take a boating safety course.

For those in the professional and amateur fishing world, this PSA packs a rhetorical punch; it works because it has Bill Dance, the superstar of the fishing world, in it. That is, its primary persuasive force is *ethos*: an appeal based on an individual's character, in this case, Bill Dance—Dance, according to his website, is a "world famous fisherman," who also produces a number of fishing shows, seminars, and a magazine. Its secondary persuasive force is the other kind of *ethos*: an appeal to what's right, and here that means "Boating Responsibly." In other words, knowing how to boat is an ethical responsibility.

And if you look more closely at the text, you see further evidence of ethos at work. Dance addresses the reader directly, but he doesn't deliver the message right away; instead, he talks about fishing: "Can't buy a strike? Try a spinnerbait . . .". By doing this, the writers of the PSA are establishing Dance's credibility as an elite fisherman.

Once the audience is reminded of his expertise, he delivers the real message: take a boating safety course. Dance is not a boating safety expert. But rhetorically, it doesn't matter: we have accepted him as an expert in one area, and so we are willing to accept his advice in this other, related, area. And even if we don't know who Bill Dance is, having the Coast Guard use him ("Bill Dance and the Coast Guard remind you . . .") in the PSA as a spokesperson builds his credibility for the non-fishing specialists in the audience.

Pathos and *Logos* in Visual Arguments

Sometimes the **pathos** and **logos** of an image also carries with it a powerfully persuasive—if not always explicit—punch, as in this political protest poster entitled "Blood Bath 2002" by artist Yossi Lemel.

The **pathos** is obvious: people are dying because the Israeli-Palestinian conflict remains unresolved. We know this, even if we know little about the conflict, because we know that a blood-bath is a terrible thing—a term used to describe a violent encounter where people are

killed indiscriminately. The image resonates with us—it appeals to our feelings of horror and sadness associated with war and death.

The *logos* is a bit harder to see, because it isn't represented visually, but *suggested*. The image suggests at least two logical appeals: 1) if the situation continues as it has, the bloodbath will continue (there is still room to fill in the tub and it could still overflow); and 2) the history of the conflict has led us to this point, a bloodbath.

What is not clear, perhaps, in this poster is *who* exactly is the source of the problem: is it the Israelis? the Palestinians? Is it American foreign policy as it affects Israel and Palestine? What is Lemel's position on the issue?

And therein lies one of the interesting aspects of visual arguments—they are more contestable, more ambiguous than verbal or textual arguments because there is less to work with. That is, looking at a *speech* entitled "The Israel-Palestine Bloodbath," you could examine the claims, evidence, underlying assumptions, word choice and so on, and come to a reasonably accurate conclusion regarding the writer's position. It's much harder to do that with a text that is primarily visual—but of course that's also the power and allure of visual argument.

WRITING ACTIVITY   Recognizing Rhetorical Appeals in Visual Texts

Locate a visual argument and analyze how the images and text work together to appeal to audiences. Develop your analysis in terms of the rhetorical appeals at work in the example you choose.

For examples to start you off, go to **WebLinks: Exploring Visual Messages** on page 106 for examples of ads and PSAs to analyze. Use the questions below to develop your analysis.

Consider the following:

1. How does the creator of the visual message establish credibility or expertise? What kinds of appeals to what is "right," "just," or "ethical" appear in the document?
2. Who would want to read this and why? Where might they read this? What situation makes the visual message important to readers now? Given the audience intended, what emotional appeals (pathos) are at work?
3. What are some of the logical appeals at work in the visuals and text? Do these make sense given the purpose and audience?
4. What visual elements are at work in the example (color, images, arrangement) and how do they resonate with the audience?

5. What kinds of appeals does the visual argument seem to rely on? Does this rhetorical strategy seem effective given the rhetor, message, and audience?

6. What is the overall message and how is it communicated—Visuals? Text? A combination?

■ ■ ■

Claims and Evidence in Visual Arguments

Recognizing claims and evidence in visual arguments can be challenging because the claims may be implied rather than stated, especially in a purely visual text (as opposed to one with both words and images).

For instance, in this image—titled "Man Controlling Globe" by artist Todd Davidson—what is the claim or argument being made? The image is a "stock photo" from a company called Getty Images who provide "digital media worldwide, creating and distributing a range of assets—from royalty-free stock photography and editorial images to footage, music and multimedia—that help communicators around the globe tell their stories." And that's the point—it can be used to communicate so many different messages that *without any text or context*, it's difficult to identify the argument being made here.

As with any text, it makes sense to start with the title. "Man Controlling Globe" suggest Davidson's intended meaning: Man (and he probably means Man as "humans") is affecting the planet directly. That much, perhaps, is obvious. But titles can only direct readers, they cannot completely contain or limit the meanings of a particular image. And that means we have to look at the entire image and try to come to some conclusions about what it means.

Some things we notice right away are the weapons being held by the globe, a missile and a gun, as well as the businessman in a suit who has a harness on the globe. So, a writer who chose to use this image might be making the claim that global business corporations, particularly men, are "pulling the reigns" or leading the world in a direction of global violence. The evidence is the details we noted.

Or the claim might be that business is trying to control or steer the world away from a direction of global terrorism, and the evidence is the expression on the face on the head of the globe and the way the suited man is using all his might to stop the "progress" of it.

Other aspects of the image suggest other claims; for instance, the background is either a nighttime setting or the sun is being obscured by dark clouds (perhaps pollution?). In either case, the claim there is negative: something bad is happening, and the details are the evidence. Another detail suggests that the man is trying to redirect the globe: notice the placement of the earth's feet: the right foot is going forward, but the left foot is perpendicular.

Although we can arrive at some reasonable conclusions about what claims the image is making, we cannot know for sure if those claims are accurate or what the main argument of the image is, because the evidence, the details of the image, are too vague. To arrive at definite conclusions, we would need to see the context in which this image appears. If we read this image in a left-leaning, environmentalist magazine, we could arrive at a particular conclusion about it; we would arrive a very different conclusion if we were to see it in a pro-business trade magazine. The latter would suggest that corporations can help to redirect the destructive path we are on, whereas the former might suggest that corporations are part of the problem.

So this image by itself does not make an argument—or at least an argument that is obvious and that most readers would agree on. Without a recognizable claim, it cannot be persuasive. When we think about claims in visual texts, we should remember that such claims are made as a result of an image within a context, including any accompanying text—we have to consider all elements of a visual text before we can begin to articulate the claims and evidence. Once we do that, we can then look at individual elements in the image to understand sub-claims being made, and, of course, to begin to critique the image itself.

GROUP ACTIVITY   Analyzing Claims in Visual Texts

Examine the two advertisements below, both for the Iron Horse Hotel in Milwaukee, WI, and identify the major claims and how the ads support those claims—the evidence used. First establish who the audience is. Then evaluate the effectiveness of those claims and evidence: in what ways are they persuasive? In what ways are they not?

When you have finished analyzing the ads, consider the following **background information** on the Iron Horse Hotel:

The Iron Horse Hotel is based in Milwaukee, WI, and on its website bills itself as "the industry's first upscale hotel geared for business travelers and motorcycle enthusiasts alike, The Iron Horse Hotel (www.theironhorsehotel.com) meets the distinct needs of both corporate and leisure guests with its special services, unparalleled amenities and 102 loft-style guest rooms." The Iron Horse Hotel is part of a larger hotel management group called Desire Hotels (www.desireshotels.com). According to their website, Desire Hotels are "High in style, unique and creative. [They are] lifestyle hotels [that] offer one of a kind architecture and interior design. Each boutique hotel has a distinct personality and its own rhythm; this is a holiday from the ordinary—no cookie cutters here. Savvy travelers looking for a lifestyle-oriented experience tailored to Your Desires need look no further. The hotels in the Desires Collection are hip, stylish and trend setting, with an unwavering commitment to service—Style with Substance."

1. To what extent do you think the two advertisements match the corporate philosophy articulated on the Iron Horse Hotel and Desire Hotels websites? How is that philosophy visually reflected?
2. What is being suggested by the name of the hotel chain (Desire Hotels)? And what about their service called "Your Desires"? What does that suggest? Go to the website and read what they intended.
3. Is the audience the same in both ads? How is the audience suggested in each?
4. In the first ad, what is "unusual" about what is being portrayed? What does this tell you about the audience? In the second ad, how is the term "warrior" being visually portrayed? How accurate is that portrayal?
5. What design elements do you notice being used to entice you to stay at these hotels?

■ ■ ■

WebLinks
Exploring Visual Messages

ADVERTISING

Advertising is a rich and creative field. To see examples of other print ads (national and international), watch television and web ads, and listen to radio ads, type the following into a search engine:

Ads of the World

Ad*Access at the Duke University Digital Archives

AdFlip

PUBLIC SERVICE ANNOUNCEMENTS (PSAS)

The Ad Council, an organization which has been producing PSAs for over 60 years, organizes PSAs by topic on its website.

Visual Design: Fonts, Color, and Arrangement

The claims and rhetorical appeals of a visual argument are generally supported and developed by some basic design elements. These elements include what sound like simple things: typefaces or fonts, colors, and the arrangement of text and visuals on the page. However, these aspects turn out to be not so simple, as any visual artist can tell you.

Let's look at an example. The following public service announcement, "Think Before You Post," was developed by the Ad Council for a campaign against the online exploitation of children, a campaign sponsored by the U.S. Department of Justice and the National Center for Missing and Exploited Children. This particular PSA is targeted at teenagers.

Looking carefully at this PSA, you might notice any number of important aspects. The young girl—a teenager, presumably—is positioned in the center of the page, and it is

to her that our attention is drawn. She is looking at us, making direct eye contact. If we try to avoid looking at her, our gaze is forced back by a number of design elements:

- The list of individuals who might see what this young girl posts online surrounds her, creating a kind of lens that focuses our attention on her. It also suggests that she is a caught in a spider's web.
- This "lens" is supported by the use of straight lines radiating from the individuals listed to the young girl—they act as "line of sight" guides to make sure we look at her and to remind us that each person listed is also looking right at her.
- The stool she sits on serves the same purpose—it points up to her, as the base is wider and the seat narrower, functioning much like an arrow.
- Finally, the laptop screen shows us what we would see if we went online: a young girl in her underwear and personal information that she is perhaps unaware she is revealing to viewers. Thus we are asked to participate in the voyeurism and the exploitation of the girl in the PSA, reinforcing the warning to the young people it is intended for: Think before you give out personal information online.

Other design elements are in play as well, not just the arrangement of the material. The basic color scheme is mostly grays and blues. The background is entirely a washed out gray, while the text surrounding the girl is a darker gray. The text does not "shout" at us, so we have to look closely to read it (in the same way, speakers might modulate their voices for effect; if someone speaks softly, the audience is forced to listen more closely). The more eye-catching colors—red (for caution, danger) and a bright blue—are reserved for the text "Think Before You Post" and "Missing & Exploited" and her underwear.

Finally, the font is also plain—there are no stylized typefaces, just blocky text. This *sans serif* font lacks the little hooks on the letters.

This is an example of a *serif* font, and This is an example of a *sans serif* font.

Generally speaking, sans serif fonts are harder to read, so they are reserved for headlines and display type. The choice to use a sans serif font in this PSA is both practical—there was not much text, so each person in the list is like a separate headline—and rhetorical—*sans serif* fonts slow us down, force us to work at reading. Furthermore, the font suggests a serious tone, which is appropriate given the subject matter. Imagine the text in the more whimsical font Curlz MT:

> Sex Offender
> Your Mom
> Your Math Teacher

The effect would be to undermine the message and, perhaps, to suggest that readers not take it seriously.

Visual Design and Visual Manipulation

Images can be easily manipulated—anyone with access to a computer and a software application like Photoshop can change visual images to suit their needs.

Photographs and other images can be changed in any number of ways: They can be cropped, color-enhanced, darkened, lightened; objects can be inserted or removed from them; and the background, foreground, and selected areas in them changed. And, of course, the image can be changed with the addition of text, as we saw earlier in the chapter.

The problem is that it's very hard to tell how an image has been changed if you don't know what the original looks like—and it's the subtle changes that are the hardest to spot and, perhaps, the most effective. Since we equate seeing with believing, we may be seeing a version of reality that does not actually exist.

Consider the photograph of O. J. Simpson taken at the Los Angeles Police Department after he was arrested for the murders of Nicole Brown Simpson and Ronald Goldman in 1994. (To see it type "mugshot and O.J. Simpson" into a search engine or go to Mugshot.org and search for it.)

While you may not have seen many mug shots before, you certainly recognize the genre, and Simpson's is fairly typical. Aside from the fact that it is a mug shot, it tells us nothing about Simpson's innocence or guilt. It simply tells us he was arrested and booked on June 17, 1994. Any meaning we attribute to it comes from the larger context: what we know about Simpson, the murders, the slow police chase in his white Ford Bronco, and our own thoughts on the idea that one is "innocent until proven guilty."

But what if we had never seen this photograph? What if we had only seen the one reprinted on the cover of *Time* magazine shortly thereafter? (To see *Time* magazine's cover of O.J. Simpson search "*Time* magazine cover and O.J. Simpson".)

You'll notice immediately that this is a very different picture, even though it is the same photograph as the one above. The editors at *Time* have obviously darkened Simpson's skin (why?) and lightened the background so that Simpson appears to be under a spotlight (why?). The changes made to Simpson's appearance—he is now a much darker skinned African American man than he actually is—change the story being told about him. The text, too, changes the story: What is the tragedy being referred to?

There are a lot questions to ask about this second image: Is *Time* suggesting he is guilty? Why did they darken his skin to make him look darker skinned than he is? Why darken the area around his mouth and cheeks so dramatically? Why the suggestion of a spotlight?

If this is the only picture we have of Simpson, if we do not have the original in front of us as well, why wouldn't we assume that this is a truthful representation of him?

Time is a trusted news source, so their message carries a great deal of weight. Their version of reality eclipses the actual, and more mundane, reality represented in the original booking photo of Simpson.

Theory into Practice: Constructing Your Own Visual Messages

WHAT WRITERS CONSIDER WHEN CONSTRUCTING VISUAL MESSAGES

In general, writers of visual messages . . .

- Establish the rhetorical situation.
- Articulate the message as clearly and precisely as possible.
- Develop claims to communicate the message, and consider which ones would benefit from repetition. They consider, too, appropriate language given the audience.
- Decide which claims need the most evidence and support. They consider how to best present that evidence through text, images, and graphics.
- Establish the connection between the text and images. They decide which ones or what kinds of elements the audience would most likely and most strongly respond to, which ones they would not respond to.
- Think about how the text and images work together. They focus on *how* the images interact with and reinforce the text of the visual message.
- Plan a layout that encourages the audience to read the visual message. They consider, too, how the layout will help reinforce their message.

Understanding how visual elements work is important for readers, as it helps them critically evaluate the text they are reading. But that same understanding is useful for writers who want to use visual elements in their writing. After all, understanding *how* certain images evoke an emotional response enables writers to use them to similar effect in their writing.

WRITING ASSIGNMENT OPTIONS

Visual Messages

For this assignment, create a visual message for an issue or topic that you feel strongly about and have a personal investment in. Think of a local or national issue or concern that you feel others need to be informed about or act upon.

As you think about topics or issues you would like to write about, consider your <u>audience</u> and <u>purpose,</u> and think about these questions:

1. Who would be interested in or most likely to read about the issue in your visual message? Why?

(continued)

2. What do you imagine your audience already knows about the issue?
3. Where would you imagine your audience would read your visual message (in a newspaper, a specialty magazine, on television, or on the web?)
4. Why are you writing this visual message? In other words, what do you hope to persuade/inform readers of?

Visual Message Assignment Options

1. Create a brochure for a local park or other recreational activity or place. Be sure to highlight why readers would want to go there, provide directions and other relevant information, and choose a visual design that reflects the content of the park or activity.
2. Create an informational brochure about a public issue that affects a particular group of people. Be sure to attend to the audiences' values, needs, and beliefs as you arrange content and visuals in the brochure.
3. Create a flyer announcing an upcoming meeting of a group you belong to (or want to belong to) and the content and purpose of the meeting. Be sure to tell your audience how to get there, who to contact, and when the meeting takes place, but also remember that you need to persuade nonmembers to attend—how would you do so?
4. Develop a PSA that focuses on a compelling issue in your community (your dorm, your campus, town, city, or any other community you belong to). Remember that who produces the PSA is as important as what they say, so be sure the group or organization generating it is clearly identified as well as their mission or philosophy.
5. Create an advertisement for a product or place that you enjoy, use, or patronize. What is the essential aspect of that place or product that you want to communicate? What kinds of visual imagery would help you do so?
6. Alternative Advertisement Assignment: Create a spoof advertisement of a product or place. The advertisement should call attention to something intrinsically wrong with the produce or place. (See www.adbusters.org for examples.)
7. Series of Visual Messages: No group, organization, or company produces just one kind of visual message; they want to get their message out to a lot of different people so they use different genres for different situations. Develop a series of visual messages—from advertisement to brochure—using the same topic but altering the purpose and audience. Which visual message accomplishes what? What specific part of a target audience does each reach? How do they each succeed differently?

Community-based Writing Option

Visual messages are often employed by local community organizations because of their brevity and design. These groups need to attract the attention of a very busy citizenry that doesn't have the time or the inclination to read a lengthy report or article. For this assignment, choose a local organization that serves some sector of your community, perhaps one you have volunteered for in the past or currently volunteer for, and construct a visual message that meets a need this organization has. For instance, you might create a brochure detailing the services offered by the local hospice chapter, or a flyer announcing the latest "build" being done by Habitat for Humanity.

PART TWO

Exploring Genres

CHAPTER 5   Public Letters   113

CHAPTER 6   Reviews   159

CHAPTER 7   Essays   205

CHAPTER 8   Memoirs   263

CHAPTER 9   Profiles   313

CHAPTER 10   Research Reports   363

CHAPTER 11   Proposals   431

CHAPTER 12   Portfolios   481

CHAPTER 5

Public Letters

Have you ever read letters to the editor in newspapers, magazines, websites, and other publications? Ever opened a letter of appeal from a charitable organization asking you to donate your money or contribute your time? Ever received a letter from a political candidate asking you to support her campaign or vote for her in an upcoming election? If so, you have read public letters.

What Is a Public Letter?

A **public letter** is a letter asking citizens to take an action or at least consider the letter writer's perspective on an issue. Letters to the editor, letters of complaint, letters of appeal, and open letters are all types of public letters. The public letter is a civic genre written for a broad audience by a writer who has a particular interest in or expertise on an issue. Usually, public letters are written about the controversial and pressing issues of the day—Martin Luther King, Jr.'s famous "Letter from Birmingham Jail," lamentations over changes in hip-hop culture and music, or calls for politicians to stop the genocide in Darfur. Public letters are an important part of public discourse; it's how everyday folk make their voices heard. And as the dominant form of public media has shifted from newspapers and magazines to the Web, the public letter has changed along with it. The **blog** (Web log) is a cousin to the public letter; it shares some characteristics of the memoir, essay, personal journal, and other genres.

Public letters, because they are a civic genre, can be written off-the-cuff, such as when the writer needs to vent about an issue and does so in the pages of a local newspaper. More commonly, public letters are informed and thoughtful, and reflect the writer's careful reasoning and thorough understanding of the issue being discussed. Public letters can be formal or informal, serious or humorous, depending on the writer, the purpose, the issue, or the audience. And though public letters come in many varieties, most are fairly brief. For instance, very few open letters present lengthy, detailed proposals for solving problems, although they might offer tentative or broad solutions to the issues they raise.

The Purpose of Public Letters

Public letters are usually persuasive, conveying a multitude of opinions and points of view on contemporary culture and topics (e.g. "Why the Curse of the Bambino Is a Myth" or "Failures in Ethics of the Clinton Presidency"). Public letter writers have many purposes: to move people to take action, to say "listen up" to readers and shed light on an issue, to advocate for a change in a given situation, or simply to be heard. Public letters usually are written because writers feel strongly about sharing their points of view and initiating dialogues about what's at stake for readers.

The Rhetorical Situation of Public Letters

Often public letter writers are directly connected to the issues in their letters; they have something at stake that triggers the writing: a personal experience, a vested interest, something to gain or lose. Although public letters may arise from personal experience, commitment, and concern, public letter writers do research—they write from their expertise on the issue, and they are informed about what has been said and what others may be saying about it. They enter (or initiate) the conversation on an issue from a well-informed standpoint.

For instance, a letter of complaint by a resident student to the dean of students about the unlivable conditions in a dorm requires that the student do research on the college's residential policies. Equally important, the student needs to research his target audience: what does the dean of students value and believe about the residential life of students? And then, the student needs to present his concerns in the letter of complaint with the dean's beliefs in mind.

As you work through this chapter, you'll read examples of different types of public letters. One type we focus on is the open letter, a genre that you are likely to have read in newspapers, magazines, or websites that cater to audiences with particular interests. An **open letter** allows a writer to muse more broadly on a subject, as Walidah Imarisha and Not4Prophet do in their open letter "Dearest Hip Hop" (pp. 115–118). While letters to the editor often respond to one particular incident or event, an open letter takes on a larger issue, asking its readers to also consider the problem or concern rather broadly, without the need for any definitive conclusion.

Reading Public Letters Critically

Public letters are a dynamic genre. They have to be, for they are a way we discuss and argue publicly over ideas. A public letter is one of the few civic genres that actively seeks to engage readers in discussion and argument. The letter itself is a response to a situation, and it asks for further feedback from readers. So when we read public letters, we need to read them knowing that they are part of an ongoing conversation and that the genre and the writer invite a response.

Thinking about the Genre

Think about the reasons why you might want to write a public letter. What would make you do so? What kinds of situation do you find yourself in every day that might make you write a public letter? What are some of the topics you might address? Who would you write to?

Examining the Genre

As you read the sample public letters, read for comprehension and to understand the *characteristics* of the genre. Look for *patterns* that might reveal something about what public letters do in general.

1. Locate the writer's position or point of view on the issue. How does the writer express this stance?
2. Who is the writer's audience(s) for the letter? Look at the kinds of examples, tone, language choices, and so on the writer uses to gain an understanding of audience.
3. Why is the writer writing the letter? What is the purpose or goal the writer hopes to accomplish?
4. What are the writer's claims or reasons to support the position?
5. What kinds of evidence does the writer use to develop the claims? Does it make sense given the audience? How much background information does the writer provide? Or is the audience familiar with the issue so not much background is necessary?

Reflecting on the Genre

After you have finished reading, explain what you think the characteristics of public letters are. Be sure to provide evidence from the letters, quoting or summarizing as necessary.

■ ■ ■

Genre Analysis: Walidah Imarisha and Not4Prophet, "Dearest Hip Hop"

"Dearest Hip Hop," a public letter written by Walidah Imarisha and Not4Prophet, was published in the collection entitled *Letters from Young Activists: Today's Rebels Speak Out.* The open letter is actually a critical analysis of both the historical role of hip-hop in the lives of urban youth and its current manifestation as a movement that has lost its way or sold out, according to the authors. Walidah Imarisha has her own website at http://www.walidah.com/ and Not4Prophet is part of Ricanstruction at http://www.ricanstruction.net.

The writers begin their letter informally—as though they where talking to a person. They also provide some background for the letter, establishing the context for readers.

Dearest Hip Hop,

What's up? It's been a minute since we had a sit down together. I mean, I still see you at shows, we give each other a pound, and sometimes we even kick it at my spot and listen to records. But it ain't like it used to be. You've changed, and I didn't want to admit it. I been thinking about it a lot lately. I see you everywhere I go, and you all up in folks' mouths that don't have no right to call you by your true name, 'cause they don't know even half the game. Sometimes it feels like you forget where you came from, or someone's trying real hard to make you forget who you were, and that you coulda been more than a contenda, back in the day.

Oftentimes, I wonder if you even remember the times when we would hang out at the cement city schoolyards in the south, South Bronx, plug into a lamppost, scratch scavenged sides simmering with stolen sounds and spit street science and inner-shitty subversion all night, and say "fuck you" to the popo as they rolled by, afraid to disturb our anti-govern-mental groove, un-regimented rhymes, and anti-authoritarian azz shaking.

You were born a bad azz bastard b-boy/girl, a historical hybrid full of as many countercultural contradictions as the project physicians that brought you into creation, built from bad breaks and basuras, cross colors and krylon. You were salvaged from garbage cans and demolition dumps, boosted in bulky parkas, and borrowed from our mom's 45 collection, scrawled on the stank subway 6 train, and plastered on piss-filled platforms and sacred play-grounds.

You were our ten-point program, our list of demands, a declaration of existence, our statement of resistance, a shout (out) from those whose tongues had been previously tied by the shitstem, a voice for those who were not supposed to be seen or heard. Because you existed, we persisted. And you were as rebellious as a riot, as insubordinate as us, a borrowed black-brown-boricua bible tribal tone poem pieced together from the samo shit talk and sabotage spanglish, a ghetto griots god-guided tour of every gutter and all-borough bombing. You were just as hard as Harlem, as bad as the Boogie Down and Brooknam, and as stunning as Strong Island, St. Albans, and Shaolin.

You were the terrible twin of punk, Afrika Bambatta in a "Never Mind the Bullocks" T-shirt and afro-hawk, Ramalzee and Lee and the urge to get free, Dondi as a spray can splash Gandhi, Grand Master Flash and The Clash, both poles of Basquiat, painting primal anti-products on barrio billboards, ex-vandals drawing skelly courts on stolen streets.

You, the eternal outlaw, couldn't/wouldn't be placed in a box, and illegal-ist artists never got paid, but still they played and sprayed on reclaimed walls and project halls liberated in the name of nobody but ourselves. We boldly emblazoned our names and claims to fame in forty-foot-high letters on pri-vate and city property. Back then, no one would give us a permission wall or permission to be (who needs their permission to be free?) so we just took it. We stole that space just like our labor, our blood, our babies, our culture had been stolen from us since foreva and eva, amen.

We couldn't afford (to pay for) instruments or attention, so we scratched on vinyl; we had no canvases, so we painted on overpasses; we had no ballet classes on these crazy calles, so we made do with our own bold (b-boy) bodies and cardboard boxes. We stole back space and sound as

---

Margin notes:

Lots of slang and "color-ful" language used—they assume their audience will understand the references and accept the profanity.

In these paragraphs, the writers are providing a kind of history of hip-hop, writing about what it used to be about.

In discussing the condi-tions of early hip-hop (and artists), the writers are also suggesting that this has all changed. The tone and language sug-gests that this change has not been for the better.

reparations for the countless creations crafted by people of color then co-opted and commandeered by culture vultures with calculators, and the DJs and MCs of the APOCalypse didn't give a damn if their utterances got any farther than that little slum schoolyard where they first plugged in their two turntables and a microphone, powered by our war-words and spit. In our cheap converses, appropriated adidas, low-budget levis, and cool co-op kangols, we created a counter culture that you couldn't get over the counter. And back then no one wanted you over the counter anywayz, not Virgin or the Tower (of Babel). Not Sony or MCA or Atlantic, BMG either. Not white (washed) boys in segregated suburbs straining to grasp slum syllables while stretching our sold salvation army skins to fit their permanent privilege. Not music moguls and mass-media mobsters who buy our muse for their amusement and market our azzes for mass consumption to the highest (and lowest) bidder.

They directly criticize what hip-hop has become.

Back then bling wasn't the thing, and the only platinum was a Piñero poem about a black woman with a blonde wig on, and there was no half-nekked salt-shakin' sistas on MTV (or BET and VH1), and fuck Bentleys, you couldn't even catch a cab on 125th street and Malcolm X Boulevard. There was no corporate conglomerate to vomit back (and forth) our surreality, and no preacher-pimp publishing company would touch you with a ten-foot bill-board.

But nowadays I see you on every (clear) channel of the tell-lie-vision, on (and off) every stage, hear you laughing (and crying) on the radio, watch you acting (and re-acting) in movies, hawking your "hip hop" franchise fashions like French fries, your basketball shoes like rhythm without the blues, soda pop and pimp juice, and a million other mega-million-dollar marketing schemes you're tied into and tied up in, and I am faced with a painful ques-tion: You started out rebelling against the system, pounding on the doors of perception, but was that only 'cause you couldn't find the key to open the door?

They question the early motives of the movement.

And now that you smacked the doorman and snatched the key, art turned alchemy, it's solid platinum, hanging from your neck like a slave chain. Sure, sometimes I think I see the old you peeking out shyly from underneath your worn kangol, a glimmer of a vision in your eye, now obscured by the "bling" and all them other material things. And I swear I can still hear you spittin' sweet sedition way left of the de-funkt dial on my battered boom box, but just when you about to bring the noise, it's inevitably drowned out in a bottle of counterfeit Courvesoir and a cup of (jim) crow. Tired of living the amerikan nightmare, you wanted the amerikan dream, so a microphone became just another way out the hood, like a basketball or a kilo or a fast car. In the end, you weren't tryna bust out of the shitstem, only bust the door down to get in.

Writers continue to develop their point about selling out, but also acknowledge that sometimes the "true" hip-hop is still present.

Yeah, you coulda been a leader for a people who will lead themselves, a real synonym for black power, the anti-nigga machine, the Moses for the massive, the true king (and better) of New York. Man, you was beautiful, full of innovation and inspiration, rebellion and redemption, energy and possibility, but never beyond belief. Because you were something to believe in, in a world with nothing left to believe in.

They use lots of cultural references—to people (Afrika Bambatta), to companies (BMG), and to movements and ideas (the maquildora—a corporation that assembles components made elsewhere).

We made ragtime and blues, jazz, be-bop, and rock-and-roll and soul and funk and ska and reggae and salsa and more, music designed to blow minds, while the Man built factories to manufacture our minds. But music does not belong to man, man belongs to music, and we thought hip hop was different anyway, because it resisted and existed outside of the maquiladora and the machine that our papis and mamis slaved in. Hip hop said fuck your factories, and FBI files too, and your idols and idea of fun. Yeah, hip hop, like Malcolm you were our shining black hope for forging our own damn future. Remember, long before the motor boats on the French Riviera, and the champagne on Thursdays, and the "cribs" designed by Trump and the R&.B hook some random chump crafted, before you was rich and famous, when a nickel bag cost a dime, you was just a semija dropped in some abandoned lot that no one ever thought would take root. But Tupac was right; roses do grow from concrete, and that rose in Spanish Harlem song wasn't as corny as we thought. You flourished, feeding off the ghetto garbage, dumpster diving and stealing from supermarkets, a rebel without a pause, and we hoped that would be enough. And for a New York minute, it was. For a minute.

Throughout the letter, the writers continue to address hip-hop as a person, rather than as a "thing."

I hope you don't get it twisted, cuz I still got mad love for you. How could I not? We been to the mountaintop and the project rooftop together, we rode and wrote on the subways and highways before we went our separate ways. We saw a promised land of free meals, free lands, free minds, free hands, and back then we really gave a damn. I still remember how we held our boom boxes and ghetto blasters high as our head and wherever the beat fell was our traveling autonomous zone. And we did it all on our own. Now that was fame. Remember?

Peace,

This was a fun letter to read, though I'm not sure I understood half of it. A lot of the references I need to look up—and some of the language, too: Brook-nam and Strong Island—Brooklyn and Long Island? I like how they address hip-hop as a person; it made this sound like a letter to an old friend whom you lost touch with, or who has changed in some way you can't accept. So they are using personification as a technique here, which is really clever. In terms of characteristics of open letters, I guess you could say "informal" for sure—lots of swearing and slang. Sounded angry at times. And they used "you" a lot too. Seems like that is appropriate given the topic and the audience. So even though the letter is addressed to "hip hop," the readers are really those who would be interested in hip-hop culture, and music in general. So open letters can have multiple readers, and might even address one person, when they really are meant to be read by others.

The writers spent a lot of time on "how it [hip-hop] used to be," so one characteristic of open letters would be providing background or history on the issue for readers. They must have done a lot of research—or known a lot about hip-hop and the music world in general already, but they didn't cite anything, so research isn't cited formally but casually, like the rest of the letter.

Michael Stinebrink and Tommy Balestracci (student), An Exchange of Letters on College Football Championships

In the following exchange, student Tommy Balestracci writes in response to a letter to the editor in *USA Today* written by Michael Stinebrink. Stinebrink's letter was itself a response to Ralph D. Russo's newspaper article "Florida Beat Michigan on Sunday in the Only Game That Mattered." In his article, Russo discusses the upcoming 2006 Bowl Championship Series (BCS) championship match between Ohio State and Florida, using it as an occasion to raise the perennial discussion about whether the bowl system in college football is fair or not.

While the letters and original article are themselves interesting, of equal importance are two other aspects: first, the time that passed between the original article and Balestracci's letter—nearly three years. A hallmark of the letter to the editor is suggested there: it is an ongoing dialogue not restricted by passage of time. Second, the geographical distance between the two—Stinebrink in Wisconsin and Balestracci in Connecticut.

Major College Football Needs Playoffs

Michael Stinebrink

Plover, Wis.
USA Today,
December 8, 2006
Posted at 12:09 AM/ET

The latest reincarnation of the Bowl Championship Series is further proof that major college football needs a playoff ("Championship bound," Cover story, Sports, Monday).

Put together a selection committee—similar to that of college basketball's national tournament—and select the top eight teams in the country for a playoff. Matching those teams up in the four biggest bowl games—Rose, Sugar, Orange and Fiesta—would allow college football to keep the pageantry of the bowl system. Then, the four winners would meet a week after New Year's Day in a football Final Four, and the national semifinal winners would play a week later for all of the marbles.

This format would add a mere three extra games to the season, would be completed before the start of second-semester classes, could be scheduled around the NFL playoffs and would result in a true national champion.

[Posted at 12:09 AM/ET, December 08, 2006 in College sports – Letters, Letter to the editor]

Tommy Balestracci

Professor Ferruci

English 100P

25 Sept. 2009

To the Editor:

College football needs a playoff tournament to determine the college football championship instead of the Bowl Championship Series (BCS) system determining the title game ("Major college football needs playoffs," Opinion, Dec. 08). Michael Stinebrink and I both agree that we need an eight team playoff to determine the champions of college football.

Stinebrink makes a good point: we need a selection committee to pick the top eight teams based on records, exactly the same way they do it for college basketball. College football can keep the major bowl games—Rose, Sugar, Orange, and Fiesta—and make that the opening round of the tournament.

I have followed college football since I was young. I know that this BCS system is unfair to other teams. Just last year the University of Utah went undefeated posting a 12–0 record for the season. The sad thing is even though they went undefeated they didn't even have the chance to fight for the title. Instead they got put in the Sugar Bowl game by the BCS system. They beat Alabama in that game for an official record of 13–0 for the 2008 season.

They should have had a chance for the title game. I mean the two teams that made the BCS Championship Game were Florida and Oklahoma. I'm not trying to be mean to their organizations or anything like that because they both are very talented teams, but Florida and Oklahoma both went 12–1 during the regular season.

A lot of people say the one loss doesn't matter because they both play in hard divisions, which is true, but that's why I want a playoff even more because then if Utah got to play one of them during the tournament, then we can see who really deserves to be in the BCS Championship Game.

That's the way I look at this situation anyway, and so do a lot of other college football fans.

Reading for Comprehension

1. What are some of the issues at stake the writers raise in this exchange of letters?
2. After reading this exchange, if you didn't know about the issues before, how do you understand them now? If you had prior knowledge, has the exchange offered you any insights that you might add to such a discussion if you were to write a response?

Analyzing the Genre

1. How do the writers in this exchange contextualize their responses? What kinds of references do they make to Russo and to the issue he discusses? What do their comments add to the discussion?
2. Does this exchange serve other purposes besides calling for responses and discussion on the issue? What kinds of readers might be inclined to offer further responses, and what might their interests, values, and ideas be?

Anne Lamott, President Obama: Healthcare; You Promised

Anne Lamott is the author of six novels and four nonfiction books, including Operating Instructions, about her struggles as a single mother, and Traveling Mercies, in which she explores her own faith. Her work is insightful and inspiring, and often very funny. In this open letter to President Obama, published in the Los Angeles Times on August 27, 2009, she uses humor to chide the president for not yet doing what he was elected to do: reform healthcare.

I am afraid there has been a misunderstanding since that election in 2008, during which 66,882,230 Americans cast their votes for you. Perhaps one of your trusted advisors has given you bum information. Maybe they told you that we voted for you—walked, marched, prayed, fund-raised and knocked on doors for you—because we hoped you would try to reunite the country. Of the total votes cast that long-ago November day, I'm guessing that about 1,575 people wanted you to try to reconcile the toxic bipartisanship that culminated in those Sarah Palin rallies.

The other 66,880,655 of us wanted universal healthcare.

You inherited a country that was in the most desperate shape since the Civil War, or the Depression, and we voted for you to heal the catastrophic wounds Bush inflicted on our country and our world. You said that you were up to that challenge.

We did not vote for you to see if you could get Chuck Grassley or Michael Enzi to date you. The spectacle of you wooing them fills us with horror and even disgust. We recoil as from hot flame at each mention of our new friends. Believe me, I know exactly how painful this can be, how reminiscent of 7th-grade yearning to be popular, because I went through it myself this summer. I did not lower my bar quite as low as you have, but I was sitting on the couch one afternoon, thinking that this adorable guy and I were totally on the same sheet of music—he had given me absolutely every indication that we were—and were moving into the kissing stage. Out of nowhere, I thought to ask him if he liked me in the same way I liked him.

He said, in so many words, no.

And Mr. President, that is what the Republicans are saying to you: They are just not that into you, sir.

This may have thrown you for such a loop that you have forgotten why you were elected—which was to lead your people back to the promises of our founding parents. Many of us no longer recognized our country after eight years of Bush and Cheney, and you gave us your word that you would help restore the great headway we had made on matters of race, equality and plain old social justice.

People, get ready, you said; there's a train a coming. And we did get ready. We hit the streets. We roared, whispered, cried, whooped and went door to door, convinced that even if Dr. Martin Luther King Jr. had not specifically dreamed of you, his dream of justice and equality and pride might come into being through your vision, your greatness, through the hope that your words gave us, through the change you promised.

He dreamed of a leader like you. Just like you. And something in the deepest part of this country's soul heard.

After eight years of Bush, and then the Palin nomination, we were battered and anguished and punch-drunk. But in rallying behind you, we came back to life, like in Ezekiel when the prophet breathes the spirit of bearing witness and caring onto the dry bones, and those bones come back to life, become living people again, cherished and tended to.

We did not know exactly how you would proceed to restore our beloved Constitution. It seemed beyond redemption, like my kitchen floor did briefly last week after my dog, Bodhi, accidentally ate 24 corn bread muffins. You said you would push back your sleeves and begin, that it would take all of us working harder than we ever had before, but that you would lead. While acknowledging the financial and moral devastation of the last eight years, you said you would start by giving your people healthcare. You would do battle with the conservatives and insurance companies. You said in your beautiful way many times that this was the overarching moral and spiritual issue of our times, and we understood this to mean that you took this to be your Selma, your Little Rock.

I hate to sound like a betrayed 7-year-old, but you said. And we believed you. Now you seem to have abandoned the dream. That is why moderates and liberals and progressives like myself all seem a little tense this summer. It is time to call your spirit back. We will be here to help when you get back from vacation. We want to help you get over the disappointment of Mr. Grassley's cold shoulder, of Mr. Enzi blowing you off, even that nice Olympia Snowe standing you up. We can and will take to the streets again, march and hold peaceful rallies, go door to door, donate to any causes that will help get out the truth of what a public option would mean. But we need you to shake off the dust of the journey and remember the promises of Dr. King, and we need you to lead us toward what is no longer so distant a shore.

Do it for Teddy Kennedy, boss. Do it for the other Kennedys too, for Dr. King, for Big Mama, for the poorest kids you met on the trail, the kids who go to emergency rooms for their healthcare, do it for their mothers and for Michelle. Just do it.

Trusting you, Mr. Obama,
Anne Lamott

Reading for Comprehension

1. About half way into the letter, Lamott makes reference to the biblical character of Ezekiel, who reportedly resurrected the dead. What is the significance of this reference? What does it reveal about the way Lamott, and those who might agree with her, sees Obama?
2. How does Lamott use cultural and historical references, and what do those add to her arguments?

Analyzing the Genre

1. Humor is always a risky rhetorical strategy, as it can easily backfire if readers think a writer is being mean rather than "poking fun." Examine the places where Lamott uses humor. How does she succeed? Are there places where she seems to take it too far?
2. Open letters are sometimes addressed to one person but are really written to a larger audience. How does Lamott include her larger audience in this letter to Obama? What strategies does she use to get readers involved in her concern?
3. What kinds of rhetorical appeals does Lamott use, and are they effective for achieving her purpose?

Christian De Graff, Science in Defense

Christian De Graff's letter to the editor was published in the monthly trade magazine National Defense, which "provides authoritative, non-partisan coverage of business and technology trends in defense and homeland security," according to the publication's website.

Thanks for writing the November 2008 article, "Scholars Give Defense Department Failing Grade." I retired from the Army a year ago and I started working for Lockheed Martin Simulations and Training Support in January 2008. Before I retired, I had seen this same short-term focus in many other areas. The reasons for this are many, and could possibly be worth a study of its own

It reminds me of the story of a group of folks setting off to drain a swamp. Everyone goes into the swamp to do their part in draining it, until they find themselves surrounded by alligators. Even the best people get consumed in fending off the attacks. The alligators keep coming and the swamp doesn't get drained. Of course, it is clear from dry land, the alligator problem would take care of itself, if they would only drain the swamp.

So, as noted in your article, perhaps a root cause of the short-term focus is a Herculean effort, by many superb people (military and civilian) to solve the latest problem—be it improvised explosive devices, better body armor, new vehicles, rotary wing missile counter measures or new tactics—for those soldiers, Marines, airmen, and sailors who are themselves, up to their neck in alligators.

We are often enamored by the latest technological widget and our procurement system is designed to buy "things," not services. The solution isn't always a better widget. Sometimes the solution is more people (such as human terrain teams, or more civil affairs, or more military intelligence) properly trained (immersed in the culture, plus survival skills, negotiation skills) and technologically enabled. Sometimes, it is use of technology to enhance training that is needed. Occasionally, the technology itself is the game changer. Unfortunately, when in the swamp, you grasp for the quick-fix solution, which as noted, is often the widget.

If one goes back to World War II, there were several big game changers sponsored by the government. The atomic bomb, radar, code breaking computers being at the top of the list. Fighting against an axis of countries, armed with similar weapons, who wore uniforms, and for the most part, followed known tactics, is quite a bit different than fighting against a foe who blends in with the populace, operates in small distributed cells, who doesn't have to kill a lot of us, just enough to stay in the news.

If one looks at the explosion of potential technical solutions, offering that quick-fix to the latest alligator attack, one can easily see how an organization can get trapped in the short-term.

Therefore, the larger question is, is there a solution? It appears that the Jasons are bemoaning both the short-term focus and a lack of respect, leading to ineffective research and a lack of viable solutions that meet Defense needs. If my interpretation is at least partially correct, perhaps this group of learned scholars, "Sitting on dry land," could put their heads together, and in addition to delivering a scathing critique, could offer a strategy that is not built on a money argument, but rather on a foundation of how steady and proper levels of funding can help the Defense Department solve both current and future challenges. Give me examples of success where 6.1 funding led to key technologies currently in use by the department.

The proof of course is in the pudding. An introspection of how defense research money is spent at universities (overhead and tuition for graduate student research assistants versus actual research) and what was delivered as usable solutions might also be in order. Research is interesting and can become an end unto itself. It might be helpful to show how much bang the Pentagon is getting for its buck. A short term focus and rapidly shifting funding priorities will impact individual research programs, but the bigger issue of net declines in the Defense Department's percentage of the free world's research funding may have root causes that lie outside the department—not the least of which is the end of the Cold War, and the strengthening of the world's economies.

Christian De Graff

Reading for Comprehension

1. Why does De Graff begin with the story about the alligators? What does he gain from doing so? How does that story connect with what he says about the short-term focus of the Defense Department?
2. What does he suggest as solutions to the problem of the department's short-term focus?

Analyzing the Genre

3. De Graff begins with some personal information about his own experiences in the military and working for Lockheed Martin. Given the focus of his letter, why do you think he thought it necessary to do so? And does the information help him achieve his purpose, or should he have provided more?
4. While he cites no research, De Graff is clearly knowledgeable about the subject. Locate those places where he draws on that knowledge. What does it add to his argument?

WRITING ASSIGNMENT OPTIONS

Public Letters

Write a persuasive open letter on a controversial issue or concern that affects a particular public audience. Think of a local issue in your town or community or one of broader national or global concern and an audience that would be interested in reading about it (e.g. college students, a group of workers, a local community, political leaders, etc.).

Public Letter Assignment Options

Your topic and purpose will help you choose the appropriate letter genre and audience. Here are some suggestions to get you started:
1. Write a letter to the editor of your state, local, or campus newspaper in which you address or respond to a topic of either local or statewide concern.
2. Write a letter of appeal to your state representative in which you call attention to concerns that their local constituents share; suggest ways that this person might address your concern.
3. Write an informative letter to a local organization or business owner about a topic or issue that you feel might improve the quality of his or her services.
4. Write a letter of complaint in which you clearly define a problem or concern, and recommend suggestions for improving the situation using appropriate research to support your claims.

Community-based Writing Option

If you have ever done community service or other kinds of volunteer work, think of an issue in the place where you served and the community you helped. Write a public letter

(continued)

in which you shed light on the activities of the organization or advocate for change based on an issue the organization represents. For instance, if you worked for a children's literacy program in your town, you might write a letter to the editor about the need for more town funding to be allocated for the program. Or you might write a letter of appeal to local residents in which you advocate for the organization's cause and ask for their support.

Writing Public Letters

Just as with any genre, public letters have particular characteristics that help writers understand what they need to say and how to say it.

> **WHAT WRITERS CONSIDER WHEN THEY WRITE PUBLIC LETTERS**
> In general, writers of public letters:
>
> - Respond to local, state, or national concerns
> - Address issues rather than topics
> - Use research to deepen their analysis and support their position
> - Generate claims that clearly support their position
> - Arrange letters in ways that help readers understand and accept their positions
> - Contextualize their letters
> - Participate in an ongoing conversation about an issue

Generating Ideas for Public Letters

Typically, the subject of a public letter arises from our public and civic lives. You wouldn't write about very personal matters in a letter to the editor … unless those personal concerns were also concerns that the public might share. For instance, you might notice that you or your parents are finding it harder and harder to make ends meet when everything from milk to health care is more expensive, and you know yours is not the only family that is struggling. So, though you know there is not much you can do about it on a national level, you feel pretty strongly that local initiatives make a difference—in particular the increasing tax burden your town has put on residents. So you write a letter to the editor of your local paper raising the issue and asking others to respond. In such a scenario, the personal is very much relevant to the public concern.

WRITING ACTIVITY   Generating Ideas for Public Letters

A good way to start generating ideas for a public letter is to focus on recent controversial issues. The reasoning is simple: Controversies are controversial because people hold different views on them, they are important, and at some level they tap into our concerns, hopes, fears, or beliefs.

With that in mind, here are some suggestions for generating ideas for a public letter.

Listing:

■ Make a list some of the news events, newspaper articles, radio news, or online news that you've heard lately that has stuck with you or ones you've had immediate reactions to. These can be national or global issues or ones that affect your life locally (your town, campus, etc.).

■ Make a list of television programs you watch or films you've seen recently and the kinds of issues they raise. Such programs or films might include the following: sports, dramas, news programs, reality shows, music and entertainment, and documentaries.

■ Make a list of local issues that interest you. Such issues might concern your community, college, town, or state, clubs or organizations you belong to, or ones related to hobbies that you have.

■ Make a list of issues that people in your life (family, friends, coworkers) discuss or face in their personal lives (e.g. lack of services for the poor, care for chronic illness, childcare, etc.).

Reading:

■ Peruse your local newspaper or newsletter; read a national paper or an online news service like MSNBC, Fox News, or CNN; or scan a blog (go to Blogs.com for a list of popular blogs). What kinds of issues do writers take up? Which of these do you feel the need to respond to? Why? Keep track of the editorials, news items, or blog entries to which you have strong reactions.

Writing:

■ Choose four possible topics (or more if you like) and write down what you already know about them and what you want to find out. Then write down who might be interested in reading about those topics and why.

GROUP ACTIVITY   Seeking the Input of Others on Letter Topics

Discuss your ideas with your group and ask them to help you figure out which idea seems the best to them and offers the most possibilities for development. Then discuss what they would like to read about this topic: What's their opinion on it? What do they know about it? What kinds of *claims* might you, the writer, make? Who is your prospective *audience*?

■ ■ ■

Focusing the Topic: Getting to the Issue

Once you have decided on a topic for the letter, the next step is to ensure that you frame it in a way that will make it suitable for the persuasive and argumentative aspects of the public letter genre. You may have noticed that we kept referring to the topic of the letter as an *issue* in the writing activity above. Generally, a writer chooses the genre of the public letter because they feel the need to respond to and explore publicly an issue that concerns them.

For example, you may be really interested in the general topic of "universal health insurance," and as a topic, that's fine, but the next step is to start thinking about what issues are involved in that more general topic.

Knowing that "health care coverage" was too broad a topic for an open letter, first-year writer Shawn Johnson narrowed it down this way:

> I want to write about the need for insurance companies to provide automatic coverage for procedures and treatments for serious, life-threatening illnesses to the underinsured. If someone needs an expensive procedure, but they are not covered for it, then they have nowhere to go—hospitals won't do the procedure if they can't pay for it or don't have insurance to cover it. I think it is wrong for someone to be denied life-saving treatment for a disease they had no control over. The open letter is a good genre to get people thinking about this need.

See Chapter 13: Research and the Rhetorical Situation for further discussion of moving from a broad topic to a focused issue.

WRITING ACTIVITY   Focusing the Topic: Getting to the Issue

A topic is a broad category, such as "universal health care," that might contain many subtopics. Issues, on the other hand, are generally more focused concerns and are often articulated as a *question*; for example, "Should the under- or uninsured with terminal illnesses have guaranteed access to all life-saving treatments regardless of cost?"

As you consider your own topic and the need to uncover the issues surrounding it, think about the following:

1. What are the concerns you or others have about your topic?
2. Where are those concerns being played out in the media, among your friends or family?
3. What questions arise from those concerns?

■　■　■

Avoiding Common Public Letter Pitfalls

Common trouble spots writers run into when choosing a topic for public letters include some of the following:

1. *Choosing to write about a topic rather than a controversy.* Topics are general categories, such as "skateboarding." But public letters are not the genre for dealing with such general topics—they are public conversations, and when we have really good conversations, we have them about *issues*. So if skateboarding appeals to you, consider the issues that surround it. You could write about the stereotyping of skateboarders by public officials and connect that to larger issues of injustice. You could argue that skateboarding is a sport that takes skill and training, and is not just a hobby.
2. *Choosing a personal versus public issue.* Readers expect to hear about writers' personal experiences with an issue, and they expect the writer to use "I," but the public letter becomes too personal when it focuses only on the writer and not on the larger issue and its effects on the public.

Thinking about Audience, Purpose, and Situation

Public letters work well for many different audiences and for different purposes; in short, they are flexible and appropriate to many different rhetorical situations. This genre, maybe more than others, allows for the expression of almost any idea, and it also allows the writer to present those ideas in any number of ways. The audience and purpose for the public letter determines, in part, how the writer will present his ideas

But what makes for a dynamic genre also makes for a challenging one. The public letter, partly because it includes a number of subgenres, does not limit the writer as other genres might. However, having choices also makes the genre challenging because you have to carefully define and understand your rhetorical situation. See Chapter 3: Analyzing and Writing Arguments to help you define your rhetorical situation.

WRITING ACTIVITY   Defining the Rhetorical Situation for Your Public Letter

Keeping in mind the issue you are writing about and the reasons you chose it, define the rhetorical situation in order to determine the kinds of claims you can make and the kinds of research you might need.

1. **Consider the situation.** What made you want to write about this particular issue? Are you responding to something someone else said? Are you initiating a discussion? Are others writing or talking about this issue? What are the circumstances that surround the issue?
2. **Consider your readers.** Who is your audience? Why are you addressing them? Who might disagree with your argument and how will you respond to them?
3. **Consider your purpose.** Why are you writing this letter? What do you hope to accomplish?
4. **Consider how to present yourself.** How will you present yourself? What kinds of information can you reveal about yourself?
5. **Consider your tone.** What tone will you take or language choices will you use? Why are those appropriate given your audience, purpose, and the subject itself?

■   ■   ■

Researching Public Letters

You may think some of the public letters you have read were written off-the-cuff. They remind you of your grandfather at the breakfast table looking up from the paper and saying, "You know what really bugs me about this guy ...," and then he's off on a tirade and you're stuck there because you were too sleepy to move faster.

Sometimes it's acceptable for a writer to respond to an issue or another letter without conducting much in the way of research—public letters are public discourse and there is no law that says you have to be an expert or even be well-informed. But often letter writers know something about the issue they are responding to.

Research for public letters draws from your experiences as well as secondary sources: newspaper articles, magazine or journal articles, credible online sites, etc.

Searching Your Experiences

Your experiences are going to fuel much that goes into your letter since your reason for writing may come from your own investment in or concern about the issue. Articulating what your experiences say about your issue helps you in two ways: It gives you material to write about, and it helps you position yourself as a writer—that is, it helps you understand the persona you'll create as you write the letter.

Doing Background Research

While the experiences you include will help you build *ethos* and connect with your audience, most audiences will want to see that you are also well-informed about the issue in more than a personal way. It's not that public letters cannot succeed if they draw solely on the writer's personal experiences; it's just that the more knowledgeable you seem, the more likely it is that people will take your ideas seriously.

Shawn Johnson, a student in a first-year writing course, was working with the issue of access to life-saving treatments for the under- and uninsured; he used his understanding of the rhetorical situation to help him come up with these questions to guide his background research for his open letter:

<u>Background Research on Open Letter</u>

The Issue: providing life-saving treatments to the underinsured who are terminally ill
1. How does being underinsured really affect access to certain treatments?
2. How big is the problem nationally? In my state?
3. Is anyone doing anything about it (elected officials, insurance companies)?

My Audience: insurance companies
1. Who is really affected (demographics)?
2. How do people who can't afford the treatments cope? What actually happens to them?
3. Why don't insurance companies already give the underinsured access?

My Purpose: to convince insurance companies to provide treatments
1. Who else could help out along with insurance companies?
2. How much would it actually cost them?
3. What have insurance companies done in the past, or already do?

WRITING ACTIVITY   Searching Your Experiences and Doing Background Research

To figure out what you might need to research in order to be well informed about your issue, you first need to be clear about what you already know based on your experiences and your understanding of the issue. Keep the rhetorical situation and your issue in mind as you respond to these questions:

1. **What do you know about the issue?** Does the issue you are writing about affect you or someone you know? What are the details of this experience with the issue? What was the outcome?
2. **Would using the experience help you meet your *purpose* in writing the letter?** Would using that experience help you connect with your *audience?* Would an anecdote be something your audience would respond to (either positively or negatively)? What other information would readers need to know about the issue to be persuaded by your arguments?
3. **What does your audience already know about your issue?** What are their beliefs about it? What kinds of differing views might they have on the issue? Knowing readers' understanding of and beliefs about the issue will help you decide what you need to research further.
4. **Have you done something relating to the issue you are writing about?** Maybe you volunteered or worked for an organization that is involved with the issue? Could those related experiences help you connect with your audience? Could they help you meet your *purpose?*

■ ■ ■

Understanding what you do and do not know can help you decide how best to conduct your research. You may need to do some field research—maybe conducting surveys or interviewing people—or you may need to read research studies, articles, and so on. Or you might need both types. Chapter 13: Research and the Rhetorical Situation will help you conduct your research.

Conducting thorough research will enable you to write an effective, persuasive public letter on the issue—to build convincing arguments and present yourself as a well-informed writer.

Drafting Public Letters

After doing background research, you probably have a good idea of what you want to say and what points you want to make in your public letter. If not, it is time to consider the claims you want to make. To read more about understanding claims, see Chapter 3: Analyzing and Writing Arguments.

Generating Claims

Claims in public letters do most of the persuasive work because letters tend to be short, written for a large, sometimes general audience, and rely less on lengthy evidence. So as you start the drafting process, you'll want to be sure that you generate the strongest claims you can. Considering the rhetorical situation again will help you do so. Let's look at an example:

Components of the Rhetorical Situation:	Possible Claims:
Issue: Is safety and security in public high schools taken seriously? Are students really safe at Memorial High School?	1) The current procedures in place are inadequate, even though the administration might think differently. 2) People are concerned with increased violence at the schools, including Memorial High School.
Audience: School officials, parents, and teachers	1) Parents are unaware of how unsafe their kids are. 2) Teachers are not given the proper training they need to adequately protect students in their classrooms.
Purpose: To convince school officials at Memorial High School to implement new security programs	1) The new security programs include security training for teachers, even though they may feel security is not part of their job, since they are the ones who are with the students the most. 2) New security programs will make students feel safer. 3) New security programs will help administrators protect students from violence on school property. 4) New security programs will help parents have peace of mind when they send their children to school.
Writer's Connection: Graduate of Memorial High School	1) I know what it is like to feel unsafe at M.H.S. 2) When I was there we heard about kids who planned to commit violent acts at the school. 3) When you feel unsafe as a student, it makes you unable to concentrate on what's happening in the classroom.

Notice that in this example all the writer did was infer from the details of the rhetorical situation what kinds of claims could be made. Each of these claims, in turn, suggests areas that might be researched.

WRITING ACTIVITY   Generating Claims for Your Public Letter

Write down your issue or concern, your audience, your purpose, and your connection to the issue.

Generate claims for each part of the rhetorical situation of your public letter. Brainstorm at least 3–4 claims in response to the details you know about each part.

1. **Issue:** What questions are raised? Why is it a concern? What claims can you make about these questions or concerns? Will others see the concerns or problems differently?
2. **Audience:** Who are the intended readers for your letter? What do you know about their beliefs and values? What do you know about their views on the issue? What parts do they disagree on? Write down the possible claims.

3. **Purpose:** What are the goals of this letter? What do you hope to gain by writing it? What claims could you make to fulfill your purpose?
4. **Writer's connection:** How are you connected to the issue? What kinds of experiences do you have with the issue? What claims can you make based on your experiences?

■   ■   ■

Organizing Public Letters

Because public letters tend to be brief, the organization of your claims is particularly important—you need to move your reader along quickly, keeping them engaged while also persuading them to see the issue from your perspective. Your claims will help you do this, but so will the order you choose to present your claims.

Options for Organizing Public Letters

1. *From most important or strongest claim to least.* This order provides readers with your strongest point first, which has the best chance of interesting them in the issue.
2. *From least important or weakest claim to most.* This order builds your argument to a crescendo or tipping point, where readers can no longer disagree with you. It also works well if you think your audience is likely to automatically disagree with you.
3. *By topic.* By grouping similar claims together, you show readers the range of connected points as well as the complexity of those points.
4. *By cause and effect.* Such an organization introduces inevitability in to your argument: If X is the case, then Y will happen (or not). But be wary of cause and effect claims as they often can lead to flaws in logic and conclusions that are unprovable.
5. *Disproving the differing views.* You might build your argument by responding to each of the key arguments made by readers you disagree with, thus showing readers you have investigated the issue in depth and can find flaws with each argument.
6. *By point/counterpoint.* Such an organization works well when you anticipate a skeptical audience, one that is already predisposed to disagree with you. By making your claim and then anticipating and responding to the counterclaims, you build ethos as a fair-minded individual and are able to show readers how your claims are stronger than the counterclaims.

Openings and Closings for Public Letters

Although openings and closings bear some similarities across genres, there are some approaches specific to public letters. One primary challenge stems from the nature of the genre; it is public, and thus there is no inherent reason why any one person might want to read the letter. Whereas a reader might search out a research report, proposal, or memoir, they may not necessarily do so with public letters. In part, this is due to how public letters are disseminated: often in a newspaper, as in the case of editorials and open letters, or in what is not so kindly called junk mail, in the case of letters of appeal.

So your challenge is to give a disinterested (at best) audience a reason to read your letter.

Write several possible openings for your public letter, keeping in mind your audience and purpose. Consider sharing your choices with other writers to get their feedback. Then choose the one that seems most appropriate.

1. **Establish the concern.** A writer may choose this opening when she thinks her readers might be unfamiliar with the issue and so needs to fill them in on the situation. Or a writer may choose it when she is entering an ongoing conversation and needs to say what she is responding to: another letter, a recent event, and so on.
2. **Address the audience and what they might be thinking or feeling.** If a writer thinks his audience will be resistant to his perspective on the issue, he may need to acknowledge their feelings or ideas. A writer might need to establish a connection with his audience by showing that he understands their concerns.
3. **Establish your credibility.** If a writer is addressing a particularly contentious issue or is asking her readers to do something, she may need to establish her credibility immediately—she needs to show her audience that she has some expertise on the issue and that they can trust her.
4. **Get to the point.** Since letters are usually brief, a writer might choose to just say what's on his mind as the best way to establish his credibility and connect with his audience.

■　■　■

Closings for public letters depend in part on the writer's purpose. If the writer is calling for some action ("write your congressperson to tell them you do not support public education budget cuts"), then the letter might be closed with a call for readers to act. Closing a public letter is also determined by the situation or context surrounding the letter writing. If the issue is about a recent controversy, chances are the writer is writing about a preexisting situation. In that case, the closing may refer readers back to the conversational thread the writer has picked up on.

The audience, purpose, and the situation of your public letter help you determine its closing. Brainstorm some possible closings for your letter using the suggestions below.

1. **Suggest an action be taken.** Depending on the writer's purpose, a letter may end with an appeal for time, money, or volunteers. Or it may ask readers to participate in a letter writing campaign, write or call their representatives to support a policy change, or engage in a civic activity.
2. **Remind readers of consequences.** A letter writer may choose to emphasize the direness of a situation to leave readers with a sense of urgency or to remind readers how they might be affected by the issue. Pathos appeals often emphasize the critical status of an issue.

3. **End with a question.** This type of closing gives readers something to think about or choices to consider. Sometimes ending a letter with a rhetorical question, one where an answer is already assumed by the writer, can emphasize the writer's position.

■ ■ ■

Revising Public Letters

Because letters are part of an ongoing conversation that neither begins nor ends with the particular letter, there are two areas that require special attention during the revision process: the audience's response and the larger context of the letter.

Anticipating Audience Response

Even if you are initiating the conversation in your local newspaper, it is unlikely that you will be telling your readers something they have never heard of. They will, instead, read your public letter with some ideas of their own—preconceptions—that they will know are true (since no one thinks what they know is false).

Preconceptions are a challenge to the writer of a public letter. The writer has to anticipate reader objections and responses to the ideas being presented and address them.

WRITING ACTIVITY   Anticipating Audience Response

Consider the issue you are writing about or what you are asking readers to do.

1. **Is the issue particularly controversial or divisive?** Will your audience have strong opinions about the issue? How can you counter those responses? How can you make use of those responses if they are in your favor?
2. **Is the issue you are writing about one that readers will be unfamiliar with?** Will you give them a brief introduction to the issue? What further background should you give them so they aren't confused about your point?

■ ■ ■

Engaging in the Conversation: Contextualizing Your Letter

Since letters are part of an ongoing conversation, it is important that letter writers acknowledge that conversation in their own letters. Sometimes this acknowledgement is as simple as noting what you are writing in response to. Such a statement communicates to readers that your letter is a response to something someone else wrote (whether a news article or other public letter) or something you saw on the television or heard on the radio.

Sometimes, though, you need to contextualize your letter more thoroughly in the ongoing conversation, and you do this by making more fully developed references to what others have said about the issue. (Please see the exchange of letters between Balestracci and Stinebrink reproduced on pages 120–121 for examples of how writers contextualize their letters.)

Engaging in the Conversation

Consider the context of your letter, and then use the prompts below to revise your draft.

1. If you are writing in response to a particular letter or writer, have you acknowledged this in your own letter? Have you fairly and accurately represented what that writer actually said?
2. Are there places in your letter where you need to more fully reference and make use of what others have said about your issue? Look for places where you can incorporate other voices in the conversation to illustrate not only your own knowledge but also to show the breadth and depth of the discussion.
3. Are there differing views that you need to respond to that you haven't? Doing so will strengthen the persuasiveness of your argument, especially if you are responding to a letter you disagree with.

■   ■   ■

PEER REVIEW   *for Public Letters*

As you read, give specific comments and suggestions that will help the writer revise the draft. (e.g. "This is confusing <u>because</u> I don't really know anything about your issue—could you provide some more background information?")

Comment in the margins on the following:

OPENING: What is the issue the writer is addressing? What is the writer's argument or perspective on the issue? Is the writer responding to another letter, writer, or a recent event? Underline the parts of the opening paragraphs where you learn the argument and to whom or what the writer is responding.

ENGAGING THE READER: How does the writer engage you as a reader in this issue or concern? Comment on the specific areas where you find yourself most involved or parts that make you want to read on.

CLOSING: Do you know what the writer wants his audience to do by the closing? Comment on the closing paragraphs to help the writer clarify the action required of readers or add other necessary information.

Finally when you have finished reading and annotating, write an endnote to the writer in which you comment on the following:

Begin by telling the writer what you enjoyed about the letter (be specific).

DEVELOPING THE ISSUE: How does the writer use evidence and details to explain and develop the issue? How could the writer better use evidence and details to develop his letter?

(continued)

ENGAGING THE AUDIENCE: How does the writer engage the audience? What kinds of appeals has the writer used to address readers' concerns and values about the issue? How could the writer address the audience better?

ADDRESS THE AUDIENCES' RESPONSES: How does the writer address the views of others? Does the writer anticipate the audience's response to his perspective? Where might he do so? Where might he include the voices of those who have written about the issue or research to show the details of those conversations?

Reflecting on the Process

Reflecting on the choices you made as a writer as you wrote your public letter may help you better understand why you made those and how they helped you to achieve your goals or not. Examining your choices critically may help you make different choices next time you find yourself writing a public letter.

WRITING ACTIVITY   Reflecting on Writing a Public Letter

Reflect on your writing process for your letter: how you generated ideas, did research, and drafted and revised your letter. Imagine you are writing this reflection for writers who have never written a public letter. What might they learn about working with the genre from you? What could you tell them that might help them as writers?

1. **Begin** by describing what aspects you are most pleased with in your letter.
2. **Analyze** your strengths and weaknesses as a writer for this letter.
3. **Explain** what you think contributed to your success in these areas.
4. **Reflect** on how you determined your purpose and audience for your letter. How did these elements influence your choice of arguments or examples?
5. **Discuss** your revision process, including how you used feedback from your readers.
6. **Conclude** by reflecting on what you learned about the genre of public letters. You might also reflect on what you might do differently the next time you write a letter.

■ ■ ■

Katie Hicks's Open Letter

Katie Hicks, a student in a first-year writing course, wrote an open letter about the need for more parental involvement in the lives of their children; she argues that lack of involvement is the root of a lot of the trouble that teenagers can find themselves in when left unsupervised and uninvolved in activities outside the high school classroom. She uses herself as an example, but she also draws on research to support and develop her points.

Generating Ideas for the Open Letter

Although Hicks ultimately decided to write about parental involvement in the lives of their children, especially teenagers, it took her a long time to focus on that issue. When she first began thinking about topics for her open letter, she was thinking primarily about the need for a skate park for teenagers in her hometown; the lack of one was the cause of some of the criminal behavior in her town. You can see the core idea that eventually became the focus of her letter, but it took her a while to get there.

Notice that Hicks has a range of ideas here, but they all seem to point to the need to get teenagers involved in positive activities.

Listing:
Why do kids need organized events outside of school?
The increasing crime rate
The need for a skate park in my town
Getting the people in town to attend important town meetings
Morals and rule of parenting and how they have changed
Underage drinking and drugs

Possible topics:
I like the idea of doing something with the crime rate, since it seems to be going up every year. I'm not really sure what I would say about it though. I know in my town it has not been that big a deal, but I live in a small town. I know firsthand that cities like Hartford and New Haven are pretty violent.

I could write about skate parks pretty easily; I have friends who skate and there really is no place for them to do it my town. There is not much of anything to do in town, so we basically just hang out most of the time. I think a skate park would really help kids out and give them a place to hang out where they can do their own thing.

I don't really have anything to say about morals and parenting. Just an idea I threw out. My parents were pretty cool, and so were my friends' parents, so I can't even make fun of them.

Lots to say about underage drinking and drug use. Happened all the time in my high school—we had nothing else to do, so we drank. Alcohol was easy to get, usually from our parents' stash.

Later, Hicks will actually find a way to bring almost all these ideas together into her open letter on parental involvement.

Thinking about Audience, Purpose, and Situation

Initially, Hicks chose to write about how the crime rate can be lowered by providing more activities for teenagers after school lets out, and we can see her here trying to articulate the rhetorical situation for that issue. But it is a big issue, and because she is still unclear about the connection between teenagers, activities, and crime, her rhetorical situation is not all that well-defined.

Notice how Hicks is still unsure about her issue—she seems to go back and forth on whether she is writing about the crime rate or what kids do after school.

Hicks contextualizes her letter in a larger, national concern, while also responding to a particular incident.

Defining the Rhetorical Situation

Topic:	Why do kids these days need organized events outside of school?
	Where are the parents?
	What percentage of kids are home alone after school?
	What are kids doing after school?
	What is the current youth crime rate?
	What is the youth crime rate from to 20 years ago?
Situation:	The increased crime rate among teenagers
	What different towns are doing to stop it
	The kid in San Diego who shot someone at school
Audience:	Parents of teens
	What will encourage them to do something about their kids
Purpose:	I'd like to generate awareness as to why the youth crime rate has risen and what we can do about it.
Writer:	A person who feels that the crime rate needs to be lowered.
	I will be serious, yet sarcastic in tone.

Drafting the Open Letter

Drawing on her understanding of the rhetorical situation, Hicks generated possible claims and used those to help her figure out what research she needed to conduct (see Chapter 13: Research and the Rhetorical Situation). She then wrote a rough draft of her open letter. Notice how her draft pinpoints the issues surrounding the recent increase in crime among adolescents that prompted her to enter what is probably an ongoing conversation among many of her readers.

She has defined a very particular audience, one she feels is in the best position to do something about the concerns she raises.

Katie Hicks
Professor Ferruci
17 Sept. 2007
English 100P

Open Letter Draft 1

Dear Parents of Teenagers:

    I am sure that recently you have picked up a newspaper or watched the news and found some headline about teenagers getting arrested or caught drinking or doing drugs. If you haven't noticed, this is an ongoing issue, and it is only going to get worse. I know what you're thinking right now, who is this girl and what does she know about parenting or raising a teen? Well I don't have any experience raising a child or parenting but I do know a whole lot about what your kids are going through because I went through it myself and am still continuing to go through it.

I don't want you to think that I am some perfect role model for what kids should be like, because I am not; in fact, I have contributed to those headlines that you read about in the paper. I started drinking when I was thirteen years old and in my 8th grade year. I participated in no after-school activities, my parents weren't there after school, and I wanted to fit in with my older friends. This led me to start drinking after school when my parents weren't home; I would just sit in my room with my friends and drink my parent's alcohol because there was no one there to tell me not to. This all caught up to me one Halloween when I drank myself into an alcohol-induced coma and didn't wake up for 12 hours. I was close to death and my blood alcohol level was more than 4 times the normal limit. This experience changed my life in a way that I never thought possible.

Because of this situation I was no longer allowed to hang out with the kids that I was with that night; this made me make all new friends going into freshman year of high school. My parents also made me get involved in an after-school activity because they did not trust me to be home alone when they weren't out of work yet. With these rules intact, I joined the chorus, soccer team, and the freshman class board. These activities kept me after school later and kept me away from being home alone to do whatever I pleased.

Now I am not saying that your child is going to end up in the situation that I was, but it could very well be something similar. What helped me was joining after-school activities; these kept me away from temptation and got me back on honor roll all the way up to my senior year where I achieved high honors. A study of over five thousand 8th graders and their parents concluded that if a child was left home for more then 11 hours a week then that child was more likely than other children to get involved in alcohol, tobacco, and marijuana.

That study is not a comfortable one to go to bed with at night, but let's face it, when you are at work you have no idea where your child is after he/she gets out of school. My friends and I were famous for lying about where we were after school when our parents would ask because we figured, which is the truth, that our parents had no way to find out what we were really doing.

I always wondered why the crime rate and teenage drug abuse is such a problem now and it wasn't, say, 50 years ago. Well, 50 years ago very few women went to college and worked. The mother was generally home taking care of the house while the husband was at work. Because the mothers were home, kids couldn't sneak alcohol in their house and go get drunk in their room. Now that women are so much more empowered and go to college and succeed in the workforce, it is difficult for them to be home when their children get off the bus, so I am not recommending being home when your kids get home. What I am recommending is to get your kids involved in an after-school activity. Don't feel that you are alone in this and that your child is the only one being left home alone. Studies show that about 3,500,000 children in America are home alone after school. The shocking part is that these children, ranging from age 5 to 12, are on their own for up to an hour a day.

Now I know that I talked briefly about my story and how I changed myself, but there are many cases where teenagers get mixed in with the wrong crowd and activities. This happened to what used to be a close friend of mine; we did everything together up until my freshman year of high school when I started noticing big changes in her. The two of us would drink occasionally on the weekends (before my incident on Halloween) and would go to parties. Then she started dating a guy who was much older and was a drug dealer; her mom had no idea because she worked at a hospital and was barely ever home. Soon smoking weed for my friend turned into doing cocaine and then to heroin and then to barely graduating high school.

Now she is two years out of high school and works at the town gas station and never made it to college and still continues to date the same guy she did when she was a freshman in high school. This is because her parents were divorced and she only stayed with her mother who was never home and she never got involved with any after-school activities to keep her away from being home alone every day from the time she was 13 until now.

Again I am not saying that this will be your child; I am just saying that it is possible for your teenager to get stuck in situations like this. It is your job to stay aware and active in your child's life and to limit their time spent alone as much as you can. Again I come to you as someone that went through these hard times and was lucky enough to have had parents who cared to fix the problem and point me on the right path of where I belonged. Staying involved in your child's life and getting them to do after-school activities is so critical in their life and they will only benefit from it in the long run.

Sincerely,
Katie Hicks

Here she uses her friend as an example of what can happen to unsupervised children. It is another extreme example.

Hicks comes back to the problem of parenting, and here she introduces the idea that a broken home is to blame, at least in part, for what happened to her.

Revising the Open Letter: Peer Review

Because public letters are conversations, Hicks wanted to have some early feedback to her letter from readers who could help her revise and improve it. Her readers gave her good feedback, but some of it was contradictory, and so she had to decide how to negotiate the differing suggestions she received. In the following excerpt we show the original draft with the reviewers' comments as well as Hicks' revisions and commentary after she revised for the peer suggestions.

Reviewer 1: I think you should get rid of this first sentence or rewrite it because it seems like you are contradicting yourself. I know you are trying to establish ethos, but maybe talk about the general experience instead of just yourself?

Reviewer 2: How did you get to the hospital? Did your friends help you? Or did you just wake up on your own? Might add some more emotional appeal to the story?

Reviewer 2: This is a great story—helps us see the problem!

Reviewer 1: Do you really need this story? Your story is more important, and I'd like to know more about you.

Dear Parents of Teenagers:

. . .

~~I don't want you to think that I am some perfect role model for what kids should be like because I am not, in fact I have contributed to those headlines that you read about in the paper.~~ *Going through high school is an extremely hard time, especially being a freshman, because you just want to fit in. I gave in to peer pressure and* started drinking when I was *fifteen* ~~thirteen I started drinking when I was thirteen years old and in my 8th grade year.~~ I participated in no after-school activities, my parents weren't there after school, and I wanted to fit in with my older friends. This led me to start drinking after school when my parents weren't home; I would just sit in my room with my friends and drink my parents' alcohol because there was no one there to tell me not to. This all caught up to me one Halloween when I drank myself into an alcohol-induced coma and didn't wake up for 12 hours. <u>I was close to death and my blood alcohol level was more than 4 times the normal limit.</u> *I was lucky enough to come out of the coma, but there were fifteen teens in the hospital that night with alcohol poisoning and three of them were not so lucky and never woke up. You might be wondering why I was so close to death and why no one had helped me sooner? Because my friends at the time didn't want to get in trouble; they would rather watch their "best friend" die than get caught for drinking. Luckily an upper classman that I didn't even know went to get help and called 911 or else I might have been one of the kids that never woke up. This experience changed my life in a way that I never thought possible.* (*I agreed with both reviews that more details were needed.*)

. . . .

~~Now I know that I talked briefly about my story and how I changed myself, but there are many cases where teenagers get mixed in with the wrong crowd and activities. This happened to what used to be a close friend of mine; we did everything together up until my freshman year of high school when I started noticing big changes in her. The two of us would drink occasionally on the weekends (before my incident on Halloween) and would go to parties. Then she started dating a guy who was much older and was a drug dealer; her mom had no idea because she worked at a hospital and was barely ever home. Soon smoking weed for my friend turned into doing cocaine and then to heroin and then to barely graduating high school.~~ (*I agreed with the second reviewer—not a necessary story.*)

Here is Hicks's discussion of how she revised in response to her peer reviewers' comments.

After meeting with my two peers, I had a lot of work to do on my paper. I decided to pick through all the comments and change what I felt needed changing. Some of the things were the opening line in my second paragraph which stated, "I don't want you to think that I am some perfect role model."

I took that line out because one of my peers said it took away from my credibility as a writer. I also added in three major paragraphs, one being about how some people who were in the hospital that night with alcohol poisoning actually did die and why it took me so long to get to the hospital. I added this information because one of my peers said that it would be a huge pathos appeal and it would help ignite my audience. Another paragraph was about the types of kids that were in the after-school activities with me and those that weren't, and how I noticed a difference in my two groups of friends. This comparison is to tell the parents that their children will most likely find good and responsible kids in after-school activities. The third major paragraph was about how much influence parents have on their kids. I felt this really helped my paper because it gave parents hope that their kids will listen to them and that parents' opinions do matter to a teenager as much as teens act like they don't. I also deleted a couple of paragraphs that told the story about my friend; one peer said he liked it, the other said she didn't, and I agreed that the focus should be on me, so I cut it.

I also revised the closing and added in a huge pathos appeal about a parent's child being in the situation that I was in and their having no idea that their child was dying. This I put at the end because I figured it would be a very strong note to leave the reader thinking about after they read it. I wanted that to be one of the last things they read so they would understand how scary it was for my parents and how scary it could be for them.

Katie Hicks (student), Dear Uninvolved Parents: An Open Letter (final draft)

Katie Hicks
Professor Ferruci
English 100P
24 Sept. 2007

Final Draft, Open Letter

Dear Uninvolved Parents:

Hicks begins by establishing the problem; she's also establishing "common cause"—she's asserting that we all know and care about this issue.

I am sure that recently you have picked up a newspaper or watched the news and found some headline about teenagers getting arrested or caught drinking or doing drugs. Just recently there was a story on the news about underage drinking and the ordinances towns are trying to pass to prevent it. If you haven't noticed, this is an ongoing issue, and it is only going to get worse.

Here she tries to antici-
pate the concerns her
audience might have
about her authority to
speak on this subject.
Does it work?

I know what you're thinking right now: Who is this girl? And what does she know about parenting or raising a teen? Well, I don't have any experience raising a child or parenting, but I do know a lot about what your kids are going through because I faced peer pressure myself and am still facing it. So I write to warn you about what could happen if you don't start becoming more involved in your child's life.

In this paragraph, Hicks
makes a connection
with her audience by
acknowledging that
the parents are not
solely to blame, but
at the same time she
reinforces the serious-
ness of the problem
by incorporating her
research.

I know it is not all your fault—part of the problem is that both parents work full time now, whereas back in the day, the mom stayed home. This meant a parent was home when their children got home, and so they got into less trouble. Kids couldn't sneak alcohol in their house and drink it in their rooms because their mothers were always home. Now with both parents working, it is very difficult for parents to be home when their children get off the bus. Your child is not the only one being left home alone. Studies show that about 3,500,000 children in America are left home alone after school. The shocking part is that these children, ranging from age 5 to 12, are left for up to an hour a day on their own. I am not recommending that you always have to be home when your kids get home; I am recommending that you get your kids involved in an after-school activity so that they are not going home to an empty house.

She works in her
research in these two
paragraphs, but notice
that it is not cited—the
genre does not require
formal citation and
the audience will not
expect it.

Research shows that children are more apt to get into trouble if their parents are not around or if their parents are divorced. This was the case of a kid from San Diego who recently opened fire in his high school. Reports say he was a child whose parents had been divorced for ten years and he was constantly unsupervised and never got any attention from his parents. Teenagers are on an emotional roller coaster; when they don't get attention, they will pretty much do whatever they can to get it. If you as a parent aren't always showing your children that you care, then they will find ways to make sure they get your attention.

I was one teenager who wanted more attention, and to get the attention I thought I deserved I started drinking when I was fifteen years old and in my freshman year. I participated in no after-school activities, my parents weren't there after school, and I wanted to fit in with my older friends. I started drinking after school when my parents weren't home; I would just sit in my room with my

This additional information helps the reader better understand what Hicks went through and further establishes both her credibility and the seriousness of the problem: This situation is every parent's nightmare.

friends and drink my parents' alcohol because there was no one there to tell me not to. This all caught up to me one Halloween at my friend's house when I drank myself into an alcohol-induced coma and didn't wake up for 12 hours. The doctors told me that if I had been left unattended for only two more hours I would have died; my blood alcohol level was more then 4 times the normal limit and my body temperature had dropped down to 92 degrees. I was lucky enough to come out of the coma, but there were fifteen teens in the hospital that night with alcohol poisoning and three of them never woke up. You might be wondering why no one had helped me sooner? Because my "friends" at the time didn't want to get in trouble. They would rather watch their "best friend" die than get caught for drinking. Luckily an upper classman that I didn't even know called 9-1-1; otherwise, I might have been one of the kids that never woke up.

Now I am not saying that your child is going to end up in the situation that I was in, but it could very well be something similar. A study of almost five thousand parents and their 8th graders showed that a child is three times as likely to get involved with alcohol, tobacco, or marijuana if he/she is left alone for more then eleven hours a week. If this statistic applies to you and your child, then right now your child is at great risk for getting involved in one of the three things mentioned. Now, that study is not a comfortable one to have on your mind before you go to bed at night, but let's face it, when you are at work you have no idea where your child is after he/she gets out of school. My friends and I were famous for lying about where we were after school when our parents would ask because we figured they had no way to find out what we were really doing. You can't honestly say that you know where your children definitely are at three or four in the afternoon. If you would like to know where your child is after school, then suggest to them the idea of a club or activity because it will give you a little more comfort knowing where they are.

Even in this final draft, you can see some of the original ideas that Hicks wanted to work with, but notice that in this version they are all focused on the need for parents' involvement in the lives of their children. This focus allows her to write about those issues in a coherent way.

You might be wondering how I turned out, how my parents reacted to the episode and what changed in my life because of it. Because of this situation and how my friends never went to get help, I was no longer allowed to hang out with those people. What my parents also made me do was to get involved in after-school activities because they did not trust me to be home alone. With these rules in place, I joined the school choir, varsity soccer team, and the freshman class board. These activities kept me after school later and kept me away from being home alone to do whatever I pleased.

Joining these after-school activities really kept me away from temptation and got me on the honor roll and eventually on high honors. Joining activities helped because it gave me somewhere to go after school, and it also connected me with other teenagers on a better path that kept me out of trouble. Also, the parents of these students were strict, so we were constantly supervised.

You might think that your kid would never go for after-school activities. It might not seem it, but as parents you have a huge influence on your children's decisions. If you strongly recommend something to your child, they will most likely do it. This is because, like in my situation, kids know their parents would only do what they believe is best for them. One way that you could make it sound more appealing is to tell your child that extracurricular activities look better for scholarships for college. Let them know that colleges don't just look at grades, but what you were involved with outside the classroom. For me, giving it a chance ended up being one of the smartest decisions I had ever made. So if you believe that your child will never be convinced to get involved with their school, at least give it a shot, because they will most likely listen to you.

It is your job as a parent to stay aware and active in your child's life and to limit their time spent alone as much as you can. Could you imagine your little girl being unconscious at a party while you're sitting in your living room watching TV thinking that everything was okay? I am telling you from personal experience that having my parents involved and being there to urge me to join activities made such a huge difference in my life; you can have the same effect on your child's life as well.

Sincerely,
A Concerned Teenager

In her conclusion, Hicks chooses to come back to the central story of her letter—her near-death experience. This repetition reinforces the consequences for her audience and allows her to make the strong statement, which begins this conclusion.

Questions for Discussion

1. How does Hicks help readers understand the issue as she sees it and the significance of it on her readers' lives?
2. How effective is Hicks's personal story in illustrating the problem? What does it add to her letter?
3. Where does Hicks draw on formal research? How effective is it? Are there areas that you felt she needed more or less research? Why?

Reflection on Writing an Open Letter

Here is an excerpt from Hicks's reflection on the process of writing the letter.

In my first draft I had a really hard time narrowing down both my subject and my audience. My topic went from wanting to get a skate park built in my hometown to why kids benefit from joining after-school activities. When I started off with the skate park idea I was unsure if my audience should be the kids in the town or the town council. I thought that my letter could either be written to persuade council members to build a skate park or my letter could persuade kids in town to speak about their need for a skate park When I finally decided what my topic was going to be, I had trouble deciding what tone to take and what style of writing to use. I wasn't sure if I should have used the casual funny approach or the serious factual approach. I ended up going with a serious approach because my audience was parents and I felt that they would respond better to that tone.

Professor Ferruci also got me thinking about the kinds of research I could use, and we talked about research on how much kids lie and how little parents know so that I could build up my credibility as a writer. With this advice I added more research and completely rearranged the order of my paragraphs, which I think added greatly to my paper.

WRITING ACTIVITY   *Evaluating One Writer's Journey*

Review Hicks' process. What can you say about the choices that she made? Do you agree with those choices? Are there places where you think she might have made different choices that could have led to a stronger letter? Do you think the final letter is complete or still needs some work?

■ ■ ■

TRANSFORMATIONS

GENRE CROSSING: From Public Letter to Research Report

Public letters are great starting places for transformations because they ask the writer to engage seriously (or at least earnestly) in an issue, require the writer to be knowledgeable about the issue and perhaps to conduct research, and require the reader to consider the issue from a civic perspective. As a result, the public letter lends itself to crossing to a number of other genres.

Sometimes, when writing a public letter, the writer finds herself wanting to say more about an issue than she has space for, since letters tend to be brief. While researching, she finds that the issue is complex and multifaceted and that a lot of people don't really understand the issue. A writer in such a position would turn to another genre, the research report, in order to inform readers about the issue. And because the research report can also be a persuasive genre, the writer can also use it to make an argument or suggest that readers take some action. For more information on the research report genre, please see Chapter 10: Research Reports.

Genre Crossing Writing Assignment

From Public Letter to Research Report

ASSIGNMENT: Write a research report by drawing on the claims you made and research you conducted for the public letter.

Consider what ideas you want to work with: You may want to focus your report on one aspect of your public letter, since a public letter can deal with a lot of related ideas briefly. A report, however, is more commonly focused on one issue in great depth.

Reevaluate the rhetorical situation for your report: You had a particular audience and purpose in mind when writing the letter, but your report will require that you rethink them. So consider why you are writing a report: To inform? Persuade? Call to action? Why does your audience need to know about this issue? What will they already know? What won't they know?

Consider the position and role from which you write: Since a report is a more formal genre than the public letter, you will likely need to rethink your role as a writer. What kinds of experiences can you or can't you draw on? Will you be able to address those directly in the report?

Consider the research you have—and what you will need to get: You will likely need to broaden your research scope as you consider who and what you are writing for. You will also likely need to conduct more research to deepen your understanding of the issue and to ensure that your information is timely and accurate.

On the following page is an example of Katie Hicks' transformation of her open letter to a research report.

Katie Hicks (student), After-School Programs: Benefits for Adolescents, Benefits for Communities (Research Report)

In her open letter, Hicks focused on the importance of parents' involvement in the lives of their children. But here she has refocused on the benefits of after school activities, a much broader aspect of her original focus.

Notice the new audience this report is focused on: the community taking action, which may include parents but also include others, such as community leaders, school officials, and kids themselves.

Katie Hicks
Professor Ferruci
English 100P
20 Oct. 2007

After-School Programs: Benefits for Adolescents, Benefits for Communities

Overview

Teenagers have always gotten into trouble and this includes not graduating, experimenting with drugs, committing violence, to name just the worst. <u>Yet there is a lot that communities can do</u> to prevent this from happening. The most effective method in decreasing teen crime and improving overall performance in school is to provide adolescents a place to go after school where they can feel safe and get off the streets and out of their basements. Reports have shown that after school 3–6 PM are the highest hours for which crime is committed by teenagers, so they need somewhere to go (Afterschool Alliance, "After School Programs"). Having after-school programs can provide important resources for teenagers and help ensure that they do well in school, but many schools cannot afford to run and staff these programs. However, other town and state offices or civic groups and organizations could also develop and run after-school programs for kids.

Facts about Teenagers and Crime

Recently, crime has been on the rise, and much of it is related to or involving teens. According to an issue brief produced by the Afterschool Alliance, adolescent crime is on the rise again after a period of long recession. There were two million aggravated crime arrests involving minors in 2005. Some of the problems result from kids being left unsupervised for over 20 hours per week; kids with such lack of supervision and activities are twice as likely to try drugs. Also kids who are not involved in after-school activities tend

Notice how the writer spends a lot of time establishing the problem for readers. Since she is trying to convince them to spend resources on the problem, she needs to establish the urgency of it.

to skip class more often than those who are in activities (Afterschool Alliance, "After School Programs"). Mary Eberstadt makes a similar argument in her article "Home-Alone America": "Recent social science makes plain ... that the connection between empty homes ... and childhood problems ... cannot possible be dismissed as coincidence" (11). Clearly, there is a need for after-school activities.

Why Do Kids Need After-School Programs?

Scholars James J. Zhang and Charles E. Byrd argue that "a great need exists for after-school activities.... Academic literature supports the idea that children and parents are well served by carefully organized and supervised youth programs during after-school hours" (3). There are many arguments in support of after-school programs; the most important one is that they are a great way for adolescents to be involved with fun, structured, and supervised activities. Programs have been known to be directly related to higher class attendance, better test scores, and a higher number of teenagers going to college ("Endangered After School Programs" 20). Furthermore, Zhang and Byrd note that after-school programs can help protect adolescents from "unhealthy environments" (3). But after-school programs also have other benefits that include inspiring a greater sense of community and encouraging a commitment by others to giving the children in that community the best opportunities possible.

Facts:

"Teens that don't participate in after school programs are three times more likely to use marijuana or other drugs." (Afterschool Alliance, "After School Programs")

"Only 17% of violent juvenile crime occurs after 10 p.m., compared with the 22% that takes place in the after-school hours." (Nifong)

Teen sexual activity is starting to rise due to lack of supervision in the home when kids get home from school. In 1988, 1 in

The writer cites ideas from multiple sources. This shows that the problem is recognized by a variety of individuals and groups who are concerned. Doing so builds her credibility by showing that she's not just relying on one source.

10 girls had engaged in sexual activities before turning 15, this number rose by 1995 to nearly 20 percent. The National Center of Health Statistics estimates now that 33% of girls 15 or under has had sexual intercourse. In 1970, less than 1 in 20 had (Ebserstadt 15).

The crime rate is starting to rise; 2004–2005 "statistics reflect the largest single-year percentage increase in violent crime in 14 years" (Afterschool Alliance, "After School Programs").

The more activities that a child is involved with increases the chances that that child will do better in school and adjust to their surroundings more efficiently (McGinn).

According to Thelma Baxter, principal of Roosevelt High School in the Bronx, NY, "To prepare to be academically successful, kids need to develop their bodies and mind" (qtd. in Archibold).

What Happens When After-School Programs Are Not Available?

If our community doesn't start putting money toward after-school programs then there is a good chance that the crime rate will do one of two things: It will either stay where it is with no improvement or it will rise. There are some people who feel that after-school programs will be too much pressure on their child or that they are not worth the cost. In their 1998 report *Quality Child Care and After-School Programs: Powerful Weapons Against Crime*, the organization Fight Crime claims that "the proof is in: Good child care and after-school youth development programs ... sharply reduce crime and help children develop the skills and values to become good neighbors and responsible adults instead of criminals. When we fail to invest in the proven programs ... we all pay an enormous price" (6). It has been shown in a recent study that the more activities a child is involved in, the better the child will do academically and socially (McGinn). Anyone who has played a sport or been part of some club knows that teenagers always do better in school when they are kept busy because it puts them on a schedule

Hicks makes a good rhetorical move here: She lays out possible consequences if the problem isn't addressed while also considering the views of those who might object to putting more resources into after school programs.

and keeps them from procrastinating. When a child is busy, then they generally don't waste as much time as they normally would because they know they have no time to spare.

Another aspect of why we need after-school activities is because crime is on the rise, "which many law enforcement officials attribute to decreased federal spending on crime prevention and more juveniles becoming involved in violent crimes" (Afterschool Alliance, "After School Programs"). According to the FBI's 2005 Uniform Crime Report, homicides, robberies, and aggravated assaults increased between 2004 and 2005 (Afterschool Alliance, "After School Programs"). "Sixteen percent (or 2 million arrests)" of all arrests were minors (Afterschool Alliance, "After School Programs").

How Effective Are After-School Programs?

In the broadest sense, after-school activities are very effective; as Harknett et al. found in the their research, "There is a strong relationship between what states spend on children and how children fare: Children tend to fare best in the states that spend the most on children and to fare worst in the states that spend the least" (122). Obviously, then, when after-school activities are provided, kids do better. Studies have shown that kids who are involved in after-school activities are less likely to skip classes, experiment with drugs, and get involved with violence (Afterschool Alliance, "After School Programs"). A recent report shows that if children are provided with early education programs—in and out of school—then every year there would be "50,000 additional high school graduates, 200 fewer murders and 5,500 fewer arrests" (Fight Crime: Invest in Kids, "New Research"). These are huge numbers and it is even more shocking that all of these facts are directly connected to after-school programs.

The Effectiveness of After-School Programs:

Case Study, Dave Jones

Dave Jones was a "hustler in Baychester, New York" when he was 17 years old. After a while on a bad path he knew his life

The case study serves as a concrete example of the benefits of having after school programs—adding also *pathos* appeals to the report.

needed to change. "I got pistol-whipped by seven dudes," he said. When his mother made him choose to either go to jail or join the Baychester Youth Council, an "after school tutoring/mentoring program," luckily he chose the program. Now at 26 years old he is a counselor for Baychester Youth Council. If he had not entered the program, he says he would "probably be locked up." This program tutors and mentors individuals but goes beyond school work and teaches them things such as how to talk properly and how to dress appropriately (Holmes).

Why Don't All Schools Have After-School Programs?

The simple answer to this question is that many schools cannot afford to pay for after-school activities. When a town budget fails, then after-school programs are usually the first things to go because they are looked at as the least priority. But the problem is also at the federal level, since so many state and local communities rely on federal funding to support after-school initiatives. According to the Afterschool Alliance, "Funding has been stalled at approximately $1 billion since Fiscal Year 2002. To make matters worse, the program has been subjected to a series of across-the-board cuts to education programs that reduced funding to $991 million in Fiscal Year 2005— a far cry from the $2 billion authorized by No Child Left Behind for that year" ("Impossible Choices"). There is one case in New York where programs are in danger of being shut down unless they can raise $30 million dollars, a near impossible task without government funding. This is happening because these programs rely on a combination of "federal, state, and city money and private donations." But the Congress and Bush administration did not fully fund the No Child Left Behind Act and so after-school providers were told that they were not going to receive any grants which they had been receiving since 2003 .In New York City alone, this leaves almost 120 after-school programs with no funding and about

This information shows the larger roots of the problem: larger cuts to federal funding— and some of its real consequences already seen in schools.

20,000 children with no where to go after school ("Endangered After-School Programs").

Who Wants After-School Programs?

The answer to this question is nearly everyone. But two groups in particular seem to support them: the kids themselves and law enforcement officials. Consequently, residents should not fear that their money would be wasted because teenagers would not use the services, and they should feel confident in knowing that their law enforcement officials see after-school programs as a way to cut down on crime.

Students' Opinions on After-School Programs

- Over half of all teenagers in high school in Chicago report having nowhere safe to go after school.

- 66% of teenagers in the country wish there were cool, fun, and safe places where they could go after school or on weekends.

- 33% of students in California reported a lack of "supervised after school activities" and two-thirds of those students claimed they would make use of programs if they existed. (Afterschool Alliance, "After School Programs")

What Other Communities Have Done

There are many states that are struggling with financial issues related to after-school programs. There are also a lot of states that are finding ways around this issue by getting grants, donations, federal funding, etc. Although the situation seems dire, the success of many states in finding funding means that it is not an impossible task for communities to solve. Listed below are things that other states and cities have done to get past the financial aspect of after-school programs, and these are very good ideas for how to help our community.

In Tulsa, OK town officials got a bank to give them $41,000 to invest in after-school programs for kids in hopes to fight the "growing gang problem" there.

This is another good rhetorical move, as it draws both on *ethos* (police think this is a good idea) and *pathos* (let's do it because our kids want it).

This information provides a larger context—the funding and development of after-school programs is happening in many states.

In Yonkers, NY the city received a $77,000 grant for "Achieving Success," which is a program designed to help kids with computer training, tutoring for over 50 adolescents, and other basic skills instruction.

In Fairfax County, VA the police department received a grant that grew into $2 million; half of the money goes to the police-run programs and the other half goes to intervention programs. A component of the program is a statewide five-day after-school program. "Since this [program] has been in place gang crime activity has dropped 39 percent and continues to decline." (Afterschool Alliance, "After School Programs")

Conclusion

After-school programs need to be in our community in order to reduce the crime rate, allow children to succeed academically, and to give children a larger sense of the social realm of things. If we do not start acting upon this now, then just like 90% of the police chiefs agreed, "We will pay for this later if we don't start making greater investments in helping the children now" (Afterschool Alliance, "After School Programs"). Below are some key points to remember about the importance of these programs and how much we need them.

In her conclusion, Hicks reiterates her main point and reminds the reader of why such programs need to be implemented.

After-school activities *will* reduce crime rates in local towns and *will* help with increasing high school graduation rates, decreasing teenage violence, and lowering drug and alcohol use.

Children of all ages *want* to join after-school activities but in a lot of cases there are none available to them.

Towns *need* funding and other resources to be able to start and run after-school activities, but other local and state government and civic organizations could develop and run the programs.

Other towns, cities, and states have started working on developing after-school initiatives because they realize that if they don't then the problem of crime and delinquency will only get worse. These kinds of after-school programs have worked in other towns and had huge impacts on high school graduation rates and city/town violence.

Works Cited

Afterschool Alliance. "After School Programs: Keeping Kids—and Communities—Safe." *After School Alert Issue Brief* 27 (April 2007). PDF. 25 Oct. 2007.

———. "Impossible Choices: How States Are Addressing the Federal Failure to Fully Fund Afterschool Programs." (2006). PDF. 25 Oct. 2007.

Archibold, Randal C. "To Improve Learning and Attendance, Schools Are Drumming Up Interest in After-School Programs." *New York Times.* New York Times, 24 Mar. 1999. Web. 27 Oct. 2007.

Eberstadt, Mary. "Home-Alone America." *Policy Review* (June 2001): 5–23. *Academic Search Premier.* Web. 19 Sept. 2007.

"Endangered After-School Program." *New York Times.* 19 June 2007, Editorial Desk: A20. *LexisNexis.* Web. 14 Oct. 2007.

Fight Crime: Invest in Kids. "New Research Shows Pre-K Programs Increase High School Graduation Rates by 10 Percentage Points, Cut Murders by 20 Percent." 21 June 2007. Web. 14 Oct. 2007.

———. "Quality Child Care and After-School Programs: Powerful Weapons against Crime. A Report from 'Fight Crime: Invest in Kids.'" 1998. *ERIC.* Web. 25 Oct. 2007.

Harknett, Kristen, et al. "Are Public Expenditures Associated with Better Child Outcomes in the U.S.? A Comparison Across 50

States." *Analyses of Social Issues and Public Policy* 5.1 (2005): 103–125. *Academic Search Premier.* Web. 29 Oct. 2007.

Holmes, Tamara E. "After-School Program Transforms Lives." *Black Enterprise* 35.1 (Aug. 2004): 126. *Academic Search Premier.* Web. 28 Oct. 2007.

McGinn, Daniel, et al. "The Benefits of Busy." *Newsweek* 148.14 (2006): 43. *Academic Search Premier.* Web. 14 Oct. 2007.

Nifong, Christina. "Not Evenings, but Idle After-School Hours Are the Prime...." *Christian Science Monitor* 8 Apr. 1997. *Academic Search Premier.* Web. 28 Oct. 2007.

Zhang, James J., and Charles E. Byrd. "Successful After-School Programs: The 21st Century of Community Learning Centers." *JOPERD: The Journal of Physical Education, Recreation & Dance* 77.8 (Oct. 2006): 3–12. *Academic Search Premier.* Web. 30 Oct. 2007.

Reading for Comprehension

1. What is Hicks's primary argument in favor of after-school programs? How do you know? How does she develop this throughout her report?
2. How does Hicks contextualize the problem and show her audience its extent? How successful is she in doing so?

Analyzing the Genre

1. Research reports make much use of repetition. What ideas does Hicks come back to? What are the different ways she makes those points?
2. Reports draw heavily on many kinds of research; how thorough is Hicks's report? Were there places where she could have used more research?
3. Read over Hicks's open letter, the original source of this report. How successful was she in transforming the open letter into a report? What ideas did she carry over? Which did she leave out? What new ideas and material are present and how do those add to your understanding of the problem?

CHAPTER 6

Reviews

Every day we give or get reviews—when we evaluate a film (that was the best/worst film ever), when we draw conclusions based on our experiences (let's go to Joker's; the fried fish sticks are amazing), and when we reflect on and analyze the value of something (that class was hard, but I learned a lot, you should take it). In all these instances, we are reviewing things in an informal way.

What Is a Review?

A *review* is an evaluative genre in which a writer's assessment or judgment of something comes across clearly and persuasively. In a review, a writer tries to convince readers that his or her judgment or evaluation of a situation, place, product, or work of art has merit and is convincing.

Sometimes reviews are positive, sometimes negative, and often they are mixed. For instance, you may have eaten at a restaurant where you liked some things (the cozy atmosphere, the soft lighting) but not others (the poor service). So a review is not an either/or genre: While some aspects of the subject under review might meet the reviewer's expectations, other aspects might be in need of improvement.

As readers, reviews help us figure out what we want to do. Before going to see a film, you might have read reviews of it on RottenTomatoes.com. Before buying a large-ticket item (a computer, for instance), you probably read reviews of the product. So we read reviews to help us make choices on what to do next, what to buy, and so on. Reviews help readers make informed, thoughtful choices.

The Purpose of Reviews

Reviews serve many purposes, depending on the audience, the subject, and the context in which the review will appear. Reviews make evaluations. They look at a subject and ask some basic questions: Is it good? Is it as good as it can be? Or the reverse: Is it bad? Is it as bad as it could have been?

While most reviews are **evaluative,** judging an item by a set of criteria it should meet, reviews may have other functions as well:

- **Analytic reviews** include a breakdown of the parts of a subject using criteria that make sense given the subject. For example, a pair of Rossignol skis might be analyzed based on the criteria of durability, performance, style, and so on. The reviewer might also *contextualize* the subject under review: Rossignol's new Attraxion XI Mutix System skis are clearly superior to last season's downhill ski release.
- **Critical reviews** usually appear in scholarly or professional journals and evaluate a subject (a scholarly text, a body of scholarship, research studies, etc.) based on an assessment particular to that field. For example, in the social sciences, a review of research might look at its validity, contributions it makes to a discipline, and so on.
- **Comparative reviews** look at subjects that are similar and evaluate them by comparing and contrasting. For example, the Sony PlayStation is good for individual gameplay, but the Xbox is best for online gaming, while the Nintendo Wii is great for parties.

So when we write reviews, we assume that the audience wants to know more on the subject and have others' judgments to consider before they act. The reader wants to find out about the subject in order to take the next step: read the book, buy the DVD, and so on.

The Rhetorical Situation of Reviews

Reviews are written for a variety of reasons. Sometimes we write reviews out of personal interest or need (we are excited by the features of the iPhone or irritated by the lack of organic produce at the Hy-Vee supermarket). Sometimes we write them out of civic commitment (we might be dedicated X-country runners and want to let our community know about the River Parks Trail in Tulsa). Sometimes we write reviews on the job (we might write performance reviews of employees or reviews of competitors' products). Finally, we may write reviews of literature, films, or other art for our humanities courses and of research studies for our social science courses.

Thus, we write reviews when a situation calls for an informed evaluation of a subject.

The Writer's Stance

Review writers are generally informed about the subject of their reviews, but their knowledge varies considerably. They may be experts, amateurs, or novices.

- An *expert* has a deep and broad knowledge of a subject; he or she knows enough about the subject and comparable items to make useful evaluations of it. Still, an expert may need to do research to be current on the subject under review. For example, you would not trust a review of the 2007 Ferrari 599 GTB Fiorano by someone who has never driven one, even if that person were a trained mechanic.
- An *amateur* knows something about the subject, but may never have studied or pursued the subject in-depth. For example, an avid cook may have experience using quality

cookware and know why he prefers one brand over another, but he does not offer a professional chef's perspective on the equipment.

■ A *novice* reviewer experiences something for the first time, often giving readers a fresh perspective on a subject. For example, a tourist in Pamplona, Spain, who reviews his first experience of the Running of the Bulls during the San Fermín festival, is a novice.

Regardless of their stance, all review writers need to know enough to develop *criteria* for their evaluation, which involves *research*.

Reading Reviews Critically

WRITING ACTIVITY   Analyzing the Genre of Reviews

Thinking About the Genre

Using a search engine, locate some online reviews on a subject of interest to you: books, films, music, products you use, services, etc.

Examining the Genre

As you read these reviews you are reading for comprehension, but you are also reading to understand the *characteristics* of the genre. Look for *patterns* that reveal something about what reviews do in general.

1. How do writers tend to introduce their subjects?
2. How is the material arranged?
3. What criteria is the writer using to evaluate the subject?
4. What can you say about the language of this review (provide some examples)? What does the language reveal about the writer's knowledge and experience?
5. How detailed is the review? How much (or how little) background material or research is provided?

Reflecting on the Genre

After you have read the reviews, *explain* the major characteristics of the genre as you understand it. Refer to specific passages, quoting where necessary.

■ ■ ■

Genre Analysis: Peter Meehan, "Will Pigs' Feet Fly?"

"Will Pigs' Feet Fly?" is a review of the Manhattan restaurant Hakata Tonton by former *New York Times* writer Peter Meehan. He was the "$25 and Under" restaurant column writer for four years. His reviews ranged from restaurants offering unique fare, such as the one featured in this review, to food sold by vendors outside the Red Hook Recreation Area or at the Brownstoner's Brooklyn Flea market. Annotated below is an analysis of Meehan's review based on some key features.

Will Pigs' Feet Fly?

Peter Meehan

New York Times online
January 23, 2008

In this age of rapidly rising restaurant prices, it's heartening to find a new place that serves a nine-course tasting menu for $40. The portions aren't Lilliputian, the folks who work there are friendly and attentive and nothing on the à la carte menu costs more than $12.

There's just one catch: nearly all the dishes, save the sweets, incorporate—and in most cases glorify—pigs' feet. Those that don't, like a pig's ear salad or an order of calf liver sashimi, aren't going to do much for those not inclined to eat pigs' feet, either.

At Hakata Tonton, Himi Okajima, the chef and an owner, has built an impressive and intimidating temple to the very strange idea that trotters are the missing ingredient in just about everything.

There are feet in the pasta carbonara. The rice in the **bibimbop** is glazed in sticky foot broth. And anybody who needs to ask if there are feet in the "healthy collagen salad"—collagen being something that pigs' feet have a lot of, especially in relation to the negligible nuggets of meat stuck in their deepest recesses—is in the wrong spot.

So with that hurdle cleared, there's the menu to navigate. **Offal** dilettantes, the curious but skeptical and those without a tested track record of enjoying foot eating should eschew the nine-course beginner's tasting menu. (An "advanced" menu, $35, actually seems far tamer.) But such a tour at such a value is hard to pass up, even if it's over this column's usual price limit.

It starts well enough, with dishes I'd order again à la carte: a summer roll and a crisp deep-fried spring roll. The foot factor is low in both: the slices of foot skin that dot the summer roll could be easily mistaken for overcooked bits of shrimp with a funny flavor; the only thing that gives away that there's something piggy about the spring roll is that unmistakable but pleasantly animal aroma of something that's been fried in pork fat.

Croquettes follow, and though creamy inside, they're not a particularly worthwhile diversion.

The grilled foot that follows is. Portions looked to be about a half foot each, split open after a good long cooking and then grilled until the skin of each was black like the brand on a football.

A dab of **yuzu rind** came perched on the rim of the bowl, **wasabilike,** and ready to be stirred into vinegar sauce in the bottom of the bowl. It freshened up the foot with its sweet, floral citrusy kick.

This is foot cookery at its minimal and beautiful best because it plays to the strength of pigs' feet: skin that will crisp to shattering, flesh-wafer goodness

---

Definitely attention grabbing. Two qualities important to the audience.

The opening includes the name of the restaurant, the chef/owner, and indicates why it is unique.

Is this language familiar to pig feet aficionados?

Will need to look this word up.

Here's the writer's nod to the cost again, something readers will want to know before they go there.

Lots of details about the kinds of foods one might expect to find at the place—and notice the language being used—you have to know your pig's foot and Asian spices to understand what he's talking about.

Lots of evaluative language to help the reader understand his judgment.

He goes into great detail to describe how the food is prepared, a characteristic of the genre of food reviews. Definitely a mixed review—this sounds absolutely disgusting.

Atmosphere is part of the reviewer's criteria for evaluation.

Speaks to the kitchy-ness of the place. . . . and the lighthearted tone of the review.

without drying out, and a lumbering flavor that can take on the brashest, most domineering condiments, like yuzu rind.

After that, the beginner's menu went astray with a chicken and pig's foot stew that was just too mysterious and murky. Dumplings—boiled, crumpled and impossibly dense and leaden—arrived garnished with pig nails. In the context of that simply grilled foot, a curved, yellowed fang of a toenail poking through the bulbous burnt stub of a toe is one thing: a fact of foot eating. Stuck into a dumpling, where it didn't need to be, it was just plain gross.

But while some might expect this to be a parlor of extreme eating, there isn't a macho vibe at the restaurant; it's quiet, even reserved. I never got the feeling that the chef was trying to put something over on the dining room, or that this was some weird experiment. The place feels honest and genuinely warm, even if it is genuinely weird.

To wit: Leaving the restaurant after my first visit, a waitress followed my friends and me outside and presented me with a sealed envelope that contained the restaurant's card and a quarter to pay me back for calling to make a reservation (which I had found necessary). Then she pulled out a Mr. Incredible PEZ dispenser and offered each of us a candy to freshen our breath before sending us off into the night.

Hakata Tonton
61 Grove Street (Bleecker Street), West Village; (212) 242-3699.
BEST DISHES Spring roll; summer roll; pig's foot "simply grilled with salt"; pig's foot with bordelaise sauce; all desserts.
PRICE RANGE All dishes, $5 to $12. Tasting menus, $35 to $40.
CREDIT CARDS All major cards.
HOURS Sunday through Thursday, 5:55 p.m. to midnight; Friday and Saturday, 5:55 p.m. to 2 a.m.
WHEELCHAIR ACCESS Up a couple of steps from the street.

I'm not sure I'm ready to eat at this restaurant any time soon, but the review was well written—Meehan really knows his stuff. And it wasn't a completely positive review, which I liked—seems like you usually get either "this was the best ever" or "this was the worst ever." While he really seemed to enjoy it, he was a little disgusted by the toe nails. Me too. Maybe Meehan wrote this review because the restaurant was so different? I guess he was probably writing it to say, "Hey, if you like out of the ordinary food that's cheap, here's a place for you."

I googled the name Hakata Tonton and found out that Hakata is a region in Japan, and the place where the chef comes from. I couldn't find tonton although I did find tonsoku which is Japanese and means "pig's feet," so perhaps tonton is Japanese for pig.

> *I'd say one of the characteristics of reviews would be lots of details—I sometimes felt like I was in the restaurant with Meehan. The introduction reveals some of the criteria Meehan used to evaluate the restaurant—price and food quality. And presentation and atmosphere also seem to be a criteria. He seems unhappy about the food that didn't look good, the "mysterious and murky stew." He also seems to think that "minimalist" is the way to go with pigs' feet.*
>
> *The audience would be newspaper readers who like cheap good food, especially those willing to try something new. But some of the language is sophisticated—bibimbop and Yuzu rind. I don't know what those are, so maybe his real audience includes food lovers. The organization, though, was pretty straightforward, so no expertise was needed to follow it; he organized the essay around the order of the meal. I don't know about research—maybe some of the background stuff on the owner? Would he have known that without research? Otherwise, I didn't really see any, except what he learned while eating there—field research.*

Tim Rutten, Review of *The Anatomist: A True Story of Gray's Anatomy*

In the following book review, columnist Tim Rutten reviews Bill Hayes' nonfiction book *The Anatomist*. Rutten, who has worked for the *Los Angeles Times* for almost thirty years and has his own column in the "View" section, has written on a range of issues from race in the California Assembly to class and the California highway system. Bill Hayes, the author of the book Rutten reviews here, has been writing since the early 1990s.

The Anatomist: A True Story of Gray's Anatomy

Bill Hayes

From the Los Angeles Times BOOK REVIEW

By Tim Rutten
Los Angeles Times Staff Writer

Author, not the book's subjects, is dissected.

There ought to be a particularly dark corner of purgatory reserved for authors who sacrifice a great idea for a book on the altar of their own narcissism.

In more judicious or scrupulous hands, "The Anatomist: A True Story of Gray's Anatomy" could have been a fascinating book. The one that San Francisco-based science writer Bill Hayes has written, however, is—by turns—cloying, irritating and wrongheaded. In fact, it's virtually a one-volume compendium of all that's wrong with the nonfiction genre these days—a syllabus of errors, particularly the pervasive fallacy that "how I got the story" is as interesting as the story itself. (The presumption that readers are interested in how the facts of the story made the author feel comes in a close second.)

This is the 150th anniversary of the first publication of *Gray's Anatomy,* a book that is to the era of scientific medicine what the works of Galen and Avicenna were to the preceding ages, that is, a foundational text. First published in 1858, the book has been continuously in print and regularly updated. Today, you can purchase it in a print edition, as a CD-ROM or download it online. Hayes' ostensible purpose is an excellent one: to give the first book-length account of the anatomy's composition and to put flesh on its obscure makers.

It's an intriguing story, starting with the fact that, while the book bears one man's name, it actually was the work of two collaborating—and equal—young physicians in Victorian Britain. Henry Gray was a newly appointed lecturer on anatomy at St. George's Hospital Medical School in London when he approached a young colleague and gifted artist, Henry Vandyke Carter, to work with him on a new anatomy text for medical students and surgeons. They collaborated intensely for 18 months, working from dissected corpses. Gray provided the text, and Carter did all the illustrations. (As medical scholars and commentators subsequently have pointed out, Gray's text was remarkably clear and authoritative, but what set the book apart was the quality—and size—of Carter's wonderfully precise illustrations.)

. . .

The two doctors

Gray was apparently the more ambitious and successful of the pair. His agreement with the publisher called for him to be paid a royalty of 150 pounds for every 1,000 copies of the text sold; Carter got a flat fee of 150 pounds and used the money to buy a microscope, which he took with him when he embarked for Bombay as a physician for the East India Co. while the book still was in galleys. Gray, who appears to have been on the fast track to a place in London's medical firmament, died not long after the book was published after contracting smallpox from a nephew he was treating.

Carter spent his entire career on the subcontinent and, despite a tumultuous and rather scandalous first marriage, retired to England as the deputy surgeon general of India and subsequently was named honorary surgeon to Queen Victoria. He made a good second marriage, had children and died in 1897. He also left rather extensive diaries, and nearly all of what's compelling and valuable in "The Anatomist" comes directly from those. They are, in fact, Hayes' only significant original source. As he admits in the book, like other researchers before him, he came up empty when seeking the historical Henry Gray, who curiously died without even an obituary or the written tributes from colleagues that were common during that era.

Confronted with that vacuum, a serious writer might have turned to a detailed reconstruction of the era, which was itself a fascinating one. Only

26 years earlier, Parliament had passed the Anatomy Act, legalizing the dissection of unclaimed corpses from the workhouses that were a ubiquitous feature of urban England. By the time Gray and Carter came along, the old private anatomy schools—holdovers from the time when study of the human body was tainted by grave robbing—were closing, and medical schools had annexed anatomy to the scientific revolution that was reshaping medicine and so much else.

.   .   .

All about the author

Look elsewhere for that information. Instead, Hayes elected to fill in the gaps by enrolling in a medical school anatomy class and telling readers all about it:

"On the first day of class, I am mistaken for a teaching assistant six times, which, on the one hand, simply tells me I'm old ... but, on the other hand, seems to imply that I look as if I belong....

"The class size is 120 (150 if you count the cadavers). We had been warned beforehand that some students are overwhelmed by the first sight of the dead bodies. And sure enough, some students clearly are. But I am more freaked out by the woman in the gas mask. What does she know that the rest of us don't?

"'Class? Hello?' comes a disembodied voice, tinnily amplified. This is Sexton Sutherland, one of the three professors for this ten-week course in gross anatomy at UCSF. ... 'Before we get started, some housekeeping rules: No eating your lunch in here.' This elicits a collective ewwwww. ..."

And so it goes, with Hayes switching back and forth between his anatomy class, various trips to the various research libraries—including digressions on the indignities of wearing used gloves when handling rare books—and extended quotations from Carter's diaries. These are often fascinating, but Hayes is like one of those dreadful dinner party guests who is only interested in what other people have to say because it reminds them of something about themselves.

Thus, when Carter—who appears to have suffered from melancholy bordering on clinical depression—agonizes over sexual desire in a rather typically Victorian sort of way, it reminds Hayes of his own struggle to "come out" as a homosexual. Why the author's sexual orientation is of the slightest interest to anybody but the writer or his intimates or what relevance it has to a historical study of "Gray's Anatomy" is anybody's guess.

Like the real life of Henry Gray, it's just one of the mysteries this annoying book leaves unsolved.

timothy.rutten@latimes.com
The Anatomist
A True Story of "Gray's Anatomy"
Bill Hayes
Ballantine: 272 pp., $24.95

Reading for Comprehension

1. What is Rutten's primary criticism of Hayes's book? Why does Rutten feel that his critique is valid?
2. What do we learn from the background information Rutten provides on Gray and Carter (the author and illustrator of *Gray's Anatomy*)? How does this material connect to the critique of Hayes's book?

Analyzing the Genre

1. How does Rutten develop his evaluative thesis? What kinds of evidence does he provide to support it?
2. Rutten spends two thirds of his review discussing the history and background of *Gray's Anatomy* and spends the last third actually writing about Hayes's book. What does this tell you about the genre of book reviews and the particular audience Rutten is writing to?
3. What are the evaluation criteria Rutten uses to review Hayes's book?

John Phillips, "2008 Maserati GranTurismo—Road Test"

John Phillips is a frequent contributor to and was once executive editor of *Car and Driver* magazine. He has a column about all things auto-related, and has written reviews of cars ranging from a Volkswagen Eurovan to Rolls-Royce Corniche. In this review, published in June 2008, Phillips brings his playful wit and acute sense of what makes for a good driving experience to bear on the Maserati GranTurismo.

2008 Maserati GranTurismo—Road Test

By John Phillips

Tracing its genetic code to the Ferrari F430, the Alfa Romeo 8C, and Andrea Pininfarina himself, Maserati's latest luxo-coupe is a Modenese masterpiece.

Of the seven Maserati brothers, six became renowned mechanics and engineers. The black sheep of the family—Mario—instead became a painter, although he left an indelible mark on the marque. Wandering about Bologna's main square one day, Mario came face to face with a statue of Neptune, whose barbed trident he promptly expropriated as the logo for his brothers' first car, the 1926 eight-cylinder Tipo 26.

Why Mario would associate a racing car with the Roman god of the sea is one of those synaptic misfires mostly appreciated by liberal-arts majors. But it proved a good choice. By the time the brothers had introduced their stunning A6GCS road car, Maserati automobiles had become associated with a distinctive concave grille with chrome vertical fillets, lending their products the countenance of a jawfish gagging on tadpoles. Voilà! The marine connection was complete.

Fast-forward to 2008. Were Mario still painting today, he'd fling his palette in joy to behold an identical aquatically themed grille, with huge chrome trident still attached, adorning Maserati's latest, greatest luxo-coupe. The GranTurismo is a Maserati Quattroporte with two fewer doors, a 4.8-inch shortening of the wheelbase, and Pininfarina styling so seductive that the kid running the Ann Arbor carwash wouldn't afford passage until he photographed it with his cell phone.

Apart from its Joe E. Brown mouth, which half our staff thinks is too large, this four-passenger coupe is the quintessence of Italian flash and panache. Its airy cockpit smells like the tack room at Balmoral, chockablock, as it is, with a sumptuous festival of buttery cowhides and burled walnut. Each chunk of wood trim is whole, rather than an amalgam of glued-together pieces. The leather is stitched with thick threads of a starkly contrasting hue, a ploy to draw your eye. Ten shades of skins are on offer, and they can be endlessly mixed and matched to upholster seats, dash, parcel shelf, trunk, steering wheel, shifter, and headliner. Maserati North America PR manager Jeff Ehoodin reckons there might be "four million combinations." If you spent one minute studying each, then selecting your GranTurismo's interior could require 2778 days. The Brembo brake calipers come in six colors. "A different shade at each corner?" we inquired. "No problem," replied Ehoodin, although special orders require a four-month wait....

.   .   .

The trunk is small—roughly 14 inches deep, 42 inches wide, and 23 inches long. Supposedly, it will hold a bag of clubs, although maybe not the latest 45-inch drivers. Perhaps Maserati meant miniature golf. The cockpit contains only two substandard items: the radio's plasticky faceplate and a bone-white accelerator scuff plate that is in jarring contrast with the rich black carpet.

Happily, ergonomics are mostly the antithesis of Italian tradition. The driver sits in proper relationship with primary and secondary controls, although the signal and wiper stalks were a little too far from our fingertips. Also, if you like "gettin' up on the wheel," as they do in NASCAR, your right leg will rub the transmission tunnel. Luckily, the steering wheel is widely adjustable for reach and rake.

The seat cushions and the seatbacks are quite firm. Some would say hard. They're great for short bursts of spirited driving but can induce some squirming in the second hour of occupancy. Sightlines are mediocre, hindered by a small backlight and the fat A- and C- pillars. Looking out over the hood, all you see is the sensuous left wheel arch delicately kicking up. And peering into the large side-view mirrors, you're rewarded with a gratifying glimpse of muscular hips comprising more compound curves than Michelangelo could muster. The rear quarter-panels look eight months pregnant with Pirelli P Zeros—not a styling cue that would occur to, say, the Germans.

The GranTurismo's V-8 is built in Maranello and for good reason. It is a 405-hp, 4.2-liter wet-sump iteration of the engine you'd normally locate in the middle of a Ferrari F430. Fitted with a unique induction system, Maserati's version offers gentle step-off, pulls seamlessly from as low as 2000 rpm, then rips to its 7250-rpm redline faster than you can say "cavallino." It is as vibrationless as a BMW inline-six. At idle, it engenders not a quiver in the dangling key fob. And the sound it makes is one-third angry cougar, one-third Ducati, and one-third Pavarotti, who, by the way, loitered frequently among Maserati's 600 Modena-based employees. Eighty dBA at wide-open whack, however, is a lot of sound. But at least it's a good sound.

Disable the traction control and the GranTurismo leaves hard. Sixty mph arrives in 4.9 seconds—0.4 second behind a Jag XKR but 0.6 second quicker than a BMW 650i. And through the quarter-mile, the Maserati is as quick as an Aston Martin V-8 Vantage.

The yowling V-8 is mated to an equally impressive ZF six-speed automatic that is telepathic about reading your intentions via throttle inputs. It knows when to hang onto gears for engine braking, and it knows when to hold a heady bundle of revs for rocketing out of turns. It is one of the most versatile transmissions extant. Feeling lazy? Just leave it in full-auto mode. Want to row? Move the shifter into its manumatic track: Push forward for downshifts, pull back for upshifts. Need both hands on the wheel? Select gears via paddle shifters behind the steering wheel—left paddle for downshifts, right for upshifts. No matter which mode you fancy, every shift is a crisp rifle shot preceded by matching revs, followed instantly by a big green LED informing what gear has been summoned. In sport mode, the shifts crack off even harder, and gears are held longer. Overall, this transmission leaves you wondering what purpose a manual clutch and linkage would serve.

In the hills, we were ever aware of this coupe's 4374-pound heft, but the car always felt stable, nicely planted, and free of extraneous body motions. Better yet, its ride, even over Michigan's ravaged roads, was appropriate to its luxo-coupe mission—firm but never intrusive. To enliven your commute, engage the sport mode, and the shocks will subjectively stiffen by about a third. Along Hogback Road, this induced all manner of jitters and shivers, but it would likely work wonders on Angeles Crest Highway in L.A.

The brakes are easy to modulate—you can maintain deceleration right on the threshold of ABS intervention—although we'd prefer the pedal were slightly firmer in its travel. In any event, 70 mph is dispelled in 157 feet, same as in a Saleen S7 Twin Turbo.

Perhaps the GranTurismo's chief flaw is its steering. It is too heavy at all speeds, there's some slop on-center, and never does it transmit much information about road textures or available grip. At least it tracks like a bloodhound, requiring few corrections. Push this GT hard and it's often the superb stability control, rather than the steering, that whispers the first word of warning.

Maseratis have traditionally been long on personality in a weird and quirky way, which always felt like an accident, as if the builders didn't really know how the car was going to turn out. In contrast, the GranTurismo feels engineered with a purpose. It is competent, solid, sumptuous, and capable of serving as a daily driver. Heck, it fired right up on a minus-six-degree Michigan morning. Yet it diverges colorfully and joyfully from its purposeful, businesslike Teutonic competitors—notably the BMW M6 and Mercedes-Benz CL550. Every editor who climbed out of the GranTurismo said, "Wow, that was refreshing."

Compared with the Germans, this Modenese masterpiece feels very much hand-tailored instead of off the rack. In an era when all four Benz CL models fetch in excess of 100 grand—yet remain almost ubiquitous on the streets of L.A. and Miami—this Maserati's $113,750 base may well persuade many a Mario to stand out from his brothers.

[http://www.caranddriver.com/reviews/hot_lists/high_performance/sports_car_central/2008_maserati_granturismo_road_test
Copyright ©2007 Hachette Filipacchi Media U.S., Inc.]

Reading for Comprehension

1. Phillips is writing a product review of the 2008 Maserati GranTurismo, a high-end foreign sports car. What do product reviews usually include, and does this one meet your expectations?
2. If you were someone who was considering buying this car, what about Phillips' review might convince you to do so or not?

Analyzing the Genre

1. What kinds of research does Phillips include in his review to inform readers about the car and to show his expertise on the subject?
2. What language choices and examples does Phillips use to let us know who the audience is for this review?

Peter Kvetko, Noora: A Golden Voice; Wah Rangiya: Passionate Punjab; Bol Ni Chakkiye: The Singing Wheel of Life

The following review was published in the winter/spring edition of *Asian Music*. On its website, the journal is described as "the leading journal devoted to ethnomusicology in Asian music, publishing all aspects of the performing arts of Asia and their cultural context." Peter Kvetko is an assistant professor of music at Salem State College in Massachusetts and has a Ph.D. in ethnomusicology (a branch of musicology that focuses on ethnic and social aspects of music in both local and global contexts).

> ***Noora: A Golden Voice***. Produced by Folk Music India Pvt. Ltd. Beat of India CCD 1012. One compact disc, 67 minutes. Includes 13 pages of liner notes, photos, transliterations, and English translations.
>
> ***Wah Rangiya: Passionate Punjab***. Produced by Folk Music India Pvt. Ltd. Beat of India CCD 1013. One compact disc, 62 minutes. Includes 13 pages of liner notes, photos, transliterations, and English translations.
>
> ***Bol Ni Chakkiye: The Singing Wheel of Life***. Produced by Folk Music India Pvt. Ltd. Beat of India CCD 1014. One compact disc, 69 minutes. Includes 17 pages of liner notes, photos, transliterations, and English translations.

Given the recent surge of globalized Punjabi pop music (witness Jay-Z's 2003 collaboration with Punjabi MC on the remixed track "Mundian To Bach Ke," and Rabbi Shergill's "Bullah Ki Jaana" as the first video shown on MTV Desi), there has been a corresponding increase of interest in traditional Punjabi music from both academic and commercial perspectives. Unfortunately, ethnomusicological sources focusing on the rich and spirited folk music of the Punjab region continue to be limited. Although Alkia Pande's book, *Folk Music and Musical Instruments of Punjab: From Mustard Fields to Disco Lights* (2000), is a colorful and handy reference, it does not fill the urgent need for ethnographically grounded scholarship. Perhaps the most relevant and useful text in that regard, and one that offers a critical background to the first disc reviewed here, is *The Female Voice in Sufi Ritual: Devotional Practices in Pakistan and India* by Shemeem Abbas (2003). In terms of recordings, resources are similarly small in number and, while the Gramophone Company of India's 5-disc set, *50 Glorious Years of Punjabi Music,* offers a generous collection of classic recordings, the majority of its tracks are commercial in nature, with abundant *filmi* orchestration and studio polish. In order to complement the wealth of materials on popular *bhangra* music in the South Asian diaspora, more research and documentation of traditional Punjabi music in India and Pakistan is sorely needed.

Beat of India's release of a three-disc series, *Gudti Punjab Di,* makes a welcome addition to the body of available recordings of traditional Punjabi music. The New Delhi-based organization quickly has built an impressive collection of recordings from across North India and targets "the global listener" with its CDs, DVDs, and downloads from their website (www.beatofindia.com). With recordings of *rasiya, kajri, hori,* and *birha* already in their catalog, Beat of India focuses on the traditional songs of Punjab with these three discs.

The first volume of the collection, *Noora: A Golden Voice,* features the rich vocals of Swarn Noora, daughter of the Sufiyana Qalam singer, Bibi Nooran.

Swarn Noora began to perform in public after her mother's death guided by her husband, a *qawwali* singer at the local All-India Radio station in Jalandhar. These recordings also feature her son, Dilbahar, on harmonium and vocals, with *dholak* and *tabla* percussion filling out the ensemble. The opening track, "Bahana Tere Tak Len De," gives the listener a good sense of Swarn Noora's powerful, open-throated vocal style as well as the formal conventions of this music: a brief introduction in free rhythm followed by verse, refrain, and instrumental sections set to a vigorous *keherwa tala*. Central to Punjabi folk singing are the stories of unrequited love, and this disc contains songs about two legendary couples, Heer-Ranjha ("Mera Ranjha Palle De Vich Pa De") and Sohni-Mahiwal ("Kaccha Vekh Na Leya"). The final two tracks directly evoke an inclusive spirituality typical of the Sufi mysticism from this region of South Asia and, unlike the earlier pieces, these two feature much more of the male vocalists singing collectively. As the disc comes to a close, Swarn Noora's magnificent voice has disappeared into the background, though fortunately for us it returns on the second disc in this collection.

Volume two, *Wah Rangiya: Passionate Punjab*, features two more tracks by Swarn Noora and three by her son, Dilbahar. The disc opens, however, with one of three tracks by Mehar Chand Mastana. A longtime member of Neelam Mansingh Choudhary's theater group, Mastana is a seasoned performer of Punjabi folktales and folk music. His recordings here include a song of separation and longing ("Aaja Ve Mahiya"), a ballad about another legendary pair of lovers (Mirza-Sahiba), and his own version of the story of Jugni (a Jugni song also concludes volume one). Originally extolled as a devotee of Ali, Jugni has become a symbol of the encounter between village purity and urban modernity as she travels far and wide, even making it to the U.S. in the form of Bikram Singh's 2005 *bhangra* pop album, *American Jugni* (VIP Records). Among the other tracks, there are two versions of challa songs worth hearing in comparison to the popular versions by Gurdas Mann and as remixed by Punjabi MC. Finally, a collection of Punjabi folk music is not complete without a song about Jagga (sung here by Swarn Noora's son, Dilbahar). Described in the liner notes as "a character like Robin Hood who robbed the rich to help the poor," Jagga embodies the "passionate Punjab" of folklore where heroes lay down their lives in the battle for justice and autonomy.

The third volume is entitled *Bol Ni Chakkiye: The Singing Wheel of Life*. Unlike the previous discs, this one evokes a survey of the wide variety of contexts for music-making in the Punjab. It contains four more tracks by Mehar Chand Mastana, including a *chakki* (grinding wheel) song of a devotional nature, sung to the Hindu god Rama ("Bol Meri Chakkiye"), and another version of the tragic love story of Sohni and Mahiwal ("Kaccha Kada"), in which Sohni drowns while trying to meet her lover by crossing a river in an unbaked clay pot. The last track by Mastana, "Dulla Bhatti," recalls the popular hero of resistance to Mughal rule. Other tracks of note on this disc include three instrumental pieces, two featuring the *been* (the reed instrument typically associated with "snake charmers") played by Sohan Nath Sapera and ensemble, and one recording of the *tumba* (small plucked lute) by Mundri Lal. Perhaps the most curious track on volume three is "Pat Ditte Tape Record Ne" by Harpal Singh Pala and party. It contains a comical conversation between villagers in which "TV" is confused with "TB," and thus the spread of mass media in the form of tape recorders and television is compared to the outbreak of an infectious disease.

Beat of India deserves much credit for this excellent collection. The sound quality of the recordings is clean and generally well-balanced, making this repertoire easily accessible to even the most novice listener. Included with each CD is a colorful booklet containing transliterations and English translations of each song. Given the importance of storytelling to most of these pieces, the complete translations are an especially valuable resource for educators. Finally, the website contains some useful supplemental materials, such as a subtitled, 13-minute interview with Swarn Noora. Individual tracks can also be downloaded for the reasonable price of US$0.69 per song.

Unfortunately, beyond providing the lyrics for each song, the booklets do not contain comprehensive liner notes and offer negligible information on the artists and settings in which the recordings were made. While the three discs do offer a glimpse into the rich variety of musical practices in the Punjab region, the collection should not be mistaken for a thorough survey, lacking, for example, traditional bhangra and giddha (which teachers might be most in need of at the moment), Sikh devotional music, and ghazal songs. The overall approach is to let the "authentic and awesome" music of Punjab speak for itself, leaving perhaps a little too much room for misunderstanding or confusion.

One final limitation of the collection concerns the discs themselves. The labels on the discs were painted on so thickly that the CDs would not play in my laptop or desktop computers, though I had no problem listening to them on a conventional CD player.

The three-disc series, Gudti Punjab Di, is a timely and useful resource that libraries should certainly acquire. Individuals, however, might consider using the Beat of India website to download a sample of tracks (such as Mehar Chand Mastana's rollicking version of "Jugni" or Swarn Noora's "Bahana Tere Tak Len De") and use the streaming video or their DVD ("Colours of Earth") when teaching.

References

Abbas, Shemeem Burney. 2003. The Female Voice in Sufi Ritual: Devotional Practices in Pakistan and India. Austin: University of Texas Press.

Pande, Alkia. 2000. Folk Music and Musical Instruments of Punjab: From Mustard Fields to Disco Lights. Middletown, NJ: Grantha Corporation.

Reading for Comprehension

1. What aspects of these three discs being reviewed make them special? What qualities does Kvetko highlight?
2. Kvetko focuses much of his discussion on the historical and cultural content of the songs. Can you think of similar cultural or historical references from our own culture? What do those references add to your understanding of the music being reviewed?

Analyzing the Genre

1. What does Kvetko's use of specialized terminology (e.g. *dholak* and *tabla*) tell you about this genre and about his intended audience? Spend some time looking those terms up (you might try CulturalIndia.net) to better understand the music and the audience intended.
2. Because ethnomusicology is his specialty, Kvetko has a lot of knowledge he can draw on, but he obviously conducted research for this review. Locate places where he has included background information and write about what it adds to the review. Are there places where you would have appreciated more research being included?

WRITING ASSIGNMENT OPTIONS

Reviews

Write an evaluative review of a film, restaurant, product, or any other subject that interests you. You do not need to be an expert in order to review a subject, though you will likely have to conduct some background research.

Review Assignment Options

1. Write an *evaluative* review of a film in which you contextualize it in its genre (e.g. *Pirates of the Caribbean* and other pirate films or other Disney live-action films). Check out the website http://imdb.com/Sections/Genres to read some film reviews categorized by genre.
2. Write a *critical* review of a scholarly article or book on a subject within your major or your profession.
3. Write an *academic review essay* in which you review a body of literature in your field of study or in your professional career.
4. Write a *comparative* review of the latest release of a product of interest to you (CD, software, etc.). Compare the current version or release to at least two previous ones.
5. Write an *analytical review* in which you contextualize a subject in terms of the genre it belongs to (e.g. a teen gross-out movie compared to others in that film genre).

(continued)

> **Community-based Writing Option**
>
> If you volunteer for a community organization or group, write an *evaluative review* about an event or program that might be interesting or useful for the population the organization serves. Inform them about it, being sure to provide information about how to get there, when it is, what it does, and so on, and evaluate it in terms of the needs and abilities of the organization's audience.

Writing Reviews

Just as with any genre, reviews have particular characteristics that help writers understand what they need to say and how to say it.

> **WHAT WRITERS CONSIDER WHEN THEY WRITE REVIEWS**
> In general, review writers:
>
> - Position themselves as expert, amateur, or novice on their chosen subject.
> - Identify criteria for evaluation.
> - Develop an evaluative thesis—implied or explicit.
> - Balance summary and description with analysis and evaluation.
> - Work with direct experience of their subjects.
> - Weigh details with audience expectations.

Avoiding Common Review Pitfalls

Remember, nearly anything can be reviewed—but this does not mean that everything *should* be reviewed. Here are two common pitfalls to avoid when choosing a subject for a review.

1. *The **Too Familiar** Subject.* Choosing a subject that most readers are already familiar with can cause difficulties from the start. For example, if you write a review about the final Harry Potter novel, *Harry Potter and the Deathly Hallows,* and there are a million other reviews of it in newspapers, magazines, and online, chances are you won't have too many new things to add to the conversation. A review should offer something new to readers, something they haven't heard before. So if you can find a different way to evaluate J. K. Rowling's last installment, do so. Otherwise, choose a different subject.

2. *The **Too Broad** Subject.* Choosing a subject that is too broad to be captured in a review can create problems for you as the writer as well as baffle your readers: What is this review *really* about? A review should be focused on a targeted subject so readers are clear about what is being reviewed. As you consider your subject ask yourself, can it be reviewed accurately and effectively in a short amount of space? Can it be dealt with in a review or would a different genre do the subject more justice?

Generating Ideas for Reviews

Review writers choose their subjects based on any number of experiences or interests they might have. For example, you find yourself so taken with a new band that you have to tell your friends about it. Or you attend a local summer festival and feel moved to tell someone about all the disappointing events, vendors, and music it has to offer.

WRITING ACTIVITY   Generating Ideas for Reviews

Reflecting

1. Consider the activities, hobbies, or interests you have. Are any of these good subjects for reviews? Would others be interested in reading about them?
2. Do you have expert knowledge about a subject or activity? Have you recently done or seen something that might make a good review subject?

Reading

1. What kinds of reviews do you (or would you) enjoy reading? What are the subjects of those reviews? Read some sample reviews to see what subjects others have written on, what interests you, and how the genre works.

Writing

1. List the kinds of films you like to watch, books you like to read, music you like to listen to, games you like to play, and performances you attend. Is there a particular subject that you know a lot about?
2. List the kinds of activities you have engaged in recently: cultural events, community gatherings, outings with friends. Would any of these make for a good review subject?
3. List the items you use on a daily basis, from cars to carrots. Would any of these be worth reviewing?

■　■　■

WebLinks

The World of Film Reviews

Examine how writers put together film reviews and identify some common characteristics of this genre. The Internet Movie Database offers reviews of current and past films, as well as a wealth of other information about the films. Search for IMDB to access the website.

Thinking about Audience, Purpose, and Situation

Since reviews can be written to inform, evaluate, critique, or compare subjects on which readers may or may not have background, your job is to know your subject, who you are writing to, your purpose, and how you want to present yourself, your *persona* as a writer—that is, you need to understand the rhetorical situation.

Consider the following questions to help you define your rhetorical situation:

1. **Consider the situation.** What made you choose the subject of your review? What circumstances surround the subject you are writing about?
2. **Consider your purpose.** Do you want to persuade your readers to purchase a product? Are you evaluating a film to convince readers to go see it? Are you informing them about the subject while simultaneously reviewing its worthiness to invest their time, money, or energy into?
3. **Consider your audience.** What will they be interested in hearing about? If you know your purpose, this will help you decide on whom you are writing to. Imagine a conversation with that audience: What will they say and how might you respond?
4. **Consider how to present yourself**. Are you an expert, amateur, or novice writing the review? Do you have any authority to speak on the subject? What examples, research, or language could you include to help build your credibility? What information about yourself, if any, should you reveal to the reader?
5. **Consider your tone**. Keep in mind the subject and the audience(s). Will a lighthearted tone capture their attention? Does the subject require a professional or serious tone?

■ ■ ■

Researching Reviews

When we talk about research and reviews, we are really thinking in terms of two different activities: background or contextual research and "field" research. As you think about conducting your research, recall the work you did earlier to establish your audience and purpose, as these will help you determine the type and amount of research you need to do.

Doing Background and Contextual Research

Whether you are an expert, amateur, or novice, research helps you connect with your audience by establishing your *ethos,* your credibility to speak on the subject and to comment with confidence about your subject.

Write down your subject (e.g. the new Apple iPhone), your audience (people unfamiliar with iPhones), your purpose (to convince people they absolutely need to buy one), and the rhetorical situation (e.g. your audience will read your review on a general website, maybe coming to it unintentionally, but will want to know whether the product is good for "everyday users" not just technophiles). Your answers to these questions will help you determine the kinds of research you'll need to do.

1. **What do you already know about your subject?** Are you new to it (and others like it)? What experience do you have with it? Have you read other writers' reviews of your subject?

2. **What don't you know about it?** Be broad in your answers to this question. For instance, if you are reviewing a film, do you know anything about cinematography? Background music?

3. **What will your audience absolutely need you to know in order for them to consider your review?** For instance, if you are reviewing a new *reggaeton* CD, your readers will expect you know about this variation of reggae music in general and how it differs from other forms of reggae music.

■ ■ ■

Developing Criteria for Evaluation

Reviews are based on *criteria* or standards that writers use to evaluate their subjects. Writers use evaluation criteria to help them focus on how they will analyze and assess a subject. They ask, "What's important to include in my evaluation? What do I value? What will my readers expect my review to contain?"

One way to develop criteria is to consider what criteria other critics apply to a similar subject. For example, as he was preparing to review Applebees, a national family-dinner chain, student Kyle Frey read a number of restaurant reviews to find out what kinds of criteria he could apply.

> Reviews on restaurants seem, as I would have guessed, to focus on the food. Specifically, they talk about things such as flavor and tenderness of meat. Also, pertaining to the food, reviewers talked about portion sizes and the drinks. The reviewers comment on whether or not the prices are reasonable, given what you get. Reviews are not always positive, and one common area that gets bashed is service. This is an important criterion because restaurants are in the service industry. A final category that seemed to be mentioned in most of these reviews was environment. That would include the noise level, décor, and the architecture.

These are not all the criteria Kyle might end up using, but his research into what others tend to comment on when reviewing restaurants allows him to predict what readers will expect to see.

WRITING ACTIVITY   Developing Your Review Criteria

Use the following prompts to help you define your review criteria.

1. Are you writing as a novice, an amateur, or an expert? What are some of the criteria that your audience would expect, given your stance?

2. What does your knowledge about and experience of the subject reveal to you about the important factors to consider in your review?

3. What is your audience's level of familiarity with your subject? What are they looking for in this review?

4. What are the ideal characteristics of your subject? (E.g. what makes for a perfect dessert?) What are the areas you believe are the most crucial to your subject? (E.g. a dessert needs to have chocolate in it.)

5. What do other reviewers of similar subjects base their evaluations on? (E.g. what do other book reviewers consider? What do other book reviews talk about in general?)

■ ■ ■

Doing Field Research for Reviews

Regardless of how familiar you are with your subject, field research is critical—you can't write a review of the Callaway Golf® FT-i drivers if you have never used them on a golf course. Nor can you review a film without actually seeing it. So your first step when conducting field research is to experience the thing for yourself. Reviewers often experience a subject many times before reviewing it for a number of reasons: to make sure their experience, good or bad, was not a fluke; to get a sense of all the subject has to offer; or to look at different aspects of the subject.

Since you have already established your criteria, you have a sense of what you need to look for as you experience the subject. Use those criteria to help you focus your observations. Reviews include details and examples, so be sure you take careful *observation notes*. For example, if you are reviewing a film, you'll want to record the details of particular scenes, the plots and subplots, characters' names, and so on. Your observation notes will help you present your audience with a detailed, interesting review of your subject.

In addition to observing your subject, you may want to talk to others about it. *Interviews* help reviewers gather firsthand information so readers understand how others experienced it: fans at a concert; people outside the theatre after a play; anime role players at the annual convention.

For more on field research, see Chapter 13: Research and the Rhetorical Situation.

Drafting Reviews

As you conduct your background and field research, you are also evaluating your subject; these evaluations will be positive, negative, mixed, or comparative. By the time you have finished your field research, you'll have an overall sense of your stance, and you may even have already articulated a *thesis,* or primary claim.

Writing Explicit and Implied Evaluative Thesis Statements

When thinking about your thesis statement, it's important to remember why people read reviews: to find out if the subject of the review is something they want to buy or experience. So readers will look for a statement that directly states or at least suggests what the writer has concluded about the subject.

Here's an example of an explicit evaluative thesis from Tim Rutten's review of *The Anatomist: A True Story of Gray's Anatomy* reproduced earlier in the chapter:

> In more judicious or scrupulous hands, "The Anatomist: A True Story of Gray's Anatomy" could have been a fascinating book. The one that San Francisco-based science writer Bill Hayes has written, however, is—by turns—cloying, irritating and wrongheaded.

Rutten is pretty clear about the book. But notice something interesting: Even though the audience is reading the review in order to decide whether to read the book, Rutten's thesis is sufficiently compelling that we want to keep reading his review. We don't want to read a book that is "cloying, irritating and wrongheaded," but we do want to find out *why Rutten thinks that* and whether we think that Rutten is right. Rutten's purpose, then, becomes in part to convince us that his evaluation is right.

Sometimes, however, review writers will include what is called an *implicit,* or *embedded, thesis*—one where the argument is suggested rather than stated directly. Implicit theses allow the reader to figure out the writer's judgment on her own through the comments and evaluative language made throughout the review.

The example below shows how one reviewer, John Phillips, indirectly weaves his evaluation throughout his review of the 2008 Maserati GranTurismo, using phrases and sentences at various points:

> Apart from its Joe E. Brown mouth, which half our staff thinks is too large, this four-passenger coupe is the quintessence of Italian **flash and panache**. . . . Looking out over the hood, all you see is **the sensuous left wheel arch delicately kicking up**. And peering into the large side-view mirrors, you're rewarded with **a gratifying glimpse** of muscular hips comprising more compound curves than Michelangelo could muster. . . . Maseratis have traditionally been long on personality in a weird and quirky way, which always felt like an accident, as if the builders didn't really know how the car was going to turn out. In contrast, the GranTurismo feels **engineered with a purpose.**

What you may notice is that Phillips uses a series of *claims* to build his evaluation of the 2008 GranTurismo rather than directly state a thesis at the start. Doing so keeps the reader interested to find out more about how all these details contribute to Phillips' evaluation of the car.

WRITING ACTIVITY   Articulating Your Thesis

Look over your notes from the field research you conducted, paying particular attention to your reactions and thoughts immediately after you finished observing and exploring your subject.

1. How would you characterize your response? Positive? Negative? Mixed? If you are writing a comparative review, how does your subject compare to similar subjects?
2. What were the key aspects of your subject that made your assessment positive, negative, or mixed, or made you want to favorably or unfavorably compare your subject to others?
3. Consider your audience and your purpose, as well as how you are positioning yourself as a writer: Will you need to state this thesis directly? Or can you suggest it indirectly?

■ ■ ■

Generating Claims for Reviews

Once you have a good idea of what your thesis will be, it's time to consider the arguments, or claims, you want to make in support of that thesis. In reviews, claims are primarily *evaluative statements*—ones that include the writer's judgment or assessment of particular aspects of the subject.

One way to get started is to look at the two areas that are ready-made to help you generate your claims: your *criteria* and your *research*. For example, suppose you are reviewing a vacuum cleaner, and during your testing, you have come to the conclusion that this particular vacuum cleaner, the Benton SV 17 model, well, sucks (or perhaps does not suck, which would be bad for a vacuum cleaner). What kinds of claims could you make to support your thesis that the Benton SV 17 is not worth the money?

Your first step is to consider your *criteria*. The criteria you established before using the Benton will help you generate claims now that you have tested it a few times.

Criteria for vacuum cleaners	*Claims: The Benton SV 17 is not worth the money, because . . .*
Should be lightweight	. . . seems as heavy as a small car, and it easily weighs ten pounds more than its nearest competitor.
Components should be easy to switch	. . . switching components takes the mathematical and spatial manipulation skills of a master architect.
Should be able to remove 95% of dirt from a white shag rug	. . . it left most of the caked-in dirt and 30% of the cookie crumbs our two-year-old assistant left in the rug.
Should have easily removable bag or cylinder, for easy cleanup	. . . the cylinder requires a two-handed release, something not easily accomplished.

Even in this hypothetical scenario, it is easy to see how our evaluations of our subject against our criteria become claims.

Your criteria are the first place to look for possible claims, but you have at least two other sources: *your own experience (your field research)* and *your formal research*.

Experience/Research	*Claims*
"I had a hard time maneuvering the Benton around the corners of my entertainment center."	The Benton is hard to maneuver.
"I found myself wishing the model came with earplugs."	The Benton is excessively noisy.
Research: New HEPA technology virtually guarantees that most allergens will be filtered out. The owner's manual states that the Benton removes 80% of allergens.	The Benton's HEPA filtration system is barely adequate—it released 20% of allergens back into the room, according to the "tech specs" in the manual.

Notice that in doing this activity, you are also generating some of the *evidence* you will need. In the last example, evidence for the claim that "The Benton's HEPA filtration system is barely adequate—it released 20% of allergens back into the room" comes from the research: "New HEPA technology virtually guarantees that most allergens will be filtered out."

Using the example above as a model, generate claims for your review. Consider three areas: criteria, experience, and research.

1. **Look over your initial criteria for evaluation.** List the ones you applied as you observed your subject. Articulate a claim for each that suggests your position on the subject.
2. **Look over your notes from your field research, observations, and initial reactions.** List those points that seem related to your criteria and to your thesis. Articulate claims for each.
3. **Look over your formal research.** List the material that reflects your position on the subject. Articulate claims that reflect that research and your position on the subject.

■ ■ ■

Writing Openings for Reviews

The primary piece of information a reader needs is what subject is being reviewed. Most reviews open by stating the specific subject being evaluated. For example, student Patrick Merrigan mentions the topic of his review, the movie *Superbad,* in his first sentence (see page 194).

However, in John Phillips' review of the 2008 Maserati GranTurismo, the first paragraph provides historical and anecdotal information about the Maserati family. Phillips can begin this way because his audience is familiar with car reviews, may be familiar with high-end lines like the Maserati, and would be interested in hearing more about the company. Indeed, he doesn't mention the specific model he is reviewing until the third paragraph.

Writing Closings for Reviews

While the closing of a review can restate the thesis or, for example, tell the reader directly to do or not do something, review writers generally conclude by finding a way to help the reader, one last time, experience the subject—whether that experience is pleasurable or not.

Let's look at the closing from the review of Hakata Tonton by Peter Meehan on page 163. You'll notice that Meehan concludes with an ***anecdote*** about the restaurant, one that he feels will convey something missing, maybe, from the review or will erase any negative impressions the reader might have gotten. This conclusion seems to suggest that the place is worth going to—if not for its food, then for its uniqueness.

Occasionally, a reviewer recommends that readers "go and eat there," "buy this car now," or something similar. You may find that such a ***direct address*** works for your closing—given your subject, purpose, and audience.

As you consider your choices for how to open and close your review, think about your audience, purpose, and how you present yourself as a writer.

1. Does your subject suggest a particular kind of opening?
2. Would an audience expect a particular kind of opening?
3. Do you need to state the thesis directly in the opening paragraphs, or can you weave it implicitly throughout your review?

4. Does your level of experience on the subject suggest an opening for you? A detailed account based on your expertise? Background on a subject you knew nothing about?
5. Does your field or background research suggest a good opening?
6. Does your opening suggest a closing to you?
7. Would your audience want you to echo what you said in the opening? Does the purpose you established in the opening require a certain kind of closing?
8. Would an anecdote or illustration make sense as a closing?
9. Does your field or background research suggest a good closing?
10. Is a direct recommendation appropriate for your closing?
11. Does your review subject warrant ending with a quick checklist of particular information for readers to refer to?

■ ■ ■

Revising Reviews

The first thing you should consider as you look over your draft is "do I need to revisit the subject of my review or do I have enough material to work with?"

Balancing Summary/Description and Analysis/Evaluation: The What and the How

Reviews need details. Details allow the reader to feel like they are experiencing the subject with you. If you are reviewing a film, for instance, chances are that readers have not yet seen it, so your review provides them with an evaluation as well as with details upon which you've based your evaluation and any other examples they'll need to understand the gist of the film. Scenes, characters, plotlines, theme, music, and other elements are just some of the details you might include to paint a full picture in your review. But just as your readers are in need of some details to illustrate your claims, they also don't want to know everything about the film—that would take away from their experience of seeing it. Knowing the right balance of information to include is the key to writing a detailed, well-developed review.

Equally important, the reviewer should balance the description and summary with analysis and evaluation of the subject. After all, readers not only want to know *about* the subject, they want to know if it's any good. Think of it this way: Summary and description tell readers *what* you are reviewing while analysis and evaluation tell readers *how* the elements of the subject work together to affect opinion or judgment.

In his review of the film *Dazed and Confused,* Ryan Reed, a student in a first-year writing class, tells us what we need to know in order to understand his analysis without telling too much. Notice how the details he provides are carefully chosen to support his analysis.

> Written and directed by Richard Linklater, this picture doesn't hold back whatsoever in this bold depiction of high school life in our society. And because of the film's controversial topics, the movie has acquired a love-hate relationship with its viewers. Released in 1993, *Dazed* has already reached cult film status, with a highly devoted but relatively small following. *Dazed and*

> *Confused* isn't another movie where the football team wins the championship, or the girl next door finally falls in love with her neighbor. This movie is not just about getting accepted, it's about not being accepted, and standing up for what you believe in. It's about all aspects of high school life, getting there, making it through and leaving.

GROUP ACTIVITY   Balancing Summary/Description with Analysis/Evaluation

Read through your group members' drafts and mark the places where the writers **summarize/describe** the subject of their reviews. Do they include enough material to help you understand the subject? Where do they need more summary or description?

Mark the places where the writers **analyze / evaluate** how the elements of the subject are working together. Where do they need more analysis or evaluation?

■ ■ ■

Entering the Conversation: Integrating Other Reviews into your Review

Reviews involve entering conversations. For example, when you sit down to dinner with friends or family and join their conversation on the latest Coldplay CD, you are adding your evaluation of the new release.

Similarly, examining what others have said about the subject of your review strengthens your analysis. Considering others' evaluations can also build your ethos, your credibility to speak on the subject and it shows you've done your research.

In his introduction (page 194), Patrick Merrigan works in a number of different film critics as he analyzes and reviews the documentary film *Superbad*. Notice how he incorporates both the material from the film and what other reviewers have said about the film in order to help us understand the directors' message which he articulates in the last sentence of the introductory paragraph.

WRITING ACTIVITY   Incorporating and Synthesizing Other Voices in Your Review

Based on your research of the subject, are there other critics' reviews that you can incorporate into yours? You can use their overall evaluations or particular arguments to:

1. Agree with your claims on the subject (e.g. "others feel similarly about the book").
2. Disagree with your claims on the subject (e.g. "the reviewer fails to look at the larger message in the documentary"), and subsequently, strengthen your argument.
3. Compare similar points critics have made about *a different subject in the same genre* (e.g. a food critic's point about another upscale restaurant).

Mark places in your review where other critics' voices would help you deepen your analysis, and use Patrick Merrigan's introduction to his review on page 194 as a guide.

■ ■ ■

As you read, give specific comments and suggestions that will help the writer revise the draft. (e.g. "This is confusing <u>because</u> I have not seen the film—could you provide some more summary of the plot?")

Provide writers with feedback on their review drafts, keeping in mind that the writers may have chosen a variety of subjects to review. Therefore, think about the subject and specific criteria for evaluation used in *this review* as you offer specific written comments.

Comment in the margins on the following:

OPENINGS: What captures your attention in the opening? Suggest concrete ways the writer could make the opening more engaging for the reader.

EVALUATIVE THESIS: What is the writer's evaluation of the subject? Is the thesis explicit or implied? Suggest ways the writer revise the thesis to make it clear.

DETAIL/SUMMARY VERSUS ANALYSIS/EVALUATION: Comment on the detail the writer provides on the subject. What more do you need to know? Where should an excess of detail be trimmed? Where should the writer include more analysis/ evaluation of the subject? Are there places the details lead into an analysis/evaluation of the subject?

Finally when you have finished reading and annotating, write an endnote to the writer in which you comment on the following:

Begin by telling the writer what you enjoyed about the letter (be specific).

DEVELOPING THE ARGUMENTS: Does the draft reflect what the writer promises to talk about in the thesis—or not? Suggest ways for the writer to revise the draft so that the thesis and arguments in the draft are developed clearly.

INCORPORATING RESEARCH: Where in the review does the writer use comments from other reviewers to deepen the evaluation of the subject? In which places does the writer use other kinds of research to deepen the reader's understanding or strengthen the argument?

ANALYZING THE AUDIENCE AND CRITERIA FOR EVALUATION: Who is the audience for the review and how do you know based on your analysis of the criteria, examples, language, and so on? Does the writer seem to know his audience's needs and expectations based on the information he provides on his subject?

Discuss your comments with the writer when you have finished.

Reflecting on the Process

We learn how to write better by writing, but we also learn by being careful critics of our own processes—looking back on the steps we have taken and the choices we have made can teach us a lot about ourselves as writers. The writing activity that follows will help you develop your skills for reflecting critically on your own writing.

___WRITING ACTIVITY___   Reflecting on Writing a Review

Reflect on your writing process for your review: how you generated and chose ideas, did research, and drafted and revised your review. Imagine you are writing this reflection to writers who have never written a review of this kind. What might they learn about working within the genre from you? What could you tell them that might help them as writers?

1. *Begin* by describing what aspects you are most pleased with in your review.
2. *Analyze* your strengths and weaknesses as a writer for this review.
3. *Explain* what you think contributed to your success in these areas
4. *Reflect* on how you determined your purpose and audience for your review. How did these elements influence your choice of arguments or examples?
5. *Discuss* your revision process, including how you used feedback from your readers.
6. *Conclude* by reflecting on what you learned about the genre of the review. You might also reflect on what you might do differently the next time you write a review.

■   ■   ■

Patrick Merrigan's Film Review

Patrick Merrigan, a student in a first-year writing course, chose to write a review of the film *Superbad,* which he identifies as an adolescent comedy. Notice how he balances the use of evaluation and analysis and summary and details; also notice how he blends in the ideas of other reviewers to make his evaluative argument. Here we show you some of the thinking and writing processes that led up to the finished review.

Thinking about Audience, Purpose, and Situation: Developing Criteria

Merrigan began by thinking about his *audience* and his *role* as the review writer.

As a novice he can write about what makes him laugh thereby helping the audience see how his response is the right one.

Merrigan defines an audience that knows a lot about films like Superbad.

> I will be writing as a novice because I am very unfamiliar with the movie-making business and the behind-the-scenes stuff that goes on. I know a fair amount about the subject because I have seen **Superbad** a few times and have seen similar movies that used the same actors, producers, and writers. I saw it in theaters, bought it on DVD, and watched it a few more times.
>
> My audience will be those who are interested in gross-out comedy movies. They will probably have a fair amount of previous knowledge because they will most likely have seen similar movies.

One of the crucial steps in writing a review is establishing the criteria by which you will judge subject. Merrigan, in his development of criteria, looked to two different sources: what he already knew about comedy films from years spent watching them, and what he learned from professional movie critics and what they thought made for a good comedy.

> My criteria for a good comedy movie:
> Good lead actor/actress
> Chemistry between the actors
> Storyline is funny but realistic
> Length has to be within 90-120 minutes
> Should have some clever parts
> Appropriate music to go with the movie
> Good camera angles to make scenes funnier

Drafting: Integrating Background Research

Merrigan was not the only person to write about *Superbad,* nor was he the first person to review an "adolescent comedy," so he did some *background research* to find out how other similar comedies were reviewed—and what those reviewers said about the *genre* of adolescent comedies. Later, when he wrote his first draft, he made reference to this material.

Merrigan uses other comedies and other reviewers to help him understand aspects of good comedy.

Here, too, we can see the source of Merrigan's criteria—the most unusual is the one about camera angles.

Readers, and Merrigan, might need some more specifics here—what makes a camera shot/angle memorable?

There are certain criteria that are used to evaluate the subject of comedy movies. One such quality is laughs that have a deeper meaning. Critic Peter Travers of www.rollingstone. com says of Judd Apatow who directed Knocked Up, "He won't settle for skin-deep. His jokes double back after the first laugh and hit you where it hurts". This is an important quality because you want the jokes to have some substance and meaning. Chemistry is equally important; Robert Ebert of www.rogerebert.com writes about The 40 Year Old Virgin and claims that "the movie works [. . .] because Steve Carell and Catherine Keener have a rare kind of chemistry that is maybe better described as a mutual sympathy". This stands out in that film and is part of what made it such a good comedy.

One important aspect to a good comedy is the use of camera angles and certain shots during specific scenes. When talking about Wedding Crashers, critic Bob Townsend of www.accessatlanta.com says that, "A cleverly shot and edited montage pictures the pair in scenes from their greatest pickups". This is the type of camera work that is vital to a good comedy movie. Finally, the actor/actress in a film is key. Critic Kenneth Turan of www. calenderlive.com writes that, "For as "Liar Liar" proves one more time, there is probably no more consistently funny performer working in film today."

Drafting: Using Evaluative Language and Tone

One of the characteristics that Merrigan noted in his genre analysis of other film reviews was the informality of the genre; as he puts it "The language of the reviews is part of what separates them from other genres. The genre seems to allow an informal tone because it asks questions and is not as formal as a research report." So one of Merrigan's goals was to write a positive, evaluative review of *Superbad* using an informal, friendly tone. But he also wanted to be taken seriously and not be dismissed as someone who simply loves the film uncritically. As you read his draft, note those places where he meets these goals.

Merrigan has tried a similar approach to the one he describes above—his opening, however, asks you to sit down with him in his room. Does it work?

In his introduction, he's also giving us a little background—about the people involved in the film and then later about the film itself.

Patrick Merrigan
Professor Ferruci
English 100P
2 Apr. 2010

Draft 1

Superbad: Super Movie or Bad Movie?

As I sat down on my bed in my dorm room and pulled down the shades I wondered to myself how a movie titled *Superbad* could be any good. The movie was "From the guys who brought you The 40-YEAR-OLD VIRGIN and KNOCKED UP" so I had a idea about what type of movie it was going to be. The previous movies that this group of "guys" made were a crude and gross-out type of comedy, but they did have some sort of substance underneath. The story of *Superbad* is one about two teenage guys who are unpopular but see their opportunity when they are invited to a party at the end of their senior year. They see this as their last chance to get with a girl before they go off to college.

The two main characters are Seth and Evan, who are named after the two writers who wrote the script. Seth, played by the hilarious Jonah Hill, is the large kid with the even larger mouth and has almost nothing to say but dirty phrases involving sex and swears. Evan, played by Michael Cera, is the more straight-laced one that seems to be afraid of his own shadow at times and especially when it comes to talking to girls. The two are given the task of getting alcohol for the entire party and are joined by their friend Fogell, played by first time actor Christoper Mintz-Plasse. Even they seem to consider Fogell a loser but they need to get alcohol and it just so happens that he is getting a fake I.D.

The scene where Fogell is in the liquor store with his fake i.d. which says that his name is McLovin the Hawaii organ donor is priceless. To make Fogell's story even funnier, he is joined on his crazy adventure by two cops, Slater and Michaels, played by Bill Hader and Seth Rogen, who seem to be more immature than the teenage guys. The three of them go on crazy misadventures from bar fights, to breathalyzer tests, to destroying their own squad car.

Jonah Hill and Michael Cera each bring a great performance to the table as best friends Seth and Evan. They play off the parts as though they have actually been best friends all their lives, as is the story with the two characters. Throughout the movie they are asked by various people how they will survive next year without one another. Evan got into Dartmouth (as did Fogell), whereas Seth is headed to state school. Their sidekick Fogell, is played by Mintz-Plasse who does a great job in his first movie role. The character of McLovin is sure to become part of high school teen comedies for a long time. The two girls of interest for Seth and Evan are Jules and Becca, played by Emma Stone and Martha MacIssac. This was also Stone's first movie but she turns out a solid performance as Seth's crush, as well as MacIssac who was Evan's crush.

The laughs continue as Seth and Evan end up at an adult party where there are alcohol, drugs, fights, and menstrual blood. Meanwhile Fogell is out with the two cops drinking a lot and causing mischief. One of the funniest scenes in the entire movie is when Michaels and Slater are having a shootout they are trying to shoot the "O" in a stop sign. Then they hear sirens so they yell "Shit! It's the cops!", run into the police car, and speed away.

The music that is in the movie Superbad is very appropriate as it even fits the title. The music is under the classification of funk. This seems to fit well in with the characters because they seem to be funky themselves as outcasts among kids in their own age group. Even Seth, who is dressed in Evan's dad's clothes, had a funky look to it. The opening credits and the first few songs have a real funk feel to them which is important because it helps set up the feeling of the movies.

The climax of the movie takes place when the three guys finally reach the party after a fight between Seth and Evan leads to Seth getting hit by a

Merrigan gives us a brief overview of the film and introduces us to the main characters. For those who have not seen the film, this is crucial, and for those who have, it reminds them of the central plot.

Merrigan is applying his criteria here. There is something special about this scene and he wants to call attention to it—this is a characteristic of the film review.

Merrigan provides details about this film, focusing on some of the more humorous parts of the storyline—the two main characters' inseparability for instance and Fogell as "McLovin."

It's a good move, here, to provide some specific examples of what makes the film so funny.

Here's another of the author's criteria—the use of music and its appropriateness given the content of the film.

One of the characteristics of a film review—especially when reviewing a current film—is not to give the ending away. In the next two paragraphs, Merrigan writes about the climax; does he succeed in giving enough background or does he give too much away?

police car. Seth shows up as the hero who brings in all the alcohol including the green beer that is in a detergent container. Meanwhile Seth is gets drunk so that he can get with the girl of his dreams, Becca. Fogell then somewhat overcomes his awkwardness and begins dancing with his crush, Nicola, played by Aviva Farber. Evan ends up in a bedroom with Becca and stops her before they go too far. At the same time Seth is trying to get with Jules but ends up passing out and head butting her right in the face and giving her a black eye. The party is then broken up by the two cops who also interrupt Fogell as he is about to have sex. Seth then tries to carry Evan to safety as the party is being broken up by Slater and Michaels.

The movie then concludes with a series of tying up loose ends. Fogell, Slater, and Michaels shoot up the police car and light it on fire to cover up all the damage they caused to it. Seth and Evan then have a heartfelt talk while in sleeping bags on the floor of Evan's basement. The next day they both head to the mall and run into Becca and Jules. After a brief talk they go their separate ways with Evan joining Becca while Seth goes off with Jules.

This sounds like Merrigan's main point.

The movie is crude and just downright gross as some point such as Seth's penis drawing addiction, a girl "periding" on Seth's leg, and when Seth is making sexual gestures at Jules during cooking class. But at its core, the movie has a heart and a good message or two. The boys being scared about the future and losing one another is an important idea that they have to come to grips with. Also, Seth learning that he doesn't have to be drunk to get with a girl like Jules is important because that is how many teenagers think. Superbad may be a gross-out high school teen comedy but its clever acting, writing, and directing make it the best of its kind.

Revising: Balancing Detail with Audience Needs

Very often after we have written a first draft, we are aware of areas that need improving. One of the challenges Merrigan faced was deciding how much detail he needed—how much could he assume his readers knew or wanted to know about the film? Merrigan returned to his first draft and revised with this in mind. In the excerpts below, notice how much material gets cut or rewritten, and how only in the second draft he articulates a thesis.

Patrick Merrigan
Draft #2

Superbad: Super movie or Bad movie?

As I sat down on my bed in my dorm room and pulled down the shades I wondered to myself how a movie titled *Superbad* could be any good. The movie was "From the guys who brought you The 40-YEAR-OLD VIRGIN and KNOCKED UP" so I had a idea about what type of movie it was going to be.

The previous movies that this group of "guys" made were a crude and gross-out type of comedy, but they did have some sort of substance underneath. The story of *Superbad* is one about two teenage guys who are unpopular but see their opportunity when they are invited to a party at the end of their senior year. They see this as their last chance to get with a girl before they go off to college.

It may be a gross-out adolescent comedy, but its clever acting, writing, and directing make it the best of its kind.

. . .

The writers, Seth Rogen and Evan Goldberg, are masterminds when it comes to writing the script. They began writing it at age 13. Unbelievable I know. They bring the same style of comedy as Knocked Up and The 40-Year-Old Virgin while making it original at the same time. Rogen actually has a supporting role in the film as one of the officers. Greg Mottola works together brilliantly with the writers as well as the actors. Mottola is the director and has also worked in numerous other films. He does a great job with directing and gets all the shots at the right angles with the right timing so that the movie turns out hilarious.

. . .

~~The climax of the movie takes place when the three guys finally reach the party after a fight between Seth and Evan leads to Seth getting hit by a police car. Seth shows up as the hero who brings in all the alcohol including the green beer that is in a detergent container. Meanwhile Seth is gets drunk so that he can get with the girl of his dreams, Becca. Fogell then somewhat overcomes his awkwardness and begins dancing with his crush, Nicola, played by Aviva Farber. Evan ends up in a bedroom with Becca and stops her before they go too far. At the same time Seth is trying to get with Jules but ends up passing out and head butting her right in the face and giving her a black eye. The party is then broken up by the two cops who also interrupt Fogell as he is about to have sex. Seth then tries to carry Evan to safety as the party is being broken up by Slater and Michaels.~~ Fix all this, but don't give it away—delete

~~The movie then concludes with a series of tying up loose ends. Fogell, Slater, and Michaels shoot up the police car and light it on fire to cover up all the damage they caused to it. Seth and Evan then have a heartfelt talk while in sleeping bags on the floor of Evan's basement. The next day they both head to the mall and run into Becca and Jules. After a brief talk they go their separate ways with Evan joining Becca while Seth goes off with Jules.~~ Get rid of.

This is a good thesis that clearly communicates the point of the review to the audience and tells them why he thinks it is a good film.

This new paragraph goes into more detail about the writers and director—so Merrigan has done some research to provide the insight into the business he says he lacks in his initial work.

This is a lot to delete, but Merrigan clearly feels that it gives too much away.

The climax of the movie takes place when the three guys finally reach the party and just when you couldn't laugh anymore because your sides hurt, you are hit again with a wave of hilarious antics that make you fall to the floor. This movie is crude and just downright gross as some point such as Seth's penis drawing addiction, a girl "perioding" on Seth's leg, and when Seth is making sexual gestures at Jules during cooking class. But at its core, the movie has a heart and a good message or two. The boys being scared about the future and losing one another is an important idea that they have to come to grips with. ~~Also, Seth learning that he doesn't have to be drunk to get with a girl like Jules is important because that is how many teenagers think.~~ We learn from the movie that it can be an exciting but also unclear time in a young adolescent's life that is full of change and the struggle of coming to grips with it. *Superbad* may be a gross-out high school teen adolescent comedy but its clever acting, writing, and directing make it the best of its kind. ← thesis! move to end of my first paragraph and be sure to talk about it in the rest of the paper.

Revising: Peer Review

Having completed his own revisions, Merrigan submitted his next draft to readers for feedback. What follows are excerpts from that draft. Notice how the readers ask Merrigan to further develop and clarify some of the points for an audience who might be unfamiliar with the film.

Patrick Merrigan
Draft 3

Superbad: Super movie or Bad movie?

    As I sat down on my bed in my dorm room and pulled down the shades I wondered to myself how a movie titled <u>Superbad</u> could be any good. The movie was "From the guys who brought you <u>The 40-YEAR-OLD VIRGIN</u> and <u>KNOCKED UP</u>," so I had an idea about what type of movie it was going to be. The previous movies that this group of "guys" made were crude and something of a gross-out type comedy but usually had some sort of substance underneath it all. The story of <u>Superbad</u> is one about two teenage guys who are unpopular but see their opportunity when they are invited to a party at the end of their senior year. They see this as their last chance to get with a girl before they go off to college. It may be a gross-out adolescent comedy but its clever acting, writing, and directing make it the best of its kind.

    · · ·

    The climax of the movie takes place when the three guys finally reach the party and just when you couldn't laugh anymore because your sides hurt,

Professor: Since you bring up the other movies, do you want to comment on what the substance of one of those was?

Professor: Good Thesis. Do you want to give some brief description of what makes it adolescent—either earlier in the paragraph or later?

Student 2: I think this sentence belongs at the end of the last paragraph—seems to fit better, and the rest of the paragraph then works better as a conclusion.

Student 2: Needs a stronger conclusion—how about "Superbad was nothing short of a super movie."

you are hit again with a wave of hilarious antics that make you fall to the floor. It ended up grossing $121,463,226 domestically and since the budget was only $20,000,000 the movie could be considered a big success. (Superbad (2007)). This movie is crude and just downright gross as some point such as Seth's penis drawing addiction, a girl "perioding" on his leg, and when he is making sexual gestures at Jules during cooking class. But at its core, the movie has a heart and a good message or two. The boys being scared about the future and losing one another is an important idea that they have to come to grips with. We learn from the movie that it can be an exciting but also unclear time in a young adolescent's life that is full of change and the struggle of coming to grips with it.

When Merrigan received his draft back from his professor and peer reviewers, he reflected on those comments. Notice, especially, that he does not simply accept the suggestions—he weighs them against his own vision and understanding of the review.

Patrick Merrigan

Peer Review Discussion

My readers gave me suggestions that will help make my paper better. Jamie and Mike had things that they liked about my paper, such as my thesis, but they also had constructive criticism for me.

A lot of the changes I made were little spelling things like "a" instead of "an." I fixed these immediately and was glad that they pointed these things out to me. Another problem that seemed to be throughout my paper was that I was not putting commas where they needed to be. Jamie put a lot in throughout my paper and I included most of them. Some of them I didn't add in because I felt as though they weren't necessary and were more of a stylistic choice. I also did some rewording at the end of the paragraph where I talk about the writers and director because it wasn't flowing very well.

I was also advised to make a few changes near the ending of my review. Mike wanted to know why I didn't say more about the "menstrual blood" scene, since it was the grossest part of the movie. I didn't know what to say about it, so I didn't change anything. Jamie suggested that I move the sentence where I talk about the climax of the movie into the previous paragraph. From there I talked about how much money the movie made so that would be the beginning of my new paragraph. Another change I added in was a suggestion from Jamie for me to add in a more conclusive sentence and she gave me an example. I felt as though this was the perfect conclusion sentence so I added it into my paper.

Patrick Merrigan, (student), Superbad: Super Movie or Just Bad? (final draft)

Patrick Merrigan

Professor Ferruci

English 100P

30 Apr. 2010

Film Review: *Superbad:* Super Movie or Just Bad?

As I sat down on my bed in my dorm room and pulled down the shades I wondered to myself how a movie titled *Superbad* could be any good. The movie was "from the guys who brought you *The 40-Year-Old Virgin* and *Knocked Up,*" so I had an idea about what type of movie it was going to be. The previous movies that this group of "guys" made were crude, gross-out types of comedy, but they usually had some sort of substance under the surface. *Knocked Up* is a good example of this kind of comedy, but according to the Internet Movie Database (*www.imdb.com*), it's also a movie with some substance. *Knocked Up* is about how "Slobby Ben and up-and-coming career girl Alison meet at a bar, and end up having a one night stand. Eight weeks later, Ben is shocked when Alison meets him and reveals that she is pregnant. Despite having little in common, the two decide that they have to at least try to make some kind of relationship work for the baby's sake." Brought to us by the same "guys," the story of *Superbad* is about two teenage guys who are unpopular but see their opportunity to get with a girl before they go off to college when they are invited to a party at the end of their senior year of high school. *Superbad* may be a gross-out adolescent comedy but its clever acting, writing, and directing make it the best of its kind.

The two main characters, Seth and Evan, are named after the two writers of the movie's script. Seth, played by the hilarious Jonah Hill, is a large kid with an even larger mouth who has almost nothing to say but dirty phrases involving sex and profanities. Evan, played by Michael Cera, is the more straightlaced one who seems to be afraid of his own shadow at times, especially when it comes to talking to girls. The two are given the task of getting alcohol for the end of the year party they were invited to and are joined by their friend Fogell, played by first-time actor Christopher Mintz-Plasse. Even Seth and Evan consider Fogell a

In his final draft, merrigan has done a good job of making the connection between the other movies and this one.

Merrigan's thesis is clear and direct.

loser, but they need to get alcohol and it just so happens that he is getting a fake driver's license saying he is older than twenty-one.

The writers, Seth Rogen and Evan Goldberg, are masterminds when it comes to the script. They began writing it at age 13. Unbelievable, I know. They use the same style of comedy in *Superbad* as in *Knocked Up* and *The 40-Year-Old Virgin,* while making it original at the same time. Rogen actually has a supporting role in the film as a police officer. The director Greg Mottola worked brilliantly with the writers as well as the actors, and has also worked in numerous other films. He does a great job with directing. He gets all the shots at the right angles with the right timing so that the movie turns out hilarious.

Mottola shows his directing brilliance in the scene where Fogell is in the liquor store with his fake license, which says that his name is "McLovin" the Hawaiian organ donor. It is priceless. To make Fogell's story even funnier, he is joined on his crazy adventure by two cops, Slater and Michaels, played by Bill Hader and Seth Rogen, who seem to be more immature than the teenage guys. The three of them go on crazy misadventures ranging from bar fights, to breathalyzer tests, to destroying their own squad car.

Jonah Hill and Michael Cera each bring a great performance to the table as best friends Seth and Evan. They play their parts as though they have actually been best friends all their lives, as is the story with the two characters. This is so believable due to the fact that Hill and Cera are such good actors and are able to feed off of one another and sometimes even improvise to make each scene funnier. Throughout the movie, they are asked by various people how they will survive next year without one another. Evan (as well as Fogell) got into Dartmouth, whereas Seth is headed to a state school. Mintz-Plasse, who plays their sidekick Fogell, does a great job in his first movie role. The character of McLovin is sure to become a legend of high school teen comedies for a long time because of his appearance and voice. The two girls of interest for Seth and Evan are Jules and Becca, played by Emma Stone and Martha MacIssac. This was also Stone's movie debut, and she turns out a solid performance as Seth's crush, as does MacIssac, who was Evan's crush.

The film's musical score, mostly a kind of "funk," is very appropriate as it even fits the title and the characters because they seem to be funky themselves

---

This paragraph is a good example of the background and context of the film.

Merrigan should provide a bit more here—actually telling us what those other films are, what they were about, how they did and how they compared to this one.

It might be so, but Merrigan should explain what makes it priceless.

One of Merrigan's qualities for what makes for a successful comedy.

Because he has already mentioned McLovin above, it ends up feeling a bit repetitious—it may have been more successful had it been incorporated above.

This is one of the more interesting of Merrigan's criteria, because a film's score is often meant to play a background role. But as the reviewer, he needed to be a bit more specific here—what exactly is "funk"?

Here's the casual tone and voice that Merrigan was going for; we feel like we are in his room with him, talking about the film. And given the audience intended for both the film and the review, it seems appropriate.

The writer's conclusion addresses a new idea: there are two other criteria that make the film a success: 1) the film's profit at the box office, and 2) "the message" and what "we learn" from a film like Superbad are important aspects of this genre.

The last sentence emphasizes what makes the film a success—its larger underlying message.

as outcasts among kids in their own age group. Even Seth, who is dressed in Evan's dad's clothes, has a funky look. People who have seen the film agree; says Amazon.com reviewer Shaffer, "This soundtrack features funk classics alongside new material by Bootsy Collins. Unlike most movie soundtracks, 'Superbad' is an instant classic that actually stands on its own without foreknowledge of the film. A fun, 'superfunky' album!" The opening credits and the first few songs have a real funk feel to them which is important because it helps set up the feeling of the movie.

The laughs continue as Seth and Evan end up at an adult party where there are alcohol, drugs, fights, and menstrual blood. Meanwhile, Fogell is out with the two cops drinking a lot and causing mischief. One of the funniest scenes in the entire movie is when Michaels and Slater are having a shootout where they are trying to shoot the "O" in a stop sign. Then they hear sirens so they yell "Shit! It's the cops!" run into the police car, and speed away. The climax of the movie takes place when the three guys finally reach the party. Just when you couldn't laugh any more because your sides hurt, you are hit again with a wave of hilarious antics that make you fall to the floor.

Superbad ended up grossing $121,463,226 domestically and since the budget was only $20,000,000 the movie could be considered a big success. This movie is crude and downright gross at some points: Seth's penis-drawing addiction, a girl "perioding" on his leg, and his sexual gestures at Jules during cooking class are just three of hundreds of examples. But at its core, the movie has a heart and a good message or two. The boys come to realize an important idea—they are scared about the future and about losing one another. Ultimately, we learn from the movie that the end of high school can be an exciting but also unclear time in a young adolescent's life that is full of change and the struggle of coming to grips with it. Overall, *Superbad* turned out to be nothing short of a super movie.

. . .

Superbad: Directed by Greg Mottola; written by Seth Rogen and Evan Goldberg; produced by Judd Apatow and Shauna Robertson; released by Columbia Pictures, 2007. Running time: 117 minutes. Rated R.

Starring: Jonah Hill (Seth), Michael Cera (Evan), Christopher Mintz-Plasse (Fogell), Seth Rogen (Officer Michaels), Bill Hader (Officer Slater), Martha MacIsaac (Becca), Emma Stone (Jules), and Aviva (Nicola).

Questions for Discussion

1. What parts of Merrigan's final review did you find effective or not? What made them so?
2. Part of review writing is balancing the writer's evaluation of the subject with details about the subject. How well does Merrigan blend these elements in his film review?
3. What do you think about his decision to write this review informally? Does this style work for you?

Reflecting on the Process

Below is an excerpt from Patrick Merrigan's reflection on the process for writing his review.

> Overall, I think I did a very good job with my review. One aspect of my paper that I think I did well on was giving specific examples from the movie to help illustrate my points. I talk about the scene where Fogell goes into the liquor store to try and purchase alcohol. I give a certain level of detail that helps show the quality of my paper, but at the same time makes sure not to give away any major plot points.
>
> Another thing I did well in writing my review was describing the actors and the characters they portrayed. I had watched the movie quite a few times so I felt like I knew the characters pretty well and I learned even more about them after I did my research. I described the primary characters of Seth, Evan, and Fogell in great detail and I also described the secondary characters such as the cops and the boys' crushes, but in lesser detail.
>
> For this paper we had to clearly identify a purpose and an audience. The purpose of writing this review was for me to talk about the film, the different aspects of it, what I thought of it, and tell the reader whether or not they should see it. My audience was those who might be interested in watching the movie and want to find out more about it.
>
> I learned about the different characteristics that make up the genre of reviews. Reviews provide an overview of the "facts," a summary of sorts. They also tend to engage the reader, possibly by asking questions. The tone is informal and reflects the subject whereas the "mood" can be negative, positive, or mixed. There is also usually a detailed explanation and analysis which assumes an interest in the subject by the reader. The characteristics seem to be loose depending on the writer and how he plans on presenting the content and who the audience is going to be.

WRITING ACTIVITY   Evaluating One Writer's Journey

Review Merrigan's process. What can you say about the choices that he made? Do you agree with his choices? Are there places where you think he might have made different choices that could have led to a more persuasive review? Do you think the final review is complete or still needs some work?

T R A N S F O R M A T I O N S

GENRE BLURRING: Rhetorical Analysis of a Documentary

Sometimes a reviewer wants to expand the focus of his review (as in a review essay, a blurring of the review and the academic essay) or he might want to narrow the focus of his review to one aspect of the subject. In this second case, the writer may choose to write a review that is a rhetorical analysis. For example, such a review seeks not to evaluate whether a film should be seen or not, but *how* the film actually succeeds at making a convincing argument—or not. A rhetorical analysis of a film shares many of the characteristics of other types of reviews, although it is more formal in tone and approach, often making many careful references to the film.

Documentary films are ripe for this kind of rhetorical analysis. The documentary genre is often assumed to be "the truth" and "factual" because it "documents" events or issues rather than fictionalizes them. Yet although the information may be factual, *how* the information is conveyed and the techniques used to persuade viewers are often similar to the ones found in television ads, advocacy ads, and drama. A writer might choose to do a rhetorical analysis of a documentary to persuade his audience to look more carefully at its rhetorical techniques and message in order to understand that a documentary film is but one version of the truth.

For more information about rhetorical analysis, please see Chapter 3: Analyzing and Writing Arguments.

Genre Blurring Writing Assignment

Rhetorical Analysis of a Documentary

Write a review of a documentary film of your choice in which you analyze and evaluate the film's rhetorical effectiveness.

Examine how the filmmaker makes the arguments: Keeping your criteria for evaluation in mind, watch the documentary a few times. The first time you are watching it to get a "feel" for it, to be clear on *what* happens, so that later you can focus on *how* it happens.

After you have viewed the entire film once, watch it again. This time look for *how* the documentary works. Take careful notes and consider the following:

- What is the argument being made, and how is it being made? Explain the film's purpose, claims, and particular point of view. To figure out the message or argument of the film, identify some of the following: rhetorical appeals (*ethos, pathos, logos*), the intended audience(s), filmmaker's purpose, claims, evidence, research, differing views, and assumptions.

- What techniques and strategies are used by the filmmaker to make convincing arguments and appeal to a target audience? (e.g. images, music, portrayal of people or "characters," storyline/plot, scene sequences, interviews, narrator's role, etc.)

(continued)

Sometimes *what is not shown* is just as important as what is for the argument, so take note of any intentional *absences* in the film.

Draft an evaluative review Write your review of how well the filmmaker conveys his message and fulfills his purpose in the documentary using your rhetorical analysis above. Be sure to provide an evaluative thesis that 1) clearly communicates to the audience whether or not the film's argument is effective, and 2) use particular examples from the film to illustrate how it is (or is not) convincing.

Below is an annotated rhetorical analysis of a documentary written by first-year writer, Kim Thomassen Strand. Strand rhetorically analyzes the film's arguments, then evaluates the film's persuasiveness. The annotations highlight *how* the writer makes her arguments.

Kim Thomassen Strand (student), There Is Nothing Called Hope in My Future: A Rhetorical Analysis of *Born Into Brothels*

Kim Thomassen Strand
Professor DeRosa
English 100P
1 Nov. 2006

There Is Nothing Called Hope in My Future: A Rhetorical
Analysis of *Born Into Brothels*

The injustice of social arrangements hinders many people from leading humane lives—ones filled with hope for a future. *Born Into Brothels,* an incredible documentary made in 2004, follows filmmakers Zana Briski and Ross Kaufman on their journey to the red light district in Calcutta, India, where they capture the lives of children of prostitutes, who are to join their parents' "careers" in the near future.

Director Briski lived among the children and their parents in Calcutta's red light district and taught photography classes to the children. She shows, in a realistic portrayal, how art and education can transform lives even in the most discouraging places. By using gripping interviews, graphic images, and impressive montages of the children, their work, and their surroundings, she puts us face to face

In the first two paragraphs, the writer introduces us to the film—providing information about the directors and a brief summary of the content, just as you would expect to see in any film review.

Here is Strand's evaluative thesis, in which she clearly states the criteria she has used in evaluating the film.

This is the beginning of her analysis—the film works because of the perspective from which it is told. It is hard for most of us to look apathetically upon the suffering of a child, so the director's choice here is a good rhetorical one.

Strand uses other review-ers to establish her own credibility—ethos—she has done some research, this tells us, not just watched the film.

Another claim about the emotional appeal of the film; she provides an example of a particular scene, its music, and use of black and white to emphasize how the argument is made by filmmakers.

The writer includes this poignant first hand account, emphasizing the filmmaker's use of pathos through interviews. Was this a good choice for the reviewer's title?

with the depressing truth while at the same time presenting a measure of hope for the viewers.

The film begins immersing viewers into the squalor of this section of Calcutta. The images of the surrounding brothels are shown through a child's perspective, thus telling us that this documentary is focused on the lives of the children of the prostitutes. This perspective makes the documentary very expressive emotionally, and it fulfills the filmmaker's goals of evoking our compassion and sympathy, pathos appeals, by emphasizing to us that these are *the children's* experiences.

What also makes this documentary so powerful emotionally is that it is told in an unsentimental way without any sugar coating. As reviewer A. O. Scott puts it, "'*Born into Brothels*' tempers its optimism with realism in a way that is both uplifting and heartbreaking" (5). We follow the children into their homes where a vicious cycle of hopelessness and dejection has taken over. There is no love in these homes. There is only work, castigation, and ruthless humiliation from the mothers. The physical and emotional abuse of these children appalls us. They are targets for aggression and frustration from the adults, and they are soon expected to join the profession. In one scene, set in slow motion, a child walks into a room, hand in hand with an older man, while dramatic music plays in the background. Because the scene is in black and white, it adds to the bleakness of the situation and reveals the future awaiting these children.

"When will you join the line?" is a question that all the young girls in the film grimly understand will soon be put to them. Briski shows us a twelve-year-old girl from her photography class who is soon to enter into prostitution in order to make money for her aunt. When asked what her dreams are, she answers, "There is nothing called hope in my future. One has to accept life as being sad and painful, that's all." Because she wants to show the hopelessness these girls face but not let us pretend they are different from the children we know in our own lives, Briski shows us scenes where they run around with the cameras, and for a moment, it appears as if they see the world with new eyes, even though we know and they know that their world is bleak.

Using impressive montages of the girls' work from her photography class, Briski is able to show throughout the film the contrasts between the depressing situations and the hope from the fun-loving kids. We are inspired as we see the montages appearing as slideshows in the documentary. Their talent is impressive, and they illustrate how such an ugly place can contain amazing beauty. It is moving to see how the children are filled with a new sense of wonder and importance and how their self-worth grows as they work together with Briski. Still, in the midst of this glimmer of hope, we constantly see contrasting images to remind us of the misery lurking in the background.

Despite the hopeful scenes of the children's photography, Briski's message is clear—there is no freedom in the lives of the children in the brothels. Kochi, a shy but wistful girl, tells us in one of several interviews, that her father would have sold her if her grandmother did not take her. An image of her grandmother's home is shown: Kochi's little brother sits chained to the wall to keep him in place. It becomes too obvious at this point that regardless of where you are, as long as you live in brothels, there is no freedom.

In addition to directing the film, Briski also serves as the narrator of the documentary. In doing so, the viewers are assured a firsthand account of the events that took place during her journey through the red light district. Throughout the course of the film, the children are interviewed or we follow Briski around while she struggles to get the children into boarding schools. But the journey was not a smooth one for Briski. Families objected to Briski's attempt to give the children better lives, and Calcutta's bureaucratic

---

Notice the writer's use of evaluative language as well as her knowledge of film-making techniques. She attends to audience's needs for details about the film while building her credibility as a documentary reviewer.

Strand's argument about the film's message is illustrated through her analysis of how the film makes its message explicit: literal images of children in chains.

Does the quote from Turan work well here? Rhetorically, it emphasizes what Strand has summarized in the paragraph, but what does he mean by "reorder the worldview" and could Strand have said more about how this may be the case?

government did not make her goal any easier. Parents objected to Briski's attempts to find boarding schools for the children because this would mean they would have to give up the only thing that keeps them going; the children provide money for the family by "joining the line." Also, the government's reluctance is demonstrated in the scenes with Briski facing countless denials and unwilling attitudes despite her great efforts to help the children. Showing these frustrations has the effect of making us side strongly with Briski, of course, and with the children, in case we had not already. As *L.A. Times* film reviewer Keith Turan claims, this is "a documentary that changes the lives of both the subjects and the filmmakers. It will reorder the worldview of whoever sees it" (E1).

Strand's uses of other reviewer's comments builds on her analysis of the film's message and strengthens her credibility as a review writer who has done her research.

Dramatic music is another persuasive element the filmmakers use throughout the film to heighten the impact of the terrible images for viewers; conversely, they also strengthen a sense of hope using upbeat, cheerful music. One scene in particular where music is used effectively is when the children run around with their cameras on a trip outside the red light district. The choice of music and corresponding images made Briski's claim about the joy and the despondency of the children's lives very powerful. As *Washington Post* reviewer Ann Hornaday points out, "The film is filled to bursting with ravishing images." When the kids dance and sing excitedly on the bus on their way home from a trip to the ocean, we are presented with an explosion of music and images. Fast shaky shots were used and a red light took over the warm pleasant light. The music becomes more dramatic and extremely loud, and the shaky shots intensify. With these elements, the director manages to show us the chaos these kids have to return to—the dismal reality of their lives.

The writer comments here on the use of music and images and how these work in particular scenes to support the filmmakers' claims about the children's lives.

To see the faces of the children is heartbreaking, because we know since the making of this film, most of them have lost their childhood forever, some their lives. Although reviewer John Petrakis

Uses a reviewer's comment to disagree with her argument about film's purpose.

Contrasts the film to other documentaries that may not show the "real story" of the subjects' lives; this reemphasizes her claim about the genre that a documentary should be accurate representation of the events it covers.

points out his disappointment that the stories of the prostitutes themselves get lost, as he would like to have known more about their lives (65), he misses Briski's intended focus and the message of the film. Although it is a touching and heartfelt story about the tiny bit of hope the children hold inside them, *Born Into Brothels* stands out as a one of a kind film because it never backs away from the realities of their lives, in which dreams take a backseat to their daily struggles to survive.

Works Cited

Born Into Brothels. Dir. Zana Briski and Ross Kauffman. Think Film, 2004. Film.

Hornaday, Ann. "*Born Into Brothels*: A Shot of Hope." *Washington Post* 18 Feb. 2005: C01. *Academic Search Premier*. Web. 31 Oct. 2006.

Petrakis, John. "Kids with Cameras." *Christian Century* 22 Feb. 2005. *Academic Search Premier*. Web. 31 Oct. 2006.

Scott, A. O. "Nurturing Talents of Children in Calcutta." *New York Times* 8 Dec. 2004. *Academic Search Premier*. Web. 31 Oct. 2006.

Turan, Kenneth. "Children Focus on the Art of Survival." *Los Angeles Times* 28 Jan. 2005: E1. *Academic Search Premier*. Web. 31 Oct. 2006.

Reading for Comprehension

1. What is Strand's evaluative thesis? How does she support this thesis throughout her analysis of the film?
2. How would you describe the tone of her review? What parts contribute to that tone?
3. Some readers may not have seen the film. Does Strand provide adequate examples and background information from the film to help her audience understand her evaluation?

Analyzing the Genre

1. How does Strand's choice of evaluation criteria help her reinforce her claims about the film? What other parts could she have discussed in her rhetorical analysis of the film?
2. How does Strand use others' reviews to develop her evaluation of the film's argument and its effectiveness?

CHAPTER 7

Essays

It is a pretty good bet that you have written an essay before. It's also a pretty good bet that if you're asked what an essay is, you might have a hard time giving a coherent definition. And you would not be alone. There are many different kinds of essays: the personal essay, the academic essay, the lyric essay, the journalistic essay, the meditative essay, the persuasive essay, and the list goes on. Writers have adapted the essay in all its various forms as a means of expression in everyday life and for professional or academic situations. The essay is quite a flexible genre.

What Is an Essay?

As writer Aldous Huxley eloquently suggests, "The essay is a literary device for saying almost everything about almost anything." Essays are exploratory writings that seek to make sense of a particular, and focused, subject. Essayists might observe the solitary confinement of a neighbor and ponder the breakdown of community, or notice the increase in recreational drug use and argue that legalizing all illegal drugs might solve the problem. They might speculate, "what-ifs" to ponder an abstract idea—patriotism, compassion, vegetarianism—to come to terms with what it means in our society. Observing behaviors, trends, or situations in the world around them and thinking deeply about them is the work of the essay and the essayist. Essays are more than interesting musings, but they are not reports on a subject either. Often they explore unusual or unexpected subjects, though they also often explore common ideas but find something new to say about them. An essay offers **commentary** on a subject and explores some **conclusions** about the subject. Those two words describe an important characteristic of essays. An essay does not (usually) provide a single answer which the author asserts is *the* answer. Instead, as the meaning of the word suggests, the essay is an attempt to provide *an* answer by giving *some* answers. Essay comes from the French verb *essayer,* which means "to try" or attempt. Essayists try out ideas and conclusions about the larger world around them. They think out loud. And thus they do more than report on a subject; they comment on it, reflect on it, and try to understand it.

The Purposes of Essays

We write essays because we want to figure things out, and we realize that the process of figuring something out may be as interesting to readers as the conclusions (tentative or concrete) we reach. Like other kinds of writing, essays often come out of our own observations, concerns, or hang-ups. We might not understand why we react in certain ways, why we think what we do, or act as we do, and we want to figure it out. Sometimes the impetus is immediate: that guy on the bus who is clearly too sick to go to work makes us wonder why going to work is so important that it overrides common sense. And sometimes what makes us want to write has nothing to do with us at all, at least not directly. Why, the essayist might ask, does a politician reference the events on September 11, 2001 so frequently? What does he gain from it? The writer then begins to explore the issue by examining her own conceptions of and experiences with it, by talking with others to find out what they think, and by conducting some formal kinds of research, for example, background on the issue or what other experts have said about it. Writers use the essay because, as you might notice, it is a genre that offers them a lot of flexibility: They can use a variety of research; use different voices; include dialogue, photographs, and charts; and even use different forms. As you work through this chapter, you'll read examples of different kinds of essays, but one type we will focus on is the personal essay, a variety that allows for many approaches.

Reading Essays Critically

Writing a successful essay requires, in part, a thorough understanding of what essays do and how they work. Once we understand the characteristics of an essay, we may be better able to choose ways of composing so we meet our audience's expectations and our purpose for writing.

WRITING ACTIVITY   Analyzing the Genre of the Essay

Thinking About Essays

Think about what situations might make you want to write an essay. What would you write about and why?

Examining the Genre

1. As you read an essay, you are reading for comprehension, but you are also reading to understand the *characteristics* of the genre. Look for *patterns* that might reveal something about what essays do in general. How does the essay begin? How is the subject introduced? What does the title suggest about the subject?
2. What do you notice about how the ideas are developed? Does the writer draw on research? Anecdotes? Examples? And so on.

3. How is the material arranged? Why has the writer chosen that arrangement?
4. What can you say about the language, tone, and voice of this essay? Provide some examples.
5. Who seems to be the audience for this essay? How do you know? Language choices, tone, and references made might give you a hint.
6. What does the writer have to say about the subject? Where and how does the writer comment on and draw conclusions about the subject?

Reflecting on the Genre

After you have read the essay, *explain* the major characteristics of the genre as you understand them. Refer to specific passages, quoting where necessary

■ ■ ■

Genre Analysis: Jo Ann Beard, "Out There"

The personal essay below by Jo Ann Beard is part of her collection of autobiographical essays, *The Boys of My Youth*. She is a Guggenheim fellow and has had her writing published in *The New Yorker* and *O, The Oprah Magazine*. Beard is on the writing faculty at Sarah Lawrence College.

The genre analysis of Beard's essay questions and responds to particular characteristics and part of the essay that stand out to the reader. In an analysis, the reader is making sense of the genre and what it is all about.

"Out There"

Jo Ann Beard

Lots of details and description in this opening. I feel like I am immediately in this scene with the narrator, and I know her personally. It also is told in the present tense as if it is happening now.

It isn't even eight A.M. and I'm hot. My rear end is welded to the seat just like it was yesterday. I'm fifty miles from the motel and about a thousand and a half from home, in a little white Mazda with 140,000 miles on it and no rust. I'm all alone in Alabama, with only a cooler and a tape deck for company. It's already in the high 80s. Yesterday, coming up from the keys through Florida, I had a day-long anxiety attack that I decided last night was really heat prostration. I was a cinder with a brain; I was actually whimpering. I kept thinking I saw alligators at the edge of the highway.

Is she hallucinating?

There were about four hundred exploded armadillos, too, but I got used to them. They were real, and real dead. The alligators weren't real or dead, but they may have been after me. I'm running away from running away from home.

Her reflection here gives readers the situation for her writing this essay—some backstory about why she's on the trip. But it also tells us how she feels at the moment.

I bolted four weeks ago, leaving my husband to tend the dogs and tool around town on his bicycle. He doesn't love me anymore, it's both trite and true. He does love himself, though. He's begun wearing cologne and staring into the mirror for long minutes, trying out smiles. He's become a politician. After thirteen years he came to realize that the more successful he got, the less he loved me. That's how he put it, late one night. He won that screaming match.

He said, gently and sadly, "I feel sort of embarrassed of you."

I said, "Of what? The way I look? The way I act?"

And he said, softly, "Everything, sort of."

And it was true. Well, I decided to take a trip to Florida. I sat on my haunches in Key West for four weeks, writing and seething and striking up conversations with strangers. I had my thirty-fifth birthday there, weeping into a basket of shrimp. I drank beer and had long involved dreams about cigarettes, I wrote nearly fifty pages on my novel. It's in my trunk at this very moment, dead and decomposing. Boy, do I need a cup of coffee.

There's not much happening this early in the morning. The highway looks interminable again. So far, no alligators. I have a box of seashells in my back seat and I reach back and get a fluted one, pale gray with a pearly interior, to put on the dashboard. I can do everything while I'm driving. At the end of this trip I will have driven 3,999 miles all alone, me and the windshield, me and the radio, me and the creepy alligators. Don't ask me why I didn't get that last mile in, driving around the block a few times or getting a tiny bit lost once. I didn't though, and there you have it. Four thousand sounds like a lot more than 3,999 does; I feel sort of embarrassed for myself.

My window is broken, the crank fell off in Tallahassee on the way down. In order to roll it up or down I have to put the crank back on and turn it slowly and carefully, using one hand to push up the glass. So, mostly I leave it down. I baked like a biscuit yesterday, my left arm is so brown it looks like a branch. Today I'm wearing a long-sleeved white shirt to protect myself. I compromised on wearing long sleeves by going naked underneath it. It's actually cooler this way, compared to yesterday when I drove in my swimming suit top with my hair stuck up like a fountain on top of my head. Plus, I'm having a nervous breakdown. I've got that wild-eyed look.

A little four-lane blacktop running through the Alabama countryside, that's what I'm on. It's pretty, too, better than Florida, which was billboards and condos built on old dump sites. This is like driving between rolling emerald carpets. You can't see the two lanes going in the opposite direction because there's a screen of trees. I'm starting to get in a good mood again. The best was Georgia, coming down. Willow trees and red dirt and snakes stretched out alongside the road. I kept thinking, that looks like a rope, and then it would be a huge snake. A few miles later I would think, that looks like a snake, and it would be some snarl of something dropped off a truck.

Little convenience store, stuck out in the middle of nothing, a stain on the carpet. I'm gassing it up, getting some coffee. My white shirt is gaping open and I have nothing on underneath it, but who cares, I'll never see these people again. What do I care what Alabama thinks about me. This is a new and unusual attitude for me. I'm practicing being snotty, in anticipation of being dumped by my husband when I get back to Iowa.

I swagger from the gas pump to the store, I don't even care if my boobs are roaming around inside my shirt, if my hair is a freaky snarl, if I look

Why is she telling us about the end of her trip?

I get a sense of this desolate place by her descriptions. It's not pleasant.

More vivid descriptions in this paragraph.

defiant and uppity. There's nothing to be embarrassed of. I bring my coffee cup along and fill it at the counter. Various men, oldish and grungy, sit at tables eating eggs with wadded-up toast. They stare at me carefully while they chew. I ignore them and pay the woman at the counter. She's smoking a cigarette so I envy her.

"Great day, huh?" I ask her. She counts out my change.

"It is, honey," she says. She reaches for her cigarette and takes a puff, blows it up above my head. "Wish I wudn't in here."

Dialogue lets me hear the voices of other people in this personal essay

"Well, it's getting hotter by the minute," I tell her. I've adopted an accent in just four weeks, an intermittent drawl that makes me think I'm not who everyone thinks I am.

"Y' all think this's hot?" she says idly. "This ain't hot."

Great simile for how she feels about going home and facing her husband.

When I leave, the men are still staring at me in a sullen way. I get in, rearrange all my junk so I have everything handy that I need, choose a Neil Young tape and pop it in the deck, fasten the belt, and then move back out on the highway. Back to the emerald carpet and the road home. Iowa is creeping toward me <u>like a panther</u>.

All I do is sing when I drive. Sing and drink: coffee, Coke, water, juice, coffee. And think. I sing and drink and think. On the way down I would sing, drink, think, and weep uncontrollably, but I'm past that now. Now I suffer bouts of free-floating hostility, which is much better. I plan to use it when I get home.

A car swings up alongside me so I pause in my singing until it goes past. People who sing in their cars always cheer me up, but I'd rather not be caught doing it. On the road, we're all singing, picking our noses, embarrassing ourselves wildly; it gets tiresome. I pause and hum, but the car sticks alongside me so I glance over. It's a guy. He grins and makes a lewd gesture with his mouth. I don't even want to say what it is, it's that disgusting. Tongue darting in and out, quickly. A python testing its food.

I hate this kind of thing. Who do they think they are, these men? I've had my fill of it. I give him the finger, slowly and deliberately. He picked the wrong day to mess with me, I think to myself. I take a sip of coffee.

He's still there.

She really builds the tension in these paragraphs by giving such strong details of the actions.

I glance over briefly and he's making the gesture with his tongue again. I can't believe this. He's from the convenience store, I realize. He has on a fishing hat with lures stuck in it. I saw him back there, but I can't remember if he was sitting with the other men or by himself. He's big, overweight, and dirty, wearing a thin unbuttoned shirt and the terrible fishing hat. His passenger-side window is down. He begins screaming at me.

He followed me from that convenience store. The road is endless, in front there is nothing, no cars, no anything, behind is the same. Just road and grass and trees. The other two lanes are still invisible behind their screen of trees. I'm all alone out here. With him. He's screaming and screaming at me, reaching out his right arm like he's throttling me. I speed up. He speeds up, too, next to me. We're only a few feet apart, my window won't roll up.

He's got slobber on his face and there's no one in either direction. I slam on my brakes and for an instant he's ahead of me, I can breathe, then he slams on his brakes and we're next to each other again. I can't even repeat what he's screaming at me. He's telling me, amid the hot wind and poor Neil Young, what he wants to do to me. He wants to kill me. He's screaming and screaming, I can't look over.

I stare straight ahead through the windshield, hands at ten and two. The front end of his car is moving into my lane. He's saying he'll cut me with a knife, how he'll do it, all that. I can't listen. The front end of his Impala is about four inches from my white Mazda, my little car. This is really my husband's car, my beloved's. My Volkswagen died a lingering death a few months ago. There is no husband, there is no Volkswagen, there is nothing. There isn't even a Jo Ann right now. Whatever I am is sitting here clenched, hands on the wheel, I've stopped being her, now I'm something else. I'm absolutely terrified. He won't stop screaming it, over and over, what he's going to do.

I refuse to give him an inch. I will not move one inch over. If I do he'll have me off the road in an instant. I will not move. I speed up, he speeds up, I slow down, he slows down, I can see him out of the corner of my eye, driving with one hand, reaching like he's grabbing me with the other. "You whore," he screams at me. "I'll kill you, I'll kill you, I'll kill you . . . "

He'll kill me.

If I give him an inch, he'll shove me off the road and get his hands on me, then the end will begin in some unimaginable, unspeakable style that will be all his. I'll be an actor in his drama. We're going too fast, I've got the pedal pressed up to 80 and it's wobbling, his old Impala can probably go 140 on a straightaway like this. There will be blood, he won't want me to die quickly.

I will not lose control. I will ride it out. I cannot let him push me over onto the gravel. His car noses less than two inches from mine; I'm getting rattled. My God, he can almost reach me through his window, he's moved over in his seat, driving just with the left hand, the right is grabbing the hot air. I move over to the edge of my seat, toward the center of the car, carefully, without swerving.

We get Beard's thoughts on what's happening as it is unfolding which makes us feel like we are part of the action.

In the rearview mirror a speck appears. Don't look, watch your front end. I glance up again; it's a truck. He can't get me. It's a trucker. Without looking at him I jerk my thumb backward to show him. He screams and screams and screams. He's not leaving. Suddenly a road appears on the right, a dirty and rutted thing leading off into the trees. He hits the brakes, drops behind, and takes it. In my rearview mirror I see that the license plate on the front of his car is buried in dried mud. That road is where he was hoping to push me. He wanted to push my car off the highway and get me on that road. He was hoping to kill me. He was hoping to do what maniacs, furious men, do to women alongside roads, in woods. I can't stop pressing too hard on the gas pedal. I'm at 85 now, and my leg is shaking uncontrollably, coffee is spilled all over the passenger seat, the atlas is wet, Neil Young is still howling on the tape deck. By force of will, I slow down to 65, eject the tape, and wait for the truck to overtake me. When it does, when it comes up alongside me. I don't look over at all, I keep my eyes straight ahead. As it moves in front of me I speed up enough to stay two car lengths behind it. It says England on the back, ornate red letters outlined in black. England.

That guy chased me on purpose, he hated me, with more passion than anyone has ever felt for me. Ever. Out there are all those decomposing bodies, all those disappeared daughters, discovered by joggers and hunters, their bodies long abandoned, the memory of final desperate moments lingering on the leaves, the trees, the mindless stumps and mushrooms. Images taped to tollbooth windows, faces pressed into the dirt alongside a path somewhere.

I want out of Alabama, I want to be in England. The air is still a blast furnace. I want to roll my window up, but I'd have to stop and get the crank out and lift it by hand. I'm too scared. He's out there still, waiting behind the screen of trees. I have to follow England until I'm out of Alabama. Green car, old Impala, unreadable license plate, lots of rust. Seat covers made out of that spongy stuff, something standing on the dashboard, a coffee cup or a sad Jesus. The fishing hat with a sweat ring around it right above the brim. Lures with feathers and barbs. I've never been so close to so much hatred in my whole life. He wanted to kill me. Think of England, with its white cows and broken-toothed farmers and dark green pastures. Think of the Beatles. I'm hugging the truck so closely now I'm almost under it. Me, of all people, he wanted to kill. Me. Everywhere I go I'm finding out new things about myself. Each way I turn, there it is. It's Jo Ann he wanted to kill.

By noon I want to kill him. I took a right somewhere and got onto the interstate, had the nerve to pee in a rest area, adrenaline running like an engine inside me, my keys threaded through my fingers in case anyone tried anything. I didn't do anything to earn it, I realize. His anger. I didn't do anything. Unless you count giving him the finger, which I don't. He earned that.

As it turned out, my husband couldn't bring himself to leave me when I got back to Iowa, so I waited awhile, and watched, then disentangled myself. History: We each got ten photo albums and six trays of slides. We took a lot of pictures in thirteen years. In the early years he looks stoned and contented, distant; in the later years he looks straight and slightly worried. In that last year he only appears by chance, near the edges, a blur of suffering, almost out of frame.

Just before we split, when we were driving somewhere, I told him about the guy in the green car. "Wow," he said. Then he turned up the radio, checked his image in the rearview mirror, and smiled sincerely at the passing landscape.

Beard begins her personal essay by using an anecdote to put readers in the scene with her. She uses the present tense and first person which makes it feel like the events are happening now. Also, there are lots of details and descriptions of the car, the heat, and the actions around her to make readers feel like they are in the moment with her. These details set up her reflection about her failing marriage—the reason for her trip. In the closing, Beard circles back to another anecdote about the outcome of her relationship with her husband after she returns, so perhaps her purpose is to make readers think about their own lives, relationships, and where they are going.

She seems to use a straightforward chronological order in this essay although she sometimes digresses and reflects on her life from the present. There seems to be two stories here: the first about her failed marriage which we learn from knowing what she's thinking, and the second about scary events with the creepy guy in the car on an Alabama highway. In both cases, we are allowed to know what she's thinking as she's thinking it which makes us feel like we are experiencing the events with her. This is probably one of the characteristics of the personal essay—to make readers feel like they can relate to the writer's experiences.

Jim Kuerschner (student), "Big Brother Is on the Facebook"

In this academic essay, student writer Jim Kuerschner explores the recent popularity of Facebook, one of a number of social networking websites, and wonders about its role as both a tool for voyeurism and, more importantly for Kuerschner, as a means of self-imposed surveillance. Kuerschner's essay and others written by New York University students appear in a publication produced by NYU's expository writing program, *Mercer Street Publications*. To read additional essays of all kinds, use a search engine and type "Mercer Street Publications" into the search box to access the website.

You see him everyday as you cross West Fourth Street. You've never spoken to him, but you know his name, his age, major, and relationship status. You've never officially met, but you know what his high school friends look like, how his spring break trip to Cozumel was, and what he looks like while under the influence. Giving him the awkward "I-know-you-but-I-probably-shouldn't-know-*this*-much-about-you-so-I'm-not-sure-if-I-say-hello-or-if-I-just-walk-on-by-and-pretend-to-not-see-you" smile, you continue on your way, wondering if you could have sparked conversation by humming one of his favorite tunes or quoting one of his favorite movies. The tension builds, you cross the street, and nothing happens. Heaving a sigh of relief that you haven't just made a fool of yourself to a complete stranger, you begin to wonder, am I a stalker? No, you reassure yourself, you are simply a member of the Facebook.

In 2004 students at Harvard created the popular website, "Facebook.com," lovingly and begrudgingly known as "The Facebook," with a grant of $500,000 from Peter Thiel, founder of PayPal. Members of Facebook, an online social network for college students, can post a personal profile and search through profiles of other students across the country, linking themselves to friends at their own school and at other schools. Eventually encompassing more and more universities, the Facebook provides access to more than 25,000 high schools and 2,000 institutions of higher learning (Naing). The creators of Facebook have continued to update and improve the web-profile service, adding the ability to display photos and join interest groups; within the past month, Facebook users have gained the ability to communicate on the Facebook via cell phone and can now search for phone numbers and other personal information from anywhere with decent cell phone reception (Yuan).With more and more features added, students spend more and more time surfing profiles, filing through pictures, and reading favorite quotes.

The constantly growing popularity of the Facebook has generated quite a bit of controversy since its inception two years ago. Current discourse on its use runs the gamut from the vehemently opposed to the insouciant to the most vocal champions of the online college-profile service. Most opinion comes from college-aged students—those who traditionally have access to the website. However, though the opinion makers are similar in age and level of education, their opinions are vastly different. Those in favor of the service include D.J. Johnson of Bowling Green State University who writes, "Facebook is the door to the worlds never explored. Millions of people have uploaded information about themselves online in an effort to be read. To be discovered." He continues, "It's an optional service, so men and women around the world are voluntarily submitting information for the pleasure of others." He claims that it is ridiculous to hide our fascination with the site as it has provided beneficial services to millions of users.

Julia James of the University of Alabama disagrees. Explaining the dangers of having your personal information on the web, she claims that "anything negative on your Facebook profile can and will be used against you." She also addresses the issue that administrators and prospective employers can view the site, which could potentially be problematic. University of Pennsylvania writer Cezary Podkul may quell James's fears. He writes that Facebook "is a Web site created for fun and amusement" and that "Penn officials have better things to do than comb through the 3.85 million registered Facebook users ... looking for incriminating material." Even if they did, as Johnson might suggest, everything posted online is done voluntarily, and students are well aware of what they are making available for public display.

Employers and college administrators have also taken a stance on the issues that Facebook presents. "It is a tricky issue," says Catherine Amory, interim director of career services at Northeastern University. "I'm not so sure that students shouldn't be free to be themselves. On the other hand, if they intend to work for a conservative institution, then they need to be more careful" (qtd. in Lewis). This phrase, however, seems to suggest that we have the freedom to express ourselves—as long as what we express is acceptable to the head of human resources at a blue-chip corporation.

Whatever stance you take, Facebook usage is here to stay. Over 10.5 million unique visitors explored the Facebook in February of 2006 alone, making it one of the most popular sites on the web (Yuan). College newspapers, as well as student sentiment and interest groups on the Facebook itself, curse its hypnotic, addicting powers, yet students are still unable to free themselves from checking the Facebook countless times a day.

Even with the knowledge of Facebook access by administrators and prospective employers, students fearlessly post incriminating pictures of themselves—some nearly softcore pornography, others more akin to Smirnoff advertisements. Clearly, college students have many better things to do with their lives than sit for hours on end examining the Facebook profiles of their friends and coming up with witty comments to post on their pages (or "walls," in Facebook lingo), yet for some reason the majority of the college populous is enamored with the Harvard-created site. Why then, when we have the ability to speak face-to-face with a vast number of college students simply by walking through our campuses, do we feel the need to use such a profile service?

The Facebook embodies the Big Brother spirit of our generation. While some post purely for viewing by their own friends (and indeed there are privacy controls that allow very limited visibility), many update their pages constantly, knowing that someone will probably see their new silly or sexy picture, perhaps inducing a message or a "poke"—one of the more strange features of the page, which allows users to send any member of the Facebook, even if you have no idea who they are, a message reading, "You have been poked by [insert real name of Creepy McCreepster here]." In a generation when Internet chat rooms and online dating services have been around for most of our lives, we are much more comfortable sending messages to those we don't know than people have been in the past. Facebook allows us to put every moment of our personal lives up for public display, if we wish. And many do.

Yet while we are okay with everyone knowing our personal affairs via Facebook, we hotly protest (and rightfully so) the ever-increasing surveillance that has been imposed on our society post-September 11th. Is there a difference? Perhaps we fall into a false sense of security, refusing to believe that anyone other than our college buddies and other university students can view what we make publicly available. Facebook's privacy policy, made available to every member, however, states that the site has the right to share information with a third party when it is "reasonably necessary to offer the service"—a quite vague description ("Privacy"). But if I'm not doing anything wrong, why do I care that someone knows what I'm doing? The problem is that added surveillance can turn into added control, especially when we are not aware of how we are being monitored. When do we draw the line between harmless monitoring of Internet profiles and constant Orwellian watch?

Surveillance and voyeurism, binaries evoked by the Facebook, have caused riffs in society for hundreds of years. "The philosopher Jeremy Bentham," writes Ellen Goodman of the *Boston Globe,* "once described the perfect prison as a 'panopticon' where prisoners were under complete surveillance and yet could not see the watcher." Would modern society feel the same way? As hundreds of thousands of people over the years have applied and auditioned for television programs such as MTV's *The Real World* or *Big Brother* on CBS, it appears as if Bentham's penitentiary would be far less frightening. On these TV shows, participants have every moment of their lives recorded and broadcast to millions of viewers across the country and the world. By freely giving away their rights to privacy, these individuals seem to illustrate a growing acceptance in today's culture of constant surveillance.

On any given day, how many times do you think you are captured on video? According to one study, reports Alexandra Marks of the *Christian Science Monitor,* a Manhattanite is caught on screen an average of 73 times. Feel like a celebrity? For millions of reality TV viewers, this could be amusing. In an article by *New York Times* writer Emily Eakin, communications professor Mark Andrejevic of the University of Iowa at Iowa City remarks, "Today, more than twice as many young people apply to MTV's 'Real World' show than to Harvard," he says. "Clearly, to a post-Cold-War generation of Americans, the prospect of living under surveillance is no longer scary but cool." Members of our generation are excited by the chance to expose themselves, to get their fifteen minutes of fame. The thought of being overwhelmed by paparazzi is considered glamorous, "an entree into the world of wealth and celebrity," as Andrejevic writes in his book, *Reality TV: The Work of Being Watched* (qtd. in Eakin). Facebook, too, offers individuals a taste of this celebrity world, as members can have a webpage totally devoted to themselves, where whatever they want to say or display can be viewed by anyone with an Internet connection. We each want a voice. We want to be heard. But do we really want every detail of our personal lives available to the public? To some, the chance to connect with other people via similar experiences, personality traits, and even through compromising pictures is worth the sacrificed security and privacy. Behind the need to display this information is a need for attention. When our need for personal relationships diminishes, so too may our desire to connect with strangers through the web.

There are other reasons to refuse to sign up for the popular profile service, though. Preserving one's online anonymity seems to be at the forefront. Surveillance, to many people, is incredibly intrusive and frightening. The thought of someone viewing personal information causes some to edit their profiles, removing all incriminating or potentially dangerous information. This self-censorship is reminiscent of George Orwell's dystopian novel, *1984*. Andrew Hultkrans writes about the power of Big Brother, the constantly scrutinizing government in Orwell's hellish world:

> Orwell's surveillance nightmare 1984 [explores] the collective insanity (and absurd paradoxes) induced by constant panoptic observation. The key to the absolute hegemony of Big Brother is not that "he" is actually watching you at all times (in fact, there is no "he" at all), but that, as in Jeremy Bentham's Panopticon prison, you come to believe he may be watching at you any time, thereby policing yourself. (Hultkrans)

The ominous thought of having our actions under perpetual watch can be frightening, and in the case of the Facebook, many are now choosing to remove their information in an attempt to free themselves from an outsider's field of vision. And while Facebook surveillance is worrisome, it alerts us to the horrifying nature of modern surveillance in our daily lives. With the Facebook, you have the option to keep away from the glare of other members by simply not signing up—the only negative effect being minor social ostracism. We cannot, however, choose when third parties read our e-mails, or whether or not we are recorded when we enter a bank, a grocery store, or a city street.

But what is more puzzling is that we cannot seem to live without the new technologies that make such surveillance possible. "Contemporary consumers," writes Hultkrans, "clamor for more ATM machines, more point-of-purchase payment options, more smart cards, digital cash, and online shopping while simultaneously decrying the invasion of privacy intrinsically connected to such cyber-cash convenience." Though we may not like that our web surfing can be monitored, it is nearly impossible to imagine a year without the Internet or the myriad of services it brings us. Moreover, in the name of security, our society has for the most part accepted the addition of surveillance devices, as long as surveillance is done in the name of security. We are comforted by the camera lens, believing no harm can come to us under its protective eye. Now, it is impossible to use government as a scapegoat when there is no protestation on a large scale from citizens. Suddenly, by allowing our every move to be monitored, we ourselves are partially to blame.

At the same time, this move towards constant surveillance is not a new one. We have been gravitating towards it since the dawn of human communication, each new technological advance slowly encroaching on our abilities to live free from the scrutiny of others. In Ancient Rome roads connecting outside provinces to the heart of the empire helped officials easily govern people not in immediate view. In Nazi-ruled Germany, the Hitler Youth became government watchdogs inside family homes. Now, video cameras in parts of the United Kingdom, the United States, and a host of other countries watch the actions of drivers, automatically sending punitive tickets to those who violate the laws of the road. In 2013 it will even be mandatory for citizens of the U.K. to be included in the National Identification Register, a database that will include biometric information from their compulsory ID cards—including fingerprints, iris scans, and digitized facial scans—along with *all* of the places of residence of *all* residents of the United Kingdom throughout their lives (United 2). U.K. Information Commissioner Richard Thomas has announced his fear that we may "sleepwalk into a surveillance society" ("Mass"). My fear is that we already have.

The purpose of surveillance, it seems, is to keep the people of a community, nation, or empire in line. If Big Brother is watching, we won't commit crimes or criticize the government. By installing cameras to monitor us, institutions are trying to simulate a hyperactive conscience—a more strictly defined sense of right and wrong. The Eastern State Penitentiary in Philadelphia, which, at the time of its construction in 1829, was the most expensive building in the United States, was designed so that each cell has anopening at the top to make the prisoner feel "penitent," giving him a renewed (or new) sense of conscience and moral standards ("Eastern"). But what about our own consciences? Some would claim that over the thousands of years of civilization we have lost our compunction and that we now require some sort of institution to tell us what we should not do. The synthetically constructed conscience, though, gives us more than rigid principles. It hinders us from asking questions that may make someone, including ourselves, uncomfortable. It stops us from investigating anything too dangerous, anything with the potential for revolution.

Government-implemented surveillance has always justified itself in terms of national preservation. Know when people are going to attack, and you can attack them first. In this case, knowledge, quite literally, is power. So this artificial conscience doesn't tell us what is good or bad at all; it only tells us what is primarily good or bad for the institution. The goal for surveillance, then, should ideally be focused on refining our existing consciences, not on creating new ones. "Liberty of conscience," as John Locke writes, "is every man's right," and surveillance-induced superegos rob us of this right ("Letter"). Though I'm sure there are those whose consciences would allow them to do things not beneficial for a society, taking away our right and obligation to decide what is acceptable strips us of our right to think and at the same time transfers responsibility to the monitoring institution. The criminal is not culpable for his actions; the failed security camera is.

We are being watched and monitored, be it through the Facebook or an ATM, an outdoor surveillance camera, or an e-mail scanning program. Still, we, the people, have freedom. We can knowingly post incriminating pictures on our websites and send furious e-mails about Presidential policy, or we can try to avoid our omnipresent observers. The problem is that our information is out there—a low profile might just mean it takes an extra week to find it.

Works Cited

Eakin, Emily. "Greeting Big Brother with Open Arms." *New York Times*. 17 Jan. 2004. *ProQuest*. Web.18 Apr. 2006.

"Eastern State Penitentiary."*Wikipedia. Wikimedia Foundation*. Web. 4 May 2006.

Goodman, Ellen. "Life Before the Cameras." *Boston Globe*. 6 Oct. 2002. *ProQuest*.Web. 18 Apr. 2006.

Hultkrans, Andrew. "Surveillance in the Cinema." *Caught Looking: Prison and Surveillance Films*. 10 Mar. 1997. Web. 18 Apr. 2006. <http://www.stim.com/Stim-x/7.1/SurvFilms/SurvFilms.html>.

James, Julia. "Leave Facebook—If You Can." *The Crimson White*. 2 Mar. 2006. *LexisNexis*. Web. 8 Apr. 2006.

Johnson, D.J. "Forget Love and Diamonds; Facebook Is Forever." *The BG News*. 16 Feb. 2006. *LexisNexis*. Web. 10 Apr. 2006.

Lewis, Diane E. "Job Applicants' Online Musings Get Hard Look." *Boston Globe*. 30 Mar. 2006. *ProQuest*. Web. 11 Apr. 2006.

Locke, John. *A Letter Concerning Toleration*. Ed. Mario Montuori. 1689. The Hague: Martinus Nijhoff, 1963. Print.

Marks, Alexandra. "Smile! You're on Hidden Camera." *Christian Science Monitor*. 22 Dec. 2000. *ProQuest*. Web. 18 Apr. 2006.

"Mass Surveillance." *Wikipedia Online Encyclopedia*. 3 May 2006. Web. 4 May 2006.

Naing, Eric. "Facebook and 'Big Brother.'" *Daily Illini*. 31 Jan. 2006. *LexisNexis*. Web. 8 Apr. 2006.

Orwell, George. *1984*. New York: Harcourt, 1949. Print.

Podkul, Cezary. "No Need to Fret Over Facebook." *Daily Pennsylvanian*. 28 Feb. 2006. *LexisNexis*. Web. 10 Apr. 2005.

"Privacy Policy." *Facebook*. 27 Feb. 2006. Web. 17 Apr. 2006. <http://nyu.facebook.com/policy.php>.

United Kingdom. Office of Public Sector Information. *Identity Cards Act 2006*. 30 Mar. 2006. PDF file. <http://www.opsi.gov.uk/ACTS/acts2006/ukpga_20060015_en.pdf>.

Yuan, Li, and Rebecca Buckman. "Social Networking Goes Mobile; Myspace, Facebook Strike Deals with Cell Companies; A New Set of Safety Concerns." *Wall Street Journal*. 4 Apr. 2006. *ProQuest*. Web. 11 Apr. 2006.

Reading for Comprehension

1. Why is Kuerschner concerned about Facebook and the way his peers use it?
2. About half-way through the essay, Kuerschner introduces the idea of surveillance in the real world, telling us about how often New Yorkers are videotaped on an average day. Why does he introduce this idea in a paper about a virtual site? What does he gain from it?

3. In his conclusion, Kuerschner suggests that we will be watched, no matter what, and that our choice whether to try to avoid being seen or to flout those who are watching ultimately makes no difference. What's your response to him?

Analyzing the Genre

1. This is an academic essay. How does Kuerschner use research to develop his claims? How does he blend his personal observations (the ideas that are driving the essay) and the formal research?
2. Academic essays are often thesis driven. Locate what you think is Kuerschner's thesis, and then, note how he develops his argument. Do you see any pattern to his approach? And do you think he has adequately supported his argument given his audience and purpose?

Jennifer Moses, "Stepping Out"

In her travel essay published in 2006 in the Washington Post, Jennifer Moses captures the essence of Louisiana's Bayou Country by exploring two types of music that emerge from that region: Cajun and zydeco. Moses, a resident of Louisiana until 2008, is the author of two books, Bagels and Grits: A Jew on the Bayou and Food and Whine: Confessions of a New Millennium Mom. Her essays, travel writing, and op-eds have appeared in the New York Times, the Washington Post, and Poets and Writers.

After settling into Louisiana's Bayou Country, her love of dance was rekindled by the Cajun and zydeco music all around her. But with a husband who likes to sit it out, what's a frustrated, toe-tapping woman to do?

It's a Saturday night, and I'm out past my bedtime. Way past my bedtime. Not only that, but I'm dancing in the arms of a killingly good-looking stranger. I'm pressed up against him among the gyrating, tapping, prancing, two-stepping, sweating bodies of couples all around us here in El Sid O's, a club with the appearance of a long-disused filling station. It's tucked away on a desolate street of modest, one-story and occasionally abandoned houses near the interstate, on the wrong side of the tracks in Lafayette, La. We've come to El Sid O's ($8 cover, $2 a beer) on this sticky Saturday night to get a taste of the real thing: the homegrown, Creole-infused meld known as zydeco, a brand of music that recently has begun to leak out past its origins in Southwest Louisiana with its irresistible, driving rhythm. And tonight's attraction, Keith Frank, is the real thing. A Creole by birth, he's a self-taught master of accordion, drums, bass, guitar, scrub board, keyboard, piano and even harmonica. His band includes his sister on bass and brother on drums.

Like just about everyone else in the world of zydeco, Frank came up—as we say in Louisiana—surrounded by musicians: his daddy, his uncle, his paw-paw. It's in his blood.

My husband and I parked in a weedy lot and threaded our way self-consciously through pickup trucks and ancient Oldsmobiles to the club's entrance. I feel even more self-conscious now, but my dancing partner, no doubt sensing my nervousness, is going gentle with me. He is tall and muscular, and at least 10 years my junior, with skin the color of sun-soaked oak and the compact, lean build of a runner. In short, he is a god. But he doesn't seem to know that, and, holding me tight, he leads with utter confidence. It's as if he's willing my feet to move and my hips to sway in time with his.

Not five feet from us, Keith Frank and the Soileau Zydeco Band is shaking the roof off the rafters with the kind of music you can't not dance to—characterized, like most zydeco, with a down rhythm as sexual as anything in music, punctuated by the frottoir (a metal washboard typically played with spoons) and the accordion. Only this isn't your old man's one-two/circus music/polka accordion. This is a squeezebox—the accordion as aphrodisiac.

I'm turning in my partner's arms—step, step, step-back—and back again, and then again. It's ecstasy.

In truth, I'm dancing with a god not because of my good luck or wily charm. Rather, when his date—a slim young woman with long hair down her back, a cowboy hat perched pertly on her head—appeared next to me at the sink in the ladies' room, I told her point-blank that I'd pay money to dance with her boyfriend. She said that he wasn't her boyfriend, but her cousin, and that she'd ask him to dance with me. Which, this being Louisiana, where people are unbelievably friendly, he did. Meanwhile, my husband sat still as a rock, utterly unaware that if I didn't get pulled onto the dance floor, and soon, something profound and deep-seated and central in me was simply going to bust. (He later told me that he doesn't do zydeco—that it's too sexual, too loud, too rhythmic. He was just as happy to let me get my ya-yas out with someone else.)

El Sid O's, which is known for, among other things, its custom of serving booze by the half-pint, is hopping. Zydeco, unlike Cajun, is mainly played by, and for, black folks, and the crowd tonight is primarily African American. The men wear cowboy hats and sharp suits or red straw boaters and matching red shoes; the women wear tall strappy sandals and sparkly slacks so tight they look poured on. Everyone is dancing: young with old, fat with skinny, ugly with gorgeous, and black with white. And why not? It was just last summer when Katrina and Rita wiped out a good swath of South Louisiana, but here in Lafayette, not only are most buildings still standing, but folks can't help themselves. Dancing is encoded in their French-African-Caribbean-Louisiana-Catholic-Native American-Baptist gene pool.

My dream dance partner's name, I learn, is Herman Stevens. He hails from Lake Charles, works as a contractor in the family business, has a wife and three kids, and learned to dance by watching his parents, grandparents, aunts and uncles. "You know, I came up that way," he says.

I wish my husband and I had come up that way, too: We're both about as East Coast as you can get, with a crushing self-consciousness about anything approaching laissez les bon temps rouler (let the good times roll). There's one major difference between us, however: I love to "hear" music in my body, and have known how to dance ever since my grandmother taught me when I was 7 years old. He hears music in his ears. Shaking his groove-thing is something that doesn't exactly come naturally to him. But having experienced this kind of exhilaration, I'm determined that my wallflower days are over. The only question is, can I keep finding willing partners, or am I ultimately going to have to dance solo?

Cajun Country—or Acadiana—is a stretch of Southwest Louisiana roughly defined by the Atchafalaya River to the east, the city of Lake Charles to the west, Highway 190 to the north and the Gulf of Mexico to the south. It is home to hundreds of dance halls, bars, clubs, restaurants and even churches, where on any given day you can find people grooving down to a live band, enjoying a crawfish boil, or both. But, for me, it's all about the music and the dancing—the ramshackle lounges in tiny towns such as Cecilia, Eunice, Mamou, Butte La Rose and Erath that don't always show up on maps. Lafayette, a small sprawl of a city with a pre-hurricane population of about 110,000, and a post-storm population of some several thousand more, is at the heart of the region. Viewed by New Orleans, some 135 miles east, as a kind of poor relation, a country bumpkin with rough manners, Lafayette has always struck me as the second-born sibling who dedicates his life to outshining the brother who came first: If big brother invented Dixie-land and modern jazz, then little brother would show him up with Cajun, zydeco and swamp-pop (a blend of New Orleans R&B, country and blues, performed with a Cajun accent). During the day, this dead-flat city of low-lying buildings, suburban neighborhoods, heavily trafficked boulevards, mom and pop shops, sprawling strip malls and crawfish stands seems like no more than an overgrown small town. Its historic downtown of two- and three-story, red- and yellow-brick buildings is still handsome and intact, but its outlying sections are somewhat dreary and have none of the charm of, for example, the famous French Quarter of New Orleans or the stately historic houses of Natchez, Miss. It's at night that the city comes alive, showcasing one of America's remaining folk cultures.

Cajun Country continues to be like no other place in the United States, with an ethos and culture unique to itself, primarily thanks to Mother Nature. The region is set apart from the rest of Louisiana geographically as well as culturally and linguistically (with Cajun French still widely spoken), with its landscape of bayou, swamp, rivers and coastal marshes. All this is courtesy of the Atchafalaya Basin, the largest freshwater swamp in the United States. For better or worse, the swamp is rich in natural resources, particularly oil, and, over the decades, more and more of the wetlands have been destroyed for profit. The wetlands are shrinking at the rate of two football fields every hour: Over the past 50 years, an area the size of Rhode Island has become part of the Gulf of Mexico. Until Interstate 10 was built across the basin in 1973, the region was almost entirely isolated, protecting its indigenous culture and allowing it to flourish without outside influences.

The original Acadians were French Catholic colonials who, having been kicked out of the Acadia province of Nova Scotia by the British in the 18th century, wound their way down to Louisiana, which in those days was still held by Catholic France. Most of the good land along the Mississippi and farther east in New Orleans was already claimed, so the settlers headed west, directly into the swampy lands of bayous, crawfish, muskrats and alligators. Today, the area is still largely Cajun (the word is a corruption of "Acadian") and, unlike North Louisiana, primarily Catholic. There is also a large Creole population of African Americans who were brought up in French-speaking families and are of Caribbean descent. Cajun French is still widely spoken, and if you tune into KRVS Lafayette or KEUN in Eunice, you'll get an earful of Cajun, zydeco and swamp-pop, with French-speaking deejays. One way or another, the culture of music is so pervasive that chances are good your hairdresser, dentist or air-conditioning repairman works nights as a musician. The music—which goes hand in hand with the dancing—is as much a part of the culture here as the heavily seasoned, flavorful food: hot and spicy, down-home and delish, nothing fancy, and everyone's welcome.

When I tell my friend Durwood in Baton Rouge about my plan to get more dancing in my life, he immediately says I have to meet Hadley Castille—an old-time Cajun fiddler. Castille has been keeping people in Cajun Country dancing for most of his life, and maybe he can give me some insight into why this music is so irresistible. So one day I drive from Grand Coteau up Interstate 49—18-wheelers, billboards, pickup trucks, wildflowers—until I get to the town of Opelousas. There I hang a right on U.S. Route 190, another right near the sign advertising same-day surgery and a final right on a quiet road threading through woods and surrounded by the buzz of a million insects. I reach Castille's comfortable, neo-Acadian cottage, which is propped up on a rise. At the door, he greets me with the kind of smile you usually reserve for long-gone children. Castille, who has a wonderfully expressive face under a mop of thick white hair, brings me inside, where my eyes are immediately drawn to his collection of fiddles, one in the shape of the state of Louisiana.

Like just about every other musician in South Louisiana, the 73-year-old Castille never had any formal instruction; he learned to play the fiddle from his uncle. He walked to dances in his bare feet so as not to ruin his one good pair of shoes, grew up speaking French and one day, when he was young, experienced a revelation. "I must have been about 11 or 12—my father brought home a radio," he says. "I tuned in and heard something I'd never heard before, Texas swing. I couldn't believe what I heard. I stayed up all night listening to that radio and wore the batteries out." Castille took the mischievous sound of Texas swing, with its teasing fiddle, darting melodies and—unlike traditional Cajun music—swaggering hints of cowboy, and turned it into what's now Cajun swing. It's played on two strings with a back-and-forth, wave-like movement of the bow, and produces a fuller, richer, more complex sound. Today Castille—who for years earned a living as a plumber—performs with his son, Blake, and teenage granddaughter, Sarah Jayde Williams.

His bow glides up and back over the strings in a demonstration for me—a black bowler on his head, his entire face alive with feeling. He keeps time by the slow tapping of his foot. "The melody? You see—it's carried by just the one string." The room fills with a wild, playful music that's so alive, so vibrant that it's as if the small instrument in his hands can barely contain the big joy inside it.

My feet are tapping, too. I long to inhabit that music, to start dancing right there in his living room. But I'm too self-conscious to get up off the sofa.

Next I head to Louisiana State University's "leisure school," on LSU's leafy green campus, under live oaks and magnolias, past the university lake, fraternity row with its big, Southern-style brick buildings, the wide expanse of the parade grounds and the massive neo-Gothic law school. In the student union, up on the third floor, is the Atchafalaya ballroom, a large, unfurnished, characterless room surrounded by dirty windows. Roland Doucet is teaching Cajun dancing to yet another group of people who somehow missed out earlier in life, and I want to see if there is anything I can glean that might help me light a fire under my husband. What I find are about 30 couples, at least half of them with a willingness to learn but no natural ability. The class is a godsend because, as Doucet says when I explain my struggle to loosen up my husband, who is a professor at LSU, "The hardest people to teach are professors and engineers, because they want to learn how to dance with their heads, and half the time don't even know where their feet are." Whereas the majority of Cajun dancers learn not by memorizing the steps but rather by copying what everyone else is doing, which is how Doucet learned to dance. Only his story has a twist: Like just about everyone else in Doucet's hometown of Vinton, his father, Haywood Doucet, played the fiddle in a Cajun band, which meant that if his mother wanted a dance partner, she had to ask one of her four sons.

As befitting his second-job persona as a dance instructor (his day job is installing and designing custom rugs; he also hosts a Cajun radio show on WXCT here in Baton Rouge), the 55-year-old Doucet addresses his mainly middle-aged students as "ladies" and "gentlemen." As in: "Gentlemen, remember that the most important thing you can do when you're dancing with this lady is to look her in the eye and say, 'Honey, I'm sorry.'" Or: "Gentlemen, make sure you're stepping back with your left foot, because she's going to be stepping forward at the same time with her right, and if your big old foot is in the way, she'll rupture you."

The secret of his classes is that he breaks the dancing down into small, manageable steps, segregating men and women on either side of the room, and repeating each move over and over until his students feel confident enough to try with their partners. At first the method seems like overkill. I mean, how many times does it take to learn how to move your right foot two inches farther to the right and then bring your left foot in to join it? On a cue from their teacher—the formerly separated couples are floating around the dance floor, the men guiding their partners in large, graceful circles, the women accommodating the husbands' and boyfriends' leads as if they've been doing it all their lives. As for me, when I see Doucet cutting in to dance with a pretty older woman with curly white hair, and the woman, in turn, relaxing into his embrace, as if she'd been waiting for him her entire life, I feel a bolt of pure envy.

Unlike zydeco, most Cajun music is sung in French—and danceable even for oldsters and young fogies. So even my husband will dance to Cajun music. Or so I'm hoping. We've come to Randol's, a big barn of a place with red-and-white checked tablecloths and a commodious dance floor in Lafayette. There are numerous other good, family-style restaurants in Acadiana where you can dance, as well as enjoy excellent high-end dining—Catahoula's in Grand Coteau and Cafe Des Amis in Breaux Bridge, with its zydeco brunch on weekends—but we've come to Randol's because we heard that the band alone is worth the trip.

Cajun music, which tends to be played by and for white people, is typically slower-moving and sweet-tempered, having evolved around the turn of the 20th century from fiddle music played at house parties to an accordion-based sound big enough to fill up old-fashioned dance halls.

All around us diners are feasting on huge platters of fried fish and potatoes, jambalaya, gumbo and spicy-hot boudin to the sounds of Kevin Naquin and the Ossun Playboys. The food of South Louisiana has a French-Creole accent: crawfish bisque (prepared in a rich roux), sauce piquant, boulette (hush puppies seasoned with onions and crawfish tails), cracklins (fried pork skin), etouffee (various kinds of seafood simmered in a rich spicy stew), dirty rice, maque choux (highly seasoned corn).

These days the place is filled with FEMA and Red Cross workers, insurance adjusters and National Guard members. But the regulars are here, too: Long-married couples, little girls with their daddies, and women with their best girlfriends dance gracefully in the typically circular pattern of the Cajun waltz and two-step. "Maybe they'll order a beer, or a cold drink, but most of 'em come for the music and dancing," says Rusty Randol, the head chef. "We see the same couples over and over again."

As usual, no sooner are we seated than I'm filled with a kind of yearning. How could it have happened that I married a man who can't dance? Doesn't he notice that my feet are tapping on the floor and my fingers are drumming on the table? How can he just sit there, when all I can think of is finding one of the many elderly gentlemen who might not mind ditching his wife for a minute or two in order to dance with me?

But then, just as I'm about to burst at the seams, my husband turns to me, takes my hand, asks me if I'd like to chance it and leads me forward. And a minute later, the two of us have joined the circle, dipping and swaying to the accordion and fiddle as best we can. The other couples glide like swans around us.

"That's it," I'm saying. "One, two, three, one, two, three." Actually, the Cajun waltz is about the easiest dance in the world to learn—you just move your feet in a simple left-right-left, right-left-right pattern, pausing slightly on the third beat for emphasis.

The song comes to an end. It's time to quit. But then something happens. As the band launches into another tune, my husband takes my right hand in his left, puts his left at my waist and begins gliding me backward. Only this time there's no need for me to count out the beats, or jump away from his feet or even make sure we don't crash into another couple. Something about the tune—its sweetness, or perhaps its pace—seems to have embraced my husband, leading him out and away from himself and landing him right smack in the middle of Acadiana. When I glance up at him, I see that he's smiling. Around and around we go, in time with the other couples but lost in our own time, too, until I no longer know where I am, how I got here, or how I got by for so long without this.

Reading for Comprehension

1. Moses uses the language of Acadiana. Look up some of the terms. How do they give you a better understanding of this culture: its people, music, food, so on?
2. What organizational patterns do you notice Moses using as she works her way through the essay and Cajun country?

Analyzing the Genre

1. What kinds of research does Moses use to give readers a sense of this place, its landscape, the people, and its cultures? How does her choice of examples and different kinds of research materials emphasize her purpose?
2. Often essays about place offer the writer's cultural commentary on the location. What is Moses commenting on about Louisiana Bayou Country and its blend of cultures? What effect does she hope to have on readers with her commentary?

James A. Banks, "Remembering Brown: Silence, Loss, Rage, and Hope"

In the following academic essay, James A. Banks, the Kerry and Linda Killinger Professor of Diversity Studies and Director of the Center for Multicultural Education at the University of Washington, Seattle, uses his personal experiences as a resident of Arkansas to analyze the reactions of his community to the landmark 1954 Supreme Court case, Brown v. Board of Education on the desegregation of public schools. Professor Banks has earned many honors for his research and scholarship in multicultural education and in social studies education, and he has written many books including *Race, Culture, and Education: The Selected Works of James A. Banks*. Professor Banks is the editor of *The Handbook of Research on Multicultural Education* in which this essay appears.

I was in the seventh grade at the Newsome Training School in Aubrey, Arkansas when the Supreme Court handed down *Brown v. Board of Education* on May 17, 1954. My most powerful memory of the *Brown* decision is that I have no memory of it being rendered or mentioned by my parents, teachers, or preachers. In my rural southern Black community, there was a conspiracy of silence about *Brown*. It was completely invisible.

A Conspiracy of Silence

I can only speculate about the meaning of the silence about *Brown* in the Arkansas delta in which racial segregation was codified in both law and custom in every aspect of our lives. The only public library in Lee County was 9 miles from our family farm in Marianna, the county seat that had a population of 4,550. Although I was an avid reader, I could not use the public library. It was for Whites only. The only time I saw the inside of the public library was when the choir from my all-Black high school entertained a White civic group in the library. We had to see second-run movies at the all-Black Blue Haven Theatre. To see first-run movies, we had to go to the White Imperial Theatre and enter the "Colored entrance." which led upstairs where the projection room was also located. We could hear the rattle of the movie projector as we tried to concentrate on the movie. Marianna and Lee County, Arkansas epitomized the institutionalized discrimination and racism that existed throughout the Deep South in the mid-1950s.

The conspiracy of silence about *Brown* in Lee County among Whites was probably caused by fear that news of *Brown* might disrupt the institutionalized racist system of segregation that had been established in Lee County in the years after Reconstruction. That system was never publicly challenged or questioned by Whites or Blacks. Black resistance to racism was deep but covert. Blacks wore a mask as they feigned contentment around Whites as their anger seethed below the surface—ready to explode. The statue of Robert E. Lee that towered above the park in the Town Square symbolized the racial oppression that gripped the community in which I—and many other southern Blacks—came of age in the 1950s and 1960s.

My teachers and preachers surely knew about the *Brown* decision and must have been quietly joyous about it. However, it must have also evoked fear in them as well—about losing their jobs and their schools. They must have quietly discussed *Brown* among themselves, out of the earshot of the children and certainly out of the earshot of Whites. The National Association for the Advancement of Colored People (NAACP) took the five cases that constituted the *Brown* decision to the Supreme Court. The White establishment throughout the Deep South regarded the NAACP as a subversive and dangerous organization. It was viewed with as much suspicion and animosity as was the Communist Party in the North. Black teachers were often fired by school boards in the South when it was learned that they were members of the NAACP. The White school boards controlled both Black and White schools. Consequently, for Black teachers to spread the word about the *Brown* decision, especially among students, it would probably have been considered a subversive and dangerous act.

Education for Black Uplift

The silence about *Brown* that haunted Lee County and the lack of actions related to it continued throughout my elementary school years (Grades I through 8) and high school years (9 to 12). I attended Newsome Training School until I graduated and then entered all-Black Robert Russa Moton High School in Marianna. Moton was a protege of Booker T. Washington who became principal of Tuskegee Institute when Washington died. Many Black schools throughout the Deep South were named for Moton.

I graduated from Moton in 1960. Throughout my elementary and high school years and without any focus on *Brown* or school desegregation, our Black teachers taught us to be citizens of both the Black community and of American society. Each day in morning exercise, we said the Pledge of Allegiance and sang both the Negro national anthem, "Lift Every Voice and Sing," and the American national anthem, "The Star Spangled Banner." The lives and triumphs of Black leaders—Booker T. Washington, Mary McLeod Bethune, Robert Russa Moton, George Washington Carver, and Marian Anderson—were interspersed throughout our curriculum. Our teachers tried hard to make us productive citizens of U.S. society as well as to instill in us a commitment to the uplift of the Black community. Yet, I can remember no explicit efforts to prepare us to function within a desegregated society—a society whose possibility my teachers had not fully imagined or grasped.

The Price They Paid

Brown had no real or specific meaning in isolated rural communities in the South until a group of Blacks organized and took on the White power structure. This was a difficult fight to take on and those Blacks who did paid a high price. When a group of Blacks in Little Rock decided to push for the desegregation of Central High School in 1957, Governor Oral Faubus used all the power of the state to resist desegregating the school. The Black civil rights activists who led the movement to desegregate Central High School, such as Daisy Bates (1987), were steadfast in their fight to end racial segregation at Central High. After a long and bitter struggle, they were successful. However, the nine Black students who desegregated Central High paid a dear price as did Mrs. Bates. The ugly racial incidents to which these students were victims left deep scars that endured. As the students walked to school each day, White mobs—which included White fathers and mothers—hurled racial epithets and rocks at them. The newspaper owned by Mrs. Bates and her husband was destroyed because the White merchants withdrew their advertising to retaliate for her actions on behalf of the students.

Hope, Rage, and Loss

Brown engendered great hope and possibilities for Southern Blacks but evoked rage and hostility among Whites. When teaching about *Brown* and its historical context, teachers should help students to understand the complex emotions, behavior, and consequences of the *Brown* decision. It is often described in brief textbook accounts in a way that can lead students to conclude that shortly after the *Brown* decision was handed down, schools throughout the South were desegregated with "all deliberate speed." The battle to desegregate Southern schools look place one at a time—from town to town and county to county.

Students need to understand that in each Southern community, there was a struggle to desegregate the schools and that the cost African Americans paid for desegregation was enormous. Blacks experienced both hope and loss with the *Brown* decision. Many African Americans were damaged—psychologically and physically—when they first entered all-White southern schools. Melba Pattillo Beals (1994), one of the Little Rock nine, wrote, "I had long dreamed of entering Central High. I could not have imagined what that privilege could cost me" (p. i). Many Black teachers who took active roles to desegregate schools or joined the NAACP lost their jobs. Other Black teachers lost their jobs when schools were desegregated and White teachers were chosen to replace them. Rather than desegregate its schools, the school board in Prince Edward County, Virginia closed its public schools and gave tuition grants to White students to attend Prince Edward Academy, a private school. There were no schools for Black children in Prince Edward County between 1959 and 1964 (Irons, 2002).

There was another kind of loss experienced when desegregation took place in the South. The Black school, like the Black church, was an important source of ethnic pride and a center of important activities in Black communities. Many of these schools, despite meager physical resources, had dedicated teachers who provided nurturing and positive educational environments for Black students who would have not experienced educational success without them. My own teachers—such as Mrs. Sadie Mae Jones, Mrs. Mary Wilson, Mrs. Verna Mae Clay, and Miss Curry—epitomized caring and committed Southern Black teachers. Teachers were important and respected people within the Black community. The loss of Black schools, as Venessa Siddle Walker (1996) pointed out in her pioneering study, *Their Highest Potential: An African American School Community in the South,* left a tremendous void in African American communities throughout the South.

Assessing *Brown*

W. E. B. Du Bois said (as cited in Kaplan, 1992), "The problem of the twentieth century is the problem of the color line" (p. 604). *Brown,* as well as the events that preceded and followed it, are manifestations of both the problems and the hope for improving race relations in America. Martin Luther King (1991) said, "[t]he American people are infected with racism—that is the peril. Paradoxically, they are also infected with democratic ideals—that is the hope" (p. 71). *Brown* was an expression of those aspects of American civic culture that articulate democratic values such as the Declaration of Independence, the Constitution, and the Bill of Rights. By ruling that *de jure* segregation was illegal because it damaged the hearts and minds of Black students, the Supreme Court gave credence to the values stated in the nation's founding documents and consequently gave Blacks hope.

There has always been—and there remains—a wide gap between America's democratic ideals and its practices. Although the spirit of *Brown* reflected the democratic values in the nation's founding documents, the efforts that were made to implement it and the White rage that it evoked were deeply American. Even the ruling itself reflected the ambivalence of the court. Chief Justice Warren had a difficult time getting the court to make a unanimous decision on *Brown* (Irons, 2002; Kluger, 1975). Rather than set a definite timetable for Southern schools to desegregate, the court set forth the ambiguous phase, "with all deliberate speed," which gave Southern school districts the license to stall and procrastinate.

The rage that *Brown* evoked among White Southern lawmakers in Congress and among their White constituencies was also deeply American. Racial progress in the United States throughout its history has always been attained through struggle. As Douglass (1857, as cited in Mullane, 1995) stated

If there is no struggle, there is no progress. Those who profess to favor freedom and yet deprecate agitation, are men who want crops without plowing up the ground, they want rain without thunder and lightning. They want the ocean without the awful roar of its many waters. This struggle may be a moral one. or it may be a physical one, and it may be both moral and physical, but it must be struggle. (pp. 118–119)

It took struggles to end slavery and lynching. It was through struggle that Blacks obtained access to public schools. Through the historical struggles to improve race relations in America, both Blacks and Whites have been changed, and we have come closer to the dream of attaining a nation with liberty and justice for all. For all of its shortcomings—and there were many both in the decision and its consequences—*Brown* brought the United States closer to its ideals. In declaring that "separate educational facilities are inherently unequal," *(Brown v Board of Education, 1954. p. 495)*, the Supreme Court enabled Blacks in tightly segregated communities such as Aubrey and Marianna to challenge a system of institutionalized racism that had been entrenched since the post-Reconstruction period.

Echoes of *Brown* finally reached Marianna years after 1960, the year that I graduated from high school and left the South to go to college in Chicago. The White rage that was unleashed when Blacks demanded an end to the entrenched system of segregation nearly destroyed the town. However. Marianna was reborn. When I visited Marianna in 1998 to give the keynote address at my high school reunion, it had a Black mayor, but the schools were segregated. Most Whites had fled to the suburbs or sent their children to private schools that were established to escape desegregated schools. Battles to desegregate schools similar to those that took place in Southern cities occurred in Northern cities such as Boston, Chicago, Detroit, and New York years later in the 1960s.

The silence, loss, rage, and hope that *Brown* evoked still simmer in Black and White communities throughout the United States. Schools throughout the nation are now resegregated (Orfield, Eaton, & the Harvard Project on School Desegragation, 1996). Blacks and Whites often remain silent to maintain the peace. Blacks feel that much of their culture has been lost and eradicated from the schools in their communities. There is White rage about affirmative action and massive immigration and Black rage about their plight in America. *Brown* gave us hope that America might one day overcome its deep and entrenched racial legacy and indicated how difficult this journey was and still is.

References

Bates. D. (1987). *The long shadow of Little Rock.* Fayetteville: University of Arkansas Press.

Beals, M. P. (1994). *Warriors don't cry: A searing memoir of the battle to integrate little Rock's Central* High. New York: Pocket Books.

Brown v. Board of Educ., 347 U.S. 483 (1954).

Irons, P. (2002). *Jim Crow's children: The broken promise of the Brown decision.* New York: Penguin.

Kaplan. J. (Ed,). (1992). *Barlett's familiar quotations* (I6th éd.). Boston: Little, Brown.

King, M. L.., Jr(1991). Showdown for nonviolence. In J. W. Washington (Ed.), *A testament of hope: The essential writing and speeches of Martin Luther King. Jr* (pp.64-72). San Francisco: HarperCollins.

Kluger, R. (1975). *Simple justice: The history of the Brown v, Board of Education and Black America's struggle for equality.* New York: Vintage.

Mullane, D. (Ed.). (1995). *Words to make my dream children live: A book of African American quotations.* New York: Doubleday.

Orfield. G. Eaton. S. E., & The Harvard Project on School Desegregation. (1996). *Dismantling desegregation: The quiet reversal of Brown v. Board of Education.* New York: The New Press.

Siddle Walker. V. (1996). *Their highest potential: An African American school community in the segregated South.* Chapel Hill: The University of North Carolina Press.

Reading for Comprehension

1. How does Banks explain the "conspiracy of silence" in his town after the *Brown* decision? Why does he think his teachers and preachers kept silent about it?

2. How familiar are you with the Brown decision? What do you learn about it from Banks? What questions does his essay raise for you?

Analyzing the Genre

1. Banks uses subheadings to organize sections of his essay. How do the different sections connect to each other and to his essay's argument?

2. Banks draws heavily on personal reflection and experience – what does this add to his discussion and analysis of the Brown decision? Where does Banks use commentary to strengthen his analysis of the issue?

Essays

For this chapter's assignment, write a personal essay on an issue, experience, or an idea that is of concern both to you and to a particular audience. Consider the larger significance of the subject you write about.

Essay Assignment Options

The essay genre has many subgenres: the academic essay, the personal essay, the segmented essay, the portrait or sketch, and so on. In each case, the rhetorical situation that drives your writing will help you choose the appropriate subgenre for your essay.

1. Write a **persuasive essay** in which you argue for a particular way of understanding a controversial issue or current trend in society. Think about situations you find yourself in everyday life, work, or your community that might intrigue others who share your concerns.

2. Write an **academic essay** in which you explore and argue for a particular interpretation of a text or set of texts (a poem, short story, visual texts such as advertisements or commercials, or another essay).

3. Write a **meditative essay** in which you explore a particular issue or concern that you personally find hard to understand or come to a conclusion about. Think about the concerns you have based on the many roles you play: father, mother, sister, son, worker, Montana rancher, urbanite, etc., to help you think of issues you care about.

4. Write an **essay in which you examine and analyze the rhetorical choices** the writer of an essay made. You can analyze another essay, an opinion piece, a film, or some visual text such as a brochure, website, or poster. Chapters 3 and 4 can help you with the rhetorical analysis, and provide you with student-written examples.

Community-Based Writing Option

The work that we do as part of our civic responsibilities can often be a good source of material for an essay. Write an essay that comments on the work of an organization, group, or other civic agency you are involved with that serves a community or particular public audience. Keep in mind your purpose as an essayist in general—to comment on the larger significance of an idea or concept—and as you write, comment on the underlying civic idea this group stands for. For instance, if you write about the work of a local homeless shelter, your essay might comment on larger issues of poverty and homelessness nationally or globally and encourage citizens' ethical and civic responsibilities to enact changes.

Writing Essays

Just as with any genre, essays have particular characteristics that help writers understand what they need to say and how they can choose to say it.

> **WHAT WRITERS CONSIDER WHEN THEY WRITE ESSAYS**
>
> In general, essay writers:
>
> - Consider subjects that are meaningful to them and to their audience
> - Evaluate the audience and their needs, as well as consider their purpose for writing
> - Conduct and use research to deepen their commentary and analysis and provide readers with background on the subject
> - Articulate and develop claims that help them explore their subject
> - Offer commentary on their subject
> - Choose an organizational pattern that reflects their purpose and subject

Generating Ideas for Essays

As we have suggested, there probably aren't many topics that wouldn't be appropriate for an essay, so consider Phillip Lopate's description of the essay writer's task: "The essayist attempts to surround a something—a subject, a mood, a problematic irritation—by coming at it from all angles, wheeling and diving like a hawk, each seemingly digressive spiral actually taking us closer to the heart of the matter." In a personal essay, this might mean trying to make sense of an experience and what it tells the writer and audience about themselves. In a more formal essay, such as a rhetorical analysis essay, this might mean trying to make sense of how another writer constructed his or her argument and why. In any case, remember that the essayist often begins with what he or she finds curious or interesting or even odd.

Avoiding Common Essay Pitfalls

Because it is such a dynamic genre, there are not many approaches or subjects that won't work for an essay. But as with all writing, there are areas where writers can get off track.

1. **The "Too Common" Subject** Because we are all human, we all share similar experiences: the first crush, the first time we learned our parents were wrong about something, the first time we won (or lost) the big game. These are subjects that "have been done already"—perhaps are even cliché. So one pitfall you should avoid is writing about a *too common* experience or observation. You should avoid writing about too common subjects not because they aren't valid—they absolutely are—but because it's hard to find a new way to write about such subjects.

2. **The Too Personal Subject** The essay invites writers to reflect on ideas from a personal perspective and to write about themselves in ways that reveal some larger idea that others can relate to. But sometimes this aspect can lead writers to write about subjects that are *too personal*. Remember that the essay is a public genre that's very different from a journal entry. Choose subjects for your essays carefully, and consider whether you can comfortably discuss personal issues with your readers.

Freewriting

1. Have you or someone you know had an experience that others would find interesting and worth reading about? Why? What is its significance?
2. Have you noticed something about an individual or a group that you find intriguing and would like to explore the meaning or significance of? Why does it intrigue you?
3. Have you ever wondered about the everyday items we use in our lives or activities we engage in and why they are so important? Or why we use them or do them at all, where they came from, and so on?
4. Have you ever encountered something irritating or something exciting and wondered why it is irritating or exciting?

Reading

1. Take a look at the essays published in journals like the *Journal of Creative Nonfiction, Fourth Genre,* or *River Teeth: A Journal of Nonfiction Narrative.* Your library may provide access to these journals through the *Project Muse* database. What kinds of topics are other writers exploring?

Writing

Choose three possible topic ideas and write a few paragraphs about each in which you address the following:

1. What is the subject you wish to write about?
2. Why is this subject of interest to you? And what do you want to say about it?
3. Who would want to read about it and what would they get out of it? (You might think about this question by asking yourself : What would readers get out of your essay that would prevent them from saying, after reading it, "So what?")

■   ■   ■

Essayists write for a broad audience, and so one way to test your ideas and to further explore and complicate them is to talk with your classmates and friends about those ideas, while you are still thinking them through. Talking with others about your ideas can help you develop them, can help you refine them, and can help you choose which one(s) you really want to pursue. The key to group work is to be an active participant—go into the group with some ideas, ones you wrote in response to the prompt above, but also questions you have about the topics or concerns you have. Having these will enable you to recieve the best possible feedback.

Thinking about Audience, Purpose, and Situation

Because it is multifaceted, the essay allows the writer to take on any number of personae. You can be witty, wry, or serious. You can present yourself as an insider or outsider, an expert or a novice. You can develop your ethos with personal anecdotes or through your use of research (or both). Similarly, your audience is less clearly defined for you than if you were writing a research report or even a brochure. In those cases, your purpose helps you define your audience. For example, the purpose of a brochure is to sell something or inform someone of something, and so the baseline audience is those who would benefit from the information or item. What other essays and essayists do, how they negotiate the rhetorical situation they are a part of, is important to understand because it reveals some of the choices that you can make. You might look back at the essays reproduced in this chapter and analyze them rhetorically, looking for how they imaged their audiences, used evidence to support and develop their commentaries, and so on. Please see Chapter 3 for a detailed discussion of rhetorical strategies. Writers begin by thinking carefully about *why* they are writing and *to whom* they are writing—their purpose and audience in a particular situation. Along the way, they consider how they might present themselves and how they want the essay to sound.

WRITING ACTIVITY   Defining the Rhetorical Situation for Your Essay

1. ***Think about the situation.*** What is the context of your essay? What made you want to write it? What situations surround the subject you are writing about? Whatever the subject, be sure that you address the rhetorical situation in your essay.
2. ***Decide on your purpose.*** Do you want to persuade your readers to be concerned about the subject of your essay? Change readers' minds about a current viewpoint? Or ask them to reconsider something about themselves? How will your essay influence the readers affected?
3. ***Decide on your audience.*** Who is your intended audience? Who would be interested in reading about your subject? Who might not know much about it or be misinformed about it? What do you know about that audience?
4. ***Decide how to present yourself.*** What kinds of information about yourself should you reveal to the reader in your essay? What examples, ideas, or personal experiences could you include to help build your credibility, or would you benefit from acknowledging ignorance? Can you make use of humor? Will you address readers directly, or take a more reserved, more removed tone?

■ ■ ■

Researching Essays

As it is with most academic and civic genres, research is an important part of essay writing; Readers have the expectation that writers will know their subject well and present them with a fresh perspective for them to think about the subject. Essay writers may do formal-research (i.e. look things up in a library or database) so as to understand their subject more deeply before writing about it, or they may mine their own experiences for examples and evidence to support their claims.

Searching Your Experiences

Depending on the kind of the essay you are writing, you may be able to draw on personal experiences to help you develop, explore, or comment on your subject. Even if you are writing one of the more formal subgenres—the academic essay, for instance—your personal experiences can help you figure out what you want to say, even if you cannot use them in the essay itself.

As you do some exploratory writing in response to the questions below, keep in mind the material you generated when you defined the *rhetorical situation*. Work here with the questions that seem relevant to your situation. Your answers to these questions will help you figure out what you already know and see where you could conduct research.

1. **Tapping the familiar.** Is the subject you are writing about familiar—an experience or observation that affects you or someone you know? Write down some of the details of that experience or observation. What was the outcome? Was this the only time it happened to you, or is the subject one that is recurring or common—one that you and readers might expect to experience again? How would using this material help clarify your purpose or connect to your audience?

2. **A circling hawk.** Essayists often come at their subject from many vantage points (keep in mind Lopate's statement about the circling hawk). Have you had other experiences or made other observations that might be connected to your subject? Do you know of others (friends, family, people in the news) who have had similar, relevant experiences or observations? How might you include those experiences or observations in your essay?

3. **Troubling the waters.** Is there something that bothers you about the experience or observation? Something you can't quite figure out? What is it? And why does it bother you? Write about what is bothersome and what is bewildering about your subject.

■ ■ ■

Doing Background Research

Sometimes when we read essays, especially personal essays, we might think that the writer did no more research than thinking hard about his or her experiences. And we even suggest that your personal experiences or observations, and those of your friends and family, are good informal research sources. But often the writer has used formal sources when it appears otherwise. For essays, at least the less academic kind, you might find it useful to talk with others, to find out what they think or believe about your subject. You can do this formally—through a survey or interviews—or you can do so more casually by talking with people you know or sitting down at the lunch table with someone and striking up a conversation. Of course, your research needs to complement your rhetorical situation. For a more formal essay, you'll want to find out what other people have written about the subject you are exploring. You can then use that material to help you develop your own ideas and tweak your purpose. You might find that you want to refute what others have said about the subject because you feel they don't understand the full scope of the problem or issue. See Chapter 13: Research and the Rhetorical Situation for more on conducting research.

Incorporating Research

Conducting research and using it in your essay is important for a number of reasons. Research helps you understand your subject well enough to draw conclusions about it that are not only meaningful to you but to your audience. It makes you an authority on the subject. And it establishes your credibility or *ethos* as the writer.

Let's look at an example so that you can see how writers can work research into an essay. The following is an excerpt from Jennifer Moses's essay, "Stepping Out" on page 221.

> Cajun Country—or Acadiana—is a stretch of Southwest Louisiana roughly defined by the Atchafalaya River to the east, the city of Lake Charles to the west, Highway 190 to the north and the Gulf of Mexico to the south. It is home to hundreds of dance halls, bars, clubs, restaurants and even churches, where on any given day you can find people grooving down to a live band, enjoying a crawfish boil, or both. But, for me, it's all about the music and the dancing—the ramshackle lounges in tiny towns such as Cecilia, Eunice, Mamou, Butte La Rose and Erath that don't always show up on maps. Lafayette, a small sprawl of a city with a pre-hurricane population of about 110,000, and a post-storm population of some several thousand more, is at the heart of the region. Viewed by New Orleans, some 135 miles east, as a kind of poor relation, a country bumpkin with rough manners, Lafayette has always struck me as the second-born sibling who dedicates his life to outshining the brother who came first: If big brother invented Dixie-land and modern jazz, then little brother would show him up with Cajun, zydeco and swamp-pop (a blend of New Orleans R&B, country and blues, performed with a Cajun accent).

Notice the casual way in which Moses integrates research and her impression of this region of Louisiana into her essay. Moses's perspective on Cajun Country—how she reacts to the landscape and people—are the focus of this excerpt. What is especially revealing about her personal reaction to the place is her personification of Lafayette; it provides readers with her subjective experiences there. You might also notice that although she uses research to comment on the area, she does not formally cite it. Other essays use formal citation, such as Jim Kuerschner's academic essay "Big Brother Is on the Facebook" (page 212). His use of formal research, and formal citation, makes sense given his subject and the particular kind of essay he is writing: an academic essay.

The essay is a genre that straddles both academic and civic genre categories. How you use research in your essay will depend on the subgenre you have chosen as well as the context of your rhetorical situation. In Chapter 14 we discuss formal citation, quotation, paraphrase, and synthesis.

Drafting Essays

As you are doing your research, you are thinking about what points—claims—you want to make. What claims you make will depend on what you want to say, your own purpose in writing the essay, and who you are writing to. (Different audiences will require you to make different claims and to support them in different ways.) Please see Chapter 3: Analyzing and Writing Arguments for a discussion of claims and evidence.

The Rhetorical Situation and Claims

The claims you might make are suggested by what you know about the rhetorical situation.

Experience: Working on your father's fishing boat during summers as a student.	Possible Claims The summer job scene in New England for college students is dismal. The demand of physical labor often has psychological impact on workers.
Audience: Others who've found themselves struggling to find money to pay for something important to them; others who found value in or new insights about the activities they struggled with, much to their own surprise.	Possible Claims "Eyes on the prize" becomes the mantra for those doing something they dislike or find boring in order to get something important. We don't always get what we expect, and sometimes that's a good thing—living means embracing the struggle and making good on it. Work or struggle reveals other rewards we don't expect.
Purpose: To remind readers that fate often plays a role in our lives.	Possible Claims Unexpected events often force us to think about what we really care about, what's important to us. Conversely, unexpected events might make us pretend that things are better than they really are.
Writer: The student who cared little about her dad's fishing boat but came to realize the importance of her relationship with her father.	Possible Claims When I first fished on the boat, I was bored, resenting my dad for not being a big exec who could get me a cushy job in an air-conditioned office for the summer. Fishing is more than a means to make a living; it's also about the traditions of those who make a living off the sea.

GROUP ACTIVITY   Developing the Claims in Your Essay

Write down your subject, your audience, your purpose, and your connection to the subject. For each of these, brainstorm three or four claims you *could* make in response to the details you know about your rhetorical situation. Then, for each claim, write down your answers to the following questions.

1. What research do you need to present in order to successfully make your claim?
2. Should your claim be separated into two or more claims?

■ ■ ■

The Commentary: Answering the Question "So What?"

Essays do more than describe an experience or report on an observation. They also say something about what the essayist has experienced, observed, or analyzed. Your commentary on the subject of your essay is the answer to the question "So what?" For example, if you are writing about your first encounter with a homeless person, the reader is going to expect that you will say something about that experience, not just describe it. In the essay, this question is answered through commentary. The commentary is often one of tentative speculation: The writer is saying, "Here's what I think it means."

In his essay on page 212, Jim Kuerschner explores the idea of social networking as self-imposed surveillance, using his commentary to extend his ideas and suggest what the new technology, namely Facebook, may mean for our society as a whole. Below is an excerpt from Kuerschner's essay:

Notice how Kuerschner uses questions to make readers think more deeply about his commentary.

The writer uses a question/response/question pattern which keeps readers thinking about the issue at stake as he provides commentary on it.

> Yet while we are okay with everyone knowing our personal affairs via Facebook, we hotly protest (and rightfully so) the ever-increasing surveillance that has been imposed on our society post-September 11th. Is there a difference? Perhaps we fall into a false sense of security, refusing to believe that anyone other than our college buddies and other university students can view what we make publicly available. Facebook's privacy policy, made available to every member, however, states that the site has the right to share information with a third party when it is "reasonably necessary to offer the service"—a quite vague description ("Privacy"). But if I'm not doing anything wrong, why do I care that someone knows what I'm doing? The problem is that added surveillance can turn into added control, especially when we are not aware of how we are being monitored. When do we draw the line between harmless monitoring of Internet profiles and constant Orwellian watch?

GUIDELINES: DEVELOPING THE COMMENTARY IN YOUR ESSAY: WHAT IF . . .?

When you consider your essay's subject, and you consider telling someone about it, what do you think the point is? Your starting point for the commentary is your answer to that question.

But *what if* there were more to your experience than that? Getting at the significance of your essay means exploring the "what if . . .?"

Do some exploratory writing in response to the questions that apply to your situation:

1. Why do you feel or think the way you do about the subject? Why do you have the reactions you do to the subject? What do those feelings or reactions tell you about yourself?

2. If you are writing about a particular behavior or practice, think about why you or others do those things. Do those reactions make *logical* or *rational* sense? If not, why are they continued to be done?

3. How does your experience or observation about your subject challenge or make readers think differently than they might normally think about the subject?

Organizing Essays

Organizational possibilities for essays are as varied as the genre itself, but the key to a successful organization strategy is the same as in any other genre: Can your audience follow it and does it help you make your point? Organization patterns are often determined by the subgenre and purpose of an essay. For example, personal essays may rely on chronological narrative patterns as you saw in Beard's "Out There" on page 207. But academic essays or persuasive ones may rely on a claim-evidence pattern or other traditional argumentative forms. For example, Jim Kuerschner's "Big Brother is on the Facebook" is an academic essay, and he uses the claim-evidence pattern to develop his purpose—to present reasons for the popularity of the social network in the context of the culture from which it emerged. After Kuerschner provides some background on Facebook.com, he launches into the controversy that surrounds this social networking tool. Having begun with a quote from a pro-Facebook researcher, Kuerschner follows up quickly with Julia James's differing view about the function and usefulness of Facebook. James's concerns are then quickly addressed with another claim and evidence example—this time from expert Cezary Podkul. In a follow-up claim, Kuerschner points to the popularity of Facebook and provides statistical evidence for his claim that its use is spreading.

WRITING ACTIVITY   Organizing Your Essay

1. **Examine the claims or points you want to make in your essay.** As you look at them, is there an obvious order that they suggest? Does one claim depend on your already having made another one? A good way to start thinking about organization is to group claims together in this way.

2. **Consider your audience.** Are there certain ideas that you need to give readers first in order to prepare them for later ideas? Will your audience be willing to continue reading if you delay some key information?

3. **Consider your purpose.** Is there a central idea or recurring image that you come back to that you can use to guide and orient your readers? An experience or example can often be broken into pieces and then used at various points in an essay. Such an approach builds tension (what's going to happen next?) and may subtly lead readers to your purpose.

4. **Consider your subject.** Does it need to be explored or explained in a particular way in order for your audience to understand it? Does it need to be explored in a way that keeps your reader from reaching the obvious conclusion when you are after one that is more complex?

■ ■ ■

Writing Openings for Essays

Your audience, the subgenre, your subject, and your purpose may all be driving factors in how you open your essay, but in general you can begin an essay any way you want. For instance, Beard's essay "Out There," begins with a detailed description of the scene she finds herself in immediately—driving down the Alabama highway in intense heat. The use of the first person and present tense coupled with thick descriptions puts readers in the car with her and makes them feel the immediacy of the moment.

> It isn't even eight A.M. and I'm hot. My rear end is welded to the seat just like it was yesterday. I'm fifty miles from the motel and about a thousand and a half from home, in a little white Mazda with 140,000 miles on it and no rust. I'm all alone in Alabama, with only a cooler and a tape deck for company. It's already in the high 80s. Yesterday, coming up from the keys through Florida, I had a day-long anxiety attack that I decided last night was really heat prostration. I was a cinder with a brain; I was actually whimpering. I kept thinking I saw alligators at the edge of the highway.

Jim Kuerschner begins his essay in a much different way: He chooses to include the audience directly in the subject by using direct address ("you"). Just as importantly, he narrates an encounter that someone on Facebook might find familiar, but suggests that there is something wrong in the encounter:

> You see him everyday as you cross West Fourth street. You've never spoken to him, but you know his name, his age, major, and relationship status. You've never officially met, but you know what his high school friends look like, how his spring break trip to Cozumel was, and what he looks like while under the influence. Giving him the awkward "I-know-you-but-I-probably-shouldn't-know-*this*-much-about-you-so-I'm-not-sure-if-I-say-hello-or-if-I-just-walk-on-by-and-pretend-to-not-see-you" smile, you continue on your way, wondering if you could have sparked conversation by humming one of his favorite tunes or quoting one of his favorite movies. The tension builds, you cross the street, and nothing happens. Heaving a sigh of relief that you haven't just made a fool of yourself to a complete stranger, you begin to wonder, am I a stalker? No, you reassure yourself, you are simply a member of the Facebook.

Kuerschner will return to this idea throughout the essay, and he will reinforce the problem the encounter suggests in his conclusion. His opening also suggests the controversy surrounding Facebook despite its popularity, part of his purpose for writing the essay. There are many ways to begin an essay, of course, and how you begin will depend on what you want to say, what your subject is, how you want to present yourself as the writer, who you are writing to and so on.

Writing Closings for Essays

Closings can vary, but generally speaking essayists don't try to sum up all their points in the closing paragraphs. There are at least two reasons for this: 1) Essays are generally not long enough to warrant a summary of what was said in the body itself; and 2) since essays are often going after a subtle and complex point, they need to keep exploring the issue, concern, and experience right until the end. Essays, then, are often open-ended.

Often personal essays are probing, and question some thoughts of the writer on a subject or particular experience she's had. For example, here is the closing to Jo Ann Beard's "Out There:"

> As it turned out, my husband couldn't bring himself to leave me when I got back to Iowa, so I waited awhile, and watched, then disentangled myself. History: We each got ten photo albums and six trays of slides. We took a lot of pictures in thirteen years. In the early years he looks stoned and contented, distant; in the later years he looks straight and slightly worried. In that last year he only appears by chance, near the edges, a blur of suffering, almost out of frame.
>
> Just before we split, when we were driving somewhere, I told him about the guy in the green car. "Wow," he said. Then he turned up the radio, checked his image in the rearview mirror, and smiled sincerely at the passing landscape.

Beard chose to close her essay with another anecdote by circling back to the narrative about her failing marriage. The ending does two things for readers: it provides us with insight about the way Beard has changed since the highway incident ("...I waited awhile, and watched, then disentangled myself") and the way her husband has remained the same as before: distant and uncaring. Second, the echo effect in the anecdote emphasizes the significance of Beard's inner thoughts to the purpose of the essay as they are revealed to readers throughout the essay.

Jim Kuerschner, in his essay "Big Brother Is on the Facebook," chose to conclude with a warning—a warning he made throughout the essay. He uses the conclusion to repeat that warning:

> We are being watched and monitored, be it through the Facebook or an ATM, an outdoor surveillance camera, or an e-mail scanning program. Still, we, the people, have freedom. We can knowingly post incriminating pictures on our websites and send furious e-mails about Presidential policy, or we can try to avoid our omnipresent observers. The problem is that our information is out there—a low profile might just mean it takes an extra week to find it.

His conclusion is particularly effective because he names the problem with Facebook which his introduction only alluded to in its narrative of a chance encounter. The connection between introduction and conclusion unifies the essay.

WRITING ACTIVITY   Thinking about Openings and Closings

1. Are you writing about something controversial or uncommon that requires you to win over your readers? Can you reveal something about yourself that establishes your credibility immediately? Can you reveal something at the end that reasserts your credibility?
2. Is there some central, defining metaphor that you can introduce and use to focus and organize your essay? In your conclusion, can you return to a central example, anecdote, or metaphor and use that to get the reader thinking about their own experiences?
3. Would it make sense for you to make your points in the opening paragraphs of your commentary? Or should you comment more fully on your subject in your conclusion, to further complicate a concern, problem, observation, or assumption? Perhaps pose a question?
4. Does your writing situation require a formal introduction where the problem is introduced and a thesis is provided, or a formal conclusion where you restate your argument and conclusion?

■ ■ ■

Revising Essays

A critical component of the essay is the commentary where a writer suggests that the subject reveals something important to us, something we might otherwise not see. To put it another way, the commentary is the "so what?" of essays. Since this is such an important component of essays, it is the focus both of a writer's revision and the feedback they receive from readers.

The "So What?" Reaction from Readers: Further Developing and Refining Your Commentary

In her essay, Mariah Leavitt, a student in a first-year writing course, explored the importance of her grandfather's death and how she ultimately decided that it was a good thing that he died since it relieved him of the pain he was suffering and released the family from distress. In this paragraph she explores the way we commonly think about the death of a loved one and how her grandfather's death allowed her to think about it differently:

> When it comes to death, we are selfish. In the hours and days after a death, we yearn for our loved one to be back with us, instead of celebrating their life. Most people see death as their prison cell; I see it as our key. To me, my grandfather's death was his relief, relieving him from the pain he felt everyday, relieving us of the challenges of his life. He was a man so full of life, but so unable to live his life to the potential he wanted. His many heart and lung problems limited his abilities, and his strained relationships with his children limited his emotions. This made him angry at the world, and to most he was just a crabby, stubborn, angry old man. It sounds so horrible to say his death was a relief, because our society sees that as insensitive, as a sign that we are unable to cope. But how can I regret his death? How can I see it as a bad thing?

Notice the hesitancy in her commentary; she seems at once sure of herself—"my grandfather's death was a relief"—but also hesitant when she asks those concluding questions, suggesting that at least part of her is still unsure. Her hesitancy suggests the focus, or point, of her essay: that the way we deal with such moments in our lives is often much more complicated, much more messy than most people admit. Leavitt had to think hard about her own feelings and the normal view of grieving in order to suggest that grieving can, all at once, be about loss, relief, and even happiness that that person has passed on.

WRITING ACTIVITY   Developing Your Commentary

Read the parts of your essay where you've provided commentary, the parts where you begin to look at your subject or experience critically. Consider the following:

1. Have you asked readers to think or feel about the subject in ways that might challenge how they do so ordinarily?
2. Are there ways you can probe their thoughts and yours on the subject even further? Perhaps ask some poignant questions, even ones that may make them or you feel uncomfortable?
3. Are there any further questions you can pose or comments you can add that may extend your insights more critically or perhaps even lead to some conclusions?

▪ ▪ ▪

PEER REVIEW   for Essays

As you read, comment as fully as you can by giving specific and suggestive feedback. Be sure to explain your comments: e.g. "This is well written, because you provide lots of rich details."

Comment in the margins using the following questions as a guide:

READ THE TITLE: What, if anything, does it reveal about the essay? From it, can you predict what the writer might be saying?

READ THE OPENING: How does the writer **engage the reader**? Are you given enough detail, or do you think more should be given? Does the essay resonate with

(continued)

you? Why or why not? Suggest ways for the writer to heighten reader interest or tension.

READ THE REST OF THE ESSAY: Focus on how the writer **develops the commentary.** Pay attention to where the writer comments on or draws conclusions about the subject of the essay, and then offer suggestions on how to deepen the commentary. Is more explanation needed? Would research of some sort help? Does the writer need to better prepare the reader for the commentary?

Finally, when you have finished reading and annotating, write an endnote to the writer in which you comment on the following:

Begin by telling the writer what you enjoyed about the letter (be specific).

ENGAGING THE AUDIENCE: How does the writer engage the reader? Does the material in the introduction get referred to later on?

ESTABLISHING A PURPOSE: Does the writer provide and develop examples that illustrate the purpose throughout the essay? Are vivid details used? Comparison/contrast examples?

EVALUATING THE WRITER'S COMMENTARY: Does the writer adequately explore the importance of the experience or observation being commented upon? Is the writer connecting the event or observation to a broader social experience?

As a reader, do you feel that you have been asked to think differently about the subject? How so? If they haven't, help the writer to do so by offering your thoughts on the subject.

Reflecting on the Process

WRITING ACTIVITY   Reflecting on Writing an Essay

Reflect on the writing process you followed to develop your essay—how you generated ideas and chose one, did research, and drafted and revised your essay.

Imagine you are addressing writers who have never written an essay of this kind. What might they learn about working within the genre from you? What could you tell them that might help them as writers?

1. *Begin* by describing what aspects of your essay you are most pleased with.
2. *Analyze* your strengths and weaknesses as an essay writer.
3. *Explain* what you think contributed to your success in these areas.
4. *Reflect* on how you determined your purpose and audience for your essay. How did these elements influence your choice of material, details, and research?
5. *Discuss* your revision process, including how you used feedback from your readers. What kinds of revisions did you make to ensure that your commentary in the essay was clear to readers?
6. *Conclude* by reflecting on what you learned about the genre of the essay. You might also reflect on what you might do differently the next time you write an essay.

■ ■ ■

Colin Keane's Personal Essay

Colin Keane, a student in a first-year writing course, wrote a personal essay about his experiences growing up in a small town and watching it grow into a busy, and sometimes unrecognizable town. In this section, we show you some of the thinking and writing processes that led up to the final draft of his essay.

Generating Ideas for the Personal Essay: Starting with What You Know

As Keane thought about ideas, he started with subjects that were important and meaningful to him. As you read his topic ideas, you'll notice how different they are, and how they could become very different kinds of personal essays. You'll also see that even this early on, he is thinking about his audience and purpose for writing.

As Keane is considering topic ideas, he is already thinking about the larger issue. His thoughts on the larger issue could become the basis for his commentary on his own experiences.

Essays often allow writers to "think big" and make connections between local and global concerns, but the proposed topic may be a bit too big for a personal essay.

Or essays might help those who haven't had a similar experience to learn about how people in other geographical locations live and what concerns they have.

Essays often comment on changes writers observe in the world around them.

Colin Keane

Ideas for the Personal Essay

<u>Possible Topic One:</u> One of the topics I wish to talk about is my last lacrosse game in high school. This is a feeling that many people get. When you know that something you love is about to end, you don't want to leave. During my last lacrosse game, I played differently; I seemed to try harder, and I felt like I was trying to slow everything down, and really pay attention to what was going on.

This subject is of interest to me, because I feel like it's a common experience. The audience would be anyone, really, but maybe mostly those who have recently graduated or are even about to.

<u>Possible Topic Two:</u> My second topic is going to be my town. I grew up in a farm town where we had, literally, fields and cows—we were even known for having more cows than people about 15 years ago. Over the last few years my town has grown, and now we have fast food restaurants everywhere. This is a problem, because it takes away from the kind of town we have always been; and it's also a problem of global warming, which I have been reading a lot about in my other classes.

The audience for this topic would be broad. Not just people from small towns but also those who grew up in the city—they might say "I have never experienced this, but it is interesting." Overdevelopment is a big part of the global warming problem, and every time I go home I see a new development or something going in. I'm seeing firsthand how this development hurts small towns.

Thinking about Audience, Purpose, and Situation

Keane chose to write about his hometown and global warming in part because the development in his town really bothered him and because he was worried that an essay about the lacrosse game would sound like just another sports piece. Once Keane had chosen his subject, he began to define the rhetorical situation. Notice that as he does so, he begins to articulate some of the claims that will later find their way into his essay.

Colin Keane

Defining the Rhetorical Situation for My Essay

Audience: The audience for my paper is kind of hard to define—I guess anyone can be interested in the changes of a small town. Maybe it is really those who have seen something similar happening in their own town; overdevelopment is everywhere these days. Some people don't want development in their towns, but others want more— so maybe this is for those two audiences?

Purpose: I want to show people what it is like to live in a small town that is going through some drastic changes because of development. It's going to reach out to others who live in towns going through similar changes.

Writer: I'm going to present myself as someone who has seen his town change for the worse; my personal experiences, and maybe those of my family and friends, will help readers see how the town has changed. Since I have lived in larger towns and cities, I can use that experience to show I know more than just where I grew up.

Tone: A little bit of humor would work well. No one wants to read about some guy complaining all the time. I will be reserved and let people who want to listen, listen. I don't want to be preachy. I will also take an informal tone, because that's what it is like to live in small town—everyone knows everyone else, and I want my readers to see that.

Larger Context: I chose to write about this situation because it is something that has happened recently, and is happening everywhere. The fact that everyone I talk to in my town doesn't like what is happening makes me wonder why it has to happen in the first place.

Here it seems the writer wants to write to an audience who is already familiar with the subject and the problems involved. What would he not need to include in that case?

The writer's thoughts on how he can use other experiences he's had makes the subject seem more significant, more inclusive.

The purpose of essays may be to challenge what we think we know, but often we come to find out as we explore a subject that what we think we know is not exactly so.

Drafting: Researching Experiences and Connecting to the Larger Issue

Before he drafted his essay, Keane first needed to articulate what he already knew about his subject and what he needed to find out. This step was especially important for Keane because he was writing about a subject that is also a national problem.

Colin Keane

Researching My Experiences

Tapping the Familiar: I know that developers are replacing farmland with housing developments. They are putting in fast food restaurants and new stores that are not needed. My town is growing, and has way too many people now. I know that the town just finished redoing my high school, and now they are talking about needing to build a new one in ten years because the population is growing.

What I Need to Research: I don't know a lot of the facts—like how many developments, how much growth, what's coming up, and so on. I don't know how these things have happened in other towns, or what has been done to stop it. I know how it affects my town, but I don't know how it actually changes the way the town works or feels. These are areas I think I need to research.

While these are brief entries, they give Keane a sense of the range of material he could write about. He does not address all of these in his final essay.

Personal essays depend on personal experience and observation, but they also make use of more formal kinds of research, including field research.

One of the problems Keane faced as he wrote his essay stemmed from his initial understanding of his subject. He wanted to write about his town in relation to the larger concern of global warming, which he had been studying, but he wasn't sure how to connect the issues in his paper. So his initial draft was very hesitant and unfocused—and almost two papers.

Colin Keane
Professor Ferruci
English 100P
6 Apr. 2010

Draft 1
Change in a Small Town

Growing up in a small farm town is something that many people do not get to experience anymore. I grew up in a town where I knew everyone in school since preschool, where you could drive down the road and know who was driving in half the cars you passed by. It was a town where there were farms everywhere, and it was normal to see someone driving a truck with a cowboy hat on. We all went to the same party after graduation; we tore down a circle in a cornfield, and had a party there and the farmer who owned the land was fine with it.

The town that I grew up in is called Ellington, where fifteen years ago we were known for having more cows than people in our town. Although

In his first line, Keane introduces the major idea in his essay, and in doing so signals to the reader what the point of his essay will be.

Such details are important for personal essays, but notice that these are rather vague.

throughout the last five years we have undergone a lot of construction that is taking away from the old hometown that I grew up in. In my town there were four gas stations, two small car dealerships, a post office, country breakfast diner, a small grocery store, and a few pizza shops, and that's about it. Recently, farmers have been losing their farms because they were having trouble paying off the expense, and so they sold their land to developers. Many of the fields that I was used to seeing are now housing developments. Two years ago we had our first big change when a national grocery chain moved in—the Big Y. It was the talk of the town, and no one wanted the Big Y to come because we had our small grocery store that everyone had been using for years; Big Y ended up buying and closing it down. A year after the Big Y came, we got a McDonald's which again no one wanted, and now there is talk of a Wal-Mart trying to buy a field just outside town. One of the big controversies dealing with more growth is global warming, which is happening because of the higher CO_2 released by more and more cars and more construction. What about you, though, are you willing to risk global warming for a fast food restaurant two minutes away instead of fifteen? These changes have erased the feeling we once had in our town, and it's something that has happened everywhere, not just my town.

I have noticed that nearly every town I drive into, I can find a McDonald's and probably many other fast food restaurants. I used to ride my dirt bike with my buddies around my town, going from field to field and crossing maybe four roads. Now it seems like we can't go anywhere without being on someone's front lawn.

The development that has gone on the past five or so years has increased at an incredible rate. New York City grew at a rate of 1,000,000 people between July 1, 2003 and July 1, 2004 and that was four years ago now. Many people who grew up in my town and wanted to start their own family came back to Ellington to raise their own children in the same environment. Ever since I was young, I remember how much of a pain it was to get stuck behind a John Deere tractor going 10 mph on the road for a few miles. Every spring, I would wait at the bus stop and have cow corn debris fall out of the trucks going by. My senior year in high school, the trucks had disappeared and fewer and fewer tractors were seen.

The fact that my town is growing and I am upset about it is not the real issue right now. The real issue is that the population growth is demanding more homes, which in turn accounts for more natural resources being used. Our forests are becoming depleted, not to mention all the pollution that has been caused. Al Gore's video *An Inconvenient Truth* says that if we don't stop polluting that our earth could reach devastation in 50 years. He talks about how we have the choice to change the way we live. The US has the highest CO_2 emissions in the world, at over 30%, and we have to be the ones to change considering we have made this a major problem. The information he

We better understand the subject Keane is writing about, but here is where the connection between overdevelopment in his town and global warming becomes unclear.

Because personal essays need to resonate with readers who have not had the same experiences as the writer, Keane knows that he needs to talk about more than his experiences. Here he attempts to do so by acknowledging that overdevelopment is not just a problem in his town.

Here, again, Keane provides us with important details, and a nice story about what it's like to live in his town or at least what it was like before the developers moved in.

Keane comments on his experiences and how others might relate to them, and he is trying to use the information from Gore's film to tie those experiences to the larger significance of his essay.

talks about really became reality when I thought about what was happening in my town. The McDonald's in my town is only fifteen minutes away from another McDonald's in any direction you drive. There was no need for that restaurant. If you go back to your hometown, you will see considerable change from when you were a child. The small changes in my town may not seem bad to anyone not living there, but small changes in a lot of towns turn into a big deal.

Revising: Focusing on the Subject, Emphasizing Commentary

For his second draft, Keane refocused his essay primarily on his experiences of growing up in a small town and the negative effects brought about by what he calls development. He is also trying to work on the **commentary**—how his personal experiences connect to a larger issue or concern for readers: the vanishing small towns of America. In the excerpt below, you can see from his reviewers' comments that his two initial focuses, his small town and global warming, are still creating a confusing essay.

Colin Keane
Professor Ferruci
English 100P
6 Apr. 2010

Draft 2 Peer Review
Big Change in a Small Town: A Personal Essay

Growing up in a small farm town is something that many people do not get to experience anymore. I grew up in a town where I knew everyone I went to school with since preschool, where you knew who drove every single car in the parking lot, including the teachers. Every year, we all went to the same graduation party; we would tear down a circle in the middle of a cornfield, and have a party there and the farmer who owned the land would be fine with it. The town that I grew up in is called Ellington, where fifteen years ago we were known for having more cows than people in our town. Throughout the last five years we have undergone a lot of construction that is taking away from the old hometown that my friends and I grew up in. Construction in small towns is not all that uncommon anymore, but it still has an impact almost everywhere.

In my town there were four gas stations, two small car dealerships, Lee's Auto Ranch and Bolles Motors, a post office, a country diner called The Chuck Wagon, the only place in town to eat-in, Ellington Supermarket, and Hometown Pizza and Holiday Pizza.

Reviewer 1: I like the details you give here. They help me see the place. I know personal essays don't have to have thesis statements, but since you have one, can you make it more direct? More meaningful?

Reviewer 2: Can you elaborate on this? I would like a little more detail about these places.

Reviewer 2: Why are you writing about NYC? Can you include statistics about Ellington instead?

I like this story!

> The development that has gone on the past five or so years has increased at an incredible rate. New York City grew at a rate of 1,000,000 people between July 1, 2003 and July 1, 2004 and was four years ago now. Many people who grew up in my town and wanted to start their own family came back to Ellington to raise their own children in the same environment. I remember how much of a pain it was to get stuck behind a John Deere tractor going 10 mph on the road for a few miles. Every spring, I would wait at the bus stop and have cow corn debris fall out of the trucks going by. My senior year, the trucks had disappeared and fewer tractors were seen.

In making his revisions, Keane considered not only the suggestions he was given but his own sense of his purpose and audience. Here is an excerpt:

Keane completely rewrites this section, recognizing from his reviewer's comment that it has nothing to do with his subject. The new material makes much more sense and gives readers an "official" version of how the town has grown.

> Colin Keane
>
> Revisions from Peer Review Draft
>
> The development that has gone on the past five or so years has increased at an incredible rate. ~~New York City grew at a rate of 1,000,000 people between July 1, 2003 and July 1, 2004 and was four years ago now. Many people who grew up in my town and wanted to start their own family came back to Ellington to raise their own children in the same environment. Ever since I was young, I remember how much of a pain it was to get stuck behind a John Deere tractor going 10mph on the road for a few miles. Every spring, I would wait at the bus stop and have cow corn debris fall out of the trucks going by. My senior year in high school, the trucks had disappeared and fewer and fewer tractors were seen.~~ <u>Between 1990 and 2000, Ellington added 1700 people to its population, but in the next six years between 2000 and 2006, it has increased already 1400 people according to the U.S. Census Bureau. The past two years we have had the most construction, so from 2006–2008, I expect another gigantic population increase. I have seen the end result of growth in neighboring towns and how populated they have become. There is more traffic on the streets day and night, people hanging around on the side of streets, and even higher crime rates.</u> `[I realized that NY has nothing to do with what I am writing, so I provided details about Ellington.]`

Colin Keane (student): Big Change in a Small Town: A Personal Essay (Final Draft)

Colin Keane
Professor Ferruci
English100P
12 Apr. 2010

Big Change in a Small Town: A Personal Essay

Growing up in a small farm town is something few people experience anymore. I grew up in a town where I graduated with the same kids I started preschool with, where you could identify the owner of every car in the high school parking lot, including most of the teachers' cars. Every year, we all went to the same graduation party; we would tear down a circle in the middle of a cornfield and have a party there and the farmer who owned the land would be fine with it. The town that I grew up in is called Ellington, a town of 13,000 residents, where fifteen years ago we were known for having more cows than people in our town. But over the last five years development and construction has been taking away from the old hometown that my friends and I grew up in. Construction in small towns is not all that uncommon anymore, but it still has an impact almost everywhere.

In my town there were four gas stations, two small car dealerships, Lee's Auto Ranch and Bolles Motors, a post office, a small mart called Ibeez, Ellington Supermarket, the only places to eat, a country diner called The Chuck Wagon, commonly referred to as The Chuck, and Hometown Pizza and Holiday Pizza. The Chuck, the post office, and Ibeez were all in the same small plaza, and my friends and I would always go there to meet up before we went anywhere or just to hang out.

Historically, much of the land in Ellington has been used for farming; the land has been locally owned and in use for as long as I can remember. But recently, farmers have lost their property because they were having trouble paying off the expenses on it, so they sold their farms to construction companies. Many of the fields I used to see are now housing developments. We had our first big change when a national grocery chain moved in—the Big

The writer hints at the problem he sees that affects not only small towns but other places as well.

Notice the use of details—names of places and nicknames—which make readers think of their own towns or neighborhoods. These were added upon the recommendation of one of his readers.

Y. It was the talk of the town, and no one wanted the Big Y to come because we had our small grocery store that everyone had been using for years; Big Y ended up buying that store and closing it down. A year ago, we got a McDonald's which, again, no one wanted, and now there is talk of a Wal-Mart trying to buy a field just outside town. These changes have erased the feeling we once had in our town, and it's something that has happened everywhere, not just my town.

The example illustrates the problem he introduces above with clarity and specificity.

Students who graduated from Ellington High School in 2005 put together a video of what was going on in our town and played it at our high school auditorium. The movie was based on our Ellington Supermarket and how the Big Y bought it and closed it down. All the students in the movie were workers at our local supermarket and were upset about what was going on. They showed how they were working, their reactions to the news that Big Y was buying the market, and what they tried to do to stop it. It didn't make a difference—Big Y still came.

The writer uses some specific examples of how the changes in landscape have affected residents for the worse, thereby supporting his claim and his purpose for writing.

I have noticed that in nearly every town I drive into, I can find a McDonald's, some big name grocery store such as Stop& Shop or Shaw's, and probably at least one or two other fast food restaurants. I used to ride my dirt bike with my buddies around my entire town, going from field to field, and crossing over maybe four roads. Now it seems like we can't go anywhere without being on someone's front lawn. I used to have a feeling of exuberance when I started my bike up, but now I don't even want to start it up anymore because I know I can barely ride it anywhere. The biggest changes I notice are when I go home from college during breaks; I'm amazed at how different my town looks. I went back over winter vacation and a new development had already gone up, and some houses were already occupied.

This paragraph uses some formal research to lead into an informal example from Keane's personal experience with rapid growth and development.

The development that has taken place over the past five years or so has increased at an incredible rate. According to the U.S. Census Bureau, between 1990 and 2000, Ellington added 1700 people, but in the next six years, between 2000 and 2006, it has already increased by 1400 people. Ellington's population is probably still on the rise. I have seen the end result of growth in neighboring towns and how populated they have become. There is more

The farming reference, appropriate to Keane's town's makeup, is recurrent throughout his essay.

traffic on the streets, day and night, people hanging around on streets at all times, and even higher crime rates. My mom grew up in Ellington and said that when she was growing up the neighboring towns were already beginning to grow rapidly. Ellington was one of the few left, so although other towns are still growing, it may not be as big a deal because they have been developed for a while. But mine has just begun. Many people who grew up in my town and wanted to start their own family came back to Ellington to raise their own children in the same environment, but doing so has increased the problem.

Ever since I was young, I remember how much of a pain it was to get stuck behind a John Deere tractor going 10 miles per hour. Every spring I would wait at the bus stop and have to dodge the cow-corn debris flying out of the trucks going by. My senior year in high school, many of the trucks disappeared, and fewer and fewer tractors were seen. Now in parts of Ellington, we are stuck in traffic jams at intersections, instead of being stuck behind a tractor. It seems somehow better to be stuck behind a tractor, though at the time I didn't think so. You can get stuck in traffic anywhere, at least I know that a tractor has a purpose, that the farmer is working to get things done. The people in the cars might be heading to McDonald's or the Big Y.

The writer suggests in his commentary here the ways we are all affected by what he sees as "meaningless" development using contrasts: tractor traffic versus fast food or big box traffic.

Anyone thinking back on the town they grew up in will see a different town than what they remember. It's a fact of life. I'll be moving to South Carolina soon. And when I come back in a few years I wonder what will have happened to the town I grew up in. I want to see how many fast food restaurants and new developments there are. I wonder if I'll recognize it, or want to live in Ellington at all. But in fairy tales, there is always a happy ending, and I'm hoping for the same.

Questions for Discussion

1. How does Keane help readers to understand the larger significance of his essay? What kinds of commentary does he provide to do so?
2. What kinds of research did Keane use and what purpose does it serve? Does the research make sense given the subject and the subgenre of Keane's essay?
3. What kinds of organization strategies does Keane use and why?

Reflecting on the Process

Here is an excerpt from Keane's reflection on writing the essay.

> Throughout the writing of this essay, I thought about what I had lived through and what meant the most to me, and I came up with this topic about my town. It was not too hard to find ideas, but it was hard to put them into a form for the essay.
>
> I'm glad I decided not to write about global warming, and I was really happy with the way I got my point across about how the changes in my town have been pretty negative. I liked where I described the town itself, and places that have always been a part of the town, places that make the town what it is.
>
> Most of the comments from my peers were about clarifying my ideas. Neither of them was from a small town, so that helped me see how others would read my essay. One comment made about not understanding the point of the essay helped me think about the problem from the perspective of those outside my town. Another comment gave me the idea to name some specific places in my town, to help readers see what was lost when the "big boxes" moved in.
>
> The personal essay is more than just about personal stuff. It can be about anything, but there has to be a point. I probably should have done more research, especially about other towns and the effects of development across America; it would have made my essay stronger, and would have connected with my audience better. I think the personal essay needs that, otherwise it's like a journal entry.

WRITING ACTIVITY Evaluating One Writer's Journey

Review Colin Keane's process for writing his essay. How would you evaluate the choices he made as he wrote? Are there places where you think he could have made different choices, and how would those choices have affected the final essay? What further revisions, if any, do you think the final essay could use?

■ ■ ■

T R A N S F O R M A T I O N S

GENRE BLURRING: The Photographic Essay

Writers sometimes blur genres when they find themselves in situations where their subject, purpose, and audience do not suggest an obvious genre, or when the genre they selected forces them to leave something important out.

An example of the latter case is when a subject needs to be shown, literally. Perhaps an essayist considering Hurricane Katrina as a subject might look around and see images that would be more powerfully portrayed in photographs. This essayist, then, might choose to write a photographic essay—an essay in which photographs are intimately, though not always directly, connected to the writer's prose. Photographic essays can also foreground the photographs, letting them tell the story while the prose takes a backseat to the visuals. When the photographs deepen the purpose of the essay, when they move readers to feel or think the way the essayist intends in order to fulfill the purpose, then the photographic essay has been effective.

WebLinks
Photo Essays on the Web

Project Muse and *Academic Search Premier,* both databases, collect material from creative writing, popular, and scholarly magazines and journals. If your library subscribes to them, do a search on "Photographic Essays" to see the range of possibilities this blurred genre offers.

Time magazine's online edition has a recurring section on "Photo Essays." Go to Time.com and click on the "Photos" tab to view them.

Shaun O'Boyle has been taking pictures of and writing photographic essays about decrepit buildings since the 1980s. Enter "Shaun O'Boyle and Modern Ruins" into a search engine to find his website.

Genre Blurring Writing Assignment

The Photographic Essay

Write a photographic essay on a subject (a place, a person, or an idea) of your choice.

Remember the essay should have some larger insights or commentary that will resonate with your intended audience and emphasize your purpose for writing. Photographs can be read in many ways, and the lens through which readers understand the purpose of your photographic essay is subjective, so you'll need to guide their reading of your essay.

You can work with photographs you have already taken or you can take new photographs that reflect and represent the central idea you are emphasizing in your essay. The number and kind of photographs you choose will depend on your subject and purpose for writing. If you use a single photograph or a series of photos, think about how they convey the central idea you are writing about. Please see Chapter 4 for a discussion of incorporating visuals in your writing.

Michael Coles, "Smash Palace—Model Four Hundred"

Michael Coles is a writer and photographer based in Montana. His work appears in magazines and newspapers, and his photoessay "Rumor from Monrovia" appeared in the nonfiction literary magazine *Fourth Genre*. The following photoessay was also published in *Fourth Genre*. To see more of his work, search for "Michael Coles and Photography" or go to his website at www.mcolesphoto.com.

My eyes get lost in a matrix of muscular hips and curvature while wandering through cemetery-like rows of timepieces. Model As and Model Ts lean and crumble on one another. Wooden spokes pop out of rusted rims. I am immersed in a stew of throwaways—Mercury Montclair, Pinto Runabout, Plymouth Cambridge, a blown out lawnmower, a broken washer, and a chunk of firewood.

Jackrabbit bounces down a line of fenders as mountain air wisps through overgrown grass on this hillside outside Butte, Montana. Entire spans of American automobile-making in this graveyard are enough to induce a nomadic trance. Yet, amidst this jumble, one particular artifact emits sparks more than others. It seduces the lens of a camera.

"No drama, take it for what it is—just another beater," I say to myself.

But I remain transfixed by this still machine. Its very sight seems a coronation of a smash palace.

"Packard 54–55?" (a speculation of the car's exact year) is scrawled beneath a back windshield rippling in cracked spider-web patterns. A hip of the car reads "Model Four Hundred." Tires are heaped on top of the hood, and typography is bleached out by years of cold rain and snow. An array of scratches and assorted dents are embedded in blotches of faded color. Bruises and slights absorbed over time start to add up and mesmerize.

Packard's advertising slogan once rang, "ASK THE MAN WHO OWNS ONE." Czars, rajahs, kings, and presidents rode in Packards. Milt Taylor, a star clown for Ringling Bros. and Barnum & Bailey Circus, drove a special edition. Poncho Villa was a Packard customer. According to Packard lore, Czar Nicholas drove a Twin Six with its front wheels substituted by skis. Perhaps a gangster out of Dashiell Hammett's Red Harvest drove this Model Four Hundred down Mercury Street in Butte.

I gaze at the silver winged-bird hood ornament. Down below, an emblem remains lodged in the radiator grill, displaying a coat of arms originating from the old English Packard family who came to America in 1638. This coat of arms has been described as "gules, a cross lozengy between four roses argent" and "a pelican in her piety, pricking blood from her breast to feed her young."

Back in a dark room I gently roll a 48-ounce film canister half-full of developer on a countertop. One reel of Kodak Techpan film is suspended in

[Margin notes:]

The writer begins with his perceptions, but does not tell the reader what he will be writing about; the writer has assumed that the audience will accept uncertainty about the content.

We now know where the writer is and why he is there.

Details about the car he is photographing. Are those adequately reinforced in the actual photo?

Notice how the details the writer observes become an occasion for discussing the history of the car and the company that built it. The photograph—the subject of this essay—takes the writer and the reader beyond what is shown in the photograph.

The writer uses the developing processes as a "vehicle" for returning to the junkyard to reflect and comment on the experience, and to invoke other writers: Wallace Stegner was a writer who captured the struggles of Western life in ways few others have.

the center between empty reels on either side serving as spacers. Kodak Tech-pan has recently been discontinued. I guess there is not enough interest for slow-speed, fine-grain emulsions in a digital age. A radio plays music as I hope something might come out of these frames I am developing.

Staring through a film loupe at negatives, I return to this auto bone-yard. The city of Butte lies across Interstate 90 from this quiet hillside of swaying grass. Mining escarpments hover in the distance, resembling a lunarscape. Wallace Stegner once described the town dump of his child-hood as a "kitchen midden of civilization." This field of cars seems such a stowaway.

My eyes become locked in the passageway of the loupe and the mind revisits. Thrusts, juts, and sharp corners of these cars offer a cubist smorgas-bord. How does one make sense of all the names and shapes, the strange memories that they can trigger? "We learn to see before we talk or write," I tell myself.

Junkyards can serve as wellsprings for unremembered pasts. "America, that surreal country, is full of found objects. Our junk has become art. Our junk has become history," the critic Susan Sontag proclaimed.

Photography is often a solitary effort. If I do not photograph alone, I will not arrive at certain places or follow hunches that lead to immersion in a par-ticular environment. Images turn out different when I am shooting alongside other photographers. And so I stand awestruck on an October afternoon, my eyes sparked by generations of twisted, mangled, and smashed automotives—an affirmation of our relentless determination to replace, rebuild, and regen-erate: to find, then to declare ourselves through metal become our displayed flesh.

Here the writer begins to comment on his reasons for taking such photographs, and he suggests that it is less about telling a new story than about reviving an old one.

Shiny immaculate Packards still ride our roads. No doubt, car collectors constantly salvage, maintain, and renew autos. Perhaps such an owner would find it strange for a photographer to be so taken with this automobile graveyard and prepossessing of me to regard a beat-up Model Four Hundred as part of an unremembered past. What would the car owners and spectators at a ritzy Pebble Beach car show think? Probably the picture taker would get laughed into the ocean.

Photographers often attempt to trace the real, even revel in historical detritus or idle in derelict corners that seem unlikely places to pay a visit. After time spent poking around these auto yard premises, I felt like I had been told a story that germinated a tune planted long ago in my head. So much momentum and style loaded into the front of one car—something from another planet; and so much of America there—all those needs fulfilled, those ambitions, dreams, and hopes given expression through cars once proudly purchased, and now discarded here for a viewer to contemplate and for the unforgiving landscape to claim as its own.

Reading for Comprehension

1. Why does Coles say he wants to photograph the Packard Model Four Hundred?
2. What does Coles want readers to think about when he quotes Susan Sontag as saying "America, that surreal country, is full of found objects. Our junk has become art. Our junk has become history"?
3. Why is the title of the essay appropriate given the way Coles writes about both the Packard and junk cars in general?

Analyzing the Genre

1. How closely tied to the text is the actual photograph of the Packard 54–55? Is the photograph primarily descriptive or does it add something to the essay that goes beyond description?
2. Toward the end of the essay, Coles steps out of his discussion of the photograph to write about himself as a photographer and of the solitary nature of taking photographs. Why does he do so? How does that aside connect with his discussion of the Packard?

CHAPTER 8

Memoirs

Memoirs are written from vivid memories, the ones that have stuck with us over the years. And from these memories, our stories emerge. Simply, we have these memories because the events that create them are meaningful to us in some way. It takes some work, however, to unearth that meaning—we have to dig around, think it over, write about it first to figure out why it's meaningful, not only for us, the writers, but for our readers as well.

What Is a Memoir?

A **memoir** is personal writing based on *real* events, memories, and experiences from a writer's past. Unlike autobiography, a similar genre which recounts the story of an individual's entire life (or at least a significant portion of it), a memoir captures a snapshot of one episode or related episodes which left a vivid impression on the writer. The writer in turn describes those episodes vividly in sensory and concrete detail to bring them to life for readers.

Memoirists unearth these memories in order *to make sense of the world around them*. Memoir is *subjective*. It's told from the perspective of the writer who experienced the event—the truth as they recall it. And while a memoir may be about very intimate events from a person's life, the writer hopes it will ring true for readers as they become engaged in the stories she has built from her memories.

Because the memoirist deals only in small, particular moments, the challenge for the writer is to craft the memoir in such a way that readers understand its *significance* in their lives—that something about the experience *resonates* for the readers. Perhaps it is an idea. Or a feeling. While memoir writers say to readers "this happened to me," they also offer readers ways to understand why "this may be important to you, too."

The Purposes of Memoirs

Most memoirists write with readers in mind, inviting them into their stories with the hope of making connections with others. Memoirists try to engage readers in their experiences to explore how they have some larger significance that relates to readers' lives. Memoirists have many purposes for writing about their lives: some take ordinary life experiences and use them to understand themselves better in relation to others; others use memoir to reflect on and make sense of culturally important experiences; and some writers choose memoir as a way to offer different versions of historical events.

When a memoirist recalls the past, she does so in the hopes of gaining new insights about the present. Looking back on the past from a present moment, or *reflection,* allows the writer to ruminate on some larger truth the memory may have to offer. For example, in Chimamanda Ngozi Adichie's memoir "Real Food" in this chapter, she takes a childhood memory about eating a traditional Nigerian food and turns it into a reflection on conflicted feelings she has about cultural identity and the importance of family ties.

As you read this chapter, you'll notice the variety of memoirs and purposes for writing them. However, they have one thing in common—making a human connection with readers and helping them relate the significance of the memoir to their own lives.

Reading Memoirs Critically

Writing memoirs that readers can relate to, ones that allow them to see the larger significance of the memory and connect it to their own lives, involves a strong understanding of how memoirs work. Reading memoirs critically, like a writer, may help you understand some of the choices other memoirists make and why they make them, as well as some of the characteristics of memoirs, which in turn, may help you write memoirs that resonate with your audience and fulfill your purpose.

WRITING ACTIVITY   Analyzing the Genre of Memoirs

Thinking about the Genre

Think about what might make you want to write a memoir. What aspects of your personal past experiences might be significant to the lives of others? What situations might you find yourself in that make you choose to write about and reflect on those experiences?

Examining the Genre

As you read some memoirs, focus on the following:

1. What kinds of openings do you notice in the memoirs? How do they make you want to keep reading?
2. How does the writer use vivid descriptions and details? What about them stands out to you?
3. How is the memoir arranged? What kinds of organization strategies are used, and to what effect, on the reader?

5. What is the writer's purpose for writing? Are there places where the writer's purpose becomes clearer to you?

6. How does the memoir appeal to or invoke the audience? How does the memoir resonate for you as a reader? What larger significance does the writer reflect on to make a connection with readers?

Reflecting on the Genre

After you have read the memoirs explain in a couple of paragraphs the major characteristics of the genre as you understand it. Give examples, refer to specific passages, and quote when necessary. This exercise will help you identify the structures and choices memoir writers make that you might want to try yourself.

■ ■ ■

Genre Analysis: Chimamanda Ngozi Adichie, "Real Food"

Chimamanda Ngozi Adichie is an award-winning fiction and nonfiction writer whose novels include *Purple Hibiscus* and *Half of a Yellow Sun*. In "Real Food," which appeared in the September 3, 2007, issue of The New Yorker, Adichie reflects on a childhood experience in which a traditional Nigerian food, garri, influences her relationships with her family and her cultural identity. More information about Adichie and her writing can be found on her website.

I like how she tells us immediately when this is, and where it is.

I don't really know what garri is, but from the writer's descriptions, I can gather what the food is like and how it is eaten.

I was nine years old, sitting stiffly at the dining table in my blue-and-white school uniform, and across from me sat my mother, who had come home from work at the university registry, elegant in her swishy skirt, smelling of Poison perfume and saying she wanted to watch me eat. I still do not know who told her that I was skipping lunch before school. Perhaps it was the houseboy, Fide. Perhaps it was my little brother Kenechukwu, who went to school in the morning and came home just before I left. The firm set of her mouth told me that I had no choice but to eat the *garri* and soup placed on the table. I made the sign of the cross. I plucked a morsel from the soft lump of *garri*. I lightly molded it with my fingers. I dipped it into the soup. I swallowed. My throat itched. I disliked all the variants of this quintessential Nigerian food, whether made from corn, cassava, or yams, whether cooked or stirred or pounded in a mortar until they became a soft mash. It was jokingly called "swallow," because one swallowed the morsels without chewing; it was easy to tell that a person chewing *garri* was a foreigner.

I like the use of
dialogue here.

Must be kind of hard
not to like any of the
foods.

She seems to have an
easygoing, loving
relationship with
her family from this
dialogue.

She's moving around in
time here, and the
descriptions that follow
show us the relation-
ship she has with her
family.

Seems like she is trying
to make sense of her
dislike of garri here. Her
reflection.

We are at a later point
in time in the narra-
tor's life and she's got
another story that
shows how garri con-
nects to her cultural
identity.

"Hurry up," my mother said. "You will be late for school." We had *garri* for lunch every day except Sunday, when we had rice and stew and sometimes a lush salad that contained everything from baked beans to boiled eggs and was served with dollops of creamy dressing. The soups gave some variety to lunch: the yellowish *egusi,* made of ground melon seeds and vegetables; *onugbu,* rich with dark-green bitterleaf; *okro,* with its sticky sauce; *nsala,* with beef chunks floating in a thin herb-filled broth. I disliked them all.

That afternoon, it was *egusi* soup. My mother's eyes were steady behind her glasses. "Are you playing with that food or eating it?" she asked. I said I was eating. Finally, I finished and said, "Mummy, thank you," as all well-brought-up Igbo children were supposed to after a meal. I had just stepped outside the carpeted dining area and onto the polished concrete floor of the passage when my stomach churned and recoiled and the *garri* and soup rushed up my throat.

"Go upstairs and rinse your mouth," my mother said.

When I came down, Fide was cleaning up the watery yellowish mess, and I was sorry he had to and I was too disgusted to look. After I told my mother that I never ate *garri* before school, that on Saturdays I waited until nobody was looking to wrap my *garri* in a piece of paper and slip it into the dustbin, I expected her to scold me. But she muttered in Igbo, "You want hunger to kill you," and then told me to get a Fanta from the fridge.

Years later, she asked me, "What does *garri* really do to you?"

"It scratches my throat," I told her, and she laughed. It became a standing line of family teasing. "Does this scratch your throat?" my brothers would ask. Following that afternoon, my mother had boiled yams, soft and white and crumbly, made for my lunch; I ate them dipped in palm oil. Sometimes she would come home with a few wraps of warm *okpa,* which remains my favorite food: a simple, orange-colored, steamed pie of white beans and palm oil that tastes best cooked in banana leaves. We didn't make it at home, per-haps because it was not native to our part of Igboland. Or perhaps because those we bought on the roadside from the women who carried them in large basins on their heads were too good to surpass.

I wish I ate *garri.* It is important to the people I love: My late grand-mother used to want to have *garri* three times a day. My brother's idea of a perfect meal is pounded yam. My father once came home from a conference in Paris, and when I asked how it had gone he said that he had missed real food. In Igbo, another word for "swallow" is simply "food," so that one might overhear a sentence like "The food was well pounded, but the soup was not tasty." My brothers, with affectionate mockery, sometimes ask whether it is possible for a person who does not eat swallow to be authentically Igbo, Nigerian, African.

On New Year's Day of the year I turned thirteen, we went to my Aunt Dede's house for lunch. "Did you remember?" my mother asked my aunt while gesturing toward me. My aunt nodded. There was a small bowl of *jollof* rice, soft-cooked in an oily tomato sauce, for me. My brothers praised the *onugbu* soup—"Auntie, this is soup that you washed your hands well before cooking"—and I wished that I, too, could say something. Then my boisterous Auntie Rosa arrived, her wrapper always seeming to be just about to slip off her waist. After she had exchanged hugs with everyone, she settled down with her pounded yam and noticed that I was eating rice. "Why are you not eating food?" she asked in Igbo. I said I did not eat swallow. She smiled and said to my mother, "Oh, you know she is not like us local people. She is foreign."

. . .

This is a sad ending—the writer seems to feel like a foreigner to her family in some ways because she can't eat garri, or swallow it, and that feeling is only reinforced by her aunt's comment.

I liked Adichie's memoir a lot; it's short, but she manages to say a lot about how garri is important to her family and to her culture, yet she cannot enjoy it. Her use of dialogue really helped me understand her relationship to her mom, especially, but also to the other members of her family. I thought it was sad at the end when her aunt made that comment about her being a foreigner, and I guess that's the point of the memoir. Adichie prepared us for that insight by using stories from different points in her life about when she did not feel connected to the people she loves for not eating garri. At one point or another I guess we all have an experience of feeling disconnected, of thinking we wished we belonged.

We also may have the experience of having food that reminds us of who we are, our culture, our traditions. So there are a few ways Adichie draws us into her story, the foods, the family connections, the feeling of being an outsider. She seems to reflect on her search for who she is, her identity, specifically her identity in relation to her cultural background. These seem to be the way she wants to engage us, even if we have no idea about garri or her background.

Adam King (student), "These Stories"

In "These Stories," student writer Adam King reflects on his experiences as an Army recruit who has twice been scheduled for deployment, once to Iraq and once to Afghanistan, and the uncertainty surrounding the situation. In his memoir, King explores the tensions involved in straddling two worlds: the world of a civilian and the world of a soldier.

Adam King

Dr. Susan DeRosa

20 Nov. 2009

Memoir

These Stories

I. 2003

Tennis elbow, for instance.

Sergeant Nugent, our squad leader, was testing a tennis elbow brace that some of the guys bought him as a joke. He was extending his arm, contemplating his elbow with the seriousness of a mathematician doing an equation. But what's funny is that he really had tennis elbow. Sergeant Nugent, the guy that karate-chopped the air and flailed his arms around to drive a point home. That's what's so funny about it, the irony of it all. But that's not all.

It's all of us, back in 2003, a year already turning black and white and fuzzy in my mind like an old home movie. We were at our mobilization station in Virginia, waiting to go die in Iraq, standing around in this room inside our barracks—this room we called the war room that had panels missing out of the walls and ceiling. It's the barracks itself, a building that was meant to be condemned and bulldozed and blown up before we took up residence in it. It's us laughing anyway, at our deaths, at Sergeant Nugent, at the war room. We were laughing at him and with him at the same time because he was ours to laugh at and nobody else's; because if anyone else laughed at him we'd stop laughing and stare them up and down.

In the corner, Private Roach sang R & B in his hip hop lounge singer voice and Sergeant Melanson—a former Drill Sergeant—was telling someone the story about when he got jumped and made abstract art out of five guys' faces with a fire extinguisher.

There's so much to tell.

To my buddies, though, I can sum it all up by saying tennis elbow, and they'll look at me and smile and know.

These stories we tell with so few words.

* * *

To write this memoir, I sit at my computer in my silent room. Every now and then I hear a car pass by. People with their own lives and stories. I try not to think of all the other things I could be doing but am not—things I'd later tell stories about.

But wait. Let me start over—at the beginning.

* * *

What better present for my twenty-first birthday than a phone call to go to war? January 8, 2003. My mother handed me the telephone with the suspicious look she got every time someone in the military called the house after the September 11th crashes. "It's your sergeant," she said. I took the phone into the kitchen.

"Hello?"

"Specialist King? This is Sergeant Dowe. You got your TA-50?"

I knew what was coming. Guard units all over the country were being mobilized and deployed overseas. I wanted to lie and tell him no, I didn't have a full TA-50 issue, not so much as a poncho.

"Yes," I said.

"Okay. You're falling in on a different unit," he said. I heard him shuffle papers around. "The 250th. You're going to Camp Rowland, building 803, okay?"* He said something about bridges and I said okay a few more times, and then we hung up, and three days later I parked my car at cold Camp Rowland, in Niantic, and stepped out onto the frozen-mud parking lot. I slammed the door shut, watched my breath rise into the air and disappear.

Building 803 was filled with people I didn't know—strange, unfamiliar faces laughing together in small clusters. I sat at a table in an empty corner and folded my hands, wishing I'd brought a book. Not that I'd get any reading done with all the noise. Sometimes it just feels good to look like you're doing something. A Staff Sergeant walked by, stopped. He looked me over. "King?" he said after checking my nametape and referring to a piece of paper. His nose was round and red.

---

* Interesting story. I got taken out of my old unit, the 242nd, to fall in on the 250th. In the mail one day, I got a company newsletter from the 242nd. Must have still been on their mailing list for some reason. Right on the front page, I saw a congratulations to me and another soldier for volunteering to go to Iraq.
Does it sound like I volunteered to you?

"Yes, Sergeant." I stood and crossed my arms behind my back in the position of parade rest. His nametape said "Nugent."

"You're in my platoon. That's Second, got that?"

"Yes, Sergeant."

He turned and walked away and I sat back down and rested my head on my arms. "What the f— is *this*?" I heard. I lifted my head to see Sergeant Nugent standing over a surprised soldier. He was pointing at the soldier's unzipped gore-tex field jacket. He said, "Military regulations," banging a fist into his palm for emphasis.

He said, "Your gore-tex zipper can be zipped up to this button, or all the way. That's it."

He said, "Fix it," and then walked away. I watched this, clenching my jaw. That guy was my new squad leader?

*   *   *

To write this, I must remove myself twice from meaningful events. I am telling a story about telling stories.

I am in my room. One ceiling, one floor, four blue walls. Above my computer monitor, a plaque with the NCO Creed. Behind me, a bed, blue.

*   *   *

The 250th Engineer Company builds bridges. That's our job. The Medium Girder Bridge, or MGB, is a steel-reinforced, British-engineered bridge that is put together kind of like Legos. Big, heavy Legos.

After arriving at our mobilization station—Fort Eustis, Virginia—we trained on the bridge twice a week, every week. We trained in gas masks and chemical suits, sweating and drinking water and sweating more. We trained in kevlar helmets and kevlar vests. We trained with M-16s strapped across our backs. We trained in the rain, in the mud, in the snow. Every once in a while, Sergeant Topliff, our platoon sergeant would arrive out of nowhere and say, "Hey Sergeant Nugent, you're dead."

We'd stop building for a minute and look up at him. He'd say, "What the f—? The mission still has to be accomplished. Sergeant Nugent's dead, who's next?" Sergeant Val or Corporal Lee would step up and take control of the bridge-build, and Sergeant Nugent would go and sit down and talk shit to us.

This was our lives. If you asked if we were ready to go to Iraq, we'd shrug and say, "Whatever."

Every Monday, we marched to the motor pool to perform maintenance on our 5-ton dump trucks. We changed oil and tires and transmission fluid. We slept in cabs when no one was looking, and underneath the trucks with our hands propped up on the axles so we looked like we were doing something. We took classes from the mechanics on field expedient vehicular maintenance. Actually, it all happened because someone was messing around during one of these classes. The smoke session,* I mean.

Second Platoon had just finished dinner chow, laughing and smoking and walking slow back to the barracks because the workday was over. It just finished raining, and the grass behind the barracks was shiny and green. Huge puddles turned the sidewalks into marshland. I was walking up the stairs to the barracks when I heard Sergeant Nugent, yelling for Second to fall the f— in. We looked at one another, confused, and started over to him

"Take your time!" he said. He stared past the grass, arms at his sides. The way he stood so straight, I could tell his body was tensed.

When we fell in, he immediately began pacing in front of the formation.

"While the NCOs were up there," he said, pointing to the barracks, "listening to Captain Novak talk about the *logistics* of a f—ing bridge-build, you were—who was it, Gallo? Rowe? You were f—ing around with this." He produced an empty bottle of Sprite from nowhere. "As I see it, there are, how many, ten, eleven Specialists in this platoon? As I see it, you need to step the f— up and take some *responsibility*. While the NCOs are gone, you guys are in charge, and not playing baseball with a soda bottle falls under *responsibility*." He looked us over. "So as I see it, all of you are responsible for Gallo and Rowe f—ing around when Sergeant Samson was trying to give you a class on 5-tons."

It never occurred to me to wonder how he found out about Gallo and Rowe. He just knew. There was no sense questioning it; the answer was

---

* In the military, there are a myriad of colorful expressions for making a soldier exercise as punishment. You get told to drop, to beat your face, to get in the front leaning rest. Push-up sessions, as well as other, more degrading exercises, all fall under the category of getting smoked.

simply that Sergeant Nugent, he always knew. You could drive yourself mad with that kind of question, sort of like the chicken and the egg, or a tree falling in the woods with no one around

He tossed the soda bottle. "Do some push-ups," he said, and we got down in the front leaning rest position, in the mud, and did push-ups while he lectured us on the finer points of responsibility.

The military has a game. "Front! Back! Go!" it's called. It's really fun as long as you're not playing. What it is is this: When the person leading the formation says, "Front!" that means you have to do push-ups. When the person says, "Back!" you have to do flutter-kicks. When they say, "Go!" you have to run in place with your arms stretched out in front of you like an idiot.

When Sergeant Nugent got tired of watching us push, we played that game until he got bored. Then he called us up, one by one, to lead the fun. Then he called Corporal Lee to lead. Then Sergeant Pare. When that got old, he made us low-crawl across the grass over and over, until there was no more grass. Until the field was a brown, slick bog and we were so dirty we were unrecognizable as human beings.

I remember getting angry. I yelled at the slower soldiers to hurry up. Crawl faster. I could feel mud down my shirt. Inside my ears and mouth. Everything smelled like earth.

Across the green, Sergeant Nugent leaned against a tree, arms folded, grinning.

* * *

PUTNAM UNIT MAY MISS TRIP

The quickness with which the war ended in Iraq could be good news for some Connecticut Guard troops scheduled for deployment overseas.

The 250th Engineering Group based in Putnam, a specialized bridge-building unit, may not be needed as part of the reconstruction effort in Iraq.

It may be heading home.

Ray Hackett
Norwich Bulletin, May 8, 2003
* * *

You come back to civilian life, where everything is hushed and subdued and real. You try to take it all in—just the freedom to go to the grocery store whenever you want is mind-blowing. Maybe all that freedom—that disorganized liberty—and all those civilians, so comfortable in the simple act of being, just get to you. Maybe, you come close to breaking, squeezing your eyes tight, breathing heavy, unable to speak.

When you're away, nothing is better than home. Your girlfriend she's never been so beautiful. Your mother is perfect. Just the thought of your bed makes your stomach twist inside you. Coming home, you watch the illusion dissipate before your eyes, and you realize that maybe, in Virginia, in the mud—dirty, sweating, miserable—you'd never been so content.

* * *

II. 2005

In August, the commander calls us into a small room. She says, "We're going to Afghanistan to get blown up," and we say, "And?"

So here I am, two months later, at drill. Camp Rowland. Again. During the day, my platoon waits in long lines to get paperwork straight so the government can send us to go die. Again.

Then nighttime comes and my platoon's alone in the barracks, no supervision, and out of nowhere everyone's wasted. Me and Baribault end up outside on the second floor landing with the night out there and cigarette smoke over here, and he's telling me how much he hates everyone one minute and trying to explain the significance of Rodriguez saying he can beat him in hockey the next.

He's like, "I was the man at hockey when I'se in high school, you know? Like, I used to totally check dudes, like—and then my jaw, and I got thrown out of the game. You know?" His face is red. He has the kind of blond hair that's almost translucent, like you can see into his head and through to the other side. He smiles, dumb, drunk.

I nod and say something like, "Hell yeah," even though I don't know. Like I don't get it. I'm a little jealous and a little sad for him at the same time because Baribault, when he was playing hockey, he found that place. And now he's trying to find it again, but really he's just wasted and he never can, and he's trying to make me understand with his words, but I never will.

Inside, someone dumps a locker over to set up a makeshift bar. I don't see this so much as hear the metal crash and the drunken laughter.

Baribault's teammates, though, they'd understand if they were here. They'd nod and be like, "Dude." But all I can do is lie to him and let him feel that glow and know he's feeling it.

Later, when we all know we should be sleeping because we have, like, three hours left until wakeup, we cheer Baribault on as he stuffs Rodriguez into a garbage can.

* * *

It's tempting to talk about the bridge as a metaphor for the connection between the members of Second Platoon, but I won't. I won't talk about its symbolic destruction when, after being called to Afghanistan, our unit became a combat engineer company specializing in explosives instead of bridges. How I was removed from my platoon to become a team leader in another platoon, a separation that felt kind of like being locked out of a house your family is inside of, and they can't let you in. I won't talk about the Afghanistan mission being scrubbed—how it was the second failure of my unit to deploy—or my unit's transfer back to doing bridge. How I'm a squad leader now and I can never get back into Second—that bridge has been severed. I won't talk about that stuff, but it's tempting.

* * *

We're waiting for drill to end, sitting at a table in the unit's armory. Moore's making a "T" with his hands. "Yo, time out, time out. Nugent told us to do that." He folds his arms behind his head. "I was just following orders."

I say, "Yeah, but Garvin was scared."

"And that's my bad?" He leans forward. "Nugent gave me an order."

I'm shaking my head, slow. "It wasn't right."

Gabriel breaks in. "Yo, King was like, *'Stop, stop!'*" Everyone laughs. Moore's like, "Ay, if Garvin talked about my wife like that—all I'm sayin'—it's a *wrap.*"

"Remember we put shaving cream on Garvin while he was doing push-ups," Gabriel chuckles. "And he was like, *'I'm a sergeant, I'm a sergeant. You can't do this to me!'* We was like, 'Shut the f— up and push!'"

Sergeant Nugent clears his throat and everyone gets quiet. He's looking down at the table. "He's lucky," he says, articulating each word precisely, "that I had you guys take care of him."

It was during last summer's annual training, and we were inside billets in South Dakota at the time. I remember telling Sergeant Nugent that what he was doing wasn't right, and him looking at me. He was so angry that he looked sad and lost. "Nobody talks about my wife," he had said, and seeing the look on his face, I shut up. Gabriel and Moore yelled at Garvin across the room. "Push!" Garvin's face was flushed and serious as he wobbled push-ups out on tired arms.

Sergeant Nugent had looked at me like he wanted to explain something complex and important. Like he needed to say something bigger than language allowed. He leaned his arms over a top bunk's metal frame. He was looking at me, but he was seeing something else.

"She's all I got," he had said, and then he studied the ceiling a second before he walked away.

* * *

Here are some more stories we tell: That chick with the man hands. That time Sackandy sh— in the rental car. That time King broke the bridge.* That time Challenor put Topliff in the Camel Clutch. Reynolds naked. The Brain—you don't want to know. Seriously.

All these phrases, they're entire stories. Each word, an image. An emotion. A moment of our lives.

* * *

56 CONNECTICUT GUARD TROOPS IN MIDDLE EAST RIGHT NOW

The 300 National Guard soldiers of the 242nd Engineer Battalion from Stratford and the 250th Engineer Company of Vernon were getting ready to go to Afghanistan to work under the 10th Mountain

---

* Moore can sum this one up in seven words: Yo, don't let King near no winches. Sergeant Nugent can sum it up in five: King, you're a f—ing idiot. I still say it wasn't me that broke that stupid bridge.

> Division. But they learned Thursday they'll remain
> at home for now. Maj. Gen. Thaddeus J. Martin, the
> Connecticut National Guard commander, credited
> "rapidly changing requirements" for part of it. Next
> year, 600 soldiers from Connecticut are due to be
> called up to serve under the 10th Mountain Division,
> but for now most of the traffic is incoming.
>
> Staff Writer
> *New London Day*, December 3, 2005
>
> * * *
>
> Awaiting orders, sir.
> Still awaiting orders.
> Sergeant King. Out.

Reading for Comprehension

1. What kind of opening has the writer chosen? What immediate effect does it have on readers?
2. As you read through the memoir, what details and descriptions engage you? How does the writer show versus tell about his experiences?

Analyzing the Genre

1. King uses segmented organization to arrange the episodes in his memoir. How do these segments build up King's purpose for writing this memoir?
2. What effect does King's use of newspaper articles in his memoir have on his audience? How do the news clips serve the story being told?
3. How does the reflection in the memoir point out the significance of the memoir even if many readers have not shared the same experiences as the writer?

David Sedaris, "Let It Snow"

David Sedaris is the author of many collections of personal essays and memoirs including When You Are Engulfed in Flames. In many of his works, he reflects on everyday events and finds ways to show readers how they resonate in their lives, even if they have never found themselves in similar situations. The following memoir was published in The New Yorker magazine in December, 2003.

Winters were frustratingly mild in North Carolina, but the year I was in the fifth grade we got lucky. Snow fell, and, for the first time in years, it accumulated. School was cancelled, and two days later we got lucky again. There were eight inches on the ground, and, rather than melting, it froze. On the fifth day of our vacation, my mother had a little breakdown. Our presence had disrupted the secret life she led while we were at school, and when she could no longer take it she threw us out. It wasn't a gentle request but something closer to an eviction. "Get the hell out of my house," she said.

We reminded her that it was our house, too, and she opened the front door and shoved us into the carport. "And stay out!" she shouted.

My sisters and I went down the hill and sledded with other children from the neighborhood. A few hours later, we returned home, surprised to find that the door was locked. "Oh, come on," we said. I rang the bell, and when no one answered we went to the window and saw our mother in the kitchen, watching television. Normally she waited until five o'clock to have a drink, but for the past few days she'd been making an exception. Drinking didn't count if you followed a glass of wine with a cup of coffee, and so she had a goblet and a mug positioned before her on the countertop.

"Hey!" we yelled. "Open the door. It's us." We knocked on the pane and, without looking in our direction, she refilled her goblet and left the room.

"That bitch," my sister Lisa said. We pounded again and again, and when our mother failed to answer we went around back and threw snowballs at her bedroom window. "You are going to be in so much trouble when Dad gets home!" we shouted, and in response my mother pulled the drapes. Dusk approached, and as it grew colder it occurred to us that we could possibly die. It happened, surely. Selfish mothers wanted the house to themselves and their children were discovered years later, frozen like mastodons in blocks of ice.

My sister Gretchen suggested that we call our father, but none of us knew his number, and he probably wouldn't have done anything anyway. He'd gone to work specifically to escape our mother, and between the weather and her mood it could be hours, or even days, before he returned home.

"One of us should get hit by a car," I said. "That would teach the both of them." I pictured Gretchen, her life hanging by a thread as my parents paced the halls of Rex Hospital, wishing they had been more attentive. It was really the perfect solution. With her out of the way, the rest of us would be more valuable and have a bit more room to spread out. "Gretchen, go lie in the street."

"Make Amy do it," she said.

Amy, in turn, pushed it off on Tiffany, who was the youngest and had no concept of death. "It's like sleeping," we told her. "Only you get a canopy bed."

Poor Tiffany. She'd do just about anything in return for a little affection. All you had to do was call her Tiff, and whatever you wanted was yours: her allowance, her dinner, the contents of her Easter basket. Her eagerness to please was absolute and naked. When we asked her to lie in the middle of the street, her only question was "Where?"

We chose a quiet dip between two hills, a spot where drivers were almost required to skid out of control. She took her place, this six-year-old in a butter-colored coat, and we gathered on the curb to watch. The first car to come along belonged to a neighbor, a fellow-Yankee who had outfitted his tires with chains and stopped a few feet from our sister's body. "Is that a person?" he asked.

"Well, sort of," Lisa said. She explained that we'd been locked out of our house, and, while the man appeared to accept it as a reasonable explanation, I'm pretty sure he was the one who told on us. Another car passed, and then we saw our mother, this puffy figure awkwardly negotiating the crest of the hill. She did not own a pair of pants, and her legs were buried to the calf in snow. We wanted to send her home, to kick her out of nature just as she had kicked us out of the house, but it was hard to stay angry at someone that pitiful-looking.

"Are you wearing your *loafers*?" Lisa asked, and in response our mother raised a bare foot.

"I *was* wearing loafers," she said. "I mean, really, it was there a second ago."

This was how things went. One moment she was locking us out of our own house and the next we were rooting around in the snow, looking for her left shoe. "Oh, forget about it," she said. "It'll turn up in a few days." Gretchen fitted her cap over my mother's foot. Lisa secured it with her scarf, and, surrounding her tightly on all sides, we made our way home.

Reading for Comprehension

1. What is your initial reaction to this memoir and to Sedaris's description of his family? Does it change after you've read through it? Explain.
2. Sedaris's memoir is told in one scene. How does he engage readers in such a brief episode from his childhood?

Analyzing the Genre

1. What is Sedaris's purpose for writing this memoir? How does he use humor to achieve that purpose?
2. How does Sedaris use description and details to help readers understand his family and their relationships?

Chitrita Banerji, "A Shared Plate"

Chitrita Banerji, born and raised in Kolkata, the capital of the Indian state of West Bengal, is the author of several books and essay collections in which she explores the relationship between Indian culture and food, including *Eating India: An Odyssey into the Food and Culture of the Land of Spices* and *Bengali Cooking: Seasons and Festivals*. Her work has appeared in many publications including the *New York Times* and *Gourmet* magazine in which the memoir below was published in 2005.

"The tatto is here, the tatto is here!" Bare feet rush down the stairs and out toward the front door as the house resonates with the blowing of conch shells and loud ululation—auspicious sounds believed to scare away evil spirits.

Staying with a friend in Calcutta to attend her daughter's wedding, I am caught up in the excitement. The tatto whose arrival is causing such a commotion is a collection of gifts—clothes, cosmetics, decorative objects, food—that the bridegroom's family sends to the home of the bride on the morning of a Bengali Hindu wedding. I haven't attended such an event in many years, but my memory flashes to long-forgotten images of the gifts sent to our house for an aunt's wedding. As a small child, I had been particularly awed by one item—an enormous carp, its silvery scales gleaming with an undertone of pink, its head patterned with turmeric and vermilion, a double garland of tuberoses twined round its ample belly. Is such a princely fish still part of the Bengali wedding tatto?

I move forward to look at the trays being unloaded from the car. Yes, one does contain a carp, although its dimensions fall short of those I remember. But the family seems pleased, to judge from their gleeful comments about the muror dal to be made with the head at lunchtime. For us fish-loving Bengalis, this is a cherished delicacy. The fish head is fried, broken into pieces, and added to roasted moong dal, its copious brain matter (like the marrow from beef bones) giving a baroque note to the redolence of turmeric, ginger, cumin, cinnamon, cardamom, and green chiles.

But amid the happy exuberance, I feel a deep sadness as I think of my own family. My mother was the eldest daughter among many siblings, and her wedding was a lavish affair. The legendary chef my grandfather hired for the occasion transformed the entire roof of the ancestral house into an enormous kitchen for three days. It was said that he prepared an akhni water—a stocklike decoction of the various spices used in making pilaf—so fragrant that the entire street was enveloped in its aroma. Every item of the spectacular meal he served was described in excruciating detail whenever any wedding was discussed in our family. It sounded like a golden affair, burnished with each retelling.

By the time I was a teenager, though, these narratives evoked only a bitter irony. The golden couple of the wedding were unrecognizable in the two adults who were my parents. A terrible sense of grievance and letdown seemed to consume them much of the time, and the most unlikely event, topic, visit, or comment could precipitate a marathon session of loud arguments and bitter reproaches, scorching words that walls and doors could not keep out. And then there were the silences—long, throbbing interludes of absolutely no conversation that lasted for hours, even days.

Joy, however, was not totally absent in our family. My conflicted parents shared one enthusiasm—food. She was a fabulous cook, a true artist, and he had a rare and subtle palate. He also enjoyed shopping for the season's best produce, fish, and meats. Through my school and college years, I took for granted the delectable offerings on our table—slow-cooked potatoes with tamarind and asafetida, carp in yogurt sauce, shrimp with ground coconut and mustard, and so many others.

Despite their constant discord, my parents were also extremely hospitable, and friends and family were frequently invited to our home for meals. Among the many classic dishes for which my mother was justly famed was muror dal. Each time she made it, she waited intently for my father's reaction. Even if they were not speaking to each other, the appreciative sniff that greeted the serving of the dal on his plate and the zestful way he sucked the juices from the head were the accolades she really looked for.

Not having the maturity to sense the complex emotions that underlaid my parents' endless conflict, I blamed the Indian system of arranged marriage that allowed families to match incompatible duos for life, since Hindus do not believe in divorce. Never, I resolved, would I be trapped like that. The only way to avoid it was to escape—and I did, as far away as the United States. I also exercised choice in my marriage.

But I could not escape destiny. In the late 1980s, I found myself, the first divorcée in my orthodox Hindu family, back in Calcutta, living with my parents in their rambling three-story house. Once again, the erupting arguments and conflicts made me ponder the nature of the marital bond that held them together. But with older eyes, I could see the deep attachment below the surface. How had it developed when they seemed to have disappointed each other right from the beginning?

One evening, when I came home from work and found them bickering viciously over a particularly insignificant matter, I lost my usual restraint. "Why didn't you get a divorce years ago?" I burst out. "At least I would have had some peace!"

Immediately, I was overcome with shame and regret. Didn't I know how impossible it was for people of their generation to even think about divorce? Hadn't I shamed them enough with mine? Guiltily, I fled upstairs. But my mother followed me. With surprising calmness, this habitually no-nonsense, even prosaic woman sat down and explained her conception of marriage.

"You didn't care for our rituals," she smiled sadly, "you married outside our religion, you had a civil marriage in America. But you've seen many Hindu weddings. You know the ceremony requires the couple to feed the fire, and then feed each other. Food is life, and by eating together, the pair bonds for life. We did that. How can you talk to us about getting a divorce?"

She spoke of ceremony and bonds. But looking at her face, and listening to her voice, I heard only the word love. I thought back to the long years of conflict, but also to the deep, shared passion for the art of cooking, eating, and offering hospitality. That daily tableau of the table, I now saw, was neither duty nor obligation—it was love, but a tormented version that found no expression except through food.

Soon after, I went away again—back to America. After my father's death, I decided to bring my mother over to join me, and for ten years I watched as time and distance failed to wipe out her regrets and sorrows. In the absence of the one person with whom she had argued and fought and eaten, she totally lost the pleasure she once took in cooking. Even her enjoyment of food seemed sadly diminished.

The wedding I am attending in Calcutta—an arranged marriage—is in the evening. By now, I am in a pensive mood. The tatto has been put away, the fish consumed by the family. In the large rented hall, a canopied enclosure has been decorated with red cloth and tuberose garlands. In front of the chief actors, seated on a carpet, is an array of items necessary for the complex Hindu ceremony. I see the bowl of snowy white popped rice, the bunch of ripe bananas, the conch-shaped sweets on a terra-cotta plate—and my mother's words ring vividly in my ears: "Marriage is a lifelong undertaking to eat together."

First the bride's father has to give her away. The priest guides him through the Sanskrit mantras, while he holds his daughter's hand and places it on top of the groom's. It is a solemn undertaking, since the "gift" is not simply a daughter but also a woman now endowed with her share of the family property. The pinched look on the father's face demonstrates the effects of a daylong fast. Earlier, I had seen him at home, closeted with the household gods and one of the priests, making sacred offerings to both gods and ancestors, asking them to bless his daughter and son-in-law.

In my mother's time, the bride, too, had to fast all day. But this 21st-century bride had been allowed a little snack in the middle of the day. Wrapped in a gold-embroidered red silk sari (red being an auspicious color in Hindu culture), decked out in intricate gold jewelry, her forehead decorated with patterns of sandalwood paste, she seems an icon of happy expectation. Had my mother, too, looked like that on her wedding day?

Once the bride has been given away, the father leaves the scene—a symbolic gesture of renunciation. Now it is the couple's turn to wind their way through further intricate rituals, guided by two priests. Several times they make offerings to the gods: flowers, leaves, unmilled rice, a type of grass called durba. But the crucial—and most spectacular—part of the ceremony comes later. The pair rise and stand, she in front. His arms come around her and he places his palms underneath hers so that they can jointly hold a plate laden with foods. One of the priests quickly builds a fire in a large copper vessel and the couple pour offerings into it. The popped rice is the first. As it falls, the flames rise up with a whooshing sound, as if Agni, the god of fire, is welcoming the tribute. Item by item, all the food is submitted to the flames. Finally, the two walk around the fire seven times, the shoulder end of her sari knotted to his shawl, reciting the Sanskrit couplets that express the undertaking of a lifelong bond. But this first day's ceremony (weddings are not complete until the end of the third day) is not over yet. Tradition requires them to feed each other sweets from the same plate. As they do so, I am struck by the tenderness with which he brushes the crumbs from her mouth.

Throughout the long ceremony, guests have come and gone, sampling the wedding feast in another room. When most people have left, the bridal pair sit down to dinner at a large table with a group of friends. I wish them happiness and say good-bye to the family. From the landing, I look back one last time. Amid the laughter and chatter of the friends, the groom is placing a spoonful of pilaf on the bride's plate. She, still feeling shy, looks down, but the flush of pleasure on her cheeks and the upward curve of her mouth are unmistakable.

Suddenly, I imagine my parents in place of this couple. In my vision, their faces are fresh, expectant, and youthful, instead of marked with half a century's wear and tear. I see my father, his handsome face topped by the conical groom's hat, serving portions of food onto his new bride's plate. I watch my habitually stern mother transformed into a bashful bride who smiles with happiness under cover of her veil.

I walk away, but as I go I wish for the young couple that today's shared communion will be allowed to blossom, that the shining bride will have the uninhibited freedom to say she loves her husband and children every time she serves a meal, and that the groom will find a way to reciprocate. I wish for them a home where two people live an ordinary life, its disappointments made bearable by the leavening of laughter and the communion of food. It does not seem too much to ask.

Reading for Comprehension

1. What are some of the rituals that Banerji recalls about Hindu wedding feasts? Why are they important to her and her family? What are some of the rituals important to understanding your family's culture?

2. In the beginning of Banerji's memoir, she sees her parents' relationship as tumultuous and flawed. What makes her change her impression of that marriage? How does she relate her realizations to her friend's daughter's wedding she is attending?

WebLinks

Creative Nonfiction and *Fourth Genre: Explorations in Nonfiction*

Although you can find memoirs in magazines like *The New Yorker* or *Atlantic Monthly,* two good places to start are in the journals *Creative Nonfiction,* one of the leading publishers of memoirs, personal essays, and other nonfiction literary genres or in *Fourth Genre: Explorations in Nonfiction.* Use a search engine to search the titles of either journal.

Analyzing the Genre

1. Banerji's memoir recalls two wedding stories, and among these stories the writer includes digressions where she reflects on conversations she has with her mother later in her life. What insights does Banerji reveal in these reflections? How does her reflection help you understand the purpose of her memoir?

2. How does Banerji help readers, who may be unfamiliar with Bengali customs, understand the significance of food to the ceremonies and to the culture?

WRITING ASSIGNMENT OPTIONS

Memoirs

For this assignment, write a memoir that is based on an experience, memory, or event from your past. It could be about an event that somehow transformed your life, a first experience, a moment of realization (or an "a ha" moment or revelation)—there are many starting points.

Memoir Assignment Options

1. Write a memoir about an important childhood experience or a place from your childhood that helps you discover some new insight about who you are.
2. Write a memoir about a family tradition (ritual, celebration, food) that shows you something significant about your cultural identity.
3. Write a memoir about an everyday experience you've had that provided you with insights on human behavior or relationships.
4. Write a memoir on an object from your past that holds great familial or cultural significance in your life.
5. Write a "sign of the times" memoir about an experience you've had that reveals something about a particular historical or political moment.

Community-based Writing Option

Write a memoir about a time when you volunteered or provided service to an organization or group in your community that helped you to better understand the issue the group stands for. Write your memoir for people who may be unfamiliar with the organization and its mission and social significance.

Writing Memoirs

Just as with any genre, memoirs have particular characteristics that help writers understand what they need to say and how to say it.

WHAT WRITERS CONSIDER WHEN THEY WRITE MEMOIRS

In general, memoir writers:

- Identify an experience or event that is meaningful to them and to readers
- Provide rich sensory details that place the reader squarely in the experience
- Define the rhetorical situation of the memoir
- Conduct background research on the people, places, and events
- Choose an organizational pattern that helps the reader understand the significance of the experience
- Reflect on that experience in order to explore its larger significance

Generating Ideas for Memoirs

Writers of memoirs mine their pasts for experiences, events, and even objects that *resonate* in their lives. Generating ideas for memoirs means a writer needs to *reflect* on past experiences, events, and memories from a *present perspective*. While initially you'll need to focus on a moment from the past, eventually you should be able to reflect on the experience to show the *larger significance* for your audience. It must ring true for them as well.

Avoiding Common Memoir Pitfalls

1. **The Confessional Memoir.** As a memoirist, you aren't pouring out your soul just to have others feel sorry for you or to join you in a celebration of how wonderful you are. Instead, there needs to be a larger, more significant purpose for your memoir. Your readers will want to understand how you have made sense of the experience or event about which you write.
2. **The Too-Common Experience.** While memoirists look for the common thread that connects their experience with their audience's, they need to also avoid simply telling a story we have already heard before. Although they may make engaging stories, some childhood first experiences are so common that it's hard to find anything new to say about them, unless there is a unique twist to the experience.

WRITING ACTIVITY   Generating Ideas for Memoirs

As you start thinking about subjects for your memoir, consider those events that have stuck with you, but don't ignore those small moments that at the time seemed insignificant, and that in retrospect are rather important.

1. **Recalling a scene.** Recall a moment from your past that influenced who you are today. Choose an episode from the past that allows you distance from it and time to reflect on it.
2. **Drawing a map.** Create a map of a neighborhood or place from your childhood. Label the places where something happened that made a lasting impression on you. Describe one of those events, how it influenced you, and why others might find it interesting.
3. **Telling stories.** Write down the kinds of stories you might tell to your friends that reveal to them something significant about you and who you are.
4. **Describing a cultural artifact.** Describe a family or cultural tradition or object that reveals something to you about who you are in relation to your family or culture. Recall a moment when that tradition or artifact was important, and write about its significance to you and your family and culture.
5. **Exploring the common.** Write about what seems an ordinary event or everyday activity that revealed something extraordinary to you about yourself and the world around you. Describe the ordinary event as it happened to you, and its importance

to you as you look back on it now. Write down how readers might also find it important in their lives.

■ ■ ■

Ethics and Memoir Writing

As you are thinking about writing your memoir, remember that although it is a recollection of your experience, it usually involves the lives of other people: family, friends, acquaintances, coworkers, and so on. So you'll need to consider some of the ethical dimensions of writing memoir to avoid revealing details and experiences about those other people who may not want them revealed.

- **Avoid revenge prose.** When you find yourself writing about others in your memoir, often it may be because you don't like them very much. But no matter how angry they made you feel, your purpose isn't to get even with them. Your purpose is to reflect on the significance of your shared experience.
- **Protect others' privacy.** You'll want to be responsible and ethical when presenting information on others in your memoir. Two suggestions for doing so include using a disclaimer or composite characters.
  - *Disclaimer.* A disclaimer is a statement that says you are changing the names of some characters to avoid exposing information on others as you tell your story—especially when your audience may know who they are.
  - *Composite Characters.* Sometimes changing the names of people in your memoir isn't enough. For instance, a coworker is not hard to identify if the writer has one assistant. Creating composite characters involves taking the characteristics of a few people and blending them into one representative character in your memoir. Writers do this to protect the privacy of several people at one time while retaining important details that are critical to the narrative.

GROUP ACTIVITY   Testing Memoir Topics on an Audience

In groups, take turns reading your possible topics for memoirs. The group should offer generous feedback, striving to help writers choose and develop the ideas that seem to make sense for a memoir and ones that interest the readers.

1. As each writer reads, the rest of the group should take notes and jot down responses to each idea.
2. Once the writer has finished, the group should discuss which ideas seem most interesting and offer the best possibilities for development. The writer should take notes on what was said in the discussion, as both oral and written feedback are useful.
3. After the writer has chosen one idea, the whole group should discuss the topic in-depth. Consider the following questions: What is interesting about it? What more do you want to know? Is there a hint of a purpose or larger significance for the memoir idea yet?
4. At the end of group work, each person should have a topic with ideas for how to develop it into a memoir. Share these ideas with the rest of the class.

■ ■ ■

Thinking about Audience, Purpose, and Situation

Writers have many reasons for writing their memoirs, but one overall goal is to get the audience to think differently (or to think for the first time) about an experience or event the writer assumes will resonate or ring true with them.

WRITING ACTIVITY   Defining the Rhetorical Situation for Your Memoir

As you work through these prompts feel free to skip around; the important thing here is not the order of the prompts but that each set of questions will help you refine and articulate the others.

1. **Think about the situation.** What made you want to write about that particular moment, experience, or event? Did something you read or hear trigger the desire to write about it now? What circumstances surround the memory you are writing about? Was this an intensely personal or private moment or was it more public?
2. **Decide on your purpose.** Your purpose in the memoir is going to be closely tied to how you reflect on the experience or event. Think about what the larger significance is for your memoir, other than simply telling readers about an experience that happened to you.
3. **Decide on your audience.** Who is your intended audience? What will they know about the experience or event you are writing about? Can you assume a similar experience on their part? What background for your memoir—cultural, familial, historical, political—do you need to provide readers with for the experience and larger significance to resonate?
4. **Decide how to present yourself.** What kinds of information about yourself should you reveal to the reader? What will the revelations accomplish for you?
5. **Think about your tone.** As you decide on appropriate style and language choices for your memoir, keep in mind the scene you are recreating, the experience you are exploring, and what you are saying about the experience. Will those things be served with humor or satire? Would a more formal, serious tone work better?

■ ■ ■

Researching Memoirs: Doing Background Research

Although it may seem like memoirs do not contain the same kind of research needed for academic writing, memoirs whose stories resonate the best with readers are those where their writers took the time to research background information and details about the experiences they wrote about. Memoirists also conduct research because the primary material—the writer's memories—are so subjective. While readers expect memoirs to be true stories, we know that truth is subjective depending on whose version of the memory is being recounted. One way that writers reassure readers that their memoir is true, though subjective, is to contextualize the experience or event by using research.

Memoirists often do background research on the places and events that surround their memory. This research establishes place and people as real and contextualizes the memory in a particular point in history. Research also adds historical or cultural significance to the memoir. That is, when writers provide readers with rich details or background of the time and place surrounding their experiences, they set up their memoirs so that they have some larger significance against the backdrop provided.

Even as they incorporate research, memoirists tend to keep the personal, conversational voice in their memoirs—the "I-happened-to-come-across-this-while-I-was-writing" voice—so that the research is woven into the fabric of the memoir smoothly.

WRITING ACTIVITY   *Researching Your Memoir*

Consider the subject you are writing about—the event or experience—and the kinds of research that might help you further develop the scene you have in mind. For example, a scene set in the late 1990s in the rural town of Charlotte, Iowa, would suggest that you need to provide some background on the town, who lives there, and so on.

1. Are there newspaper articles on the event or time period that could deepen readers' understanding of the historical moment of your story?
2. Is there background you could provide on places, people, or groups you mention in the story that would help readers better understand the event?
3. Could you provide cultural, historical, or political references that would help readers understand the landscape that surrounds your memoir?

■ ■ ■

Drafting Memoirs

Because memoirs rely so heavily on sensory descriptions to place the reader in the scene, a good way to start drafting of a memoir is by taking notes on and perhaps writing the key scenes of your memoir.

Developing Sensory Descriptions and Concrete Details

When readers read a memoir, they expect to be drawn into the writer's world, to connect with the emotions, ideas, and experiences of the memoirist through concrete detail, vivid descriptions, and sensory images. So it is very important that the writer give the readers enough material for them to experience the scene or event.

One way writers immerse readers in their memoirs is through the use of **sensory descriptions**: sight, sound, smell, taste, and touch. Appealing to the five senses creates time and place for readers. Without rich details, the writer has a short, bland story that goes nowhere. With concrete details, the writer tells a richly evoked narrative that places the reader front and center in the writer's experiences.

GUIDELINES: DEVELOPING SENSORY DESCRIPTIONS

1. **Describe the immediate moment of the event or experience.** Is it the dog days of August heat that you recall? Is it morning or evening? Is the scene happening outside on a city street or along a rural country road? On a baseball field? At a house? Use spatial description to show readers the surrounding landscape or to take them on a tour of the rooms, colors, smells, and items in a kitchen or basement.

(continued)

2. **Describe the place.** Immerse readers in the physical setting for your scene. Be specific and include street names, landmarks, names of particular places (schools, bars, stores, famous sites, etc.), and climate. Show how the place evokes a particular emotion or feeling. For particular time periods, make references to pop culture, political happenings, or historical events so readers get a feel for this time and place.

3. **Describe the people.** Reveal characters' personalities by describing how they move, their mannerisms, or their facial features or other physical attributes. What do they look like? What do they sound like? Dialogue adds details about peoples' dialects, temperament, and speech patterns and rhythms. Dialogue portrays people vividly for readers and establishes relationships between people. (Look at the use of dialogue in King's "These Stories.") Action also helps readers visualize people. What are they doing in your scene?

Once you have the pieces of your scene in mind, and perhaps sketched out on paper some descriptions and details of people and places, begin to think about how to organize your memoir.

Organizing Memoirs

There are two issues to consider as you structure your memoir. First, memory is confusing, and when we share memories with others, it is important to give readers a lot of cues about how the material is arranged. Second, a memoir's organization needs primarily to serve the *reflection* component (see page 290 for a discussion of reflection). That is, you want to organize your material so that you lead your readers to the *larger significance* of the experience, in some cases, weaving it like a thread throughout your memoir.

Ultimately, your goal is to keep the reader on track with what is happening, where it is happening, and when it is happening—to situate them in your experience and take them along for the ride. There are several ways to do this.

Chronological order. Memoirists use this common pattern to arrange their narratives along a timeline. Think about when your friend asks you how your day was. You tell the story in *time order* and take them through the interesting highlights from beginning to end. Narrating a story from the past often lends itself to chronological arrangement because it is retrospective. The writer looks back on an experience, describes important actions, and builds up to a particular moment of importance or climax or turning point.

Digression. Sometimes memoirists step out of the chronological pattern. They begin the memoir with a critical scene, then step back in time to provide readers with backstory, or how they got to that climatic scene. If memoirists move out of a strict chronological order, then they need to signal to readers that they are doing so. One simple way writers can show readers that they have moved around in chronological order is to use signal phrases that indicate a time shift: "In the summer of my fourteenth year…." or "In September 1998…" (For more on signal phrases, see page 291 on "Moving Around Through Time.")

Segmentation. This memoir structure involves creating a narrative made up of building blocks: scenes or explanatory passages that play off each other and when linked together form the whole narrative. Segmented memoirs are broken up by subheadings, extra white space breaks, or another typeface that signifies a shift in the narrative. Segmentation reinforces the subjective nature of memoirs—the visual aspect of the white space suggests that the memory is not complete or that it has been pieced together.

Openings for Memoirs

The opening of a memoir often determines whether readers will keep reading or not. Engaging the reader from the start is critical for memoir; if they can't find a way into your story, they may ask the dreaded question "so what?" or think "why should I care?" So keeping readers "hooked" from the start is one way to think about openings. In general you have lots of choices for opening your memoir depending on your purpose for writing and the larger significance you want to convey to readers.

The *in media res* opening. *In media res* is Latin for "in the middle of things," and when using this opening, that's what you do—you start somewhere other than at the beginning of the memory you are writing about. There are many reasons writers choose this kind of opening: Maybe the actual beginning isn't the important part, and so they decide to give that material to the reader later. Maybe they want to begin with a climatic or critical scene to put readers immediately in the action, leaving the rest of the memoir to tell how scene came about. A perfect example of an *in media res* opening is King's "These Stories." He not only begins in the middle of things but actually in mid thought: "Tennis elbow, for instance." The opening scene reflects clearly being in the thick of things: We don't know where we will end up, how things will turn out, or how we will feel about it, but we are actually living the experience.

The meditative opening. Writers using a meditative opening call immediate attention to the so-what—the larger significance—of their memoir. They are looking back from a present perspective on a past event and making sense of it. By doing so, writers are in effect telling readers how they want them to read their memoir. You might choose a meditative opening if you think your readers will too easily dismiss your subject, assuming it isn't important enough to read about. Or you might use the technique if you think the subject of your memoir is too controversial, too difficult, or too complex for readers to work through without some initial guidance.

Closings for Memoirs

Closings in memoir writing may function in many different ways depending on the complexity and depth of the story being told. Because most real life events are not always so simple that they can be "summed up" in the end, the memoirist needs to think carefully about how they end their memoir. Here are some examples of possibilities for closing your memoir.

The open-ended closing. Most memoirs, like our life experiences, do not end up with a neatly packaged ending or a firm resolution to the events in the story, so often the closing will be open ended. Many memoirists choose to write about the experiences that have left them wondering or thinking "what if" things had happened differently or about the possibilities of making other choices in their lives. The open-ended closing will leave readers thinking about how the memoir in some way touches their own lives, or asking questions about their own life experiences in light of the writer's story. For an example of the open-ended closing, see King's "These Stories" page 267.

The reflective closing. Memoirists may decide to do some of their reflecting on an experience in the closing. It is here they will address the experience's larger significance: What does it mean, how do they look at the experience now, and what has changed? Does this experience tell readers or the memoirists anything about themselves? This closing, too, needs to be set up. So at various points in your memoir, you will hint at what you will say in the closing, just as novelists and directors foreshadow later events.

WRITING ACTIVITY   Openings and Closings
_____

Use the following prompts to help you consider your purpose in writing a memoir about an experience or event and how to open and close your narrative.

1. Does your audience or your purpose for writing about the experience or event suggest a particular way of opening and closing it? For example, do you need to prepare your readers for the larger significance of your memoir?
2. How might your opening engage your readers immediately? How does it keep them wanting to read on?
3. Does your subject call for a certain kind of opening or closing?
4. Do you want your readers to feel or react in a certain way at the end of the memoir? How about at the start?

■   ■   ■

Revising Memoirs

When revising your memoir, pay particular attention to the element of reflection and to your narrative's organization.

Reflection: Pointing Out the Larger Significance

The central element of a memoir is *reflection,* where the writer looks back on and analyzes her experiences or the events in order to explore their meaning. Reflection in memoir is also done so that the reader can better understand the larger significance of the story—the broader cultural implications or human connections. Sometimes writers digress from the main narrative of the memoir and comment on their past experiences from a present perspective. Think of it as a detour on the memoir's narrative "road." Digression, then, is a form of reflection.

For example, in her memoir "Real Food" (page 265), Chimamanda Ngozi Adichie reflects on the importance of *garri* to her Igbo culture:

> I wish I ate *garri*. It is important to the people I love: My late grandmother used to want to have *garri* three times a day. My brother's idea of a perfect meal is pounded yam. My father once came home from a conference in Paris, and when I asked how it had gone he said that he had missed real food. In Igbo, another word for "swallow" is simply "food," so that one might overhear a sentence like "The food was well pounded, but the soup was not tasty." My brothers, with affectionate mockery, sometimes ask whether it is possible for a person who does not eat swallow to be authentically Igbo, Nigerian, African.

Adichie moves back and forth in time in this short passage to help build her reflection: She uses the memory of her father (set in the far past) and the memory of her brothers' commentary (in the present, but also continuous) to show readers how she pieced together over time an understanding of the cultural significance of *garri* to her family.

WRITING ACTIVITY   Developing Reflection in Your Memoir

Now that you have a working draft of your memoir, you can more easily consider the larger significance of the experience or event you're writing about—what memoirist Patricia Hampl calls "the human connection."

1. What makes the experience described in your memoir significant for you? What does the experience reveal to you about yourself now that time has elapsed since it occurred?
2. Is there a moment in the memoir where you recognize something important that the experience reveals to you? Is this moment clear to readers?
3. What do you want readers to understand about the experience? In other words, why should readers care about it? How might they relate it to their lives?
4. Does your memoir have any cultural or historical significance? Is it a sign of the times? A political commentary? Does it show us something about who we are as a nation? As humans?

■   ■   ■

Moving Around in Space and Time

Because memoir writers reflect on experiences and events from the past, they often move among different points in time and place. In order to do so, writers make creative use of *time and place markers* or *signal or transition words*. Signaling to readers *when* something is happening in time or *where* it occurred is especially important when writers disrupt the chronological order by using flash-backs or flash-forwards, or when they interrupt the narrative with backstory or reflection. Words that signal readers where the story is in time are also important, especially when writers switch tenses, moving from past to present to past again.

Notice the use of time and place markers in Eliza Poulos's memoir, "Lucky?" in the One Writer's Journey section later in this chapter. The chronologically organized memoir takes place in different locations which are clearly indicated by *transitions* used by Poulos to keep readers oriented.

It started off like any normal Saturday. I had slept in because I had a big soccer game the night before and I was wiped out....

Later that night, I was eating dinner with my family ...

When my mother and I arrived at the mall ...

After the lunch with my fellow contestants ...

Read through your memoir draft and locate places where the time and place markers need to be clarified so readers know where and when the events are happening. Revise those sections using descriptive and specific language that helps readers better understand your memoir.

■ ■ ■

PEER REVIEW *for Memoirs*

As you read, comment as fully as you can on the writer's draft. Be sure to explain your comments (i.e. "I get confused in this part because you jump around in time here. . .") and give specific examples of how the writer could revise.

Comment in the margins on the following:

OPENING: How does the writer immediately capture your attention in the opening paragraphs (e.g. make a bold statement, put the reader in an important scene, tell an anecdote, reflect on a past experience)? What do you expect the memoir to be about?

SENSORY DESCRIPTIONS AND CONCRETE DETAILS: Where does the writer include descriptive writing, showing you the person, place, or thing being described and explored? Mark the places where you think the writer could provide more sensory and concrete details to bring the people and places to life for readers.

After you have finished, write an endnote to the writer in which you comment on the following:

- Begin by telling the writer what you enjoyed about the memoir.
- Describe what you think is the purpose of the memoir. Where does the writer *reflect* on experiences to point out the significance of the memoir? Is there reflection on a universal idea or feeling?
- Comment on the places where you feel the memoir resonates with you and the intended readers. What strategies does the writer use to make those connections with readers?
- Can you follow the narrative or do you get confused in parts? Suggest revisions for **organizing** the narrative more clearly, perhaps to clarify time and place of the story.
- Where does the writer use vivid descriptions and details to put you in the scene of the memoir? How could the writer develop those parts further to immerse readers in the memoir?
- What type of **closing** has the writer chosen? Do the opening and closing make sense *together*? Do they make sense given the content of the memoir? Suggest how the writer could revise the opening or closing to engage readers from start to finish.

Reflecting on the Process

Reflect on your writing process for your memoir. How did you generate ideas, do research, and draft and revise your memoir? Imagine you are writing this reflection to writers who have never written a memoir. What might they learn about working within the genre from you? What could you tell them that might help them as writers?

1. *Begin* by describing what aspects you are most pleased with in your memoir. *Analyze* your strengths and weaknesses as a writer for this memoir.
2. *Reflect* on how you established the scene of your memoir. How did developing the scene help you determine your purpose and audience? How did your purpose and audience influence your choice of material? How did you develop your reflection?
3. *Discuss* your revision process, including how you used feedback from your readers.
4. *Conclude* by reflecting on what you learned about the genre of memoirs. You might also reflect on what you might do differently the next time you write a memoir.

■ ■ ■

Eliza Poulos's Memoir

When first-year writing student Eliza Poulos started to think about ideas for her memoir, she knew she had to choose a topic that would resonate with her audience. She had a few ideas to start, and after working with a group of students in class, she narrowed down her choices to a memory about the time she entered a celebrity look-alike contest at a local mall.

Generating Ideas for the Memoir: Recalling Past Experiences

Often memoirists write about past experiences that have had an emotional impact on them or that have changed them or their outlooks on life. Poulos begins exploring topics for a memoir by thinking about personal experiences that have influenced her and how much detail she can remember about the events.

> *Generating Ideas: Memoir*
>
> *Eliza Poulos*
>
> *Memoir Topic #1:*
>
>   *An event that I can remember vividly from my childhood was when I was in eighth grade, I entered a mall concert and had a chance to win $5,000 to the furniture store Ethan Allen. The contest was a significant turning point in my life because I realized how much family and friends mean, and how they are willing to go the extra mile to help and support me. Readers might read my memoir and think about what they are lucky for in their lives, and so I'll need to make it clear just how the whole experience changed me at a time when most young kids are influenced by what their friends think, or do, or how they act.*
>
> *Memoir Topic #2:*
>
>   *I could write about my grandfather and his ukulele playing. I can remember him playing the ukulele and my Great Aunt playing the piano as they sang. My family would get together and play music and eat pizzelle. Most of my memories are family based and this helps me understand how my past is such an important part of who I am, and how I want to hold on to it. I think readers will think of their family histories and how their backgrounds influenced who they are and will become later in life.*

Poulos is thinking about the importance of this experience in her life and how it will resonate with her audience.

Here, Poulos thinks through how her purpose might be to have readers think about the ways family background shapes their identities.

Thinking about Audience, Purpose and Situation

Poulos chose to write about the contest at the local mall because she claims it made such an impression on her at a young age. She also thought that since it was an unusual experience, it might pique her readers' interest and get them to think about her purpose a bit more carefully. After she chose her subject, Poulos began to think about the rhetorical

ONE WRITER'S JOURNEY

situation. The excerpt below shows how she begins to flesh out some of the *reflection* she will include in the memoir draft.

Audience and Purpose for the Memoir

<u>Audience:</u> Since really anyone might be interested in reading a memoir about some kid winning a contest, if it was a good story, I think I need to be clear that I'm writing it for maybe those young people who don't think they are especially lucky or thankful for what they have in their lives. Not really a lecture ("be thankful"), but instead get them to think about their lives more thoughtfully.

<u>Purpose:</u> My purpose really has to do with showing how this experience made me rethink things around me, like other people always wanting to look like famous stars or look like some beautiful model and think that's the most important thing. But really, what I think made this contest stick in my mind was how my family and friends stood by me, and how that's really what makes a person lucky, so there's kind of a double meaning in the title I chose.

Drafting the Memoir: Choosing Details and Specifics

As the writer, Poulos's job is to recall the experience by choosing details and specifics that are relevant to moving the narrative forward. In doing so, she must show, versus tell, how the story unfolded, allowing readers to feel like they are experiencing it as the writer did.

Eliza Poulos
Professor DeRosa
English 100P
17 Dec. 2009

Memoir Draft 1

It started off like any normal Saturday. I had slept in because I had a big soccer game the night before and I was wiped out. When I went downstairs my mom was sitting at the dinner table wearing my dad's glasses, thick brown frames that looked as though they belonged on someone twice my parent's age. She sometimes used them to read the newspaper, despite how unattractive I told her they were. I sat down next to her and she folded the newspaper down to look at my face.

"You know," she said, her brown eyes peering over the rims of my dad's glasses, "there's a celebrity look-a-like contest at Westfarms Mall and the winner gets $5000 from Ethan Allen." Her voice was so excited it was if I had already won.

I stared at her like she was crazy.

Poulos's opening does a fairly good job putting readers in a particular time and place of the memoir.

Poulos sets up the event that is the focus of her memoir, and at the same time provides background on it. Notice the details she uses to help readers visualize her mother's expression.

The opening sets a "scene" for readers to enter: We are introduced to the contest, and dialogue shows us some of the relationship between Poulos and her mom.

"No way that I'll win. Do you know the odds of getting chosen for a contest like that?" I said.

She glared at me, crinkled her face, and both hands went up in the air. You know it is going to be bad when an Italian woman starts talking with her hands.

"So what?" she said, arms waving, "You should enter the contest anyway."

I shook her off telling her I definitely would not win.

The next day my mom was still asking me to sign up online, so I did just so she would stop nagging me. The online form took me about two minutes, but the rules and terms took me about twenty to read. I never signed or agreed to something before I read it. After I applied the whole thing slipped my mind, I did not think or really care about the contest, I did not even check the date that the contest winner(s) would be announced. That's why you can see how surprised I was when . . .

How does this humor work for you as a reader? What does it add to the narrative, the story being told in the memoir?

. . . I got a phone call from Geico asking me If I wanted to save a bunch of money by switching my insurance. I declined this fantastic offer and to be able to hang up the phone I decided to act as though my mom was calling me. That's always the way it goes with telemarketers, we always make up different excuses, like "sorry my television's on got to go" or "just heading out," or when they mispronounce your name and you say "no one here by that name."

Later that night, while I was eating dinner with my family the phone rang, and my dad told me it was for me. The woman on the phone told me that I had been selected as one of the three finalists for the Westfarms contest and that the next day we would meet at the mall . . .

* * *

Poulos manages to weave into the memoir the details of the contest.

This leaves us wanting some background or fuller details.

When my mother and I arrived at the mall we were seated with the other two girls and their mothers. Both the girls were extremely pretty and I feared that I did not have a chance to win this contest, none the less I was still excited to be there. The manager of Westfarms arrived and I could tell by her voice it was the same lady with whom I had spoken on the phone the day before. She sat down and we ordered lunch. While we were waiting for the food to arrive she explained how the whole contest was going to work. She said that we would pick a celebrity to resemble and do this by picking out clothes, getting our hair done and having accessories to accent who we were trying to portray. I can remember thinking to myself, oh great like I have a chance in hell over this blonde girl who looks like Britney Spears and this brunette whose legs looked as though they could be a mile long and she resembled Jennifer Love Hewitt. And there I was sitting in my jeans and t-shirt, not resembling anyone besides myself. Feeling defeated, I perked up when she said that the winner would be determined by applause and that we could bring as many people as we wanted to support us.

Again, a good time marker to keep readers focused on the chronological organization of the memoir.

After the lunch with my fellow potential contest winners we were each given $300 to spend on our outfit. I went to the GAP and bought a pair of

Can readers visualize how she looks?

Again here, it seems like this may be a place for the writer to reflect, emphasizing for readers her purpose for choosing to write about the contest, on how she was feeling at the time.

dark wash jeans and a matching jacket. Next, we went to American Eagle where I bought a shirt that had a guitar on it, which was practically perfect because the person that I decided to "attempt" to resemble was Michelle Branch, a singer, songwriter and an avid guitar player. I tried very hard to pick out clothes that she herself would wear; I bought a pair of plain sneakers and a crazy scarf. I also bought a khaki colored bag to carry as an accessory, and I still use it today. When we were done shopping I had to get my hair cut so that it would look like Michelle's. Luckily, she had long hair so they did not cut mine all that much. I felt so important that day, the way I imagine a celebrity does every day. [. . .]

Revising: Developing Reflection in the Memoir

A challenging problem a memoirist faces is how to show the audience the significance of the memoir, or make it resonate with readers. Poulos faced this challenge in her second draft, which was peer-reviewed by her classmates. You'll notice that the reviewers' comments are similar; both ask for Poulos's deeper reflection on her childhood experience and suggest places where she might develop a reflective voice—one that looks back on the events of the story and provides insights on the memoir's larger significance.

The following excerpt includes the reviewers' comments and Poulos's revisions, as well as her explanation for why she made those changes.

Eliza Poulos
Professor DeRosa
English 100P
19 Dec. 2009

Lucky?

Reviewer 1: Add a title that hooks the reader into your memoir.

[I added the title as my reviewer suggested, and I put a question mark to make readers think about it.]

It started off like any normal Saturday. I had slept in because I had a big soccer game the night before and I was wiped out. When I went downstairs my mom was sitting at the dinner table wearing my dad's glasses, thick brown frames that looked as though they belonged on someone twice my mother's age. She sometimes used them to read the newspaper, despite how unattractive I told her they were. I sat down next to her and she folded the newspaper down to look at my face.

Reviewer 2: I like the opening. It tells me what the story is about and leaves me wondering what's going to happen to her. . . .

"You know," she said, her brown eyes peering over the rims of my dad's glasses, "there's a celebrity look-a-like contest at Westfarms Mall and the winner gets $5000 from Ethan Allen." Her voice was so excited it was if I had already won.

I stared at her like she was crazy.

"No way that I'll win. Do you know the odds of getting chosen for a contest like that?" I said.

She glared at me, crinkled her face, and both hands went up in the air. You know it is going to be bad when an Italian woman starts talking with her hands.

"So what?" she said, arms waving. "You should enter the contest anyway."

I shook her off telling her I definitely would not win.

The next day my mom was still asking me to sign up online, so I did just so she would stop nagging me. The online form took me about two minutes, but the rules and terms took me about twenty to read. I never sign or agree to something before I read it. After I applied ~~the whole thing slipped my mind.~~ [cut some repetition] I did not think or really care about the contest. I did not even check the date that the contest winner(s) would be announced. That's why you can see how surprised I was when . . . I got a phone call that afternoon from Geico asking me if I wanted to save a bunch of money by switching my car insurance. I declined this fantastic offer and <u>just so I could</u> hang up the phone, I decided to act as though my mom was calling me. That's always the way it goes with telemarketers, <u>and I</u> always make up different excuses, like "sorry my television's on got to go" or "just heading out," or when they mispronounce your name and you say "no one here by that name." <u>They have to have the worst job in the world, with people hanging up on them all the time, and they're lucky if someone even bothers to listen to their sales pitch or even say goodbye before hanging up on them.</u>[I added this because the reviewers asked me to say why I used the example, which was to throw in some suspense and humor at the same time.]. . . .

When my mother and I arrived at the mall we were seated with the other two girls and their mothers. Both the girls were extremely pretty and I feared that I did not have a chance to win this contest. <u>Still</u> none the less I was still excited to be there. The manager of Westfarms arrived and I could tell by her voice it was the same lady whom I had spoken on the phone to the day before. She sat down and we ordered lunch. [cut, it was obvious] While we were waiting for the food to arrive she explained how the whole contest was going to work. She said that we would pick a celebrity to resemble and do this by picking out clothes, getting our hair done and having accessories to accent who we were trying to portray. I can remember thinking to myself, oh great like I have a chance in hell over this blonde girl who looks just like Britney Spears <u>with long blonde hair and glowing (unnaturally) white teeth,</u> and the <u>brunette who resembled Jennifer Love Hewitt and</u> whose legs looked as though they could be a mile long and she resembled Jennifer Love Hewitt. And there I was sitting in my jeans and tie-dyed t-shirt, not resembling anyone besides myself. Feeling defeated, I perked up when <u>the manager</u> she said that the winner would be determined by applause and that we could bring as many people as we wanted

Reviewer 1: Why did you write this?

Reviewer 2: This is funny, I do this too, but it ends kind of abruptly. Maybe add a transition to the next part or something?

Reviewer 1: This part makes me want to know more about what the writer was thinking, like why she felt bad then perked up. Maybe add how you feel about it today to make it clearer.

to support us. <u>It was then I realized that I might, just maybe, have a shot at winning the contest, or at least not losing miserably since I could probably convince my friends and family to show up on the day of the contest. Now, of course, I realize that I had something much better than the glamour of being a celebrity look-alike.</u> `[I added this because the reviewer's comment made sense. I reflected on why it was an important moment in my experience.]. . . .`

After they had calibrated the results of the crowd, the judges determined a winner. A giant check appeared on stage with the decorator that the winner would also receive to help them pick out which furniture to buy. The DJ came over the microphone and said that the winner was ... me! I could not believe it. I had won against girls who I thought were for certain better, more beautiful than I and that one of them was definitely going to be the winner. <u>And when I wear that colorful scarf today, I think about what the contest was about back then, the imitation of famous people, the transformation of us "ordinary" girls into extraordinary, glamorous, celebrities. But I know how lucky I am, and how I can be myself and be just as rich.</u> `[I added this reflection in the memoir because both reviewers said my closing wasn't good, and I tried to drive home my purpose for writing so readers would really get thinking about how they could look differently at their own lives and what it means to really be lucky.]`

> Reviewer 1: You need to add more to the ending, like how you feel about the contest now, and what you think about the way you did back then.

> Reviewer 2: This doesn't really seem finished. I think you should think about what you want to say about that day and how it changed you.

Eliza Poulos (student), Lucky? (final draft)

Eliza Poulos

Professor DeRosa

English 100P

20 Dec. 2009

Lucky?

It started off like any normal Saturday. I had slept in because I had a big soccer game at my middle school the night before and I was wiped out. When I went downstairs, my mom was sitting at the dinner table wearing my dad's glasses, thick brown frames that looked as though they belonged on someone twice my mother's age. She sometimes used them to read the newspaper, despite how unattractive I told her they were. I sat down next to her and she folded the newspaper down to look at my face.

The dialogue helps to establish the writer's relationship with her mother as well as advance the storyline of the memoir.

The humorous voice of the writer is continued here. We hear it in the opening as she describes her mother's gestures. What purpose does it serve in this digression?

"You know," she said, her brown eyes peering over the rims of my dad's glasses, "there's a celebrity look-alike contest at Westfarms Mall and the winner gets $5000 from Ethan Allen." Her voice was so excited it was if I had already won.

I stared at her like she was crazy.

"No way that I'll win. Do you know the odds of getting chosen for a contest like that?" I said.

She glared at me, crinkled her face, and both hands went up in the air. You know it is going to be bad when an Italian woman starts talking with her hands.

"So what?" she said, arms waving. "You should enter the contest anyway."

I shook her off telling her I definitely would not win.

The next day my mom was still asking me to sign up online, so I did just so she would stop nagging me. The online form took me about two minutes, but the rules and terms took me about twenty to read. I never sign or agree to something before I read it. After I applied I did not think about the contest. I did not even check the date that the contest winner(s) would be announced. That's why you can see how surprised I was when ... I got a phone call that afternoon from Geico asking me if I wanted to save a bunch of money by switching my car insurance. I declined this fantastic offer and just so I could hang up the phone, I decided to act as though my mom was calling me. That's always the way it goes with telemarketers, and I always make up different excuses, like "sorry my television's on got to go" or "just heading out," or when they mispronounce your name and you say "no one here by that name." They have to have the worst job in the world with people hanging up on them all the time, and they're lucky if someone even bothers to listen to their sales pitch or even say goodbye before hanging up on them.

Later that night, while I was eating dinner with my family the phone rang, and my dad told me it was for me. I was surprised and took the phone into the other room, because my parents do not like it when people call during dinner. The woman on the phone told me that I had been selected as one of the three finalists for a celebrity look-alike contest and we'd meet at the mall the next day to discuss the details. My mouth was still dropped open when I returned to the table.

I choked out the words to my parents.

My mom stood up and clapped her hands. "I told you to apply." She turned to my dad. "See Dale, didn't I tell her?

"Thanks mom," I said. I rolled my eyes. But my heart was pounding in my chest, and I could barely hear what my mom was saying.

> *The writer has divided the memoir into sections, this one ending with an echo effect of the dialogue in the opening with her mother.*

Lunch at the Mall

When my mother and I arrived at the mall we were seated with the other two girls and their mothers. Both the girls were extremely pretty and I feared that I did not have a chance to win this contest. Still I was excited to be there. The manager of Westfarms arrived and I could tell by her voice it was the same lady whom I had spoken on the phone to the day before. While we were waiting for the food to arrive she explained how the whole contest was going to work. She said that we would pick a celebrity to resemble, choose our clothes and accessories, and have our hair cut to imitate the people we were trying to portray. I can remember thinking to myself, oh great, like I have a chance in hell over this girl who looked just like Britney Spears with long blonde hair and glowing (unnaturally) white teeth and the brunette who resembled Jenifer Love Hewitt and whose legs looked as though they could be a mile long. And there I was in my jeans and tie-dyed t-shirt, not resembling anyone besides myself. But I perked up when the manager said that the winner would be determined by applause and that we could bring as many people as we wanted to support us. It was then I realized that I might, just maybe, have a shot at winning the contest, or at least not losing miserably since I could probably convince my friends and family to show up on the day of the contest. Now, of course, I realize that I had something much better than the glamour of looking like a celebrity.

> *Notice how the writer begins to reflect on her experiences in the memoir.*

After the lunch with my fellow contestants, we were each given $300 to spend on our outfit. I went to the GAP and bought a pair of dark wash jeans and a matching jacket. Next, I went to American Eagle where I bought a shirt with a guitar on it, which was practically perfect because the person that I decided to "attempt" to resemble was Michelle Branch, a singer, songwriter

The writer continues her reflection on the experience and what it means to her today.

and an avid guitar player. I tried very hard to pick out clothes that she herself would wear. I bought a pair of plain white Converse sneakers and a crazy scarf with a rainbow of colors woven through it. When we were done shopping I had to get my hair cut so that it would look like Michelle's. Luckily, she had long hair so they did not cut mine all that much. I felt so important, the way I imagine a celebrity does every day.

Imagine this: every day, you, the celebrity, are special. Every day, you are important just because you are famous, "beautiful," or because of some talent you may have. That's not to say that talented people shouldn't be celebrated. But we get stuck on this stuff because we can't see what's important in our own lives that we already might have.

As I hold the colorfully woven scarf in my hands today, I know I will treasure it forever.

How do the subheadings affect your reading of the memoir?

Contest Day

In the words of the great rock and roll star Bobby Lewis, "I couldn't sleep at all last night!" And it was true. I did not get any sleep the night before the contest.

In the mall, the stage was set up for the contest. There were chairs for us contestants to sit on so people could judge whether or not we looked like the celebrities we were trying to imitate. I could hear the DJ from Kiss 95.7 (a Connecticut radio station) announcing our entrance. Everyone started clapping. My heart began pounding in my chest. It was very strange to be the center of everyone's attention.

Notice how the details build tension of the moment.

We stepped on the stage, and the bright lights shone in my face. The host, a DJ from KISS 95.7, revealed a before and after photo of each contestant. She did this for the three of us, then the DJ was supposed to raise her hand over our heads and depending on the screams of the crowd, determine the winner. She started with the girl who was supposed to look like Britney Spears, next was Jenifer Love Hewitt, then me. I told myself just breathe as the DJ raised her hand over my head, then I felt comfort as I looked out into the crowd. My family and friends had driven from all over the state to see me and held up signs that read "You go Eliza!" and others that said "You're already a winner!"

ONE WRITER'S JOURNEY

And at that moment, I felt like one.

After they had calibrated the results of the crowd, the judges determined a winner. A giant check appeared on stage, the kind you see in the Publishers Clearinghouse commercials, and brightly colored balloon floated in the air. The DJ announced that the winner was . . . Eliza Poulos. Me! I could not believe it. I had won over the other girls who I thought for certain were more beautiful than me.

And when I wear that colorful scarf today, I think back to what that contest was all about: the imitation of famous people, the transformation of "ordinary" girls into extraordinary, glamorous celebrities. That's kind of weird to think about. But I realize how lucky I am, and how I can be myself and be just as rich—or richer—for it.

The scarf is a recurrent image the writer has chosen to weave throughout the memoir.

Questions for Discussion

1. How does Poulos's reflection help readers understand the purpose of her memoir? What about the use of humor in her comments?
2. Memoirs show, versus tell, readers about an experience. Are there places where Poulos's use of details and descriptions presents readers with a vivid picture of her experience?
3. Notice the use of subheadings the writer has included. How do they help the organization of the narrative? What other organization techniques does the writer use to keep readers oriented?

Reflecting on the Process

Below is an excerpt from Poulos's reflection on the process for writing her memoir.

Writing a memoir is more complicated than it seems at first. Out of a couple of topics I chose the celebrity look-alike contest I entered when I was younger since I thought I could build tension and write it like a story where readers would be interested in finding out who won. I wanted to make sure that readers saw the humor in my memoir, so I tried to add things in like my mother's talking with her hands and the Geico telemarketer. There was some sarcasm about how the other girls looked like the celebrities, too. One thing that writing a memoir has taught me is it is important to give your writing a voice. A memoir should always have significance about a memorable event you will never forget, but it doesn't always have to be serious.

Peer reviewers told me I needed to reflect much more in my memoir because no one seemed to know why I was writing about the contest. So I tried to add little bits of reflection throughout, and the reviewers suggested places where I thought it made sense, too. So it was a "scene—reflection—scene" pattern. My peers also helped me see where I needed to do more showing versus telling and add description and detail, like in the part where I add details about what the contestants look like: "like I have a chance in hell over this girl who looked just like Britney Spears . . . ." I think these details tell readers how I saw the people and what I felt about them. Writing a memoir has shown me that it's more than just a story from your life. If I want people to care about what happened to me, I need to make them see how my story relates to their lives, too. I wouldn't want anyone to read it and say, "who cares?" What I'd probably do differently is try to make it funnier, because the whole contest on stage was really funny, and I think I may have made it sound a little too serious.

WRITING ACTIVITY   Evaluating One Writer's Journey

Review Poulos's process for writing her memoir. How would you evaluate the choices she made as she wrote? Are there places where you think she could have made different choices, and how would those choices have affected the final memoir? What further revisions, if any, do you think the final memoir could use?

■ ■ ■

TRANSFORMATIONS

GENRE BLURRING: The Travel Memoir

Memoirists often blur genres when they want to work with material in a new way, or if the material or subject lends itself to such blurring For instance, many memoirists today write about their experiences with the foods or culinary aspects of the cultures they visit and explore all of these elements in a "food memoir."

Another example of a blurred genre is the travel memoir. A recent critically acclaimed travel memoir is Elizabeth Gilbert's *Eat, Pray Love: One Woman's Search for Everything Across Italy, India, and Indonesia*. But travel memoirs have a long-standing history since traveling and/or exploring new places and writing about those travels is not something new.

Travel memoir writers do in fact travel to places and describe them, but more so, these writers reflect (after the journey and sometimes throughout it) on how that place led to new insights about their lives, the world around them and how to live in it (perhaps in a new way). Travel memoir readers also pause to think about the ways place shapes them, their identities, their lives.

Genre Blurring Writing Assignment

The Travel Memoir

Write a travel memoir about a trip or series of trips you took which changed, in some way, your perspective on yourself or others, or perhaps changed the ways in which you behave toward others. The location of the trip does not have to be "far away" or "exotic;" travel memoirists often explore the ordinary places and in their explorations, the ordinary becomes extraordinary. A travel memoir should not only richly describe the place or places you traveled to but should also provide insights into that experience that readers can understand and share. Since photographs are often part of (and almost required of) our trips, consider including some in the memoir, being sure that they serve a clear purpose.

Ted Conover, "On the Trail of Poppa's Alaska"

Ted Conover is a Distinguished Writer in Residence at New York University. He is the author of many nonfiction books, including Newjack: Guarding Sing Sing, *about the famous maximum security prison. The book won the New York Book Critics Circle Award in 2001 and was a finalist for the Pulitzer Prize. A self-described literary journalist, Conover writes nonfiction pieces for publications such as* National Geographic *and* Travel and Leisure Magazine, *in which the travel memoir below appeared in 1997.*

Eighty years ago his grandfather set out to explore uncharted land on horseback. Then the horses ran off. Ted Conover and his father attempt to wrestle the same route.

The writer opens by putting the reader right into the action of the place using details and descriptions.

Smoke from an unseen forest fire cleared as we crossed the White Mountains through Windy Gap, our string of horses clopping toward a far slope. Ahead of me rode my father, and ahead of him our guide, Keith, and his assistant, Hans, each leading a pair of packhorses. The animals, with their slipping packs and saddles, had been a headache so far. But at Windy Gap I patted mine and praised the rest, for it was near here that my grandfather and his party, in 1915, had lost all their mounts and pack animals and been stranded—without cell phone or emergency locator beacon—a long way from anywhere. And our horses were still with us.

Some backstory adds to the significance of the travel memoir for the writer.

I had conceived of this trip, a retracing of Poppa's journey, as a tribute to my grandfather, as a way to spend some time outdoors with my dad, and as an introduction to that mythic land, Alaska. Of all the many places my grandfather explored in his life, Alaska—kept unspoiled by its vast distances and long winter, and by federal land ownership—was perhaps the only one that might be essentially the same 81 years later. It is still possible to travel there like a pioneer.

The far Northwest had intrigued me ever since, as a boy, I heard my grandfather recite the Robert Service poem "The Cremation of Sam McGee": "There are strange things done in the midnight sun / By the men who moil for gold. . . ." But I didn't learn the details of Poppa's Alaska trip until I was in college, when he answered a letter I had written asking how he'd decided on his career as a mining engineer. The response, an 18-page typewritten epic, described how his geology professor had needed a field assistant for a summer expedition to the Alaska Territory, as it was then known. The U.S. Geological Survey sponsored the trip, because though gold had been discovered near Fairbanks and Dawson a few years earlier and miners were streaming in, large areas remained unmapped.

Near the end of my grandfather's life, I was given a photo album Poppa had made of his trip; when he died in 1993, I inherited the diary that went with it. Poppa was always scrupulous about details, and using these two documents I was able to chart his route fairly precisely on a present-day U.S.G.S. map. A Fairbanks-area backcountry guide, Keith Koontz, told me the trip would be feasible with his horses; Keith had homesteaded and lived as a trapper in the very White Mountains region we would explore—most of it now Bureau of Land Management country.

Keith proposed taking us by van from Fairbanks to the town of Circle, on the Yukon River (and nearly on the Arctic Circle), where my grandfather and his professor had alighted from a riverboat and hired a cook and a "packer." From there we would drive the Steese Highway—much of it a bumpy dirt road—back toward Fairbanks, pausing at the ruins of Miller House, an outpost where the 1915 party had hired four tired horses and three mules. Like my grandfather, we would then leave the main route, making our way on horseback and on foot to the gleaming White Mountains, some 60 miles away, and to Windy Gap, the pass that leads through a range of sawtoothed mountains.

On the far side of Windy Gap—I don't think it's a coincidence—the modern map shows a Lost Horse Creek. After my grandfather's party lost their horses somewhere nearby, they carried their gear in three trips to Beaver Creek, where they built two log rafts. Keith would leave my father and me at Beaver Creek with provisions and an inflatable raft. A week or so of floating would carry us to the confluence with Victoria Creek, at the mouth of which Keith's old cabin still stood. We hoped to spend the last night of our trip there. The next day, a bush pilot would land on a long gravel bar nearby and carry us out.

Dad and I were thrilled by the sight of Keith's eight strong horses when we awoke our first morning. Keith and Hans, a 50-ish East German army veteran, had arrived late the night before, owing to truck trouble, and were still asleep in Keith's tall green tent. By noon, Dad and I were dying of impatience. Not to worry, Keith reassured us when finally he got up: "We'll be there by sundown!"

This, of course, in the land of the midnight sun, meant about 2 a.m., but we weren't concerned. Compared with Poppa's entourage, we had every creature comfort—waterproof boots, sunscreen, mosquito repellent, Gore-Tex gear, fishing rods, and small cameras. The horses carried a huge quantity of food, in addition to a Global Positioning System and a .45 Magnum to ward off bears. Soon it was sunny, with the temperature at 60 degrees. Best of all, Dad was in a great mood, in love with his little horse, Hannibal, and raring to go. I was proud and pleased that Dad, a robust 63, was willing to brave these mountains with me.

By mid-afternoon the horses carried us up a wide valley of spruce stands and meadows, over a stream capped with late-melting, crusty snow, and across a forest floor strewn with fallen logs, bluebells, pink wild roses, and white Labrador tea. The difficulty of the Alaska backcountry also revealed itself: thick underbrush that our mounts strained to pass through; the wet footing of mossy muskeg; and dense clouds of mosquitoes. ("To fit any more into the same space," Poppa had written, "you would have to make them smaller.") I was fairly well protected by repellent, but a swipe along my horse's neck left my palm red with blood.

In the golden light of 11 p.m., we climbed past the timberline, losing the mosquitoes to the breeze and altitude, and ourselves to a stunning view of green-brown mountaintops succeeding one another in the distance. Three caribou caught sight of our train and gamboled along for a quarter-mile or so, looking like big, awkward dogs off a leash. Poppa's group, upon seeing almost any animal, had unholstered their guns and aimed to get supper; we,

Details add to the significance of their journey—the modern technology these men carry with them versus the "roughing it" that Poppa did on his trip.

The trip has significance for the writer in his personal relationship with his father.

Vivid landscape details here: harshness and beauty of Alaska's backcountry.

Poppa's voice is included by the excerpts from his letters to the author.

in possession of canned cattle from lower elevations, could afford to appreciate the caribou just for their looks.

Unfortunately, we didn't make camp until 3 a.m., when all of us, not least the horses, were exhausted. Having searched quite a while for a better place, we settled on a small, grassy patch amid big clumps of willows that left one feeling hemmed in. My father, despite our being outdoors in the most sparsely populated state in the Union, awoke at 7 a.m. with an attack of claustrophobia. It was caused partly by our tent, partly by the willows, and largely, we soon agreed, by the feeling that we were trapped by our guide.

Keith, it became increasingly clear, had a somewhat fuzzy memory of the terrain. The brush was thicker than he'd recalled, and in setting the itinerary he had significantly underestimated how long each day's travel would take. This meant we'd have a lot of long days.

Impatient and distracted, Keith proved unwilling to let us know when he was about to mount after a break. As anyone who has ridden in a string of horses knows, the animals don't appreciate being left behind—they'll try to keep up with their fellows whether there's a rider in the saddle or not. This put Dad and me in a bad spot, because we were often slow to climb aboard. The second day, after half an hour of grazing the horses, Keith and Hans disappeared up a heavily wooded slope before Dad could mount. I kept my horse, Clem, back as long as I could, the animal rearing and neighing over his lost companions. Finally, Clem charged ahead, unwilling to wait any longer.

"Why the hell can't you give us two minutes' notice?" I shouted to Keith. Nonplussed, he said only, "You gotta learn to hold your horse back." A minute later, Hannibal arrived without Dad. I was livid. I dismounted, walked back, found Dad, and led him to the group. He was fine, he said as we walked—he'd just given up in the face of overwhelming odds. Keith was like a ski instructor, Dad said, who took his beginners to the top of an expert slope and then skied off without them.

Despair ensued but soon faded: there was nothing for it. One boon was the constant comparison with how things had been for Poppa. Every morning, seated around a cook fire sipping coffee and wiping clean our metal plates of bannock bread, eggs—and, if there was a stream nearby, breaded grayling—we read from the pages in Poppa's diary that matched where we were. We could figure out that their animals had terrible saddle and cinch sores, that everyone's boots were constantly soaked, and that the weather was cold—but Poppa hardly complained. "In morn. Prof. B. and I started down the creek. Found some fragments of Cambrian trilobite, first fossils in this part of country . . . spent most of morn. cracking them out. Cold drizzle . . . found a few more fossils& pretty near froze getting them out with wind blowing thru us. Made fire to warm up, then went back to camp. . . . A.& M. had moved camp over to spruce grove& put up fly& made a swell table of logs."

Poppa's notes serve to emphasize the hardships of his journey, a contrast to the "hardships" the writer and his father endure.

With each fresh comparison to our experiences, the diary took on new life: Poppa battling mosquitoes with citronella; the hardtack and tea and rationed lumps of sugar that constituted his breakfast; the blued screws he put in his boot soles for traction; and the climbing and note-taking he did with his professor in addition to the daily trek. My grandfather's exuberance was fabulous to behold. I wondered if at age 19 I could have kept up with him.

Though Dad was tired, he was tough, and in traveling together under difficult circumstances, we grew closer. Until the time I left for grad school we had done a lot together outdoors: bicycle tours, backpacking trips, even some freight-hopping. But in the years since, with me in New York and him in Denver, our shared experience had seen a drought. This journey was refilling the well.

It felt particularly so one afternoon, atop a mountain ridge after an especially hard climb, on a day when Keith for his own reasons had ceased speaking to all of us. Following a brief shower, the sun appeared and framed our route in a double rainbow: Alaska spread out on every side of us, the horizon so low, because of our elevation, that the world was 80 percent sky. Hannibal seemed to prance across the granite and turf, and Dad was ebullient. Nothing could overwhelm us now, we felt; the heavens were with us.

The final 50 feet we traveled with Keith proved disastrous. It was 10 days since we'd begun, and following a long afternoon on the western side of Windy Gap, we'd finally come down to Beaver Creek—its name a modest one for a surging river more than 100 feet wide, its banks lined with trees brought down during spring flooding. Between our packtrain and a meadow on the riverbank lay a wet gully maybe five feet wide. We stopped and waited as the horse Keith was riding gingerly slipped down the near slope of the gully, then scrambled up the far side. His second horse, however, attached by a short leash to Keith's saddle horn, decided not to walk but to jump. He made it, barely; the catastrophe began when huge Dolly, the third horse in the string, found herself at the brink of the gully without enough rope and was forced to jump. Dolly wasn't built for jumping, and I winced as I saw her front legs make the far bank, and then the huge weight of her pack boxes pull her backward, into the gully, as her rope snapped. The huge animal lay on her back in the mud, neighing pathetically as we looked on in horror and Keith looked on in disgust.

"Get down there and hold her head up so she don't drown," Keith barked at Hans, who soon was up to his thighs in mud. Keith ordered us to cross the gully at a narrower spot and bring our horses to him. Then, with his horse in the lead, he fashioned a multihorse tow system, tying the rope at the end to Dolly's harness. "Git!" he cried, whacking the rearmost animal, and the chain of horses strained forward. With a sucking noise, Dolly was slowly brought free of the muck, tilting forward in a motion I thought would break her. Then she popped out and was pulled up onto the bank; in a few seconds she was on her feet. Keith had brought her through, with not insignificant discomfort. Dad and I could relate.

Our adventure began in earnest when we boarded the raft at Beaver Creek. Even as Dad and I floated off, waving to Keith and Hans, we realized that our vessel was inadequate for the job; only eight feet long, it was barely big enough to hold both us and our gear. To sit on the sides, as planned, was absurd—even with the raft fully inflated, water rushed in, and on shallow stretches we scraped the river bottom. The first afternoon, my plastic paddle came apart from its aluminum handle, and just as we finished taping it together we noticed that the rear half of the raft was slowly sinking into the creek. We made a beeline for the shore to fix it.

But despite these worries, we felt a sense of freedom, for we could start and stop and sleep as we liked. We could eat a leisurely breakfast, pause for fishing, bathe in the evening (chilly!), and focus on each other's company.

And talk about Poppa. My favorite picture of him was taken somewhere along Beaver Creek. Nineteen years old, my grandfather stands on a big log raft between Ashby, the cook, and Morton, the packer, who man the sweeps at either end. Behind them is the lost-horse fiasco; ahead are three weeks (more, for all they know) down an uncharted creek that they hope will reunite them with the mighty Yukon, and civilization. Morton and Ashby look strained. But my grandfather, during one of the most trying times of his young life, wears a big grin.

My father was like Poppa in many ways. Dad loved travel and the West and adventure, too—after all, he was game enough to try this harebrained journey. And accounts: in the back of Poppa's diary was the penny-by-penny expense list his father had required him to keep ("leggings 1.25, hdkchfs .25, tip .10, drayage and wharfage on trunk, .75"). My father had asked the same of me at college.

The writer reflects on the significance of the journey and the closeness it brings between him and his father—and Poppa.

Now, though, as we aged, roles were starting to shift; my father was ceding certain kinds of authority to me. How to handle Keith, for example: I had done the discussing, then the yelling. Which way to approach the rapids we encountered as the river meandered north, where to set up the tent—these, now, were my decisions to make. But in return, I had to keep my father well.

Animals occupied our attention as we drifted: a cow moose standing directly in our path (as nervous about a meeting, thankfully, as we were); a wolf that slinked off a gravel bar as we approached, then reemerged to appraise us as we drifted away; eagles that dive-bombed us. Our presence caused a herd of some 30 Dall sheep drinking at the river to dash uphill.

Bears eluded us, though each time we stopped at soft sand it was marked with their prints.

Smoke continued to rise from the forest. Later we learned that 13 fires were burning along the western flank of the White Mountains as we floated by, some just a few acres large, some several square miles. They were part of a natural cycle, and most would run their course in a few slow-burning days—but the smoke they produced was dramatic. More than once we were unable to see across the river; twice we saw live flames licking the riverbank and a landscape of blackened, smoldering trunks beyond.

Finally, eight days down Beaver Creek, we saw our first sign of human habitation—a cabin, Keith Koontz's original homestead. We dragged our ailing raft from the water and looked around. The present owners had posted a sign on the door (next to strips of grizzly hide placed there to scare bears away) asking visitors not to stay in the cabin, but inviting them to use the smaller one a hundred yards away. We explored this offer and found it very much to our liking. It would be two and a half days before our plane arrived, and now we wouldn't have to spend this time in a tent dodging mosquitoes. Instead we read, fished, photographed, cooked, and talked. My father and I are poorer for the distance we live apart. These days in Alaska were money in the bank.

Poppa, to conclude his trip, had floated two more weeks down Beaver Creek. Lack of wind and the slow going made his party easy prey for insects, and their food dwindled to practically nothing. Finally, though, they reached the Yukon River, and were soon pleasantly ensconced in the stateroom of a steamer aiming for the Lower 48.

Our exit from the wilderness was more sudden. Outside early on the appointed day, we didn't have to wait long for our plane—and a sweet sight it was, for even with Keith's landmark to guide us, we were not absolutely sure of our whereabouts. The short, wide-winged plane buzzed over our gravel bar three times before setting down. The pilot didn't want to risk taking off with a fully loaded plane from this little strip, so he ferried us one at a time downriver to a safer gravel bar. He could have told us to sit upside down and we would have done it, so glad were we to see him.

Yet, as we shot over the mountains toward hotel rooms, cold beers, and hot showers, I felt a loss: the skills we had honed for Alaska would not be needed now. Dinner no longer would involve catching a fish. It would be weeks or months—perhaps forever—before I would spend this kind of time with my dad again. And part of me would yearn to be back on my grandfather's trail.

Ending seems to emphasize a sense of nostalgia for a lost time when the Alaskan backcountry was "wilder".

Reading for Comprehension

1. What is your initial reaction to the places in Alaska that Conover describes? How does your reaction change as you read through the travel memoir?
2. Conover is going to Alaska to retrace part of the journey his grandfather made across the backcountry, an unspoiled wilderness. How does the trip prove to be similar to or different from his grandfather's? Does it meet the writer's expectations?

Analyzing the Genre

1. What insights about the place, himself, and others does Conover's travel memoir offer readers?
2. What effect does Conover's use of excerpts from Poppa's notes have on the purpose of his memoir?

CHAPTER 9

Profiles

It's human nature to be curious about the lives of other people, whether it is the kid down the hall who just scored the highest points ever on the retro arcade game Galaga, the latest film star, or a neighbor who suddenly appears on the evening news for winning the local Iron Man competition. We are curious about how people think, how they feel, what they do for a living or for fun, and we like to read about why they live the kinds of lives they do.

What Is a Profile?

So it is no wonder that the profile is a popular feature throughout the media. Pick up the latest *Rolling Stone* and you will be sure to find a profile of the Shins or a rock group from the 1980s making a comeback. Open your local newspaper and chances are you will find a profile of a philanthropic or community organization, such as Literacy Volunteers of America. Or check any social networking site like Facebook and you'll find profiles of people and groups of every variety presenting themselves in persuasive or informative ways. While many profiles focus on interesting people or groups, there are also profiles written about places—some unusual or remote (as seen in *National Geographic*) and others more mundane (like the local town square). The point is, profiles come in many varieties.

Profiles are *civic* genres that reveal a particular *angle* on an individual, group, or place. A profile offers readers a focal point through which to understand or envision the subject, one which is unique to the way the writer sees the person or group or place. And so while one writer may write a profile about the significance of the changing architecture of Washington Square Park in Greenwich Village, New York, another may profile the place in terms of the performers and artists who frequent it daily—the cultural landscape of the park.

Profiles are written from a subjective viewpoint or perspective; profile writers *choose* to profile a particular place (or person, or group) *as they see* their subject.

Thus, profiles are not objective or neutrally written genres. Nor is a profile a biography or a report. A profile does not explain the complete person, place, or group or describe its history. For that we would read a biography, history, or geography text.

The Purposes of Profiles

There are a number of reasons a writer would want to profile a person, place, or group. He wants to tell others about this wonderful but unknown person or group because they reflect some larger aspect of our culture. Perhaps the person has done something few of us can imagine doing, or something we have all done, but done it differently. Maybe that person has overcome a challenge that might inspire the rest of us, or maybe failed to overcome something (failure can be just as interesting as success). A writer might also profile a place because it, like a person, holds something unique or special. A profile of Bayard, West Virginia, for instance, might highlight long years of struggle but suggest that things are starting to improve.

A profile is a snapshot of a subject, not the whole history of the person, place, or group, and the subject is framed by through the writer perspective on it. The writer zooms in on the part of the subject that's been unnoticed, undiscovered. The writer's angle focuses the purpose of the profile for readers.

Writers, then, think about their angle or perspective with a particular readership in mind. They ask themselves: Who would want to read a profile about a man who stormed the beaches of Normandy during World War II? Who would want to read a profile about a single teenage parent who challenges stereotypes about single parents? Who would want to read a profile about a soup kitchen where students do community service?

Understanding your subject, the reasons you want to write about that subject, and why others would want to read about it, is the work of the profile writer.

Reading Profiles Critically

WRITING ACTIVITY   Analyzing the Genre of Profiles

As you read the profile(s), read not only for comprehension but also to understand the *characteristics* of the genre. Look for *patterns* that might reveal what profiles in general do.

Thinking about the Genre

What does the title tell you about the angle the writer has taken on the subject? Skim the first few paragraphs. Frequently writers will provide scenes, anecdotes, or descriptions early in the profile that tell readers about the focus the writer has chosen. What do the first couple of paragraphs reveal about the subject?

Examining the Genre

1. What angle does the writer take on the subject? What details or examples does the writer use to show the angle? How does the writer establish his perspective on the subject from the beginning?
2. How does the writer organize the profile? How does the writer use different kinds of information to develop the angle of his subject? What kinds of information does the writer use to present the angle of his subject?

3. Profile writers do not usually include interview questions in the profile; instead writers *suggest* the questions asked of the subject. What questions do you think the writer asked of his subject(s) based on the material revealed in the profile?

Reflecting on the Genre.

After you have read the profiles(s), explain in a couple of paragraphs the major characteristics of the genre as you understand it, quoting from the profile(s) as necessary.

■ ■ ■

Profiles are written about so many different subjects and for a variety of purposes—people, groups, places. Because of their diversity, they are fun and interesting to read as well as write. While we look at one profile of an individual below, you should also look at other kinds of profiles to understand the genre fully.

Genre Analysis: Larry Rohter, "Part of the Carnival Show: The Man Behind the Masks"

Larry Rohter is an American journalist who was the Brazil-based South America bureau chief for the *New York Times* from 1999 to 2007. He has also worked as a journalist for the *Times* in the Caribbean and Latin America. The profile below was published in the *New York Times* online section, the "Saturday Profile, which includes profiles of individuals from around the globe and of international interest.

"Part of the Carnival Show: The Man Behind the Masks"

Larry Rohter

When Sílvio Botelho de Almeida was 13, he became the apprentice of a local designer of Carnival masks. His father, Alvaro, an appliance salesman, wanted his three children to become doctors or lawyers, and was not pleased.

Draws readers in because it's a common story, and the quote emphasizes the point.

"I didn't take drugs or drink, but he would still mock and ridicule and punish me," Mr. Botelho recalled ruefully. "He thought I would never be able to make a living from Carnival. He used to say to me, 'Are you planning on eating only once a year?' "

Today eating is hardly a problem. Mr. Botelho designs giant puppets, some standing more than 20 feet high and weighing more than 60 pounds, that are so popular he gets requests for them year-round. His fame for this elaborate craftsmanship has spread throughout Brazil and beyond.

Good details about the popularity/success of Botelho and his work.

He has been invited to show his work in Argentina, Cuba, France and the United States. At this year's Carnival, which starts officially at midnight on Feb. 21, Mr. Botelho, now 47, is commemorating the 30th anniversary of the creation of the first of his startlingly lifelike satirical puppets, ''The Afternoon Kid,'' still his personal favorite.

In turn, local Carnival neighborhood groups are celebrating him, both for his contribution to Brazilian popular culture and for helping make Carnival in this languid city of 375,000 people, on the northeast coast of Brazil, one of the best known in a nation that adores the annual pre-Lenten festival like no other.

"For as long as I can remember, I was always fascinated by Carnival and the playful force it embodies," Mr. Botelho said in an interview during his harried final week before the revelry began. "Even as a little boy, the adrenaline would rise and the mere thought of Carnival would take form and force in my head. So I knew that I had something to give and had to have a life that was related in some way to Carnival."

That childhood, he recalled, "was very humble, or to put it more bluntly, poor." But poverty bred in him an ingenuity for expression with simple materials.

"My amusements as a kid were to play with things I found and recycled," he said, "and so I always felt connected in some way to arts and crafts, whether it was drawing on paper or making sculptures out of pieces of wood or clay."

But to please his father, Mr. Botelho said, he took the entrance exam for medical school anyway, five times in fact. He hoped to be a plastic surgeon, if only because he perceived a similarity to the craft he so loved, but he could never score quite high enough to be admitted.

"I tried to become a plastic surgeon, and now I'm a plastic artist," he said, laughing. "Instead of operating on people's faces, I transform them into papier-mâché, and so far, no one has complained."

Far from complaining, they line up for orders. This year there is a backlog because the weather has been unusually humid, which both complicates and slows his work.

A puppet can take two weeks to make, requiring the application of layer upon layer of paper. He has nearly a dozen helpers, but tends to do the most delicate and meticulous work himself, like the actual painting of the puppet's face.

This being an election year in Brazil, Mr. Botelho is swamped with requests that go beyond even the enormous demands of Carnival. Local politicians are among his best customers: they order puppets in their own images, to put at the head of street processions, with a live band following, in order to draw voters to rallies.

"I accept orders from all the parties, big or small, right or left," he said. "It's just a question of my time and their money."

All over Brazil, the most popular Carnival masks worn by revelers the past couple of years have been of George W. Bush, Saddam Hussein and Osama bin Laden. Mr. Botelho has refused to portray any of them, preferring instead to reproduce the images of local celebrities, like a fondly remembered waiter who died in 1997, a coconut vendor, a singer and a radio soccer broadcaster.

"Negative forces gain strength and energy when they are let loose," he explained. "I don't want to criticize people for the wrong things they do, because that is something that ought to be forgotten, not mentioned."

This anecdote explains his upbringing and its influences on his art choices: poverty, class and importance of family.

He isn't bitter; he has a sense of humor.

Pride in his work.

Gives me a sense of Botelho's philosophy on his art and its purposes.

By his own count, Mr. Botelho says, he has made 478 different puppets, some of which he stores in his workshop between one Carnival and the next. People approach him on the street, he said, to ask when he will portray them, or to say their father, uncle or spouse would be a perfect subject.

He likes the prestige, attention and power that goes with his craft, Mr. Botelho admits. But there is one subject he says he absolutely refuses to depict: himself.

"I would never be so vain and narcissistic as to do a self-portrait," he said firmly. "I've already obtained more respect and acceptance than I ever thought would be possible, so why should I deprive someone else of the privilege of being honored with a puppet?"

Mr. Botelho was honored a few years ago by a samba school in Rio de Janeiro, some 1,250 miles south. But he has resisted all entreaties to move there.

Rio's festivities, he says, have been hijacked by television networks, beer companies and other commercial interests. He called it a "spectacle" for tourists.

"Carnival in Rio is like going to the theater just as a spectator and leaving as soon as the play ends," he said, "whereas here you are part of the show that's going on out on the street."

The intensely competitive aspect of Rio's parade, with one samba school walking away with all the glory, also strikes Mr. Botelho as contrary to the spirit of Carnival. He prefers the collegial atmosphere of the "Encounter of the Giant Puppets," a celebration he sponsors on Carnival Tuesday in honor of all the local puppet makers, which has become a highlight of the festivities here.

Mr. Botelho's father died six years ago, still unreconciled to his son's success, though his mother, Maria Dolores, 72, is an admirer of his work. His own marriage, Mr. Botelho said, fell apart because his wife complained that he spent "20 hours a day thinking of Carnival and only four hours thinking of her."

Mr. Botelho acknowledged that he might have time for other pursuits if he could only find a proper heir to his craft. He has a 10-year-old son, Túlio César, who shares his enthusiasm for Carnival, but it is too early to tell if the boy also has the talent, Mr. Botelho said. As for the apprentices he hires, well, they just do not show the same dedication that he demands of himself.

"Most of them are slow to pick things up, and even the one or two who have come along and appear to have the gift, they have been easily distracted by other things, like soccer or music," Mr. Botelho grumbled. "It's not enough to have the ability; you also have to have the commitment."

The writer seems to want readers to get an understanding of how Botelho's views on life are at least partially reflected in his puppetry and artistry. He gives us lots to think about: details to show Botelho's success (he's become internationally known), anecdotes on the influences of his devotion to the puppets and to Carnival itself, and many quotes that allow readers to hear Botelho's passion for his work. The organization is loosely chronological: begins with some info on his childhood influences, to his early work and career, to current day success, and finally a look to the future of his art. But in between, lots of quotes from Botelho himself looking back on those stories from his past.

I wasn't sure why we don't get a clear picture of what Botelho himself looks like—maybe because Botelho himself refuses self-portraiture in his puppets? Seems like the focus or angle is on what drives the artist and the uniqueness of his puppets. But clearly Rohter wants us to feel the almost obsessive quality that Botelho has for creating these giant puppets—certainly a unique career—based on the quotes he includes, and that he doesn't really do it for fame or money, but more so for his love of Carnival as a child and now, plus his desire to celebrate the locals—ordinary people—by creating their images and telling their stories in his puppets. That quality, making something extraordinary from something that appears ordinary, seems like the angle of the profile.

Charlie LeDuff, "End of the Line"

Charlie LeDuff is a writer for the Detroit News. In 2001 he won the Pulitzer Prize for a series of articles in the New York Times called "How Race Is Lived in America." He is the author of two books, was the host and co-producer of the BBC series "The Gates of America," and hosted the series "Only in America" for the Discovery Times channel. In this profile of Janesville, Wisconsin, published in the monthly magazine Mother Jones, LeDuff explores the repercussions of General Motors' failure on the town and the people in it.

GM GUARANTEED THE PEOPLE OF JANESVILLE, WISCONSIN GOOD WAGE FOR A HARD JOB. THOSE WERE THE DAYS.

Driving through Janesville, Wisconsin, in a downpour, looking past the wipers and through windows fogged up with cigarette smoke, Main Street appears to be melting away. The rain falls hard and makes a lonesome going-away sound like a river sucking downstream. And the old hotel, without a single light, tells you that the best days around here are gone. I always smoke when I go to funerals. I work in Detroit. And when I look out the windshield or into people's eyes here, I see a little Detroit in the making.

A sleepy place of 60,483 souls—if the welcome sign on the east side of town is still to be believed—Janesville lies off Interstate 90 between the electric lights of Chicago and the sedate streets of Madison. It is one of those Middle-Western places that outsiders pay no mind. It is where the farm meets the factory, where the soil collides with the smokestack. Except the last GM truck rolled off the line December 23, 2008. Merry Christmas Janesville. Happy New Year.

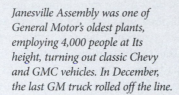

Janesville Assembly was one of General Motor's oldest plants, employing 4,000 people at Its height, turning out classic Chevy and GMC vehicles. In December, the last GM truck rolled off the line.

The Janesville Assembly Plant was everything here, they say. It was a birthright. It was a job for life and it was that way for four generations. This was one of General Motors' oldest factories—opened in 1919. This was one of its biggest—almost 5 million square feet. Nobody in town dared drive anything but a Chevy or a GMC. Back then GM was the largest industrial corporation in the world, the largest carmaker, the very symbol of American power. Ike's man at the Pentagon—a former GM exec himself—famously said, What "was good for our country was good for General Motors, and vice versa." Kennedy, Johnson, Obama, they all campaigned here. People here can tell you of their grandparents who came from places like Norway and Poland and Alabama to build tractors and even ammunition during the Big War. Then came the Impalas and the Camaros. In the end they were cranking out big machines like the Suburban and the Tahoe, those high-strung, gas-guzzling hounds of the American Good Times.

Today, some $50 billion in bailouts later, GM is on life support and there is a sinking feeling that the country is going down with it. Those grandchildren are considering moving to Texas or Tennessee or Vegas. Who is to blame? Detroit? Wall Street? Management? Labor? NAFTA? Does it matter? Come to Janesville and see what we've thrown away.

For years, the people here heard rumors that the plant was on its way out. But no one ever believed it, really. Something always came along to save it. Gas prices went down or cheap Chinese money floated in. Janesville was too big to ignore. Too big to close.

And then they closed it.

The local UAW union hall is quiet now. A photograph from a 1925 company picnic hangs there. The whole town is assembled near the factory, the women in petticoats, the children in patent leather, the men in woolen bowlers. The caption reads, "Were you there Charlie?"

Todd Brien's name still hangs in the wall cabinet—Recording Secretary, it reads. But that is just a leftover like a coin in a cushion. Brien, 41, moved to Arlington, Texas, to take a temp job in a GM plant down there in April. He left his family up here. He is one of the lucky ones. Most of the other 2,700 still employed after rounds of downsizing had no factory to go to. But now, what with the bankruptcy of GM, he's temporarily laid off from Texas, and back in Janesville to gather his family and head south.

"It was always in the back of my mind around here ... They can take it away," Brien says. "Well, they did. Now what? Can't sell my house. Main Street's boarding up. The kids around here are getting into drugs. You wonder when's the last train leaving this station? I just never believed it was going to happen." Today, freight trains leaving from Janesville's loading docks take auctioned bits and pieces of the plant to faraway places: welding robots, milling machines, chop saws, drill presses, pipe-threaders, drafting tables, salt and pepper shakers.

Janesville is still a nice place. They still cut the grass along the riverbank. The churches are still full on Sunday. The farmers still get up before dawn. But there are the little telltale signs, the details, the darkening clouds.

The strip club across the street from the plant is now an Alcoholics Anonymous joint. There are too many people in the welfare line who never would have imagined themselves there. Dim prospects and empty buildings. A motel where the neon "Vacancy" sign never seems to say "No Vacancy."

The owner is Pragnesh Patel. He is 36, looks a dozen years older. He left a good job near Ahmedabad, India, as a supervisor in a television factory, he says. He came to try his luck in America. He got a job in a little factory in Janesville that makes electronic components for GM. He also bought the motel just up the hill from the assembly plant. Now with the plant closed, he's down to three shifts a week at the components factory and having to make $2,500 monthly payments on his motel on Highway 51. He charges 45 bucks a night and today it's mostly the crackheads and the down-at-their-heels who come in for a crash landing. Welcome to America, except Patel has to raise his children amid this decay. "I'm trying, really trying to survive," he says. "I don't know anymore. I mean, I'm an American. I cast my lot here. But I have to tell you, on many days, I regret that I ever came."

There is a bar on the factory grounds that has become a funeral parlor. Yes, a bar on the factory grounds, not 500 feet from the time clock! Genius! It has been here since at least the Depression if the yellowed receipt from 1937 is to be believed. Five cases of beer for 8 dollars and 30 cents.

And in some way, that bar on the factory grounds might explain what happened here. "We used to have a drive-through window," says one of the former UAW workers gathered at Zoxx 411 Club and drinking a long, cool glass of liquor at three in the afternoon. He is about 50, about the age when a man begins to understand his own obsolescence. "Used to put two or three down and go back to work. Now those were the days, yes-siree."

You feel sorry for that autoworker until you hear he draws nearly three-quarters of his old salary for the first year of his layoff and half his salary for the second year of his layoff—plus benefits.

"It don't make sense to work," says the autoworker, buying one for the stranger.

If he finds a job, he says, they'll take his big check away.

"There ain't no job around here for $21 an hour," the autoworker says. "I might as well drink."

A taxpayer-funded wake. Good for him. Except you get the feeling that it's not good for a man to drink all day. Two years comes faster than a man thinks.

A little Detroit in the making, except Detroit has General Motors and Ford and Chrysler. Detroit is an industry town. Janesville had only General Motors. Janesville was a company town. You didn't have to go to college—but you might be able to send your kid there—because there was always GM. GM—Gimme Mine. GM—Grandma Moo, the golden cow. Now GM has Gone Missing. GM has Gone to Mexico.

"We took it for granted," says Nancy Nienhuis, 76, a retired factory nurse who farms on the outskirts of town. She did everything at that plant a nurse could do: tended to amputations, heart attacks, shotgun wounds inflicted by a jilted lover, even performed an exorcism of spiders from a crazy man's stomach. Whatever it took to keep those lines moving.

"The rumor would start, they're talking about closing the plant. No one would believe it. Then you saw the Toyota dealership open on the east side of town and still they didn't believe it. The manager and the worker sat next to each other in church, you see? They went to high school together. Understand? The good worker got no recognition over the bad worker. Nobody made waves about a guy drunk or out fishing on the clock. In the end, the last few years, management rode them pretty good. But by then it was a little too late."

Richard, a former welder at the plant, puts a pastry box in Nurse Nancy's car. Richard begins to weep. He looks over his shoulder, wipes his nose on his sleeve and says, "I don't want my wife to see this. I'm 62 and I'm delivering doughnuts. What am I going to do?"

Desperation comes in subtler ways than a grown man crying. The winner of the cakewalk at the local fair got not a cake—but a single, solitary cupcake. Parents don't come to the PTA as much anymore. A lot of kids will have left by the beginning of the school year, the superintendent says. Unemployment here is near 15 percent. The police blotter is a mix of Mayberry and Big City: Truancy, Truancy, Shots Fired at 2 p.m., Dog Barking, Burglary at 5 p.m., Burglary at 6 p.m.

At 7 p.m. they fry fish at the VFW hall. Beers 2 bucks. Two-piece plate of cod $6.95. Charlie Larson runs the place. You can see the factory from Charlie's parking lot, the Rock River running lazily beside it. Charlie tried the factory in 1966. His father got him in, but he was drafted into the jungles of Nam in 1967. "It's a discouraging thing," Charlie, 61, says of the plant closing down, smoothing a plastic tablecloth. "It was the lifeblood of this town. It was the identity of this town. Now we have nothing, nothing but worry. Aw, there's going to be hell to pay when those unemployment checks stop coming."

Blame the factory worker if you must. Blame the union man who asked too much and waited too long to give some back. Blame the guy for drinking at lunch or cutting out early. But factory work is a 9-to-5 sort of dying. The monotony, the accidents. "You're a machine," says Marty Wopat. He put bumpers on trucks. A six-foot man stooping in a four-foot hole, lining up a four-foot bumper. Three bolts, three washers, three nuts. One every minute over an eight-hour shift. Wopat, 62, has bad shoulders, bad knees, bad memories. "You got nightmares," he says. "You missed a vehicle or you couldn't get the bolt on. You just went home thinking nothing except the work tomorrow and your whole life spent down in that hole. And you thinking how you're going to get out. Well, now it's gone and alls we're thinking about is wanting to have it back."

And maybe they will have it back. The recession is loosening its grip, some say. Some towns will rebound. Some plants will retrofit. Wind, solar, electric—that's the future, Washington says. But you get a pain-in-the-throat feeling that it is not the future. Not really. At least not as good a future as the past. There's no 28 bucks an hour for life in that future. No two-car garage. No bennies. No boat on Lake Michigan. Because in the new world they can build that windmill, or a solar panel, or an electric battery in India, where the minimum pay is less than $3 a day. Just ask Patel, the motel owner living at the edge of a dead factory in Janesville, Wisconsin. "You cannot compete with poverty unless you are poor."

Janesville still looks like Heartland, USA— a giant fiberglass cow even marks the entrance into town. But restaurants are all but empty, and school enrollment is down.

Janesville was a company town, where generations of GM workers met at the VFW to cap off a hard day's work. A town of Cooties and 4-Hers is now also a town of moving trucks and permanent yard sales.

Unemployment in Janesville is now the highest in Wisconsin. The local food bank serves 10 percent more people than it did a year ago.

Motel owner Pragnesh Patel says he wishes he'd never come from India.

Reading for Comprehension

1. Early on in the profile, LeDuff writes that a job with GM "was a birthright. It was a job for life and it was that way for four generations." How does LeDuff show that that is no longer the case?
2. LeDuff offers a lot of reasons for why Janesville has the problems it does, but where does he ultimately suggest the blame belongs?

Analyzing the Genre

1. How do the photographs of Janesville help LeDuff portray the town? How do the photographs help him communicate or suggest the angle he has taken on the town?
2. Part of what profile writers do is present the subject from a particular perspective or angle. How does LeDuff use the voices of townspeople to accomplish this? How does he use his own voice?

Elaine Miller, "Being Rosie the Riveter"

Elaine Miller's profile was published in 2009 in the weekly magazine *American Profile*, which describes itself as a "magazine that celebrates hometown American life." On its website, you can find profiles of individuals, groups, and places—from a profile of Berdine's Five & Dime in Harrisville, West Virginia, to one of an emerald miner in North Carolina. In "Being Rosie the Riveter," Miller profiles Fran Carter, a woman who helped build B-29 bombers during World War II.

When Fran Carter, 86, dons blue coveralls, a red and white bandana, rubber-soled shoes and red lipstick to portray Rosie the Riveter—the cultural icon of the working American women of World War II—she knows and plays the part by heart.

In the 1940s, Carter riveted sheet metal onto the fuselages of B-29 bombers at an aircraft factory in Birmingham, Ala. Today, when she puts on the uniform usually associated with Rosie, she does so to honor the legacy and contributions of the millions of women who manned the factories and fields when the men went overseas to fight.

"We weren't women's libbers," says Carter, founder and executive director of the 3,000-member American Rosie the Riveter Association. "We just wanted to get the boys back home so we could marry them. A lot of us did it because we thought the country was worth fighting for."

Several times each month, Carter and her husband, John, 87, visit schools, churches and veterans organizations to share the story of Rosie the

Riveter, the fictional character—celebrated in song and popularized on period posters—who represented the 6 million to 10 million women who contributed to the war effort between 1942 and 1945.

During the war, real-life Rosies built 297,000 airplanes, 88,000 warships, 102,000 tanks and 372,000 artillery pieces, and produced 47 million tons of artillery munitions and 44 billion rounds of small arms munitions. They made uniforms in cotton mills, farmed, drove buses or taxis, worked in defense agencies or did volunteer work. Some served as pilots, ferrying fighter planes and other aircraft from the factories to the training fields.

"Rosie could have been Wanda the Welder or Mabel the Machinist, but a song, along with movies about Rosie, made her the icon," says John, wearing his World War II paratrooper uniform. "Her legacy is the jobs open to women that weren't open to them before the war."

Fran had been a schoolteacher in Thaxton, Miss., when she moved to Birmingham in 1943 to work at the Betchel, McCombs and Parsons Airplane Modification Center. Wearing her factory's uniform of gray coveralls, goggles and a hairnet, she drove rivets through sheet metal, while a woman on the other side of the airplane pressed a brick against the metal to flatten and secure each rivet.

After the war, Fran and John married, had two children, and became professors at Samford University in Birmingham. She taught home economics, and he was dean of the school of education. Now retired, they live in Homewood, Ala. (pop. 25,403), a Birmingham suburb.

Fran was inspired to start the American Rosie the Riveter Association (ARRA) after attending a program in 1997 that featured a dramatic portrayal of the lives of five females employed during the Second World War. The program, conducted annually at the Little White House State Historic Site in Warm Springs, Ga., honored Fran and other real-life Rosies.

"I decided we had a legacy to leave, and the best way to do it was to form an organization," says Carter, who first portrayed Rosie the Riveter in 2001.

ARRA was founded on Pearl Harbor Day, Dec. 7, 1998. The organization has members in 48 states, has published three books of personal Rosie stories and a cookbook, and convenes each June to commemorate and preserve the legacy of the working women of World War II. Any woman who did what traditionally was men's work during the war qualifies as a Rosie. Female descendants may join as Rosebuds. Husbands, brothers and male descendants may join as Rivets.

"Time is against us," Fran says. "Most of the Rosies have already passed away, and we have a hard time locating the ones that are still here because most places didn't keep the employment records of the women. It's important that we get their stories before they all die."

Reading for Comprehension

1. In the third paragraph, Carter claims that "We weren't women's libbers." What does that suggest about her view of women who worked during WWII? What does that reveal about her?

2. What does Miller mean when she describes Rosie the Riveter as a cultural icon? Can you think of any other female figures who have been considered icons in American culture?

Analyzing the Genre

1. What lasting impression of Fran Carter does Miller want to leave readers with? What strategies does Miller use to develop this angle in the profile?

2. What kinds of research does Miller use in this profile? How does that information add to the angle of the profile?

3. How do the opening and closing in this profile both engage readers and emphasize the purpose of the profile?

Mary O. Parker, "Bingo!"

In her profile, also published in American Profile (see author information above for a description of the magazine), Mary O. Parker takes a close look at a popular American pastime, at least among a certain demographic. Bingo, originally called "beano," has been played in some form for centuries, and in her profile, Parker explores why people play it so passionately.

Vella Garrett, 80, the self-proclaimed "bingo queen" of Smithville, Texas (pop. 3,901), insists that bingo is the thing to do on a small-town Saturday night. "It's what I look forward to all week long. And just look at all them other folks who feel like me!" she says, gesturing to the packed room in Smithville's VFW hall.

Sitting at a table with friends and munching on pimiento cheese sandwiches made by volunteers, Garrett studies the emerging patterns on her bingo card as caller Bill Zimmerhanzel announces one letter-number combination after another.

"B-12! G-49! N-32!" Zimmerhanzel calls out between sips from a water bottle as he pulls pingpong-size balls bearing the combinations from a faux-wooden box.

"I don't play real serious, not for the money," says Garrett, who has played bingo at the Veterans of Foreign Wars hall each Saturday night for more than 20 years. It's the friendship and fellowship with local townsfolk that draw her to the game.

Indeed, old-fashioned bingo is the game of both choice and chance in small towns across America, where players of all ages congregate regularly in churches, community centers, firehouses, fraternal lodges and other venues in search of lighthearted fun and social interaction—all while helping organizations raise money for local charities.

"Sure beats staying home and staring at the four walls!" says Pat Werlein, 79, another Smithville regular who sits at the same table every week with a group of friends dubbed the "Widows Club."

"Yep, we go to bingo every chance we get," adds Della Mae Urban, 78, between giggles with the other Widows Club members.

Gladys Susen, 87, has played bingo at Smithville's VFW hall since the 1950s, when corn kernels served as markers. These days, players use ink daubers to mark their cards, and Susen brings along six—including one with an image of Betty Boop—plus her rabbit's foot and a lucky horseshoe. "But don't let that fool you," she insists, dispelling the power of her lucky charms. "If I bingo, I bingo; if I don't, I don't."

From Beano! to Bingo!

New York toy salesman Edwin S. Lowe is credited with creating today's version of the game in 1929 after seeing its Italian-born forerunner played at a carnival in Atlanta. The game used beans as markers, and the winner called out "Beano!" to signal a winning card. Lowe renamed the game after he overheard a player mistakenly yell "Bingo!" and then asked Columbia University math professor Carl Leffler to increase the number of possible bingo card combinations. By 1930, Leffler had devised 6,000 different cards, and churches across the country quickly adopted the game as a fun and effective way to raise money for charity.

Even with the introduction of electronic versions online and at gambling casinos, playing bingo the old-fashioned way hasn't lost its charm. Traditional bingo "still dominates the market and is spread across the nation," says Steven Fingold, vice president of sales at American Games Inc., which manufactures bingo supplies in Council Bluffs, Iowa (pop. 58,268). "Bingo is a game that brings people together to socialize and have fun. Electronics take away from the typical bingo social environment."

Kathy Horn, a worker with the South Carolina Charitable Bingo Association, likens community bingo halls to second homes for many players. "Everybody knows everybody," Horn says. "They like to meet and greet everyone. And if they don't get a chance to do that, they feel like they've really missed out."

At the Moose Lodge in La Pine, Ore. (pop. 5,799), the weekly Wednesday night game has drawn a crowd for 25 years. "Some people have been coming about that long to play here," says Dave Lea, lodge administrator. "Players have friends they sit with every week."

Playing for Others

The fact that proceeds are used to help fund community projects—from sprucing up Little League fields to helping pay for equipment and building improvements at local schools and hospitals—is another impetus for the game's popularity.

"People come to bingo to have a good night and fellowship with friends," says Charles Garthwaite, president of Ledyard Lions Club in Gales Ferry, Conn. (pop. 6,837). "But I think they also like knowing that the money goes back into the community."

Last year alone, the Ledyard Lions Club used bingo income to provide more than $12,000 in college scholarships to Ledyard High School graduates and raised $10,000 to take 96 families Christmas shopping. "Another thing we do with the money is get eyeglasses for those who need them and can't afford to get their own," Garthwaite says.

The Moose Lodge in La Pine also puts its bingo money back into the community. "The high school basketball team might need help buying their uniforms or an individual might need help with medical bills. We'll use the money for things like that," Lea says.

In Smithville, bingo proceeds are used to buy flags that fly in the town on patriotic holidays and school supplies for children, among other things. Volunteer Joe Sulak, 80, says charity bingo is an all-American pastime because of the way the game is used to help others. "I think that's the best part," he says, before dashing from table to table to supply players with fresh cards.

Bingo's goodwill goes far beyond dollars and cents, however. "Our son's dying of cancer," confides Barbara Villegas, 73. "This lets me forget about it for awhile and be around nice people," she says as her husband, Edward, 81, nods in agreement while playing by her side.

Nearby, Melissa Borja, 43, plays from her wheelchair. "I've got RSD (reflex sympathetic dystrophy) and this helps me take my mind off the pain," she says of her neurological condition. Borja flashes a smile across the table to April Wolfe, 46, her bingo buddy who faithfully picks her up and brings her to the VFW hall each Saturday.

"As far as I'm concerned, bingo's the only game in town!" she says.

Reading for Comprehension

1. Why, according to Parker, do people play bingo? What do they get out of it?
2. As Parker describes it, bingo has long been an American cultural pastime. Are there characteristics or values associated with the game that Parker reveals as particularly American?

Analyzing the Genre

1. While Parker is profiling a group—bingo players—she relies on individuals to help her develop the angle on that group. What impression of the group does she convey to readers through her use of their individual stories? What strategies does she use to give this group a voice in the profile?
2. Parker makes use of some research in her profile. How important is that background material to her portrayal of bingo players? What does it add to our understanding of bingo players?

WRITING ASSIGNMENT OPTIONS

Profiles

Write a **profile of a person** who has made a difference in society because of their talents, philosophy on life, outreach to others, work or hobbies. If the person has been profiled before, write the profile for a different audience and purpose and with a unique angle.

Profile Writing Options

1. Write a **profile of a group or organization** that does interesting work or has a unique focus, or one that is not well understood or well known.
2. Write a **profile of a place** to reveal its character. You can choose a public place, like a park or a bus, or a private place, such as someone's home, or even a virtual place, such the online worlds of World of Warcraft or Second Life. The personality of the place is what makes it interesting.
3. Write a **profile on a person or company** in a field you are in or might pursue. Inform readers about the unique aspects of that career, the practitioner, or the company.

Community-based Writing Option

Many community-focused organizations lack funding to publicize their need for volunteers, yet these are the very organizations that need volunteers to keep running. These organizations need to reach the population they serve, too, but again cannot afford to publicize their services. One way organizations reach out to volunteers or the local population is through word of mouth. A profile of an organization published in a local newspaper would attract volunteers and clients who read the piece or heard about it from another reader.

Write a profile of a community organization you volunteer for or know about in order to inform readers of its mission and attract attention to its services. For your angle, focus on the people who use it, the people who run it, or another aspect of the organization.

Writing Profiles

Just as with any genre, profiles have particular characteristics that help writers understand what they need to say and how to say it.

> **WHAT WRITERS CONSIDER WHEN THEY WRITE PROFILES**
> In general, profile writers:
>
> - Choose subjects that are unique, misunderstood, outstanding, or challenge readers' ways of thinking about them
> - Conduct background and/or field research of their subjects
> - Develop an angle on their subject by choosing significant quotes, details, anecdotes from field research
> - Incorporate the subject's voice into the profile
> - Choose an organizational pattern appropriate to their angle and purpose

Avoiding Common Profile Pitfalls

Not every person, group, or place will make a good subject for a profile. In fact, there are some subject types you should definitely avoid:

1. *The way-too-busy subject.* Sadly, the people who are most likely to be "way too busy" subjects are exactly the kinds of people we are drawn to write about: They are dynamic, motivated, and interesting. But they often cannot find time to talk with the profile writer. To avoid running into this kind of difficulty, carefully examine each person before you decide to profile her. If you decide to go ahead anyway, set clear guidelines about what time commitments you will need—if she finds these too demanding, she will back out.

2. *The private subject.* Sometimes individuals belong to organizations that restrict what they can say. For instance, a student decided to profile an honor guard at Arlington National Cemetery, but a problem arose when the officer's supervisor had to approve both the questions being asked *and* the answers the officer provided. As a result the profile writer's work was delayed and she could not include many of the more interesting aspects of the honor guard's duties and responsibilities. Similarly, if you want to interview a sorority sister or a member of the Skull and Bones Society, you should keep in mind that members of such groups often cannot reveal the most interesting aspects of their organizations. So ask about restrictions before committing to profile such a group or its members.

Generating Ideas for Profiles

The best place to get ideas for a profile is from your own experiences. You know numerous people: family members, friends, roommates, other students, coworkers. You, most likely, are connected to groups or organizations: the Boy Scouts, church choir, swim team, an employer. And you've been to lots of

WebLinks

The Genre of Profiles

Profiles can be found in many newspapers and magazines (e.g. *Sports Illustrated, Washington Post,* and the *New Yorker*). The *New York Times'* online "Saturday Profile" section includes profiles of people from around the globe who have made a difference in society or have unique careers, hobbies, or personalities. To go to the site, use a search engine to search the words "New York Times Saturday Profiles."

places—even if you haven't traveled extensively: the place you grew up, the coffee shop you frequent daily on your way to work, the amusement park where you spent every weekend.

Given all the possible choices, how do you decide which one is best? One way that writers choose is to consider what they know about the subject already and what they want to say about him or her (or it). They think, too, about potential audiences: Who would want to read about this person, group, or place? What would they want to know? Profile writers consider the angle they might take and then focus on the aspect that is most interesting, revealing, or uncommon.

WRITING ACTIVITY   Generating Ideas for Profiles

Listing:

Write down at least ten possible topic ideas. Use the prompts below to guide your brainstorming.

- Do any individuals or groups have an interesting or unique career or hobby or lifestyle that interests you?
- Do any individuals, groups, or places illustrate a larger social issue (i.e. an environmental activist, a gang member, the local soup kitchen, campus Habitat for Humanity)?
- Do any individuals or groups challenge a stereotype or have unconventional methods of doing things?
- Do any individuals or groups represent those who have lived through particularly challenging events, historic moments, or time periods?
- Do any places encourage certain kinds of behavior? Are any of them well known but little used? Are any secret or exclusive? Do any attract certain kinds of people?
- Do any of these places, on closer observation of the people and settings, cause you to think about the social, political, or cultural issues going on there?

Brainstorming:

Think about your reasons for choosing a subject. For each of the possible (or likely) subjects you generated above, freewrite about the following:

- Why are you interested in profiling this subject? Who else besides you would be interested in reading about the subject of your profile? Why?
- What do you hope your profile will accomplish for readers? What message will it convey about your subject?

■ ■ ■

Thinking about Audience, Purpose, and Situation

As in most writing situations, it helps to have a really clear sense of who your audience is. Think of it this way: Would your grandparents really be interested in a profile of 50cent? Would your spouse or partner want to read a profile about your fellow hobbyists? Probably not, unless they share the same interests. So you'll want to have a sense of who your audience is before choosing your subject.

One way of deciding on the audience is to think about where your profile might be published. If you want to see your profile published in an issue of *Teen*, then you'll need to choose a subject the magazine's audience might want to read about. The readers of *Teen*, tween and teenage girls, have particular interests.

Understanding and carefully articulating your audience will also help you figure out your purpose: Why are you writing about this particular subject? Do you want to inform an audience about an individual they are not likely to have encountered? Do you want to challenge a stereotype or misconception about a particular group or place?

WRITING ACTIVITY   Defining the Rhetorical Situation for Your Profile

1. Who would want to read your profile? And where would they read it—website? Newspaper? Magazine?
2. What are your intended readers like? What are they interested in? What might they already know about your subject (person, group, place)?
3. What is your purpose in writing the profile? What do you hope to accomplish?
4. What do you want your audience to think and feel after reading it? How should they react?
5. What made you choose the subject of your profile? What situation or circumstances surround the subject you are writing about?

■ ■ ■

Researching Profiles: Background Research, Interviewing, and Observing

Profile writers gather most of their material from their subjects by immersing themselves in their subject's world. To do so, they conduct field research by interviewing and observing their subjects. But in order for writers to familiarize themselves with their subjects before they interview or observe them, they first need to conduct background research.

Doing Your Homework: Background Research

Conducting background research is absolutely essential for profile writers. Background research helps profile readers better understand the subject before they start writing about it. Doing research helps writers learn more about their subjects and enlarges the context in which they think about their subjects. For example, notice how Charlie LeDuff uses background research on the town of Janesville and the role that GM played in shaping the town and its residents in order to underscore how the town was devastated when GM left.

Background research also helps writers develop thoughtful interview questions. If your subject is a volunteer, for instance, you could conduct background research on "volunteerism" to help you better understand your subject and ask interview questions that yield thoughtful and quotable responses from interviewees. Please see Chapter 13: Research and the Rhetorical Situation, pages 501–539, for more on conducting background research.

Developing Interview Questions and Conducting Interviews

While background information helps writers prepare for interviews, the interviews are often the primary means of gathering information on a subject; just as importantly, that information leads to quotes for the profile written in the subject's own voice. And though writers do use background research in their profiles, they want the subject's voice to tell readers about the details. Often an interviewee's perspective is more interesting than what formal research might relay.

Interviews often serve another purpose: Writers can use the interview to create the conditions necessary to getting the subject to open up. One way to do this is to ask carefully crafted and well-organized questions. For example, you wouldn't want to start by asking the subject, say the chef of an award-winning restaurant, which awards he earned this past year. These are details you should already know from the background research you did *before* you went to the interview. So you might reframe the question: "I know you won a few awards last year, including the world-renowned Golden Ladle Award, but is there one that was more meaningful to you than the rest?" This question lets the chef (interviewee) know you are truly interested in him and his talents and sets the tone for a good interview.

A second way to spur your subject to talk is to ask questions that require more than a "yes/no" answer. Open-ended questions encourage interviewees to tell stories about their lives or give examples when they respond. Such dialog leads to more interesting profile material.

And finally, remember that you may be doing more than one interview of the same person, so if you forget to ask a question or if you find you need to ask some follow-up questions, you can always do a second interview by phone or email. See Field Research in Chapter 13 for information on constructing and conducting interviews.

WRITING ACTIVITY   Generating and Organizing Interview Questions

Generating Interview Questions. With background information about your subject in mind, develop open-ended interview questions that require more than yes/no answers.

1. Does your prior knowledge about your subject suggest any questions which would deepen or clarify your understanding of the person?
2. Does your prior knowledge reveal any gaps you could explore further?
3. What would you like to learn about your subject?
4. What might your intended audience be interested in knowing about the subject?
5. What kinds of open-ended questions will you need to ask in order to fulfill your purpose for writing the profile?

Organizing Interview Questions. Organize your interview questions under topic headings. Grouping your questions will help you avoid jumping around from topic to topic during the interview and ensure you leave with good material for your profile.

■   ■   ■

Observing People and Places

Including detailed observations of the subject allows readers to feel like they are a part of the experience: They are with the writer as she is witnessing the people and places of the profile. To observe well, you need to use all your senses to look for details that are interesting or unique, or reveal something about your subject. What you see, hear, smell, and so on when observing your subject can be quite revealing to readers who later read your descriptions.

In the following excerpt, LeDuff describes the town of Janesville. His description helps us see not only the place but also the people who live there:

> A sleepy place of 60,483 souls—if the welcome sign on the east side of town is still to be believed—Janesville lies off Interstate 90 between the electric lights of Chicago and the sedate streets of Madison. It is one of those Middle-Western places that outsiders pay no mind. It is where the farm meets the factory, where the soil collides with the smokestack. Except the last GM truck rolled off the line December 23, 2008. Merry Christmas Janesville. Happy New Year.

Calling the townsfolk "souls" rather people is reflected later as we come to see them as "lost souls." The sense he gives us of Janesville as a place between other places, a place that is neither one thing nor another, helps LeDuff later make the claim that these kinds of places are all too real. Without careful observation, profile writers miss out on important aspects of their subjects. For more about making observations, see Field Research in Chapter 13, pages 501–539.

Drafting Profiles

Generally, profile writers begin by taking stock of the material they have gathered from their interviews, observations, and background research.

Taking Stock: Sorting Through Field Research

In the process of interviewing, observing, and researching your subject, you will generate a lot of material. And that means you will need to choose what to include, since you won't want to include it all—remember this is not a report on the subject or a biography; you are writing to reveal a particular angle on your subject, so not all the material you gathered will be relevant. Furthermore, not all of the material will be interesting to readers; you will choose the best of what you have. As you sort through your material to decide which information to include or cut, you will begin to frame the angle of your profile because some aspects of your subject will emerge as more relevant.

WRITING ACTIVITY   Taking Stock: What Does Your Field Research Reveal?

1. Write down your current perspective on your subject. What makes the subject "profile-worthy" and why do you think others would be interested in reading about it? Choose interesting anecdotes or quotes that stand out—ones that seem to be leading you toward *your perspective* of your subject that you wish to present to readers. Circle or highlight these on your field research notes.
2. Review your observation notes as well with the same goal—to find material that seems to develop your purpose for choosing the subject.
3. Cluster the information you've circled or highlighted under subheadings—ones that reveal a particular aspect of your subject. Grouping these ideas under subheadings may help you to organize your thoughts and the focus of your profile.
4. Finally, determine what the information you've chosen reveals about your subject. Does it change your perspective or lead you to a particular focus or angle for your profile?

■   ■   ■

Framing Your Angle

Although you may have started out with one idea for the angle of your profile, after you've done some field research and reviewed your notes, you may find yourself changing the angle or zooming in on it in more focused ways. Sometimes angles may emerge from your research notes. Remember, a profile is based on your perspective—your subjective vision—of the person, group, or place, and that vision is the lens through which you see your subject—and ultimately how you decide you want readers to see it, too.

Indeed, profile writing is not objective reportage. Instead, with a clear purpose and audience in mind, profile writers persuade readers to see the subject the way they do: from a particular point of view or angle.

WRITING ACTIVITY   Framing Your Angle

1. What aspects of your subject stand out most, after you have sifted through your research?
2. Are there any particular words or adjectives that describe your subject and reflect your angle?
3. Having gone through all your research, how has your original purpose changed? How have your initial thoughts on what makes this person (or group, or place) interesting changed?
4. What is the impression you want to leave readers with about your subject? What can they get out of reading your profile?
5. Finally, what will readers find important about the person, group, or place you've profiled? How can they relate to the subject in their lives?

■ ■ ■

Showing Versus Telling Your Angle

Unlike a thesis statement in formal academic genres, the angle of a profile is usually *implied* rather than stated explicitly. In part, this method is stylistic. The profile genre is suggestive rather than direct, so readers expect to come to understand the subject gradually, not be told directly in a thesis statement.

As a profile writer, you need to consider how you will make your angle apparent to readers without actually stating it outright. The research you've gathered—anecdotes and quotes from interviews, descriptions and details from observations— will help you "show" the angle rather than "tell" readers what you want them to think about your subject.

Notice how Larry Rohter suggests the artist Botelho's success in the material he chose to include in his profile:

> Mr. Botelho designs giant puppets, some standing more than 20 feet high and weighing more than 60 pounds, that are so popular he gets requests for them year-round. His fame for this elaborate craftsmanship has spread throughout Brazil and beyond.
>
> He has been invited to show his work in Argentina, Cuba, France and the United States. At this year's Carnival, which starts officially at midnight on Feb. 21, Mr. Botelho, now 47, is commemorating the 30th anniversary of the creation of the first of his startlingly lifelike satirical puppets, ''The Afternoon Kid,'' still his personal favorite.

Another way to show the angle is by using "thick description" of your subject; that is by including sensory details (sight, sound, taste, touch, and smell). Sensory details fill in the portrait of your subject and immerse readers in the subject's world. Even if your reader is familiar with your subject, you can describe it in a way that offers a fresh perspective they may not have noticed before.

So, for example, instead of writing "the weather was miserable but people showed up on the day of the championship softball game," you can show the miserable weather: "Rain pelted down on the metal stands like nails on a tin roof while faithful fans gathered, covered head to toe in their bright yellow slickers, to watch the championship game of State College's women's softball team." This description immerses the reader in the scene and experiences of the subject.

Writing Openings for Profiles

Profile writers craft opening paragraphs that engage readers immediately, suggesting the angle, and piquing the readers' interest with a quote, anecdote, description of a scene, and so on. Openings of profiles are often the first glimpse readers have ever had of the subject, and writers aim to crack open the door of a subject's world, so to speak, so readers can step inside.

One way a profile writer might do this is by putting readers in a scene that is significant to the subject's environment and captures the subject's essence. Setting the scene often involves thick descriptions filled with such details as the surroundings, the actions taking place, the people, and sensory impressions.

For example, Brian Hiatt's profile for *Rolling Stone* magazine, "The Second Coming of Pearl Jam," uses thick descriptions and details to convey a particular impression to readers about the lead singer, Eddie Vedder.

> "Hey, Eddie!" It's after midnight on Cleveland's sleepy waterfront, and Eddie Vedder—carrying a worn suitcase and wearing a thin corduroy jacket—is walking in his hunched posture toward the Ritz-Carlton hotel. He hears someone shout his name, and turns.
>
> A mean-eyed young Republican steps from the shadows, barking, "Bush 2008! Bush 2008! Bush 2008! Jeb's running!" Then the guy grins at Vedder—who was one of the headliners of 2004's pro-Kerry Vote for Change Tour—gives him a sarcastic thumbs-up sign and prepares to watch the dour, volatile lead singer of Pearl Jam freak out.
>
> Vedder stares for a moment. Then he just shrugs, mumbles, "OK, man," and heads inside. The heckler looks crushed....

We learn a lot about Vedder from these two short paragraphs: He's rich enough to stay at the Ritz, yet he wears a "thin corduroy jacket," carries a "worn suitcase," and doesn't react to the taunts of the "mean-eyed Republican"—he keeps his cool. The impressions about Vedder suggested in this opening are developed throughout the profile. Hiatt's angle on Vedder—as the world-weary and *changed* rock star—is clearly communicated.

WRITING ACTIVITY   Openings for Profiles

Consider one of these strategies to open your profile.

■ **Create a striking image.** Use descriptions and details to show the personality of your subject as Rohter does in "Part of the Carnival Show: The Man Behind the Masks."

■ **Introduce the subject's voice.** Use a quote from your subject (or from someone talking about your subject) that reveals his or her personality and suggests the angle for your profile.

- **Use an anecdote.** A story told by your interviewee might be used to introduce your subject's personality and what makes her interesting. Often, a short story will suggest the angle that is carried on throughout the profile.
- **Set the scene.** Pull readers into one situation in the subject's world. Describe important places or surroundings to create your angle or impression of the subject: a workplace setting, a football field, or the inside of the subject's house. Describe the subject in action in those settings or scenes doing a job, hobby, talking to others, and so on.
- **Ask a question.** Pique readers' interest by posing an intriguing question—one that relates to your subject and the angle you are trying to convey.

■ ■ ■

Writing Closings for Profiles

Because the point of a profile—the angle on your subject and what you want to say about it—is woven into the profile itself, the closing does not need to summarize the profile or restate your major "points." Instead, the closing of a profile is a chance for the writer to reinforce the angle taken on the subject.

In the profile "Part of the Carnival Show: The Man Behind the Masks," Rohter chose to use Botelho's own voice to close. He uses a quotation that emphasizes Botelho's passion for his art. Instead of trying to tell us how Botelho feels about the future of his art, he *shows* us; and in doing so, he emphasizes Botelho's dedication to his work—despite the sacrifices he's made.

> Mr. Botelho acknowledged that he might have time for other pursuits if he could only find a proper heir to his craft. He has a 10-year-old son, Túlio César, who shares his enthusiasm for Carnival, but it is too early to tell if the boy also has the talent, Mr. Botelho said. As for the apprentices he hires, well, they just do not show the same dedication that he demands of himself.
>
> "Most of them are slow to pick things up, and even the one or two who have come along and appear to have the gift, they have been easily distracted by other things, like soccer or music," Mr. Botelho grumbled. "It's not enough to have the ability; you also have to have the commitment."

WRITING ACTIVITY   Closings for Profiles

- **Create an echo effect.** Close with a quote or anecdote or description that echoes or reinforces the ideas or images in the opening of the profile and reemphasizes the angle you've chosen.
- **Describe a lasting image.** Use thick description of a place, an action, or so on, that conveys the lasting impression you want to leave readers with.
- **Provide a commentary.** Include a subjective commentary about the subject (either your own or someone else's you interviewed who knows the subject) that reveals to readers a commonality with or significance of the subject in your profile.

■ ■ ■

Organizing Your Profile

Two common patterns of organization in profile writing are narration and topical (or open-ended) organization.

Narration. Narration is usually done in chronological order, but it doesn't necessarily have to be. A writer may move back and forth in time or in place while maintaining a strong narrative thread. For instance, a writer who wants to create tension or suspense may start with a particularly compelling story in one section, but not finish it until later in the profile.

In his profile "The Man Behind the Masks," Rohter uses a loose chronological organization pattern. Although the writer begins the profile with a paragraph about Botelho's boyhood apprenticeship, he quickly shifts to a quote of the artist today and how his father's disapproval of his work affected him. The chronological narrative thread of the profile is interrupted by the writer as he weaves commentary and background information about Rohter's experiences throughout his life as an artist.

Topical Organization. Another organizational strategy used by many profile writers is topical organization. In earlier writing activities, you clustered similar information under topics you noticed emerging from your research. Taken together these topics or traits of your subject create a composite sketch that may illuminate the angle of your profile.

Suppose you decide to profile the director of a local soup kitchen. In researching your subject, you shadow the director for a day, observing and recording what you see and experience. You also talk to some of the men and women who eat at the soup kitchen, to volunteers, and to the director's ex-husband, who still volunteers at the kitchen. After considering the information you've gathered, you realize that the best way to show who the director is, is to create sections of the profile based on recurring topics: her commitment to the kitchen, her estrangement from her husband and family, her early influences in volunteerism, the comments about her by the people who frequent the soup kitchen, and so on.

Often topics become headings for subsections in the profile that build on each other. Subheadings can help writers develop an angle that makes a lasting impression of the subject on readers.

Revising Profiles

During the revision process the profile writer is often adding material that emphasizes the angle, and cutting information that, although interesting, is irrelevant to the profile's focus. Clarifying, focusing, and further developing the angle are key to revising profiles.

Rethinking the Angle

What often happens in profile writing is that the angle we think we are taking on our subject turns out, in the end, to be different from what we actually write. To put it another way, we learn what's important about our subject in the process of writing about that subject, and so our purpose changes.

This means profile writers need to return to their drafts and look critically at the choices they have made about how to portray their subject. Sometimes focusing more clearly on the subject is a matter of tweaking what is already in the draft. But more often the angle needs to be rethought in light of what was discovered while drafting the profile, conducting follow-up interviews, and getting reader feedback.

For example, one student profiled his uncle, a recovering alcoholic, whom the family often referred to as a drunk. This writer realized that his uncle still retained some of the characteristics of an alcoholic but was also trying to make amends. Since not all of the characteristics of this student's subject were as important as others, he chose to develop an angle on his uncle in which he emphasized his alcoholism more than his other, more positive characteristics. Doing so, the writer established a 3 to 2 ratio, focusing more on alcoholism and sharpening this angle in his profile.

WRITING ACTIVITY Sharpening the Angle

1. Write down the primary characteristics of the subject that you want to highlight—this is the core of your angle. Then decide how you want to weight some characteristics versus others—the ratio for emphasizing some aspects of your subject over others.
2. Find the places in your draft where you *show* those characteristics already and label them (e.g. "shy" or "annoyingly opinionated") in the margins.
3. Next, look over your research notes, the material you did not use, and label them using the same characteristics as you used on your draft. If you find material that doesn't seem to fit any of the identified characteristics, generate a new characteristic and flag that material for later consideration.
4. Here's the ruthless part. Ask yourself whether the material you have in the draft really does illustrate each characteristic in the best possible way or if some of your other material might do a better job.

■ ■ ■

Incorporating the Writer's Voice

As a profile writer you should write subjectively, looking at your subject from your own perspective and choosing how to present that subject to readers. When revising, be sure you have put yourself in the profile, sharing your perspective on what you saw and heard and felt as you did your field research. Incorporating your voice immerses readers in the subject's world as well as sharpens the angle you want to convey.

Briggita Schwartz, a first-year student who profiled a woman who had worked for the FBI, weaves both the subject's voice and her own commentary into the scene that opens her profile.

> As you enter her house, there is a sense of loneliness, that is, until her three cats greet you. Her house is fairly bare, there are very few pictures hung, but her old couches and love seat give the house some life. The antenna for the television is wrapped in tinfoil, but the TV does not work. "Come in and have a seat, would you like to sit on the couch or chair?" she asks with a smile on her face. Her 88-year-old body slowly makes its way to the couch, which is covered with a towel to prevent cat hair from getting on it. As she plops herself on the couch, she slightly winces in pain because she recently broke her tailbone when she fell at church. As she readjusts herself, one of her cats hops onto her lap. "Looks like Tootsie came to join us today."
>
> Because of her demeanor, one would not expect her to be a retired FBI agent. There is no evidence in her house of her past. She does not appear to be secretive. [Subject] knows I'm eager to hear about when she worked for the FBI. She seems excited to talk about it too. "I'll start with the basics. I went to school for 3 years, my main focus was Journalism." She sipped her steaming hot tea....

Another way profile writers incorporate their voice into the profile is to use "I" as they comment on their subjects. For example, look at how Charlie LeDuff's profile "End of the Line" includes his comments on the feel of the town as he drives through it.

> Driving through Janesville, Wisconsin, in a downpour, looking past the wipers and through windows fogged up with cigarette smoke, Main Street appears to be melting away. The rain falls hard and makes a lonesome going-away sound like a river sucking downstream. And the old hotel, without a single light, tells you that the best days around here are gone. I always smoke when I go to funerals. I work in Detroit. And when I look out the windshield or into people's eyes here, I see a little Detroit in the making.

LeDuff's subjective perspective and his commentary emphasize how he wants readers to see the town: he is smoking as he is driving, and since he only smokes at funerals, we know that he wants us to see what's happening in Janesville as a funeral, or perhaps the wake as he suggests later in the profile. Notice, though, that he "intrudes" on the town and describes it only minimally; he relies primarily on the voices of those living there to provide color.

WRITING ACTIVITY   Incorporating Your Voice in the Profile

1. What is your perspective on your subject, now that you've done your research on it?
2. Where in the profile would inserting your commentary emphasize your perspective, the angle, or your purpose for writing?

■   ■   ■

Incorporating the Subject's Voice

Another common characteristic of profiles is the incorporation of the subject's voice. The subject's voice often gets lost in the movement from field research to drafting. But voice is one powerful way to make your reader feel like they *know* your subject by the time they get done reading your profile, so don't underestimate the importance of quoting your subject. As you revise, look for places where you can replace a paraphrase of what the subject said with what he or she actually did say. Use direct quotes from your interviews.

Visual Rhetoric and Profiles

Including photos as part of the text of your profile can contribute to the angle of your profile. So ask yourself, "What visuals, photos, images would help enhance the angle and purpose of my profile?"

For instance, a profile of a student who is a star pitcher for the women's softball team at her college and challenges the "dumb jock" stereotype by becoming a scholar-athlete may warrant a photo of her receiving some academic awards in addition to photos of her throwing the winning pitch that helped her team win the Division III softball championship.

As you read, make specific comments and suggestions that will help the writer revise (e.g. "I like how you describe the subject, but I wonder if you could give some details that show him in action?").

Comment in the margins on the following:

READ THE OPENING: How does the writer begin? By setting the scene? Using a revealing quote? Telling an anecdote? Asking a question? Another way? How does the opening engage you as a reader? Make suggestions for how the opening might better engage readers.

READ THE REST OF THE PROFILE: Pay attention to the level of detail and description. Do parts seem to skimp on details or description? Can you suggest ways the writer could make these people, places, or objects more vivid to readers (including background research, more material from the interviews, etc.)?

Finally when you have finished reading and annotating, write an endnote to the writer in which you comment on the following:

- Developing the angle. Tell the writer what you think the angle is and how you know. Suggest how the writer could further develop the angle. Mark paragraphs where the writer could include anecdotes, quotes, examples, and so on to better convey the angle.

- Incorporating the subject's voice. Where could the writer add more quotations from the subject?

- Incorporating the writer's voice. Where could the writer comment on the subject and strengthen the angle?

- Patterns of organization. How is the draft organized (topically, chronologically)? Where could the writer use transitions to move from topic to topic, paragraph to paragraph, or move through time?

- Use of visuals. If the writer uses visuals, how do they add to the angle of the profile? Do the visuals appear next to paragraphs that describe them? Do they have descriptive captions ?

Reflecting on the Process

Reflecting critically on your writing process may help you better understand why you made the choices you did to create your profile.

Reflect on your writing process for your profile. How did you choose your subject, generate interview questions, do research, and draft and revise your profile?

Imagine you are writing this reflection for writers who have never written a profile. What might they learn from your experiences? What could you tell them that might help them as writers?

Begin by describing what aspects you are most pleased with in your profile.

Analyze your strengths and weaknesses as a writer for this profile. *Explain* what you think contributed to your success in these areas.

Reflect on how you determined your purpose and audience for your profile. How did these elements influence your choice of angle? Comment on the interview and/or observation process: How well did it go? What would you do differently next time?

Discuss your revision process, including how you used feedback from your readers.

Conclude by reflecting on what you learned about the genre of the profile. You might also reflect on what you might do differently the next time you write a profile.

■   ■   ■

Brynna Williams's Profile

First-year writing student Brynna Williams decided to profile the organization Simply Smiles, an organization that works to improve the lives of children and families in Oaxaca, Mexico. She had worked for them in the past and wanted to bring attention to their work. She knew a lot about the organization and so could draw on her own experiences as well as the material she gathered in her interviews with the director.

Generating Ideas for the Profile

Williams was pretty sure she would profile Simply Smiles from the start, and you can see right away that what is driving her to write this profile is her concern that people, especially those her own age, are not volunteering for worthy causes. As she works through the drafting process, you can see how this concern gets developed.

Williams considers why others might want to read a profile about someone who is so selfless.

Williams points out what she believes will be a common thought in her readers' minds and would make the profile intriguing to them.

> *Brynna Williams*
> *Generating Ideas for Profiles*
>
> *Subject One: One person who I could profile would be a guy I know who started an organization called Simply Smiles, a volunteer group that improves the lives of children and their families living in places like Oaxaca, Mexico, by building houses, providing schooling and basic health care to them. This subject is interesting because in this day and age, there aren't too many people who want to help others, especially young people, mostly because they are so busy struggling to keep their own lives together.*
>
> *Subject Two: Another idea I had for a profile was to write about a church in my town that does lots of community service in nearby towns. They have a large group of young people interested in helping in soup kitchens and tutoring in schools....*

Thinking about Audience, Purpose, and Situation

After considering her two possible subjects further, Williams chose the first subject but changed her focus slightly. Instead of writing just about the person who started Simply Smiles, she decided to write about the organization itself. She narrowed her focus as she thought about the audience and purpose, and came up with some rough ideas about her angle as well.

> *Brynna Williams*
>
> *Potential Readers: I think my audience would include people who are interested in reading about humanitarian groups. Especially today, young people are really involved*

Williams considers the timely situation that readers may find themselves in: the context, their experiences, their lifestyles.

Williams gets at the angle a bit here: to persuade readers that not everyone is ignoring society's problems.

She clearly wants readers to not only feel inspired but also to take some action.

more in community service either because they got involved in high school or they know the experience could help them later in their jobs. Serving the community is a national issue.

Why Write This Profile: A few reasons for writing this profile might be to motivate others to get involved, maybe not with this group particularly, but with other organizations and issues they find interesting or to point out that there are people who are taking a stand and doing something to help others in need—we aren't just ignoring the issues.

My Purpose: I want readers to think "I could do something like this" and help out on issues that interest them. This is a "feel good" profile, so readers might react by joining some organization that stands for issues important to them.

Drafting: Gathering Research, Organizing Ideas, and Discovering the Angle

Williams had a lot of past experience to draw on, and she was able to use this experience to decide what to ask in her interviews; that knowledge and her background research helped her to organize her questions into general topics.

Profiles rely heavily on field research, including interviews and observations of the subject.

Williams clearly has access to her subject.

Some of Williams's categories and interview questions introduce her "angle-in-progress" for the profile—why the group is significant.

Brynna Williams
Background Information and Interview Questions

What I Know about My Subject. I know the group Simply Smiles was started in 2003 by Bryan Nurnberger who wanted to make a difference and change the lives at an orphanage called Casa Hogar in Oaxaca, Mexico, after seeing the poverty the children live in. I went there with Simply Smiles as a volunteer.

What Can be Researched and Why. I should interview Bryan Nurnberger and some of the volunteers who have gone to Oaxaca from Simply Smiles. Lots of my observations of the place and the people, what it looks like and what happens there, will help my readers feel like they are there with me at Casa Hogar. Readers need to understand the importance of the work that Simply Smiles does, and realize how they transform lives.

Possible Interview Questions and Topics

Background: Simply Smiles
What is the group about? Who do they help?
Where did the name come from?
How did it get started?
Who are the people who volunteer in Simply Smiles?

Transforming Lives

What kinds of service projects do they do to help people?

Are there any projects that show the best work of the group?

Influences

What made you start the organization Simply Smiles?

What got you interested in volunteering?

What are some of your most memorable experiences working with SS?

Can you describe some of the most difficult times working with SS? What kept you going?

Future Projects

What does the future look like for the group?

What kinds of projects do they have coming up?

Williams had a good sense of why she wanted to profile Simply Smiles but had some problems organizing her information. She also struggled with how to include both the interview responses and background research *with* her own personal experiences and keep it sounding like a profile instead of a memoir. She knew that balancing these elements would help her zero in on the angle of the group in her profile.

Brynna Williams

Professor DeRosa

English 100P

10 Oct. 2009

Profile Draft 1 (Excerpts)

Simply Smiles

Williams starts the profile with a quote from Nurnberger, but without any context. Is this engaging for readers or confusing?

"I realized that I wanted to do this—help kids like these—for my life, and I wanted to do it on a scale that demanded that I start an organization. I named it Simply Smiles so that I would always remember that this work is about creating moments that make people smile," said Bryan Nurnberger, when he was asked about what made him build the organization he started in 2003. Simply Smiles is a program that helps needy kids in Oaxaca, Mexico. Oaxaca is a busy city of street vendors selling colorful rugs and painted statues, tourists with their fanny packs and cameras, and beautiful buildings. The same city where violent crimes happen such as school buses getting raided on the way to school with no warning and where hundreds of sick dogs roam the dirt roads and lay dead against the one room, dirt wall shacks people call their homes. The city of Oaxaca is the state capitol is located at the bottom of Mexico.

Bryan had seen poverty before. But that poverty he saw could be categorized as disturbing poverty. You would think that an orphanage in this poor part of Oaxaca City that uncomfortably housed 80 plus children would show sad, unshowered, unfed kids whose eyes tell you that they crave something as simple as a plate of food and a bed to be able to sleep in. Yet when Bryan started living with them he discovered something amazing that he didn't expect. "I saw how bad they had it, and how happy they were anyway." I know how he feels.

I had gone to Casa Hogar for the first time in 2005. I had expected to see sick, coughing, weak, fighting, crying children. But I was pleasantly surprised to see children running around playing with a very much loved soccer ball that was torn and only half inflated. Some girls were washing the clothes belonging to all the children, while singing and laughing. I was instantly drawn to a little girl named Luz. She had beautiful chocolate colored eyes that glistened when she smiled, and her smile could light up a whole room. With the connection he had made with the kids and from observing the life they were living and still holding their little heads up, he wanted to do something for them. "I wanted to help them because I knew and loved those kids, not because of statistics or because the Bible or something was telling me to do so, it came from a human being to human being connection." ...

Welcome to Casa Hogar

Casa Hogar is home to just over 80 children. It is run by Carol and Francisco Marin. There are no age maximums for the residents and the orphanage focuses on children who have special needs such as Cerebral Palsy, blindness, deafness, seizures, developmental, learning and emotional problems. ...

Notice here the abrupt shift from interviews with Nurnberger to her personal experiences at Casa Hogar.

Williams makes another abrupt shift from her first time at Casa Hogar to Nurn-berger's reason for starting Simply Smiles. Where could this quote work better to empha-size Nurnberger's commitment?

Revising: Framing the Angle, Emphasizing the Writer's Perspective

Williams's second draft, read by two peer reviewers, shows some comments she received on the draft's organization and its effect on how readers understood the angle of her profile—in this case, how the group Simply Smiles has transformed the lives of the people they help and in turn, how the volunteers have been changed as well by their experience. In her second draft, she concentrates on how she can emphasize her perspective to the group and include her personal experiences without the profile becoming too much like a memoir.

Brynna Williams
Professor DeRosa
English 100P
12 Oct. 2009

Profile Draft 2 (Excerpts)

Simply Smiles

"I realized that I wanted to do this—help kids like these—for my life, and I wanted to do it on a scale that demanded that I start an organization. I named it Simply Smiles so that I would always remember that this work is about creating moments that make people smile," said Bryan Nurnberger, when he was asked about what made him build the organization he started in 2003. Simply Smiles is a program that helps needy kids in Oaxaca, Mexico. Oaxaca is a busy city of street vendors selling colorful rugs and painted statues, tourists with their fanny packs and cameras, and beautiful buildings. It is also the city where men in uniforms hold guns and ride tanks through the streets. The same city where violent crimes happen such as school buses getting raided on the way to school with no warning and where hundreds of sick dogs roam the dirt roads and lay dead against the one room, dirt wall shacks people call their homes. The city of Oaxaca is the state capitol is located at the bottom of Mexico.

Bryan had seen poverty before. But that poverty he saw could be categorized as disturbing poverty. You would think that an orphanage in this poor part of Oaxaca City that uncomfortably housed 80 plus children would show sad, unshowered, unfed kids whose eyes tell you that they crave something as simple as a plate of food and a bed to be able to sleep in. Yet when Bryan started living with them he discovered something amazing that he didn't expect. "I saw how bad they had it, and how happy they were anyway." I know how he feels.

…

I had gone to Casa Hogar for the first time in 2005. I had expected to see sick, coughing, weak, fighting, crying children. But I was pleasantly surprised to see children running around playing with a very much loved soccer ball that was torn and only half inflated. Some girls were washing the clothes belonging to all the children, while singing and laughing. I was instantly drawn to a little girl named Luz. She had beautiful chocolate colored eyes that glistened when she smiled, and her smile could light up a whole room. I could see that they didn't have many toys or activities to do, tables to sit at or even music to listen to, but that didn't seem to bother them much at all. It was rare to see a child cry. "I wanted to help them because I knew and loved those kids, not because of statistics or because the Bible or something was telling me to do so, it came from a human being to human being connection."

Reviewer 1: I like the quote, inspirational. But it seems out of place since this is all about Oaxaca.

Reviewer 2: This seems out of order here. Also I don't think the description of the city and Nurnberger's quote make sense together.

Reviewer 1: Why is Nurnberger living with them? Can you give more background?

Reviewer 2: I really like the way you add your personal experience. But then the part about Nurnberger seems like it doesn't go here—maybe put it where Nurnberger is talking about his experience in Oaxaca?

> Reviewer 1: Remember, you don't have to put the question you asked him in the profile. Just introduce the quote.

I asked Bryan faced many challenges when he started the organization assuming he would have a lot to say about what he went through and he said "The challenges for us have been 99% good ones because they have been surrounding us, trying to keep up with the excitement that people have to support us." Bryan is such a positive man and it's great to see a guy like him doing something about poverty of children living in this world, but this lifestyle wasn't always what he imagined for himself....

The peer review draft below includes some revisions Williams made to the first part of her profile based on her peers' comments. Williams's comments on *why* she made those revisions are in parentheses next to her changes.

Brynna Williams

Revisions from Peer Review Draft (Excerpts)

<u>The dogs are barking, the birds are singing and the roosters are crowing at the crack of dawn. I roll off of a worn out mattress with mismatched linens. I tip-toe across the squeaky wood floor boards that separate me from the workers below me. The rest of my group is still sleeping in cramped bunk beds of the hot attic-like room we stay in. I pass the jammed open window that looks out to the mountains for Oaxaca, Mexico. I can see children playing soccer, skating on roller skates with missing wheels, and laughing while Nacho, one of the blind kids, rolls down the hill without bumping into anything. I giggle and continue to the bathroom to ease my bladder. I have to remember not to flush the toilet paper because in Mexico the pipes are only two inches wide compared to the eight inch pipes in the States. Just something I have to get used to during my stay at the Casa Hogar Children's Home as a volunteer for the group Simply Smiles.</u> `[I added this because both reviewers said the opening was confusing so I used the quote from Bryan later. They both liked the descriptions of Oaxaca but I didn't want to begin there because it isn't about the city. So I thought I could put the readers at Casa Hogar by describing it and my experience as a volunteer for the group.]`

> The new organization has improved transitions that set up the next section's topic for readers.

Simply Smiles, ~~is~~ a nonprofit organization that helps needy kids in Oaxaca, Mexico, <u>was started by a man from Westport Connecticut, Bryan Nurnberger, in 2003</u>. "I realized that I wanted to do this—help kids like these—for my life, and I wanted to do it on a scale that demanded that I start an organization," Bryan said during an interview. "I named it Simply Smiles so that I would always remember that this work is about creating moments that make people smile." `[Moved up from below to put the focus on Simply Smiles so readers know it is the subject.`

ONE WRITER'S JOURNEY

The quote by Bryan that reviewers like adds some background about the group.]

...

I know how he feels. (Moved into separate paragraph for better transition.)

I had gone to Casa Hogar for the first time in 2005. I had expected to see sick, coughing, weak, fighting, crying children when I got there. But I was pleasantly surprised to see children running around playing with a very much loved soccer ball that was torn and only half inflated. [...] It was rare to see a child cry at Casa Hogar. They had learned to be happy with the torn shirt they had been wearing for a week, or the flip-flops that had been worn so much that their heels could be seen from the bottom. ~~With the connection he had made with the kids and from observing the life they were living and still holding their little heads up, he wanted to do something for them. "I wanted to help them because I knew and loved those kids, not because of statistics or because the Bible or something was telling me to do so, it came from a human being to human being connection." I asked~~ [Cut this per peer reviewer comment about question/answer format.] Bryan faced many challenges when he started ~~the organization~~ Simply Smiles ~~assuming he would have a lot to say about what he went through.~~ "The challenges for us have been 99% good ones because they have been trying to keep up with the excitement that people have to support us." Although Bryan is such a positive man ~~and it's great to see a guy like him doing something~~ with lots of energy to do something [added in to sound less like just like my opinion] about poverty of children living in this world, but this lifestyle wasn't always what he imagined for himself. Bryan used to be an active rock climber. "I was willing to die climbing because I thought that living a life how I wanted to was a virtuous way to spend your life and a virtuous way to maybe die. However, I see now that the most human fulfilling life is one that works to improve humanity in some small way."

The revisions here not only bring Williams's text more in line with the genre but also clarify her purpose and enable readers to see Casa Hogar and Nurnberger, rather than being told about them.

Brynna Williams (student), "Simply Smiles" (final draft)

Williams's new opening sets the scene with thick descriptions of her experience and puts the readers in the place.

Brynna Williams
Professor DeRosa
English 100P
14 Oct. 2009

Simply Smiles

The dogs are barking, the birds are singing and the roosters are crowing at the crack of dawn. I roll off of a worn-out mattress with mismatched linens. I tip-toe across the squeaky wood floorboards that separate me from the workers below. The rest of my group is still sleeping in the cramped bunk beds of the hot attic-like room we stay in. I pass the jammed-open window that looks out to the mountains for Oaxaca, Mexico. I can see children playing soccer, skating on roller skates with missing wheels, and laughing while Nacho, one of the blind kids, rolls down the hill without bumping into anything. I giggle and continue to the bathroom to ease my bladder. I have to remember not to flush the toilet paper because in Mexico the pipes are only two inches wide compared to the eight-inch pipes in the States. Just something I have to get used to during my stay at the Casa Hogar Children's Home as a volunteer for the group Simply Smiles.

Simply Smiles, a nonprofit organization that helps needy kids in Oaxaca, Mexico, was started by Westport, Connecticut, native, Bryan Nurnberger, in 2003. "I realized that I wanted to do this—help kids like these—for my life, and I wanted to do it on a scale that demanded that I start an organization," Bryan says. "I named it Simply Smiles so that I would always remember that this work is about creating moments that make people smile." He sits in the choir room of First Church of Bethlehem, UCC, in Bethlehem, Connecticut, in well-worn Birkenstock sandals, khaki pants and a simple blue t-shirt. Bryan sips on Red Bull, which made me recall how he drank them every morning at Casa Hogar.

Oaxaca is a busy city of street vendors selling colorful rugs and painted statues, tourists with their fanny packs and cameras, and beautiful buildings. It is also the city where men in uniforms hold guns and ride tanks through the streets. The same city where violent crimes happen such as school buses getting raided on the way to school and where hundreds of sick dogs roam the dirt roads or lay dead against the one room, dirt-wall shacks people call their homes.

You would think that a small orphanage in this poor part of Oaxaca City that housed 80-plus children would include sad, unshowered, unfed kids who just want some food and a clean bed to sleep in. Yet when Bryan started living with them, he discovered something amazing that he didn't expect. "I saw how bad they had it, and how happy they were anyway." He made a connection with the kids and from observing the lives they were living and still holding their little heads up, he wanted to do something for them.

Some background on the organization and its history.

Presents details about Nurnberger and a quote to show his personality.

An interesting way to describe the writer's feeling of ambiguity about Oaxaca.

"I wanted to help them because I knew and loved those kids, not because of statistics or because the Bible or something was telling me to do so, it came from a human being to human being connection." I know how he feels.

When I had traveled to Casa Hogar for the first time in 2005, I expected to see sick, coughing, weak, fighting, crying children. But I was surprised to see laughing kids running and chasing a much loved, half-inflated soccer ball. Some girls were washing the other children's clothes, singing and laughing. I was instantly drawn to a little girl named Luz. She had beautiful chocolate-colored eyes that glistened when she smiled, and her smile ... well, it could light up a whole room. There weren't many toys or music or activities, and few tables to sit at, but that didn't seem to bother them. It was rare to see a child cry at Casa Hogar, despite the torn shirts or well-worn flip-flops they wore.

Although Bryan is a positive man with lots of energy to end the poverty of children, it wasn't the lifestyle that he imagined for himself. Before he founded Simply Smiles, Bryan used to be an active rock climber. "I was willing to die climbing because I thought that living a life how I wanted to was a virtuous way to spend your life and a virtuous way to maybe die. However, I see now that the most fulfilling life is one that works to improve humanity in some small way." His commitment shows in the lives of those who live and work at Casa Hogar.

Welcome to Casa Hogar

Casa Hogar is home to just over 80 children. There are no age maximums for the residents, and the orphanage focuses on children who have special needs such as cerebral palsy and blindness, or those with developmental, learning, or emotional problems. This place is their home where they get so much support. I remember watching a young girl in a wheelchair, held in with straps and a divider for her legs to fit snug and keep them immobile. She was being fed by a worker, who struggled to keep the food from falling onto the girl's pink shirt. It was hard to watch because I could feel the frustration of both of them. Then there is Luis and Marta, 12-year-old twins who are mute. They are the funniest kids at the orphanage. Talk about getting some perspective.

Williams gives us a hint about Nurnberger's lifestyle before Simply Smiles. Does she want to leave readers wanting more about Nurnberger's motivation for starting the group?

Williams provides lots of spatial descriptions of Casa Hogar and details about the children. Notice how she shifts to "you" when describing the place. How does that affect your reading of the section?

When you enter the orphanage compound you first notice a small stucco church. You can see the rest of Casa Hogar at one glance. To the left of the church is a small blue building containing a room with books, coloring books and crayons and also a computer, and a makeshift desk, which the children use to write thank you notes to their sponsors. Also in that building is a kitchen and a guest room for visitors. Upstairs is a crowded room where the teenage boys sleep and another small room for visitors.

Outside the building is a dirt field where there are two rusted basketball rims with no nets and the van that transports the handicapped children to school. Past the field is the almost square-shaped building that houses the younger children; on its walls hang paintings of Jesus embracing a young Mexican boy, Tiger and Winnie-the-Pooh, and flowers and trees. When volunteer Pam Williams came to Casa Hogar, one of the first projects she worked on was to have all the children paint a tile and put them around the room. "The tiles created a border and it was cool for them to see all their artwork up there," said Pam, "especially since many of them hadn't ever used paint before." In the "cafeteria" there are plain, cracked walls, four picnic tables and the "kitchen." Long clothing lines of colorful socks, pants and shirts hang in a zigzag behind the lunch room.

Tiny one-room shacks are tightly lined up; dirt roads and barking dogs surround Casa Hogar; and the heart of Oaxaca is just down the main dirt road. The sun beats down hard and the dust is always in the air from the cars and trucks going by. Because of the living conditions, it isn't uncommon for a child to be born with a problem. "Many children are deaf or blind as a result of being born in a village with bright sun, dust, poor soil for growing food, etc.," says Bryan.

Transforming Lives

On the other side of a rusted, squeaky gate that protects the lives of the children in Oaxaca is a place to call home for all of those once abandoned. Casa Hogar is like a resort some of the kids have never dreamed about, and because of Simply Smiles, it's a safe haven.

Williams uses subheadings to group information by topic and also to build on her angle for the profile.

Examples and specific details show versus tell readers about the work of the group.

But change doesn't happen without hard work. One of the projects the First Church of Bethlehem was involved with at Casa Hogar was called the "bus project," which involved buying a school bus in Connecticut, loading it up with toys, stuffed animals, medical supplies, toiletries, clothes and linens for the kids, and driving it down to Oaxaca. Bryan and his girlfriend willingly took this life-changing journey. "We were like hippies with a mission or something. It took us months to cross the border," Bryan recalls. "But I learned that even horrible situations can have an upside. In this case, we got so much media attention for being stuck and sticking with it, that it thrust Simply Smiles into a position where people knew who we were and recognized our name and work because of that bus trip."

The "bus project" was my first visit to the orphanage, and my first excursion with Simply Smiles. At Casa Hogar, I walked around on cracked cement, dirt grounds. There was no grass, one worn picnic table, and an unstable steel staircase in the sleeping quarters. The teenage boys would sleep in a cockroach-infested, stifling room with a slanted roof with nails protruding through it. Dogs barked in the shacks and streets surrounding the compound. The children had the same meal every day and children drank coffee in the morning and sometimes at lunch or dinner. They hardly got enough help for homework, and there was a time when some of the kids could not go to school because they couldn't get the uniforms needed to attend.

Bryan remembers that people and kids who lived outside of Casa Hogar used to make fun of the "poor" kids, "and now [they] are jealous because of the bus, the nice backpacks for school, the soccer court, and high-speed Internet." The kids now are distracted by the air hockey table that keeps them from doing their homework, whereas they were once distracted because they were always hungry. The kids work in a new computer lab inside an igloo-shaped room equipped with Internet, where before they didn't know what a computer was.

Pam Williams, a volunteer, thinks Bryan has profoundly changed the lives of the children. "Bryan is solely responsible for completely transforming their lives. By bringing their plight to the attention of others in the States and by

This quote adds to Williams's angle on the group—the transformation of lives through actions.

continuing to champion their cause, and building their support system, Bryan has insured that they have nourishing and plentiful food every day, an education, a safe and comfortable place to live, and a few joys and treasures," says Pam. "Bryan has given these children not only a home, but a future and most especially the knowledge that they are loved. He has given them hope...."

Perhaps it's obvious how Simply Smiles changes the lives of the children, but the volunteers' lives have been changed as well by Casa Hogar and its children. My younger sister, Erica, came along on a Simply Smiles trip when she was 12 years old. She was mature for her age, and confident she could handle what she saw there. Now almost 15, Erica recalls that experience at the orphanage. "I really got a good look at the lives of children at Casa Hogar who aren't so lucky to have a life like mine. They don't have the basic things I take for granted every day, such as three meals and clean clothes, but I realized how much people care for and dedicate themselves to these kids."

Just a Smile

Williams's commentary points to the larger significance of the profile: to change the way readers may think about volunteerism.

Many people think that doing volunteer work in another country might require rigorous training or plenty of funding and supplies, but that's just one perspective. When I went to Mexico with Bryan and the other volunteers in my sophomore year of high school, I came back with a totally different mindset.

So in my senior year, I made a second trip to Casa Hogar with Bryan and the group to do my final senior project. I wanted to bring art back into the children's lives at the orphanage, so I planned to have them paint pictures on canvas board that I cut from scraps and collected from art stores around my town. And, although I had a firm vision for what the project would involve, the kids had their own ideas. I envisioned them painting beautiful pictures. I tried my hardest to explain my vision of the project to them in my broken Spanish. While they didn't follow my instructions exactly, they all jumped right in eagerly. Twenty kids were having a blast. They were mixing every paint color together, spilling it all over the floor, and using their hands to smear paint on the canvas, tables and walls. In the end, there were 50 paintings (about 10 that were actual pictures) from smiling, laughing kids, many of whom hadn't ever used paints before.

Williams's choice to include this memory adds details about the project and gives readers insight into her relationship with the children.

Sometimes even the best-made plans turn into different and better ones when you trust the people around you.

Smiles for the Future

Simply Smiles and the children have accomplished so much, but there is more to be done. One current project is called "The Dump Project." Bryan discovered that people were living in the dump, really just a place where trash was, well, dumped, and these people were treated as modern-day untouchables or lepers. "We in turn befriended these men, women, children, and began trying to give our new friends better lives," recalls Bryan. They started out providing people with clothes and sandwiches, and once they earned their friendship and trust, the volunteers asked if they could build them houses. "Because we started out as friends, and tried so hard to develop that kind of relationship, the work is done in a way that preserves their dignity." And that dignity is key.

Simply Smiles has different ongoing projects in other places as well. The one thing that keeps the organization going is the people who take an interest in it and want to help. Bryan agrees. "The biggest thing is to tell people. Give them the website. Give them my email. We get most of our support from word of mouth. Speaking in one church or school almost always has a huge impact on the people we support." As with any grassroots, nonprofit group, it holds true for Simply Smiles that people helping people can only happen through awareness. More information about Simply Smiles can be found on the website www.simplysmiles.org. It isn't just the satisfaction we get from helping others that motivates the volunteers. It's the ways this work changes our lives and attitudes forever—and of course, makes us all smile.

Williams reminds readers about the rewards of serving others and closes with how readers can get more information on the group.

Questions for Discussion

1. How does Williams help readers understand the angle and purpose for her profile?
2. What kinds of research did Williams use and for what purpose? How do the research and the ways she includes it in the profile emphasize her angle?
3. What organizational strategies does Williams use to help readers follow her profile of the group?

Reflecting on the Process

In the following excerpt, Brynna Williams reflects on the process she used to write her profile.

Writing this profile reminded me how much I loved working with Simply Smiles and the kids at Casa Hogar. The hardest parts for me were not making it sound like a memoir, putting in other peoples' quotes and not including interview questions, and of course, making sure my angle was clear to readers. I had so much reorganization to do based on the feedback I got from peers and my professor that I was constantly changing the order of things. But I think working on the organization helped me clarify the key points I wanted to get across; it helped me highlight the group and its work, not just my feelings about it. The subheadings helped me organize the tons of information I had and made it easier to write the profile in sections.

I got lots of comments from my peers to make it stronger. They wanted clarification and more detail about what I saw there like the sleeping quarters and the children descriptions. I think I added more spatial descriptions of the place and tried to include little mini profiles of the kids in some parts. With these details, I hoped readers would feel like they knew the people and were in the place.

I didn't want to highlight all the horrible things that the kids and families went through in Oaxaca so that people would just think it was a "pity profile." I wanted the work that Simply Smiles does to change lives to be highlighted so that readers could see that making a difference is possible, and that you change too in surprising ways from the experience.

WRITING ACTIVITY   Evaluating One Writer's Journey

Review Brynna Williams's process for writing her profile. How would you evaluate the choices she made as she wrote? Are there places where you think she could have made different choices, and how would those choices have affected the final profile? What further revisions, if any, do you think the final profile could use?

■ ■ ■

T R A N S F O R M A T I O N S

GENRE CROSSING: From Profile to Brochure

The profile is a *civic genre,* the purpose of which is to highlight and explore an aspect of an individual, group, or place. The **brochure,** also a *civic genre,* has a different purpose; the purpose of the brochure is to sell something or inform an audience, though it can and often does do both. Brochures are intended to provide usable information or brief talking points to readers about a subject. Brochures have a clear purpose and focus—a message, similar to the angle of a profile. It should be obvious to readers why they want to read a brochure and how it is important to their experiences.

A writer might create a brochure to provide brief how-to information or to move readers to take action on a subject. Brochures are a portable genre that readers can pick up and read on buses, subways, while they sit in a doctor's waiting room, or at home. Readers expect a lot less detail in brochures than in profiles—just the basics and where to go to read more about the subject.

Brochures also depend heavily on a strong visual design that reinforces the message and encourages potential readers to interrupt their busy lives and pick them up. Consult Chapter 4: Analyzing Visual Rhetoric for a discussion of how to apply principles of visual rhetoric and design to your brochure.

Genre Crossing Writing Assignment

From Profile to Brochure

Write a brochure that has a clear purpose and targets a particular audience on the subject or some aspect of the subject you wrote about in your profile. For instance, if you wrote a profile about a retired coal miner who suffered from chronic lung illness, you could develop a brochure on treatment options for those with similar ailments using the profile subject as a case study or testimony.

Your brochure might target a different audience and have a different purpose, but you can use appropriate research material from your profile to create it. However, you may need to use a different tone and language given your audience's expectations and your purpose. Also remember that the brochure is a brief genre, one that also relies on visuals to convey its message.

Transformation Questions to Ask

- What is the message I want to communicate? What aspect(s) of my profile will I focus on?
- Who is my audience for this brochure? What will they do with the brochure?
- What is my purpose?
- What material can I use (including quotations and research) given my audience and purpose?

- What new research do I need to do given my new rhetorical situation?
- How can I communicate some of that material through the use of visuals or graphics?

Brynna Williams "Simply Smiles: Transforming Lives of Impoverished Peoples" (brochure)

Brynna Williams transformed her profile of Simply Smiles into a brochure about the organization. While the profile informed readers about the work of this nonprofit group and celebrated its accomplishments, the brochure has a different message: It urges readers to take some action to help ensure the continued success of Simply Smiles and its projects.

Simply Smiles

Transforming the Lives of Impoverished Peoples

We are dedicated to building bright futures while improving the lives of impoverished families and children around the world

"We believe creating just one smile on a child's face can change their life forever. We've seen it a thousand times, and we cherish each and every time a child...simply smiles."

—Bryan Nurnberger

For more information on Simply Smiles or how you can contribute, please go to the website: www.simplysmiles.org

For general information, send an email: bryan@simplysmiles.org. or contact:

Bryan Nurnberger, President
1771 Post Road East
Westport, CT 06880
Phone: 203-910-6209

Additional Resources:
Group Helping Children In Mexico
Borough man's organization to build orphanages
08/19/07—*Waterbury Republican-American*

Everyday Heroes: Bryan Nurnberger
Man's Mexican Vacation Becomes Life-Saving
Mission 05/18/07—*WFSB Eyewitness News*

What You Can Do to Help

✓ Visit the Simply Smiles website

✓ Consider making a donation

✓ Contact Bryan Nurnberger to find out how you can contribute

✓ Come with us on our next trip

✓ Tell your friends and family about Simply Smiles

"The biggest way to help is by spreading the word"

—Bryan Nurnberger

Who We Are

Simply Smiles, Inc. is a nonprofit organization founded in 2003 and committed to improving the lives of children living in poverty. The organization is funded mostly by donations and relies on the hard work and dedication of its volunteers.

With the help of our volunteers and with your help, we have continued to achieve our goals of improving the lives of impoverished children.

"Helping these children really made me open my eyes to just how good we have it. The experience left me with the urge to never stop giving."
—Erica Williams, volunteer

How Simply Smiles Works

CASA Hogar, Oaxaca, Mexico

Casa Hogar is home to 80 plus children ranging in age from 2–18 years. Many of these children have physical, emotional, or learning disabilities, and most of them have been abandoned. Improving the quality of life for the children at Casa Hogar was the first project Simply Smiles initiated in 2003.

With the hard work of volunteers, the children at Casa Hogar have improved living conditions such as three meals a day, clean clothing, access to education, and a loving supportive environment in which to live and thrive.

http://www.simplysmiles.org/casahogar_ch.cfm

Transforming Lives

The DumP Project, Oaxaca Mexico

People helping people. That is what Simply Smiles is all about.

One recent project that Simply Smiles has undertaken is to build proper houses for the more than 30 families who currently live at and off of the Oaxaca Dump. These people rely on their sustenance from scraps of food and earn money from recycled bottles and cans they find at the dump.

But Simply Smiles is helping to change their lives. The Housing Project is an initiative the group undertook in 2007 to build adequate homes for the 120 people living at the dump.

Further proof that the people helping people philosophy works becomes apparent in the work done by the children of Casa Hogar. When they heard that families were living at the dump, they created a Meals Program, in which they prepared and delivered meals to the families themselves.

http://www.simplysmiles.org/dumpproject.cfm

Reading for Comprehension

1. When you first read this brochure, what was your initial reaction? What part(s) captured your attention first?
2. How does the brochure inform you about Simply Smiles? What kinds of information does it give you?

Analyzing the Genre

1. What is the message of the brochure? How do the text and visuals work together to convey this message?
2. What kinds of choices did Williams make as a brochure writer that were different from those she made as a proposal writer? Was she successful in her transformation or was something important lost?

CHAPTER 10

Research Reports

You might be thinking to yourself something like, "Oh, no . . . the research paper. I wrote one of those in my history course and I ended up throwing a bunch of quotes from some sources together just to show the teacher that I had done the research." Although it might be fair to say that this is a pretty common experience for some writers, the genre of the *research report* is much more dynamic than you might think. If you look at the ways you come across research reports in your daily life, you might gain a whole new perspective on the genre. For instance, you might pick up a research report while waiting in the doctor's office: "What Is Pulmonary Heart Disease and How You Can Avoid It." Or you might come across one while sitting in a mechanic's waiting room: "The New Generation Hybrid Car: More Technology, Better Savings." Or on a gaming website: "The Architecture of Online Gaming Experiences: A Report on the Reality of the Virtual Places of the Halo Series." As you can see, reports are a part of our private, public, and academic lives.

What Is a Research Report?

Reports are informative genres that are written not only in academic situations but in everyday life and for audiences with special interests. So if you find yourself seeking information about a topic on maintaining your health and well-being or on a hobby like gaming, it's likely you'll find what you're looking for in a report written by an expert on the topic.

As some of the report titles above suggest, reports are simultaneously persuasive. If you're reading a report on saving money by driving a hybrid, chances are it will be touting the benefits of hybrids to potential consumers. You might notice how the title even has the words "The New Generation . . . Better Savings" which perhaps make you think that if you want to be part of this new breed, you'll take a look at what the report has to say about hybrids. A research report, as the name suggests, discusses current research on a particular subject or issue. It provides readers with an overview of what has already been said about a subject, brief background, a discussion of the issue, and sometimes an analysis of the issue.

In your daily life or in school, you may have read or written reports: news reports, lab reports, research reports for many different academic subjects. Similarly, in your community, you may belong to an organization or community group that produces updates or reports on its ongoing activities with the purpose of informing the public about decisions on issues that affect the community. For example, your local board of education most likely produces reports that inform residents of developments that affect your local school system. And in workplaces, employees write progress reports or project reports to update employers or to provide ongoing information to the rest of the company. But like so many academic and civic genres (and a report may be both), what the report ends up looking like, what the content is, and how it is all put together varies greatly depending on the audience for and purpose of the report.

The Purposes of Research Reports

A research report can serve multiple purposes: to inform a particular group of something; to outline a problem and suggest some ways of solving that problem; and to sway an audience in some way. While we tend to think of research reports as objective and factual, and as in the example that started this chapter, as dry recitation of information, reports are dynamic and can in fact be (and often are) persuasive as well. For instance, the local chapter of the American Red Cross might produce a report on how to motivate people to join the blood drives sponsored in their area. Other public organizations, such as government agencies, public interest groups, and political organizations, generate policy reports or investigative research reports that try to persuade concerned citizens to adopt a new policy or take action on an issue. So you might see a report from Mothers Against Drunk Driving (MADD) that details the progress made by your state for curbing teen drunk driving through educating young people on its dangers.

You can expect to find research reports just about anywhere a person might need to know information on a particular issue or subject. And just like any genre, they can be used for different purposes: to inform, to propose, or to persuade. The characteristics of the research report make it versatile and highly useful for a range of rhetorical situations as we'll see as we examine them in more detail throughout the chapter.

Reading Research Reports Critically

WRITING ACTIVITY   Analyzing the Genre of Research Reports

Writing research reports that inform readers and address their concerns requires a strong understanding of how the genre works. Reading reports critically may help writers understand some of the choices other writers make and why they make them, as well as some of the characteristics of research reports.

Thinking about the Genre

Do some background research on the organization or group that has written or produced a report from one of the readings that follow. Knowing who produced the report will help you better understand the report's purpose and its arguments. Keep in mind that sometimes a report is sponsored or requested by another group or organization (for example, the Pew Charitable Trust may sponsor the writing of a report by the Pennsylvania Medicaid Policy Center).

Examining the Genre

As you read the research report, read for comprehension as well as to understand the characteristics of the genre. Look for *patterns* that might reveal something about what research reports in general do.

1. What characteristics do you notice immediately about the report?
2. How is the material arranged? How is the report organized? What do the title and subheadings suggest about the content and focus?
3. What rhetorical situation is addressed in the report? What purpose does the report seem to serve?
4. What kinds of information is in the report? What kinds of research are used to fulfill the goals of the report?
5. Who might be the audience for the report? Notice the language choices, tone, examples, and references being used to understand who might read the report.
6. How are visuals being used in the report?

Reflecting on the Genre

After you have read the report, explain in a couple of paragraphs the major characteristics of the genre as you understand it, using the questions above as a guide. Give examples, refer to specific passages, and quote when necessary. Reflecting on the genre in this way will help you keep track of the kinds of choices writers make that you might want to try when you write your report.

■ ■ ■

Genre Analysis: RI–PIRG, "Rhode Island's Food Safety Net: Ensuring Safe Food from Production to Consumption"

"Rhode Island's Food Safety Net" is a research report produced for the Rhode Island chapter of US-PIRG, an advocacy group for public health concerns. The report examines the steps that Rhode Island has taken in protecting its residents from food-related illnesses and asserts that although the federal government has been unable to ensure food safety for the nation, Rhode Island has done an excellent job in doing so. The report concludes by claiming that the responsibility for food safety will increasingly fall to the individual states.

Okay, so they are defining the problem here - do they need, though, to tell us that we expect it to work well? Isn't that a given?

Overview

Protecting the safety and integrity of the food supply is one of the oldest functions of government, one that the American people expect their government to perform and perform well.

The current food safety regulatory system in the United States is the shared responsibility of local, state and federal partners. In some cases, the federal government has delegated the responsibility for ensuring food safety to states and municipalities, which are often more nimble and able to respond quickly to localized public health problems. Approximately 80% of food safety inspections in the nation, for example, are completed at state and local levels. All 50 states hold the primary responsibility for ensuring the safety of milk and the sanitary operation of restaurants. In other areas, states have passed unique food safety standards that address local concerns or fill important gaps in food safety regulation left open by the U.S. Food and Drug Administration (FDA) and other regulatory agencies. As federal agencies become increasingly under-funded and influenced by powerful corporate interests, the states' role in maintaining the food safety net grows ever-more important.

The following are just a few examples of how the state of Rhode Island has enacted standards to ensure the safety of the food supply in Rhode Island and protect the health of its residents.

Milk and Other Dairy Products

In the early 20th century, adulterated and spoiled milk caused a range of diseases and illness, including tuberculosis and diphtheria. States and municipalities responded to this problem by passing standards for how the dairy industry gathered, processed, distributed and sold milk in the United States. To this day, the states hold the primary responsibility for milk safety. FDA provides guidance to the states in the form of model codes,[1] and the states may adopt these codes voluntarily. But the federal government has not established any mandatory national safety standards for Grade A milk; no national law even regulates the sale of raw unpasteurized milk. That has been left up to states and localities, which are best equipped to regulate, monitor and inspect the local dairy industry and respond to local reports of adulterated milk.

Okay, so they are defining the problem here - do they need, though, to tell us that we expect it to work well? Isn't that a given?

I didn't know any of this, so I'm glad it's here; I haven't ever really thought about food safety, and it never occurred to me that States were primarily responsible.

Rhode Island's milk safety standards regulate the sale of milk, milk products, raw milk and raw milk products; the production, processing, labeling, storing, handling and transportation of milk and milk products; and the sanitary conditions at any dairy or other facility and in any truck or other vehicle in which milk or milk products are produced, processed, handled or transported.[2] The Rhode Island Department of Health, under the auspices of the Office of Food Protection's Dairy Industry Program, conducts inspections of fluid milk production and processing facilities; performs pasteurization equipment testing; and collects product samples for laboratory analysis.[3] Rhode Island's milk standards protect the state's residents from the outbreaks of milk-borne diseases that were common in the early 20th century.

A key component of state milk safety standards, including Rhode Island's standards, is the provision empowering the state to prevent the sale of contaminated or adulterated milk. Whether milk becomes contaminated or adulterated by accident or intent, the state's authority to remove these products from the marketplace is critical for public health.

Food Safety in Restaurants and Other Food Establishments

Almost everyone experiences a food-borne illness or food "poisoning" at least once in their lifetimes after eating out at a restaurant or other food service establishment. These food-borne illnesses, caused most often by inadequate cooking, improper holding temperatures, poor personal hygiene, contaminated equipment and food from unsafe sources,[4] can cause symptoms ranging from the uncomfortable to the life-threatening, particularly for the elderly and those with compromised immune systems. The Centers for Disease Control estimates that food-borne disease causes 325,000 hospitalizations and 5,000 deaths each year.[5]

The federal government has promulgated no mandatory requirements for the safety of restaurant and food service establishment food, devolving this responsibility to the states. All 50 states—generally through their health, small business or agriculture departments—regulate and inspect restaurants, schools, nursing homes, and other food service establishments to ensure the safety of food served. State and local agencies are the main line of defense against food-borne disease.

Rhode Island has established statutes to protect the public from food contaminated by food service establishments or retail food stores during storage, preparation, service, or display and to ensure that food service establishments and retail food stores have adequate facilities for the storage, preparation, service, or display of food.[6] The Rhode Island Department of Health's Office of Food Protection works to prevent disease by assuring the safety and quality of the food supply by inspecting food establishments and investigating complaints and foodborne disease outbreaks.[7]

Shellfish

Shellfish are filter feeders; they get food and oxygen by pumping large quantities of water across their gills. During feeding, shellfish take in bacteria, viruses and chemical contaminants, which can bioaccumulate in their bodies. As a result, some shellfish harvested from polluted areas may pose a health hazard if consumed, causing diseases such as typhoid, hepatitis and salmonellosis.

Here, too, they seem to be trying to frighten us. But then they point out how great a job RI is doing. You'd almost think they were writing this for the RI Department of Health.

No federal laws exist to regulate shellfish harvesters and processors to ensure that shellfish are safe; as such, states are responsible for adopting laws and regulations to ensure that shellfish are grown, harvested and processed in a safe and sanitary manner. FDA's National Shellfish Sanitation Program has created a model ordinance for states, but this serves only as guidance and is not mandatory.[8]

Approximately 16 states have adopted shellfish safety standards, including Rhode Island. Rather than simply adopting FDA's model ordinance on shellfish, Rhode Island decided to tailor it to better fit the state's harvesting methods and focus on hard shell clams.[9] Rhode Island's regulations outline sanitation and permitting requirements for shellfish processors, handlers and transporters; require shellfish dealers to conduct a hazard analysis; and prohibit the sale of any shellfish that have not been processed, labeled, or transported in compliance with the state's standards.[10] Rhode Island also prohibits the sale of all unprocessed and/or uncooked fish, shellfish, and scallops by retail markets and other retailers without a label indicating whether the fish, shellfish, or scallops have ever been frozen.[11]

The federal government has not established similar mandatory standards for shellfish; FDA regulations merely prohibit the interstate transport of shellfish that are likely to contribute to the spread of communicable disease from one state to another.[12]

Conclusion

The Rhode Island food safety standards discussed here and others are important for several reasons:

- They help protect public health from food-borne illnesses and other risks by filling gaps left in federal law;
- They give consumers the power to make informed choices about the food and beverages they purchase for themselves and their families; and
- They help protect local industries by ensuring the safety and purity of their products.

The FDA and other federal agencies do not have the resources—and often do not have the political will—to monitor all aspects of food safety. In fact, the number of full-time FDA employees dealing with food safety has fallen steadily from 3,167 in FY 2003 to 2,843 in FY 2006; the president's proposed FY 2007 budget for FDA would further reduce that number to 2,757.[13] As such, states will continue to play a pivotal role in ensuring that America's food supply remains among the safest in the world.

End Notes

[1]See U.S. FDA, Center for Food Safety and Applied Nutrition, National Conference on Interstate Milk Shipments (NCIMS) Model Documents, accessed March 21, 2006 at http://www.cfsan.fda.gov/~ear/p-nci.html.

[2]Rhode Island Milk Sanitation Code, Title 21, Chapter 21-2.

[3]Rhode Island Department of Health, Office of Food Protection's Dairy Industry Program, accessed March 23, 2006 at http://www.health.state.ri.us/environment/food/dairv/dairvhome.php.

[4]U.S. FDA, FDA Report on the Occurrence of Foodborne Illness Risk Factors in Selected Institutional Foodservice, Restaurant, and Retail Food Store Facility Types, 2004.

So here are the citations - I guess for this genre it's sometimes okay to reference sources this way. Near as I can tell the sources look good - I like that they are working with the actual laws in RI, not someone else's reports on those laws.

[5]Centers for Disease Control, Division of Bacterial and Mycotic Diseases, îFoodborne Illnessî fact sheet, accessed March 22, 2006 at http://www.cdc.gov/ ncidod/dbmd/diseaseinfo/files/foodborne_illness_FAQ.pdf.

[6]Rhode Island General Laws, Title 21, Chapter 21-27, ßß21-27-1- 21-27-11.13.

[7]Rhode Island Department of Health, Office of Food Protection, accessed March 22, 2006 at http://www.health.state.ri.us/environment/food/index.php.

[8]FDA, Center for Food Safety and Applied Nutrition, National Shellfish Sanitation Program Model Ordinance, accessed March 30, 2006 at http://www.cfsan.fda.gov/~ear/nsspotoc.html.

[9]Personal communication with John Mullen, Rhode Island Department of Health, March 30, 2006.

[10]Rhode Island Department of Health, Office of Food Protection, Shellfish Inspection Program, Rhode Island Shellfish Regulation R21-14SB, accessed March 21, 2006 at.

[11]Rhode Island FDCA, ß21-31-3(13), available at.

[12]See U.S. FDA, 21 CFR 1240.60.

[13]FDA, Office of Management Budget Formulation and Presentation, îFoods,î accessed March 30, 2006 at http://origin.www.fda.gov/oc/oms/ofm/budget/2007/HTML/lFoods.htm.

I learned a lot from this report. I didn't know anything at all about food safety, but I have never had food poisoning, so there was no reason I should. I like that the report was so methodical—each section was set up the same way: here's some history on the subtopic, here's what the federal government is not doing, and here's what RI does and does well. I was a little confused by the lack of citations, but I saw at the end that there were footnotes, so clearly this is based on research. Aside from the cover page, there was not much in the way of visual interest in the report—some photos might have made the reading more interesting, but maybe the authors wanted to be sure we took this issue seriously, and too many pictures of kids eating might have sent the wrong message?

I am a little suspicious; I guess RI could be as great as they make it sound, but it seems like there would be some issues or areas for improvement. But maybe that wasn't the purpose of the report. The reason that I bring it up is that I did some research on PIRG, and this is what they say about themselves on their website: "U.S. PIRG, the federation of state Public Interest Research Groups (PIRGs), takes on powerful interests on behalf of the American public working to win concrete results for our health and our well-being. With a strong network of researchers, advocates, organizers and students in state capitols and population centers across the country, we stand up to powerful special interests on issues to promote clean air and water, protect open space, stop identity theft, fight political corruption, provide safe and affordable prescription drugs, and strengthen voting rights." I guess I wonder how this fits in with the standing "up to powerful special interests"?

Rich Morin, "Black–White Conflict Isn't Society's Largest: The Public Assesses Social Divisions"

Rich Morin's report "Black-White Conflict Isn't Society's Largest" was written for the Pew Research Center's Social and Demographic Trends project and published on September 29, 2009. The Pew Research Center is "a nonpartisan 'fact tank' that provides information on the issues, attitudes and trends shaping America and the world." It has many projects including the Pew Research Center for the People and the Press and the Project for Excellence in Journalism. The Social and Demographic Trends project studies "behaviors and attitudes of Americans in key realms of their lives, including family, community, health, finance, work and leisure."

It may surprise anyone following the charges of racism that have flared up during the debate over President Obama's health care proposals, but a survey taken this summer found that fewer people perceived there are strong conflicts between blacks and whites than saw strong conflicts between immigrants and the native born, or between rich people and poor people.

A majority (55%) of adults said there are "very strong" or "strong" conflicts between immigrants and people born in the United States. Nearly as many—47%—said the same about conflicts between rich people and poor people, according to a nationally representative survey by the Pew Research Center Social & Demographic Trends project.

The survey found that about four-in-ten (39%) believe there are serious conflicts between blacks and whites, and only a quarter (26%) see major generational divisions between the young and old.[1]

The findings come at a time when discussions about the role of racism in American society has featured heavily in media coverage of Obama's presidency—triggered first by the arrest in July of a prominent African-American Harvard professor in his own home, and more recently by the assertion by former President Jimmy Carter that much of the opposition to Obama's policies is racially motivated. The Pew Research survey was conducted from July 20 to Aug. 2, shortly after the Harvard incident but before President Carter's recent comments.

Different Groups See Different Levels of Conflict

The survey found some notable demographic patterns in the public's perceptions of social conflicts. For example, blacks, Hispanics and women are significantly more likely than whites and men to say major conflicts exist between groups in at least three of the four areas tested in the survey. Blacks, in particular, consistently see more social conflict than do other demographic groups. But not even blacks believe that racial conflict is the most prevalent

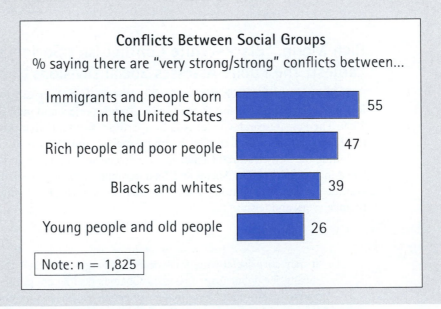

Conflicts Between Social Groups

% saying there are "very strong/strong" conflicts between...

Immigrants and people born in the United States   55

Rich people and poor people   47

Blacks and whites   39

Young people and old people   26

Note: n = 1,825

kind of conflict in the country today. A bare majority of blacks (53%) say there are "very strong/strong" conflicts between blacks and whites. At the same time, nearly two-thirds of blacks (65%) say there are significant conflicts between the rich and poor, and 61% say there are significant conflicts between immigrants and the native born. Blacks also are twice as likely as whites to see major generational conflicts (42% vs. 21%).

The pattern is mixed among other groups. Older adults are significantly less likely than younger people to see strong conflicts between immigrants and native born and between the rich and the poor, but just as likely to see serious generational differences and racial disputes.

Similarly, half of all Democrats (46%) but a only third of Republicans (33%) say there are serious conflicts between blacks and whites. The partisan perceptions gap is even bigger on perceptions of conflicts between the rich and poor: a 55% majority of Democrats see very serious or serious conflicts between haves and have-nots, compared with 38% of Republicans. At the same time, there is no significant difference by party affiliation in perceptions about conflicts between immigrants and native born or between the generations.

Social Conflict in American Life

To measure perceptions of social conflict, a total of 1,815 persons age 16 and older were interviewed July 20–Aug. 2, 2009. Respondents were asked in separate questions "In all countries, there are differences or conflicts between different social groups. In your opinion, in America, how much conflict is there between . . . " blacks and whites, the poor and the rich, young people and older people, and immigrants and people born in the United States. Respondents were then given these answer options: "very strong conflicts, strong conflicts, not very strong conflicts, there are not conflicts" for each domain.[2]

Disagreements between immigrants and native-born Americans emerge as the most prevalent and serious type of social conflict among those tested in the survey. A clear majority (55%) of adults say there are "very strong" or "strong" conflicts between these groups, including 18% who say there are "very strong" conflicts and 37% who describe them as "strong."

Hispanics in particular see serious clashes between these groups: nearly seven-in-ten (68%) say there are major conflicts between immigrants and the native born, a view shared by half of whites (53%) and six-in-ten blacks (61%).

At the same time, those born outside the United States are no more likely than the native born to say there are serious conflicts between immigrants and people born in the U.S. (56% for native born vs. 53% for foreign born).

Perceptions of Social Conflicts

% who characterize conflicts between each social group as "very strong" or "strong"...

	Blacks/ whites	Rich/ poor	Immigrants/ native-born	Young/ old
Total	39	47	55	26
Gender				
Men	38	43	52	23
Women	40	51	59	29
Race/Ethnicity				
White	35	43	53	21
Black	53	65	61	42
Hispanic	47	55	68	39
Age				
16–29	36	50	56	28
30–49	42	52	61	25
50–64	39	45	55	24
65+	36	36	44	26
Income				
$100,00+	47	46	60	20
$50–99k	38	50	55	22
$30–49k	38	45	58	25
LT $30k	39	47	54	23
Party				
Democrat	16	55	56	28
Republican	33	38	57	24
Independent	35	45	54	23
Nativity				
Native born	32	47	56	25
Foreign born	42	49	53	35

Note: "Don't know/refused" not shown.

Q: In your opinion, in America, how much conflict is there between (groups): Very strong conflicts, strong conflicts, not very strong conflicts, there are not conflicts?

Nearly half of respondents (47%) say there are serious conflicts between the rich and poor—a double-digit decline in perceptions of economic-class-based conflict from 1987 when the General Social Survey found that 59% saw "very strong" or "strong" conflicts between the two groups.

In the Pew Research survey, adults older than age 65 are significantly less likely than people under the age of 50 to see serious divisions by economic class (36% vs. 51%). Blacks, Hispanics, Democrats and women also are more likely than other groups to perceive major disputes between economic classes. Perhaps surprisingly, income seems to have little relationship with perceptions of rich-poor conflicts. Slightly less than half (46%) of those with annual family incomes of $100,000 or more say there are serious conflicts

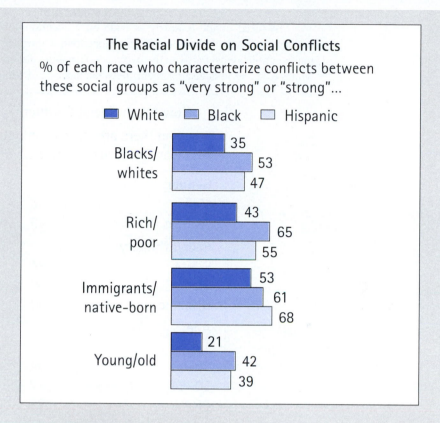

The Racial Divide on Social Conflicts

% of each race who characterterize conflicts between these social groups as "very strong" or "strong"...

■ White   ▨ Black   □ Hispanic

Blacks/whites
- White: 35
- Black: 53
- Hispanic: 47

Rich/poor
- White: 43
- Black: 65
- Hispanic: 55

Immigrants/native-born
- White: 53
- Black: 61
- Hispanic: 68

Young/old
- White: 21
- Black: 42
- Hispanic: 39

between the rich and poor—and so does a virtually identical share (47%) of those earning less than $30,000.

About four-in-ten Americans see major conflicts between blacks and whites, including 53% of blacks and 47% of Hispanics, but a significantly smaller share of whites (35%).

Only 26% see major conflicts between young people and older adults—a view shared by virtually identical proportions of older (26%) and younger adults (28%). As with the rich-poor divide, the proportion of Americans who see a great deal of generational conflict has declined substantially: In the 1992 GSS survey, fully 42% saw major divisions between the old and young.

Race and Perceptions of Social Conflicts

Blacks were more likely than whites to see "very strong" or "strong" conflicts in three of the four areas. In the fourth domain—disagreements between immigrants and native born—the difference also was large but fell just short of statistical significance (61%for blacks vs. 53% for whites). Nearly two-thirds (65%) of blacks but 43% of whites say major disagreements exist between rich people and poor people, a view shared by 55% of Hispanics.

The racial divide is nearly as wide on perceptions of racial conflict. A majority of blacks (53%) but slightly more than a third of whites (35%) say major conflicts exist between the two races. Hispanics also are more likely than whites to see serious disagreements between blacks and whites (47% vs. 35%).

How Much Social Conflict?	
% saying there are strong conflicts in at least three areas tested...	
Gender	
Men	26
Women	33
Race/Ethnicity	
White	24
Black	50
Hispanic	43
Age	
16–29	31
30–49	34
50–64	27
65+	23
Income	
$100,00+	33
$50–99k	28
$30–49k	26
LT $30k	32
Party	
Republican	22
Democrat	36
Independent	26
Ideology	
Conservative	26
Moderate	30
Liberal	34
Note: Hispanics may be of any race	

The gap is narrowest between blacks and whites on conflicts between immigrants and the foreign born, 61% vs. 53%, an eight-point gap. But there is a 15-point gap between Hispanics (68%) and whites (53%) on this question. There is also a sizable gap in views about generational conflicts: blacks are twice as likely as whites to see major conflicts between the generations (42% vs. 21%), a view shared by 39% of Hispanics.

The Politics of Social Conflict

The issue of race has been thrust onto center-stage of American politics this summer. In July, President Obama hosted a "beer summit" at the White House to try to smooth over a controversy he helped to fuel with his comments at a press conference regarding the arrest of a black Harvard professor by a white Cambridge policeman. More recently, prominent Democrats such as former President Carter have publicly speculated that race—and, by implication, racism—is behind some of the attacks on President Obama at venues ranging from town-hall meetings to the floor of Congress. Meanwhile, Republicans accuse Democrats of playing the race card to deflect legitimate criticisms of the president's policies.

The Pew Research survey suggests these very different views on black-white relations reflect deeper partisan and ideological differences. Nearly half of Democrats say there are "very strong conflicts" (10%) or "strong conflicts" (36%) between blacks and whites. In contrast, only about a third of Republicans say racial disputes are as serious (7% say these conflicts are "very strong" while 26% characterize them as "strong").

At the same time, nearly six-in-ten Republicans (59%) say there are no major areas of contention between the races, a view shared by 48% of Democrats. Conservative Republicans are significantly more likely than liberal Democrats to see relatively few racial conflicts (63% vs. 50%). But their counterparts on the left—self-described liberal Democrats—are no more likely than other Democrats to say major conflicts exist between blacks and whites (48% for liberal Democrats vs. 45% for moderate or conservative Democrats).[3]

This partisan divide on social conflicts also exists on another issue tested in the survey. A majority of Democrats (55%) but just 38% of Republicans see serious conflicts between the rich and poor.

However, the partisan-perception gap does not extend to other areas of American life. An equal share of Republicans (57%) and Democrats (56%) say major conflicts exist between immigrants and native-born Americans. Similarly, roughly a quarter of each party believe there are major conflicts between the young and older generations.

Big Majority Sees at Least One Area of Major Social Conflicts

To provide an overview of public attitudes toward social conflicts, a simple scale was created based on the four types of conflicts measured in the survey—rich and poor, black and white, immigrants and native born and young people and older adults. The scale totaled the number of realms in which each respondent believes "very strong" or "strong conflicts' currently exist. For example, if a respondent says very strong or strong conflicts exist in all four areas, the respondent's score would be four. If a respondent reports no strong conflicts in response to all four questions, his or her score would be zero.

Overall, fully three-quarters of those surveyed (76%) say that serious conflicts currently exist in at least one of the four areas tested. About half (51%) report major conflicts in two or more areas.

At the same time, nearly a quarter (24%) say there are no major disputes between groups, while, at the other extreme, only about one-in-ten say there are serious conflicts in all four domains.

Blacks are more than twice as likely as whites and somewhat more likely than Hispanics to see major conflicts in three or more areas (50% for blacks vs. 24% for whites and 43% for Hispanics).

Democrats, too, are more likely than Republicans (36% vs. 22%) or political independents (26%) to see three or more areas of serious disagreement. Political liberals saw more disagreements overall than conservatives (34% vs. 26%).

The perceptions gaps are smaller among other demographic groups. Women (33%) are more likely than men (26%) to see three or more areas of serious conflict while the foreign born are more likely than people born in the U.S. to see multiple areas of disagreement (37% vs. 29%).

---

[1] *For a more extensive analysis of generational conflict, see "Forty Years After Woodstock, A Gentler Generation Gap."*

[2] *This basic question and answer scale has been used three times since 1987 in the General Social Survey, conducted by the National Opinion Research Center at the University of Chicago. However, the GSS did not ask about conflicts between blacks and whites, or between immigrants and the native born, but has asked about rich-poor and young-old conflicts.*

[3] *As shown in the previous section, blacks are significantly more likely than whites to see conflict between the races. Since blacks disproportionately identify themselves as Democrats, might the partisan differences vanish if the racial makeup of the two parties is taken into account? The survey suggests that the answer is no. White Democrats are still significantly more likely than white Republicans to say there are strong disagreements between whites and blacks (41% vs. 31%).*

Reading for Comprehension

1. Why does this report seem timely given the political and social context it describes in America? How does your impression of race relations in the United States match what the report finds?
2. What kinds of evidence are used by the writer to draw conclusions about racial conflict in America? Do you agree with the conclusions of the survey? What do you base your agreement or disagreement on?

Analyzing the Genre

1. What audiences might find interesting or useful the results of the research conducted for this report? What might those readers say? How might they react differently to Morin's conclusions?
2. What purpose do the visuals used in Morin's report serve?

Steven Clark, M.D., Alicia Mangram, M.D., Ernest Dunn, M.D., "Car Surfing: Case Studies of a Growing Dangerous Phenomenon"

From Methodist Health and Hospital System, Dallas, Texas

In their brief report, physicians Steven Clark, Alicia Mangram, and Ernest Dunn write about car surfing (lying or sitting on a car while someone drives it), which they declare a "dangerous new pastime for American youth." Their report was published in the journal the American Surgeon, which "brings up to date clinical advances in surgical knowledge in a popular reference format."

Car surfing is a dangerous new pastime for American youth. Car surfing is an activity that is defined as standing (or lying) on a vehicle while it is being driven. This activity frequently results in severe injuries that often require significant surgical intervention. Despite its destructive nature, however, there are many Internet sites that encourage this behavior and view it as amusing. As a result, car surfing is becoming increasingly popular. We conducted a retrospective chart review of all patients injured as a result of car surfing over the last 4 years at our Urban Level II trauma center. Data collected included Injury Severity Score (ISS), Revised Trauma Score (RTS), age, gender, injury pattern, surgical intervention, and length of stay. Eight car surfers were identified. The average age was 17. The average Revised Trauma Score was 6.8 with an average Injury Severity Score of 16.9. Five patients were admitted to the intensive care unit. Four of these five patients needed to be intubated for ventilatory support. Five of the eight patients had significant intracranial injuries. Two patients had epidural hematomas that required evacuation. Two other patients had subdural hematomas that were treated nonoperatively, and one patient had a subarachnoid hemorrhage that was also treated nonoperatively. Four of the eight patients required surgical intervention. There were no deaths in this study. Car surfing leads to severe injuries that can result in significant morbidity. American youth have access to Internet sites that project this activity as an acceptable behavior. Five of our eight patients had a significant intracranial injury. Trauma surgeons need to be more aware of this injury phenomenon.

* * *

A DANGEROUS JUVENILE GAME is growing in popularity in the United States. Car surfing has become an increasingly popular mechanism for vehicular trauma during the last 15 years. Car surfing is an activity that is defined as standing or lying on a vehicle while another party is driving. Participants position themselves on the hood, roof, or truck bed while the vehicle is in motion. In a similar activity known as "ghost riding," individuals leave their vehicles unmanned while they dance next to the vehicle or on the hood. Both car surfing and ghost riding have become popular teen pastimes around the nation. The popularity is increasing as American youths are now filming and posting images of themselves car surfing on a variety of Internet sites. As can be expected, significant bodily harm occurs when participants accidentally fall or are thrown from their vehicles. We looked at all of the car surfing incidents that occurred over the last 5 years at our urban Level II Trauma center to better define this problem.

Case Studies

The medical records of eight trauma patients admitted within a 5-year period (2000 to 2005) from injuries related to car surfing at Methodist Dallas Medical Center located in Dallas, Texas, were identified. The charts were reviewed for Injury Severity Score (ISS), Revised Trauma Score (RTS), age, gender, intracranial and other injuries, surgical intervention, need for mechanical ventilation, intensive care unit admissions, duration of hospital stay, and mortality.

Over the 5-year period, eight patients were admitted to our Level II trauma center for injuries related to car surfing. The average ISS was 16.8 and the average RTS was 6.78. The average age of the patients was 17 years and males were predominant, encompassing 63 per cent of the studied population. Five of the eight patients were admitted to the intensive care unit and

Address correspondence and reprint requests to Steven Clark, M.D., Methodist Hospital, Office of Medical Education, c/o Berta Turner, 1441 N. Beckley, Dallas, TX 75203. E-mail BertaTurner@MHD.com.

four of those five patients required intubation and ventilatory support. Five patients had an intracranial injury: two patients had epidural hematomas, two patients had subdural hematomas, and one patient had a subarachnoid hemorrhage. Both patients with epidural hematomas required emergent surgical evacuations; one of these two individuals had a concomitant orthopedic injury that required additional surgical intervention. The three other patients with intracranial injuries did not require neurosurgical intervention. Overall, half of the patients required some type of surgical intervention. Two patients had isolated musculoskeletal injuries that required orthopedic surgical procedures. The average length of stay for these patients was 6.5 days. The shortest length of stay was 1 day and the longest was 13 days. There was no mortality in this study.

Discussion

As our data shows, car surfing is an extremely dangerous and costly activity. Although no institution reports more than a few admissions from car surfing, all institutions agree that patients who are admitted tend to have severe injuries.[1–4] In Carey's survey of 35 patients admitted with injuries from car surfing over a 15-year period, 82 per cent of those studied had head injuries.[1] Traumatic brain injuries seem to be the most common reason for admission with patients injured from car surfing. Geiger's joint study with patients from both Ann Arbor, Michigan, and Toledo, Ohio, noted that severe brain injury was the most common injury pattern seen in that group. Twenty-two of the 26 patients in the study had closed head injuries with 85 per cent of those studied requiring long-term rehabilitation.[3]

Four of the eight patients we studied needed operative management of their injuries, and five of the eight patients required admission to the intensive care unit. Five of the eight patients in our study had traumatic brain injuries. Estimated costs of traumatic brain injuries reach $56.3 billion annually.[6] Car surfing is costing patients, hospitals, and the general public significant healthcare dollars from an easily preventable action.

Car surfing has been reported in numerous states such as Ohio, California, Michigan, Indiana, and Texas.[1, 2, 5, 6] Oddly enough, although substance abuse has been reported with car surfing, the majority of the youth involved with this dangerous activity are not under the influence of alcohol or drugs.[2, 3, 7] In the age of the World Wide Web, teenage children can surf the Internet and learn how to car surf from sites as basic as Google at video.google.com. By searching "car surfing" on the extremely popular MySpace.com and YouTube.com, hundreds of profiles appear with teens and young adults expressing their love of the "hobby" of car surfing. These are just two examples. There are also many obscure Internet sites that have clips of teens car surfing. Some sites identify car surfing as unintelligent behavior, but others simply view the car surfing clips as amusing.

Conclusion

Car surfing is a dangerous phenomenon, which is now being seen in many states. The mechanism of injury predisposes these young people to significant intracranial injuries as well as orthopedic injuries. Trauma surgeons may see this type of behavior increase as youth emulate behavior seen on the Internet.

References

1. Carey J, McCarthy MC, Ekeh AP, et al. Car-surfing in southwest Ohio: Incidence and injuries. J Trauma 2005;59:734–6.
2. Peterson T, Timberlake G, Yeager A, et al. Car surfing: An uncommon cause of traumatic injury. Ann Emerg Med 1999;33: 192–4.
3. Geiger JD, Newsted J, Drongowski RA, et al. Car surfing: An underreported mechanism of serious injury in children and adolescents. J Pediatr Surg 2001;36:232–4.
4. Kohr RM. Car surfing in Indiana—An unusual form of motor vehicle fatality. J Forensic Sci 1992;37:1693–6.
5. Thurman D. The epidemiology and economics of head trauma. In: Miller L, Hayes R, eds. Head Trauma: Basic, Preclinical, and Clinical Directions. New York: Wiley and Sons, 2001.
6. Hooft PJ, van de Voorde HP. Reckless behaviour related to the use of 3, 4-methylenedioxymethamphetamine (ecstasy): Apropos of a fatal accident during car-surfing. Int J Legal Med 1994; 106:328–9.

Reading for Comprehension

1. The authors note that car surfing is increasingly popular among youth. How popular is it? Research the subject using your library's databases or an Internet search engine to get a sense of who is doing it and where.
2. What can happen to people car surfing? How serious are the injuries? Look up terms and injuries that you are unfamiliar with.

Analyzing the Genre

1. The authors draw on rather limited data for their study. How do they supplement that data? Does the supplemented data add or detract from the persuasiveness of their report for their audience?
2. This report relies primarily on the case studies the authors examined. What do readers learn about those individuals in that section that emphasizes the authors' purpose? What information is missing about the individuals and how might that information be useful?

COL Elspeth Cameron Ritchie, MC USA Contributors: Robert Andrew Cardona, MD*; COL Elspeth Cameron Ritchie, MC USA†, "U.S. Military Enlisted Accession Mental Health Screening: History and Current Practice"

Colonel Ritchie and Dr. Cardona's report appeared in the January 2007 issue of Military Medicine, the official journal of the Association of Military Surgeons of the United States (AMSUS). The journal has been in publication since 1892, when it was called the Military Surgeon.

Through the stimulus of war and concerns about neuropsychiatric disability, the U.S. military developed methods to rapidly screen the mental health of World War I and II draftees. Intelligence testing and brief psychiatric screening expanded the accession physical examination and underwent revision to identify only gross mental health disability. Supplemental psychiatric evaluations and written psychological screening tools were abandoned after postwar assessments; they demonstrated poor predictive power in evaluating recruit service capacity for combat environments. Currently, only three mental health accession tools are used to screen applicants before their entrance into military service, namely, educational achievement, cognitive testing, and a cursory psychiatric evaluation. The Navy and Air Force use a fourth screening measure during entry-level training. Educational attainment with high school graduation has been the strongest predictor of finishing a service term. The purpose of this article is to provide both a historical review and a review of testing efforts.

Introduction

Interest in reducing attrition was renewed in the middle to late 1990s as attrition rates reached new highs. Over the past two decades, first-term enlisted attrition rates consistently averaged 30%. By 1997, 4-year attrition rates peaked at 37%.[1] This sparked a variety of activities to investigate causation and to identify potential remedies.[2] One such activity was the Accession/ Recruit Mental Health Symposium held in Chicago on September 12 to 13, 2000. The symposium was

* Community Mental Health Service, Reynolds Army Community Hospital, Fort Sill, OK 73503-6300.

†Psychiatry Consultant, Office of the Surgeon General, 5109 Leesburg Pike, Suite 689, Falls Church, VA 22041-3206.

The views expressed in this article are those of the authors and do not reflect the official policy or position of the Department of the Army, the Department of Defense, or the U.S. government.

This manuscript was received for review in April 2003. The revised manuscript was accepted for publication in June 2006.

sponsored by the Office of the Assistant Secretary of Defense (Force Management Policy) and represented a tri-service working group of mental health professionals, which reviewed recruit attrition issues related to mental health.

In preparation for that conference, it became clear that a recent historical review of military psychological screening did not exist. This history provides insight into the contributions and limitations of mental health screening for military attrition.

This article outlines the 85-year history of accession mental health screening and current screening practices. Civilian psychological testing initially served as a template for the military, leading to the development of accession screening tools. Intelligence testing materialized in World War I, psychiatric qualification became the focus during World War II, and then a variety of personality and motivation measures were explored. There are three accession tools that are currently used to screen military service applicants. The Navy and Air Force use a secondary screening measure during entry-level training.

The Origins of Psychological Testing

In the late 19th century, the study of individual differences led to interest in the quantification of human qualities. Francis Galton, who is ascribed as the father of psychological testing, administered the first measurement battery to thousands at the International Health Exhibit in England in 1884.

In 1897, Alfred Binet began work on measuring and testing individual differences by studying children in the Paris public school system. Binet and a physician, Theodore Simon, developed the Simon-Binet test of intelligence in 1905, to select students needing remedial education.

By 1908, Henry Goddard had translated the test into English for U.S. consumers. As intelligence testing increased in popularity, this test underwent multiple revisions, with Lewis Terman standardizing the test for U.S. children in 1916. It is known today as the Stanford-Binet test. In 1917, Robert Woodworth developed the Personal Data Sheet, which was briefly used to screen military recruits. This was the first group personality test and was the forerunner off the current Minnesota Multiphasic Personality Inventory.

As the country headed into World War I, efficient methods of screening vast numbers of drafted men were sought to support the war effort. The war provided a major stimulus in the further development of cognitive testing and novel screening efforts.

World War I and Intelligence Testing

From 1909 to 1915, 83% of all military service applicants were rejected. Because of the war effort, the applicant pool was expanded with modification of a few physical requirements and reduction of the age requirement from 21 years to 18 years. World War I medical screening produced 468 defective men per 1,000. Mental health defects represented 6% of all rejections, with the majority being intelligence deficiencies.[3]

Dr. Robert Yerkes, then president of the American Psychological Association, proposed blanket intelligence testing for military recruits. The Surgeon General of the Army considered his proposal, whereas the Navy turned him away. Dr. Yerkes was appointed director of the U.S. Army Psychological Testing Corps and headed a task force of psychologists.

The expansion of draftee screening brought hundreds of psychologists into the service to perform testing. They processed draftees at the rate of several thousand per day through each induction station. A paper-and-pencil survey was developed and correlated with the standardized Stanford-Binet test. Testing was designed to screen for intellectual defectiveness and to assist in appropriate career placement, where a recruit could render maximal military service.[4] In 1917, Dr. Yerkes, with the help of Lewis Terman, David Wechsler, and others, developed the Army Alpha and Beta tests (Alpha for those who were literate and Beta for those who illiterate).

Approximately 2 million draftees were administered the tests. Line officers found the ratings useful in the formation of training groups and noted a predictive element regarding the draftee's capacity to make training progress at 2, 4, and 6 months. The civilian sector, particularly universities, demonstrated interest in adopting similar entrance screening procedures.

After the war, interest persisted in the development of cognitive testing at recruit evaluation stations. The military committed to expanding the role of psychological testing, with the expectation of further developing screening methods. Despite this interest, minimal research occurred during the 1920s and 1930s.

A significant lesson from World War I included the recognition that war elicited a significant number of neuropsychiatric casualties. Although only 10% of all disabilities were attributed to neuropsychiatric conditions, it was noted that a large percentage of these casualties had preexisting symptoms.[3] Questions were raised about whether additional screening efforts could assist in minimizing future neuropsychiatric casualties.

Costs of medical care and disability from the war reached ~1 billion dollars for the 2.3 million World War I veterans.[5] Interest in reducing economic and personnel expenditures became the focus of mental health screening as the United States headed into World War II.

World War II and Psychiatric Qualification

Screening Goal

Rapid testing and classification of new recruits were critical to the rapid build-up of U.S. forces after the attack on Pearl Harbor. The usefulness of intelligence testing was fully accepted, and attention turned toward issues of mental health fitness through psychiatric qualification. Selection standards were high before the declaration of war. All men with actual psychiatric disorders or character flaws were screened out, creating a psychiatric rejection rate of 10 to 15%.[6]

To minimize neuropsychiatric casualties, the goal was to reject all men who had a greater than average likelihood of having difficulty adjusting to military conditions. It was thought that adjustment difficulties and psychiatric conditions were rarely treatable and patients should be exempted from military service.

A Divergence of Opinion

Opinions varied regarding the ability of psychiatric screening measures to adequately qualify draftees for service. Many took a moderate view, citing the reasonable ability to detect applicants with existing neuropsychiatric disabilities but doubting the capacity to identify soldiers who would break down under combat conditions.[7] Different screening proposals arose from diverse philosophies, including acceptance of borderline cases for probationary training and acceptance of antisocial applicants for specific service assignments.

Bowan[8] cited information from World War I indicating a 5% general psychiatric rate (with subsequent review, it was found to be 3%), but less than one-half of cases were detected in the selection process. That author was convinced that more could have been detected if a complete history had been obtained. He recommended that local draft boards obtain additional historical records from hospitals, schools, courts, and social service agencies. Others disagreed that personal history, or even the presence of significant personality abnormalities, would be efficiently predictive of nonadaptability to military service.[9] It was repeatedly cited that recruits who were maladjusted in their premilitary life, and even those with a history of psychiatric treatment, could and did accommodate well to military service.[10]

Harry Stack Sullivan was appointed as psychiatric consultant to the Selective Service in 1941. He directed the planning of draftee psychiatric examinations to aid medical examiners at draft boards. Local community physicians first evaluated draftees in a screening medical examination. Those found to be fit were advanced to an induction station for final evaluation, including standardized intelligence testing.

Civilian psychiatrists were frequently used, because of military psychiatrist shortages, and conducted up to 50 examinations each day. Screening in many instances required only 2 to 3 minutes per applicant, in the setting of good school and work records. Consequently, more time was made available for consideration of men for whom there was less certainty, with an average examination time of 6 minutes. If a decision could not be reached in 15 minutes, then further observation was performed in a hospital setting.

Screening philosophies and testing differences emerged in the dual systems of the local draft board and induction stations. Ultimately, they were amalgamated into one examination standard, which underwent several revisions throughout the duration of the war.

Sliding Accession Screening Standards

After the United States entered the war in 1942, a large Army was required, resulting in the lowering of stringent screening standards. Examiners shifted rigid or liberal interpretations of existing induction standards to reflect manpower needs. The Navy tended to be more rigid in its enlistment standards and was prone to reject more than the Army psychiatrists. Registrants were not considered fixed in one category but were constantly reevaluated. In April 1944, a War Department directive emphasized accumulating evidence that many individuals with minor psychiatric conditions or personality flaws could be of service.[10] Many who had been screened out earlier were later reconsidered and placed into service. They were found to provide the war effort with good performance.[11]

Medical Survey Program and Longitudinal Functioning

Significant emphasis was placed on obtaining historical and functionally based material for review when screening a draftee. This material included legal, medical, educational, and mental health records. Screening selection methods would be considered ineffective if based solely on a brief examination. The Medical Survey Program was developed in 1943 to set procedures for obtaining historical information. For this endeavor, Department of Selective Service Form 212 (Medical and Social History) was created.[6] Completion of the form depended on the activity of social workers, who were limited in number. Information was obtained and forwarded to the induction station medical examiner.

Many of the forms used by psychiatrists in screening potential service members were incomplete and addressed only pathological histories. Even if fully completed, they were too lengthy to be useful. To improve efficiency, a trained psychiatric social worker was placed in each induction station to review the forms and to summarize information on a face sheet. However, because of persistent deficits in completion of the forms, this program was downscaled and used only when the local board had reason to suspect significant deficits. Despite the program's shortcomings, psychiatrists were unanimous regarding the potential effectiveness of such a program in the selection process.[6]

Because of insufficient numbers of psychiatrists to provide thorough routine evaluations, many general practitioners were pulled into service as psychiatric examiners. A group screening measure was contemplated, to reduce the number of inductees to undergo the psychiatric interview and to improve personnel utilization. Several induction station psychiatrists devised their own homemade tests and screened for past and present symptoms, antisocial behavior, and psychosomatic manifestations.[6]

Neuropsychiatric Screening Adjunct

Dr. John Appel, chief of preventative psychiatry in the neuropsychiatry consultants division of the Office of the Surgeon General, made an effort to validate a single screening device. A 15-item screening test was developed for the most common psychiatric problems. Eight questions were added to screen for psychosis and antisocial dispositions. Those with poor scores underwent individual psychiatric examination. The uniform measure was named the neuropsychiatric screening adjunct (NSA) and was adopted for use at all induction stations by the end of 1944.[12]

The NSA never replaced the psychiatric interview and was administered to augment this process. NSA scores successfully selected 80% of those diagnosed as psychiatrically impaired in interviews.[13] The authors of the test concluded that the screen could have served an important role in selection efficiency, but they acknowledged the need for better standardization.

A follow-up study evaluated the effectiveness of the selection process by reviewing hospitalization rates. For neuropsychiatric disorders, 53% had the diagnosis of psychoneurosis. A large percentage of these had worksheets at the induction station with evidence of deficiencies or had undergone more-extensive examination at the time of induction. Those with a diagnosis of schizophrenia or bipolar disorder were consistently free of this evidence.[14] Many of the service members who manifested disciplinary problems were administratively discharged and were not included in the review. An investigation was made by the Office of the Surgeon General to evaluate the predictive power of the NSA for neuropsychiatric disabilities. A poor association was noted.[6]

Department of Defense Review of Neuropsychiatric Screening
Several postwar studies reviewed the overall efforts of neuropsychiatric screening. Psychiatric screening was considered inefficient and failed as a primary method of preventing the great majority of losses caused by neuropsychiatric disorders.[11,15] However, induction screening did serve a useful purpose in eliminating from service those with overt psychosis, mental retardation, or severe psychoneurosis.[16]

World War II accession standards were recognized as excessive and resulted in unnecessary loss of potential service members. The mental health criteria used in determining suitability were seen as being inadequate for predicting service performance.[6] Screening processes were unable to evaluate the most important factors influencing the adjustment of a soldier, including the leadership he would receive, his degree of motivation, the type of position and unit assigned, and the degree of external stress to which he would be exposed. It was advocated that greater proficiency of evaluating service suitability would be accomplished by evaluating recruits under military conditions, rather than by using extensive induction screening procedures.

Recognition of induction screening limitations led to secondary screening efforts at initial training centers under military conditions. This effort expanded into individual and group preventative psychiatric interventions.[17,18] Mental hygiene and life skill lectures were standardized. Experimental retraining units were created for selected soldiers and were supported by commanding generals. Approximately 70% successfully transitioned into military service, and the rest were separated.[5]

By the end of the war in 1945, experience accumulated from training centers and line commands that fundamentally changed the views regarding the ability of individuals to withstand war stress. As manpower needs liberalized some of the induction standards, it became evident that individuals with minor psychiatric symptoms were able to provide effective service in a war setting. Emphasis was placed on the importance of longitudinal information in establishing the suitability of applicants. Unsuitability needed to rest on clear evidence of sustained and incapacitating dysfunction, supporting the openness to trial service.[6,10]

Liaison with classification sections afforded the opportunity to place inductees in assignments for which they were best suited. This also provided the capacity to place those into service who might otherwise have been rejected during entry screening. Upon receipt of ongoing screening findings in War Department Technical Bulletin 33, many induction stations reexamined their applicants and found that >50% were acceptable and subsequently inducted. One study investigated attrition of these reconsidered soldiers and found that 80% remained in service after 1 year.[6] Many were found to serve for long periods with satisfactory performance.[19]

Post-World War II Screening Policy

From these postwar assessments, screening procedures were modified. Psychiatric evaluation was integrated into the general medical examination, with the intention of identifying and disqualifying only gross psychiatric disability. Supplemental psychiatric screening aids were discontinued. If there was a question regarding an applicant's suitability, then a full psychiatric evaluation was sought through consultation, for final service determination. Similarly, any personality flaws that had not incapacitated an applicant in civilian life were acceptable for service. As a result of further developing policy in accordance with field findings, the disqualification rate for psychiatric causes decreased from 5.5 cases per 1,000 applicants to 1.9 cases per 1,000 applicants in the 1950s.[20]

Post-Korean War Screening Efforts

After the Korean War, efforts resumed in further developing and improving accession screening measures. Cognitive and general psychiatric screening had been fully accepted and integrated into the accession process. The focus turned to developing measures that identified personality characteristics that were predictive of satisfactory military service. Examples of these efforts follow.

Danielson and Clark[21] designed a screening tool in 1954, the Fort Ord Inventory. They tested 15,000 Army recruits, finding four scales that differentiated between those with poor adjustment qualities and those with leadership potential. In 1961, Jenson[22] used a 82-item questionnaire with >9,000 male Air Force recruits and also found areas related to training failure.

In 1962, Plag[23] published testing results with a 195-item questionnaire for 20,000 Navy recruits and found several variables linked to successful training. In 1965, Plag[24] published another study in which 134 Navy recruits who were thought to be mentally unsuitable for military service were specifically retained, trained, and then placed in the fleet. Approximately 70% of that group remained functional on active duty at the 2-year follow-up assessment, compared with 86% for a control group matched with respect to age, intellect, and educational experience. The author thought that the capacity for successful duty for this group was related to their achieving emotional growth within the military environment, with the fleet being able to match specific services with skills of marginal enlistees, and that initial training difficulties tended to be transient.

In 1974, Lachar et al.[25] used two testing measures, the Psychological Screening Inventory and the History, Opinion, and Interest Form, for ~15,000 male Air Force recruits. They identified a high-risk group with the adaptation index, which demonstrated 50% accuracy in identifying recruits who did not complete basic training. Those authors promoted a tiered approach in screening and used screening not only to determine unsuitability but also to identify potential recruits who would respond to training modalities that integrated behavioral modification and group dynamics.

In 1975, the Air Force used the History, Opinion, and Interest Form as part of a research screening program conducted over the course of 1 year. The product was the Air Force Medical Evaluation Test Program (AFMET), which involved a three-phase screening program. Additional modifications produced the AFMET used in the Air Force and Navy secondary screening programs today. During the same time, educational selection was integrated into general accession screening procedures. The AFMET and educational selection processes are discussed below.

In 1988, a study of ~340 enlisted airmen referred for command-directed evaluation was reported by McGraw and Bearden.[26] They underscored the need for early identification and separation of unsuitable recruits, to minimize increasing technical training costs. These airmen were described as being unmotivated for continued service and refractory to therapeutic interventions. Early indications of reduced adaptability were present in mental health evaluations during basic training.

Efforts were made to supplement or to replace reliance on education credentials for service determination in the 1980s. Biographical and temperament indications increasingly became favored. The Army developed a self-reporting instrument named the Assessment of Background and Life Experiences. It screened motivational factors and was reported to correlate with first-term attrition and performance. It tended to produce false-negative results and was never put into pilot implementation. With further development, a "fake-resistant" 30-minute self-report model called the Assessment of Individual Motivation (AIM) was created.[27] It was reported that findings showed little overlap with the Armed Services Vocational Aptitude Battery (ASVAB) or educational achievement. The Army implemented it as a pilot program and successfully demonstrated that if a recruit scored high on the AIM, despite lower educational achievement or ASVAB scoring, attrition risk remained stable during the first year of service. Its development provides an inclusionary screening instrument, consistent with historical lessons against screening out potential recruits capable of providing good military service. The implementation of AIM is currently being expanded and further examined for longer-term outcome data.

Current Accession Mental Health Screening

To sustain today's military force, an annual recruitment of ~200,000 enlisted recruits occurs. Currently, there are three components of mental health screening used in the accession of military applicants. The first involves assessing aptitude with the ASVAB, which was put into place in 1976. Four of the 10 ASVAB subtests are grouped into the Armed Forces Qualification Test (AFQT) score, which estimates a recruit's intelligence capacity. Scores are also used to place applicants in work assignments where they are most likely to succeed.

The second screening measure is the determination of educational achievement, specifically high school graduation or an equivalent achievement level. The U.S. Congress sets accession quality standards, based on a Department of Defense attrition mathematical model that links educational attainment, aptitude, and recruiting resources to job performance within a cost setting. This model is based on performance, using a standard obtained for the 1990 enlisted recruit cohort during the last national engagement in large-scale combat. Educational attainment with high school graduation has been the strongest predictor of finishing a service term, followed by an AFQT score in the upper 50%.[28]

"High-quality" recruits are defined as having a high school diploma and scoring in the top 50% on the AFQT. Since 1973, accessions for high-quality recruits have increased from 30 to 60% across services to 60 to 80%. In 1994, those with a high school diploma and 50% AFQT score were 68% of all recruits accessed.[29] Historical evidence indicates that, if the Department of Defense did not target these higher-quality recruits, then attrition rates would be higher, resulting in an overall lower level of service performance.[30]

The third screening measure consists of a review of medical screening forms and a general psychiatric evaluation, which is integrated into the entrance physical examination at military entrance processing stations. Beyond these three screening measures, there are no specific tools used in assessing personality or other psychological dimensions before accession into any military service. The Air Force and Navy conduct secondary psychological screening of recruits upon arrival at entry-level training sites, as mentioned above. Special Forces applicants also undergo specialized accession screening.

Conclusions

Military accession screening expanded to respond to the war effort needs of World War I and World War II. Intelligence testing was developed from civilian advancements in cognitive testing. Supplemental psychiatric evaluations and written screening tools were abandoned after postwar assessments. These assessments demonstrated their poor predictive power in evaluating the service capacity of recruits for a combat environment. Psychiatric screening was integrated into the induction physical examination, to identify only gross mental health deficits. Longitudinal functional histories and assessment of capacity under realistic military conditions were considered more reliable.

Current accession screening continues to reflect these principles by identifying only gross mental health disability and assessing functional capacity as educational achievement. In the past few decades, efforts have again focused on evaluating personality characteristics and psychiatric symptoms by using written screening tools. The U.S. Navy and Air Force use a secondary psychological screening measure during entry-level training. The U.S. Army does not use secondary screening tools, because of their historical failure to reduce neuropsychiatric casualties and to predict combat military performance.

References

1. Cekala S, Smith E, Schladt B, et al: Military Attrition: DoD Could Save Millions by Better Screening Enlisted Personnel. Report GAO/NSIAD-97-39. Washington, DC, U.S. General Accounting Office, 1997.

2. U.S. Senate Committee on Armed Services, Subcommittee on Personnel: Sustaining the all volunteer force and reserve component issues: U.S. Senate Committee on Armed Services, Subcommittee on Personnel, Congressional hearing testimony, March 17, 2000.

3. Office of the Surgeon General, U.S. Army: Annual Report of the Surgeon General, U.S. Army, pp 210–21, 279–81. Washington, DC, U.S. Government Printing Office, 1920.

4. Fancher RE: The Intelligence Men: Makers of the IQ Controversy. New York, Norton, 1985.

5. Menninger WC: Psychiatry in a Troubled World, p 267. New York, MacMillan, 1948.

6. Glass AJ, Bernucci RJ, Anderson RS: Neuropsychiatry in World War II, pp 153–91. Washington, DC, Office of the Surgeon General, U.S. Army, 1966.

7. Porter WC: The military psychiatrist at work. Am J Psychiatry 1941; 98: 317–23.

8. Bowan KM: Psychiatric examination in the Armed Forces. War Med 1941; 1: 213–8.

9. Menninger WC: Condensed neuropsychiatric examination for use by Selective Service boards. War Med 1941; 1: 843–53.

10. U.S. War Department: Induction Station Neuropsychiatric Examination. War Department Technical Bulletin 33. Washington, DC, U.S. Government Printing Office, 1944.

11. Eagan JR, Jackson L, Eanes RH: A study of neuropsychiatric rejectees. JAMA 1951; 145: 466–9.

12. U.S. War Department: Adjutant General memorandum 40–44. Washington, DC, U.S. War Department, 1944.

13. Stougger SA, Guttman L, Suchman E: Studies in Social Psychology in World War II, pp 549–67. Princeton, NJ, Princeton University Press, 1950.

14. Solomon HC, Yakovlev PI: Manual of Military Neuropsychiatry, pp 19–26. Saunders, 1945.

15. Brill NQ, Beebe GW: Psychoneurosis: military applications of a follow-up study. US Armed Forces Med J 1952; 3: 15–33.

16. Glass AJ: Psychiatric prediction and military effectiveness. US Armed Forces Med J 1956; 7: 1427–43.

17. Kraimes SH: Managing Men: Preventative Psychiatry, Denver, CO, Hirshfeld Press, 1946.

18. Kraimes SH: The Advisor system: prophylactic psychiatry on a mass scale. Ment Hyg 1943; 27: 592–607.

19. Eanes RH: Standards Used by Selective Service and a Follow-Up on Neuropsychiatric Rejectees in World War II: Selection of Military Manpower, pp 149–56. Washington, DC, National Research Council, 1951.

20. Karpinos BD: Qualification of American Youths for Military Service. Washington, DC, Office of the Surgeon General, Department of the Army, 1962.

21. Danielson JR, Clark JH: A personality inventory for induction screening. J Clin Psychol 1954; 10: 137–43.

22. Jensen MB: Adjustive and non-adjustive reactions to basic training in the Air Force. J Soc Psychol 1961; 55: 33–41.

23. Plag JA: Pre-enlistment variables related to the performance and adjustment of Navy recruits. J Clin Psychol 1962; 19: 168–71.

24. Plag JA, Arthur RJ: Psychiatric re-examination of unsuitable naval recruits: a two-year follow-up study. Am J Psychiatry 1965; 122: 534–41.

25. Lachar D. Sparks JC, Larsen RM: Psychometric prediction of behavioral criteria of adaptation for USAF basic trainees. J Community Psychol 1974; 2: 268–77.

26. McCraw RK, Bearden DL: Personality factors in failure to adapt to the military. Milit Med 1990; 155: 127–30.

27. U.S. Army Research Institute for the Behavioral and Social Sciences: Army Research Institute Newsletter 15, pp 10–2. Arlington. VA, U.S. Army Research Institute for the Behavioral and Social Sciences, 1999.

28. Accession Medical Standards Analysis and Research Activity: Annual Report. Washington, DC. Division of Preventative Medicine, Walter Reed Army Institute of Research, 1999.

29. Laurence JH: Does education credential still predict attrition? Current research issues in accession policy. Presented at the 105th Annual Convention of the American Psychological Association, November 7, 1997, Chicago, IL.

30. Office of the Assistant Secretary of Defense: Report to Congress from the Office of the Assistant Secretary of Defense (Force Management Policy): Educational Enlistment Standards: Recruiting Equity for GED Certificates. Washington, DC, Office of the Assistant Secretary of Defense, 1996.

Reading for Comprehension

1. Ritchie and Cardona divide up the research report into sections that correspond more or less with the major wars and conflicts of the twentieth century. For each of the sections, summarize the major focus of mental health screening and what the tests aimed to reveal.

2. What is the current accession mental health screening and in what ways is it similar to and different from past screening approaches?

Analyzing the Genre

1. The authors of this report chose to organize the material chronologically, even though there are some overlaps in both approach and theory among the time periods. What did they gain by organizing it this way? What other possible organization patterns could they have used?

2. This report is clearly intended for an audience of specialists, but the authors do make an effort to explain concepts so that an audience unfamiliar with psychological testing can follow the report. Locate those places where the authors seem to have in mind a nonspecialist audience. How to do they make the technical concepts understandable for that audience?

Please see Chapter 1: Introduction to Genre for another example of a research report.

WebLinks

Exploring the World of Research Reports

Entering the phrase "reports and nonprofit organizations" into an Internet search engine will reveal research reports produced for the public by government and nonprofit bodies, including the Pew Research Center and the National Institutes of Health (NIH).

WRITING ASSIGNMENT OPTIONS

Research Reports

For this chapter's assignment, write an informative research report on a current issue. In the report, carefully explain the issue or concern, provide some background on the issue, and draw conclusions based on your research about the issue.

Research Report Assignment Options

1. Write a **persuasive research report** on an issue or controversy that requires some action on the part of your audience. Be sure to clearly establish the problem and offer clear reasons for why your audience should act and how they might do so.

2. Write a **policy research report** in which you analyze a current policy, the rhetorical situation surrounding it, and how the policy has been implemented. Research what others have said about the policy to enhance your understanding of it and to support your claims for policy reform.

3. Write a **research report on a product or service** that includes a detailed discussion of that product or service and how it meets or fails to meet expectations or official or advertised requirements.

(continued)

4. Write a **report that informs readers of a recent trend**. Analyze how the trend evolved, its cultural significance, and how it has changed the way society looks at the issues surrounding it. Suggest what questions are raised by the trend or its future implications rather than draw any concrete conclusions.

5. Write a **progress report** on your local or state government's attempts to deal with a particular problem or concern. What is the problem and how has it been addressed so far? Has the government's attempts to deal with the problem been successful? How does the government plan to continue the plan to address the problem?

Community-based Writing Option

Many civic and nonprofit organizations produce reports about the group's goals and missions, recent developments, or ongoing projects and efforts to serve the public. You may have worked of volunteered for such an organization. For this assignment, write a report on an organization or group whose purpose is to serve a particular population of people or which has a particular issue it advocates for. Research the organization by conducting interviews of staff and clients, observing the group's work in action, and gathering information written about and by the organization. Depending on the group's current situation, your report may detail new developments and projects, update ongoing projects, or be an action brief on recent issue of concern the group addressed.

Writing Research Reports

Writers of research reports have a lot of options, but there are certain characteristics of reports that all writers should be aware of. Understanding these characteristics can help writers make choices about what to say and how to say it.

WHAT WRITERS CONSIDER WHEN THEY WRITE RESEARCH REPORTS

In general, research report writers do the following:

- Identify a researchable *issue* to explore
- Locate relevant research which reflects the complexity of the issue and rhetorical situation
- Develop and organize claims
- Integrate and synthesize sources to show the complexity of the issue and to clarify it
- Consider using visual aids and design
- Balance historical context, contemporary research, and commentary

Generating Ideas for Research Reports

Ideas for research reports come from a writer's own sense of what is important, controversial, in need of attention, or just plain interesting. Research report writers are often responding to the perceived need of a particular audience. Research reports address a wide range of topics and issues, but they all stem from a concern, need, or a problem.

Avoiding Common Research Report Pitfalls

There are several things to avoid when choosing a topic for a research report.

1. *Readerless topics.* Reports respond to the concerns and needs of particular audiences. But sometimes insecure writers produce reports that lack a clear purpose and intended audience, and so they read like encyclopedia entries. To avoid writing an unfocused report, analyze the rhetorical situation driving your report. What is the social context of the report? Who will read it? Why are you writing the report? Doing so may help you think further about why the report is important and who it is important for at the time it is being produced.

2. *Polarizing or overdone topics.* Polarizing topics are those that people have an immediate and emotional response to. Abortion and gun control, for instance, are topics which most people already have strong opinions about. They are also ones that people have thought, or at least heard, a lot about. So the problem with these topics is that few of us are open to seeing these issues differently than we already do. And the problem with these topics is exacerbated by the sheer volume of material written about them. Narrowing a topic down to an issue that is more interesting to you and one that can be investigated can yield research that is specific and focused.

WRITING ACTIVITY   Generating Ideas for Research Report

To generate an idea for your research report, you might begin with your own observations, your interests and the interests of others to help you generate a list of possible topics.

Observe Your Personal Experiences

1. Make a list of the subjects you are interested in, the activities you participate in, and the hobbies (e.g. rock climbing) you have. Also list any difficulties and challenges you and friends and family members have faced (e.g. a grandmother who cannot afford her medication).
2. Make a list of controversies or issues that concern you (e.g. the No Child Left Behind Act; water rights in Los Angeles County). What are you and others worried about or talking about right now?
3. Make a list of your daily activities, including current or past employment. What kinds of things did you, or do you, encounter on a daily basis that you imagine people could benefit from learning about (e.g. the disposal of paint and other toxic chemicals at the local hardware store)?

Observe the World Around You

1. Watch or listen to broadcast news, skim newspapers, or view online news sites. What are some issues that repeatedly come up that affect you or others you know? Jot down some notes on those issues and why they are important to you or why they would be important to others at this moment in time. Observe cultural trends happening around you. What are recent developments in music, food, technology, or art? What's a current

hobby or interest among your friends? Are these trends generation- or age-specific? Write down trends of interest to you.

■ ■ ■

Focusing on Researchable Issues and Questions

Having a list of topics you could write a research report on is a good start, but you will need to narrow down the topic you choose to determine the *issue at stake*.

A *topic* is a broad subject (e.g. Health Care) that can be looked at in a number of different, specific ways. For instance, the history of health care coverage, the role of the state in providing health care, and the cost of health care are just some of the issues connected to the topic of health care. The way you decide to examine your topic is determined by the rhetorical situation of the report and, of course, the writing assignment you've been given. In other words, you need to narrow your research report topic down to a researchable, specific *issue*.

Issues are specific concerns that any individual or group might have about the topic. An issue is arguable, specific, and researchable. In other words, an issue is a focused idea that prompts questions (maybe similar to the ones you already generated) and has a clearly defined audience and purpose.

Chapter 13: Research and the Rhetorical Situation discusses narrowing a topic to its related issues.

WRITING ACTIVITY   The Issues at Stake in Your Topic

Make a list of all the specific issues or concerns connected to your topic (see page 502 in Chapter 13 for an example).

■ Which of these issues seems most relevant or important for your rhetorical situation?
■ Which seems more likely to generate interest among a broad audience?
■ When you examine the issues, which seem likely to be researchable? Do any allow you to think about the kinds of research that might be useful in the report?

Your answers may eventually become the focus of your research report.

■ ■ ■

Once you have a list of possible issues, the next step is to consider which ones lend themselves best to a research report. One of your first considerations when evaluating potential issues should be your personal interests. Your interest in the issue will spur you to learn more about it (and share what you learn with others); your interest will also keep you motivated as you conduct your research, draft and refine your claims and evidence, and so on.

But how do you know which issue of interest to you will be most workable for a research report? One way to sort through issues is to generate questions that might be answered in your report.

For example, if you are thinking about writing a report on the issue of health care costs, here are some questions you might ask:

1. What is the cost of health care for a typical family of four?
2. Why is health care so costly?

3. Is anything being done about health care costs?

4. If people don't have health care coverage, what do they do when they are injured or even for routine health care?

Notice that using this brainstorming method we quickly generated a series of questions you *could* explore in a research report. You may not use them all, but they suggest the many directions you could take with this topic that would also be of interest to others.

<hr>

WRITING ACTIVITY   Generating Questions

Circle those issues you generated earlier that you are most interested in—ones you may know a lot about or ones you are interested in learning more about. Try to limit your choices here to three or four.

Next, generate a list of possible questions you could ask about each issue. Begin with the obvious—no question is too obvious for this activity—and gradually move to more specific questions. Write at least ten questions for each issue.

Which issues seem to lend themselves to more questions? What does that tell you about your interest in the issue?

Having a long list of *possible* questions that you could answer allows you some flexibility and recourse as you wind your way through the drafting and researching processes.

■ ■ ■

Thinking about Audience, Purpose, and Situation

Understanding the purpose and audience for your research report is crucial to its success. If you have already articulated the issue at stake in your topic, then you also already have some valuable insight into your audience and purpose. Please see Chapter 13: Research and the Rhetorical Situation, pages 501–539, for a discussion of defining your rhetorical situation.

As you work on defining your rhetorical situation, keep in mind what you have learned about research reports so far—your understanding of the genre will help you define some of the elements of the rhetorical situation.

<hr>

WRITING ACTIVITY   Defining the Rhetorical Situation for Your Report

Your Audience

Look back over the list of issues at stake you created earlier in the chapter. Decide which issue you would like to write about and answer the question "Who would care?" Write down a list of possible audiences for your issue, and take notes on *why* they might care about it. What interests would they have?

Your Purpose

List again the potential audiences you imagined earlier. For each, answer the following questions in as much detail as you can.

- Is the issue something that potential audiences will know something about?
- Is the issue something that potential audiences might be misinformed about?
- Is the issue something that potential audiences can act on?

Your Role as the Writer

As the writer of this report, you are the organization, or a member of it, who has produced the report. This means you need to decide what organization or group might be appropriate to the issue you've chosen to write about.

As you answer the following questions, you will begin to articulate your role as the writer of a research report.

- Conduct <u>web research</u> to locate a few organizations concerned with your general topic or issue. They need not have published information about your actual issue.
- <u>Analyze</u> their mission statements or the information they provide in the "about" section of their websites.
- <u>Question</u> whether one of the organizations reflects a viewpoint you share.
- <u>Write</u> about the position one of the organizations would take (or takes) on your issue. How would it view the problem? Who would its audience be? Why would it want to produce a report on the problem in the first place?

The Situation

Look again at the organizations or groups you found in your initial web search.

- Question why the issue is being talked about and written about now.
- Conduct a <u>web search</u> to see whether the issue is a concern that any state or government agencies have taken up. What about other groups or organizations?

Your answers to these questions will help you figure out the larger social context in which the issue is being discussed, as well as help you clarify your report's purpose (e.g. fill a gap in the discussion or to inform an ignored subgroup).

■ ■ ■

Researching Research Reports

A research report depends on high-quality, timely, and well-chosen research. Once you have chosen an issue, your job is pretty clear: Find out as much as you can about the issue you are writing on. You will use your research to help you develop a broad understanding of the issue, establish your credibility to readers, support and develop your claims, and possibly to generate additional claims. Depending on the focus of your report, most (perhaps all) of your research will come from library holdings and databases, though you may also find that reputable websites such as those by state or federal governments might also be useful.

See Chapter 13: Research and the Rhetorical Situation for more specific guidance in conducting research and evaluating sources.

GROUP ACTIVITY   Identifying Necessary Research

The Writer

Write down your topic and the issue at stake that you identified earlier. Write down all that you know about your audience, purpose, and the larger situation. If you are still vague on any of these areas, define them as best you can, but be sure to ask your group for help on that as well. When everyone has finished writing, take turns reading what you have written to the group.

The Group

1. Listen to and take notes on the writer's topic, issue, and rhetorical situation.
2. Write down which aspects of the writer's topic and issue can be researched and try to come up with four or five additional areas. Write your suggestions as research questions.

The Writer

As the group gives you their ideas, take notes and ask questions. Asking a question such as why they think that a particular area should be researched will reveal assumptions about the subject that you might be able to use in your research report.

■ ■ ■

Drafting Research Reports

As you conduct your research and do your background reading, you will start thinking about the *claims* that you want to make in your research report.

Drafting and Organizing Claims

Indeed, as you worked on identifying research questions, you were also identifying potential claims and subtopics that you can address in the report. For example, in our list of questions for the issue of health care costs below, we came up with several questions that even without the benefit of research we could generate into viable claims and eventually refine with research.

Questions concerning the issue of health care costs:	Potentially viable claims that we would eventually refine with research:
What is the cost of health care for a typical family of four? Nationally? In my state? What about for a single man or woman? Does age make a difference?	The cost of health care for a family of four is on the rise. The elderly seem to be struggling with paying for health care.
Why is health care so costly? What is the role of insurance companies in this cost? How much of the cost has to do with doctors and medical facilities?	Insurance companies have more control over cost than most of us suspect (or they have less control). Doctors contribute to the cost by ordering unnecessary procedures or tests.
Is anything being done about the cost of health care?	Many states have enacted laws to limit the cost of health insurance for poor families. Many states have created special health care programs for children to make sure they have adequate medical attention.
If people don't have health care coverage, what do they do when they are injured or even for routine health care? What are the consequences for those people: Do they cut back in other areas? Go without routine care?	Families who cannot afford basic health care often wait until a problem is severe to visit the emergency room.

Audience and Purpose: Clues to Claims

Because different audiences have different expectations and needs, understanding who your audience is may suggest the claims you need to make in your report. Similarly, understanding your purpose will help you generate claims.

- What does your audience need to be informed about? What *won't* they know?
- What claims do you need to make given the purpose of your report?

Research: Another Clue to Claims

Research provides you with material to support your claims, but it can also suggest those claims as well. When you learn something you didn't know, for example, chances are that your audience will also be unfamiliar with that information. Thus, your claim becomes the announcement of that new information (e.g. Parkour, or "freerunning," requires both physical and mental conditioning).

What has your research revealed to you about your *issue* that you didn't know before?

■ ■ ■

As you consider the claims you want to make, how they address the needs of your audience, how they help you meet your purpose, you should think, too, about how you might develop a section around a claim or set of claims.

A research report is no different than other genres when it comes to the arrangement of your ideas. You structure your report by thinking rhetorically and logically: What do my readers need to know first? Which of my claims are the strongest? Which claims belong together? And so on. Research reports are often organized into subsections. Would your research report benefit from subsections which group claims together? Look again at the samples provided earlier in the chapter for some ideas, or in the reports you found on your own.

The Writer

Explain to your group the issue of your report and your audience and purpose. Discuss the claims you have identified so far.

The Group

Can you suggest other claims that the writer can make? What would you want or need to know about the writer's issue?

The Writer

Identify the major claims, and then list subclaims underneath each major claim. Then discuss with your group possible arrangements for those claims:

- What claims need to come first and why? Are there claims that need to come first because other claims build on them?

■ Which are your strongest claims? Which are your weakest?

■ What are the benefits and drawbacks to one arrangement versus another?

■ ■ ■

Using Your Research

One of the keys to a successful research report is the *synthesis* of your research—in other words, how you connect your own ideas with those from sources. It is not enough to develop one claim with one source, another claim with a different source, and so on. Instead, you need to incorporate your research so it appears your sources are having a conversation with each other about the issue.

Synthesizing research requires careful reading, careful note taking, a clear understanding of purpose and audience, and a general sense of the claims you want to make. Luckily, there is a relatively simple tool that you can use to organize your research so that the synthesis is easier to see—a *research chart*. This useful tool helps writers see *how* their research can help them support and develop their claims. (See Chapter 14: Using and Citing Sources page 557–559 for help constructing a research chart.)

Here is how student Kyle Frey synthesized his research for one particular claim in his report entitled "Inter-country Adoption and the Problems We Face":

> Availability seems to be the main reason for adopting outside the United States. Babies born in America only meet between 50 to 65% of the total number of babies desired for adoption here (Kapstein 1). In America there is a growing trend of single moms deciding to keep their children instead of giving them up to an adoption agency. This has caused a scarcity of healthy infants for adults looking to adopt (Sherry 1). The lower number of children being put up for adoption in nations with a greater economy is not mirrored by countries such as China and others which are not as developed. These higher numbers of births, along with a lack of money, result in a great number of children who urgently need a good place to live (Norman 1). Coker reaches a similar point, as she says that the depleting economy of the former Soviet Union has left large numbers of children without parents and Americans are willing to adopt them (1). There simply is not the availability of babies in the United States as there is around the globe.

Notice in this short paragraph that Frey has used four different sources to develop the single claim that "Availability seems to be the main reason for adopting outside the United States." The use of multiple sources here works to his advantage in a number of ways:

1. it allows him to show that this is a complicated problem;
2. it communicates to the reader that is it a concern that many people share;
3. it shows the reader that the writer has done his homework, that he's knowledgeable about the issue;
4. it builds the writer's *ethos,* his credibility.

WRITING ACTIVITY   Creating a Research Chart and Synthesis

A research chart helps you develop your claims by letting you see how you can use multiple sources to support, refute, or contradict their points.

List your claims in the order you plan on using them; you may also list them by section, if this makes sense for your purpose. Using the model and instructions in Chapter 14, pages 557–559, construct a research chart to organize your research on each of your claims.

- How are your sources working together to support each claim?
- Are there any counterpoints that you need to address for each claim?

Use your research chart to draft a paragraph or section in your report draft that develops a claim and synthesizes your research from several sources to support the claim.

■ ■ ■

Openings for Research Reports

While you can start drafting your report at any part, sometimes writing the executive summary (also called an abstract or just a summary) early in your writing process will help you figure our what you you already know or what you want to discover in your research process; it may also reveal potential gaps in your research report. An executive summary is a condensed version of your report which gives readers a basic understanding of your report, and many readers use the executive summary to decide if they want or need to read the entire report. It highlights the most important claims and conclusions. So even if your report doesn't call for a summary, writing one is still a useful process because it helps you fully understand your subject and uncover where more research is needed.

Here is an executive summary by student Colin Keane for his report "The Aftermath of September 11: Rescuers and Citizens Not Out of Danger Yet."

Keane states the issue directly in the first sentence and communicates its extent in the rest of the paragraph.

Keane concludes the summary with the core of the problem his report addresses: not just the consequences to the workers, but the lack of support they have been given. This last sentence also suggests what should be done about the problem.

Colin Keane
Executive Summary

Workers and first-responders to the September 11th attacks have struggled to regain their health after being exposed to the dust during that day of horror and the nine-month cleanup that followed. Unimaginable cases of respiratory problems have occurred, usually a few months after first exposure to the dust; these problems have made the lives of these first-responders worse in many ways. An estimated twelve years have been subtracted from their life expectancy as a result of inhaling toxic particles. Worker and first-responders are remembered as heroes for their courageous acts, but now many are losing their lives and others are suffering long-term illnesses including post-traumatic stress disorder and what has come to be known as "World Trade Center cough." Many organizations and individuals are trying to assist them, while others are seeking cures for the physical problems, yet monetary support has fallen off, which is preventing some from getting the help they deserve.

Even if your report includes an executive summary, you will still need to prepare an introduction. Report introductions get right to the gist of the report and what it will focus on; the introduction to Rich Morin's report on race begins by identifying the issue immediately and describing what it is briefly. Introductions can be a paragraph or they can extend for a few paragraphs, depending on the report's purpose, audience, and the complexity of the issue being addressed. Reports are expected to provide details and specific examples throughout, so the introduction provides a synopsis, a brief version, of the issue.

WRITING ACTIVITY   Summaries and Other Openings for Reports

Summaries are short, so include only what is most important about your report. Answer the following questions as you write your summary, limiting yourself to one or two sentences at most for each.

■ What is the issue your report addresses?

■ Why is the issue a problem?

■ What has been done to solve the problem or address the issue?

■ Why has the solution been successful or not?

■ What are the major claims you make to inform or persuade the audience?

■ What do you conclude?

Openings in reports get right to the point and rarely do they try to hook the reader with startling facts, emotional examples, and so on. Instead, they assume readers want to understand the problem or issue right away.

■ What is the most important aspect of the issue you are writing about?

■ Who does the issue affect and why is it important for your audience to care about it?

■ What is already being done about the issue? How is that response sufficient or insufficient?

■ What conclusions have you reached about what must be done regarding the issue?

■ ■ ■

Closings for Research Reports

The primary purpose of a research report is to inform, and so the closing section represents the author's last chance to communicate the essential point the report is making. Closings in research reports are fairly standard. One common way to close a report is to summarize and repeat that essential information while also using the most striking or relevant research to drive home the point one last time.

For example, the report by RI-PIRG concludes in this way:

RI-PIRG concludes by reminding the reader of key points made in the report; this ensures that readers come away with the most important information.

The Rhode Island food safety standards discussed here and others are important for several reasons:

■ They help protect public health from food-borne illnesses and other risk by filling gaps left in federal law;

The writers remind us of the problem by citing the most relevant statistics to be sure that we accept their conclusion.

> - They give consumers the power to make informed choices about the food and beverages they purchase for themselves and their families; and
> - They help protect local industries by ensuring the safety and purity of their products.

The writers reiterate their main claim. They also reassure the audience about overall food safety.

>   The FDA and other federal agencies do not have the resources—and often do not have the political will—to monitor all aspects of food safety. In fact, the number of full-time FDA employees dealing with food safety has fallen steadily from 3,167 in FY 2003 to 2,843 in FY 2006; the president's proposed FY 2007 budget for FDA would further reduce that number to 2,757. As such, states will continue to play a pivotal role in ensuring that America's food supply remains among the safest in the world.

WRITING ACTIVITY   Closings for Research Reports

How you choose to conclude your report depends largely on your audience, purpose, and the complexity of the issue you have addressed. Use your understanding of the rhetorical situation to inform what you write in your conclusion.

- What are the key points you need your readers to understand? How would summarizing the main points of your report add / not offer anything for readers to think about?
- Do the ideas and information from your report lend itself to a closing that poses questions for future research?
- Can you use a particularly compelling example to reinforce the importance or seriousness of your issue?
- Do you need to offer policy suggestions for how to address the issue?
- Are you asking your audience to do something?
- Should you raise the consequences for not addressing the issue? Or the likely outcome if the issue is addressed?

■ ■ ■

Revising Research Reports

In the drafting process you conducted research, listed claims, and used a research chart to develop and expand claims. Now with the revision process you have a chance to refine and further develop your claims, as well as attend to some of the visual aspects of your report.

Just as it was in the drafting process, research is the most important aspect of the revision process. The difference here is that you are doing two things: looking for gaps in your research (those claims that are unsupported or insufficiently supported) and looking at how you integrated the material into your report.

Identifying Gaps in Your Research

Since you created a research chart to identify how your research will help you make and develop your claims, you have already given a lot of thought to your claims and may have a sense of what areas need support. Seeing the gaps in your research is difficult, because those gaps result from your familiarity with the material; in other words, you fill in those gaps with your own knowledge. The problem is that your audience does not share that knowledge.

<u>WRITING ACTIVITY</u>   Identifying Gaps in Your Research

First, write down again your audience and purpose. As clearly as you can, answer the following two questions: 1) What does your audience know and not know about the issue? 2) What kinds of information would they need to know in order to fully understand the issue?

Compare your answer to the second question with your answer to the first. Comparing what they don't know and what they need to know will help you pinpoint the *likely* gaps in your research.

Look over your draft, paying particular attention to the claims you make which reflect the aspects of your issue that the audience won't know much about it.

- Does the research fully address the concerns or questions your audience might have?
- Is the specialized information fully explained given your audience's familiarity with the issue?
- Do you use multiple sources to help reassure your audience that you know what you are talking about?
- Are there any claims that are not supported at all?

Address gaps by revising and rewriting as necessary. You may need to conduct further research or go back to the research you collected to help fill in those gaps

■ ■ ■

Integrating Your Sources

Research reports depend on good research. But a research report is not just research—it is your synthesis and explanation of the research, your use of it to support what you want to claim. Thus, how you use your research is as important as what that research is.

Integrating research is the process of incorporating source material smoothly and intelligently into your own writing. You do this by introducing sources; making connections between the sources and the surrounding material, including other sources; accurately quoting, paraphrasing, or summarizing that material; and then correctly citing it.

When you integrate a source into your paper, you are claiming that source is important to your point, that you have checked to be sure the source is valid—that it can be trusted, that it is accurate, and so on. How you introduce and integrate sources in your reports can be a rhetorical move; that is, you can subtly (or not so subtly) suggest how you would like your audience to understand the material you are integrating.

Please refer to Chapter 14 for a more detailed discussion of integrating sources.

Working with a reasonably complete draft, do the following:

1. Go through your report and mark every time you use a source—whether you are directly quoting, paraphrasing, or summarizing it.
2. Make sure that you have introduced each source, and where you have not, do so. Often you can introduce a source by providing the author and title as well as using a verb that tells the audience about how to read the significance of the source. You should choose the words you use to introduce your sources carefully, being sure that you are accurately reflecting the content of the material and how readers should understand it. Review instances where you used multiple sources to develop your claims. In these cases, you should introduce the first source as described above, and for the others, make sure to show the connections between or among the sources.
3. Verify that you have cited all sources appropriately.

Continue working on introducing your sources until you are satisfied they help you communicate and support your claims.

■ ■ ■

Design and Layout: Color, Charts, and Other Visuals

You might have noticed that some of the research reports you have read have important visual components to them: charts and graphs, pictures and graphics, borders and other organizing devices.

Some material is best presented in chart form, and some material needs to be in both narrative and chart form. Difficult concepts might need to be reinforced with a graphic or picture; and line drawings might be useful in directing readers to particular pieces of information. In this book, for instance, we make liberal use of text boxes or call-outs to highlight particular pieces of information.

Reports make use of visuals for other reasons, too. Many readers have an aversion to reading a research report or material that seems difficult. So writers have to consider those readers' need for simpler access to the research when they put their reports together and make them more visually appealing.

As you read through your report, consider again your purpose and audience, as well as the issue you are writing about. Be clear about why you want to include visuals and how you want them to work. Random-seeming or misplaced visuals can weaken your argument.

1. Does the issue lend itself in general to the use of visuals? Will your audience appreciate visuals or consider them frivolous? Would visuals help you meet your purpose?
2. Is there information that could be shown in a visual way? Is there a list of statistics that might be shown as a graph or chart? A fact that could be supported by a photograph or picture?
3. If you are writing on behalf of a particular organization, does it use a certain color scheme on its written materials? Could you use the same colors in your report? Would

your report look and read better if it were formatted differently? In columns, for instance?

4. If you use section headings, could those be in a different (but consistent overall) font?
5. Look at the sample reports included at the start of the chapter and elsewhere for ideas. Also refer to Chapter 4 for a discussion of visual rhetoric.

Peer Review

During the drafting of your report, your peers gave you feedback that helped you narrow or focus your topic, come up with claims, and develop adequate support for them. Now it is time to ask them to help you revise your report as a whole and to read it as an actual audience with fresh perspective.

PEER REVIEW *for Research Reports*

Since this genre requires lots of research, focus on how the writer has used the research and organized it (including any charts, visuals, and graphs) in his or her report.

READ THE INTRODUCTION. Comment in the margins about what you think the problem or issue is in this report. Are you given enough information to understand the problem or issue? What else could the writer provide? What else can the writer do to engage the reader?

READ THE BODY. Underline the writer's **claims**. Does each claim make sense given the problem identified in the introduction? For each claim, examine the **research** used to support it. Comment in the margins about the quality and effectiveness of that material: Does it develop the claim sufficiently? Would a different kind of research help?

If the writer has used **visual design elements,** comment on their purpose. Do they help you understand the material better? How?

READ THE CLOSING. Does the conclusion make sense given the genre and the purpose of this research report? Can you suggest ways to develop it? Write your comments in the margin.

WRITE AN ENDNOTE to the writer.

- Begin by telling the writer what you enjoyed about their research report.
- Identify who the **audience** is based on what the writer has written and the kinds of evidence and claims provided.
- Comment on whether the writer has (or has not) addressed the audience's concerns, values, and ideas.
- State what you think was the **writer's purpose.** Was the writer successful in meeting his or her purpose? Why or why not?
- Comment on the **style** and **tone** of the report. Are they appropriate? Why or why not?
- Make suggestions for **revision.** Tell the writer which parts you think need to be developed further or could be moved for clarity or to make the argument stronger. Is there anything you would suggest the writer get rid of? Why?

Reflecting on the Process

We learn how to write better by writing, but we also learn by looking back on the steps we have taken and the choices we have made. Knowing which choices ultimately made sense and which led you someplace else is crucial to becoming a more fluent writer.

WRITING ACTIVITY   Reflecting on Writing a Research Report

Reflect on your writing process for your report: how you generated ideas and chose one, did research, and drafted and revised your report. Imagine you are writing this reflection to writers who have never written a report of this kind. What might they learn about working within the genre from you? What could you tell them that might help them as writers?

1. *Begin* by describing what you are most pleased with in your report. You can point out more than one area of the paper. *Explain* what you think contributed to your success in these areas.
2. *Reflect* on how you determined your purpose and appropriate audience for your report. Why did you make the claims you did given that audience and purpose? How did you use visuals to connect with your audience and meet your purpose?
3. *Discuss* your revision process, including how you used feedback from your readers.
4. *Conclude* by reflecting on what you learned about the genre of research reports overall. You might also reflect on what you'd do differently next time you find yourself writing a report.

■   ■   ■

Patrick Merrigan's Research Report

Patrick Merrigan, a student in a first-year writing course, was assigned to write a research report on a subject or issue of his choosing. While he had many ideas at the start, he ultimately chose to write about the lack of civic awareness and responsibility among his peers. It was a rather unconventional choice, and he ran into a few problems when trying to sift through all the sources he found, but he ended up writing an engaging and informative report.

Generating Ideas for the Research Report

Merrigan began by brainstorming about subjects that interested him, issues that concerned him, and activities that he engaged in. He came up with a range of possible topics, and so he had a lot to choose from.

> *Patrick Merrigan*
> *Possible Topics for Research Reports*
> > *1. Subjects that interest me:*
> > *History*
> > *Politics*
> > *Food*
> > *Camping*
> > *2. Issues that concern me:*
> > *Civic duties involving college students*
> > *The Afghanistan War*
> > *The price of oil*
> > *3. Daily activities:*
> > *People who are heavily medicated*
> > *How cafeteria food is prepared*
> > *The types of people hired at a grocery store*

Merrigan chose three topics from that list: those that he thought he would most like to write about; those that he was most interested in learning more about himself. Note, though, that this early in the process he is still unsure about what he wants to say or really focus on, and so what he writes is pretty general.

> <u>Brainstorming Possible Ideas for Reports</u>
>
> *Patrick Merrigan*
> > *1. History teaching is a topic of interest to me because it is what I like to study and I plan to teach it in high school as a profession. Others might be interested in it because they would want to know what is currently being taught and*

maybe what students are actually learning. I already know this topic because I have read many books and taken many classes about it.

2. *Civic duties involving teens is a topic that I relate to. I find it interesting because college students in earlier generations were eager to vote and serve jury duty. Now, people are avoiding jury duty and many kids aren't even registered. This should interest people because it shows a growing problem with today's youth. I know about this because I fit right into this category.*

3. *The types of people who work at a grocery store are very interesting because they come in all shapes and sizes. People would be interested in this because they go to the supermarket on a regular basis so they interact with these people. I have experience in this because I worked at Stop & Shop for three and a half years.*

Notice that Merrigan is thinking about these possible topics in terms of the audience (who would want to read about them and why) and what he already knows about the subjects. By writing even a little bit about what he knows and who would want to read it, he is laying the groundwork for later research.

Thinking about Audience, Purpose, and Situation: Writing a Research Proposal

Once he decided on a topic—civic responsibility and college students—Merrigan's next step was to write a research proposal. Doing so helped him think more carefully about what he wanted to focus on; it also helped him to think critically about his audience. You'll notice, though, that he is still tentative about his subject and what he actually wants to say about it. (You can read about how to write a research proposal in Chapter 13: Research and the Rhetorical Situation on pages 501–539.)

The working title helps Merrigan figure out what the issue is. In this version, he connects civic duty with patriotism.

Merrigan begins his discussion of Purpose and Audience by articulating the problem he sees. He is still tentative about the issue since he has not yet done any research.

Research Proposal
Patrick Merrigan
Professor Ferruci
English 100P
14 Feb. 2008

1. Title of Project:
Civic Duties and College Students: Is Patriotism Dead?

2. Statement of Purpose and Audience:
There seems to be less involvement of college students in their civic duties than ever. My purpose in writing this report is to help inform and persuade college students to become involved on all sorts of levels. I want to show them that civic duties are important. I want to find out if there are fewer college students registering to vote, showing up for jury duty, and registering for the draft than ever before and what has caused this decline. College students are my intended audience, because this issue directly affects them and I think that if they realize that not participating is a mistake then maybe

The statement also defines his audience and why they are the audience he has chosen.

they will change their actions. Most college students are aware that most of them aren't serving their civic duties but I think that most of them don't even care. College students should read this report because it will inform them about the mistake they are making by not getting involved and the effects it will have on the future.

3. Background:

Merrigan explores the reasons why he wants to write this report. We can also see how his own background might be useful in his research, for example, his knowledge of the connection between being uninformed and not taking civic responsibilities seriously.

I am interested in this topic because I enjoy politics and history. Unlike many people my age, I have registered to vote. I have taken many history and political science classes that explained our rights and responsibilities as U.S. Citizens. These are the same rights that are being taken for granted by today's college students. I know that many kids my age don't seem to be well informed on today's events, so they might not understand why civic duties are so important. These are the kids that don't know what is going on the world and don't seem to care or want to know. I have had a lot of experience with this and that attitude is the problem itself being addressed in this report.

4. Possible Research Questions:

Merrigan poses a range of questions. After he does some research, he can refine these questions and ask more focused ones.

- What is the definition of "civic duties"?
- What are the civic duties of college students?
- Why are these civic duties so important?
- What percentage of kids are registered to vote?
- What percentage of kids would skip jury duty if they could?
- Why do college students not fulfill these duties?
- What has caused this decrease in involvement?
- Why is this a bigger problem with college students than adults?

Researching the Research Report: Writing the Annotated Bibliography

Because he had many research questions, Merrigan was able to find quite a number of possible sources. He narrowed the number of sources to ten by reading through the abstracts of all the sources he found. For the ten most useful, he wrote an annotated bibliography to help him think about *how* he might use them. See Chapter 13 (pages 538–539) for a discussion of how to construct an annotated bibliography.

Here is an excerpt from Merrigan's annotated bibliography.

Each entry is fully cited in MLA format.

Boulard, Garry. "Citizens in Training." *State Legislatures* 29.7 (July 2003): 44–49. *Academic Search Premier*. Web. 20 Feb. 2008.

Boulard discusses various ways that youth can get involved in politics. One of his main objectives is to help give these kids some civic education. He begins

Merrigan provides only a general sense of the content of the article. His purpose in writing this annotation is to establish that the source could be useful.

by commenting on how young people don't care about politics and aren't interested in voting. He provides statistics that support his view that kids do not care about the government. He then discusses solutions and says that volunteering seems to be part of the solution to this problem. He concludes by telling about how legislators can help create more interest about government and politics.

Esser, Frank, and Claes H. De Vreese. "Comparing Young Voters' Political Engagement in the United States and Europe." *American Behavioral Scientist* 50.9 (May 2007): 1195–1213. *Academic Search Premier*. Web. 20 Feb. 2008.

Esser and De Vreese compare the young voter's political participation in Europe with that in the United States. They discuss how the decrease in youth involvement in politics is not just in the United States, but globally. They then explain the aim of the study, both the US and European perspectives, and a hypothesis of what will come out of this study. They provide a chart showing the different levels of youth voting turn out (systematic, institutional, and individual) and then breakdown each of the levels. They conclude that economic status plays a large role in whether someone will vote, and that mass media also plays a role in the participation of youth in voting.

Drafting: Writing the Introductory Material

In his first draft, Merrigan focused on arranging his claims and making sure that he had enough support to develop them. At this point in the drafting process, he was primarily focused on figuring out what he wanted to say, and you can see that in the rough introductory paragraphs.

Patrick Merrigan
Professor Ferruci
English 100P
1 Mar. 2008
Draft 1

Merrigan is guided by his working title, but there is little evidence that he's addressing this issue.

Merrigan does not mention civic duties, the subject of his report.

Civic Duties and 18-24 Year Olds: Do They Still Care?

People who are at the ages of 18-24 are at a very important time in their life. Many consider it to be the best time of a person's life. This is the time when someone transitions from being in high school and very dependent to adulthood when they are entirely on their own. People in this age group learn about who they are, and what they are about. This transformation that takes place is a big part of what shapes a person.

These are all important claims to make, but they may overwhelm a reader.

Notice that in this draft, he relies primarily on *direct quotation*.

Civic duties are important even though the youth do not care

A major problem is that 18-24 year olds are not interested in their civic duties and government. This is the type of problem that can have many dangerous implications in the future. This seems to be general knowledge for most people yet it is not discussed and there seems to be few efforts to make improve the situation. In Jamal Watson's well written article "Voting should be a top priority among America's youth", he illustrates his concern when he says, "The lack of voter participation among youth is particularly disturbing, especially in light of the number of iconic figures who encouraged youth voting in this year's election" (13). He is talking about how there is still little political interest among the youth despite efforts from many celebrities to help increase participation. He notes that this problem is "disturbing" which is a correct word to describe the situation because it seems like this has the potential to get worse. . . .

Revising the Research Report: Working with Sources

By his second draft, Merrigan had refined his focus and clarified his subject, which is reflected in part by a change in the subtitle. He also worked more on integrating his sources. This draft was given to two of his classmates. In the margins are his reviewers' comments, and you can see how he responded to them.

Patrick Merrigan
Professor Ferruci
English 100P
3 Mar. 2008
Draft 2

Civic Duties and 18-24 Year Olds: How this age group
no longer cares about politics and government and the ways
to solve the problem

People who are at the ages of 18-24 are at a very important time in their lives. Many in fact, consider it to be the best time of their life. This is the time when someone transitions from being in high school and very dependent to adulthood when they are entirely on their own. People in this age group learn about who they are, and what they are about. This transformation that takes place is a big part of what shapes a person. Part of what shapes a person are civic duties which include voting, jury duty, and being involved in politics. These are important at this point because a person forms habits and opinions now that stay with them for the rest of their lives. [One of my reviewers suggested that I say more about why it's

Student 1: I know this report is about Civic Duties, but what exactly is the problem? I say that because it is not introduced here.

a problem, but I think my title communicates it, so I'm not going to add anything here.]

Civic duties are important even though the youth do not care

A major problem is that 18-24 year olds are not interested in their civic duties and government. This is the type of problem that can have many dangerous implications in the future. [Another of my reviewers wanted an example here: "For example, if this age group remains ignorant and not informed, they will not be able to run the country as effectively."] This seems to be general knowledge for most people yet it is not discussed and there seems to be few efforts to help improve the situation. In Jamal Watson's well written article "Voting should be a top priority among America's youth", he illustrates his concern when he says that for the 2004 presidential election many celebrities came out to promote adolescent involvement in politics and voting. The fact that these young adults have not been active in their voting duties despite all these efforts is causing concern among many (13). He notes that this problem is "disturbing" which is a correct word to describe the situation because it seems like this has the potential to get worse.

[A reviewer commented that I use too many sources, so I'll cut this one.] ~~Garry Boulard wrote an excellent article titled "Citizens in Training" in which he agrees with Watson that much research has suggested that the younger generation is not interested in the way the country is run no matter where the laws are coming from (44). This shows that the disinterest is throughout the youth and it does not matter where the politics and government are based. There are many components to these civic duties that the youth seems to not want to be involved in.~~

Student 2: Like? Can you provide an example of this? I think the audience would need to know what the "implications" are, especially if they don't agree it's a problem.

Student 1: All right, I read the whole paper and I feel like you have a lot of good sources, but that maybe you use too many of them? Do you need them all?

Patrick Merrigan (student), "Civic Duties and Young Adults" (final draft)

Merrigan's final research report is formatted in the style of the Modern Language Association (MLA). For more on MLA style, see Chapter 14.

Patrick Merrigan

Professor Ferruci

English 100P

8 Mar. 2008

Civic Duties and Young Adults: How 18–24-Year-Olds No Longer Care
about Politics and Government and the Ways to Solve the Problem

Young adults between the ages of 18 and 24 are at a very important time in
their lives. Many in fact consider it to be the best time of their lives, because
it is a time of transformation, when they go from high school and dependency
to adulthood and independency. They learn about who they are, and what
they are about, and maybe what they really believe in. As a result, this
transformation is a big part of what shapes a person. And part of what shapes
a person are civic duties which include voting, jury duty, and being involved in
the political process, whether local, state, or national. These are important
because a person forms habits and opinions between the ages of 18 to 24
that stay with them for the rest of their lives.

Civic Duties Are Important Even Though Young Adults Do Not Care

A major problem is that 18- to 24-year-olds are not interested in their civic
duties and functioning of government. Even in terms of something simple,
such as voting, young adults seem not to care. Jamal Watson, in "Voting
Should Be a Top Priority Among America's Youth," illustrates this concern
when he says that for the 2004 presidential election many celebrities came
out to promote adolescent involvement in politics and voting. The fact that
these young adults have not been active in their voting duties despite all
these efforts is causing concern among many (13). He notes that this problem
is "disturbing," which is an accurate description because it seems like this has
the potential to only get worse; it's particularly disturbing because we assume
that celebrities and sports stars have a lot of influence, but in this case, it
seems not. Lack of civic participation can have many dangerous implications
in the future.

Garry Boulard, in "Citizens in Training," agrees with Watson that much
research has suggested that the younger generation is not interested in the

Merrigan's purpose here is establish that civic duties are important to the "transformation" from adolescence to adulthood. Does he do a good job of establishing the problem?

Merrigan is going into much more detail here about the problem and why we need to be concerned about it.

This paragraph was deleted in response to a reviewers sug-gestions—does he gain anything by putting it back in?

Notice how Merrigan works with more than one source to develop this point. By doing so he is better able to show its complexity, and at the same time he establishes his own ethos.

Here, again, Merri-gan draws on multiple sources.

way the country is run no matter where the laws are coming from (44). In other words, young adults are equally uninterested in national, state, and local government.

The problem is that our civic responsibilities and duties are what help solidify the American idea of democracy. The editors of the journal *Dissent* argue that people nowadays do not do much in terms of civil actions for our country, such as serving jury duty ("We, the Jury . . . " 19). We actually do very little to contribute to the government in the form of working together and serving our obligations to our democracy. As far back as 1835, Alexis de Tocqueville expressed his opinion of how vital jury duty was when he said how jury duty was one of the important building blocks that helped establish this nation's government (qtd. in "We, the Jury . . . " 19). Despite its importance, people never seem to want to go. In "A Call to Justice: The Importance of Civic Education," Lewis elaborates on this point, explaining that for the average U.S. citizen, we fear going into jury duty and a minute number engage in the voting process (14). What these authors tell us is that these duties are important but are neglected by many Americans. This is a problem that is even larger among young adults.

And it is a problem because, in some ways, participation in civic duties should be higher among young adults, because there has been an increase in volunteering among adolescents and teenagers in recent years. Delchad and Crosby explain the connection between youth volunteering and youth voting when they talk about a report by the Center for Information and Research on Civic Learning and Engagement saying that adolescents volunteering is on the rise. Yet this same age group is very low in its involvement with civic duties and our government (3). This is a good sign in that youth volunteering is high which is important because that is a crucial civic duty, but the fact that they are falling behind in political participation is a bad sign.

Even when there are issues that concern them directly, young adults are reluctant to participate in civic life. Jamal Watson provides an example specifically for this age group when he writes that people who are between

Merrigan makes use of subheadings to help the reader focus. Are they successful? Do they reflect the content of the sections?

the ages of 18 and 24 should be seriously concerned with the cost of higher education, as those costs are rising yearly (13). If asked, an 18-year-old who doesn't vote might reply by saying "because my vote doesn't count." Yet, Felchner found that "according to statistics provided by Youth Vote, the youth demographic comprises 14.4 percent of the total voting age population" (8). Given the closeness of most elections, a 14.4 percent swing in one direction or another could determine who is elected. It could also change the discussion about other issues that concern them, as Watson pointed out.

Civic Education and the Youth of the Past

Civic education was once an important part of education but it is now almost nonexistent. Fred Lewis writes in his report "A Call to Justice: The Importance of Civic Education" about a number of frightening statistics. One of these statistics he lists reports that "just over half of all Americans can correctly identify the three branches of government" (13). This staggering statistic is alarming and surely calls attention to the lack of civic education being taught in schools around the country.

The background he provides here is important in understanding the issue? Does the audience need to know this sooner, so that they are more likely to accept this problem Merrigan is addressing?

Historically, this age group was much more involved in government and politics. Lewis says that "in sharp contrast to Americans today, the earliest American citizens likely viewed their civic duties as opportunities for self-governance" (14). One of those times, as Watson points out, was the 1960s and 1970s, where students spoke out about and marched for the civil rights of African Americans and later protested the Vietnam war (13). And according to Sean Yoes, they weren't just involved in activism:

> "In 1972, more than half of the nation's 18- to 24-year-olds went to the polls. However, only 36 percent of America's 26.8 million citizens between 18 and 24 voted in the presidential election in 2000" (20).

These numbers prove that in the last thirty years, youth participation has decreased in politics in comparison to other generations.

Young Adult Voting and Factors Causing the Decrease

Voting is the number one civic duty because it is so easy; the most talked about, and potentially has the biggest effect. In an article titled "We, the Jury . . . ," there is a mention of people's feeling about jury duty versus voting when it states that most people throughout the nation would be less likely to serve on juries than to vote if given the choice because jury duty is longer and requires more effort (19). Presumably, then, more people would rather vote. Yet that doesn't seem to be the case with young adults. In "Youth Voting in the 2004 Election," the authors write that studies show that this age group's representation has remained under ten percent in the last two presidential elections.

There are certain factors that have caused this decrease in interest among the youth ages 18 to 24. Watson claims that the older generations try to justify this adolescent disinterest in voting by saying that no issues concern them and they have no voice (13). Knowing this is not a viable excuse, he goes on to provide examples of why this is not true such as the rising cost of higher education. So why don't they vote when the issues affect them? Fred Lewis suggests that reality television is a major guilty pleasure of many 18- to 24-year-olds that is changing the principles of these kids (13). This may be true in some respects because young people are more interested in reality television and the coolest new gadgets that are out there for their cell phones or iPods. Scott Beale, a regional director of Youth Venture, a nonprofit organization for adolescents starting their own businesses, has his own reason for why kids do not vote: "The big reason young people don't vote is because they don't think their vote will make a difference" (qtd. in Felchner 8).

Groups Helping Out and Other Possible Solutions

While the problem is complex, the solution appears to be pretty simple: provide civic education early on. Moore observes that "young people who have taken a civics course are two to three times more likely to vote, follow government news and contact a public official about an issue that concerns them" (34). This shows that those who actually take civic classes usually get more involved in these types of civic duties. There seems to be a direct correlation between civic education and fulfilling civic duties.

There are various groups out there that are trying to increase awareness and participation among the youth. Keshia Crosby details one of these groups: "In an effort to introduce the concepts of government and civic education early, Kids Voting USA helps students become more involved in

Because his purpose is to get his audience to take action, Merrigan offers some solutions. Notice that he still has to develop and support these claims—his audience will not simply take his word for it.

politics and encourages them to realize the importance of voting when eighteen" (4). This group is helpful because its focus is to instill civic education at a young age so by the time a person is eighteen, they will have the right thought process to go and get involved in politics and government.

Education, whether in the schools or through such groups as Kids Voting USA, is one approach, but Garry Boulard argues that volunteering can help, too. He writes:

> "Based upon a survey conducted by the International Association for Evaluation of Education, the authors note that more than 80 percent of high school seniors in 2000 were engaged in some form of volunteer activity" (45).

If volunteering is very high among today's youth, then maybe by volunteering, teenagers and young adults will realize that they can make a difference that extends beyond their own lives.

But what about those who don't volunteer or don't want to get involved in groups like Kids Voting USA? Jamal Watson argues that "perhaps there ought to be a requirement that goes something like this: all high schools students must register to vote before they receive their diploma. Or better yet, voter registration is required before one can obtain a driver's license" (13). This is a type of solution that would affect every person who tried to get his or her license or graduate which would exponentially increase voter registration.

Ultimately, the solution to this problem is through civic education. If the youth are educated about their civic responsibilities and are taught the importance of these duties, then they will be more likely to get involved. It is statistically proven that young adults who take civic education classes are more likely to be interested in government and politics.

Works Cited

Boulard, Garry. "Citizens in Training." *State Legislatures* 29.7
(July 2003): 44–49. *Academic Search Premier.* Web. 20 Feb.
2008.

Crosby, Keshia. "Presidential Election Sparks Youth Participation in
Politics." *Nation's Cities Weekly* 27.41 (11 Oct. 2004): 4, 7.
Academic Search Premier. Web. 20 Feb. 2008.

Delchad, Lena, and Keshia Crosby. "Democratic Governance
Opportunity for Youth Involvement." *Nation's Cities Weekly* 28.7
(14 Feb. 2005): 3. *General OneFile.* Web. 27 Feb. 2008.

Felchner, Morgan E. "Wanted: Young Voters." *Campaigns & Elections*
24.10 (Oct. 2003): 8–9. *Academic Search Premier.* Web. 20 Feb.
2008.

Lewis, R. Fred. "A Call to Justice: The Importance of Civic Education."
Florida Bar Journal 80.10 (Nov. 2006): 12–17. *Academic Search
Premier.* Web. 20 Feb. 2008.

Moore, Nicole. "Whatever Happened to Civics?" *State Legislatures*
29.10 (Dec. 2003): 32–34. *Academic Search Premier.* Web. 20
Feb. 2008.

Watson, Jamal E. "Voting Should Become a Priority among America's
Youth." *New York Amsterdam News* 95.45 (4 Nov. 2004): 13.
Academic Search Premier. Web. 20 Feb. 2008.

"We, the Jury . . ." *Dissent* 55.1 (Winter 2008): 19–20. *Academic
Search Premier.* Web. 27 Feb. 2008.

Yoes, Sean. "Registering Young Voters Has Yielded Mixed Results."
New York Amsterdam News 95.39 (23 Sept. 2004): 20. *Academic
Search Premier.* Web. 20 Feb. 2008.

"Youth Voting in the 2004 Election: The Staff of the Center for
Information and Research on Civic Learning and Engagement
(1)." *Social Education* 69.1 (Jan. –Feb. 2005): 33. *General
OneFile.* Web. 20 Feb. 2008.

Questions for Discussion

1. How does Merrigan help readers understand the problem as he sees it? What kinds of conclusions does he draw about why young people are not interested in civic life?

2. What kinds of evidence (research) does Merrigan use to support his claims that civic duty is an important concept for young people believe in?

3. How does Merrigan convince readers that young people can be motivated to make civic contributions? How could he make his arguments more convincing?

Reflecting on the Process

I was very happy with how my research report turned out and I think I did a lot of good writing to make my ideas come together. The issue that I chose was civic duties and how they are being neglected by 18- to 24-year-olds. I had a list of ten claims that I wanted to discuss in my report and organized them into four different categories that became the four parts to my paper.

One of the parts of my report that I was most pleased with was my use of research. For most of my points I paraphrased my sources to help get my point across and make it credible. Some of my evidence was statistical figures that may cause the reader to stop and think for a minute.

Another aspect of my paper that I really liked was my discussion of possible solutions to the problem. I provided other possible solutions to this problem but spoke about civic education being the real answer.

WRITING ACTIVITY   Evaluating One Writer's Journey

Look back over Merrigan's process for writing his research report. How would you evaluate the choices he made as he wrote? Are there places where you think he could have made different choices, and how would those choices have affected the final report? What further revisions, if any, do you think the final report could use?

▪ ▪ ▪

T R A N S F O R M A T I O N S

GENRE CROSSING: From Report to Proposal

The research report is the genre equivalent of a lump of clay; that is, a lot of transformations are possible from this one genre. The reason is simple: Once you have conducted the research necessary to write a credible and well-informed report, you have accumulated considerable material and knowledge about the issue. Because of this storehouse, you may choose to write more about your topic in any of several other genres.

One relatively common crossing from the report genre is to a proposal. Proposals ask writers to define and explore a problem and offer a well thought-out solution. (See Chapter 11: Proposals) A proposal requires that the author be very well informed about the issue or problem. Thus, a research report serves as an excellent starting point for a proposal.

Genre Crossing Writing Assignment

From Report to Proposal

Write a proposal that defines a particular problem, explores how that problem has come about and what has been done (if anything) about it, refutes negative responses to the solution(s) being proposed, and proposes a workable solution to address the problem.

Review your issue. What part of that issue or topic presents a problem needing a solution? What practical and workable solutions could reasonably solve the problem? You'll need to narrow down the problem for a specific audience. If you are writing about a problem that seems to affect people on a national level, you might examine it at the local level and propose a solution for the problem in your community, workplace, or school.

Review your research materials. You may need to conduct further research in order to define the problem in your proposal and create a convincing solution (i.e. to support your arguments and show your plan for solving the problem will benefit people and can be done). Research is also needed to explore the ideas of those who might reject your proposal.

Draft a convincing proposal. Your proposal should persuade readers to rethink ideas about the issue and take action.

- Have you defined the problem clearly? In what ways does your solution or plan address the problem?
- Are you considering the audience's concerns and possible objections to your solution?
- What can you say to convince people to support or implement your proposed plan?
- Why should people who might not care about the problem take part in solving it?

Transformation from Report to Proposal: Patrick Merrigan, "Civic Duties: Fixing the Problem of Civic Engagement in Two Easy Steps"

Patrick Merrigan
Professor Ferruci
English 100P
24 Mar. 2008

Civic Duties: Fixing the Problem of Civic Engagement
in Two Easy Steps

Notice how Merrigan gets right to the problem and then quickly provides some evidence to back that claim up.

There are many problems in today's world, but one that is of increasing concern is the lack of involvement of youth in the civic life of our country and their knowledge of our government. As of 2003, less than fifty percent know their governor's political party whereas four out of five people younger than twenty-seven know Ruben Studdard won the second American Idol show (Moore 33). This is obviously a problem that can be divided into two parts: first, young people seem uninterested in government, politics, or their civic duties; and second, they lack a civic education. This second part is a big reason why the youth are uniformed when it comes to the government and their duties to the government. This is a relatively recent problem, because kids are so concerned with iPods, video games, or television that they are neglecting the responsibilities that helped make this country become what it is today.

Merrigan then provides some context for the problem, helping the readers to see it the way he does. Without this context, the audience might ignore the recommendations because they do not see the problem in the same way.

Up to and during the Vietnam War, youth voting and political participation was very high. Since that time it has been on a steady decline. Fred Lewis claims that "in sharp contrast to Americans today, the earliest American citizens likely viewed their civic duties as opportunities for self-governance" (14). Lewis points out that the average U.S. citizen fears going into jury duty and only a small number engage in the voting process (14). This tells us that it is not just the youth that are neglectful of their duties but it is U.S. citizens in

Merrigan continues to define the problem, using some of the same material from the research report, but not all of it. Should he have drawn more heavily here on his research?

general. So while this is primarily a problem of the youth, it obviously affects other age groups as well—those kids grow up, after all.

Obviously, this apathy is a problem because government participation, political participation, and civic duties are important. Serving the country on jury duty, in the armed forces or national guard, getting involved in local government and volunteering in the community are important civic responsibilities.

In order to get high participation once again, Lewis advocates a solution to the problem of Florida's youth called "Justice Teaching." Lewis says that in the Justice Teaching program "judges, lawyers, and other professionals will be trained in educational methods to effectively convey knowledge of our constitutional structure and the judicial system to students in a manner that provides an exciting, interactive educational experience" (16). By implementing this program, Lewis believes that the youth of Florida will be better educated and better able to participate in the governance of our country.

Writers of proposals need to contend with differing views; they cannot assume that their audience will agree with them. Here Merrigan articulates a counter-position to his and then refutes it.

What Lewis's work suggests is that in general 18- to 24-year-olds do not care about civic duties because of the lack of education and awareness. Some claim that kids are not interested because they simply do not care about their duties or the government. That may be. More likely, though, this is just an excuse for not doing something about it. One major reason: young people "don't think their vote will make a difference," says Scott Beale of Youth Venture, "a nonprofit organization for young people starting their own businesses" (Felchner 8). Beale is not the only one who thinks this way. Journalist Garry Boulard cites a National Association of Secretary of States report that claims "nine out of ten are certain that government is run 'by a few big interests'" (44). This type of hopeless thinking is a roadblock for getting youth involved. Young people feel as though the they make up such a small number that

they could not possibly have a voice, and learn not to care about
their civic duties or the government.

Although this conclusion seems to make sense, it is not actually
true. Morgan Felchner reports that "the youth demographic
comprises 14.4 percent of the total voting age population" (8). A
14.4 percent swing in one direction or another could determine who
the next president would be, and is enough to have an effect on
local and statewide elections.

So while the problem might seem too complex to address, the
solutions are actually straightforward and workable. In "Leave No
Voter Behind: Seeking 100 Percent Voter Registration and Effective
Civic Education," Robert Richie explains the possible reason behind
this problem: It is "a general lack of knowledge and interest
concerning the intricacies of our electoral system" (43). The first
step, then, would be to propose state legislation to create more civic
education in high schools and colleges. As part of this, Richie
suggests that "schools should establish a brief but required voting
education component for all enrolled students" and "the curriculum
in civics class or even a grade-wide plenary session would involve an
overview of the electoral process" (43). Some readers might be thinking
that it would cost too much more to implement these programs. It's
true that making room for a real civics education would require
hiring more teachers and developing new curriculum. But in the end
it would be worth it because of the long-term effects it will have. As
Nicole Moore tells us, an individual who has taken a civics class is
"two to three times more likely" to be involved in local, state, and
national politics (34). Thus having such a course in place, and making
the course mean something, would encourage civic involvement.

Education in schools would address one part of the problem, but
we would also need to increase interest and awareness from outside
the school systems. The solution would be to have state or national
government-funded groups and organizations target teenagers and

Having defined the problem, Merrigan now offers his solutions. Notice that he is still working with his research, since even if his audience accepts the way he sees the problem, readers might not agree with his solutions.

Again, Merrigan contends with differing views. And in this case, notice that he agrees with the concern.

Merrigan introduces the second solution, making sure to tie it to the first. Both, he says, need to happen.

those in their early twenties. The organizations would develop programs that engaged the target audience in various aspects of civic responsibility, and they would work with the schools as well as working on their own to get students involved. The organizations would be located in strategic places such as malls and would also go to schools to give presentations. In *Phi Delta Kaplan*, D. R. Woolf lists a number of groups already in existence; one, the National Alliance for Civic Education, "provides resource materials to groups and individuals in order to help citizens across the United States better understand the significance of effective civic education for a well-functioning democracy" (288). Groups such as this one serve an important function, and they need to be more fully funded directly by the state or national government.

Some might argue that these groups don't work—teenagers don't respond to them, they can't make a difference because students are forced to listen, and so on. Many would also worry that it would cost too much to maintain these groups. Yet these are all misconceptions and stem from a lack of understanding about how these groups and organizations function. Looking closely at just one group reveals how effective they can be. Kids Voting "offers civic education and activities for students in grade school through high school that can work with the curricula that teachers already have in place." Kids Voting is in "thirty states, reaching more than 4.3 million students and their families," and communities involved with Kids Voting have "a voting rate for registered 18-year-olds that was 14 percentage points higher than non-participating communities" (Crosby 4). This group is helpful because its focus is to instill civic understanding at a young age so by the time a person is eighteen, he or she will understand how to get involved in politics and government and why it is important to do so.

These organizations will help solve the problem of civic involvement by young people which is caused by a lack of civic

Rather than simply repeat what he has said throughout, Merrigan asks the reader to consider the consequences of not doing anything. Do you think this is an effective concluding strategy?

education in our school systems. The two-part solution to this problem is to create more civic education through legislation and to create and further fund organizations to increase awareness about these duties. Lewis writes about a shocking statistic: "Just over half of all Americans can correctly identify the three branches of government" (13). This type of statistics raises an alarm and shows the urgency of the issue. If this problem is not addressed then there could be severe consequences in the future. Imagine a country where only a few really understand how government works, and only a few understand what our rights really are? In order to preserve those rights, we have to first understand them, and we have to understand that they are earned through civic engagement and responsibility.

Works Cited

Boulard, Garry. "Citizens in Training." *State Legislatures* 29.7 (July 2003): 44–49. *Academic Search Premier.* Web. 20 Feb. 2008.

Crosby, Keshia. "Presidential Election Sparks Youth Participation in Politics." *Nation's Cities Weekly* 27.41 (11 Oct. 2004): 4, 7. *Academic Search Premier.* Web. 20 Feb. 2008.

Felchner, Morgan E. "Wanted: Young Voters." *Campaigns & Elections* 24.10 (Oct. 2003): 8–9. *Academic Search Premier.* Web. 20 Feb. 2008.

Lewis, R. Fred. "A Call to Justice: The Importance of Civic Education." *Florida Bar Journal* 80.10 (Nov. 2006): 12–17. *Academic Search Premier.* Web. 20 Feb. 2008.

Moore, Nicole. "Whatever Happened to Civics?" *State Legislatures* 29.10 (Dec. 2003): 32–34. *Academic Search Premier.* Web. 20 Feb. 2008.

Richie, Robert. "Leave No Voter Behind: Seeking 100 Percent Voter Registration and Effective Civic Education." *National Civic*

Review 96.3 (Fall 2007): 39–45. *Academic Search Premier*. Web.

26 Mar. 2008.

Woolf, D. R. "Organizations Promoting Civic Education." *Phi Delta*

Kappan 89.4 (Dec. 2007): 288. *Academic Search Premier*. Web.

26 Mar. 2008.

Reading for Comprehension

1. What did you read in this proposal that helped you understand the writer's vision of the problem?
2. Would you be inclined to accept this proposal? What might convince you to do so?

Analyzing the Genre

1. Given the audience for the proposal, how effective is the writer's use of claims and evidence to define the problem and to persuade readers to take action?
2. What kinds of choices did Merrigan make to appeal to his readers? Are his appeals convincing to his intended readers? Why or why not?

CHAPTER 11

Proposals

In everyday life, you may have been asked by a friend to solve a problem (*where will we eat tonight*?) and put a plan into action (*we'll eat at home and save money to go to the movies*). You were making a proposal, even if you were just talking about your plans for the evening. Wherever problems arise and must be solved, proposals are made, whether at home, work, school, or in the larger community.

What Is a Proposal?

A proposal is an action-oriented genre of writing. A writer takes action to address a problem or issue that affects an audience; in turn, the audience takes action if they are persuaded to do so by reading the proposal. A small business owner may write a proposal to potential consumers to persuade them to utilize the business's services. Or a novelist may write a literary proposal to convince a publisher of the value of, and market for, his book. Other kinds of proposals might address a community issue. For example, in your town, you want to address the lack of recreational activities for teenagers. This problem begins with what seems like a simple question: What will teenagers do after school? That question in turn leads to other concerns: How can teens keep active in ways that prevent them from getting into trouble? Who will finance, organize, and supervise teen activities? And where can they take place? These questions reveal the *assumptions* about the potential audience—the town's adults—that teenagers want and need such structured activities or they *will* get into trouble. The course of action you propose must consider the particular audience involved and their needs. And the proposed solution should address the problem at hand and be convincing so people want to adopt it.

As you can see, proposals are *persuasive genres* in which writers address a problem and develop well thought-out, reasonable solutions. Proposals often have their genesis in an individual or group that has found a way to look at an issue from a new angle or create a plausible solution to a problem. The proposed plan of action, of course, depends on the situation and the group of people affected by it. In order to be successful, a proposal must define a problem, offer a solution, and persuade its audience to act.

- **Defining a problem.** It's hard to motivate people to rethink old ideas or consider new ones if they do not recognize a problem or understand the consequences of *not* taking action. So proposal writers first need to define the problem clearly for readers, since not everyone sees a problem in exactly the same way. In the example above, is the problem that teens have nowhere to go or is it that there are no activities? That is, is the problem a lack of space or a lack of programs? Often when we make proposals we are asking the audience to make a commitment of time and money. Given a choice between the two, many people would choose to provide time, so getting volunteers to initiate after-school activities is probably easier than raising taxes to pay for a recreation center and ensure its continuing success (a building with no activities won't accomplish much).

- **Suggesting a workable solution.** Once you've defined the problem, you'll need to develop a solution that adequately addresses the issues facing the group or community that led to the problem. That is, will the solution offered meet the audience's needs and expectations? Does it match the problem? For instance, a solution that offers teens more programs but doesn't find ways to motivate them to attend those programs would not really work. Similarly, opening a new building would not necessarily move teenagers to participate in activities. However, a plan that engages teenagers (perhaps involving them in creating programs they are interested in versus adult-planned programs) would boost their investment in the after-school activities. So a carefully crafted proposal ensures that the solution matches the problem and fulfills the needs of those who are affected by the problem and those involved in the solution.

- **Persuading people to act.** Not only will carefully identifying the problem help ensure the proposal's success but considering the audience and possible objections to your solution will also help you see alternative views on the problem. Not everyone will agree with your description of the problem or your proposed solutions, but if you can come up with a plan that considers many views, you're more likely to get people to at least listen to your proposal. What you say should convince people to support or implement your plan, so you need to show them how they are affected by the situation and how they will benefit from your proposal.

The Purpose of Proposals

Although the basic aim of a proposal is to persuade, people write proposals for many different reasons: to get readers to rethink a problem, to alter a policy, or to change a plan that improves the situation of their target audience. Proposals are also written to implement a new plan, to get funding or resources for a program, and to argue for support for a research project.

- **Proposals to solve a problem.** For example, suppose the recycling bins in the business where you work are always full to the brim, causing people to dump their empty soda cans or water bottles in the regular trash. You propose two things. First, employees should take turns taking recyclables to the collection center once a week. Second, with the money collected for the recyclables, your group will treat itself to lunch out once a month. Your plan, thus, solves the overflow problem by sharing the responsibility of recycling and motivates workers to take part in the plan by rewarding them with a "free" lunch.

- **Proposals to change an existing policy or to create a new poli**cy. For example, the residence halls at your school have smoking zones, but smoke still permeates the buildings. You propose a policy that prohibits smoking in the dorms altogether and sets a certain distance from the buildings smokers must stand while smoking. This solution addresses the needs of both smokers and nonsmokers.
- **Proposals to redefine an issue**. For example, consider again the discussion above about after-school activities for teenagers. Residents might have begun the discussion by assuming that the problem was a lack of activities for teenagers after school. But one astute resident noted that in fact there were dozens of after-school activities being offered by the town and wondered why they were not being utilized. After some thought, she identified the problem as one of audience, interest, and access: Mostly younger teenagers needed after-school activities because older teens were generally working; the younger teens weren't interested in the kinds of programs being offered; and, finally, because they couldn't drive yet, the younger teenagers had no way of getting to activities. So the problem needs to be redefined to address the concerns of all those affected by it, and those who might benefit from a solution.

The Rhetorical Situation of Proposals

As you can see, proposal writers have to take into account the social situation driving the proposal. To put it another way, different members of the audience may see the problem in a different way and their perception of the problem—and how it affects them—will largely determine whether they will find the solution reasonable or not. In addition, proposal writers must do research to better understand the different facets of the problem that affects a particular audience. For example, if a town planning committee opposes the introduction of "big box" stores into its community, it must research how other towns have successfully opposed such efforts. The committee must also figure out what people in the community value (small-town atmosphere versus convenience of shopping) and then propose the most persuasive plan to address the people's needs and desires. The committee might research the company and find out about its business practices (will the store be built in a retrofitted space or a new strip mall?) or the infrastructure needs (will the current roads be able to handle the traffic flow?). If the company promises to create new jobs locally, will there be a desire for such jobs, even if they pay minimum wage? And will the economic cost of development offset any gains in taxes?

You can see that proposal writing takes some in-depth analysis and research to create a feasible plan. This chapter will explore some choices writers make as they find themselves in situations that warrant proposal writing.

Reading Proposals Critically

WRITING ACTIVITY   Analyzing the Genre of Proposals

Thinking about the genre.

Before you read the proposals in this chapter, think about a problematic situation that might make you want to write a proposal. Understanding your own reasons for writing can often help you better understand and critically evaluate another writer's proposal.

Examining the genre.

As you read the following proposals, you are reading not only for comprehension but to also understand the *characteristics* of the genre. Look for *patterns* that reveal how proposals work in general.

1. What are the characteristics you notice immediately about proposals?
2. What kind of information goes into the introduction of a proposal? How do writers introduce readers to the problem or issue?
3. How is the proposal organized? What are some of the parts?
4. Why is the writer writing this proposal? What situations make writers write proposals? What purposes do they serve?
5. How does the writer develop a feasible solution to match the problem? Is the solution persuasive? Why or why not?
6. What kinds of evidence or research do you notice the writer using to support claims?
7. Who might be the audience the writer is addressing in the proposal? Language choices, tone, examples, or references might give you a hint.

Reflecting on the genre.

After you have read the proposals, explain in a couple of paragraphs the major characteristics of the genre as you understand it. Refer to specific passages and quote when necessary. Reflection helps you keep track of the kinds of choices writers make that you may want to try when you write a proposal.

■   ■   ■

Genre Analysis: Women's Committee of 100, "An Immodest Proposal: Rewarding Women's Work to End Poverty"

The Women's Committee of 100 defines itself in its mission statement as "a group of feminist academics, professionals, and activists who are concerned with the relationship between women, economic survival, and the work of caregiving." In "An Immodest Proposal," the group advocates for reevaluation of caregiving as work and suggests reforms to the current welfare system in order to eradicate the poverty and discrimination faced by caregivers. A link to this proposal can be found on the group's website.

An Immodest Proposal: Rewarding Women's Work to End Poverty

By the Women's Committee of 100/Project 2002

The current funding for welfare reform – officially called Temporary Aid to Needy Families (TANF) – ends in fall of 2002. At that time, Congress will make major decisions about how much money to spend on welfare and which

In the first sentence, I think I know the problem – or at least the situation that they are responding to.

of TANF's punitive rules it will keep or replace. As the national debate on welfare reauthorization heats up, the Women's Committee of 100 – a group of feminist academics, professionals, and activists concerned with the relationship between women, economic survival, and the work of caregiving – hopes to encourage consideration of bolder new initiatives.

So the WC 100 want some change—bold new initiatives they call them. So they are about to give us the solutions—already? Seems like we need more of the problem.

Families, communities, and the economy all depend heavily on caregiving work. Yet our economic system undervalues paid caregiving in the workforce and penalizes unpaid caregivers in the home. Research also shows that caregiving work exposes many women to low wages, part-time jobs, sex discrimination, lower Social Security and Unemployment Insurance benefits, the double day, and other forms of gender inequality and stress.

Caregivers' poverty clearly has a woman's face. But because poverty is not color-blind, that face often belongs to a woman of color. Since race and racial discrimination also create unfavorable conditions for caretaking, while addressing the shared vulnerabilities of ALL women, social reform must begin with the needs of the poorest caregivers, especially poor women of color.

So the problem is that the rules affect this particular group: caregivers, especially women, and women of color.

Our Project 2002 proposal calls for replacing TANF with a set of policies that address the economic plight faced by those doing the work of caregiving – most of whom are women:

End the Caregiver's Penalty: As a crucial first step toward ending poverty, we call for social policies that reward the work of caring for dependents. At a minimum, this means repealing the following TANF provisions:

- Mandatory work outside the home
- Arbitrary time limits
- Child exclusion policies ("family cap")

Create a Caregiver's Allowance: In place of welfare reform that punishes caregiving, we favor a guaranteed income for caregivers of minor children and other family members who need sustained care. A Caregiver's Allowance would:

I like how the solutions are presented—it looks like a list, easy to read, and important points are bulleted. Because the audience is busy?

- Provide regular, automatic, and guaranteed support, without government intrusion into the personal lives of beneficiaries. Just like Social Security benefits for surviving parents and minor children, there would be no oversight or employment requirements.

- Go to all primary caregivers (not only those eligible for TANF) and be tied to care work rather than the caregivers' race, class, gender, or marital status. Payments would vary by total household income.

- Allow only the caregivers to decide how to spend the grant, whether they are caring for dependents themselves, purchasing caregiving services while working for wages or getting more education/training, or combining care work with other pursuits

- Be counted when calculating Social Security retirement benefits, along with time spent on care work for dependents, since this benefit is based on both income earned and years of work.

As an interim measure, the current child tax credit could be expanded into a refundable Caregiver Tax Credit for all caregivers with dependents needing sustained care.

Develop Additional Supports: Since real choice about caregiving requires more than income support, all caregiving should have access to:

- High-quality care for infants, school-age children, elders, and the availability of non-custodial care for incapacitated dependents. These services should be universally available; federally funded; and based on national wage, training, and fringe benefit standards, as well as input from caregivers.

- Just compensation, respite provisions, adequate retirement, health insurance, and other basic benefits.

Improve Wages and Working Conditions: Ending women's poverty requires valuing women's work and providing the following protections and supports:

- A shorter work week for both women and men so they can meet family caregiving responsibilities.

- The right to unionize.

- A living wage, which should be a universal right and could be achieved in part through an automatically indexed minimum wage.

- Equal pay for work of comparable value or worth, to correct the low wages assigned to jobs/occupations filled mostly by women.

- Affirmative Action remedies that open up higher paying jobs and redress gender, race, age, and ability discrimination.

- Paid family and medical leave.

- The end of both discrimination against workers because of their caregiving responsibilities and employment conditions that unreasonably interfere with those responsibilities (such as overtime as a condition of employment).

Respect Our lives: To enhance the quality of life of women and their families and to ensure that caregiving takes place in safety and with dignity, we also support:

- Unemployment insurance for part-time, very low-waged, and intermittent as well as full-time workers.

- Universal access to higher education and skill-building programs that prepare women for better-paying occupations. Like the GI Bill, this would include free education and training, cost-of-living stipends, and help with caregiving for students caring for dependents.

- Health care as a universal right.

Their solutions are pretty far-reaching—they see the problem as pretty complex, I guess, since the solutions are pretty detailed and cover a lot of different aspects. And a lot of people would need to be on-board, not just Congress, but also employers, insurance companies, etc.

- Broadly defined disability insurance to protect those who cannot be employed, are not caregivers, or are not retired.
- 24-hour emergency assistance, temporary shelter, and priority in subsidized housing, for victims of domestic abuse.
- Strong enforcement of child support by non-custodial parents, if requested by custodial parents.
- Federal support for affordable housing in economically and racially integrated communities.
- Expanded public transportation to include customized service to remote, especially rural, areas, and latenight service for night-shift workers.

For an unabridged version of this proposal, see www.welfare2002.org. To endorse this proposal email: wc100project2002@aol.com.

For The WC 100/Project 2002

Mimi Abramovitz (Hunter school of social Work, CUNY)	Cynthia Harrison (George Washington University)	Dorothy Roberts (Northwestern University school of Law)
Randy Albelda (University of Massachusetts-Boston)	Eva Feder Kittay (SUNY at Stony Brook)	Rickie Solinger (Historian, Boulder, Colorado)
Eileen Boris (University of Virginia)	Sonya Michel (University of Illinois-Urbana/Champaign)	Jean Verber (Welfare advocate/activist, Milwaukee, WI)
Ruth Brandwein (SUNY at Stony Brook)	Gwendolyn Mink (University of California-Santa Cruz)	Guida West (Actrvist and author, Montclair, New Jersey)
Nancy Fraser (New School University)	Frances Fox Piven (Graduate Center, CUNY)	Ann Withorn (University of Massachusetts-Boston)

It's pretty clear who this group is and where they stand on the issue—they identify themselves and include their mission statement in the introduction. That's ethos for you. I get a clear sense of what they are proposing right away and the urgency of it happening now—"the current funding for welfare reform—officially called TANF— ends in the fall of 2002." So obviously, this proposal was responding to policy changes happening at the time. Some obvious characteristics of proposals are they identify and describe a problem, in this case a social problem related to a policy. This proposal only briefly identifies the problem of caregivers being discriminated against ". . . research also shows that caregiving work exposes many women to low wages, part time jobs, sex discrimination . . ." and facing poverty. . . ."caregivers' poverty clearly has a woman's face" . . . because of the welfare system's inadequacies, then it jumps right into what WC100 wants to do to change this.

I notice the writers spend a lot of time developing the solutions—each one has its own subheading followed by suggestions. And they arrange them from specific "End the caregiver's penalty" to general "Respect our lives." They seem to know what they are talking about since they include research in the form of examples: they say "create a caregiver's allowance," then explain how it would sustain caregivers and their families, and provide examples. The audience seems to be those people who can make policy changes happen, like Congress, as reforms are made to a replacement for TANF; there are phrases like "developing additional supports" and "improving wages and working conditions" and "respect our lives," which are appealing to readers' sense of fairness, justice, and equality, so that they understand what their readers value.

Brian Halweil, "A Community Farm for Stanford"

Brian Halweil's proposal, written in 1996, argues that a community farm would revive Stanford University's curriculum on agriculture and restore some of the land to its original function. He also claims that students will benefit by becoming more environmentally conscious as they engage in practices of a working food production farm. Today, the Stanford Community Farm is located on the campus of Stanford University in Palo Alto, California, and it is run by Stanford students, faculty, and staff. You can read more about the farm by going to its website.

"Education, cultivated thought, can best be combined with agricultural labor, on the principle of thorough work, and thorough work again renders sufficient the smallest quantity of ground to each man, and this again conforms to what must occur in a world less inclined to war, and more devoted to the arts of peace, than heretofore."

—Abraham Lincoln

"To forget how to dig the earth and tend the soil is to forget ourselves."

—Gandhi

"Farming is the production of peanuts from the land; agriculture is the production of peanut butter from petroleum."

—Robert Lewontin

Over 100 years ago, a farm was converted into Stanford University. Since then all but a trivial amount of the University's land have been taken out of food production. Over the same period, the University has all but eliminated the study of agriculture and practice of farming from its curriculum. Without too much trouble, one can find an economics class which examines agricultural economics or a political science class on agricultural policy or an engineering class on soil science or a biology class on plant genetics. Yet, one would be hard-pressed to find a class on farming techniques or horticulture or soil preparation or how to grow one's own food. In an effort to provide students with an environment in which they can learn, study and practice farming techniques involved in small-scale food production, I propose the founding of the Stanford Student Farm.

On a deeper level, the farm will serve as an environment in which students could develop an ecological conscientiousness. Modern agricultural practices are at the root of many of the world's most pressing and far-reaching environmental problems, including deforestation, desertification, soil erosion, water and air pollution, ozone depletion and global climate change. The farm will provide students with an environment in which to discuss the ecological, socio-economic, political, cultural and spiritual ramifications of different agricultural systems. Furthermore, the student farm will be devoted to practicing, demonstrating and refining sustainable and organic farming techniques. The farm will minimize external inputs of agricultural amendments (such as organic fertilizers), by recycling nutrients and producing its own compost. The farm will avoid the use of toxic chemicals for pest and disease prevention by using agroecological techniques such as Integrated Pest Management and crop rotation. The farm will promote soil conservation, utilizing techniques which prevent erosion and build topsoil. The farm will demonstrate water conservation (in a region of the nation which is perennially susceptible to drought) by building soil structure and minimizing water use. In summary, the farm will serve as a model of alternative food production methods which are at the same time environmentally benign (or environmentally beneficial) and high-yielding.

Currently, there are three student-run gardens at Stanford (the Columbae, Synergy and Chi Theta Chi gardens). These gardens are worked almost exclusively by residents of these three campus co-ops. In addition, there are a few other gardens or growing areas on campus at which students can work, including the experimental plots maintained by the Carnegie Institute for Plant Research and the Biology Department. Unless a student chooses to obtain housing or land off-campus, there are few opportunities afforded for practicing the art of food production on any scale. Most major universities in California have student farms, run by students, for students (this includes all of the UC and CS schools). From personal experiences, I know that these farms provide indispensable sources of pleasure for students and other members of the university community. When one considers the national and global prowess of California agriculture it seems odd that there would be a California university which would not at least provide students with some land on which to grow food.

In modern times, the study of agriculture has been isolated in research institutions and further isolated in technical disciplines with the overriding goal of increasing productivity. As a result, the study of agriculture (what is now known as the agricultural sciences) has been separated from its community, cultural and ecological context. On the other hand, a Stanford student farm would enjoy the unique situation of being accessible to students with diverse academic interests and backgrounds (in both technical and non-technical disciplines). With a more holistic foundation, students may learn "to see farming not as a production problem to be fixed, but as a more complex activity, at once cultural, ethical, ecological and political."[2] There is an abundance of agricultural professionals and a dearth of people who understand farming in its larger social and environmental context. Along these same lines, Aldo Leopold feels that "the goal of liberal education is not merely a dilute dosage of technical education, but rather to teach the student to see the land, to understand what he sees, and enjoy what he understands."[3] Finally, the student farm will help to remedy "the debilitating separation of abstract intellect and practical intelligence" found at many modern universities.[4] Year round, agencies such as WWOF and the Land Institute (organizations which help arrange student internships on farms) are bombarded with hopeful inquiries from students (attending highly-regarded universities such as Stanford) who are deficient in practical experiences and yearn to learn out of doors. Students need an on-campus alternative. Several short-term and long-term benefits of a student farm will include, but will not be limited to the following:

1. A student farm at Stanford would provide essential and wonderful experiences which are rarely available to students from predominantly urban and non-agricultural backgrounds.

2. A student farm at Stanford would potentially serve as a multidisciplinary laboratory for the study of agroforestry, animal husbandry, botany, business operations, ecology, entomology, land restoration, landscape design, philosophy, rural sociology, soil science, solar technology, sustainable agriculture and zoology.[5]

3. In addition to serving as an educational tool and providing an outlet for desires to work the earth, a student farm at Stanford would function as a community outreach tool to work in conjunction with such Stanford organizations as SHAC and SEAS and such non-university organizations as Second Harvest Food Bank, the Palo Alto community farm and the East Palo Alto community farm.

4. A Stanford student farm would be used to preserve biological diversity in constant jeopardy of being paved over.

5. A Stanford student farm would reduce carbon emissions involved in fossil fuel burning by sequestering carbon through agroforestry (tree cropping).

6. A student farm at Stanford would provide campus food service, self-ops and co-ops with a local vendor of fresh, organic produce. (This is done successfully on many campuses throughout the nation which provide students with a food co-op.) Additionally, a student farm at Stanford would "close waste loops by composting all campus organic wastes and incorporating these as soil amendments." (In a destructive trend, universities function more and more like small cities, importing almost all food and energy and exporting enormous quantities of related wastes.)[6]

7. "By participating in the design and operation of" the Stanford student farm, "students could learn that our problems are not beyond intelligent solutions; that solutions are close by; and that institutions that often seem to be inflexible, unimaginative, and remote from the effort to build sustainable society can be otherwise."[7]

At this point in time, the Student Farm is recognized by the University as an official student organization, with a listing in the directory and eligible for possible funding. There is considerable student interest in the farm (even in its hypothetical state), ensuring that there will not be a lack of willing hands. In an increasingly virtual culture, in which humans are separated from (and largely ignorant of) the production of the houses they inhabit, the clothes they wear and the food they consume, farming needs to be included as a part of a complete liberal arts education.

All references are made to: Orr, David W. 1994. Earth in Mind: On Education, Environment, and the Human Prospect. Island Press: Washington, D.C.

Reading for Comprehension

1. Why does Halweil suggest that developing an "ecological consciousness" among students at Stanford is a logical reason to create the Stanford Community Farm?

2. According to Halweil, how will students benefit from having a community farm on the campus? Does his plan seem reasonable? Feasible?

Analyzing the Genre

1. What are some appeals that Halweil makes to convince his audience that the community garden is a worthy project in which to invest resources?

2. Halweil does not attend to any "differing views" in his proposal. To what extent do you think this weakens his argument? What are some of the possible counterarguments to his argument?

James Jay Carafano, Ph.D. "Fighting Terrorism, Addressing Liability: A Global Proposal"

James Jay Carafano is the director of the Allison Center for Foreign Policy Studies and the deputy director of the Kathryn and Shelby Cullom Davis Institute for International Studies at the Heritage Foundation. He was a lieutenant colonel in the Army before retiring, and holds degrees from Georgetown University and the U.S. Army War College. Since 2003 he has worked for the Heritage Foundation, which is "is a research and educational institution . . . whose mission is to formulate and promote conservative public policies based on the principles of free enterprise, limited government, individual freedom, traditional American values, and a strong national defense."

Homeland security is a global enterprise. Almost every aspect of keeping Americans safe, free, and prosperous in the face of transnational terrorism requires cooperation with friends and allies.

In some cases, this collaboration requires joint programs in which nations learn from each other by sharing best practices. The challenges are to make this cooperation efficient and effective without compromising the sovereignty of individual nations or impinging on the rights and liberties of their citizens. One area that is ripe for enhanced international cooperation is third-party liability for terrorist attacks.

The recent bitter debate between Congress and the Administration about whether to extend immunity from civil suits to telecommunications companies that cooperated with a classified government surveillance program highlights one of the knotty challenges involved in promoting public—private cooperation in the fight against terrorism.[1] Whether companies act or fail to act to prevent an act of terrorism, the courts may be asked to hold someone accountable for any damages.

In contrast to its attitude toward telecom companies, after the terrorist attacks of September 11, 2001, Congress became so concerned about rampant lawsuits over alleged failure to prevent the attacks, as well as claims of contributing to the catastrophic losses suffered in their aftermath, that it quickly passed legislation that limited third-party liability. Congress extended these protections to the airlines involved, the New York Port Authority, and the city government as well as the Dulles, Portland, and Boston airports.

In addition, Congress established a Victim Compensation Fund for individuals (or their families) and businesses for death, injury, and losses result-

---

1. See James Jay Carafano, Robert Alt, and Andrew M. Grossman, "Congress Must Stop Playing Politics with FISA and National Security," Heritage Foundation *WebMemo* No. 1791, January 31, 2008, at *http://www.heritage.org/Research/LegalIssues/wm1791.cfm*.

ing directly from the attacks or the response at the scene. Businesses received the largest share of compensation—62 percent of the payments.[2]

These very different responses from Congress regarding third-party liability reflect the struggle within government over how best to deal with the thorny issues that surround the nation's response to terrorist threats.

Since 9/11, Congress has acted decisively and to good effect in one area of liability protection: The Support Anti-Terrorism by Fostering Effective Technologies (SAFETY) Act lowered the liability risks of manufacturers that provide products and services used in combating terrorism. The act, passed in 2002, protects the incentive to produce products that the Secretary of Homeland Security designates as "Qualified Anti-Terrorism Technologies." The Department of Homeland Security (DHS) has made a concerted effort to implement the program, and about 200 companies have obtained SAFETY Act certification.

The SAFETY Act provides protections to "sellers" (manufacturers, distributors, and providers) for cases under the jurisdiction of U.S. courts. Terrorism, however, is a global threat, and homeland security is a global mission. From securing the border to protecting global supply chains, virtually every aspect of preventing terrorist attacks has an international dimension that requires the United States to work effectively with friends and allies.[3] Other countries should consider similar liability-protection regimes to provide the industrial base of all free nations with incentives to develop and adopt the best tools to fight terrorism no matter where they are manufactured or employed.

The best way to promote effective international cooperation is on a bilateral basis. Nations bear the primary responsibility for protecting their citizens. In turn, nations must collaborate with one another to protect their mutual interests. The United States can contribute to this cause most effectively by continuing to develop and strengthen the implementation of the SAFETY Act and by sharing best practices and lessons learned with other countries. Meanwhile, other nations should establish their own liability-protection regimes.

Acting Safe

Since 9/11, insurance premiums for all terrorism-related risks have skyrocketed, and a gradually increasing number of firms have stopped offering terrorism insurance.[4] Many companies proved hesitant to market anti-terrorism

2. Lloyd Dixon and Rachel Kaganoff Stern, *Compensation for Losses from the 9/11 Attacks* (Santa Monica, Cal.: RAND, 2004).

3. James Jay Carafano and Richard Weitz, "Enhancing International Collaboration for Homeland Security and Counterterrorism," Heritage Foundation *Backgrounder* No. 2078, October 18, 2007, at *http://www.heritage.org/Research/HomelandDefense/bg2078.cfm*.

4. Richard Hillman, "Terrorism Insurance: Rising Uninsured Exposure to Attacks Heightens Potential Economic Vulnerabilities," testimony before the Subcommittee on Oversight and Investigations, Committee on Financial Services, U.S. House of Representatives, February 27, 2002, at *http://www.gao.gov/new.items/d02472t.pdf* (May 14, 2008).

technologies because of two concerns: the costs of potentially devastating jury verdicts should the technologies fail and the costs and scarcity of adequate liability insurance.

Congress intended the SAFETY Act to serve as a critical tool for promoting the creation, proliferation, and use of technologies to fight terrorism.[5] The act provides risk- and litigation-management protections for producers of Qualified Anti-Terrorism Technologies and other providers in the supply and distribution chain. Specifically, it created liability limitation from third-party claims for losses resulting from an act of terrorism where the technologies were deployed to help identify, deter, defend against, respond to, or mitigate the danger of a terrorist attack.

The term "Qualified Anti-Terrorism Technologies" covers a broad spectrum of products and services. Certification eligibility can be extended to:

- Threat and vulnerability assessment,
- Detection systems,
- Blast-mitigation materials,
- Screening services,
- Sensors and sensor integration,
- Threatening-object detectors,
- Decision-support software,
- Security services, and
- Crisis-management services.

The SAFETY Act also encourages the development of software and other forms of intellectual property. In 2007, certification was awarded to IBM for a software application that improves the accuracy of name searching and identity verification. Overall, the certifications that have been awarded have a broad and significant impact on the everyday security of Americans.

The certification program is managed by the DHS Directorate for Science and Technology. The Office of SAFETY Act Implementation will conduct the application review using statutory criteria to assess various technologies:

- *Technical capabilities and efficacy.* The department must establish the suitability and limitations of the product or service.

- *Economic effects of deployment vs. non-deployment.* DHS must perform a risk assessment to determine how vital deployment might be in fighting terrorism.

---

5. *Federal Register,* Vol. 71, No. 110 (June 8, 2006), pp. 33147–33168, at *http://a257.g.akamaitech. net/7/257/2422/01jan20061800/edocket.access.gpo.gov/2006/06-5223.htm* (May 13, 2008).

- *Evaluation of insurance needs.* Before a technology receives a rating as a Qualified Anti-Terrorism Technology, DHS must evaluate the amount of liability insurance to be maintained for coverage of the technology and certify that it is appropriate to satisfy claims that result from an act of terrorism. The SAFETY Act also stipulates that providers are not required to obtain insurance in excess of the maximum reasonable amount. The cost of insurance should not unreasonably distort the sales price of the technology.

The office also maintains a pre-application process so that businesses can get a fast initial opinion about whether they have the potential for certification before they undertake the time and expense of the full application process. The pre-application assessment is done at no cost to the business.

In assessing the applications, DHS considers a number of factors:

- Results from operational tests that demonstrate products' real-world performance,
- Documentation of product performance on previous deployments,
- Assessments by experts,
- Feedback from customers,
- Quality-assurance plans, and
- Audit results.

Throughout the assessment process, DHS employs safeguards to protect proprietary information and sensitive data.

The SAFETY Act provides two different levels of liability protection: designation and certification. The seller's liability for products or services that are deemed "designated technologies" is limited to the amount of liability insurance that the Department of Homeland Security determines the seller must maintain. Designation can also be obtained for promising anti-terrorism technologies that are undergoing testing and evaluation.

In addition to the benefits provided under designation, certification allows a seller of an antiterrorism technology to assert the "government contractor defense" (if the government is immune from a lawsuit, the private contractor is too) for claims arising from acts of terrorism. Technologies that receive certification will be placed on DHS's Approved Products List for Homeland Security.[6]

SAFETY Act protection provides a number of advantages. If claims are made against Qualified Anti-Terrorism Technologies that have received a

---

6. Regulations Implementing the Support Anti-Terrorism by Fostering Effective Technologies Act of 2002, "Benefits to Your Company," June 6, 2006, at *https://www.safetyact.gov* (May 14, 2008).

"designation," the claims can be made only in a federal court. Even if the court rules against the defendant, the plaintiff can recover damages only in proportion to the degree of fault of the technology for failure to prevent the attack. In other words, companies may only be liable for the percentage of damages proportionate to their responsibility for the harm done. Thus, if the court finds a terrorist cell 50 percent responsible for a successful attack and the technology 50 percent responsible for failing to prevent the attack, then the company providing the technology must pay only half of the damages. Plaintiffs also cannot sue for punitive damages.

Technologies that receive a "certification" have an established claim to complete liability immunity for manufacturers and their customers. They are allowed to claim the government contractor defense. SAFETY Act certification applies whether the provider delivers goods or services to government or private clients. Plaintiffs challenging this defense would have to prove the defendant guilty of "fraudulent or willful misconduct."

Keeping the SAFETY Act Safe

Although the protections of the SAFETY Act have yet to be tested in court, there are many signs that the law is working as intended. DHS took a "crawl, walk, run" approach to implementing the certification process. In its first year and a half of operation, the program approved six certifications. In fiscal year 2007, the program approved 81 applications, an 83 percent increase over all approvals attained over the previous three years. In February 2008, DHS gave its 200th approval.[7] As companies learn about the program and understand the application process and protections offered, they are lining up in growing numbers to apply—surely a sign that the private sector is gaining confidence in the program and remains keenly interested in bringing new counterterrorism technologies to the marketplace.

To satisfy the increasing demand, the Office of SAFETY Act Implementation has expanded. About 420 experts are now available to review applications, including 90 trained reviewers in seven threat areas: in cyberspace and the economy, as well as chemical, biological, explosive, radiological, and human threats.

Despite the progress that has been made, however, the future of the SAFETY Act is not secure. Congress has engaged in a bitter debate over providing immunity protections to telecommunication companies that voluntarily cooperated with the U.S. government in the Terrorist Surveillance Program.[8] Six years after 9/11, Congress has demonstrated its increasing reluctance to

---

7. U.S. Department of Homeland Security, Office of SAFETY Act Implementation, *The SAFETY Act*, p. 11, at *https://www.safetyact.gov* (May 14, 2008).

8. For program description, see Jeffrey W. Seifert, "Data Mining and Homeland Security: An Overview," Congressional Research Service *Report for Congress Update*, January 18, 2007, pp. 18–20, at *http://www.fas.org/sgp/crs/intel/RL31798.pdf* (May 14, 2008).

limit tort action—even for the purpose of reducing the threat of terrorist attacks. Opposition to a proposed Senate bill, the Protect America Act, may presage an effort to roll back private-sector liability protections.[9]

Another issue of concern is the controversy that surrounded the September 11 Victim Compensation Fund of 2001, intended to compensate victims or their families in exchange for their agreement not to sue private-sector entities.[10] After the next terrorist attack, Congress might prove reluctant to rely on similar solutions. A RAND study concluded that, "while the government programs put in place after 9/11 create a precedent for programs that might be adopted after a future attack, there is no guarantee that similar programs will be adopted in the future."[11] The next time, rather than providing tort liability protections to the private sector, Congress might prove anxious to place the issue in the hands of civil courts, which would likely result in bitter, protracted, and expensive litigation battles.

Neither DHS nor the private sector can assume that Congress will allow the SAFETY Act to stand over time. In order to keep the program moving forward and to fight off the special-interest tort lawyers who would prefer an "open field" for litigation, DHS must continue to improve the program and demonstrate its efficacy. To this end, the Department of Homeland Security should:

- **Encourage** new entrants into the SAFETY Act process, including owners of critical infrastructure facilities and operators of "soft" targets like sports stadiums, shopping malls, and amusement parks.

- **Continue** to refine the assessment process and maintain a thorough but not unduly burdensome auditing program to demonstrate the efficacy of DHS certifications.

- **Ensure** that the certification process also addresses civil liberty and privacy concerns, since many technologies are used in the surveillance and screening of U.S. citizens.

- **Carefully implement** the Developmental Testing and Evaluation Designations to avoid undermining the credibility of the SAFETY Act protections. This level of liability protection was added in the 2006 DHS final rule to give companies an incentive to invest in research and development and the testing, evaluation, and marketing of products not yet fully developed.[12]

9. Andrew M. Grossman, "FISA Modernization Is Not About 'Warrantless Wiretapping,'" Heritage Foundation *WebMemo* No. 1847, March 12, 2008, at *http://www.heritage.org/Research/LegalIssues/wm1847.cfm.*

10. James R. Copland, "Tragic Solutions: The 9/11 Victim Compensation Fund, Historical Antecedents, and Lessons for Tort Reform," Manhattan Institute, Center for Legal Policy, January 13, 2005, pp. 22–24, at *http://www.manhattan-institute.org/pdf/clpwp_01-13-05.pdf* (May 14, 2008).

11. Dixon and Stern, *Compensation for Losses from the 9/11 Attacks,* p. 140.

12. Federal Register, Vol. 71, No. 110.

Implementing these measures quickly and with due diligence would both enhance the credibility of the certification process and encourage more and more companies to seek SAFETY Act protections. The more widely it is employed, the less likely it is that Congress will try to scale back the program.

Going Global

In addition to moving the program forward, DHS should make a concerted effort to document best practices and lessons learned in order to share them with America's allies. In addition, other nations should establish their own liability protections. The U.S. Department of State should collaborate with the Department of Homeland Security to establish a deliberate and effective outreach program.

One potential source of outreach might be the Technical Cooperation Program (TTCP), an international organization that collaborates in defense-related scientific and technical information exchange and shared research activities with Australia, Canada, New Zealand, the United Kingdom, and the United States. TTCP is one of the world's largest collaborative science and technology forums.

Outreach might focus initially on U.S. partners in Asia including Japan, Australia, New Zealand, Taiwan, South Korea, India, Hong Kong, and Singapore. Singapore is the United States' 15th-largest trading partner and ninth-largest export market. Foreign direct investment in Singapore is concentrated largely in technical service sectors; manufacturing; information; and professional scientific knowledge, skills, and processes.[13]

As national liability protection proliferates, new opportunities for international cooperation will emerge. Countries that adopt verifiably similar liability protections should extend reciprocal privileges to one another.

An expanding global web of liability protection will facilitate the proliferation of anti-terrorism technologies. The benefits would likely include:

- Security-assistance sales, lease, and grant programs that would allow DHS to assist other countries in obtaining equipment, support services, and financing for homeland security functions.

- Increased international collaboration for research, development, and sharing of security technologies, coordinated by the DHS Directorate of Science and Technology, through such instrumentalities as a new international clearinghouse for technical information.

Promoting liability-protection programs should be the centerpiece of a comprehensive global homeland security outreach program.[14]

---

13. Office of the U.S. Trade Representative, "Singapore," at *http://www.ustr.gov/World_Regions/Southeast_Asia_Pacific/Singapore/Section_Index.html* (March 7, 2008).

14. For specific recommendations, see James Jay Carafano, Jonah J. Czerwinski, and Richard Weitz, "Homeland Security Technology, Global Partnerships, and Winning the Long War," Heritage Foundation *Backgrounder* No. 1977, October 5, 2006, at *http://www.heritage.org/Research/HomelandSecurity/bg1977.cfm*

Conclusion

For the makers of anti-terrorism technologies and their suppliers and customers, the SAFETY Act provides the means to reduce the burden of liability insurance by lowering potential liability payments from claims resulting from a terrorist attack. At the same time, the SAFETY Act program encourages businesses to engage and do what they do best—create and innovate.

The Department of Homeland Security should continue to invest in this program. Congress should fully fund the activities of the Office of SAFETY Act Implementation and not alter the authorities of DHS under the act. Finally, DHS and the State Department should work as a team to engage other nations in a serious dialogue on expanding the umbrella of liability protection for effective antiterrorism technologies to all free nations.

—James Jay Carafano, Ph.D., is Assistant Director of the Kathryn and Shelby Cullom Davis Institute for International Studies and Senior Research Fellow for National Security and Homeland Security in the Douglas and Sarah Allison Center for Foreign Policy Studies at The Heritage Foundation. Heritage intern Gabriela Herrera contributed to this paper.

Reading for Comprehension

1. Carafano is focusing on one aspect of the global war on terrorism and that is the "third-party liability for terrorist attacks." What does he mean by this statement?
2. Carafano discusses the Support Anti-Terrorism by Fostering Effective Technologies (SAFETY) Act at some length. What is the SAFETY Act and what is its purpose?
3. On page 445, Carafano explains that "the SAFETY Act provides two different levels of liability protection: designation and certification." Explain those different levels.

Analyzing the Genre

1. How does Carafano establish the problem? What does the way he discusses the problem assume about his audience?
2. Carafano never really addresses differing views, instead making the assumption that his audience will largely accept what he says. Given the kinds of support he provides and the manner in which he discusses the issue, is his assumption a safe one? Why?

Patricia Sulak, MD, "Adolescent Sexual Health"

Patricia Sulak is a professor of obstetrics and gynecology at Texas A&M University Health Science Center College of Medicine in Temple, Texas. She has published numerous articles on adolescent sexuality and the use of contraception. This report appeared in the July 2004 issue of the *Journal of Family Practice*. That journal, according to its website, publishes current research for physicians, aiming to provide "the results of the most relevant, valid research into a form useful to practicing family physicians."

Teenage sexual activity has significant consequences: sexually transmitted diseases (STDs), pregnancy, social and economic disruption, and legal implications. Of the 15 million new cases of STDs that occur each year in the United States, 10 million occur in people aged 15 to 24.[1] Each year, over 400,000 infants are born to teenagers: more than 146,000 are born to those 17 years of age or younger.[2] In 2000, 18% of reported abortions in the United States were performed on teenagers.[3]

STDs in Adolescents

Adolescents aged 10 to 19 years of age are at a higher risk than adults for acquiring STDs because of the likelihood of having multiple and high-risk sexual partners and because adolescents are more susceptible to infection.[4]

Bacterial infections often lead to pelvic inflammatory disease (PID). Although no symptoms may be present initially, the end result may be pelvic pain, infertility, tubal pregnancy, and increased risk of acquiring human immunodeficiency virus (HIV) infection. Viral infections, such as herpes simplex virus (HSV) and HIV, cause severe disease, disability, or fatality in newborns. Significantly, the highest rates of HSV occur with intercourse before age 18 and multiple sexual partners.[5,6]

Similarly, genital human papillomavirus (HPV) infection, the most common STD, is most common among women who become sexually active in the midadolescent years and have multiple sexual partners[7]: 50% to 75% of sexually active women have been infected, and approximately 15% show evidence of current infection. These adolescents often have abnormal Papanicolaou (Pap) smears.[8] In a study of 80 sexually active adolescents younger than 20 years of age, 90% had HPV evidence in their cervix and 75% in their urine: 38% had abnormal Pap smears. Other STDs were frequent: 15% had chlamydial infection, 6.3% gonorrhea, and 11.3% trichomonal infection.[9,10] Genital HPV is a precursor for cancer of the vulva, cervix, and anus. One in 4 individuals newly infected with HPV is younger than 22 years.[11]

Adolescents and Pregnancy

Sexually active adolescents account for approximately 10% of all births.[12] The consequences are profound. Children of adolescent mothers are more likely than those of older women to be premature and of low birthweight, have poor health, grow up in a household without a father, run away from home, be physically abused, and be abandoned or neglected. Daughters are more likely to become teenage mothers; sons are more likely to be imprisoned than are children born to older women. The economic impact has been estimated at $29 billion per year.[13]

Birth control devices and hormonal formulations are often an ineffective solution in this age-group. Teens have higher pregnancy rates with all birth control methods when compared with adults. Hormonal methods do not protect against STDs. Condoms have a high failure rate for preventing pregnancy, so the rate of failure in protecting against STDs also should be assumed to be high. Additionally, STDs can infect areas of the body not covered by condoms.

Delaying Onset of Sexual Activity

Adolescents who are sexually active should be encouraged to seek medical care.

Data suggest that family and school connectedness are associated with delayed onset of sexual activity.[14] Recent surveys by the National Campaign to Prevent Teen Pregnancy revealed that teens regard parents as more influential than friends, religious leaders, teachers, sex educators, the media, and others.[15] These surveys also have consistently shown that most sexually active adolescents wish they had waited to have sex.

Fortunately, fewer teenagers are having sexual intercourse. In a 2001 survey, 42.9% of high-school females reported that they had had intercourse, compared with 50.8% in 1991.[16] The birth rate for teenagers declined 5% between 2001 and 2002, dropping to the lowest level in 60 years.[12]

Healthcare professionals can help their adolescent patients make intelligent decisions to delay sexual activity by talking to their patients, giving accurate information, and becoming involved in providing sex education within their communities to help adolescents understand that sexual activity is not limited to intercourse (ie, STDs can be spread by a variety of contacts) and to be aware of the long-term risks and consequences of adolescent sexual activity.

References

1. American Social Health Association/Kaiser Family Foundation. *Sexually Transmitted Diseases in America: How Many Cases and at What Cost?* Menlo Park, Calif: Kaiser Family Foundation; 1998.

2. Martin JA, Hamilton BE, Sutton PD, et al. Births: final data for 2002. *Natl Vital Stat Rep.* 2003;52:1-113.

3. Elam-Evans LD, Strauss LT, Herndon J, et al. Abortion surveillance-United States, 2000. *MMWR Surveill Summ.* 2003;52:1-32.

4. Division of STD Prevention. *Sexually Transmitted Disease Surveillance, 1997.* US Department of Health and Human Services, Public Health Service. Atlanta, Ga: Centers for Disease Control and Prevention. 1998:62.

5. Fleming DT, McQuillan GM, Johnson RE, et al. Herpes simplex virus type 2 in the United States, 1976 to 1994. *N Engl J Med.* 1997;337:1105-1111.

6. Wald A, Zeh J, Selke S, et al. Reactivation of genital herpes simplex virus type 2 infection in asymptomatic seropositive persons. *N Engl J Med.* 2000;342:844-850.

7. DiSaia PJ, Creasman WT, eds. *Clinical Gynecologic Oncology,* 5th ed. St. Louis. Mo: Mosby: 1989.

8. Ho GY, Bierman R, Beardsley L, et al. Natural history of cervicovaginal papillomavirus infection in young women. *N Engl J Med.* 1998; 338: 423-428.

9. Jacobson DL, Womack SD, Peralta L, et al. Concordance of human papillomavirus in the cervix and urine among inner city adolescents. *Pediatr Infect Dis J.* 2000;19:722-728.

10. Koutsky L, Epidemiology of genital human papillomavirus infection. *Am J Med.* 1997:102:3-8.

11. National Institutes of Health. *HIV Infection in Adolescents and Young Adults.* May 2004. Available at: http://www.niaid.nih.gov/factsheets/ hivadolescent.htm. Accessed June 16, 2004.

12. The Alan Guttmacher Institute. *Facts in Brief: Teen Sex and Pregnancy.* 1999. Available at http://www.agi-usa.org. Accessed June 16, 2004.

13. Maynard R. *Kids Having Kids: A Robin Hood Foundation Special Report on the Costs of Adolescent Childbearing.* New York, NY: Robin Hood Foundation; 1996:20.

14. Resnick MD, Bearman PS, Blum RW, et al. Protecting adolescents from harm. Findings from the National Longitudinal Study on Adolescent Health. *JAMA.* 1997;278:823-832.

15. National Campaign to Prevent Teen Pregnancy. With One Voice 2003: Americas' Adults and Teens Sound Off About Teen Pregnancy. December 2003. Available at http://www.teenpregnancy.org/resources/data/ pdf/ wov2003.pdf.

16. Grunbaum JA, Kann L, Kinchen SA, et al. Youth risk behavior surveillance—United States, 2001. *MMWR Surveill Summ.* 2002:51:1-64.

Reading for Comprehension

1. What are the health consequences for teens who have acquired a sexually transmitted disease?
2. Why does Sulak say that "birth control devices and hormonal formulations" are not effective?
3. How does Sulak claim health care professionals can help teens?

Analyzing the Genre

1. Why does Sulak begin her proposal with an introduction almost entirely comprised of statistics?
2. In her conclusion, Sulak notes that the teen pregnancy rate is decreasing. Why does she wait until the end to reveal this to her audience? Why not include it in the introduction?

For examples of other proposals, see Patrick Merrigan's research proposal, "Civic Duties: Fixing the Problem of Civic Engagement in Two Easy Steps" (pages 415–421) and Jay Weiner's editorial, "Sports Centered" (pages 42–44).

Proposals

Write a proposal that defines a problem facing a particular audience (community, workplace, school, etc.) and proposes a workable solution to the problem. Conduct research to define and explore the problem and offer a well-developed, feasible solution. The issue must be a public concern; that is, it must affect an audience that would read the proposal and be called upon to take action.

Proposal Assignment Options

1. Write an academic proposal to secure funds for an academic research project. Identify the questions or problems your grant will research and the need for such work to be done in the project's field.
2. Write a research proposal for an academic paper in your discipline of study. Be sure to include your research questions, your methods to conduct the research, your resources, and why the study is significant and to whom. Include a reference list of works cited in your proposal.
3. Write a proposal for a novel or nonfiction book for submission to a publisher. Include a brief biography of yourself, an overview of the plot or argument of the book, what makes your book unique (or different), how it compares to other, similar books, who the intended audience is, what the tone will be, and what readers will get from reading it.
4. Write a business proposal in which you bid on a job or service to be provided for a customer. Include an explanation of why you'd be the best person to perform the service, a budget outlining the costs, and a timeline for when the job would get done.
5. Write a proposal in which you position yourself as a member of a particular advocacy group or organization. In the proposal, clearly delineate the issue or problem your group addresses for an audience that may be unfamiliar with the group and propose a solution to the problem.

Community-based Writing Option

No matter the community you live in or belong to—college dormitory, sprawling suburban town, local advocacy group—problems abound. Locate a local problem that interests you and affects a particular local audience (e.g. an assisted living community with a population of residents who have no family in the area, a literacy program in your town that is about to lose their funding, and so on). Research the problem and identify and develop a workable solution. Consult with the people affected by the problem and the people who have the abilities to implement the plan you describe in your proposal.

Writing Proposals

Writers of proposals have a lot of options, but there are certain characteristics of proposals that all writers should be aware of. Understanding these characteristics can help writers make choices about what to say and how to say it.

WHAT WRITERS CONSIDER WHEN WRITING PROPOSALS

In general, proposal writers do the following:

- Consider issues that are arguable, specific, and researchable
- Define the issue as a problem or concern in need of a solution
- Consider the rhetorical situation
- Use research to define and understand the problem or concern
- Understand and refute opposing viewpoints
- Provide a feasible, workable, and reasonable solution

Generating Ideas for Proposals

Imagining ideas for proposals isn't difficult—there are many possibilities in the social, political, and cultural issues that you already care about, hear about in the news, or witness in your own communities. As you consider what you want to write about, first think about concerns that you or those around you have. Working with a subject that reflects your own interests and groups you belong to increases your chances of developing the most persuasive and feasible proposal that you can.

Avoiding Common Proposal Pitfalls

There are several things to avoid when choosing a proposal topic.

1. *The unwieldy proposal.* Often writers take on problems that may be too great in scope—or perhaps too costly or too time-consuming—to address adequately in a proposal. In turn, the proposal readers would not be persuaded to adopt it. So when considering the issue or problem for your proposal, narrow down the particular problem to one your proposal solutions can handle. Think about the feasibility, resources available, and so on.

2. *The vague proposal.* Since proposals aim to solve problems facing particular communities or groups about issues affecting them, the problem in a proposal should be defined specifically. Readers expect a detailed account of the problem and *why* it is in fact a problem for them, and perhaps even want to know the consequences if the problem is not addressed. Solutions cannot be carried out by readers if they do not have a clear understanding of the issue at stake. Vague problem statements lead to vague solutions, or ones that readers cannot imagine doing anything about.

WRITING ACTIVITY   Generating Ideas for Proposals

When thinking of topics for persuasive genres like proposals, writers must think about the particular audience that would be affected by the proposal and offer solutions that meet their needs and address their concerns. As you generate topics, consider some problems faced by the people you encounter each day, the issues faced by others on a national or global level, or local problems that affect particular communities.

Strategies for Generating Ideas

- Make a list of problems you observe in your everyday experiences. The places you go often (e.g. work, swim team practice, etc.), the people you encounter frequently (family, coworkers, etc.), and the groups or organizations you belong to (hobbyists, community organizations, etc.) all may face problems. What kinds of issues do these people or groups face? How does your relationship to these groups enable you to offer a solution to a problem they have?
- Make a list of the issues or concerns that come up in the material you read for classes or on your own. How do they affect you or others?
- Make a list of current national or global problems that interest or concern you. How do these national or global issues affect your life *locally* (in your state or town)?
- Make a list of policies or programs that you are involved with and think need to be changed. Write a list of the issues that the policies or programs are concerned with. How do these policies or programs affect the lives of people involved directly?

Thinking Through the Problems and Solutions

Choose three possible problems from your lists above and write responses to the following:

1. What do you already know about the problems and what do you want to find out?
2. What possible solutions to the problems can you imagine? Which seem feasible?
3. Whose lives would these problems affect? Who might be able to carry out the proposed solutions?

■ ■ ■

Narrowing Your Focus: From Topic to Issue

While you'll begin developing your proposal by selecting a topic, you'll need to narrow it down into *issues*. A **topic** is a broad concept that needs defining; its audience and purpose are vague, and it isn't arguable.

An **issue,** however, is more focused and prompts specific questions by writers and readers alike. Issues are specific, researchable, and arguable. For issues, the audience and purpose, the *who* and *why,* are clearly defined and explicitly articulated.

Take a broad topic . . .	*. . . and ask a question to reveal an issue:*
Assessment in public schools	Are we assessing our students too early in their schooling?
Global warming	How can local communities reduce their overall carbon emissions?
Illegal immigration	How can we encourage local businesses to hire legal immigrants or naturalized citizens?

Notice how asking a question about a topic reveals *an issue* at stake. That question leads, in turn, to *other questions* that we could consider in a proposal to address the issue. For example:

- Is the current plan to assess high school student learning necessary?
- Does assessment tell us what we want to find out about student learning?
- Should the policy of funding public schools based on assessment outcomes or test scores be changed?

These issues are narrow, specific, and arguable; they are suitable subject matter for proposals. See Chapter 13: Research and the Rhetorical Situation (pages 501–539) for further discussion on topics and issues.

WRITING ACTIVITY   From Broad Topic to Focused Issue

Choose a proposal topic, and then respond to the following questions to narrow the focus of your topic to a manageable issue.

1. What are the problems, concerns, or questions associated with your topic?
2. Why is your topic important? In other words, why do people care about it? What are they saying about it?
3. Who would benefit from or could implement the proposed solution?

■ ■ ■

Thinking about Audience, Purpose, and Situation

Thinking about the larger rhetorical and social context of your issue can be a great help in both refining the issue and coming up with solutions. Since a problem or issue is read and understood differently by different groups or individuals, it's also important to be clear about who you are writing to and why before you get too far along in the writing process.

Audience and the Issue

One way to think about your audience is to imagine readers who do not already see the problem the way you do and your job is to help them do so. In the example earlier in this chapter about after-school activities for teenagers, two *problems* were identified: activities that didn't interest teenagers; and lack of transportation preventing teens from participating because they had no way to get to where the activities are held. But your audience might not agree with your definition of the problem. For example, some residents of the town opposed to creating after-school programs for teenagers might assume that the problem is not that teenagers have nothing to do, it's that some parents are not taking care of their kids, and so why should the town overcome *their* bad parenting by offering activities? You can see the gulf that exists between your view and theirs, but as the proposal writer, you have to find a way to bridge that gulf or your solution won't be considered. Thus thinking about audience more critically helps you to see the issue from perspectives on the problem different from your own.

Purpose and Issue

Defining your audience in turn leads to refining your purpose. While your purpose may seem straightforward, it is generally more complex than you think. As a proposal writer, you may think your purpose is to convince your audience that your *solution* is good and should be implemented. But you must first clarify the problem so your audience understands it. Your purpose, then, is to present the problem in an accurate, comprehensive, and fair way. Only after you have defined the problem can you turn to your solutions as the logical way to proceed.

Situation and Issue

Your audience doesn't exist in a vacuum. Its members have real needs, opinions, and interests within the *larger* social situation in which the proposal is being written: the time and place; the cultural climate, and the values and beliefs important to the audience and the writer. And the local, immediate situation also drives the proposal: the audience the problem affects and the solution that benefits them; and readers who can carry out the proposed solutions.

In the scenario about teen after-school programs, the more that is known about the immediate situation, the more the issue—and thus the problem the writer addresses—changes. For example, if there has been a rash of crimes recently in the community, residents might be looking to blame someone—so why not those unruly teenagers? Knowing this would change the way the problem and solution are presented. Or recent budget cuts might have resulted in fewer public services (plowing, garbage pickup), and so residents might balk at having to pay for transporting teenagers to activities or even funding such activities. All of this information would change the way the proposal is written.

WRITING ACTIVITY   Defining the Rhetorical Situation for Your Proposal
_____

Understanding the larger rhetorical situation of your proposal will help you not only develop the problem and the solution, but also to anticipate possible opposition to the proposal.

1. What social situation is driving the proposal to be written? That is, why is this situation a problem that needs a solution (or solutions) *now*?
2. Who is talking about the issue? What are they saying?
3. Who is the audience for the proposal? Why this audience for this particular issue? What values, concerns, and interests of the audience should you pay attention to?
4. What can your audience do about the issue or problem? Why would they want to?
5. What is the message or purpose of the proposal?
6. Will your audience automatically agree with your understanding of the problem or is part of your work going to be to define the problem differently for them? What is the focus of the proposal?

■　■　■

Here's how one student, Jamie Morello, answered these questions about her issue of sexual assault of women in college. Notice how tentative her answers are—this is, after all, early in the writing process. But also notice how she works through the questions so that by the time she answers the question about purpose, she is more clearly identifying the social situation.

Jamie Morello
Defining Audience, Purpose, and Situation

Proposal Topic: Rape and Sexual Assault on College Campuses

The social situation driving the issue of alcohol related rapes/sexual assaults on college campuses is that it's a very large problem that affects many people—not just the women who are assaulted. These are big issues, and not much is being done about them for college students, at least from my experience. There are not enough prevention programs, and women don't always know how to protect themselves. They also don't know how to report the crimes or even if they should report them, because alcohol was involved.

The audience would be a school board, administration, or something along those lines, because they would be the ones that I have to convince to implement a prevention program or hire a new counselor specifically for rape victims.

My purpose is to convince administrators to have a sexual assault prevention program for students just coming into college where they learn preventative methods against rape and sexual assault. I may be able to incorporate the idea of having counselors specific to those who have been raped because that would go along with the program, but the main purpose would be to convince college administrators to implement a prevention program.

Morello's initial writing reveals a lot of connected issues.

Notice how Morello is working out some solutions to the problem early on.

Arriving at a Solution

Defining a problem is only part of the work of a proposal—the other is offering a workable and reasonable solution given the audience (who will be helped by it and who will implement it) and the problem itself. A solution needs to actually address the problem and not create bigger problems in the process. Thus, you'll want to think about your solution rhetorically, just as you did the problem.

Let's return to the example of a lack of after-school activities for teenagers. The possible solutions were 1) after-school programs; 2) places for teenagers to go; and 3) transportation. Given how we have defined our audience and the problem, these seem like pretty good solutions. Let's say that upon further research, we discover that there are already existing programs and places for them to happen. The town can consolidate them and all we need to do is get the kids there—the transportation. So we propose that the town provide transportation to the facilities free of charge. End of story.

Creating Solutions That Address the Problem

But what we have failed to consider are the following about our solution: 1) Who will drive the busses? The current bus drivers? Will their contract allow it? 2) What kind of insurance is going to be needed to cover any injuries or mishaps and to protect the town from lawsuits? 3) Who will supervise all these "new" kids swarming into the old programs and buildings? 4) Will parents have to pick their kids up at the program center or will they be returned to school? And so on.

So even seemingly straightforward solutions can lead to more problems. This is not to say that this particular solution is not workable, but it does suggest that this proposal writer needs to acknowledge—if not solve—the attendant problems.

In your proposal, you will need to give your audience a clear definition of the problem, possible consequences of your solution (and how those might be addressed), and how the solution will be implemented. As you offer the solution(s), consider the details readers need to know to carry out the plan successfully. Make sure your readers know that your solution matches the problem and doesn't cause other ones to arise.

WRITING ACTIVITY   Finding Possible Solutions to the Problem

Once you have identified the problem, it's time to consider possible solutions. At this stage of your proposal writing, you should feel free to be as creative as you can.

1. *Consider the obvious solutions first.* Does your issue or problem suggest any immediate solutions?
2. *Consider stock solutions that you might modify for your issue.* For example, can a new program be implemented or an old one ended? Can taxes be raised? Can a policy be changed?
3. *Consider desired solutions.* If you were personally suffering from the problem, what would you *need* to have done to improve it? What would you *want* to have done? If you know someone suffering from the problem or affected by the issue, what do they need to adequately face the problem or deal with the issue?
4. *Consider the effects of solutions.* Who will be positively affected by your solution? Who might be *adversely* affected?
5. *Consider the merit of solutions.* Given your current understanding of the problem and your audience, are your solutions *feasible* and *workable*?
6. *Consider the comprehensiveness of solutions.* Given your current understanding of the problem and your audience, are your solutions sufficiently *complex*?

■ ■ ■

Researching Proposals

It might go without saying, but a proposal is a genre that requires research for the simple reason that we need to understand what the problem is before we can solve it, and we need to know that the solution we offer is based on sound reasoning. You've spent some time thinking about the problem and possible solutions, now turn to research to help you develop your understanding of the problem. You'll want to explore what others think about the problem, what they have done about it, what they have suggested as solutions, and whether or not those solutions worked. Finally, you need to know how others might view the problem differently so that you can *refute* their *counterarguments*. All of this takes research.

Conducting Background Research

To write a well thought-out proposal, you'll need to conduct background research: first, to expand your understanding of the problem so you can fully explain it to your audience; and second, to help you develop your solution and test it against what others have tried.

WRITING ACTIVITY   Identifying Necessary Research

Write down your issue or problem, and then answer the following questions. As you work through the questions, come up with a series of questions pertinent to your issue or problem.

1. What do you already know about the social situation of your issue? (For instance, why is it an issue? How long have people been concerned about it? What are others saying about it?)
2. What do you need to know about the problem? (For instance, has it affected other communities? How have they handled it?)
3. What does your audience need to know about the problem to understand it as you do?
4. What research should you do to fulfill your purpose or accomplish your goals in your proposal?
5. What types of research would fill in the gaps in your knowledge and provide supporting evidence for your claims?

See Chapter 13: Research and the Rhetorical Situation for instruction on conducting research.

■ ■ ■

Drafting Proposals

You've already defined a problem, come up with a solution, and conducted initial research for your proposal. You've also been thinking about what you want to say and how you can develop your ideas. As you begin to draft your proposal, you'll want to think about the kinds of arguments, or *claims,* you might make given your issue, purpose, and audience. The claims you provide to define the problem and offer a workable solution should consider the rhetorical situation in which the proposal is being written. Claims identify that the problem is in fact a problem that must be addressed. (For a detailed discussion of claims in an argument, see Chapter 3: Analyzing and Writing Arguments.) If your purpose is to change a policy, then your claims would show how the current policy is ineffective. If you are redefining or rethinking an issue for the audience, your claims would show how a new angle on the issue is worth considering. For example, in "An Immodest Proposal," the writers establish the problem early on by claiming the following:

> **Claim:** Families, communities, and the economy all depend heavily on caregiving work. Yet our economic system undervalues paid caregiving in the workforce and penalizes unpaid caregivers in the home.

Obviously, the argument that caregiving is undervalued must be supported by research that supports the claim. It needs evidence: How is caregiving undervalued? Are there attitudes reflected in policies that show this? Are there expert opinions that illustrate that point? The *how* question prompted by this claim warrants further evidence to develop the writers' statement. For each claim you make in your proposal, you need to develop the argument or point with supporting evidence. The type of evidence required depends on your issue and the solution you are proposing. For example, in "An Immodest Proposal," the claim above is supported with evidence that shows the problem causes impoverished conditions for caregivers.

> **Evidence:** Research also shows that unpaid caregiving work exposes many women to low wages, part-time jobs, sex discrimination, lower Social Security and unemployment insurance benefits, the double day, and other forms of gender inequality and stress.

The rhetorical situation for your proposal will determine the claims and evidence you use. For example, if you are arguing that SUVs are not as safe as American drivers think they are, then your evidence would provide information to show how perception of safety is flawed.

Topic:	SUVs and safety
Issue:	Are SUVs as safe as Americans are led to believe by car companies?
Audience:	The wary consumer
Purpose:	To persuade consumers to reconsider the safety of SUVs and reconsider purchasing one.
Claim:	Americans who believe that driving SUVs is safer than driving a sedan are being misled by car companies into a false sense of security.
Evidence:	A recent study by the NHSA published in *Consumer Reports* shows that more SUV accidents resulted in serious injury or death than reported accidents in sedans or station wagons.

For more on how to decide which claims are appropriate for the rhetorical situation of your writing, see Chapter 3: Analyzing and Writing Arguments.

WRITING ACTIVITY   Generating Claims

After you've done some background research and identified your audience and purpose for your proposal, make a list of possible claims to define the problem and create a workable solution.

Audience and Purpose: A Clue to Claims

What arguments will you need to make that concern your audience and their needs? What does your purpose suggest about the kinds of claims you need to make?

Differing Views and Claims

For those who differ with you about what the problem is and how to address it, what are some claims they might suggest? How might they understand the problem and suggest ways to fix it?

Research: Another Clue to Claims

What has your research revealed to you about your issue that you didn't know before? What kinds of claims will you need to develop to fill in readers on this information?

■   ■   ■

Addressing Differing Views

Some of the claims you make will be in response to what other people—those in your audience—might think about your proposal, including disagreeing with it. It's necessary for you to address their *differing views* because it shows you are a fair-minded writer and have seriously thought about the opinions of others. Furthermore, by addressing differing views you may show readers the flaws in their logic and convince them to reconsider your proposed solutions. Finally, examining differing views will help you to understand the problem from a wider perspective and, thus, allow you to think through the solution with more care and in greater depth. Your proposal will be stronger for doing so.

There are several ways to address differing views.

Refutation: When you refute a differing view, you disavow it entirely; you are saying, essentially, that the differing view is wrong, or inaccurate, and so on. This approach works best when the differing view is clearly opposite to your own. The risk you run, however, is alienating readers who may not be inclined to listen to your ideas if you say that they are wrong—so be wary about dismissing ideas unless you can point out clearly flawed logic or inaccuracy.

Concession: Often, though, differing views are not completely inaccurate, but instead have pieces that are useful, applicable, and even worth considering. So when you approach a differing view from a standpoint of concession, you are acknowledging that the author has some good points to make but maybe they are short-sighted or incompletely thought-out or are not entirely applicable to your situation, and so on.

Common ground: If you are entering into a discussion about an issue that you know is contentious, you should assume that your audience is aware of that contention and may perhaps be tired of the bickering. In this situation, the best approach might be to seek common ground with those who disagree with you. This approach might seem similar to "concession," but in this case you are actively seeking to bring the opposing group into your camp. You would do so by addressing the areas you agree on in order to find ways to move forward.

For examples of how writers work with differing views, please see Christina Schirone's proposal "Union University Students Need Our Help" on pages 471–476 and Patrick Merrigan's proposal "Civic Duties: Fixing the Problem of Civic Engagement in Two Easy Steps" on pages 415–421. For further instruction in differing views see Chapter 3 pages 61–88.

Organizing Proposals

Generally, proposals first identify a problem and then offer a solution. There are, however, other ways to organize your proposal, and you may decide to use a different organization pattern based on your audience and purpose. Writers often ask what does my audience need to know first? What should come after that?

Balancing the Proposal: Emphasizing the Issue or the Problem

Depending on the audience and purpose for the proposal, a writer might choose to provide a lot of background information to establish the problem, or to minimize background information and get straight to the solution. If the audience is already well informed about the situation, then the writer may spend more time on the solution, referring readers to information on the problem as arguments are being developed along with the solution.

For example, the writers of "An Immodest Proposal" assume the audience already is familiar with these policies and what they say, yet they take the time to remind readers of the situation driving the proposal:

> TANF is about to be reconsidered by Congress. The current funding for welfare reform—officially called Temporary Aid to Needy Families—ends in the fall of 2002. At that time, Congress will make major decisions about how much money to spend on welfare. . . .

So the writers, WC100, see this as an opportunity to reform the welfare policies affecting caregivers. The situation drives how they organize their opening. The writers organize their proposal by beginning with a brief introduction to establish the problem and exigency, then move right into their arguments for change in their solution:

> Our Project 2002 proposal calls for replacing TANF with a set of policies that address the economic plight faced by those doing the work of caregiving—most of whom are women. . . .

Each new subheading introduces a new argument solution, a new claim:

> **End the Caregiver's Penalty** . . . At a minimum, this means repealing the following TANF provisions: mandatory work outside the home, arbitrary time limits, child exclusion policies (family cap)

You'll notice how this argument is a very specific claim attending to particular parts of the current TANF policy that is about to end.

The final claim extends outward to more general arguments in the proposal:

> **Respect our Lives**. . . . unemployment insurance for part time workers, . . . universal access to higher education . . . etc.

This pattern of organization *emphasizing the solution* makes sense given the *audience* for the proposal, both legislators and caregivers themselves, who will be familiar with particular policies and current problems with TANF and other welfare legislation.

Writing Openings for Proposals

As with any writing you do, it's important to take into consideration what you know about your audience and purpose to help you figure out how to begin your proposal. One of the ways writers choose to begin their proposals is by explaining the *exigency* of the problem, or why the situation *demands* immediate action. Part of persuading people to either act, listen, or rethink the issue at stake involves showing them how they are affected and *what* might happen if nothing is done. So to open a proposal a writer might establish that the problem is actually a problem and get readers to see how they (or people they know) are affected by it.

For example, in "An Immodest Proposal," the topic is welfare reform—but the introduction lets readers know two things right away. First, the *exigency* of the social and political situation driving the proposal is the end of TANF (the current funding for welfare) in October 2002 and Congress's impending decisions on how to spend money on welfare policies. The writers see this moment as an opportunity for change in the welfare system. Second, WC100 writes the proposal in order to interject their ideas on how to re-envision the issue. So establishing the exigency and focusing readers on the issue as the writers see it are two ways the problem is established in the proposal's opening.

Openings could do any or all of the following *depending on the rhetorical situation*. Consider the questions below as you write your opening.

- How might you convince readers to keep reading your proposal by emphasizing the exigency of the situation? Is the problem urgent for readers to address or pay attention to? Openings often involve identifying the situation and the critical nature of it.
- Since a problem can be described in many different ways, how do you as the writer wish to describe the problem from your perspective?
- Might you show readers how others see the problem in your opening to give them a broad critical perspective of the issue?
- Would using an example or anecdote offer the readers some insights into the problem?
- How might you move the reader to listen to your proposal right away by establishing the consequences of the problem if it is left unaddressed? What are their needs and beliefs you might tap into here?

■ ■ ■

Writing Closings for Proposals

Because proposals are a "call-to-action" genre, your readers will expect you to do just that as you close your proposal. You'll want to motivate your audience to accept your solution, to remind them why they should care (or, for a really difficult audience, try one last time to get them to care in the first place), and to carry out the solution you have provided.

Depending on the rhetorical situation of your proposal, write your closing by using some of the questions below to help you think about your closing.

- Could you offer an anecdote that suggests the importance to readers of acting on your solution?
- Should your closing outline the consequences of what might happen if the problem is ignored?
- Would reminding the audience of why they should care about the problem help to convince them to act on your solutions?
- Could reminding the readers of your credentials as the writer of the proposal—who you are and why your expertise is worth listening to— suggest that you know firsthand that this solution can work?
- Would providing details in your closing about how the audience can get involved specifically (e.g. read a website, call a number, write a letter, etc.) prompt them to take action?

■ ■ ■

Revising Proposals

Your revision might involve revisiting your development of the problem, the research you use to support your claims, and the clarity and practicality of your solution. But there is one area that requires particular attention during the revision process because it is so central to the genre of proposals: the attention to differing views.

Addressing Differing Views

Differing views are important in proposals because they show readers that you have considered what others who disagree with you might think about a problem. Addressing differing views fairly builds the writer's credibility—readers perceive that the writer has researched the issue thoroughly and is well-informed about it. Fairness and credibility are important characteristics for proposal writers because they hope to gain readers' support.

GROUP ACTIVITY   *Understanding Differing Views*

The successful use of differing views is often difficult for a proposal writer to assess without some assistance from outside readers. In groups, examine the differing views being addressed by each writer and offer suggestions for revision.

Presenting Differing Views

Writer: Explain to your group briefly the problem and solution of your proposal, as well as its audience and purpose. Read one of the sections where you address the differing views others might have about the problem or the solution you've described.

Group: Do you think the differing views (what *others* have to say, not what the writer says) are adequately expressed? Does the kind of differing view the writer has chosen to include and address seem logical in the context of the paragraph? Does it make sense given the audience and purpose?

Responding to Differing Views

Writer: Read a section where you have responded to the differing views in the proposal.

Group: Are the responses effective and logical given the audience? Suggest ways the writer could better develop responses or counterarguments. What additional claims can the writer make in response to the differing views?

■　■　■

Matching Solutions to the Problems

As you revise your proposal, check for two important elements: First, the solutions should match the problems you've identified so that your readers will think your proposal is logical and they'll be persuaded to act on or adopt your plan. Second, your solutions should be feasible so readers know they can be carried out with reasonable effort and resources.

Ensuring that your solutions match the problems you've defined in your proposal often takes a second (or third) look. In groups, examine the solutions each writer has offered and determine if they address the problems defined and can be carried out by proposal readers.

Writer: Explain briefly to the group your problem and solution. If you defined a problem that has multiple parts, take one at a time and read the solution that you've offered.

Group: Does the solution offered address the problem (or part of the problem) the writer has defined? Does it make sense given the audience and purpose? Does it seem detailed enough and workable so readers can carry it out? Suggest ways to revise the solutions offered to make them match the problem(s) and seem feasible and reasonable for the readers to act on.

■ ■ ■

Peer Review

Proposal readers play a particularly important role in ensuring that a proposal is persuasive. Because they are usually fully committed to their issue, proposal writers may have tunnel vision and believe that they've thought through all the possibilities for a problem's solution and come up with a "best plan." However, readers may introduce new ideas for the proposal that writers had not yet thought of and should consider if they want the proposal to be as effective as possible.

PEER REVIEW *for Proposals*

As you read the proposal, make specific comments and suggestions that will help the writer revise. (e.g. "This solution seems feasible because. . . .")

Comment in the margins on the following:

THE RHETORICAL SITUATION: Notice the issue of the proposal and the writer's purpose for writing about it. For instance, is it a community proposal arguing for a new program for a town group? Who would be affected? What is the rhetorical situation driving the proposal?

CLAIMS AND EVIDENCE: As you read the proposal, comment on the writer's claims and supporting evidence.

IDENTIFY THE CLAIMS: Do they help you understand the problem? Do they help you understand the solution?

IDENTIFY THE EVIDENCE USED TO SUPPORT THE CLAIMS: Does it fully support the claim? Can you suggest other kinds of evidence that would help the writer further develop the claim?

(continued)

Finally when you have finished reading and annotating, write an endnote to the writer in which you comment on the following:

SETTING UP THE PROBLEM: Does the writer make clear what the problem is and how it affects the intended audience? How so or not so? Suggest ways the writer can further develop the problem.

OFFERING SOLUTIONS: Do the solutions make sense given the problem the writer has defined? Do the solutions seem feasible and workable? How so or not so? Suggest other kinds of evidence that would strengthen the writer's solutions.

ADDRESSING DIFFERING VIEWS: Does the writer successfully raise and address differing views? How so or not so? Suggest ways the writer could strengthen or provide claims to address readers whose ideas about the problem or the solution differ from his or her own.

Reflecting on the Process

After you've completed your proposal, reflect on your experiences working in this genre. Critical reflection is an important strategy for writers to develop to better understand the choices they make as they move through various genres. Recognizing what they do well, and how they do it, and what they need to improve upon will help them develop a repertoire of writing strategies. See Christina Schirone's reflection on her proposal on pages 476–477.

WRITING ACTIVITY   Reflecting on Writing a Proposal

Reflect on your writing process for your proposal. How did you generate ideas and chose one, do research, and draft and revise your proposal? Imagine you are writing this reflection to writers who have never written a proposal of this kind. What might they learn about working within the genre from you? What could you tell them that might help them as writers?

1. *Begin* by describing what you are most pleased with in your proposal. You can point out more than one area of the paper.
2. *Explain* what you think contributed to your success in these areas.
3. *Reflect* on how you identified and developed the problem and offered a solution using claims and research. How did you develop these arguments in your proposal to meet your purpose and audience expectations?
4. *Discuss* your revision process, including how you used feedback from your readers.
5. *Conclude* by reflecting on what you learned about the genre of proposals overall. You might also reflect on what you'd do differently next time you find yourself writing a proposal.

■ ■ ■

Christina Schirone's Proposal

Christina Schirone, a student in a first-year writing course, chose to write a proposal to persuade her audience of fellow students to donate time or money to support students at Union University whose campus was nearly destroyed by a tornado.

Generating Claims for the Proposal

Schirone began her writing process by thinking about what she wanted to say about a problem she saw on campus—Eastern Connecticut State University's lack of involvement in Union University's recovery effort. She then used her understanding of the issue, her audience, and her purpose to generate claims for her proposal.

Christina Schirone

Generating Claims and the Rhetorical Situation

Topic:	Union University Destruction
Issue:	Eastern Connecticut State University isn't contributing the most they can to the recovery effort.
Audience:	Eastern students who feel they can't contribute significantly or who feel they just don't have any money to contribute to the cause.
Purpose:	To convince Eastern students that they each have enough money to donate because even pocket change goes a very long way, and there are many effective ways to fundraise.

Schirone's analysis reveals what she needs to do in her proposal; just as importantly, it helps her think about why it's important that she do those things.

<u>My understanding of the rhetorical situation tells me two things:</u>

I need to help Eastern students form a connection to Union students so that Eastern students feel sympathetic to them. (This will encourage them to take part in fundraising efforts.)

I need to know why Eastern students feel they can't make an effective donation. (This will allow me to refute and change that belief by offering them effective and practical ways to fundraise, which don't necessarily mean giving money, but rather time and effort which can lead to raising money for the cause.)

Claim 1:	Union University was hit hard by the tornadoes which struck the South early February and they are in need of financial support. (To establish the problem and validate that it is urgent.)
Claim 2:	Eastern students are similar to Union students and we need to help fellow college students who are in need. (To make the audience care about the problem and feel connected to the problem.)

Not only does Schirone list her claims, but she articulates why those claims are necessary and what they will do for her.

She starts to think of the kinds of evidence she will need to support her solutions.

Claim 3:   There are practical, wallet-friendly ways to fundraise a significant amount of money to donate to Union University. Basically, there are alternatives to just dumping out college students' already thin wallets into donation envelopes. (How Eastern students can help Union students because now hopefully they care and want to!)

Claim 4:   (Possible Solutions)

Putting on a Rock-in-Rescue Charity Concert

Meal Exchange

Contribute Pocket Change (avg. 35 cents)

*I will work these possible solutions out with hypothetical numbers to show hypothetical results.

Differing Views

In acknowledging the possible differing views, she also predicts the kinds of research she will need to refute those views.

Some Eastern students may not care that college students at Union University lost most to all of their personal possessions when the tornadoes tore through their dormitories. What if an unexpected natural disaster affected Eastern? Wouldn't we want other colleges/universities to help us financially? (Research: are there any precedents?)

Some Eastern students feel they barely have enough money for their own necessities, how can they be expected to give money to a cause that doesn't directly affect their daily/immediate lives?

Drafting: Developing Differing Views

Because Schirone knew that her audience, students at her university, might have real objections to her solutions to the problem, she devoted a lot of time to thinking of ways to help her audience accept her proposal—she was after all asking them to donate money and time which are two things students usually have little of.

Christina Schirone
Developing Differing Views
Proposal (excerpt)

Schirone predicted resistance to her solutions since students don't have a lot of money. So she came up with ways to help her audience see how they could participate painlessly.

Purpose: To get students to donate money to the relief aid.

Problem/
Differing View: Students don't have a lot of money.

Claim: My solutions will be effective and the financial burden on students will be minimal.

Solution:	Let students cash in their unused meal tickets.
Possible Resistance:	Students might not want to give up their meals. So I will suggest a "meal exchange" where students who go away for the weekend or who otherwise miss a meal can sign a form to let the fundraiser group cash in the missed meal. This appeals to students who don't have cash on them and who rely on the dining hall for food.
Solution:	Collect spare change from students.
Possible Resistance:	A person might not have a dollar on them or not like the idea of giving a dollar. So asking for spare change will make it easier to give—"it's just what's in your pocket."
Solution:	Put on a walkathon.
Possible Resistance:	Students may feel like they have nothing to give to the relief effort and so will not do anything. But a walkathon is ideal because students can participate by volunteering their time or by raising money and walking. Participation does not mean giving money, there are lots of ways to make a difference.

Her solutions allow students to donate time or money, and don't ask a lot of any individual students.

Revising: Addressing the Audience's Concerns

Schirone provided an early draft to her peers for feedback. Because she had spent so much time working on her claims and developing and incorporating evidence for them, she was confident about her proposal. However, she knew that her readers (college students themselves) could give her a real sense of how well her ideas were presented and how likely it would be that students would accept her solutions. In the margins are her reviewers' comments, and you can see how she attempted to respond to them with the material she added (in italics).

Christina Schirone

Draft 1 Proposal (excerpt)

Student 1: Can you actually describe the damage? Or maybe use some research to show it?

The damage to the university was extensive. *As for physical damage of the campus, Union University President David S. Dockery claimed, "Nearly eight percent of Union's dorms were destroyed by the tornado and seventeen buildings sustained damaged.* President Dockery estimated the damages will total at least $40 million (Howerton 2). To help paint a picture of what $40 million in damage to a university campus looks like, it is crucial to repeat that Alabama rescue worker Johnny Burnette paid a visit to Union's campus and said, "It looked like a war zone." Similarly, Steven Atkinson of the DeSoto County sheriff's department in Mississippi said, "The best way to describe it is it looks like a bomb went off" (Nicholas 1). When I viewed pictures of Union

> University's destroyed campus, I got the chills imagining what it would be like if that was Eastern. *The pictures and these quotes support the fact that Union University is in urgent need of financial support.*
>
> . . .
>
> In conclusion, it is critical for Eastern students to realize that Union University students will never be able to replace everything they lost, but sizeable monetary donations such as the hypothetical $10,566.80 would take a lot of stress off the students. *In fact, if each Union University student spent $225 on textbooks for the current spring semester like I did, then Eastern's donation could replace this semester's textbooks for 47 Union students which got destroyed by the tornados.* Take a moment to close your eyes and imagine you were a Union University student. How much would you appreciate a donation from a college or university like Eastern that could help you buy your new lap top, lucky sneakers, or favorite pair of jeans that were unexpectedly destroyed in a natural disaster? Now open your eyes and ask yourself, how much time, effort and money do you have to donate to Union University students and the relief fund?

Student 2: I'm not sure what claim you are making here: why are the pictures and your reaction important?

Student 2: I like this example, but maybe you could show us what this would do for Union University? What would this mean, really?

After she got her proposal back from her readers, Schirone looked over the responses and considered how to revise from the suggestions her peers gave her. You can see some of her reflections on how to revise based on peer review suggestions in the following excerpt:

> Sarah suggested something I totally missed; she noticed that the second paragraph in my proposal lacked a direct claim. So, to fix this I added a concluding sentence which emphasized that Union University is in need of urgent support and we can provide that aid in the form of a monetary donation. Garrity suggested using the hypothetical total raised ($10,566.80) to show how many students could buy books with that amount. So, I went to the campus bookstore and the Office of Institutional Research, but neither had information on what the average student at Eastern spends on books per semester. Since I wanted to incorporate Garrity's suggestion, I decided to use $225 (the amount I spent on books this semester) and divided the hypothetical total donation by $225 and realized that our donation could buy textbooks for 47 Union students.

In Chapter 12: Portfolios, Schirone reflects on further revisions she made to her proposal based on another peer reviewer's comments in order to strengthen its appeals to her intended audience.

Christina Schirone, "Union University Needs Our Help" (final draft)

In the final version of her proposal, Schirone tightened the language and focused on rhetorical appeals in order to clarify her purpose and argument for her audience. Her solutions also emphasize their feasibility and the benefits to those involved.

The opening paragraphs include a lot of information on the situation at Union following the tornado—*what* happened—and explain the exigency of the situation.

Schirone incorporates her research early on—this signals to readers that she knows about her subject.

But also notice that she relies on parenthetical references instead of announcing the author before the paraphrase; this method makes the citation less intrusive and is in line with how research is incorporated in this genre.

Christina Schirone
Professor DeRosa
English 100P
3 Mar. 2008

Proposal: Union University Students Need Our Help

On February 5, 2008, at 7:02 p.m., an EF-4 category tornado unexpectedly struck Union University, a private, Baptist-affiliated, four-year liberal arts college in Jackson, Tennessee. The tornado packed winds between 207 and 264 mph. Union University students recall seeing flashes of green light followed by an orange glow as the tornado shattered residence complexes and academic buildings on their beloved college campus (Wood and Yates 2). According to Collegeboard.com, Union has just over 2,000 students, and over half of them, nearly 1,200 students, were on campus when the storm hit (Howerton 1). Several Union University students that were interviewed in the days following the tragedy recalled everyone they were with crying and screaming, not sure of how to get out. Luke Burleson, a sophomore at Union University, said, "The noise of bursting and shattering glass filled our ears, as we were thrown against the wall" (qtd. in Wood and Yates 2). Miraculously, no one was killed by the tornado; however, fifty-one students were treated at Jackson-Madison County General Hospital. While most Union students were not physically injured, two Union University student news reporters noted, "The effects of the tornado left them [Union University students] emotionally and mentally drained" (qtd. in Wood and Yates 1).

As for physical damage to the campus, Union University President David S. Dockery reported that "nearly eighty percent of Union's dorms were destroyed by the tornado and seventeen buildings sustained damaged. The only building that was not touched by the storm was the Fesmire Field House." Dockery estimated the damages at $40 million (qtd. in Howerton 2). To understand what $40 million in damage to a university campus looks like, it is crucial to repeat that Alabama rescue worker Johnny Burnette said, "It looked like a war zone." Similarly, Steven Atkinson of the DeSoto County sheriff's department in Mississippi said, ". . . it looks like a bomb went off" (qtd. in Nicholas 1). When I viewed pictures of Union University's destroyed

The writer appeals to her readers' sense of empathy by using quotes from students and details about the damage. She also uses eyewitness accounts about the psychological and physical damage caused by the tornado because she wants to engage readers in the students' plight.

This paragraph helps readers see that nothing is being asked of them that isn't being asked of others—an "if they can do it, so can we" kind of logic. It also helps the writer build her argument that "every little bit helps."

campus, I got the chills imagining what it would be like if that was Eastern. The pictures and these quotes support the fact that Union University is in urgent need of financial support.

Unfortunately, many Eastern Connecticut State University students may not be aware that college students at a university which is over 1,000 miles away had an unexpected break in their education and lost most if not all of their personal possessions. As college students, we clearly value education. So what if something similar happened at Eastern? Just imagine what it would be like if a natural disaster affected Eastern. How would we obtain the education that we pay for? Wouldn't we hope that other colleges and universities would help us out financially?

Fortunately, colleges and universities across the country have stepped up to lend a hand to help Union University recover from the devastation inflicted by the tornado. In fact, according to Union University records, more than eighty different colleges and universities have sent some form of aid to Union University (McBroom 1). Eastern Connecticut State University should be and can be one of those schools that makes a difference.

Here Schirone addresses the concerns—the differing views—of her audience. By doing so, she builds her ethos; she respects the difficulties her audience faces.

It is common knowledge that most college students are on a very fixed budget, oftentimes barely having enough to afford the bare necessities. Therefore, it is understandable why Eastern students may feel they can't donate to a cause like the Union University tornado relief fund. I want to change this misconception because there are practical, wallet-friendly ways to fundraise a significant amount of money for Union University students. There are alternatives rather to emptying our already thin wallets into donation envelopes.

First off, a donation doesn't have to be big to make an impact. At the very least every student has pocket change. Let's say that on average each student on campus has 35 cents in their pocket. According to Lauren Friedman, a research analyst at Eastern, 4,826 undergraduates are enrolled either full time or part time. If you do the math, each student donating just their spare coins would raise $1,698.10! It is critical to note that a Crest toothbrush only costs $2.19 from CVS Pharmacy; therefore the money from just this one

In this paragraph, Schirone draws on local research: She talked to Eastern's administration and conducted "field research" on how meal plans work and what they cost per meal. This familiar research appeals to the audience.

fundraiser alone could buy more than one-third of the Union University students, or exactly 771 students, a toothbrush.

Even if students don't have spare change there are other forms of donations. For example, according to Giesel T. Stancil, Eastern's Director of Auxiliary Services, exactly 1,563 students currently have a meal plan. Students with meal plans generally don't use all their meals, especially freshmen and upperclassmen living in Niejadlik Hall who are required to pay for the Silver meal plan, which is unlimited swipes into Hurley's cafeteria. I propose that when students go home for the weekend, knowing they will be leaving campus, or skipping a meal for whatever reason, they fill out a form with the number of meals that they will be missing and allow the Union University relief fund to cash those meals to donate to Union University. To eat at Hurley, breakfast costs $5.95, continental costs $4.50, lunch costs $8.15, dinner costs $9.90 and premium dinner costs $10.70. Therefore, if a mere 5 percent of Silver meal plan holding students, which is 78 students, each exchange two meals (one breakfast and one dinner) that would raise a whopping $1,298.70 for the Union University relief fund.

Another possible fundraiser would be to charge a dollar admission for Eastern Connecticut State University's very popular spring concert put on by the Campus Activity Board (CAB). According to Mike McKenzie, the Campus Activity Board office manager, 723 students attended the spring concert last year. This year the band selection is Third Eye Blind. So for argument's sake let's say that one in every five full-time students attend the concert this year and pay the $1 admission. That would raise $795.

As a fourth option, Eastern could do what Murray State did: hold a Rock-In Rescue, which is a rock band tournament using the Guitar Hero video game (Phelps 1). Specifically, Eastern students would form teams of four people and the cost per team to participate would be $25. Teams would sign up in advance, and it could be held in the Student Center Café so that other Eastern students could watch and cheer. Admittance for nonparticipants would be $2 a student. If twenty-five teams sign up to participate and seventy five students attend the event, then that would raise $775.

Thus, using these four simple solutions, Eastern Connecticut State University would raise $4,566.80. This enormous sum added to the $6,000, which junior and Occum Resident Assistant, Jim Acres, who is spearheading the Union University relief effort here at Eastern already collected in raw donations from faculty, staff, student organizations and Willimantic community members, equals $10,566.80. He said, "It was a little hard getting all the students involved and many didn't participate but in the end it was worth it!" All Eastern students have what it takes to get involved. If you don't have money to donate then give your time. Help coordinate fundraisers so they run smoothly and are effective. For example, work the Rock-In Rescue. Keep track of the scores teams earn, or collect the $2 admission fee at the door. If the night of the Rock-In Rescue isn't convenient for you, maybe you'll be available to work the table at Hurley and encourage people to sign up for meal exchange. If your schedule is tight then on your free time go around collecting spare change. In terms of fundraising, money is just as valuable as time and effort of participants.

It is critical for Eastern students to realize that Union University students will never be able to replace everything they lost, but sizeable monetary donations such as the hypothetical $10,566.80 would take a lot of stress off the students. In fact, if each Union University student spent $225 on textbooks for the current spring semester like I did, then Eastern's donation could replace this semester's textbooks for 47 Union students. Take a moment to close your eyes and imagine you were a Union University student. How much would you appreciate a donation from a college or university like Eastern that could help you buy your new laptop, lucky sneakers, or favorite pair of jeans that were unexpectedly destroyed in a natural disaster? Now open your eyes and ask yourself, how much time, effort and money do you have to donate to Union University students and the relief fund?

Contact Jim Acres to get involved today because it is never too late to help!

ONE WRITER'S JOURNEY

Works Cited

Acres, Jim. Email interview. 27 Feb. 2008.

Friedman, Lauren. Personal interview. 25 Feb. 2008.

Howerton, Brittany. "Government Officials Visit Union Following Tragic Tornado." *Union News.* Union University, 8 Feb. 2008. Web. 21 Feb. 2008.

McBroom, Sarah. "Colleges, Universities, Support Union Through Donations." *Cardinal and Cream.* UWIRE, 21. Feb. 2008. Web. 25 Feb. 2008.

McKenzie, Michael. Personal interview. 25 Feb. 2008.

Nichols, Adam. "'Looked Like a Warzone,' Rescue Worker Exclaims." *Daily News* 7 Feb. 2008: 13. *LexisNexis.* Web. 21 Feb. 2008.

Phelps, Robin. "Student Organizations Support Tornado Victims." *The Murray State News.* Murray State University, 15 Feb. 2008. Web. 25 Feb. 2008.

Stencil, Gisele T. Personal interview. 25 Feb. 2008.

"Union University." *Collegeboard.* Web. 27 Feb. 2008.

Wood, Elizabeth, and Clair Yates. "Union Students Recall Shock of Tragic Tornado." *Union News.* Union University, 8 Feb. 2008. Web. 21 Feb. 2008.

Questions for Discussion

1. How does Schirone help readers understand the problem as she sees it and the significance of it on her readers' lives?
2. What kinds of arguments does Schirone make to anticipate how her readers might react to her proposal? What kinds of research does she use to make them rethink their views?
3. How does Schirone try to make her solution seem feasible to readers? Does she succeed, or could she have offered other ideas that would make her readers more likely to take action on the problem?

Reflecting on the Process

Christina Schirone

Reflection on the Proposal

Overall, the aspect of my proposal which I am really pleased with is my issue. I feel I chose an important subject, and it was interesting to research. As far as content, I thought I formulated practical and effective solutions and explained them thoroughly showing hypothetical how much could be raised, and then how that money could be used by Union University students.

Identifying and developing the problem is a critical part to a proposal. If the problem isn't significant then readers will not care about it and the proposal will be ineffective. Also, if the problem doesn't come across as urgent then readers will not follow through on your solutions. I used facts and quotations from students, the university's president and those who visited the campus after the natural disaster to validate the problem and its urgency.

After making your readers connect with the problem, it is crucial to have solid solutions which they feel will work. Without a doubt you must recognize opposing views and then refute them. My target audience was Eastern students, so I had to appeal to them. I stated how I am a fellow college student and understand we don't have extra money to donate to a cause that doesn't affect us directly, but then I illustrated the result of everyone just contributing pocket change.

WRITING ACTIVITY   Evaluating One Writer's Journey

Review Schirone's process for writing her proposal. How would you evaluate the choices she made as she wrote? Are there places where you think she could have made different choices, and how would those choices have affected the final proposal? What further revisions, if any, do you think the final proposal could use?

■ ■ ■

T R A N S F O R M A T I O N S

GENRE CROSSING: From Proposal to Public Service Announcement

The proposal serves as a good base for transforming the material you have developed into other genres, and one that serves particularly well is the public service announcement (PSA) because both are action-oriented genres. One obvious difference between the two is length: a PSA is short. Video and radio PSAs are usually 15-second spots, and print PSAs, the kind we ask you to write here, are generally one page or less. In fact, some PSAs are barely a paragraph. (See Chapter 4: Visual Arguments for more discussion of PSAs.)

PSAs contain a public service or educational message that persuades a particular public audience to become aware of or act on an issue of public concern. PSAs often make creative use of visuals, and those visuals are often chosen for their evocative power. In other words, because of very limited time or space everything in a PSA has to have high impact.

Genre Crossing Writing Assignment

From Proposal to Public Service Announcement

Write a public service announcement using your proposal as a resource.

Select important ideas. First, read over your proposal and choose important ideas and points to use in your PSA. Think about the situation that drives your PSA: What circumstances make the PSA important now to public audiences? What's happening around readers in their social, political, cultural life that calls for a PSA on this issue? Where might this PSA be read?

Decide on audience and purpose. Second, decide on your new audience and purpose and determine which ideas from your proposal you'll use and what other research you'll need to gather.

Do additional research. You may find that some of the research from your proposal is useful, while other information is not given the new rhetorical situation. You'll want to gather missing information that will allow you to address the concerns and values of your new audience and fulfill the purpose of the PSA.

Plan your presentation. You'll also need to decide on a balance of text and visuals, arrangement, colors, and fonts to create an effective PSA for your reader. Ultimately, the success of a PSA is determined by all the elements working together well: text, visuals, graphics, color, and arrangement.

Transformation from Proposal to PSA: Christina Schirone, "Make a Difference"

Christina Schirone's PSA is shown on page 479, and her reflection on the challenges she faced is shown on page 480.

YOU Can Help Rebuild the Union University Campus
>Get Involved & Fundraise Today<

MAKE A DIFFERENCE

http://en.wikipedia.org/wiki/Image:UnionDorm.jpg

"Everything had to be replaced, so I started with rebuying my underwear and went on from there," said Union sophomore Jordon Thompson.

- Feb. 5th, 2008, 7:02pm tornado strikes Union University
- 1,200 students on campus
- 80% of dorms destroyed
- $40 million total damage

WHAT IF THIS WAS OUR CAMPUS?

The Union University Relief Organization encourages you to **Donate** your **Time, Effort and/or Money.**

Every Little Bit Counts: **35¢** pocket change **X** 4,826 undergraduates = $1,698 + $6,000 already raised = **$7,698**

For more information contact Jim Acres student leader of the Union University Tornado Relief Fund or visit Eastern's Union University Tornado Relief Organization web site

Christina Schirone
Prof. DeRosa
English 100P
13 March 2008
Final PSA

Reflection: Transforming a Proposal to a PSA

Reusing the material for my PSA from my proposal was hard. My proposal was a five full pages and I found it difficult to express everything about my topic in such a limited space for the PSA. Regardless, I chose to "reuse" specific details of the tragic event such as the date, time, location, estimated damage, and percent of dorms destroyed due to the tornado. These details evoked pathos, something I needed in such a brief genre. Luckily, my purpose and audience didn't change from my proposal to my PSA. In both, I strived to encourage my audience, Eastern students, to want to get involved and fundraise money to donate to Union University students who are in urgent need. With that being said, I did do new research to find opinions of Union students about rebuilding their campus and re-buying their personal belongings.

Notice the writer's consideration of how she can best appeal to readers within the PSA.

The writer's transformation to a PSA sent her to find further research to better appeal to her readers.

Reading for Comprehension

1. When you first read this PSA, what was your reaction? What part(s) captures your attention first?
2. How does the PSA make you aware of the problem at hand?

Analyzing the Genre

1. How does the writer use text and visuals to persuade readers of the message in the PSA?
2. How does the writer use arrangement, colors, and fonts to persuade readers to understand the problem or to take action? Do you think these are effective? Why or why not?
3. How does a PSA seem to influence readers? What kinds of choices do PSA writers make that are different from those of other genre writers?

12

Portfolios

What Is a Writing Portfolio?

A portfolio is a collection of an individual's work. Artists, designers, writers, actors, and other professionals collect, revise, and organize their work in order to showcase their abilities and achievements. The pieces individuals choose to include in their portfolios are usually representative of who they are (as artists, writers, professionals) and show the scope and direction of their work. However, a portfolio can be designed for a specific audience and can focus on just one aspect of an individual's work. For example, an artist seeking a commission to paint a landscape may include mostly landscapes in her portfolio even though her work also includes portraits and abstracts. Similarly, a writer's portfolio could revolve around a particular theme. For example, a writer in a college course might choose to include different texts she has written about a particular place or about a specific issue of interest to her, perhaps one related to her field of study. While some writing portfolios are course-based, designed to showcase the work of a writer in a particular course, others are university writing portfolios containing work spanning the academic career of the student. Portfolios written for writing classes, which we will focus on in this chapter, include a selection of pieces as well as reflective writing in which writers explain the choices they made, evaluate those choices, and discuss how they have developed as writers. Writing portfolios usually reveal the writer's development over a period of time. And while writers may highlight their best work, they do not ignore or gloss over their less successful work, but assess all of it. Thus portfolio writers select their writings; contextualize their work; comment on how texts were created; show the evolution of their texts; rethink and revise parts of their writing; and reflect on the processes involved in creating their texts.

The Purpose of a Writing Portfolio

The purpose of a writing portfolio is to provide writers with opportunities to present themselves *as* writers and show how they envisioned themselves at particular periods in their writing lives. What they include in their portfolios, how they arrange the works, and what they say in their reflective writing all affect how the portfolio readers perceive the writers' abilities. A portfolio is a showcase for a writer's *ethos* (see Chapter 3: Analyzing and Writing Arguments). Is he taking on the role as an academic writer in his field of study? Does he present himself as a writer engrossed in public issues of the day? Perhaps he presents himself as a reluctant or uninterested writer? These are all valid positions to take. Whatever roles the writer chooses, he wants to responsibly and accurately portray himself in the portfolio writing choices he's made.

In their portfolios, writers also *make connections* to other areas of their academic and personal lives and project into the future: How has the work in one course connected to work in another? What will the writer be working on next? How will those projects build on the ones already completed? For instance, you might be planning on majoring in business management, or may already be working in the field, so you would want to include in your portfolio writings in your chosen profession. Portfolios are multilayered, ongoing collections of writers' works. They are fluid and changing, and how they are presented depends on the writer's purpose and the rhetorical situation in which the portfolios are constructed.

Increasingly, *electronic portfolios* (or e-portfolios, sometimes also called Web portfolios) are replacing traditional print versions. While in many ways e-portfolios serve the same purpose, they also offer some unique opportunities for writers and their construction requires some additional considerations. In an e-portfolio you can present yourself, your work, and your media experience by creating connections between and among your writing and other media including video, art, photography, visual designs, or Web links. Because the portfolio is a self-representation of the writer in a particular rhetorical context, the portfolio (or e-portfolio) writer's choices determine how that self-representation plays out.

The Rhetorical Situation of a Writing Portfolio

As you think about what to include in your portfolio, you'll need to concentrate on how you want your audience—in many cases, your instructor or other faculty members who read and assess portfolios—to see you as a writer. The way that you position yourself as a writer helps readers understand choices you have made not only in the selection of material for the portfolio but also in the content of those texts. For example, the audience would look for evidence of a struggle to articulate ideas in the work of a writer who positions herself as a reluctant, or hesitant, writer. Remember the point of a portfolio is to show readers how you honestly see yourself as a writer, not to show them what you think they want to see. Unless specifically asked to do so by your instructor, you won't include all of your writing in your portfolio. That would negate the point of learning how to make critical choices about what writing best represents you and your work. Instead, the selections you include in your portfolio will depend, in part, on the rhetorical situation. For example, if you are compiling a portfolio for a college writing course, your instructor may have particular writing goals for the course that she will want to see that you've accomplished. Those goals will guide your choices of which pieces to include. Or if the portfolio is being judged based on how the writer met particular evaluative criteria for writing, such as a university writing program's standards for its writers, then you will include texts meeting those standards.

Constructing Writing Portfolios

When writers construct portfolios, they need to think about what to include, why they want to include it, and how to arrange the material—all while keeping in mind their purpose and audience. In the next sections are examples of the various kinds of content that writers might include in their portfolios. You should realize, though, that other genres might be included also. What goes into your portfolio will depend on your instructor's guidelines and/or the rhetorical situation for the writing portfolio.

WHAT WRITERS CONSIDER WHEN PREPARING PORTFOLIOS

In general, portfolio writers:

- Consider the rhetorical situation of the portfolio
- Choose texts that represent who they are as writers
- Reflect on their portfolio writing and contextualize it for their audiences
- Evaluate their progress as writers and reflect on their abilities
- Revise selections of their writing to meet the rhetorical situation
- Create a case study of writing assignments in the portfolio to showcase their writing abilities
- Arrange material to reflect their purposes

Writing a Reflective Letter

Reflective letters (also sometimes called cover letters or reflective narratives) are often included in portfolios to explain the purpose of the portfolio and introduce the writer. A reflective letter is like the cover letter highlighting your accomplishments that you submit along with other materials when you apply for a job. That cover letter also makes an argument for *why* the employer should call you in for an interview. Similarly, a portfolio cover letter serves as an introduction to you and your work. But just as the cover letter is more than an introduction, the reflective letter is an argument for how your readers should read and understand your work. The writer does in-depth *critical reflection and evaluation* of the portfolio contents in order to write a reflective letter that persuades the audience to read selections as intended by the writer.

GUIDELINES: WRITING A REFLECTIVE LETTER

- Comment on the goals you met, such as course objectives or evaluation criteria
- Review your selections and explain what you included and why
- Show examples from the portfolio that illustrate your claims
- Include brief rhetorical analyses of particular pieces of writing
- Comment on your development as a writer or tell anecdotes of your writing history—both within the specific course and prior to it
- Provide insights about yourself as a writer now and explain your objectives for the future

---

Christina Schirone, Reflective Portfolio Letter

In her college writing class, Christina Schirone was required to submit a portfolio of her work at the end of the semester. As part of that assignment, she was asked to write a reflective letter in which she contextualized her writing for multiple readers, including the instructor and other writing instructors in the university's first-year writing program. A tough audience! As you read Schirone's reflective letter, notice how she pays attention to the rhetorical situation and comments on how it influenced her choices as a writer. Her reflection emphasizes *how* she kept in mind the audience and purposes for her works. In fact, because her audience includes other writing professors besides her own, she is careful to attend to their needs by briefly describing each assignment and including examples to illustrate her points.

For more examples of Schirone's reflection on her writing, please see Chapter 11: Proposals, One Writer's Journey.

Schirone's opening helps the reader understand a little about her previous writing experiences; the reader expects her reflection to provide details and examples of how she developed as a writer.

Christina Schirone
Professor DeRosa
English 100P
15 May 2008

Dear Professor DeRosa and Other College Writing Professors:

In the spring semester of my freshman year, I enrolled in English 100P. I was very nervous to do so because I didn't know what to expect from a college writing course. I thought the class might consist of pointless essays and long, boring writing assignments. Fortunately, this assumption was completely wrong. In English 100P I learned to write in several different genres and to use a wide variety of writing strategies and research skills, which helped me develop as a writer.

Schirone gives examples from her papers to illustrate her points about writing for different purposes and rhetorical situations.

As a writer, I have learned to pay attention to audiences, purposes, writing contexts, and the many roles writers assume as they work in different genres. For example, in my public service announcement my purpose was to make Eastern students aware of the tornado that hit Union University and the severe damage that resulted. I used visuals and text to appeal to Eastern students to get involved and to fundraise so that Eastern could donate a significant amount of money to help the Union University students in need. In my profile I had to establish my credibility and explain Bikram Yoga to an audience unfamiliar with it by using in-depth descriptions of a yoga session and field and library research. For that profile my purpose was to persuade others to practice Bikram Yoga so they too could reap the mental and physical benefits.

In addition to learning about purpose, I learned about three different rhetorical appeals used to persuade audiences: *ethos, pathos,* and *logos.* In my proposal to persuade other college students to participate in various activities

Schirone shows her understanding of using rhetorical appeals to fulfill her purpose: moving her audience to take action.

to help Union University students whose campus had been devastated by a tornado, I wrote: "Take a moment to close your eyes and imagine you were a Union University student. How much would you appreciate a donation from a college or university like Eastern that could help you buy your new laptop, lucky sneakers, or favorite pair of jeans that were unexpectedly destroyed in a natural disaster?" This is an example of a pathos appeal which I hoped would motivate my readers to take part in the fundraisers and other humanitarian efforts for Union students.

Other parts of the class that facilitated my progress as a writer included a central focus of the course, peer review and revision. Specifically, the better I am at assessing my classmate's works, the more accurately and critically I am able to edit and revise my own pieces of writing. Also, luckily for me, the targeted audiences for many of my papers were college students, so peer reviewers represented my larger audience. That is one major reason why their comments and suggestions affected my choices as a writer so much. For example, in my profile about Bikram Yoga, two peer reviewers suggested I include photos of people doing Bikram Yoga to illustrate the intensity of it, and to enhance the descriptions of the poses. I went back to the Bikram Yoga studio and asked permission to take pictures and then included them in my essay.

Schirone's reflection on peer review provides readers with her insights on its benefits for her as a writer and reader.

In my portfolio, I include the four major works in order of my most favorite to my least favorite: proposal, public service announcement, profile, and memoir. Each project in the portfolio shows the progress I made as a writer. For example, the proposal required me to produce a well-researched, feasible solution or alternative plan of action for a problem of public significance—I chose to write about how college students should participate in their campus's activities to serve others in need; I focused on Union University's needs after a natural disaster. In addition to sharpening my argument writing skills and learning about rhetorical appeals, I sharpened my abilities to use in-text documentation, MLA citations, and online library databases for research. I include the first and final drafts of my proposal to show the improvement I made within just this one assignment.

Schirone's examples provide readers with an understanding of why she made the choices to include the works in her portfolio.

Schirone reflects on how visual rhetoric builds on her growing rhetorical awareness in new ways; her challenge is how to get visuals and text to work together to create a persuasive message.

Working with the research and ideas of the proposal paper, our next assignment asked us to transform that proposal into a public service announcement. We had to figure out how to use text and visuals and additional research to target a specific public audience with a clear message and call to action, two characteristics of the genre. I learned that the use of visual rhetoric to persuade readers was challenging for me as a writer. I originally began with a picture of a sad student and the Union University symbol. Then, I changed it to a picture of the campus's destruction with the sad student and the school symbol minimized in the corners to refocus the audience on the pathos appeal of the devastation to people there rather than the school itself. The argument was that the reader could help those like the sad student in the photograph—and since they were students themselves,

Here Schirone is thinking rhetorically: She wants readers to feel **sympathy and identify** with the students of Union. Her decision to deemphasize Union's logo, she thinks, strengthened the PSA's pathos.

Schirone uses the language of a field researcher to explain how observations and descriptions persuade audiences and emphasize her purpose for the travel essay.

Schirone demonstrates awareness of her portfolio's audiences by providing examples of her thick descriptions.

Because Schirone has some distance, she is able to consider other choices she could have made to emphasize the "larger significance" of her memoir for readers.

they should do so. As my visuals changed, so did the words on the PSA. I think my PSA shows how I successfully made visuals and text work together to persuade readers to take action for the cause.

I also learned to use field research, as well as library and Internet research, to write a profile about a particular place. The place had to be one we could visit frequently, so my topic, a Bikram Yoga studio, came easily to me. I used library databases to research the history and background of Bikram Yoga. I also needed to make observations about what I saw, smelled, tasted, heard and felt while at Bikram Yoga class. These notes allowed me to formulate thick descriptions: "The studio has a front wall covered with mirrors, three white walls and a white ceiling, and a dull, gray, thinly carpeted floor," to put readers in the scene and experience with me a Bikram Yoga class. I also used descriptions of the people in class to support my purpose: Bikram Yoga is for people of all ages, races, genders, and levels of fitness, and it benefits the body physically as well as mentally. For instance, "I can't keep from staring at the middle-aged Caucasian man in the front row, shirtless, sweaty and covered with black chest and back hair trying hard to hold Tadasana. He needs to pull up his shorts" and "Despite the intense heat, an elderly woman about seventy with a beauty salon perm starts the next pose in sequence, 'Bhurjangasana,' commonly known as cobra pose, before the instructor, a testament to her commitment to stay healthy."

As is true for all the other pieces of writing, my memoir had to be written for a particular audience and with a purpose or larger significance that went beyond my own self-interest. Of all my papers for this course, I think my memoir was my weakest. I had a tough time reflecting on my topic, my high school graduation, and it was also hard to make the paper significant for others. Thinking about it, though, I might have asked a question like, "What significance do rituals like high school graduation have for American teen culture today?" Since it was my first writing assignment, now I have more practice doing critical reflection on my topics than I did then.

English 100P made me aware of my strengths and weaknesses as a writer. For instance, picking a topic and getting started is what stumps me with every project. Reflecting is another hurdle I have trouble jumping. I excel at incorporating research and quotes to support my claims. Overall I think I have improved the clarity of thoughts in my writing which wasn't evident in my prior work. Before this class, I wrote for me or to fulfill assignment guidelines. I never before took into consideration my targeted audience or the potential publisher for my piece—or the rhetorical situation. Thinking through audience and purpose will help me in my writing for other courses. Most of all, the class made me confident in my writing.

Sincerely,
Christina Schirone

Reflective Portfolio Letter

For this chapter's assignment, introduce your portfolio by including a reflective letter. In most cases, your audience for a course-based writing portfolio is the instructor, but if there are others reading it, you'll need to attend to those readers' expectations, too. Depending on your purpose, audience, and the guidelines your instructor provides, you should:

1. Reflect on your progress as a writer. Referring to examples from your writing portfolio, discuss the selections that best represent who you are as a writer and the progress you've made during the course. Explain why you made some of the choices you did in your writings: How was the rhetorical situation influencing your choices as you wrote, for instance? How did the feedback you received from readers affect your choices along the way?

2. Provide arguments and supporting evidence for how you met the learning outcomes for the course in your portfolio. Your purpose is to persuade readers that you have met whatever criteria were indicated on the course syllabus and that you have progressed as a writer. If the portfolio assignment has particular writing criteria, be sure to address each one in your arguments and explain how your work meets the criteria, or how you might have revised the writing to meet the criteria if you were given another opportunity.

3. Include an analysis of the audience(s), purpose(s), and decisions you made on what to include in your portfolio that might help you in the future as a writer. For instance, how will some of the writing you've included be relevant as you pursue your major or conduct a job search? In this case, your audience is people in your field of study or your future employers. For example, if your analysis is about writing in your major, readers will want to know how you've progressed as a writer in that discipline or how you understand the rhetorical conventions of the discipline. If the audience is people who might work with you, they will want to know how your writing illustrates your understanding of the writing done by professionals in that career.

Writing an Introductory Paragraph for Each Item

An introductory paragraph may precede each selection in a portfolio. Typically, these introductions accomplish two things: 1) They let the reader know the writer's interpretation of the writing assignment; and 2) they offer the writer's reflection on the assignment, explaining what the writer learned, how he or she benefited, as well as what he or she might have done differently.

> **GUIDELINES:** WRITING INTRODUCTORY PARAGRAPHS
> Depending on your rhetorical situation, consider doing all or some of the following:
> - Provide a description of the writing assignment you are introducing
> - Include your reflections on how you approached the assignment. Consider whether or not your interpretation of the assignment changed as you drafted and revised
>
> *(continued)*

- Point out the particular parts of the assignment you'd like readers to pay attention to
- Reflect on why you included the piece of writing: How does it show your progress as a writer or who you as a writer are at this moment? What are your challenges as a writer?

Lisa Warford (student): Introductory Paragraph for a Portfolio Selection

Lisa Warford included the following introductory paragraph with the first item in her portfolio, a personal essay about her grandmother.

Warford begins by explaining the assignment for readers outside the course.

She then explains its position in her portfolio and why it is a good example of her work.

She concludes by discussing what this text reveals about her abilities.

The assignment for paper one was to write a personal essay about an event or experience from our lives and recreate it for our readers. The essay encourages us, as writers, to question, explore and comment on our experience, and then apply it or connect it to our shared cultural experiences. We were asked to write about an event that had an impact on who we are (or how we see ourselves) and how we see the world. I chose to write about the experience of losing my grandmother, something that I'm sure many of my readers could relate to. I placed this essay first in my portfolio because, even though it was the first assignment of the semester, I felt that it was some of my best work. This was partly because of the subject—I could write about someone I loved, whereas other assignments asked for more formal subjects. When writing this essay, the words just seemed to flow out easily, and overall I felt like I met my goals in writing this (to pay respect to my grandmother and explore the impact she had on me) and I think I met the course goals as well (commentary, careful and creative description, etc.). I was able to take an event and engage the reader in it, and I was also able to connect my experience to the larger cultural experience of dealing with an elderly and ill relative.

WRITING ACTIVITY Introductory Paragraphs

For each of the selections in your portfolio, write a short paragraph in which you contextualize the writing and discuss the choices you made while writing it. Conclude the paragraph with why you chose to include the piece and why it appears where it does in your portfolio.

■ ■ ■

Preparing a Case Study

A case study is a focused, critical analysis of the choices a writer has made during the drafting and revising of one particular text. Case studies cover each stage of the writing process: topic generating, exploratory writing, first drafts, peer reviews, revised drafts, and final drafts. And just as writers do initial, exploratory writing (brainstorming, defining the rhetorical situation, etc.) before generating a formal draft, they also may do "post-writing," or what is commonly called a *reflective narrative,* after they have completed an assignment. This narrative, too, might be included in a case study. Case studies allow writers to analyze and comment on the choices they made for specific assignments and reflect on them critically after having some time away from the writing. A case study *commentary* presents detailed analyses of the selected piece so that readers might see how well the writer's claims are supported by, for instance, the examples.

GUIDELINES: WRITING A CASE STUDY

Choose a piece of your writing that you feel offers further potential for substantive revision—perhaps one that you wrote early on in the semester.

Analyzing the Choices You Made

Revisit any initial brainstorming, notes you made, and the earlier drafts to get a sense of your purpose and what you'd hoped to accomplish. Is there material from the notes and earlier drafts that you omitted but that you think should be worked into a new draft? Review your earlier drafts and take notes on the choices you made *as you drafted*. Why did you choose to include some material? Why did you choose to organize the draft the way you did? How did you imagine your audience and purpose as you were writing?

Revising Your Writing

Reread the original final draft. In the margins make notes on what you think is working well, but also pay attention to areas that you would like to revise. Are there places that need more detail? If there is research, is it integrated and synthesized? Are examples given and are they relevant to your point or thesis? Ask questions of your own text the way you would another writer's, keeping the original assignment and your sense of audience and purpose in mind. Look over the feedback you received as you drafted the paper. Are there comments that you were unable or unwilling to respond to and that you now feel should be addressed in your revision? Were there suggestions that you overlooked?

Writing the Case Study Commentary

Your particular rhetorical situation and what you actually found when you looked back over your earlier drafts will determine what you write in your commentary. But the following are some questions to consider as you write:

1. Why did you choose to revise this particular piece?
2. What was your original writing process of this paper like? Where did you struggle? Where do you think you succeeded?
3. As you reread the earlier drafts and commentary, how did you decide what to revise and what to leave alone?
4. What changes did you make? Refer to specific changes in your discussion.
5. How do you think the revisions you made improved the paper?

Revising Your Writing

Revising your writing for the portfolio allows you to reflect in critical ways on how to move to the next version of a draft you thought was "final." Revising your work also provides an opportunity to showcase for readers your ability to substantially revise. Within the genre chapters of this book, you've had many experiences with revision strategies; drawing upon these experiences may help you decide which pieces in your portfolio to revise and what parts to continue working on. The case study below is an example of one student writer's revision work in her portfolio.

Lisa Warford, Portfolio Case Study with Revisions

Lisa Warford
Dr. Ferruci
English 100P
10 May 2009

Case Study Commentary

I chose to revise my third paper titled "Visibility at Any Cost," which is a rhetorical analysis and evaluation of the documentary *Celluloid Closet*. Most of the changes that I made to my final draft were in response to the suggestions of my peers and Dr. Ferruci concerning the need for more analysis of the documentary. To initially write this paper we were asked to view a documentary and evaluate what the director's intent of the film was and what he or she wanted the audience to take from the film. I chose to view *Celluloid Closet,* a film that outlined the depiction of homosexuality in film throughout the past century. In order to write this paper we had to first view the film like a normal viewer and just watch it like a movie. During the next few viewings of the film we were asked to take careful notes and to carefully view the structure and organization of the film. In our analysis we were asked to critically evaluate the effectiveness of the film by drawing on our own observations and formal research.

I first corrected the basic grammar and punctuation flaws in order to improve the quality of my paper. I also had small changes that made my wording less confusing or allowed areas to flow together. I then began to move onto more substantive changes, following the critiques provided by Dr. Ferruci.

I attempted to analyze *why* the directors chose the format that they did (chronologically) and what their overall purpose was when putting the film together. I did this by expanding on my explanation of why the directors presented the movie in a chronological structure. Although in my original final draft I had given reasons as to why they would do this, I had not in a concrete way provided an explanation of what this accomplishes or how it impacts the audience. I believe that this change improves my paper because it

Warford gives us background on the assignment in order to help us understand how her changes have helped to improve the paper.

just doesn't summarize the flow of the film but explains how its structure guides the audience to the intended purpose of the film, which is to show how homosexuality has progressed in film throughout the century and the hardships that homosexuals have faced.

In the original final draft, the section where I discussed the use of chronology ended with the material in normal font; the sentences in italics are part of what I added:

> By using chronological order, Epstein and Friedman were able to successfully show the hardships that the gay community in Hollywood has had to struggle against. *Homosexuality was at first something accepted but unacknowledged, then was forced underground as a perversion, later homosexuals were depicted as victimizers, and more recently, depictions of gays have slowly become more realistic. The directors have organized the film chronologically in order to illustrate that slow development; if the film were organized differently, then that struggle and slow change might have been lost. Chronology also allows the viewers to see how different time periods have had different views on gays. We see that what is accepted and what is not by society changes.*

My next change was expanding my explanation as to why those interviewed were chosen. The directors chose to interview gay and straight famous people, and I argued that they do so because they reflect our society; they are a variety of people with different views, beliefs, and background, yet they all were impacted by homosexuality in film in a multitude of ways. I showed that the directors' use of famous individuals helps them present their argument that we learn from what society allows us to see.

In the original final draft, the section where I discussed the use of interviews is in normal font, and part of what I added to this section is in italics:

> The interviews are numerous throughout the film, placed at various sequences throughout the documentary, focusing first on the personal impact film had on the interviewee's life as a whole, and then on the impact of specific scenes not only on themselves but also on society. This was a successful way to integrate commentary, *because it allows the audience to develop a relationship with those interviewed, to see them as individuals, not just movie stars, and to reflect on their own experiences. Through the narrative of those interviewed, we can see a scene depicting homosexuality in a new light, seeing something we might have missed because we are not gay ourselves. This also supports the directors' argument that society as portrayed in film teaches us what to think, because we learn how those interviewed were affected by what they saw in film.*

Finally, another change I made was to expand on a quotation by Harvey Fierstein where he claims he would rather homosexuality be depicted as humor than to not see it at all. I expanded my discussion to show how this reflects the pressures of society: if we cannot see it, it does not exist. By not showing homosexuality in film we are making the concept invisible. We are showing

Warford first describes what she changed, and then provides an example—this is important because it ensures that her readers will actually see what she did.

She also chose to highlight just the most important changes she made, and to provide examples from only two of those. The point of this case study is to show the reader what the writer has been able to do, not overwhelm them with all the changes she made.

that it is not something that happens by ignoring it. By portraying gays in film, even if used as a pun or joke, the directors show us that it does exist. And just as importantly, it shows those individuals who are striving to see a reflection of themselves that they are not alone, that they are not invisible.

I believe that the changes I provided improve my paper. Specifically, they help to change my paper from mostly summary to a paper that analyzes *how* the directors are making an argument about homosexuality. I had found areas in my paper confusing where I just summarized the concepts but did not explain their intent. I noticed that many areas of my writings were almost story-like, so by adding an explanation of why ideas or certain structures are placed in the documentary I move my paper from primarily summary to an evaluation and analysis.

I placed the case study as my third entry into my portfolio because although I feel it is a strong paper, especially now that I have revised it, it was not my favorite essay because it lacked the personal attachment of the first two papers. It was an amazing topic to delve into and I was able to see many films that I have already viewed in a new light. It allowed me also to see the struggles that homosexuals have faced and the discrimination they face in society.

Here Warford summarizes why she feels her changes have improved the paper.

She concludes by writing a bit about the paper's placement in the portfolio and why she put it there, as well as comments on her own interest in the assignment and film.

Reflecting on Peer Review Commentary for Case Studies

When writers are given the opportunity to revise a piece of writing for a portfolio after it has already been evaluated, they sometimes seek out others' advice for how to revise.

First-year writer Christina Schirone chose to revise her proposal "Making a Difference" based on some peer review comments she received. She included her reflection on the comments she received in the case study section for her proposal in her portfolio.

Christina Schirone, Portfolio Case Study with Peer Review

Schirone's proposal calls for her student audience to "make a difference" by donating time or helping with fundraising efforts for Union University college students whose campus was devastated by a tornado (see Chapter 11 pages 471–476). The excerpts below include peer reviewer Elizabeth's comments to Schirone, followed by Schirone's reflection on why she made additional revisions to her proposal based on Elizabeth's feedback.

Elizabeth's comments on Schirone's proposal:

I think if you show them how bad things are for students at Union, they will be more likely to understand and feel sorry for them. You do in the introduction and then by asking readers how they might feel and what they might want others to do to help out if it happened on their own campus. You could add to that later by saying that you know it is hard for them to give money when they feel like they have so little. . . . You could add examples of how other colleges have helped out Union by doing different fundraising

> events and donating time or collecting money. This research would make readers see that other students had helped out and so should we, and they could see how other colleges did it to get some ideas of their own going. So it would make them feel like they had a responsibility to help and that they could do it more easily than they think they can.

Schirone's reflection on Elizabeth's peer review:

> College students were the targeted audience for my proposal, and I was trying in particular to convince Eastern students that they should do something to help with the relief funds set up for students at Union University who were tornado victims earlier in the year. Although I had tried to use some rhetorical appeals to do this, Elizabeth's comment made me sure that I had to do more revisions to make my pathos appeals clearer, especially by showing that I realized that most college students have little time or money to donate. I know I don't.
>
> Elizabeth pointed out that I also might want to show them that I wasn't just talking out of nowhere, that other campuses across the country and even our own campus had already started to help out in creative ways. So I added a section using a logos appeal: others had already stepped up in different ways and they were college students just like my readers; if they could do it, so could we. I had to get them thinking about rallying around my cause, and make it seem like a do-able thing.

Schirone's reflection shows both her own and her peer reviewer's rhetorical awareness of the situation: She sums up Elizabeth's comments on attending to her audience's needs, and she says why building on those rhetorical appeals would make the proposal more persuasive for readers. For a complete version of the revisions Schirone made to her proposal, see the One Writer's Journey section of Chapter 11: Proposals (pages 468–477).

Arranging a Writing Portfolio

The way writers arrange their work in a portfolio depends on the rhetorical situation and the specific guidelines of the portfolio assignment. Ultimately, the arrangement should emphasize the purpose of the portfolio and the way the writers want to present themselves.

For instance, some writers choose to show their progress as a writer from the start of the semester to the end, thus organizing their portfolios chronologically. The reason behind this organization might be to reveal to readers how the writer learned new writing strategies and took chances by trying them out in various pieces of writing later in the semester.

Other writers choose to arrange their works from what they believe is their strongest piece to their weakest one, which they feel highlights their best work for readers. Still another way writers arrange material in their portfolios is from favorite piece to least favorite piece, along with a reflection on why they classified their writing that way and why it was important for them to do so.

Jenna Clark (student), Arrangement of Portfolio Items

Jenna Clark, a student in a first-year writing course, has this to say about her choices in arranging her material for the portfolio:

Clark tells the reader immediately how she has organized her portfolio and why.

> The papers in my portfolio are not ordered from best grade to worst grade or worst to best, but instead I arranged them by which papers I enjoyed writing the most. I did this because I think those that I enjoyed the most really show my abilities the best, even though in some cases, I didn't get the best grade on them. I started my portfolio off with my brochure about becoming a paraprofessional—this was a transformation from my profile, and I really enjoyed writing it. Graphic design is one of my favorite things to do, and it was a challenge to take the material from my profile and turn it into a visual message. The second piece in my portfolio is the research report. Although it was one of the hardest to write because of the amount of research needed, and because we had to synthesize our research, I feel like I learned the most from it. It was also neat to organize the report as if you would see it in a magazine, using different textboxes and callouts, and graphics to help readers make sense of the material. Third was the open letter; I enjoyed writing it because I could include personal experiences, but I felt it was too similar to a persuasive essay I wrote in high school. I don't think I ever really understood how it was different, except it was addressed to someone. Finally, I put the profile last, because it was the hardest for me to organize and write. Maybe this is because I chose to write about someone I knew very well—my mom and her career as a paraprofessional—maybe it would have been easier writing about someone I didn't already know. But, I think it would have been hard no matter what.

Throughout she contextualizes her papers—telling the reader what made them successful for her.

Clark's honest about her struggle with some of the assignments.

GUIDELINES: ARRANGING PORTFOLIO ITEMS

Reflect on the requirements of the course or a particular theme in your writing. Keep the purpose of the portfolio in mind as you arrange the pieces you've chosen to include.

Analyze selections for patterns. As you look over your works is there an obvious arrangement to them? Do you see, for instance, how the papers might show a particular kind of development in your writing? Consider whether the pieces might reflect a particular struggle that you have had, one that you have overcome perhaps, or one that you still have. Consider whether you enjoyed writing some of the papers more than others. Could this suggest something about you as a writer?

Preparing a Table of Contents

Many portfolios contain a table of contents that lists the items in the portfolio. The table of contents is a brief outline that reveals to readers at a glance the logic behind the writer's choices for arrangement and also shows connections among the writings. Some tables of contents are also descriptive; they provide readers with a brief abstract of the content of each piece. The audience and purpose for your portfolio might make doing this a good choice.

Christina Schirone, Portfolio Table of Contents

The following example is the table of contents for Christina Schirone's portfolio. Part of the logic behind her choices for arrangement had to do with genre transformations she made from proposal to public service announcement. You will notice that after each project she includes a reflective narrative in which she explains her understanding of the genre and her work as a writer of that genre. The arrangement reflected in her table of contents also shows her purpose: to demonstrate to readers the revisions in her work. She includes final drafts and rough drafts of some of her selections. Notably, the memoir was the first assignment she wrote and the last in her portfolio. Her decision to include it last signals to readers that she begins with the papers she felt were her strongest; however, she did choose to revise the memoir for her portfolio based on additional feedback from her peers.

Table of Contents

Reflective Portfolio Letter

Case Study: Proposal: "Union University Students Need Our Help"
    Commentary for Case Study
    Final Draft with Revisions for Portfolio
    Rough Draft #3
    Peer Review
    Rough Draft #2
    Rough Draft #1
    Rough Draft
    Audience and Purpose for Proposal
    Topics for Proposal
    Reflective Narrative for Proposal

Public Service Announcement (*transformation* from Proposal): "Make a Difference in the Lives of Students"
    Final Draft
    Rough Draft
    Reflective Narrative for PSA

Profile: "Bikram Yoga: My Antidrug"
    Final Draft
    Reflective Narrative on the Profile

Memoir: "Town and Gown"
    Final Draft
    Reflective Narrative for Memoir

> **GUIDELINES:** CONSTRUCTING A TABLE OF CONTENTS
>
> A table of contents is an outline that prepares readers for how the text, in this case a writer's portfolio, is organized. At a glance, a reader should know what to expect for content in your portfolio. As you write your table of contents, consider the following:
>
> - Why are you choosing to arrange the portfolio in the order you have? Does the first item seem appropriate, for instance, for the purpose and audience of your portfolio?
> - Does the order of the table of contents reflect how you are presenting yourself as a writer in the portfolio?
> - Does the order of the table of contents indicate some pattern of your progress as a writer?

Preparing an Electronic Portfolio

The **electronic portfolio** (or online portfolio) differs in a few ways from the print portfolio. E-portfolios are multimodal, often including artwork, photography, video, and audio, as well as links to websites that can function as both background to written texts and as annotation of written texts. For instance, instead of writing a reflection on a piece of writing, you might prepare the reflection as a video clip to post in your e-portfolio. To take another example, a writer who has written a profile of a place, say their residence hall at college, can include recorded interviews with residents; still images of the residence hall in a collage or slide show; or video clips of dorm activities. Or the writer can record herself reading the profile so that the readers' experience of the piece is both visual and aural. One of the exciting things about e-portfolios is that they call attention to the *social* nature of writing. For example, as you were writing about genetically modified foods for a research report, you had experiences related to your topic: You ate in your dining hall which may serve such foods; you took an anthropology class in which the diet of aboriginal peoples was explored; and so on. But there was no way to include the interconnected issues brought up by these experiences in your actual report. In a print portfolio, you would have a hard time, too, showing those inter-connections. You could mention them in the cover letter, but that's about it.

In an e-portfolio, you can include links to websites that address the related issues, you can write blog entries, and you can link to news footage about the issues. E-portfolios, in other words, can help you better show the complexity of your thought process on any given paper; they can also become an *active* experience for your readers. Instead of reading just what you have written, e-portfolios, by including live links to other sites, sources, and media can encourage your readers to explore the issues with you. E-portfolios are also multilayered and afford more reading options than a print portfolio, which is generally read from beginning to end. All readers might *enter* your e-portfolio on the same page, as it were, but once there they can select from a series of links to your writings or other content and read your portfolio however they want and in whatever way they want. Effective

WebLinks

To find examples of e-portfolios on the web, type "student e-portfolios" into a search engine or search for the following specific universities:

"Penn State and e-portfolios"—this site for Penn State students offers sample e-portfolios as well as short video clips that highlight important aspects of constructing an e-portfolio.

"Electronic portfolios in first-year composition at NIU"—Michael Day, a professor at Northern Illinois University, has created a site that links to student e-portfolios for first year and advanced writing courses.

"LaGuardia Community College and e-portfolios"—an extensive and useful site that provides information on how to construct an e-portfolio as well as many student examples.

e-portfolios, then, must help the audience understand how all the layers are connected. Some would argue creating an e-portfolio is a more complex and challenging rhetorical task for writers than that required for print portfolios. When compiling your e-portfolio, you need to determine if you have developed your e-portfolio in a way that ensures your readers will read it all. For example, if you have external links, how will you ensure they come back to you? Or, if you are presenting yourself as a certain kind of writer (for example, as one whose strengths lie in creativity), will readers actually see you that way no matter in what order they read your work?

Since e-portfolios are nonlinear, the connections you make among the various components must be very clear. For example, if you add a video montage to your writing, you need to be clear about why you included it and what it adds to your piece. Thus, the connections you make between the links must be obvious so that no matter where the readers go next, they understand how the parts relate and how they accomplish the writer's purpose.

More and more universities are encouraging or requiring students to construct e-portoflios; sometimes these are done for specific classes (e.g. first year writing), but increasingly these are "university requirements" and the portfolios are exit portfolios, meant to reflect what students have learned and done over the course of their college careers. Many samples of e-portfolios written by college students are available on the web. Your own university may even have samples posted on its web page if constructing an e-portfolio is an option or requirement for students there.

GUIDELINES: CONSTRUCTING AN E-PORTFOLIO

Consider the rhetorical situation of your e-portfolio. Does it call for particular kinds of texts or information? Does it suggest a particular layout or organization? Does your university have its own guidelines?

1. Beyond the texts you will include, what other kinds of material (images, video, graphics, etc.) would help you show your readers the kind of writer you are?

2. What connections do you see among the pieces of your writing? Could you make connections by providing hyperlinks that connect terms and ideas among many pieces of writing? You might also provide a narrative or commentary on why those connections are important or how they add to the experience or meaning of the original text

3. What connections do you see between your writing and the work you have done for other classes, your job, or on your own? Could that material be included? What would it show the reader?

PART THREE

Research Methods and Sources

CHAPTER 13   Research and the Rhetorical
             Situation   501

CHAPTER 14   Using and Citing Sources   541

Research and the Rhetorical Situation

When most of us think about research, one of two images comes to mind: sitting on the third floor of a library surrounded by dusty books last checked out in 1952, or firing up our Web browser and heading to Google or Wikipedia. Neither, of course, really reflects what research is all about. Simply put, research is the process of finding out more than you already know.

Why Writers Do Research

Research is an integral part of all writing. For instance, you may not think a personal, creative genre like the memoir would require research. But if you are writing a memoir about a time in your life when you felt like an outsider, you'll have to explore your own memories, and maybe those of friends and family who knew you during that period, and you may need to read more on what it means to be an outsider in order to say something meaningful about it. Each of these activities is a kind of research. Writers do research for all sorts of reasons, but whatever their reasons, they must consider the rhetorical situation that drives their research: purpose, audience, genre, and the writer.

Research and the Rhetorical Situation

Say you decide to write an opinion piece for your local paper about what to do with all the waste material at the landfill. An opinion piece in the local paper is an appropriate genre given the issue is a local one and your letter will make people aware of the problem while engaging them in a public discussion. You are concerned that as the town grows, the amount of waste generated will force the town to either increase the size of the landfill or ship the waste someplace else. In both cases, taxes will need to be raised to pay for the solution. Given the current level of taxation and the rising cost of living, this option does not sit well with you or with others in town. You decide that two workable and easily adopted solutions to this problem are 1) to encourage residents to compost their vegetable waste, and 2) to reuse containers as much as possible and buy only recyclable plastic containers. Simply looking at that rhetorical situation will let you know the kinds of research you might consider doing:

Research for an Opinion Piece about Waste Management in the Local Paper

Rhetorical Situation	Research Questions	Where to Find Information
Topic: What to do with the waste generated by residents in the town.	What is currently being done?	Town officials/website
	What have other towns similar to ours done?	Other towns' officials/town websites
		Scholarly or popular articles on landfills and recycling
Audience: The townspeople	What do they think about the current system?	Interviews and surveys
	What would they like to see changed?	
Purpose: To persuade residents to compost vegetable waste, reuse containers, and buy only recyclable plastics.	How will composting help? Have other towns done something similar?	Operators of the landfill; books on composting and waste management; relevant databases at library
	How much will reusing containers reduce the amount of waste?	Books on recycling or the "green movement"; subject-specific databases (e.g. Energy Citations or Science Direct); government websites such as the EPA; community organizations such as the Ecology Center
	Which kinds of plastics are recyclable?	Same as above, but also the Plastics Trade Association website; local government officials
Writer: A resident of the town who wants to prevent an increase in taxes for waste management and do something good for the environment at the same time.	What has been my experience with recycling?	Personal experiences with recycling and managing waste at home
	How have I been affected by the cost of the landfill?	Interviews with parents, siblings, children
	Why do I care now?	

With just a basic understanding of the rhetorical situation, you can quickly get an excellent sense of what you need to know in order to write, in this case, a successful opinion piece. Of course, you might not research *all* of the areas above. That's the point: Research should be driven by the situation in which you find yourself and the need to establish a particular kind of *ethos,* or credibility, as the writer. There are, for example, many genres and situations where you need to do no, or very minimal, research. The letter to the editor may be one such genre—after all, there is nothing that says a letter *has to be* well informed, logical, or even accurate. However, if you consider that you write a public letter to convince others to at least listen to what you have to say, then you want to be sure you are writing convincingly, accurately, and with the best information to serve your audience and purpose. That's where research will help you to strengthen your writing.

WHY DO RESEARCH?

Writers conduct research for all sorts of reasons, including the following:

- To enter a conversation on a subject.
- To take a stand on a controversial issue.
- To understand what's been said by experts.
- To develop a solution to a problem or provide alternatives to existing ones.
- To challenge historical or scientific knowledge in light of new research.
- To pose new questions or expand current thinking on a subject.

Making Research Meaningful

You may find yourself in situations where research is needed in your academic, civic, or professional life. Naturally, when you choose a topic that interests you, research is less daunting, even enjoyable. But there are many situations where the topic may be chosen for you: a professor assigns a research report topic you know little about, or your team leader requires you to conduct research for a report she has to deliver to her department head. In such situations, you may simply have to work with what you have been given. But sometimes, when writers find themselves in situations where the topic is challenging, they can rethink the topic or the assignment to make the research process, and thus, the writing, more meaningful to them.

GUIDELINES: MAKING RESEARCH MEANINGFUL

1. **Find an angle.** If you have been assigned a topic that is uninteresting to you, think of an angle on the topic that would make it more interesting. Of course, check with the person who has given the assignment to be sure this is allowed.

2. **Think about genre.** Will you be able to repurpose the research to use in other writing? If you have been asked to write a report on community-based volunteer programs, can you use that material to generate a brochure for your town? If you have some flexibility with genre for the assignment, tailor it to fit the audience and purpose, and to make it more interesting for you.

3. **Imagine a larger significance.** Can you imagine ways in which the topic or the research process itself might help you in other courses, other areas of your life, or in your current or future career? If you are assigned a research project

(continued)

on the benefits and drawbacks of online courses versus traditional courses, can you use what you learn when you sign up for future college courses.

4. **Redefine research.** Some forms of research other than traditional library research can make searching for background information more interesting. For example, you can talk to people and make observations about your topic or issue in field research.

Thinking About Research

Whether you are given a topic or have chosen your own, the first steps in the research process are to assess what you already know about the subject, what you want to know to fulfill your purpose for writing, and what your audience needs to know or expects to learn.

Assessing the Topic

Before beginning any research, you'll want to make sure you are thinking in terms of *issue* rather than *topic*. A topic is a general category or broad idea—say, terrorism or speed dating. But an issue is a specific angle on a much broader topic; so terrorism might become "the effect of terrorism on university study-abroad programs." Speed dating becomes "the benefits and dangers of speed dating."

Topic	*Possible Issues*
Terrorism	Effects of terrorism on university study-abroad programs
	Racial profiling and U.S. policies as a result of terrorism
	Effects of terrorism on international travel industry
Speed dating	Gender factors: who chooses speed dating and why?
	Benefits and dangers of speed dating
	Psychosocial effects of speed dating

As you may notice in the above examples, a topic often yields many different issues. As a writer considering the rhetorical situation, it's up to you to determine which issue you'll work with as you begin your research. And, of course, you'll want to make sure your issue is appropriate for the assignment. Notice that in each case, the issue is *specific*—this is especially good for researchers. It is much easier to find useful and relevant information when you have a specific focus in mind. Moving from topic to issue involves thinking in terms of problems or concerns connected with the topic. For example, with a little thought we can articulate several issues connected to the general topic of health care:

- It costs too much.
- The state needs to pay for everyone's health care.

- Or the federal government should pay for everyone's health care.
- It's not fair that some people have health insurance coverage and others do not.
- Elected officials don't seem to be addressing health care issues; if they are, they are not doing enough.
- Some procedures are covered by health insurance, others are not. Why is that? Who decides what is covered by policies?
- There is disparity between coverage for women and men.
- So-called elective procedures are not covered.

<u>WRITING ACTIVITY</u>   Moving from Broad Topic to Focused Issue

1. Make a list of the possible issues your topic yields. You might think of these as subtopics, themes, or questions raised by the broad topic. Keep in mind your assignment, the audience and purpose, and the situation for writing. Also consider some of the specific subtopics that arise given the social situation for your writing.
2. Discuss your topic with others in class. What do they find interesting? What do they know about your topic? What questions do they have and what issues do they see connected with the topic? List all the possibilities.
3. Look at your assignment again in light of the issues you've identified for your topic. Which issue makes sense given the audience and purpose? Which interests you the most and why?

■　■　■

Considering Your Purpose, Audience, and Genre

Thinking through the rhetorical situation *before* doing research helps you narrow the focus of your topic and direction for your research. Once you know why you are doing your research, you can then consider where and how to find the information you need. The key to effective, relevant, and enjoyable research is to be clear about *why* you are researching in the first place. Simply doing research because you have to does not generally provide you with good material—it's like buying a pair of shoes without knowing how big your feet are and what you will use the shoes for. In discussing how to use the rhetorical situation to focus your research, we will use the genre of a research report, but what we suggest here will work equally well for other genres, both academic and civic. So for example, if you were to write a research report on the issue that health care costs too much, you might ask the simple question: Who would care that it costs too much? Possible answers include:

1. People who have to pay for their own health care
2. People who have to pay to cover the health care costs of those who cannot afford insurance—in other words, taxpayers
3. People who have to find ways to pay for the health care costs of those who cannot afford insurance—in other words, our elected officials

Asking who would care reveals three potential audiences, but none of them is exclusive of the others. That is, choosing one as your primary audience does not rule out the other audiences from benefiting from your report. Examining the issue and potential audience will in turn help clarify your purpose. By asking three key questions about the relationship between your potential audience and issue, you can clarify your purpose. To understand your purpose in writing about health care costs for those who have to pay for their own health care, you can again ask three straightforward questions:

■ *Is the issue something that potential audiences will know something about?*

Yes, they will be painfully aware of the problem because they have to pay for insurance (or not)—but they may not be aware of why it is so high or if there are other alternatives.

■ *Is the issue something that potential audiences might be misinformed about?*

Yes, as they might think that the costs are high because insurance companies are trying to maximize profit. They might not be aware that there are many more forces at work than just greed—cost of research and development, cost of malpractice insurance, local concerns such as proximity to certain kinds of doctors, and so on.

■ *Is the issue something that potential audiences can act on?*

Well, yes, in a limited way if they knew of other alternatives, and certainly they could contact their congressional representatives and urge them to do something about it. But audiences could not directly effect that kind of change.

Note that the answers suggest some possible refinement of focus and research. If your audience isn't aware of why health care costs so much, you can inform them; if they aren't aware of their choices, you can provide those as well. These ideas in turn suggest areas that you are going to have to research. Having defined the audience and purpose, you now need to think more about your role as the writer by considering the social situation of the report itself. In some genres, you can position yourself as antagonistic, humorous, sarcastic, earnest, or playful. You can be over the top and in your face, or reserved and serious. With the research report, your choices of approach are limited. Research reports are informative genres; they are written so that the audience can make an informed decision about an issue. Thus, as the writer of a report you will strive for formality and objectivity, and may even remove yourself from the text (no use of first person, for instance).

WRITING ACTIVITY   Defining the Rhetorical Situation and Genre for Research

Developing a clear understanding of the rhetorical situation can help you identify what kinds of research you might need and where you may need to go to find it. Consider the following:

1. Have your subject, purpose, and audience been defined for you by your instructor? If so, write a detailed description of them in your own words.

2. If they have not been defined for you:

   ■ What is the *topic* you are writing about? Can it be narrowed down to a focused issue? Write a phrase that captures the focus of your topic.

   ■ Who would care about the issue and why? Who would want to know about it or do something about it?

- Why do you want to write about it? What do you want your audience to do or think as a result of reading your text? Is what they know about the issue accurate?
- What is the situation surrounding the writing? That is, what social scenario is driving the writing (e.g. a recent controversy, a growing or renewed interest in the topic)?

3. Genre and rhetorical situation are interconnected, so it makes a difference if you are writing a research report or an open letter. Genre can give you some clues about what kinds of research you may need. Consider the following:
   - Can you choose the genre? If so, which genres seem to work best given the rhetorical situation you have identified? What genre would best convey your message and fulfill your purpose?
   - Does the rhetorical situation call for a formal or informal genre such as a research report or brochure, respectively?
   - Even if you cannot choose the genre, consider what you know about the rhetorical situation and the characteristics of the genre. What types of research do the rhetorical situation and the genre call for? Do the situation and genre allow for the use of field research such as interviews and questionnaires? Is formal academic research necessary or would informal research (e.g. a Web search) be appropriate?

■ ■ ■

Conducting Preliminary Research

Preliminary research is the process of investigating your issue to find out more about it before you begin writing. Preliminary research may lead you to think of some questions for your research project and give you ideas about how to approach your subject.

Establishing what you know. One of the best ways to begin your preliminary research is to establish what you already know about your subject. Mining your past experiences and current knowledge on a subject is a form of research itself. Before you begin to research, write down as much as you are able about your issue. This step can help you narrow the focus of your research, understand research's purpose in your writing, and establish what you don't know and need to find out.

For example, as she started thinking about her topic for an open letter about the poor and dangerous condition of her high school building, Jenna Clark wrote down what she already knew about the situation, including some of her own experiences. You'll notice how in writing about what she knows, Clark also begins to define her reasons for writing about this issue:

> The issue I chose to write about is the building of a new high school in Guilford. The construction of a new high school is current and timely because the problems of this building, and others like it around the state, are becoming more serious every year. Year after year, residents of Guilford shoot down the idea of a new high school because they do not want taxes to rise. Yet, over the summer, a new turf field was put in for our sports teams. It's amazing to me that the new field is more important than a school. Our school was built in the 1930s, and it feels like it hasn't been renovated since then! This problem needs to be addressed because the condition of the school has

> an impact on the students' education and their futures. I know from
> experience that it's a disgusting, unhealthy environment. There is mold
> because the ceiling leaks; mold is a serious health hazard. As a past student
> of Guilford High, I'm concerned about the students who are still there.

WRITING ACTIVITY   Preliminary Research: Establishing What You Know

Do some informal writing before you begin your research. Below are some strategies to get
you started.

1. **Brainstorming**: Write down everything you already know about your issue. Imagine
   you are explaining the issue to someone who knows less than you do about it.
2. **Listing**: What do you want to know about the issue? Be as general or as specific as you
   need to be depending on your current knowledge of the issue. You could include questions,
   words, or phrases you've heard that are related to the issue, or any ideas that come to mind.
3. **Discussing**: Talk with your classmates, roommates, family members, or coworkers.
   What do they know about the issue and what do they want to know more about? What
   questions do they have?

■ ■ ■

Conducting Background Research

Regardless of whether you have chosen your issue or been assigned one, background research
can help you find out what's already been said about the issue, how it is currently being discussed, or provide definitions and clarify concepts that emerge on the subject. As you conduct background research, keep a list of the sources and websites you find and of the people
you speak with so you can return to them later. Also take notes on information from your
sources to help you refine your issue or subject and to prompt questions for your research.

GUIDELINES: BACKGROUND RESEARCH SOURCES

The following is an overview of the most common places to look for background
information on your issue:

- **Books, magazines, newspapers.** Search your library's databases to find
  information from books or periodicals on your issue. Look online to the
  archives of newspapers or magazines and search for information on your issue.
- **Encyclopedias.** Your library may provide access to both general and specialized
  encyclopedias. Britannica Online, Encarta, and other online encyclopedias are
  useful preliminary research tools, but because they are general resources, they
  are best for preliminary research. Be cautious of material found on Wikipedia
  or other wikis (websites that allow users to add, edit, and revise material) as it's
  hard to verify accuracy.
- **Search engines.** Google and other search engines enable you to locate Internet-
  based information on your issue. Web searches often yield links to the sites of
  organizations and groups in a subject area.   *(continued)*

■ **Friends, family, experts, or experienced others.** Talking to people about your issue can yield interesting insights and ideas that will take your research in unique directions. Discussing your issue will help you learn about different opinions people have and why, and lead to questions about your issue you hadn't thought of before.

■ **Media.** Don't overlook television programs and radio shows that engage in discussions of public issues as research sources. They often broadcast documentaries, news reports, and interviews with experts on a variety of current subjects.

Asking Questions

It's a good idea to think about your research in terms of questions you need to have answered. *Research questions* help writers to narrow the scope of their research to make it manageable. Such questions also allow writers to think about what it is they want to discover about an issue through their research and writing. Research questions will help you later, too, as you begin to do the research itself by providing you with some of the search terms you can use to find that research.

Research is best accomplished with a clear agenda in mind. The more precise your research agenda, the easier your actual research will be. That is, when you know your purpose, audience, and issue, you can simply ask, What about each of those areas do I need to research? Let's consider again your topic of the high cost of health care. You defined your audience as those individuals and families who have to pay for healthcare expenses out-of-pocket, and decided your purpose was to inform this audience of why the costs are so high and what alternatives (or assistance) are available.

Possible research questions:

■ What is the cost of health care for a typical family of four? Nationwide? In my state? What about for a single man or woman? Does age make a difference?

■ Why is health care so costly? What is the role of insurance companies in this cost? How much of the cost has to do with doctors and medical facilities?

■ Is anything being done about the high cost of health care?

■ What are the consequences of the high costs of health care for families and individuals? Do they cut back in other areas? Go without routine care?

■ Do any programs exist to help these groups? Are there organizations that might serve these groups?

You could probably come up with more questions, but you can see that all of the questions follow from the rhetorical situation.

> **GUIDELINES:** USING THE RHETORICAL SITUATION TO DEVELOP RESEARCH QUESTIONS
> Use the following questions as guidelines to help you focus on questions you'd like to explore in your research:
>
> **Purpose:** What do you need to know in order to meet your purpose?
>
> *(continued)*

> **Audience:** What do you need to know in order to meet the expectations of your audience? What do you need to know in order to convince, persuade, or inform your audience?
>
> **Writer:** What do you need to know in order to successfully establish your ethos (your authority to write about the subject)?
>
> **Genre:** What do the characteristics of the genre require that you know (e.g. a research report will require more specific knowledge while a letter to the editor requires more general knowledge)?

Developing Keyword Search Terms

Once you have defined your audience and purpose, explored your subject, and established some of the characteristics of the genre, you are ready to generate the initial list of terms that you will use in your research. You'll add to your initial list once you get into your research and encounter other terms you can use and other questions you can ask. For her research report, Abby Radzimirski, a student in a first-year writing course, decided to write about child labor laws in the United States as they affect teenagers working part-time jobs. As part of her planning, she generated a list of possible search terms and phrases to help her find the material she would need; she then revised that list to better reflect her audience and purpose.

Key Terms	Key Terms Revised
Minors at work	Guidelines for employing teenagers
Labor laws	Labor laws *and* teenagers
Children working	Labor laws *and* adolescents
Labor laws protecting children	Labor laws *and* high school students
Child labor	Labor laws *and* underage workers
Manual labor	Labor—manual, skilled, retail
Underage workers	Regulations *and* teenage employees
Department of Labor	Minors *and* work
Working and school-age children	Teenagers *and* work
Cost of child labor	High school students *and* work and education
Regulations and teenage workers	Rights—adolescents, teenagers, high school students *and* work
Minors	
High school students	

Notice how in the Key Terms Revised list she has combined terms and used the same terms in different ways. Using *and* refines her search for databases and search engines, which will search these now linked terms and yield results in which both terms appear.

WRITING ACTIVITY   Generating Search Terms

Look over the answers you provided to the questions about purpose, audience, and genre, as well as the research questions you generated above. What terms are associated with your answers and questions? Write down as many terms as you can; consult a thesaurus and your classmates to come up with different ways of saying the same thing (e.g. "environmentalist," "tree hugger," "hippie," "green," and so on). Generate as many search terms as you can. More is better, because as you'll find out, not all sources categorize subjects using the same terms.

■ ■ ■

Creating a Research Plan

A *research plan* helps writers identify their purposes for conducting research and writing and indicates the importance of their work—why others would find it significant and want to read it. That is, a research plan suggests how the research may contribute in some meaningful way to the larger ongoing discussions about the issue. Finally, a research plan may help writers articulate what they've discovered so far and how they might use it, what direction they want to go in next, and even to sketch out a working outline. Research plans can also help writers see where there are gaps in their research, thus sending them back to sources to find out more. Research and writing is a cyclical process, despite the fact that a research plan may *look* like a linear document.

As you write your research plan, you'll want to remember: 1) It is a *working plan—one subject to revision,* so plan on moving items around, cutting and adding new ideas, as you write. 2) The more you research, the more likely you are to *refine and change* your plan to fit your purpose and audience. (See Chapter 10: Research Reports pages 411–412 for an example of a research plan.)

WRITING ACTIVITY   The Research Plan

One way to set up a research plan is to include the elements below. Each section can help you figure out what you need to research (the more detailed you can be here, the better).

1. Title of Project:

   Give your project a working title. This name does not have to be the actual title of your paper, but it should reflect how you are currently thinking about your paper. For example:

   Rural Youth and Oxycontin: When Boredom Meets Access

2. Statement of purpose and audience:

   Describe your issue. Explain what you hope your research will reveal. Who do you imagine will be the intended audience? Why them? Who are they? What do you believe or already think or know about your topic? Why would they want to or why would they need to read your text? What do you want them to do, think, or feel as a result of reading your text? Here is an example:

> Oxycontin abuse is a problem, especially in rural schools. This report will inform readers of the recent problems in the local CT schools; it will be distributed to high school and college administrators to inform them of the problem and how it has been addressed in other regions (maybe other states). My audience is likely to know a lot about teenage drug use, but they might not know about Oxycontin. Cutting off access and increasing awareness of its consequences seem like reasonable ways to decrease Oxycontin use among youth in rural areas. The consequences of Oxycontin abuse are life-threatening, so something needs to be done now.

3. Background:

Explain why you are writing about this issue. Have you done any previous research on the issue or on a related topic or issue? Have you taken any classes, seen films, or read books about the issue? Do you have any personal experience that is relevant? For example:

> I took a class on addiction, and I had to write a paper about teenage addiction, but I don't know much about Oxycontin. I had a friend who took Oxycontin in H.S. because he got a head injury during a soccer game. But then he started to take it all the time. I also had an aunt who was hooked on Vicodin, and she had to go into treatment. That was 10 years ago, but she still struggles with her addiction.

4. Research Questions:

Effective research is driven by questions you want to find the answers to. These questions will reflect your purpose in writing the text and the audience you are addressing. Some of these questions may be ones you know the answers to but need to support with research. Others will be questions you don't know the answers to. Some will be background questions, others will be factual, and so on. Some examples:

> What is Oxycontin?
> How does it work on the body?
> How is Oxycontin used legally? Medically?
> What have people studying the problem of Oxycontin abuse said about its spread among youth?
> Where is Oxycontin most heavily used?
> What has been done about the problem (at state or national level, by law enforcement, etc.)?

5. Locating Research:

Part of effective research is also know where to look for the information you need; consider not only standard sources but also those individuals in your life who might be able to provide you with information.

Do you know of specific databases that would contain the information you need? Are there particular individuals you could talk to? Are there specialized collections that would be useful?

> I can talk to my uncle, since he's in the State Police.
> I can use the database Academic Search Premier, and search other databases like MedLine or SocINDEX.

■ ■ ■

Gathering Information: Where to Go and Why

One of the most useful skills that effective researchers have is knowing where to go for what kinds of information. Reference librarians are the best resource for help during the research process, but here we would like to give you a general sense of what is available and how to use it.

Types of Sources: Primary and Secondary Sources

Information gathered from research can be broken down into two general categories: primary and secondary sources.

Distinguishing Primary and Secondary Sources

Primary sources include information the writer has gathered firsthand or from sources that are in their original forms: interviews, surveys, historical documents, letters, works of art, photographs, diaries and journals, video footage, and other information that is not analyzed by experts, scholars, or others. It consists of data that is considered raw or unfiltered. **Secondary sources** include information that has been interpreted and synthesized and analyzed by scholars, experts, and other individuals interested in the subject. These sources might include scholarly articles, texts, reviews, magazine or newspaper articles, or just about anything that has not been gathered firsthand by the writer/researcher herself.

For example, a letter written by President Lincoln to Henry Pierce in 1859 would be considered a primary source; an analysis of or commentary on that same letter would be considered a secondary source. Transcripts from court proceedings would be a primary source, whereas a reporter's account of those same proceedings would be a secondary source.

Depending on what you are writing and why, you may find that secondary sources will not be available or appropriate, in which case you'll turn to primary sources for your research. You may need to analyze the actual transcripts from your state legislature's last meeting. Or you may need to conduct a survey for a newspaper article you are writing to determine how residents in your town want the new budget to be divided among various projects; this information will not be available in print form (unless someone has already done this particular survey). However, if you are writing a proposal to the town council on how to allocate funds for the new budget, you might find yourself turning to secondary sources. The point is, often the rhetorical situation calls for particular kinds of research.

Scholarly and General Secondary Sources

As you research, you'll come across a wide range of secondary sources on your issue written for general audiences as well as specialized audiences. *It's up to you, the writer,* to decide if the subject and the assignment call for material published in both kinds of sources or if the subject lends itself to research from one type of publication.

While it can sometimes be easy to tell the difference between scholarly and general publications just by looking at the title (e.g. *Journal of the American Medical Association* is obviously scholarly), sometimes it is not that easy to recognize what type of source you've come across. Here are some characteristics that differentiate publications:

Scholarly Publications	*General Publications*
Audience: Specialized/expert readers in a particular discipline or field	**Audience**: Nonspecialized readers; little specialized knowledge of a subject
Writers: Specialized/expert in a particular discipline or field	**Writers**: Credible writers, some with specialization in a discipline, others who are journalists, commentators, etc., and whose credentials may be diverse and span many subjects
Topics/Material: Articles on a particular subject(s) or field of study that demonstrate extensive research (e.g. *Chronicle of Higher Education* contains material on subjects related to issues in higher education.)	**Topics/Material**: Articles on many subjects (e.g. *Time Magazine* covers history, politics, science, etc.)
Language/Style: Language geared toward people with specialized disciplinary knowledge; jargon related to the field; style appropriate to the discipline	**Language/Style**: Language geared toward nonspecialized readers; specialized jargon and concepts defined for readers; style in line with publication format

Media Sources: Film, Television, and Radio

Scholarly articles, letters from important people, general reference texts are all useful material for the researcher. But not everything that's important for the writer's rhetorical situation can be found in the world of print media—not *everything* has been written about, some things are talked about or shown. Nonprint media offer us a way to experience something immediately and viscerally. We can learn something different when watching, for instance, a documentary on a local contest to win a truck versus reading about that same contest in a newspaper article or a scholarly analysis of *why* people participate in such contests. What you learn in those three cases is important, but you do learn something different from each. In a documentary called *Hands on a Hard Body,* for instance, you would learn how a group of individuals think about their willingness to stand for over twenty hours next to a hard body truck – during which time they must remain in contact with the truck, otherwise they lose the contest: no sleeping, no sitting, with only a few short breaks every few hours. As one of the individuals says, it's about human drama. You might not get that sense from reading a news report about the event.

Researchers view photographs to deepen their understanding of events or historical moments or cultural movements of an era. Sometimes researchers analyze media itself. For instance, if you were conducting research to write an analytical essay on the ways the news media portrayed the events of September 11, 2001, you might look at newspaper and magazine photographs to examine trends in the photos: Were ordinary citizens' reactions shown? Rescue workers in action? What do these images tell you about how media coverage of the day influenced the messages the public received? Other times just seeing something for yourself gives you greater insight into why you are writing about it in the first place. In both cases, visual material can add depth to your research, either directly, by providing material you can reference, or indirectly, by maintaining and extending interest in the issue.

Similarly, audio sources, such as radio broadcasts, offer something you can't find in print—the voice of the individual. To hear John F. Kennedy, Malcolm X, or Mahatma Gandhi speak, to hear how they used their voices, could give you a greater understanding of how that material connects to what you are writing about, or give you a different angle on your subject entirely. And more practically, some material is only available as sound recordings—from the music we listen to (classical, R&B, ska) to voice recordings of those who survived the Holocaust. There are also many public-interest broadcasts on the radio, such as National Public Radio's programs, the president's weekly radio addresses, and local and national talk shows. Listening to interviews with specialists', hobbyists', or experts' commentary on a subject provides researchers with current information on significant topics of the day—what the public is talking about and interested in—from political elections, to the war in Iraq, to cooking authentic Greek food. All of these are valid and potentially important sources for researchers.

As you work through your research topics, think about how these forms of media research may be useful for you, the writer, and how they might help you think through your purpose, rhetorical situation, the genre, and the research agenda you have in mind.

WebLinks

The Internet Archive

The Internet Archive is an online resource that "includes texts, audio, moving images, and software as well as archived web pages." Search the web for "Internet archive."

Locating Sources

You would think, given the ease with which we can search the Web, that finding suitable research would be an easy task. Unfortunately, there is often so much information—on the Web, in the library, stored in databases—that it is sometimes hard to know where to start. As a rule of thumb, your school's library is the place to start. Knowing the difference between what your library actually has on its shelves and what is contained in its databases is a crucial first step. When you use your library, you'll be searching either the library's actual holdings (books shelved in the stacks, articles in the periodicals section, items on microfiche, microfilm, or in special collections) or its virtual holdings (subscription databases made accessible to patrons).

Of course, no matter what types of library resources you are working with, it's necessary to evaluate their *relevance* to your subject and assignment. (For guidelines on evaluating sources, see "Evaluating Sources" on page 533.)

Library Holdings	Database Content
Scholarly books, reports, and monographs; periodicals (scholarly journals, newspapers, and magazines); documents (books and articles) on microfilm and microfiche; video and audio media. Some libraries have special collections on particular subjects (e.g. Canadian studies). Because print and microform materials must be physically stored onsite, holdings are always limited, even in the largest of libraries.	Citations and/or abstracts for books, monographs, articles, and reports. The full text of some articles is downloadable. Databases are organized by discipline, area, or subject (e.g. medicine, humanities, current affairs, newspapers, etc.). Not all databases have full-text articles, so you may still need to order a copy through your library's interlibrary loan program. Books are rarely available in databases.

Archive Holdings	Web Content
Specialized collections often of historical material. For example, a university library might have archived all the teaching material of its faculty from the early part of the twentieth century. Or it might contain print material relevant to the region: old maps, newspapers, town reports, and so on. One famous archive is the Fortunoff Video Archive for Holocaust Testimonies at Yale University, which contains firsthand testimony of individuals who survived the Holocaust. Field research archives include interviews, surveys, and observations. Since these are usually physically stored in the library, holdings are limited and specialized. Similarly, access is sometimes restricted as the material is one of a kind.	Nearly everything imaginable—from scholarly and popular books available at Google Books to individual Web pages, to government resources. Unlike traditional repositories of information, the Web has nearly limitless capacity. The problem is, little of the material is organized efficiently and there is no restriction on who can say what, so verifying information from a Web source is tricky but absolutely necessary.

Searching Library Catalogs

When you search your library's catalog, usually the best way to start is to perform a "keyword" search rather than looking for specific titles or authors (if you know of some, then by all means search for them as well). Simply enter the key search terms you generated earlier to find relevant material. It's worth repeating that having a good list of key terms—more than you think are necessary and synonyms and antonyms for important terms—is essential. Without this list you're basically wandering in the dark hoping to stumble upon what you need. Say you are writing that opinion piece we mentioned earlier in this chapter about your town's landfill problems. You want to get some background information on landfills so that you are sure you fully understand the history and current concerns regarding landfills. Your first step is to look at what your library has in its catalog.

For example, a simple search of CONSULS (the Catalog of the Connecticut State University Libraries and the State Library) using the phrase "landfill and environment" yields the results shown here:

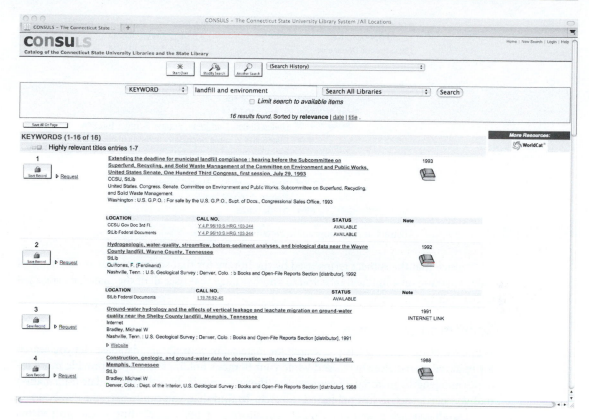

Results of Library Catalog Search for "Landfill" and "Environment"

Every library has its own catalog system, so you'll want to make use of your library's help section and reference desk to learn how to search it efficiently. Still, three basic rules usually apply to catalog searches:

1. Use multiple terms and many different arrangements.
2. Search broadly at first, and narrowly later.
3. Flag (or save) potential sources as you sift through the results.

It is important to note that library collections are organized under broad subject terms, which you can search for in the catalog. Subject terms may be different from the keyword terms on your list. Luckily, it's fairly easy to find out the subject term associated with a keyword. If we clicked on the first item in the search results shown above, we would be taken to a page that provides the abstract and bibliographic details for the source (see page 518).

LOCATION	CALL NO.
CCSU Gov Doc 3rd Fl.	Y 4.P 96/10:S.HRG.103-244
StLib Federal Documents	Y 4.P 96/10:S.HRG.103-244

Persistent link to this record: http://www.consuls.org.80/record=b2093165~S16

Description	iii, 71 p. ; 24 cm
Series Statement	S. hrg. ; 103-244
Series Tracing	United States. Congress. Senate. S. hrg. ; 103-244
Note	Distributed to some depository libraries in microfiche
	Shipping list no.: 93-0649-P
Bibliog.	Includes bibliographical references
Subject	Sanitary landfills -- United States
	Refuse disposal facilities -- United States
ISBN	0160416825

Abstract and Bibliographic Details for a Source

Notice that the subject terms used by the library for that source appear on the page as links. Clicking on a link will take you to another page that lists all of the material cataloged under that subject term.

Searching Databases

While the library catalog lets you search for material in your library, databases let you search for material stored elsewhere. And while your library's holdings will often provide more in-depth and lengthy material on your subject, they may not include the up-to-date information that you need, such as just published research. To find that, you can turn to the databases.

Databases are essentially digital repositories of texts (including audio and visual material) stored in bibliographic format and sometimes in full-text format. In other words, all databases will give you information about a text (author, title, an abstract, etc.), and some databases will give you a digitized version of the text itself. Some databases are *generalized*—they provide access to periodical content on many different subjects and from a variety of fields of study. One example is Academic Search Premier. Other databases are *specialized* —they provide access to periodical contents in a specific discipline. One example is PsychINFO, which contains information from periodicals specific to the discipline of psychology. The first step is to find out which databases you need to search. Many libraries make it easy for users by organizing databases into broad categories. Check the categories to find out which databases make sense for your project. And if you still can't find a database related to your subject, ask your library's reference librarians for help.

In most cases, unless you are researching within a very specific discipline, you'll probably find all the information you need in one of the comprehensive databases. For example, Academic Search Premier gives you access to thousands of topical journals as well as magazines and newspapers written for and read by general audiences. So it is a good place to begin your research. The search screen for Academic Search Premier is straightforward, as you can see on the next page.

Notice that you can select specific databases if you want, and you can also set the search parameters: find all search terms, some of them, related words, and so on. You can also limit your search to material from a specific time period—say published in the last five years. To find information on your topic, you will have to do some sifting and

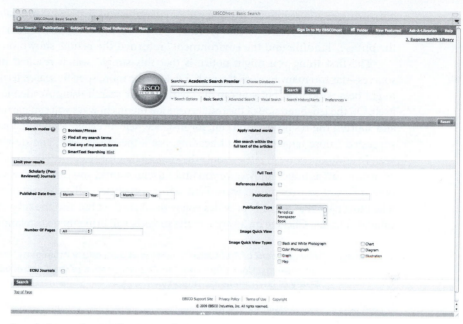

Search Screen for Academic Search Premier Database

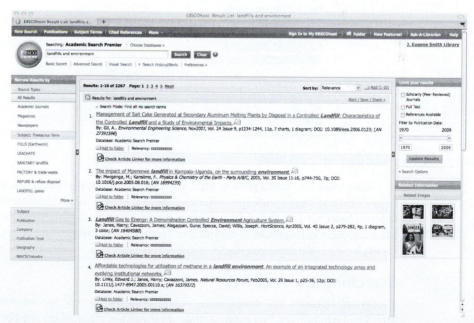

Search Results for "Landfills and the Environment"

narrowing as you search for just the right material—and that's why you have come up with a lot of different search terms. A search of Academic Search Premier database using the phrase "landfills and the environment" returned the results shown on page 519.

The first thing you might notice is that this simple search resulted in 2,267 possible sources—far too many to work through. Looking for more specific search terms from your list might be a good idea, but you can also narrow your search using Academic Search Premier itself. On the left-hand side of the results page are menus of ways you can narrow your search— and shorten the results list. You can, for instance, select certain academic journals, click on a suggested (more targeted) subject heading, use a thesaurus term, and designate publication year. In addition, you can retrieve only the sources that list references or provide the full text of an article. Just as importantly, once you find a useful source, you can use that source to find still other relevant sources in two ways. First, when you click on the abstract of a source, you are taken to a page that not only provides you with an abstract but also the subject(s) the source is cataloged under. Clicking on any one of the subjects will bring up texts relating to that subject.

Title:	***Management of Salt Cake* Generated at Secondary Aluminum Melting Plants by Disposal in a Controlled Landfill: Characteristics *of* the Controlled Landfill and a Study *of* Environmental Impacts.**
Authors:	Gil, A.1 *andoni@unavarra.es*
Source:	Environmental Engineering Science; Nov2007, Vol. 24 Issue 9, p1234-1244, 11p, 1 Diagram, 7 Charts
Document Type:	Article
Subject Terms:	*SODIUM sulfate *ALUMINUM *FILLS (Earthwork) *ENVIRONMENTAL engineering *FACTORY & trade waste *BILLS, Legislative *REFUSE & refuse disposal *QUANTITATIVE research *ENVIRONMENTAL impact analysis
Author-Supplied Keywords:	controlled landfill environmental impact assessment salt cake secondary aluminum waste reassessment

Information Screen for the First Search Result

Also, once you find a good source, you can use that text's references, which likely will be relevant and can provide you with more specific information on different aspects of your subject. Searching databases is in essence no different from searching the library catalog, but database search protocols do differ, so familiarize yourself with the particular requirements for each database you use.

Searching the Archives

University libraries and many large public libraries have a special section called the archives. Generally, archives collect material about the place where the library resides. For instance, a university archive might be responsible for collecting and cataloging all of the official documents produced by university administration, faculty, and students (from memos to syllabi to copies of the student newspaper). But the archive might also collect material from the larger community in the form of newspapers, historical documents, maps, and so on. The materials collected in archives are usually **primary sources**. At a university library, you would expect to find addresses by the presidents of the university, memoranda about major college initiatives, and so on. You might also find material relating to individuals important to the college, such as letters written by a major donor.

Searching an archive requires a particular approach. For one thing, archival material is rarely digitized, so you cannot search the holdings as you would a database. That means you'll have to go to the archive to read the material. While collections (e.g. the provost's correspondence) within the archive will be cataloged, materials within the collections are not always entirely indexed—which means the only way to find something is to read through a lot of material in order to find that one item you are looking for.

Increasingly, archives useful to researchers are being collected on the Web. Sometimes these archives are collected and developed by hobbyists or individuals with no specialization but simply an interest in particular areas. Other Web archives are compiled by organizations and foundations that seek to preserve and make available particular kinds of information. The website American Rhetoric is an online archive of print, audio, and visual speeches by some of the world's best orators (from presidents to rock stars). Generally speaking, researchers use archives when the material there cannot be found anyplace else. Imagine writing a proposal to your town officials to start a community volunteer program for the elderly; money is tight and you know that officials and residents will be reluctant to fund new programs, even worthy ones. So the rhetorical situation is tough, but as you search through the archives you discover that your town once had such a program, that it was started by one of the town founders in the early-1800s and flourished until 1930. Being able to show that such a program was once an integral part of the community will bolster the claims in your proposal.

Researching on the World Wide Web

In some respects, using the Web to do research is a little like using a chainsaw to slice a piece of pie—sure, you get results, but what a mess. It's not that the Web is a bad place to find things out, it's just not efficient. A Web search might return millions of hits, which might seem like a good thing at first, except that the only way to figure out if a site is worthwhile is to visit it, look around, and try to evaluate it (Who put it together? Are they experts? Can they be trusted?). However, there are some reasons to use the Web for research. Think about the Web as a huge encyclopedia rather than as a source for in-depth material on a particular subject. In other words, you might turn to the Web when you need to get some background knowledge on a subject before settling on a particular focus for your project. For example, a Google search using the search phrase "landfills and the environment" yields the results shown on the following page.

You might have noticed that Google returned just over two million web pages—far too many to look through, and impossible to establish their relevance or reliability without visiting each one, reading the "about" page, then checking to make sure the information given there is accurate, and so on. But notice that the first few hits are for websites that introduce the environmental concerns connected to landfills. These sites might be useful if you know something about landfills but want to know more about their dangers. And those sites themselves might in turn lead you to other useful sites or to scholarly

Web   Images   Videos   Maps   News   Shopping   Gmail   more ▼   Sign in

Google | landfills and the environment | (Search)   Advanced Search
Preferences

Web   Show options...   Results **1 - 10** of about **2,060,000** for <u>landfills</u> and the <u>environment</u>. (0.22 seconds)

                                                                    Sponsored Links

LANDFILLS
Alliance For a Clean **Environment** (ACE)- This Pennsylvania group has collected a significant   **Landfills**
amount of information on **landfill** gas. ...   Reduce waste to help the earth
www.zerowasteamerica.org/**Landfills**.htm - <u>Cached</u> - <u>Similar</u>   **and help Keep America Beautiful.**
                                                                                                     www.kab.org
Landfills
Mar 15, 2000 ... **Landfills** present a clear and present potential threat to human health as well
as a threat to our **environment**. ...
www.iun.edu/~environw/**landfills**.html - <u>Cached</u> - <u>Similar</u>

LANDFILLS: Hazardous to the Environment
The earth is a limited space. Creating waste is unsustainable. If we continue to build **landfills**,
we will eventually run out of land - although it may take ...
www.beachbrowser.com/.../**Environment**/.../**LANDFILLS**-Hazardous-to-**Environment**.htm -
<u>Cached</u> - <u>Similar</u>

Environment - Waste
The Directive is intended to prevent or reduce the adverse effects of the **landfill** of waste on
the **environment**, in particular on surface water, groundwater, ...
ec.europa.eu/**environment**/waste/**landfill**_index.htm - <u>Cached</u> - <u>Similar</u>

Our bodies, our **landfills**? - Your **Environment**- msnbc.com
Two recent studies cast dramatic light on the extent to which Americans are absorbing toxic
chemicals into their bodies as a part of everyday life.
www.msnbc.msn.com/id/3076636/ - <u>Cached</u> - <u>Similar</u>

EIA Kids Page - Waste to **Landfill**
To protect the **environment** even more, the **landfill** is divided into a series of individual cells.
Only a few cells of the site (called the working face) are ...
www.eia.doe.gov/kids/energyfacts/saving/.../**landfiller**.html - <u>Cached</u> - <u>Similar</u>

The Basics of **Landfills**
Mar 26, 2003 ... RESOURCES ON **LANDFILLS**. ORGANIZATIONS AND JOURNALS: Center
for Health, **Environment** & Justice P.O. Box 6806. Falls Church, VA 22040 ...
www.ejnet.org/**landfills**/ - <u>Cached</u> - <u>Similar</u>

Texas Campaign for the **Environment: Landfill**
Texas Campaign for the **Environment** (TCE) is working with Texans, in particular people who
live near existing or proposed **landfills** to strengthen and enforce ...
www.texasenvironment.org/**landfills**.cfm - <u>Cached</u> - <u>Similar</u>

Google Search Results for "Landfills and the Environment"

material. You can use Google and other search engines to limit what you search for. On the top of the Google search page there is a link called "Show options." Clicking on that link opens a sidebar where you can set further parameters for your search. You can limit it by the kind of material and source (images, video, news, blogs) and by time frame, and have the search results in formats that might help you locate useful material more quickly.

The final concern with research using the Web is that material you find there may not be suitable for use in formal academic genres and should be used sparingly in even the more informal genres. As a writer you need to establish your ethos, your credibility. So which sounds better: "Oh, I read it on some Web page" or "In the latest issue of the *New England Journal of Medicine*"? The bottom line is you need to be sure that your Web source is reliable, relevant, accurate, and appropriate for your research: If you can't decide, don't use it.

Please see Evaluating Sources later in this chapter, beginning on page 533.

Conducting Field Research

Field research (interviews, surveys, observations) is conducted firsthand by writers. For example, your field research for an article on public transportation might involve interviewing people riding a bus, distributing a survey or questionnaire to workers at the Public Transit Authority, or observing the patterns of bus use along major routes in the city.

Why Do Field Research?

Sometimes, the support that you need is not available in print or digital form anywhere in a database, library, archive, or on the Web. Sometimes, the information or insight that you need in order to negotiate the rhetorical situation is available only directly from **primary sources**. In such cases, you will need to interview a person or a group, survey a group, or observe people and places in action. Certain genres almost necessitate that you conduct field research: profiles of people and places, for instance. Readers of these genres expect that the writer has had direct contact with the subject through interviews and observations. Other genres, such as a research report, can be written without the writer conducting field research. But reports, too, can benefit from field research, especially when the topic is both current and local. For example, a report on the effect of the rising cost of gas on the average Missourian should contain some information about what that effect really is. So the writer develops a survey and distributes it at local coffee shops, or conducts interviews of customers at the local gas station. Field research can fill in gaps in the research. Thus, field research provides writers and readers with primary source material that is recent, relevant, and often specifically related to particular people, places, and subjects of study.

Subjectivity and Field Research

In field research, the writer is observing, interviewing, and presenting the information on the subject based on her particular experience with it. Consequently, field research can lend credibility to a text and to the writer; it can, in other words, help establish *ethos*. One could argue that observation is subjective because the writer/researcher observes what he or she sees from his or her perspective and records information through that lens. Similarly, interview questions may be written with a particular angle in mind. So field research is not objective in the literal sense of the word. Typically, however, readers accept field research as accurate and valid because they assume that the researcher has gathered and interpreted the material ethically. They trust, in other words, that what the researcher says happened, happened.

GUIDELINES: ETHICAL FIELD RESEARCH

As you conduct your own field research, keep these guidelines in mind:

Interviews

- When developing interview questions, be sure you base them on information found in accurate and credible sources.
- Consider taping your interviews to ensure for accuracy of quotations. Get permission from the interviewees before taping.

(continued)

■ Avoid gotcha-style interviews. Your purpose is to get the best information you can, not to catch someone in a lie or expose some horrid truth. Treat your subject with respect regardless of how you might personally feel about him, her, or them.

■ If a subject is particularly controversial or personal, it is considered good ethics to send the person/s copies of their interview responses before publication or submission. This courtesy allows you and the interviewee to address any discrepancies.

■ Provide the interviewees with copies of the finished writing after it is published (or submitted for a class assignment). Consider sending them a thank-you note as well.

Observations

■ Observe what is there, not what you want to see. Record accurately what is going on, but avoid editorializing or analyzing what you see until your observations are concluded. If you start drawing conclusions as you observe, you are likely to start seeing what you want to see.

■ When possible, observe your subject on more than one occasion. And acknowledge in your text how long and where the observation was done.

Surveys

■ Because surveys are meant to give a broad view of a particular group's perceptions on a topic, do not cherry-pick your respondents. You should choose a group and survey them all or a representative, randomized sample.

■ Be sure your questions are not framed to give you the answers you want (e.g. leading questions).

■ Make sure the length of your survey is reasonable given the subject and your audience. Be clear about how long you expect the average respondent will take to complete it.

Interviews

Interviewing individuals, group members, or experts provides original information on a subject that isn't available from other sources. For example, if your issue is how students at Colorado State University are dealing with recent tuition hikes, talking directly to students as they stand in line to pay their tuition bills at the Bursar's Office or speaking to Financial Aid staff members might yield interesting insights on the hike that cannot be gleaned from print sources. Secondary sources might provide background information on what led up to the tuition increases, while the interviews will serve as the principle sources of research for the report. Depending on your subject, interviews may uncover information that provides a different perspective than one presented in secondary print sources. For instance, historical texts may offer the "official" versions of local reactions to the events of September 11, 2001, whereas talking directly to people who were part of the events at the Pentagon, World Trade Center, or near the plane crash site in Pennsylvania may offer new and different information about effects on those individuals on that tragic day. Thus, interviews may provide alternate perspectives on history that add new insights on the subject of your research. As you can see, interviews may serve as a sole source of research or a supplemental form of information, depending on your project and your subject.

Understanding How Interviews Work

Interviewing is not as easy as it looks, especially when you are asking a person or a group to talk about issues that they would not normally discuss with someone they don't know or with someone who is going to make public what they say. This can create a tough situation. Think about the interviewing process a form of "wooing." You are trying to woo your subject and convince them that they should trust you enough to tell you something interesting about themselves or the subject you are writing about. After all, one goal of an interview may be to find out what you could not find out any other way.

One way to encourage your subject to answer your questions fully is to carefully craft and organize those questions. Well-crafted questions will show the subject that you have thought carefully and critically about them or the subject you are asking them about and that you respect their time enough to have fully prepared for the interview. Think of it this way: If you are out on a first date and you start talking about marriage, your date is probably going to start looking for a quick exit. Yet if that subject came up after your relationship was well established, your partner might be open to such a conversation. The same principle applies to your interviews.

Doing Your Research Before the Interview

Conducting an interview is a form of research; but as with other kinds of research, you need to do some work prior to the interview if you want it to be successful. Say you are writing a profile about a local businesswoman who runs an adventure excursion business in Provo, Utah. Through preliminary research on your subject, you find out that she likes to go "caving." So you do some research on caving and discover that one of the hardest cave systems to explore is Neilson's Cave in Utah. Now when you interview the businesswoman, you can ask her about her interest in caving and open up the conversation further by asking whether or not she has ever explored those particular caves. In doing that little bit of research you accomplished quite a few things: 1) you came to understand your subject a little better; 2) you generated interesting questions that she, presumably, would enjoy answering; 3) you have impressed and complimented her by asking questions that revealed her interest and respected her time. Consequently, she is more likely to answer your questions fully, giving you the material you need and then some. Now that's the power of research.

Designing Interview Questions

Doing background research helps you design open ended interview questions that encourage your subject to respond to them. This is true whether you are interviewing one person or many. If you are interviewing multiple subjects, you'll ask some the same set of questions; others you'll ask questions tailored to their particular expertise or role they serve in your research. For instance, if you are writing a profile on the Division III winning baseball team at your college, you'll want to question the coaches about the strategies and philosophy for a successful team. But your questions may shift gears a bit when you talk to the fans—or even the players may warrant a different set of questions. What's important is that you keep the focus of your interview questions on what you want to find out about your subject through research.

Asking open-ended questions. There are two basic premises for developing questions for your interview: 1) Don't ask questions that you could look up the answer to (unless you specifically want the interviewee to confirm something); and 2) don't ask questions that will give you "yes" or "no" or very short answers (unless that's what you want). For example, you could ask, "Do you like to go caving?" To which your subject replies, "Yep." End of discussion. Much more effective would be to frame your question this way: "I've read somewhere that people go caving because it makes them feel as though they have left the world behind, almost like they have stepped out of time. Why do you go caving?" Notice that in this example you are communicating that you are interested enough in the interviewee to have found out what her passions are and resourceful enough to have found out something about those passions. But the way you framed this question also models for your subject the kind of answer you would like to get. Had you just asked her why she goes caving, she might have simply said, "Well, because I enjoy it." But because you have given her an example of how another caver thinks of the activity, you are more likely to get a thoughtful answer. Be careful, however, of the **leading question,** that is, a question framed in such a way to get the answer you want, not the answer that is an honest reflection of what the subject thinks or feels. In the example above, there is room for the subject to respond in a number of ways, including, "Well, no, I just go because it's one of the only ways I get exercise."

Balancing questions. The kinds of questions you ask will reflect your purpose in conducting the interview in the first place. If you are writing an open letter in which you want to expose some issue, then your questions will be written to uncover that kind of information. But no matter the reason for interviewing someone, you will want to balance your interview by having "easy" and "hard" questions. Generally speaking, your interviews will not be confrontational, so your "hard" and "easy" questions might be those, for instance, that allow a subject to talk about what they know well and those that ask them to speculate on areas they are less familiar with.

Asking specific or general questions. Depending on your subject and your research agenda, you may want to ask a balance of specific and general questions in your interview. For example, if you are interviewing the head of the state Department of Health on causes of the recent *E. coli* outbreak among elementary school children in your state, you may ask more *specific questions*: "Reports indicate a contamination in milk products provided by local dairies may have caused the outbreak. What is your perspective on the source of the outbreak?" However, your questions may be more *general* if your subject includes the four living WWII veterans in Pittsfield, Massachusetts: "What was it like to leave your families and go to war?" General questions yield more "storytelling" or anecdotes from your subject, which is what you may want if your research is about what life was like for those for those young men and women to leave their families behind.

Organizing questions logically. As you develop your questions, think, too, about their order. Jumping around from topic to topic during your interview may confuse your subject. Questions that naturally lead from one to the other in some sensible order may lead the interviewee to provide thoughtful responses—ones that make for engaging writing on your part. You can organize your questions in the following ways:

■ *Thematically.* This order will help you avoid jumping around topically, and get your interviewee in a groove talking about one topic.

- *From objective to personal.* Beginning with less personal questions helps interviewees open up to talking about a topic—and perhaps later, give more personal answers.
- *From "easy" to "hard."* Questions that are fairly challenging or controversial should be tabled until later in the interview when you have established a rapport with the interviewee.
- *In a causal sequence.* A causal sequence is one in which each question builds on the one that preceded it (e.g. "Why do you believe that . . . .?" followed by "Then can you explain why you voted the way you did?"). Logical organization of questions helps keep the interviewee on track and leads to potential follow-up questions and responses.

Of course, interviewees may go off on tangents during interviews, but these new directions may lead to some of the most interesting material. Don't cut them off. Prepare a list of questions but be flexible and know you'll probably deviate from that list during the interview.

Analyzing Interview Transcripts

Interviews are harder to conduct than you might think, and it takes a lot of practice to get good at them. But as likely as not your interviewees have given you some useful material, and the task now is to find out what they said about your subject and how it will help you negotiate the rhetorical situation.

When analyzing an interview transcript, take the following steps:

- *Recall the rhetorical situation of your writing.* Having your audience and purpose in mind—as well as the role you want to take as a writer—will help you identify important statements by your subject.
- *Consider the genre.* Thinking about genre will help you choose which material to use. A formal report might not be the place for the subject's long, rambling anecdote about the time he got lost in the woods.
- *Highlight or underline significant material.* Identify quotations, anecdotes, or comments, as well as off-handed remarks, made by your interviewee that contribute to your overall purpose. Pay attention for something the interviewee said that was profound, striking, humorous, poignant, and so on.
- *Identify follow-up points.* Read for answers that you might need to follow up on. For example, you have just interviewed a soldier in the Veterans Affairs hospital about her time in Iraq, but in looking at your notes, you realize that her statement about Sadr City being a "vibrant ghost town" doesn't really make sense to you. You flag her response for either follow-up with her or for further research to answer the questions What is Sadr City like? What is its history?

GUIDELINES: CONDUCTING INTERVIEWS
Before you begin . . .

- Write down all of the background information that you already know about your subject.
- Make a list of the topics you think you want to cover in your interview. Doing so will help you prepare for the interview and write relevant and specific interview questions.

(continued)

Library and Online Research

- Find out as much as you can about the person or group you are interviewing. Locate websites of groups or organizations to find out their goals, mission statements, policies, issues they stand for, philosophy, or politics.
- Find articles, books, websites that provide information about the kind of work your subject does or interests your subject has.
- Find out if biographies, profiles, or interviews have been published on your subject. Skim through these. What information could you use in your interviews? What questions does the material raise?
- If you are interviewing someone about a particular topic, find out as much as you can about the topic beforehand and find out how this person is involved with the topic.

Writing Interview Questions

- Design **open-ended questions**—ones that will get more than a "yes" or "no" or short response.
- Develop questions that cite specific articles, studies, and other appropriate research sources that show you take your subject's time and expertise seriously.
- Group or cluster your questions in a logical order.

Interviews

- Decide if you will conduct phone, email, or in-person interviews.
- Set up dates, times, and locations for your interviews.
- Have your questions prepared ahead of time.
- Take thorough notes or record your interviews. Ask permission to record *before* you do so.
- Take time to thank your interviewees by following up with a note or email.

Observations

Observing the world around you may be something you take for granted because you see people, places, and activities that surround you as you go through your day. Still, looking at the world around you with a particular focus in mind may introduce you to a new way of observing: noticing and analyzing the meaning in the everydayness of your surroundings. Such analysis and the conclusions you draw from observation is a form of field research. Many disciplines use observation as a form of research: Anthropologists observe peoples and cultures; educators observe classroom activities, teachers, and students; scientists observe the natural world; and journalists observe the details of events they report on. Think of the reports that were published by journalists on Hurricane Katrina, for example. Observing the details of what they saw, heard, and experienced was crucial for journalists to report on that natural disaster and its aftereffects. What you see, hear, feel, and otherwise sense are elements of your observation skills. So using your senses and being aware of what's happening around you are important to working with observation as a form of field research.

Looking with keen eyes. When you look with keen eyes you attend to the details of your surroundings, recording and thinking about even insignificant details because those details can often reveal quite a bit.

For instance, you may be profiling the new drama professor at your university. As you step into his office for the interview, you see framed posters of plays he's directed, awards, decorations, photos, knickknacks, and books that provide you with some insight into the kind of person he is. These are the kinds of details that require keen eyes. What do these details reveal about him?

Looking with keen eyes requires that you use your five senses well. What you observe around you, what you hear, smell, and so on in the setting you find yourself with your subject can be quite revealing to readers who later read your descriptions. Say you are profiling the college's baseball team that is vying for the division championship. When you attend a practice or a game, what does the situation feel like? What does it sound like? What kinds of details do you observe of the players, coaches, fans, parents in the stands? All of these details create a scene for readers to put them in the "reality" of your profiled subject.

Observing what isn't there. When observing what isn't there, you are literally taking note of what is *not* in the picture that maybe should be. For example, you might note in interviewing a successful businessman that there are no pictures of his family or friends in his office or, more bizarrely, that he does not seem to have a computer, a Blackberry, or any other electronic gadget we might expect him to have. But seeing what is not there also applies to *who* might be missing. This includes group members who are not present and unrepresented people. For example, in observing a student men's organization called M.A.L.E.S. (Men Achieving Leadership, Excellence and Success), one student noticed that though the group was open to all men, no white males were represented. Was this, the student wondered, a reflection on this organization? On the college? Or was this just a one-time occurrence?

Analyzing your observations. Besides simply recording the information you see and describing it in detail, you need to analyze *what* it means, *how* it means, and *how* it applies to your subject. As you look at your notes, then, you are looking to see which details seem important given your purpose and audience. If your purpose is to highlight the living conditions that low-income elderly face when living in a retirement home, then you would look for details in your notes that reflect this: peeling paint, a particular smell, the apparent obliviousness of the staff, and so on.

GUIDELINES: OBSERVING

■ Take observation notes of the subject you are interviewing, event you are watching, and so on.

■ Observe the **surroundings.** Record the details of the environment or scene. Write down descriptions of the surroundings, including objects, artifacts, and photos—all convey information that will provide context for your readers. Note as much sensory data as you can: What does it sound like? What does it smell like? What's going on in the background or down the street? Does any of this affect your subject?

(continued)

- Observe the person or group **in action** (at home, work, performing, group meetings, school, practice, teaching, and interacting with other people). Is their life hectic, busy, fun?
- Record **descriptions.** Describe physical appearances, gestures, expressions, distinctive characteristics; conditions of the surroundings.
- Record attitudes of those around you in relation to where you are and how they interact with you or with others.

Surveys

Sometimes you need to find out what a lot of people think about a particular, usually current, issue. For example, think of the surveys of voter attitudes during election cycles. Such surveys are meant to get a general snapshot of how people are thinking. Other kinds of surveys may strive for deeper, more nuanced insight, such as surveys that seek to understand how people understand a particular issue, say stem cell research, or what potential customers want in a catering service. As a writer, you may conduct a survey when you feel your subject is not adequately covered or reflected in published research (e.g. what do voters in your district *really* feel their elected representatives should be doing about the condition of town roads). Or you might conduct a survey when you feel that a particular group has been neglected (e.g. the impressions tweens have of current issues that affect them). Surveys, like interviews, are harder to conduct than they seem from the outside. They, too, require background research and some careful thought about the kinds of questions you ask. You want to make sure, first, that you understand the issue or topic fully enough to ask important, critical questions; and you want to make sure that your questions are not leading respondents to give you the answers you want.

Purpose and Audience and Surveys

As you develop your survey, you need to fully understand why you are conducting this research—do you want to *discover* new information (exploratory) or do you want to *confirm* what you believe is actually the case (confirmatory)? Knowing which it is will help you design effective questions. You also want to think very carefully about *who* will be taking your survey. Consider what your audience for the survey is likely to know. Consider, too, what they are not likely to know, since respondents cannot provide a useful answer if they do not understand the background informing the question. Finally, consider the language the audience is familiar with. You may be studying cellular biology, but if you are surveying those who are not, avoid jargon.

Developing Survey Questions

Nearly all surveys ask *demographic questions* at the beginning of the survey. Demographic questions ask respondents to identify themselves in particular ways. They might be asked their age, gender, where they are from, whether they are liberal or conservative, homosexual or heterosexual, and so on. What you ask depends on *why* you are circulating the survey. For example, if you are asking respondents about the role of religion in their lives, then it makes sense to first ask them to identify their particular faith, their age, and gender so that you can draw conclusions about what they believe and its connection to those variables. After demographic questions, survey writers have a number of choices when they are constructing their questions. In broad terms, they can ask either *open-ended* or *close-ended* questions or a mixture of both. *Open-ended questions* allow a respondent to answer as they see fit. Such questions are useful for a writer because respondents sometimes give answers that take the research in a new direction or reveal something the writer had never considered. Of course, the reverse is true, too; the respondent might not reveal anything new or interesting. Exploratory surveys (those designed to uncover new information) often rely primarily on open-ended questions. Such questions generally get longer responses. These responses are qualitative and subjective, providing a respondent's feelings or thoughts on an issue, for instance. For example, on a survey about political attitudes, you might ask a question like "What party do you feel most connected to?" A respondent could simply write "Republican" or she might take the opportunity to provide a more complicated answer: "Well, I was raised in a family of anarchist Independents, but I have found over my fifty years on this earth that . . . ." *Close-ended questions* limit a respondent to a series of possible answers. For example, a respondent might be asked to rate his dislike of a product on a scale of one to five. This quantitative response allows you to count and put the information you receive into ratios: "8 out of 10 respondents agreed . . . ." Confirmatory surveys (those designed to confirm the researcher's assumptions or information) often use close-ended questions. Close-ended questions come in five different forms: Likert scale, multiple choice, categorical, ordinal, and numerical; all forms provide researchers with short, quantitative answers.

Likert scale questions ask respondents to rate something on a scale. These kinds of questions are most useful when you want to find out how someone feels or thinks about an issue.

Question: How would you rate the quality of the support staff at Hotel International?
Terrible   ○ 1   ○ 2   ○ 3   ○ 4   ○ 5   Excellent

Multiple choice questions narrow respondents' possible answers and ask them to choose the one that fits them best.

Question: Which political party best reflects your beliefs and values?
○ Democrat
○ Republican
○ Green
○ Other _____

Categorical questions, like multiple-choice questions, ask respondents to identify themselves in particular ways predetermined by the researcher. Categorical questions, as the name suggests, are questions that ask respondents to place themselves into a category: male/female, married/single, and so on.

Question: What is your current U.S. residency status?
○ Citizen
○ Permanent resident
○ Legalized alien

WebLinks

Designing and Using Surveys and Questionnaires

For more on developing and working with survey and questionnaire data, use a search engine to search for "Free Management Library" or search for "surveys" or "questionnaires."

For surveys on current social and political issues, see the Pew Research Center website.

Ordinal questions ask respondents to rank their responses in order of importance. Ordinal questions allow researchers to make claims about what people really value.

Question: Please rank the following categories in importance for a university president (fill in your order in the space provided using the numbers 1–5, with 1 being the most important and 5 being the least):

- ☐ Fund raising experience
- ☐ Teaching experience
- ☐ Administrative experience
- ☐ Community development experience
- ☐ Corporate experience at a higher managerial level (VP or above)

Numerical questions require a number for an answer.

Question: On average, how many books do you read a month?

- ○ Less than one
- ○ One
- ○ More than one but less than five
- ○ Between five and ten
- ○ More than ten

Finally, as you develop your survey remember to write a short cover letter explaining the survey and its purpose. This introduction will help orient the people taking it and ensure that they understand how to take it, why they are taking it, and what to do when they are finished. The memo also serves another important purpose: It may motivate an otherwise unwilling (or lazy!) individual to take the survey.

Analyzing Survey Material

When you analyze your data, you are looking for *patterns* (many respondents saying the same thing or something similar) and *correlation* (a connection between one *variable*—say, age—and another variable—the answers to particular questions). Both of these elements will allow you to make claims based on the data you received. A lack of correlation or lack of discernable patterns is also possible. Let's say you surveyed your town's residents to find out what they think of the town's plan to level the old shopping plaza and put in a park. You are writing an open letter to the residents of your town taking the position that they should not support the initiative. In your survey, you begin by asking a few close-ended questions: In what part of town do you live? Gender? Age? Are you married, single, divorced? Do you have kids? And so on. You then ask open-ended questions about whether they think the proposal is a good idea, whether there is some better purpose the land could be put to, and so on. In looking over the survey, you notice a pattern—lots of people are talking about a lack of shopping choices since the grocery store at the shopping plaza closed down a decade ago. They wish there was someplace closer than the store in the next town over. Looking more closely at your responses, you notice that the people making these comments are by and large married couples with kids. That data and the correlation you found allow you to support the claim that the town should use that space more productively: Townsfolk do not want another park; they want and need easy access to shopping. Of course, this example is a particular kind of survey, but no matter why you develop a survey or questionnaire, you should keep in mind your purpose and audience, as well as your major claims, and look for patterns among the responses, and then correlations between who the respondents are and what they are saying.

GUIDELINES: SURVEYS

Developing Surveys

- Identify your purpose and audience. Is your survey confirmatory or exploratory? What do you know about the people taking the survey?
- Identify demographic information that you think will be important.
- Identify the kind of material you want. Do you need qualitative data (longer, unscripted answers to your questions) or quantitative data (can be measured, expressed in numerical form) or a mix of both?
- Decide which kinds of questions will work for your purpose.
- Write questions that will be easily understood by your audience, deal with only one concept at a time, and do not use double negatives (e.g. not "Are you not in disagreement with the need to raise taxes to pay for needed road repairs?" but "Do you agree with the need to raise taxes to pay for needed road repairs?")
- Organize your questions logically. Choose categories for your questions, or move from concrete or abstract, objective to subjective, impersonal to personal, and so on.
- Test your survey before sending it out.
- Write a brief cover letter explaining the survey and what you will do with the information you receive.

Analyzing Survey Data

Start by examining the reasons you conducted the survey.

- What was my purpose in conducting the survey in the first place?
- How do I hope to use the data?

Then look at the data itself.

- Which were the most important questions?
- How were those questions answered? Do the responses form a pattern? Did a majority respond in a particular way? What do these patterns tell me?
- Is there a correlation among any of the questions? What does this correlation tell me?

Evaluating Sources

All the research in the world will be useless (or nearly so) if it isn't accurate, timely, and relevant. Different genres, different purposes, and different audiences all require different kinds of research and materials, but all of them require that those sources and that material be in some way relevant and accurate.

Evaluating Print Sources

Using credible and accurate sources that are up-to-date will provide you with information that is more persuasive for your arguments and for your readers. In other words, it will help your research be more convincing and interesting for the rhetorical situation involved. To evaluate print sources, check whether or not they meet the following criteria *before* using them.

Are the sources RELIABLE?

Sources are **reliable** when they are written by authors with expertise on the topic. Information that originates from researchers or specialists in particular disciplines, for instance, is usually reliable. Determine if the author is **credible** by checking their background—see what their credentials are or what affiliations with organizations or groups they list; check for a reference or works cited page at the end of the article to see what sources they drew information from. Be aware of the **author's bias**. Does the writer seem to have allegiances to particular groups or organizations? If so, does the writer use a balance of source materials to address this bias (e.g. are the sources drawn from many different authors or does the writer rely on one or two sources)? Does the article appear in a **credible journal** or magazine? Please see Chapter 2 for guidelines for checking a source's reliability. Reliable sources may include the following:

- Journals (discipline specific)
- Magazines (general topics; check reliability and references)
- Interviews (check expertise)
- Newspapers
- Government documents
- Reference books
- Media (documentaries, speeches, films)

Be cautious of using nameless sources as authorities or experts. If you come across an article that does not include an author name or does not name the experts or sources it cites within it, be wary of the information. (One notable exception are reports from newswire services such as Reuters, which often do not provide a byline; similarly, the well-respected weekly *The Economist* does not list authors for its articles.) Depending on the genre, most writers will credit information sources because it adds a sense of authority and expertise to their own persona as writers—it makes their writing more convincing. For example, a statement that begins with "According to researchers. . ." or "Researchers believe. . ." leads a reader to question: *"Who are these researchers?" "Are they credible sources of information?" "Where does their information come from?"*

QUESTIONS TO ASK ABOUT THE RELIABILITY OF YOUR SOURCES

- Who is the author? Does the author have expertise on the topic?
- Are there references cited in the source?

(continued)

> - Does the writer seem to have allegiances to particular groups or organizations?
> - Is there a balance of source materials?
> - Does the article appear in a credible journal or magazine?

Is the material RELEVANT to your topic?

Relevant material is information that relates to the ideas, position, or reasons you are trying to develop in your paper. The material from articles you find serves as evidence, background information, examples to expand your ideas, or views of others who have written about or discussed your topic. This information should enhance your paper's persuasive or informative purpose.

> **QUESTIONS TO ASK ABOUT THE RELEVANCY OF YOUR SOURCES**
>
> - How will you use the information from your sources? (As supporting evidence, background, differing views, etc.?)
> - Where will the information be useful in your paper?
> - What kinds of information does the source provide you with on your topic? (Expert opinion, statistics, definitions, case studies, etc.?)

Is the source RECENT or timely?

Check the **publication date** of your sources. Generally you will use current information. **Current information** ensures that no dramatic changes have occurred related to your topic that you've left unexamined. For example, a paper about the latest trends in computer technology certainly needs to examine recent sources since new types of computer technology are developed so quickly; a source from five years ago would be outdated. Sometimes, however, you will want to use older material. Your rhetorical situation will help you decide if older articles will be useful. For example, if you are showing your audience a change in perception or understanding of an issue, then using older sources makes sense.

Is the material ACCURATE?

If your information comes from a reliable source, most likely the information present is accurate. Of course you may find information that counters or contradicts the facts (just look at the debates between John McCain and Barack Obama on "the facts" during the 2008 presidential campaigns) or ideas in one source or another depending on the researcher's study.

> **QUESTIONS TO ASK ABOUT THE ACCURACY OF YOUR SOURCES**
>
> - Does the author rely on different sources?
> - Does the author cite the sources used?
> - Does the author make claims and points different from what you have found in other sources?

Evaluating Web Sources

When considering Web sources, you want to be sure that your rhetorical situation allows for their use (for example, a proposal for a research grant drawing on various websites might not appeal to the audience). And so, too, you want to consider the genre and make sure that the characteristics of the genre allow for the less scholarly sources you are likely to find on the Web. If you decide that Web sources are in your best rhetorical interests, you still want to make sure they are relevant, timely, accurate, and so on. In other words, you still need to evaluate them, and more so, because, as you know, anyone can say anything on the Web.

Reliable Web sources may include the following:

■ Government agency websites (e.g. Department of Education and Environmental Protection Agency)
■ Educational websites (e.g. colleges and universities; libraries and museums)
■ Online journals, magazines, and newspapers (e.g. *The New York Times* and *The New England Journal of Medicine*)
■ Nonprofit organizations (e.g. Pew Research Forum and American Lung Association)

If you have a website you think will work, the first step is to evaluate it, because even a reliable source takes a particular perspective on issues. For example, the conservative think tank the American Enterprise Institute for Public Policy Research (AEI) offers a different take on issues than its liberal counterpart, the Brookings Institute. Be sure to provide evidence for your evaluation; if you claim the website is biased, locate an example of such bias.

GUIDELINES: EVALUATING WEBSITES

As a rule of thumb, if you can't find answers to many of the questions below, then don't trust the website.

Is it reliable?

■ Who wrote or runs the website? What can you find out about its producer (the individual or group that created it or that is responsible for its content)?
■ Whose website is it? Who is the sponsor of the website (the group that supports the website or that creates its content—sometimes the sponsor and the producer are the same)? The domain name (.edu, .com, .net, .gov) will give you a clue.
■ Is the author objective or biased? Look at the tone of the pages and information provided. Is it accurate? Check to see if the facts are credible and complete. Are sources given?

Is the source relevant?

■ What's the purpose of the website? Is it trying to sell or inform or persuade or what? How can you tell?

Is the source recent?

■ Is the website content current and up to date? How can you tell?

A final word of advice, save your Web sources. Often websites change URLs or vanish completely. If they move or disappear, you may not be able to find them again. Print paper copies of Web sources or save them as a file so you have all the information (the date it was updated, the URL, etc.) on hand when you write your document.

Sample Evaluation of the Institute for Policy Studies Website

It's sometimes hard to evaluate a website because most look pretty professional these days. But once you look beyond the glossy front page, you can generally evaluate a source with a good degree of accuracy. In the following example, we show the home page for the *Institute for Policy Studies* website. The initial evaluation of the home page will help us decide whether the site is reputable, and if we decide it is, we would then do some further analysis by examining the "About" page to decide whether the material the site publishes is appropriate for our rhetorical situation.

We can tell a lot about the website from this first page. The title itself suggests that it is reputable – it's an institute that puts "ideas into Action for Peace, Justice, and the Environment." Unfortunately, that could mean just about anything, so it's not immediately useful. Along the left side of the page readers are provided with ways to get further information – we can sign up for Twitter feeds from them, for instance.

In the middle of the page, we see a brief article on a report that the IPS institute produced on the need for a "unified security budget for the United States." While we might not know what that means, we do learn that this organization produces its own material – that is, this Institute is not a just a clearinghouse for other people's ideas, but conducts its own research. By itself, this does not tell us whether the site is reputable, but it does give a clue: good, accurate research is expensive to conduct and gather, so at the very least this institute has invested some time and money in its publications.

At the bottom of the page, we can see the broad areas that the institute covers: Peace, Justice, and the Environment, and under each are links to various texts about those issues. Clicking on the "op-ed" under "Peace" takes us to an article written by John Feffer. We also learn that this op-ed was published on a different website (38 North, a website focused on analysis of North Korea). Clicking on the commentary under "Justice," however, takes readers to an article written specifically for this website. So not only does IPS produce its own material, it also collects relevant material from other sources. That they do so might suggest that they seek out material to support and supplement what they produce – presumably adding depth to their readers' understanding of the issues IPS covers.

It's hard, though, to get a sense of this website's position, its slant – is it conservative, liberal, nonpartisan? The only real sense we get is from the announcement in the upper right corner – the "Next Event." Reading that, we learn we can listen to a panel of anti-war activists and policy analysts. That suggests a left-leaning bias. Such a bias would not make this an unreliable source, but we would have to account for the bias when we use the material.

WebLinks

Duke University Research Guide

For a discussion of how to examine a website, please visit the research guide developed by Duke University. This site takes you through a series of questions for evaluating websites, and you might want to use the guidelines for research projects you do in other classes. To go to the site, type Duke University Research Guide into a search engine.

So to truly evaluate the website we would need to do at least two more things: read their "About" statement to find out how they position themselves and explore the website to get a sense of the sorts of material they produce and collect.

You should be wary of any website that makes it hard to find out anything about them, but in the case of IPS, the "About" link is prominently displayed. Clicking on it, we learn that "IPS is a community of public scholars and organizers linking peace, justice, and the environment in the U.S. and globally. We work with social movements to promote true democracy and challenge concentrated wealth, corporate influence, and military power." The language, particularly their work to "challenge concentrated wealth," reveals their left-leaning bias, as that has become a liberal cause. To their credit, IPS is direct about their goals and agenda, as they label themselves a "progressive multi-issue think tank."

Our analysis of this website reveals the complexity of doing such analysis. The fact that there is a bias does not invalidate the material you would find on this website. As a writer, you would need to account for it by acknowledging it, and also by balancing the material you use from this website with material from other sources.

Writing an Annotated Bibliography

One way to get a good sense of which sources will be useful and relevant to your project is to construct an *annotated bibliography,* a summary of each of the sources you think you will use in your paper. Scholars make use of annotated bibliographies all the time—it is an important genre in helping researchers and writers identify key sources, so you might actually come across annotated bibliographies in your own research.

For writers, constructing an annotated bibliography is an important tool for identifying sources that will be useful and for helping them see connections among their sources and between sources and what they are writing about. In an annotated bibliography, writers list the citation information for each source with a brief annotation about the source (see Chapter 14 for instruction on writing citations).

An *annotation* is simply an overview or description of what a source is about. Annotations should give readers a clear understanding of what the sources are about and whether or not they are worth reading in their entirety. An *evaluative annotated bibliography* is similar to a standard annotated bibliography except that the writer focuses on the source's usefulness and relevance to their own project. A *critical annotated bibliography* begins with a summary of the text's major ideas and argument, but also critiques the writer's argument or understanding of the content.

WRITING ASSIGNMENT   Creating an Annotated Bibliography

For each source, list the bibliographic information in the form appropriate to your citation guidelines (e.g. MLA or APA). Begin by informing the reader about the source and what it is about. Then summarize briefly the content of the article. You may provide brief and direct quotation, but most of the text should be your own paraphrase or summary, that is, your own language.

Alternative: Evaluative Annotated Bibliography

In addition to summarizing the content of the article or book, you should also consider its usefulness. How is the source interesting and/or helpful given your project? How does it help you make your claims? You should be more precise here than "I liked it" or "it contained good information." And remember that not all your sources need to agree with what you want to say.

Alternative: Critical Annotated Bibliography

In addition to summarizing the content of the article or book, you should also critique the argument. Is it well developed? Is it accurate? Has the author left important aspects out? Does the author's bias affect the argument? (See Chapters 2 & 3 for guidelines on analyzing a writer's argument.) For an example of an annotated bibliography, see Chapter 10: Research Reports, pages 412–413.

■   ■   ■

14

Using and Citing Sources

We conduct research for all sorts of reasons: To learn more about a subject, to answer specific questions, to prove our ideas or disprove others' ideas, and so on. When it comes time to *use* that material, though, our reasons become increasingly rhetorical. In fact, the rhetorical situation will suggest how we acknowledge or *cite* those sources. This chapter will show you how to make the best use of your research and cite it properly.

Using Sources

We use research to deepen and extend our analysis. But we also use sources to position ourselves as experts or at least as knowledgeable (creating *ethos*), to meet our purposes, and to fulfill the expectations and needs of our audiences.

Using Research for Rhetorical Effects

Imagine you have been asked by the director of a downtown homeless shelter to write a press release announcing an upcoming fundraiser. Your audience is community members who can provide support for the shelter in the form of food and money, and so your purpose is to convince them that donating is not only the right thing to do morally and ethically, but it is also absolutely critical at this time, even though they might feel like the economy is going downhill. In this scenario, your rhetorical situation is pretty complex since you have to convince an audience to give at a time when they might not feel particularly generous. In the process of getting ready to write the press release, you conducted research about *who* the shelter serves, *what* the shelter needs financially for upkeep and salaries, and *why* shelters are an important, critical aspect of a social services safety net. How you *use* that material might look something like this:

Research findings	Use and rhetorical effect
The shelter serves primarily single mothers, many of whom are fleeing from abusive relationships.	This material will "put a face" on the shelter, showing potential donors whom they will be supporting.
The shelter also serves a local homeless population which has steadily increased over the last decade.	This material could be used to show the inevitable consequences (*logos*) of not funding the shelter; a failure to fund the shelter would mean that the number of homeless would increase, becoming a greater drain on city resources.
The shelter serves about 1,200 individuals on a weekly basis and houses, temporarily, a dozen individuals or small families.	Statistics like this can really drive home the problem—1,200 people is a lot to serve.
The shelter pays the director a salary of $20,000 a year and pays the assistant director $15,000; it relies primarily on volunteers for staffing.	These salaries are not a lot of money, which reminds potential donors that those who work in shelters are "donating" a lot, too. This information can be shown as a commitment to social justice (*pathos* appeal).
One woman who came to the shelter was able to turn her life around and land a job with a local plumbing company; she will appear as a guest speaker at the fundraiser.	This anecdote could be used to "prove" to the audience that shelters work—they reintegrate hardworking citizens who got a bad break.

As you can see, you need to decide how to use sources based on why you are writing, who you are writing to, your role as a writer, and what you want to do with the source (for example, use it to refute another's claims). So just as you thought about *which* sources to use based on your rhetorical situation, you can now consider *how* to use them based on the rhetorical situation and the genre.

Why Writers Use Sources

Writers cannot use all the information they find in their research. Thus writers must be good critical readers in order to select information that will serve their purposes for writing and their audiences' needs and expectations. Writers use their research findings to:

- **Give background information to the audience**. Readers are not always familiar with the subject or as familiar as the writer is, so writers need to give them some information. Writers also provide background information when they want the audience to understand a subject or issue in a *particular* way—the way the writer does.
- **Deepen the audience's understanding of an issue**. Most of us want to make complex issues simple, to put them into black and white. But most issues aren't simple, so a writer can use research to help readers see that an issue they thought was straightforward (opposing a ban on stem cells derived from a fetus because those stem cells are critical to finding cures for a host of diseases) is actually more complex (current

research suggests that stem cells from other sources are just as viable and current technologies allow them to be more easily extracted).

- **Understand what others have said about a subject**. Sometimes writers write to make sense of an issue or event. For example, a writer working on a personal essay about how being adopted has affected her life and worldview would need to research the experiences of other adoptees.
- **Support claims or points**. This might be the most obvious use of research for writers. Claims, particularly those that are new or controversial, will need adequate support if the audience is going to accept them as valid.
- **Provide examples or anecdotes to illustrate ideas**. Research can fill in the blanks by giving the writer material that the audience can connect to easily. A writer exploring the technical aspects of a free market economy might use research to illustrate how such an economy affects working families by providing an anecdote about one particular family.
- **Disagree or negotiate with others' ideas**. Writers often take on another writer's ideas either as the focus for their text or as part of a larger argument they are making. In this case research helps the writers to fully and accurately understand the other writer's position as well as to successfully articulate and defend their own. (For a detailed discussion of working with differing views, see Chapter 11, page 465.)
- **Raise further questions on a subject**. When a topic or issue is controversial or when there is concern that an audience has too easily accepted the "truth" of an issue, a writer can ask the audience to reconsider their positions in light of the research the writer has done.
- **Draw conclusions.** Writers also use their research to draw conclusions, to understand what others have said, and to further develop, comment on, or question those ideas.

Genre and Using Sources

How you use and acknowledge your sources depends in part on whether you are writing an academic or a civic genre, and it also depends on the genre itself: A proposal written for an academic purpose requires citation of sources, while a proposal written as a newspaper opinion piece does not. But even when writers work in civic genres that do not require documentation of sources, they need to be careful not to **plagiarize,** or use someone else's work or ideas without crediting them. For example, a writer of a letter to the editor does not include formal citation but instead makes reference to the ideas of others in informal ways, such as a direct quote from a person connected to the letter's subject: "Social activist and consumer advocate Ralph Nader suggests. . . ." While the writer has included Nader's name as the person whose idea she is using in her letter, she doesn't cite exactly *where* she read or heard the quotation; instead, she just mentions Nader's name. In a letter to the editor, the writer attempts to build her credibility by incorporating an expert's ideas on the issue and blending them with her own. On the other hand, a writer preparing a research report on the effects of toxic groundwater in communities along the Long Island Sound will summarize findings from various environmental agency studies and cite the complete publication information for each study using a formal citation format. Readers expect that research reports reference and cite current and relevant research. Casual references to research would make readers suspicious, and they might begin to question the accuracy and truthfulness of the report. Examining the genre—coming to understand its characteristics—will help you decide how to use and cite your sources.

Using Quotations, Paraphrases, and Summaries

There are three different ways to work with sources in your writing: (1) directly quote the source; (2) paraphrase the source; or (3) summarize the source. How, why, and when to use each depends on the rhetorical situation and your reasons for using a particular source, as well as on the genre you are working in. Perhaps it goes without saying, but you cannot effectively use your research if you are not clear on what the source is actually saying. When gathering sources, the temptation is to skim a source and cherry-pick the parts that seem to work. There are many problems with that method, of course, but the main problem is that you are selecting material without being sure you fully understand the context; thus, you may be misrepresenting the author's meaning or intent. We see misrepresentation all the time during elections—one candidate says something and another candidate takes one sentence and misconstrues it, ignoring the context in which the first candidate made the statement. So before using research material in your writing, your first step is to make sure you fully understand the entire source and the writer's argument, claims, and how they are supported. One way to do this step is to construct an annotated bibliography of the sources you want to use. Doing so will ensure not only that they are appropriate but that you understand them fully. (See Chapter 13: Research and the Rhetorical Situation for how to construct an annotated bibliography.) Even if you don't write an annotated bibliography, it's a good idea to take notes and *summarize* the main arguments and claims of a source before choosing passages to work with. Then, when you do work with a particular passage, you will be able to say how it connects to the larger point the source is making.

Direct Quotation

A **direct quotation** is a word-for-word passage from a source with no changes made in the original text by the writer. Writers use direct quotation when the author's exact words need to be preserved to achieve a particular effect. Writers want to preserve the original language when the author has phrased something with a particular rhetorical appeal: the language is beautifully crafted, or it's poorly phrased, or it hides or confuses the facts, and so on.

Here's an example of a direct quotation from Jay Weiner's article "Sports Centered" (the entire article is reproduced in Chapter 2):

The signal phrase introduces the writer's name, expertise, and title.

> Jay Weiner, sportswriter for the Minneapolis newspaper *The Star Tribune*, argues:

A block quotation is more than four lines and is separated from the main text and indented. Block quotations do not require quotation marks, and no page number is given because the source did not have them.

The writer then offers his interpretation of the quotation.

> > The power of sports and sports heroes to mirror our own aspirations has also contributed to the sorry state of the institution today. The women's sports movement Billie Jean King helped create proved a great leap forward for female athletes, but it also created a new generation of fitness consumers, whose appetite for Nikes and Reeboks created a new generation of Asian sweatshops.
> >
> > Weiner suggests that for all the good that sports figures have contributed to society, our greed and consumerism have resulted in other serious social problems that reflect our cultural values.

Quotation is best used when there is either something about the original language that is worth retaining (a particular turn of phrase or style) and commenting on or if paraphrasing the material would require you to use language that is unclear or potentially misleading. However, there are drawbacks to quoting something directly. The writer must make sense of and explain the quotation to the reader after they have already read it, which often forces the reader to return to the quotation a second time. For that reason, a quotation does less work for you—you have to simultaneously explain the quotation and show its relevance to your argument and convince your reader that you are the expert, not the author of the original quotation.

Consequently, paraphrasing (see pages 547–548) is often the better option.

Here's an example of one writer's choice to use direct quotation for the impact it has on readers. First-year writer Cory Tobler's proposal on the merits of installing seat belts on school buses was prompted by the debate surrounding a 2010 bill introduced by Connecticut legislators, which reopened the issue for public debate. The debate resurfaced after a fatal school bus crash in Hartford, which killed a high school student.

> Connecticut State Representative Tony Guerrera, who is also the Democratic co-chair of the Transportation Committee, authored the recent bill that would make mandatory "a three-point safety restraint system" on school buses by January 2011. Guerrera told ABC News that the lack of a system seems illogical given our society's emphasis on vehicular safety. "Every day we put our children on a school bus, and the school bus drivers, they have seat belts. . . . You and I travel to work in vehicles that have seat belts and air bags. But for some reason, when it comes to the children, we don't have a mechanism in place that would prevent a tragedy . . ." (Ellerson).

What is in question here is not the quotation itself—the statement from Guerrera makes sense and helps Tobler make his point. However, there is nothing special about Guerrera's statement, and Tobler has to first explain the quotation and then provide the quotation, which ends up saying in more words what Tobler stated more briefly. So in this case, a paraphrase of Guerrera would work better than the direct quotation.

GUIDELINES: DIRECT QUOTATIONS

- Quote sparingly, depending on the genre.
- Use quotations to capture the original language of the text when it will have a particular effect on readers. Quote key words, phrases, and sentences of the original text.
- Use a *signal phrase* to introduce a direct quotation in order to clue readers that the writer's ideas have stopped and a source's ideas have begun.

(continued)

> ■ Use quotation marks around short quotations, and use block quotation format (without quotation marks) for quotations of four or more lines for MLA format or quotations of more than 40 words for APA format.
> ■ Cite the source, and then interpret it.

Look over some of the research material you've chosen to use in your draft. Decide which passages might warrant direct quotation using the guidelines above. Do any of the passages have a particular effect on readers that would change if you paraphrased them?

Once you decide which material necessitates direct quotation, remember to introduce it using a signal phrase and to cite the information and interpret it for readers.

■ ■ ■

Pitfall: Stringing Together Direct Quotations

Sometimes writers include a series of quotations from the same or different sources without introducing the source of the material and with little or no interpretation of what they mean. Readers will have no idea how to read this information or why the information is relevant to the writer's purpose.

First-year writing student Cory Tobler wrote a proposal that argues for the installation of seat belts on school buses in Connecticut. In the excerpt from an early draft, Cory strings together direct quotations from the same source without introducing the source or interpreting the information for readers. In the revised version, Tobler is much more effective in connecting the research to the point he is making.

Direct Quotations Strung Together:

The writer does not use an introductory phrase to set up the quotations or tell readers their source.

The writer strings together two quotations without interpreting how they connect to the point he is making or to each other.

"The National Highway Traffic Safety Administration (NHTSA), which sets national standards for school bus safety, does not require seat belts on large school buses, which comprise more than 80% of the nation's school bus fleet. However, individual states and school districts can require large buses to have seat belts" (Frisman). "The Connecticut legislature has considered 23 proposals to equip school buses with seat belts in the past 21 years. While the Transportation Committee held public hearings on a number of these bills, most recently in 2006, it has not reported any of them favorably."

Revised Direct Quotation with Introduction and Interpretation:

The writer introduces the quotation by providing source information.

According to a 2009 report from the Connecticut Office of Legislative Research, "The National Highway Traffic Safety Administration (NHTSA), which sets national standards for school bus safety, does not require seat belts on large school buses, which comprise more than 80% of the nation's

The writer introduces the second quotation by interpreting it and suggests how it relates to his position.

school bus fleet. However, individual states and school districts can require large buses to have seat belts" (Frisman). Despite the fact that states can choose to adopt such legislation, Connecticut has not done so—yet. "The Connecticut legislature has considered 23 proposals to equip school buses with seat belts in the past 21 years. While the Transportation Committee held public hearings on a number of these bills, most recently in 2006, it has not reported any of them favorably" (Frisman). With all this discussion among lawmakers, it seems like it is time for Connecticut to take action and change the seat belt laws for school buses. Perhaps the recent fatality of a high school student will cause Connecticut legislators to stop procrastinating.

The writer discusses the quotation and suggests how it relates to his position on the issue.

Paraphrase

A **paraphrase** is a restatement of the words and ideas from a source *in your own words*. Paraphrases are roughly the same length as the original texts, and represent closely the author's original ideas. When you paraphrase you must preserve the author's intended meaning in the original source. However, you may change the sentence order or structures of the original material. A paraphrase, like a direct quotation, needs to be integrated and cited. Writers paraphrase when they want to clarify the ideas of a complicated text in their own words, or to rearrange the order to emphasize a point. Writers also paraphrase when they do not need to preserve the language of the original passage. In general, a paraphrase is a more efficient way of working with your sources, because you have done some of the work of *interpreting the ideas* of the source by putting the material in your own words. As you paraphrase, you should make connections from the ideas of the paraphrased material back to your own points. Finally, be sure not to change the original meaning of a source.

Let's look at a paraphrase of the same passage from Jay Weiner's proposal again:

Even when paraphrasing be sure to credit the source.

At the end of the paraphrase, the page number is provided; this signals the end of the paraphrase.

By linking the impact of Billie Jean King and other women in sports and their contribution to increasing consumer demand to the terrible labor conditions in sweatshops across Asia, **Jay Weiner, sportswriter for the Minneapolis newspaper** *The Star Tribune*, not only argues that our own greed and consumerism are to blame for those conditions and the deplorable condition of professional and amateur sports programs but he also suggests that the blame rests most squarely on women and their entrance into professional sports.

You can see here the appeal of paraphrasing—it allows the writer to comment on and *interpret* the source while paraphrasing. In contrast, when you use direct quotation, you have to interpret before or after the quotation, which often feels awkward to readers. (After all, you are asking them to accept your interpretation *before* they have read the original or *after*, and in both cases, the readers are likely to have to reread either your interpretation or the source to be sure they understand your interpretation.) But because the interpretation comes along with the paraphrase, there is little of the awkwardness.

Paraphrasing Difficulties

Although paraphrasing is often a better option than using direct quotation, it is also harder. The writer of the original has taken what often looks like the best words, and you are left with the rest. A thesaurus is a must in these cases. But sometimes there is material in the original that seems impossible to paraphrase. There are some rules of thumb to help you in these situations.

What you do not need to paraphrase: You do not need to paraphrase technical terms such as bacteria, thermonuclear, and deciduous; articles (the, an, a); or proper nouns (Moscow, George Michael).

Paraphrasing numerical information: Numbers, ratios, and statistics would at first glance seem impossible to paraphrase; 50% is 50% and that's that. And sometimes, yes, it will be very difficult (or not worth the effort) to paraphrase certain kinds of numerical information. But often it is fairly easy. For instance, if a source says that "50% of Americans support X," you can paraphrase that percentage to "1 out of 2 Americans are in favor of X" or "half of all Americans are in favor of X." If a source claims that "4767 people voted no on last year's referendum," you could paraphrase that as "nearly 5000 residents rejected Proposition 72." If a source states "most people in their 40s are depressed," then that could be paraphrased as "a large percentage of men and women at mid-life suffer from depression." When you cannot find any way to paraphrase part of a sentence, put the part you cannot paraphrase in quotation marks:

> Most people believe that early adolescent angst is just a convenient excuse for bad behavior, but researchers have found that a "volatile cocktail of chemicals" may be the reason why so many young teenagers seem to seek out drama (Smith 21).

GUIDELINES: PARAPHRASING

- Read the source a few times to be sure you fully understand it.
- List the major points, trying to use your own words. Remember not to leave out any ideas. If any idea contradicts what you want to say, you will need to address that idea directly.
- Change the order of the points, if necessary, to reflect what you want to emphasize.
- Write out the paraphrase and then check to be sure none of the original language remains.
- Introduce the paraphrase using a signal phrase and cite it (if appropriate for the genre).

Summary

A **summary** is a *brief, condensed version* of an entire original text or a substantial portion of it. Writers use their own words to capture the main idea of the original text. Generally, writers include a summary when they need to orient readers on a particular issue or text so that the readers can then appreciate or understand what they have to say.

A summary of an article can be as brief as a paragraph, so it's important that you understand the main ideas of the text you are summarizing. When you summarize, you might be gleaning the key points of a long article to highlight the gist of what the author is saying. As you summarize, you'll use your own words while simultaneously retaining the ideas of the original text. Don't change the meaning of the original text to fit your argument. If the source makes claims that run counter to yours, you will need to address the different perspective in your text. For an example of a summary, see Chapter 2: Critical Reading and Analysis Strategies, pages 37–38.

GUIDELINES: SUMMARIZING

- Read the text to be summarized closely, annotating the main ideas and evidence.
- List the writer's argument and the main ideas and evidence used to develop the argument.
- Write the summary of the major ideas using your own words exclusively. If you do use any of the original language, place it in quotation marks.
- Introduce the summary using a signal phrase and make sure to fully attribute the ideas to the original source.

WRITING ACTIVITY   Summary and Paraphrase Practice

What follows are two paragraphs from "An Immodest Proposal" by the Women's Committee of 100 which appears in Chapter 11: Proposals (pages 434–437). After carefully reading the two paragraphs, do the following:

Summarize the main arguments of the paragraphs. What does the Women's Committee see as the problems with current views and support of caregivers? Remember, a summary is written in your own words and captures in brief the main ideas of the original text.

Paraphrase the paragraphs from the Women's Committee proposal using the Guidelines for Paraphrasing (page 548) for direction.

■ ■ ■

Families, communities, and the economy all depend heavily on caregiving work. Yet our economic system undervalues paid caregiving in the workforce and penalizes unpaid caregivers in the home. Research also shows that caregiving work exposes many women to low wages, part-time jobs, sex discrimination, lower Social Security and Unemployment Insurance benefits, and other forms of gender inequality and stress.

Caregivers' poverty clearly has a woman's face. But because poverty is not color-blind, that face often belongs to women of color. Since race and racial discrimination also create unfavorable conditions for caretaking, while addressing the shared vulnerabilities of ALL women, society must begin with the needs of the poorest caregivers, especially poor women of color.

Integrating and Introducing Sources

When you work with sources you have to be especially attentive as to how the audience will read the information. You have to, in other words, carefully integrate the source into your text and introduce it in ways that prepare the audience for it. Think of introducing and integrating in terms of giving a party. Not everyone will know everyone else, so as the host you will have to introduce people: "Grandma, I'd like you to meet Sean Finley. You remember I talked about him? He's the guy I met working at Staples who helped me get a job at Roman & Roman Law." Once you have introduced them—in this case Sean to your Grandmother—both now know a little bit about each other and they each know the other's relationship to you. As you introduce everyone, you begin integrating them as well: you remind your Grandmother that both she and Sean share a passion for New Orleans-style jazz. Thus, the connection among the three of you is established and why you are all at the same party together (because you all share similar but not identical interests) is clear. Working with sources is like being a host at the party: Your job is to establish the connections and relationships between and among your sources and your claims and to introduce your audience to those sources.

Integrating Sources

The temptation when working with research material is to let it speak for itself. The problem is that it can't. Without your guidance for *how* to read material from a source, readers will read it the way they want to or ignore it—neither of which is good for you, since you are using the material to help readers see an issue or idea from a particular perspective. Writers guide their readers by carefully **integrating** their research material into their own ideas and text. When we talk about integrating a source, we mean two things: (1) making sure the material actually connects smoothly to what we are saying; and (2) interpreting the material. This second piece, interpreting, is sometimes difficult but always necessary. You want to show your readers what the source *means,* not assume that they will simply get it—because they may not. Let's look at an example of a writer dumping their research into a paper without giving readers a clue as to how they should read it. In Jenna Clark's report on the physical conditions of public schools, she argues that physical conditions need to be addressed because they affect student learning. Here is the introduction from an early draft, before Clark had fully integrated her research and before she herself fully realized what she wanted to say in the report:

This statement is vague. Is the report about schools or all public buildings?

Since the source is not introduced, we don't know where the material is from or why it is relevant.

This quotation is also not introduced.

When a public building, such as a school, reaches a certain age, it needs to undergo some kind of renovation. "Tens of thousands of public schools urgently need repairs, renovation or new construction because of health and capacity issues" (7). They continue on saying that teachers and students spend a majority of their time in a school building, and they are at serious risk of getting sick, injured, or seriously distracted (7). Having them in such a disgusting atmosphere may affect the students' learning capabilities and/or the teachers' work strength. "Three-quarters of schools reported in a 1999 federal study that they needed funds for repairs, renovations, and modernization to upgrade their school's overall condition to 'good'" (7).

It's unclear what Clark wants to do with the sources she uses here, and as a result, her readers won't know for sure how to interpret the sources. Are they reputable? Relevant? And because Clark has not integrated them into her larger argument, they won't know why Clark is using them or how they connect to her argument. In short, when readers are done reading this paragraph, they have no reason to believe that Clark is going to tell them something worthwhile and no reason to trust her. And just as seriously, because she has not properly cited her sources, this paragraph has plagiarism implications as well. Clark went on to revise this introduction, using MLA citation format and paying much more attention to her larger point and to the way she used her sources. (For an example of how research is integrated into a paper using APA format, see Gloria Ramos' report "A Report on Same-Sex Marriage in America: A Human Right, a Family Right" in Chapter 1.)

Here is what the introduction looked like in Clark's final draft.

> The introductory material helps to set the stage for the problem Clark addresses.

We think of public schools and public education in terms of what students learn, and every few years there are changes made in what students are taught and how teachers teach. But of equal importance is where students are taught and the conditions of the buildings in which they learn and teachers work. Despite that importance, the physical conditions of our public schools are rarely updated and improved. According to Lynn Davis and Ben Tyson, "forty years" is about how long a school building lasts. In their report, they state that the National Center for Educational Statistics showed the "average public school is 42 years old" (1). As a result, "tens of thousands of public schools urgently need repairs, renovation, or new construction because of health and capacity issues," claims a report by the American Federation of Teachers (3). The report argues that because teachers and students spend a majority of their time in a school building, they are at serious risk of getting ill, hurt, or very distracted (3). In other words, being in such a hazardous atmosphere may affect the ability of students to learn and of teachers to work. According to the U.S. Department of Education, "three-quarters of schools reported in a 1999 federal study that they needed funds for repairs, renovations, and modernization to upgrade their school's overall condition to 'good'" (qtd. in American Federation of Teachers 3).

> In this version, readers are told who the source's authors are.
>
> This transition material helps readers see how the pieces of the source fit together, and it helps Clark make her point.
>
> Clark makes the connection between poor building conditions and learning by interpreting the material.

Let's look at one other example of how other writers integrate their research into their papers. This example is from Gregory Geib, a student in a first-year writing course. In his open letter to the Connecticut Board of Education, Geib argues that cutting funding for after-school sports programs is a risky choice. Here, Geib makes the claim that after-school sports programs help to keep kids safe and occupied while also building important skills. Notice how he integrates his research to support and develop that claim (and that because this is an open letter, Geib has not provided formal citation of his sources).

Then, of course, there is always the most common and obvious of all arguments for the importance of after-school programs: teenagers who have something to do after school are a lot less likely to get themselves into trouble or start using

Geib uses this signal phrase to tell us where the following material comes from.

drugs. According to the U.S. Census Bureau, at least seven million kids return to an empty house on any given afternoon. When left unsupervised, kids are most at risk of getting into trouble between 2 and 6 pm, claims a U.S. Department of Justice study. It is during these hours that kids are most likely to commit a crime, to smoke, drink or use drugs, or engage in sexual activity. After-school programs have been proven in a variety of studies to decrease juvenile crime and violence, reduce drug use, cut smoking, and decrease teen pregnancy. **As if that wasn't enough,** research also shows that children who participate in after-school programs have higher standardized test scores and are less likely to be absent or tardy to classes compared to their unsupervised peers. I've known so many kids who instead of participating in such programs have done things like started smoking marijuana and getting into pointless trouble because they are bored and have nothing better to do. . . .

Geib uses this transitional expression to illustrate that the problem is more complex and more dire than most readers might think.

Notice how all the research Geib uses connects to his original claim that sports programs can help keep kids from getting involved in risky behaviors and might actually help students academically, which in turns bolsters his main argument that cutting funding for sports programs is a bad idea.

> **GUIDELINES:** INTEGRATING SOURCES
>
> 1. Be clear on what *you* are saying. Look at the paragraph or section where you are using the source and paraphrase your point in a sentence. If you cannot do that, you probably are not clear yourself about what you want to say.
>
> 2. Examine the source material. If you are using a direct quotation, make sure you understand not only what the passage is saying but how it connects to your larger point. You might write a sentence explaining what the passage means and why you are using it. If you have paraphrased or summarized a source, you should already be clear about the meaning and context of the passage you are using.
>
> 3. Articulate for yourself why you want to use a particular source. How will it help you make your point?

Introducing Sources

As we discussed on page 550, you need to introduce your sources so that readers know *what* they are about to read and perhaps *how* they should read (for example, is the author "stating" something or "arguing" something? Is the author angry or being humorous?). Introducing your sources is relatively easy, but you will want to keep in mind your audience's needs, the genre, and, of course, why you are using the source in the first place. Generally speaking, you will always state the author's name when you introduce the source—just as you would say a person's name when you introduce them to someone new (and if you are using APA style, you also need to include the year of publication). As a writer, you have the choice of including other kinds of information as well, such as the title of the work you are citing, the profession of the author, where the author works, what else the author has done or written, if relevant, and so on. Your decision of what to include when you introduce a source depends on the genre and the rhetorical situation. (See pages 570–573 for MLA guidelines for in-text citations and pages 580–587 for APA guidelines.)

Writers use *signal words* and *phrases* to orient their readers to the purpose of a source and why they are using it. Sometimes writers use signal verbs to communicate an important piece of information about what the author of the source is doing:

> Jones **argues** . . .
> In his article, "Topiary Art," Roger Smith **claims** . . .
> Susan Kline **states** . . .
> Loman (1999) **reports** . . .

Sometimes, though, writers want to provide a bit more information to readers; they want to show readers what *they* are doing with the source and how *they* view the source. In those cases, writers might use longer signal phrases or even sentences to introduce a source. Notice that even when writers use longer phrases, they still include a signal phrase verb and the name of the author.

Consider these examples:

Longer Signal Phrases	Rhetorical Effect
"Jones argues, passionately and truthfully, that . . ."	The inclusion of those two adverbs tells the reader a lot about the writer's opinion of Jones: He is truthful and passionate. So as readers, we will then read the quote or paraphrase of Jones in that light.
"Although Jones draws on many sources to support his central claim, we are often left feeling less than convinced of his accuracy, as in the following, somewhat off-handed remark . . ."	The writer communicates that we should not trust what Jones is saying; we should be suspicious, in fact. And so, as a result, we will read the quotation from Jones in that light.

Here's an example of a signal phrase used by Cory Tobler in his proposal arguing for seat belts to be installed in Connecticut school buses.

Signal phrase introduces a quote.

Parenthetical citation is in MLA format for an online source with no page numbers.

> **According to a 2009 report from the Connecticut Office of Legislative Research,** "The National Highway Traffic Safety Administration (NHTSA), which sets national standards for school bus safety, does not require seat belts on large school buses, which comprise more than 80% of the nation's school bus fleet. However, individual states and school districts can require large buses to have seat belts" (Frisman).

Notice in Cory's example above how he emphasizes the report's origin, a state government office, and the recent date of publication to show readers that his information is credible and up to date.

GUIDELINES: INTRODUCING SOURCES

You will generally provide the author's name when introducing a source. Sometimes you might just provide the last name; sometimes you might also provide the title of the source. Your choice will depend on your reasons for using the source, the genre, and the audience. In APA style, when you introduce a source with the author's name, you must follow it with the year of publication in parenthesis.

You can also Introduce Sources by Doing the Following

1. Provide the author's name and some background information about her expertise or experience, other work she has done, and so on.

2. Summarize the main argument the author is making and show how what you are about to cite connects to that main argument. For example, "Smith argues that any taxation is inherently unfair, and he uses the example of a middle class family from Iowa and one from Florida to drive home that point (12)."

3. Show the connection between the source's point and the one that you are making.

4. Suggest what is good, accurate, and insightful about the source; conversely, suggest what is bad, inaccurate, or close-minded or clichéd about the source (avoid making such comments about the writer directly, unless there is good reason to do so, and there rarely is).

5. Provide background information or context on the subject or issue the source is addressing.

Incorporating Visual Sources

There are many occasions where you might want to include visual sources in your text. Some genres, such as the profile, encourage it, while for other genres it is almost a requirement—research reports, for instance, often contain graphs and charts, as well as photographs.

Just as when working with print sources, when you work with visual sources you should be sure that they are relevant and reputable. The crucial difference between visual sources and textual sources is that visual sources are often secondary to the content—that is, they serve to support textual evidence. For example, a graph often visually represents the same or similar data being discussed in the text; a photograph, say of the devastation wrought by Hurricane Katrina, serves to support the written descriptions in the text. See Chapter 4: Analyzing Visual Rhetoric for further discussion of how to incorporate visual material into your writing.

> **GUIDELINES:** INCORPORATING VISUAL SOURCES
>
> 1. Choose visual sources that are appropriate for the genre and for your purpose and audience.
>
> 2. Place the visual near where you discuss the idea or issue being illustrated in the visual.
>
> 3. When appropriate, refer directly to the visual source and provide information regarding its author and source. If you have used a visual created by someone else, you may need to provide a source line directly beneath it (for an example, see Chapter 4, page 100).

Synthesizing Your Research

We have been talking about sources as though you would be using one source for each claim you make, but in reality you will likely be using multiple sources to support each of your claims. In a sense, you want to have a dialogue among your claims and the sources you use to develop and support them. *Synthesis* connects ideas from several sources and shows how they relate to each other and to your purpose for writing. There are a few reasons to synthesize your sources:

1. Many issues are complex enough that one source cannot fully account for their many aspects.
2. It's easy for a reader to disregard one source if they disagree with it; it's much harder to disregard three or more different sources saying the same thing.
3. A reader wants to see that you have done comprehensive research. It's easy to *find* one source that agrees with the point you are trying to make; it takes more work and time to find multiple sources. By using multiple sources you are building *ethos.*
4. A reader also wants to see that you have contended with *differing views*—research that contradicts or questions your claims. By contending with differing views fairly and respectfully, you build *ethos* and communicate the complexity of the issue.

But building connections among ideas from sources is not an easy task for many writers. It takes lots of practice and revision to make sure (1) the relationships among sources are clear and (2) the sources support the writer's purpose for writing.

Pitfall: Using Multiple Sources without Synthesizing

A common pitfall writers encounter when they are working with multiple sources is that they fail to build relationships or make connections among the ideas. A reader should not have to try to figure out how sources relate to claims; instead, the writer should clearly establish links and provide a clear interpretation or analysis of the material.

Here's an example of *problematic synthesis* taken from first-year writer Cory Tobler's proposal arguing for legislation to add seat belts on school buses. Tobler's sources, while all relevant to the issue, are jumbled up and offer no connectivity, or synthesis, among the ideas from multiple sources.

Notice how the two differing views on seat belt safety on school buses are lumped together without explanation by the writer of these competing arguments.

Here, the writer merges the direct quotes about two different arguments on seat belts: one, a pathos appeal and claim committing funds to buses with belts, the other discussing liability issues for bus drivers.

This quote is another pathos appeal to the responsibility of state legislators to support the Connecticut bill in favor of seat belts on buses.

The seat belt debate continues nationwide. "Seat belt advocates, including the American Academy of Pediatrics and the National Coalition for School Bus Safety, argue that seat belts **would reduce injuries and deaths to school bus passengers**" (Frisman). "**The National Association of State Directors of Pupil Transportation Services and the National Association of School Transportation, among others, contend that school buses are already the safest way to travel** to and from school and that seat belts would add little or no improvement at significant expense" (Frisman). CT Gov. Jodi Rell recently said, "We need to do the right thing for our children . . . promising to allocate funds toward school bus replacements. When the state orders these new buses, they must come equipped with seat **belts**" (Ellerson). "**We're concerned about who will be responsible** for ensuring that the children put belts on," Connecticut School Transportation Association executive director Bill Moore told ABC News. "Is the driver going to be liable for the injuries received whether or not children are wearing seat belts or if they're not wearing them properly?" Moore asked (Ellerson). However, others disagree. "As a legislator, I think it's important that we become proactive and sometimes we don't act that way in this building," said state Rep. Antonio Guerrera, D-Rocky Hill, who proposed the bill. "I do not want another death on a school bus to happen again" (O'Leary).

GUIDELINES: SYNTHESIZING SOURCES

1. Read your sources critically, taking notes and summarizing the key points. Or review the summaries in your annotated bibliography.

2. Decide on your purpose for synthesizing and how the ideas from the sources relate to your purpose.

3. Write a rough draft of your synthesis including the summaries of sources and your interpretations of them. As you draft, identify the relationships between ideas for your readers.

4. Reread the synthesis to ensure the connections between sources are clear. If your connections between ideas are clear, extend the synthesis by providing your interpretation of the ideas.

5. Cite the sources that you use appropriately for the genre.

WRITING ACTIVITY   Revising for Better Synthesis

Using an example from your own draft that includes ideas from multiple sources, locate a problematic synthesis and use the guidelines above to be sure that the passage serves your purpose, makes a clear argument, and shows strong connections among ideas. Be sure to paraphrase when needed, and to cite the sources appropriately.

■ ■ ■

Constructing a Research Chart and Synthesis

It's hard, sometimes, to see how your sources all work together. In those cases it's especially helpful to construct a *research chart*. Essentially, this useful tool is a grid on which you list your claims, sources, and the passages you plan to use from those sources in order to establish how you can use them to develop your claims. One of the key features of the chart is the space given to a brief explanation of how the sources are working together.

Here is an example from Jamie Morello, a student in a first-year writing course, who constructed a research chart for her research report on the connections between drinking and rape among women in college.

Jamie Morello

Professor Ferruci

English 100P

Research Chart

Research Report: "Caution—Harmful to Women: Men, Alcohol, and College"

Sources:	Loiselle, "Alcohol's Effects on Women's Risk Detection in a Date Rape Vignette"	French et al., "Alcohol Is the New Date 'Rape Drug'"	"Alcohol and Sexual Assault on Campus: New Findings"	Cochrane, "Drunk Girls—No Big Deal"	Norris et al, "Women's Responses to Unwanted Sexual Advances: The Role of Alcohol and Inhibition Conflict"	Hindmarch and Brinkmann, "Trends in Use of Alcohol and Other Drugs in Cases of Sexual Assaults"	Abbey and Zawacki, "Alcohol and Sexual Assault"	Felson and Burchfield, "Alcohol and the Risk of Physical and Sexual Assault Victimization"	Explanation of how sources work together
Claims: Women don't think sexual assaults can happen to them while they're drinking. They're more likely to get raped if they're intoxicated.	"... women are likely to underestimate the role of alcohol as a personal risk factor for sexual assault." 261				"Several studies have indicated that at least half of all acquaintance sexual assaults involve the consumption of alcohol." 333		"... although a woman's alcohol consumption may place her at increased risk of sexual assault, she is in no way responsible for the assault." 43		All three sources agree that alcohol is a risk for sexual assault and that more women tend to get raped when under the influence.

Claims					
Claims: Women who have been drinking are at risk for rape because rapists target them.	"Alcohol may impair a woman's ability to resist unwanted sexual advances." 261	"70% of the victims reported they were too intoxicated at the time of their assault to give consent or refuse." 8	"Well, yes, there certainly is evidence that opportunist rapists target drunk women, and no doubt we should all look out for each other accordingly." 33	"One scenario ... is engaging in consensual sexual contact with a dating partner even though sexual intercourse is not ultimately desired." 333	The Cochrane article is my primary source here, and I want to use the others to support the idea that drunk women are targeted because their judgment is impaired.
Claims: Most victims do not know that alcohol and date rape drugs are involved in rapes on college campuses.	"Alcohol is frequently cited as a risk factor for date rape." 261	"If any drug deserves the title 'rape drug' it's alcohol." 26	"Recent media coverage has raised awareness of the involvement of drugs, both licit and illicit, in the crime of 'date' rape or 'acquaintance' rape." 225	"Drinking may play a causal role in victimization because it leads to provocative or risky behavior." 837	The authors agree that men use drugs and alcohol as aides in their rapes, or that they just feel like they can take advantage of women under the influence.

- Begin by writing down your audience, your purpose, and your role as the writer. Knowing these will help you figure out how to use your sources. You can use the Table function in your word processor or you can write the chart out by hand.
- In the first row of your table or across the top of the page, write down the author and title of each source you are using in individual columns.
- List the claims you want to make in the far left-hand column.
- Working claim by claim, write out the passage you want to use from each source to support the claim in the appropriate column. Not every claim needs to be supported by all the sources, so choose the ones that work best. Be sure to provide the page number. If the passage is long, provide enough of it so that the point being made is clear.
- When all material for a claim is listed, explain briefly both how you want to use those sources and how they are working together in the far right-hand column. Remember that the sources do not have to agree either with one another or with your claim.

■ ■ ■

Here's how Jamie Morello ended up developing the material she put in her research chart:

Morello uses the material in her research chart to develop the claim, quoting and paraphrasing as needed. Notice how all the sources are not used equally.

Morello uses the paraphrase to show that awareness may be increasing and to introduce the idea that not only illegal drugs are being used. This introduces ideas from other sources about alcohol being a "drug" used in date rape cases.

> Alcohol and date-rape drugs—any drug given to a woman to get rid of her inhibitions and make her recollection of what has occurred fuzzy—are very likely to be involved with rapes committed on college campuses. Most victims do not seem to know this, though studies show that legal and illegal drugs have been involved with occurrences of acquaintance or date rape, and television and radio reports have begun to spark some recognition of the problem (Hindmarch and Brinkmann 225). The most common way for a date rape drug to be given is for the perpetrator to drop it into the victim's drink. And as Kathy French and Caryl Beynon, from Liverpool John Moores University, and Jo Delaforce, from King's College Hospital London, claim, "if any drug deserves the title 'rape drug,' it's alcohol" (26). Loiselle concurs. This is so because when a woman is victimized because of her "risky behavior," it is often the consumption of alcohol that encourages her to act provocatively in the first place (Felson and Burchfield 837).

Write down the claim you want to develop.

1. Examine the research you are using to support the claim. Which source best supports, explains, or develops the claim you are making? Do other sources further define or develop the claim effectively?

2. Decide on your purpose for using the sources. Do the other sources agree or disagree with each other or with your claim? How will you address them? Are there sources that connect to the next claim or paragraph you want to develop?

3. Address readers' expectations or concerns. Are the sources notably biased or balanced? Would readers expect you, the writer, to examine the biases fairly and comment on them? Would they expect you to balance out the bias with other perspectives?

■　■　■

Avoiding Plagiarism

Plagiarism is taking someone else's ideas or words, or even a writer's sentence structure, and using them as your own without giving that person credit. It's pretty simple, really: If you get an idea from someone else, you should give them credit. If you use someone else's words, you should give them credit. When in doubt, cite the source. Writers sometimes plagiarize *unintentionally*; that is, they forget to cite the source, or mistakenly attribute a quotation to the wrong source. This usually happens when writers get sloppy working with their sources. Or sometimes they do not take careful notes of who said what in their sources, and after reading so many, they begin to think that an idea was all their own. Again, these are sloppy research techniques. One way to avoid plagiarism caused by errors is to keep careful notes on your sources and document where you get any material during the course of your research. Another form of *unintentional plagiarism* occurs when writers don't know *how* or *why* to cite sources accurately. Generally speaking, most people know that they must cite direct quotations, but they get confused about the need to cite paraphrased or summarized material from sources. Whenever the ideas or information or structure (written or visual) is not your own, you must cite the source. To help you better understand how to avoid plagiarism, let's look at an excerpt from the book *Suburban Nation: The Rise of Sprawl and the Decline of the American Dream,* by Andres Duany, Elizabeth Plater-Zyberk, and Jeff Speck, followed by a plagiarized paraphrase and a revised version of the paraphrase.

Original Material:

Almost without exception, the message we have heard, a message of deep concern, has been the same: the American Dream just doesn't seem to be coming true anymore. Life at the dawn of the millennium isn't what it should be. It seems that our economic and technological progress has not succeeded in bringing about the good society. A higher standard of living has somehow failed to result in a better quality of life. And from mayors to average citizens, we have heard expressed a shared belief in a direct causal relationship between the character of the physical environment and the social health of families and the community at large. For all of the household conveniences, cars and shopping malls, life seems less satisfying to most Americans, particularly in the ubiquitous middle-class suburbs, where a sprawling, repetitive, and forgettable landscape has supplanted the original promise of suburban life with a hollow imitation. . . . (from *Suburban Nation: The Rise of Sprawl and the Decline of the American Dream,* by Andres Duany, Elizabeth Plater-Zyberk, and Jeff Speck, pages xii–xiii).

Plagiarized Paraphrase:

The writer doesn't put quotation marks around an exact phrase from authors' original.

In *Suburban Nation: The Rise of Sprawl and the Decline of the American Dream,* a book about suburban sprawl and its effects on the American families and communities, the authors argue that the promise of <u>the American dream just doesn't seem to be coming true anymore</u>. An improved standard of living does not necessarily result in a better lifestyle as Americans might expect. Many people agree that there is <u>a direct causal relationship between physical environment and the social health of families and the community at large</u>. Despite middle class suburban advantages—from the products purchased to the malls that dot the landscape, people seem less content with life. <u>A sprawling, repetitive, and forgettable landscape has</u> arisen so that the version of suburban life promised by the American dream has been substituted with a <u>hollow imitation</u>. . . . (Duany, Plater-Zyberk, and Speck).

The writer neglects to put quotation marks around the authors' exact words.

Because the writer has not accurately cited the sources being used, a reader cannot tell which are the writer's own ideas and which are the ideas borrowed from sources.

Despite the fact that the writer includes the authors' names at the end of the paragraph, the missing quotation marks and page numbers make this paragraph plagiarized.

Paraphrase Revised to Avoid Plagiarism:

In *Suburban Nation: The Rise of Sprawl and the Decline of the American Dream,* a book about suburban sprawl and its effects on American families and communities, the authors argue that **"the promise of the American dream just doesn't seem to be coming true anymore."** An improved standard of living does not necessarily result in a better lifestyle as Americans might expect. Many people agree that there is **"a direct causal relationship"** between physical environment and the **"social health of families and communities"** in America. Despite middle class suburban advantages—from the products purchased to the malls that dot the landscape, people seem less content with life. A **"sprawling, repetitive, and forgettable landscape"** has arisen so that the version of suburban life promised by the American dream has been substituted with a **"hollow imitation"** . . . (Duany, Plater-Zyberk, and Speck xii–xiii).

The writer has done three things throughout: (1) put quotation marks around exact, word for word phrases of the authors; (2) paraphrased the rest of the authors' ideas accurately without changing their intended meaning; and (3) correctly cited the authors in parentheses at the end of the paraphrase using MLA format.

> **GUIDELINES:** WHAT TO CITE
> **Direct quotations:** Word-for-word paragraphs, sentences, phrases taken from a source (print, electronic, Web, or field research)
>
> *(continued)*

Paraphrases and summaries: The ideas of a source, unique sentence structure, or another writer's interpretation of information that are put in the writer's own words and form

Field research data: Interviews, observations, or survey materials from others' research—either referenced informally or quoted, paraphrased or summarized

Visuals: Photos, artwork, graphs, charts, graphics, logos, speeches, performances, and so on from sources, either print, online, or live

Online communications: Email, blogs, and so on

Procrastination and Intentional Plagiarism

Sometimes writers get caught in a situation where plagiarism seems like the easy way out. They have a paper due the next day (or hour) and didn't begin in time to write something of their own. Thus, they plagiarize to speed their writing.

This is intentional plagiarism, and it is unethical. The writer who plagiarizes intentionally has stolen the ideas of another and pretended that they are his own. Plagiarism is a serious offense with penalties ranging from paper or course failure to university dismissal. Remember this: A quick Web search on the writer's part may yield what seems like a perfect solution to procrastination (any number of websites sell papers), but most instructors know too well a student's writing style and voice not to recognize when a paper isn't the student's own. They may also be familiar with the sources the writer used and realize the ideas presented are not the writer's own. One way to avoid this trap is to start your writing projects early, giving yourself enough time to complete your research and writing on a manageable schedule.

GUIDELINES: AVOIDING PLAGIARISM

- Ask your instructor for help; most writers plagiarize because they may be confused about an assignment, they might be unable to figure out how to write something; they get frustrated and take the quick way out.

- Keep careful notes and document sources throughout the research process. For each source, write down the author(s), title, page number(s), and if the source is online, the URL (see pages 565–568 for other bibliographic information you will need to cite a source accurately). As you draft your paper and discover you don't have complete bibliographic details for a source, don't use information from that source unless you get the missing details.

- When working with genres that do not require formal documentation, be sure to introduce the speaker of a quotation or the author of a paraphrased idea you've used in your draft. Informally crediting or attributing a source in a civic genre, such as a public letter, helps a writer establish her credibility.

- Begin your writing projects allowing enough time to reread difficult sources so you can paraphrase them accurately. Start early to avoid writing

(continued)

under pressure, which can lead to intentional plagiarism or unintentional plagiarism.

■ If you are unsure of how to cite something, ask your instructor, the writing center, reference librarian, or peer. Or consult a reference manual. Don't just omit the citation.

■ Recheck paraphrases and summaries after you've written them. Compare them side-by-side to make sure you haven't mistakenly borrowed the language of the original.

■ Recheck paraphrases and summaries to be sure you have not changed the meaning of an author's ideas or opinions to better fit your ideas.

■ Check your draft to be sure you included authors, page numbers (when available), and any other information readers need to know about the source of the original material. Be sure to include accurate citation information; double-check the sources and the page numbers.

■ Check your university library to familiarize yourself with the plagiarism policy and to see what information they have to help you avoid unintentional plagiarism in your writing.

WRITING ACTIVITY   Revising to Avoid Plagiarism

Revise the paraphrase below so that it does not plagiarize the original text. Use the bibliographic material in parentheses to help you accurately introduce and cite the source (refer to pages 570–580 for MLA citation formatting and pages 580–589 for APA citation formatting).

WebLinks

Avoiding Plagiarism

Purdue University's Online Writing Lab website offers good information on how to recognize and avoid plagiarism as well as practice exercises to work on. Search for Purdue University's Online Writing Lab.

Original Text

Teenage sexual activity has significant consequences: sexually transmitted diseases (STDs), pregnancy, social and economic disruption, and legal implications. Of the 15 million new cases of STDs that occur each year in the United States, 10 million occur in people aged 15 to 24. Each year, over 400,000 infants are born to teenagers; more than 146,000 are born to those 17 years of age or younger. In 2000, 18% of reported abortions in the United States were performed on teenagers. (From "Adolescent Sexual Health," Supplement to the *Journal of Family Practice*, by Patricia J. Sulak, M.D., July 2004, page 53.)

Plagiarized Paraphrase

According to a 2004 report published in a supplement to the *Journal of Family Practice*, there are many serious side effects of sexual activity among teenagers including STDs, pregnancy, and other social, economic and legal consequences. For example, more than 15 million new cases of STDs happen each year in the U.S. and 10 million of those include people between the ages of 15 and 24. Another problem sexually active adolescents face is the number of babies born to teenagers overall each year is 400,000 each year, and teenagers aged 17 years or younger are giving birth to 146,000 of those babies. As a result, many teens who become pregnant are getting abortions. In the U.S. in 2000, 18% of reported abortions were performed on teens.

■ ■ ■

Documenting Sources

When you document the sources you use, you are simply providing your audience with information that will help them find the sources if they want to read, listen to, or view the original material themselves. But when we talk about documenting sources, we have to always remember that different genres have different expectations for how writers should use and document their source material. For example, in a letter to the editor you are not likely to find formal documentation for the sources the writer used; instead, you might see the writer refer to a specific author or text. In more formal genres, such as a research report, and certainly when writing academic genres, the expectation is that the writer will formally document the sources used. In each of the genre chapters, we discuss the expectations for citing sources in that genre. There are many reasons why writers document sources, but there are four basic ones:

1. To acknowledge and give credit to those whose work has informed the writer's own work. What you have written is part of a larger and ongoing conversation; your contribution builds on what others have said, and it's courteous and ethical to recognize that.
2. To provide a trail for those readers who would like to follow the writer's research. If you have done your job as a writer, your readers are engaged and interested in the subject; they may want to find out more, and the references or works cited list gives them a place to start.
3. To establish and develop their own credibility. Most readers will not simply accept a writer's argument without some support, unless they are already familiar with and trust that writer. Drawing on reputable research helps writers build that trust with readers.
4. To avoid plagiarizing.

Making Note of Bibliographic Information

When you document sources, you provide readers with specific information about the text that is referred to as bibliographic information. For documentation purposes, bibliographic information includes the author(s), title, publisher or name of the publication, date of publication, volume and issue, if applicable, and page number(s). Other details are included for electronic sources. Where do you find the bibliographic information you need for documenting your sources? It depends on the source, but in most cases it's easy to find.

Finding Bibliographic Information in a Book

Finding bibliographic information for a book is as easy as opening the book itself. All that you need can be found on the title page and the copyright page, as shown in the figure below.

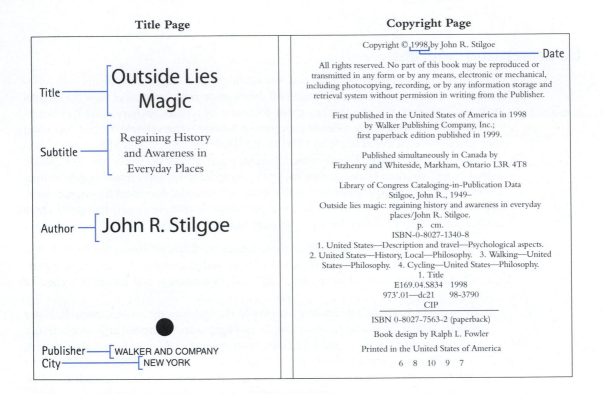

Title Page

Title — **Outside Lies Magic**

Subtitle — Regaining History and Awareness in Everyday Places

Author — **John R. Stilgoe**

Publisher — WALKER AND COMPANY
City — NEW YORK

Copyright Page

Copyright © 1998 by John R. Stilgoe — Date

All rights reserved. No part of this book may be reproduced or transmitted in any form or by any means, electronic or mechanical, including photocopying, recording, or by any information storage and retrieval system without permission in writing from the Publisher.

First published in the United States of America in 1998 by Walker Publishing Company, Inc.; first paperback edition published in 1999.

Published simultaneously in Canada by Fitzhenry and Whiteside, Markham, Ontario L3R 4T8

Library of Congress Cataloging-in-Publication Data
Stilgoe, John R., 1949–
Outside lies magic: regaining history and awareness in everyday places/John R. Stilgoe.
p.   cm.
ISBN-0-8027-1340-8
1. United States—Description and travel—Psychological aspects.
2. United States—History, Local—Philosophy.   3. Walking—United States—Philosophy.   4. Cycling—United States—Philosophy.
1. Title
E169.04.S834   1998
973'.01—dc21   98-3790
CIP

ISBN 0-8027-7563-2 (paperback)

Book design by Ralph L. Fowler

Printed in the United States of America

6   8   10   9   7

Finding Bibliographic Information for an Abstracted Article

If you have collected abstracts in the process of doing research (see Chapter 13), then much of the information you need to document your sources can be found there, as shown in the following abstract.

Title of the article

Author of the article

Name of the journal or magazine, when it was published, volume and issue, and pages

Title: The OxyContin epidemic and crime panic in rural Kentucky.
Author: Tunnell, Kenneth D.
Source: Contemporary Drug Problems; Summer 2005, Vol. 32 Issue 2, p225–258, 341p
Document Type: Article

Abstract: During the late 1990s in the United States, rural Kentucky (and rural pockets of nearby states) witnessed the emergence of a new pharmaceutical drug of abuse. The powerful oxycodone OxyContin, first manufactured in 1996 and designed for time-release pain relief, found a ready population in rural hamlets and mountain communities. Intended for patients in pain associated with terminal disease, it became a drug of abuse as it was overprescribed and trafficked within newly developed black markets. This paper describes the takeoff of this new drug of abuse, its antecedents, its effects on rural communities, and coordinated efforts at containing it. Following the trends in use and abuse, this paper presents evidence of an epidemic created in part by organizations in both the private and the public sectors. The paper also describes the much publicized and alleged relationship between Oxycontin use and increasing crime rates in Kentucky (and the surrounding Appalachian region). This paper shows that this drug-crime connection, propagated by media and government sources, has been socially constructed and bears little resemblance to empirical reality. [ABSTRACT FROM AUTHOR]

Finding Bibliographic Information for an Article

While databases will give you all of the bibliographic information you need in the abstract, if you use an article or essay from a magazine or journal (or a photocopy of one), then you'll need to locate the information yourself. Most of the information you need is given on the first page of the article, as in the example on page 568. Sometimes you'll need simply to look at the cover or the table of contents of the journal or magazine to get the necessary bibliographic material.

Finding Bibliographic Information for a Web Page

The bibliographic information you need for a website differs somewhat from that for a print source and isn't always easily located. You need the author(s), title of the page, title of the site if different from the title of the page, the version or edition of the site (if relevant), the publisher of the site, and the date of publication. Since not all websites provide all this information, the rule of thumb is *provide what you can find*. See the illustration on page 569.

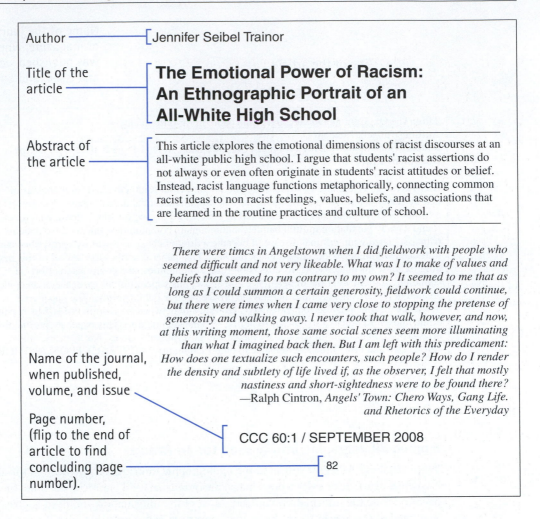

Author — Jennifer Seibel Trainor

Title of the article —

The Emotional Power of Racism: An Ethnographic Portrait of an All-White High School

Abstract of the article —

This article explores the emotional dimensions of racist discourses at an all-white public high school. I argue that students' racist assertions do not always or even often originate in students' racist attitudes or belief. Instead, racist language functions metaphorically, connecting common racist ideas to non racist feelings, values, beliefs, and associations that are learned in the routine practices and culture of school.

There were times in Angelstown when I did fieldwork with people who seemed difficult and not very likeable. What was I to make of values and beliefs that seemed to run contrary to my own? It seemed to me that as long as I could summon a certain generosity, fieldwork could continue, but there were times when I came very close to stopping the pretense of generosity and walking away. I never took that walk, however, and now, at this writing moment, those same social scenes seem more illuminating than what I imagined back then. But I am left with this predicament: How does one textualize such encounters, such people? How do I render the density and subtlety of life lived if, as the observer, I felt that mostly nastiness and short-sightedness were to be found there?
—Ralph Cintron, *Angels' Town: Chero Ways, Gang Life. and Rhetorics of the Everyday*

Name of the journal, when published, volume, and issue —

CCC 60:1 / SEPTEMBER 2008

Page number, (flip to the end of article to find concluding page number). —

82

In the example from the website sfparkour.com shown on the next page, no author is provided, which is common for websites, and the title of the Web page and the website itself are the same. The title of the website will appear in the navigation bar of your browser, but it can also be found at the top of the page (sometimes referred to as the "masthead" or "nameplate"). At the bottom of the page the version, publisher, and date of publication may be found. In the sfparkour example, only the publishers and dates are present.

MLA and APA Documentation Formats

If you look at any of the style manuals, such as the Modern Language Association's *Handbook for Writers of Research Papers* (MLA), the *Publication Manual of the American Psychological Association* (APA), or *The Chicago Manual of Style* (CMS), documenting and

Title of website

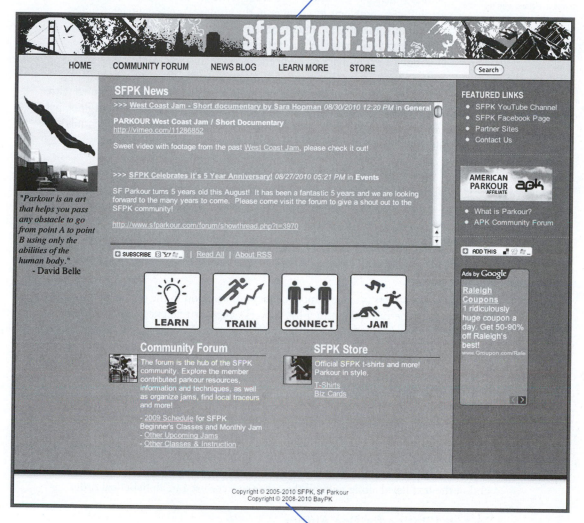

Publisher and date of publication

citing your sources can seem daunting, with a different way of citing almost every book or article. And in some cases it can be confusing. But essentially all you need to provide for a source is who wrote it, what it was called, where it was published, and when it was published. In the two most common academic styles, MLA and APA, that information is provided in two places: In the body of the text using a **parenthetical citation** (also called an **in-text citation**) and in a list at the end of the text (called **Works Cited** in MLA format and **References** in APA format).

Let's look at a brief example from a research report written by Jessica Lenares, "School Violence: Causes and Consequences." In this report she uses MLA citation format.

Lenares provides the last names of the authors of the source along with the page number. A reader can turn to the end of her report and find the entire reference in the Works Cited.

Lenares chose to tell us who the author is and what the name of the text is in the introduction to the quote. At the end of the reference she provides the page number.

The Works Cited list at the end of the paper contains the complete references for sources cited in the text.

School violence is not always the students' fault; some school violence can be attributed to problems at home or in the students' personal lives. Studies show that these play an important role in school violence; the National School Boards Association, for instance, reported that changes in family situations are a primary cause of the increase in school violence (Kerr and Benny 4). For example, according to Kevin Butler in his article "Tragic Lessons," "a fifteen-year old student walked into Weston School, armed with a shotgun and handgun. . . . The student used the handgun to shoot Principal Klang." According to the superintendent, "The guns came from the family's gun cabinet" (58).

Works Cited

Butler, Kevin. "Tragic Lessons." *District Administration* 43.5 (May 2007): 56–60. *Academic Search Premier*. Web. 13 Oct. 2007.

Kerr, Thomas, and Daniel Benny. "Combating School Violence." *School and College* 33.2 (Feb. 1994): 19–24. *Academic Search Premier*. Web. 13 Oct. 2007.

As you can see, writers provide limited citation information in the text, which the reader can use to look up the full citation in a list of works cited or references. The following sections provide details about how to create in-text and bibliographic entries. MLA in-text citations and Works Cited references are covered first, followed by APA in-text citations and References.

MLA In-text Citations

In-text citations identify material that a writer uses from a source right in the text—whether an article in a popular magazine, a report in scholarly journal, a website, or a film. It's useful to think about in-text citations as a kind of shorthand: The writer is signaling that the ideas being discussed have been borrowed from another source, and if the reader wants to read, view, watch, or listen to the original, there is a complete citation to the source at the end of the text listed along with all the other sources used in alphabetical order.

In-text Citation for One Author

Let's look again at Lenares' use of Kevin Butler's article.

For example, according to Kevin Butler in his article "Tragic Lessons," "a fifteen-year-old student walked into Weston School, armed with a shotgun and handgun. . . . The student used the handgun to shoot Principal Klang." According to to the superintendent, "The guns came from the family's gun cabinet" (58).

MLA requires that you give the name of the author for the source you are using. In this case, Lenares also chose to include the title of the article. The author's name here signals the beginning of Lenares' use of this source material. The second piece of information that MLA requires is the page number, given in parentheses, on which the quoted or paraphrased material can be found. If you were to turn to page 58 of Butler's article, you would find what Lenares has quoted here. The parenthetical reference signals the end of the citation: It tells the reader that the author has stopped working with this source for now. Notice that the parenthetical reference comes after the quotation mark and before the period.

In MLA format, writers have the option of including both author and page number in the parenthetical citation; when sources are cited this way, only the last name of the author is provided. In this rewritten example from Lenares' report, she has quoted the source and introduced it without the author's name. Thus she must place the author's name and the page number in parentheses.

> For example, "a fifteen-year old student walked into Weston School, armed with a shotgun and handgun. . . . The student used the handgun to shoot Principal Klang." According to the superintendent, "The guns came from the family's gun cabinet" (Butler 58).

In-text Citation for Sources with More Than One Author

List one or two authors in the citation, but if there are more than three, replace all but the first name with "et al." ("and others").

> Lena Delchad and Keshia Crosby explain the connection between youth volunteering and youth voting when they talk about a report by the Center for Information and Research on Civic Learning and Engagement saying that adolescents' volunteering is on the rise (3).
>
> Darya Smith et al. argue that preteens who are taught basic economics are less likely to get into financial difficulty later in life (23).

In-text Citation for More Than One Source from the Same Author

When using multiple sources from the same author, include the abbreviated title in quotation marks in the parenthetical reference.

> Detective fiction is thus "more preoccupied with the character of its hero, the society he investigates, and the adventures he encounters, than with the central mystery, which gets pushed aside by individual scenes and situations" (Grella, "Hard-Boiled" 115).

In-text Citation for Two Works by the Same Author in the Same Passage

In cases where more than one work from the same author is used in the same passage, include the author's name in the first parenthetical reference along with the abbreviated title of the source in quotation marks and page number. Subsequent references have only the abbreviated title and page number.

> It is now commonly accepted that "students who are involved in campus activities are more likely to do well in their classes" (Huson, "Keys" 21). However, acceptance of this idea by faculty and

administrators does not automatically translate into a "student body dedicated to participation in

college activities as a means to self-improvement and career success" ("Implementing" 231).

In-text Citation for Authors Who Share the Same Last Name

For authors with the same last name, provide the first initial of each author; if they share the same initial, provide their full first names.

When choosing running shoes, it is best to be professionally fitted at a store specializing in

athletic shoes (K. Mitchell 23); however, for the recreational runner, it is probably okay to "buy

off the rack" (M. Mitchell 12).

In-text Citation for Sources with Unknown Author

When no author name is present, use the title of the source.

In an article titled "We, the Jury . . ." there is a mention of people's feeling about jury duty versus

voting when it states that most people throughout the nation would be less likely to serve

on juries than to vote if given the choice because jury duty is longer and requires more effort (19).

In-text Citation for Sources with Organization, Corporate, or Government Author

MLA treats the organization, group, or governmental agency as the author, so include the entity's name as you would an author's.

Human Rights Watch reminds us in their 2009 report, "Impairing Education: Corporal Punish-

ment of Students with Disabilities in US Public Schools," that "human rights law protects stu-

dents with disabilities from violence and cruel and inhuman treatment, and guarantees them

non-discriminatory access to an inclusive education" (2).

In-text Citation for Sources without Page Numbers (Electronic Sources)

Because online documents and Web pages often do not have page numbers, MLA suggests that writers include the name of the author in the text rather than in parentheses.

According to the United Nations document *Universal Declaration of Human Rights,* "Men and

women of full age, without any limitation due to race, nationality or religion, have the right to

marry and to found a family. They are entitled to equal rights, as to marriage, during marriage,

and at its dissolution."

In-text Citation for Multivolume Works

The volume number of a source in a multivolume work is placed in the parentheses, followed by a colon and the page number(s).

In *A History of Everything,* Stephens argues for a radical interpretation of "man's" place in the universe (2: 72–73).

In-text Citation for an Entire Work

Provide the author's name (full or last) as part of the signal phrase when using an entire work as a source. Page numbers are unnecessary in this case.

Donaldson clearly argues for renewed support of civic education in the public schools.

In-text Citation for Indirect Quotations

An indirect source is a source you found in another source. When you wish to use such a source, you should first try to locate the original and quote directly from it. When that is impossible, credit the original source in the text and use "qtd. in" (for "quoted in") and the name of the source you found it in, in the parenthetical citation.

Scott Beale, a regional director of Youth Venture, a nonprofit organization for adolescents starting their own businesses, has his own reason for why kids do not vote and says, "The big reason young people don't vote is because they don't think their vote will make a difference" (qtd. in Felchner 8).

In-text Citation for More Than One Work

When more than one source makes the same claim or provides the same information, cite all the sources as you would a single source and separate them with a semicolon. (Smithson 23; Clarkson 45).

In-text Citation for the Bible

Since there are many versions of the Bible, you'll want to be clear which version you are using. In the citation, italicize the version and the abbreviated name of the book (do not underline or italicize) and then chapter and verse.

The book of Revelation in the Bible is full of passages that modern readers find hard to interpret; for instance: "In the center, around the throne, were four living creatures, and they were covered with eyes, in front and in back. The first living creature was like a lion, the second was like an ox, the third had a face like a man, the fourth was like a flying eagle" (*New International Version,* Rev. 4. 7–8).

In-text Citation for Nonprint Sources

When citing a nonprint source, including CDs and films, make sure that you cite the source by the first piece of information that will be listed on the Works Cited page. Usually this will be the author, the director, or the artist of the work.

WebLinks

MLA and APA Citation Guides

The Online Writing Lab at Purdue University offers extensive and clear guidelines for many citation styles, including MLA and APA. Find them online by searching for Purdue OWL.

> In the documentary *This Is Nowhere,* the subculture of RV campers is explored, with particular attention being given to their tendency to spend their nights in Walmart parking lots (Hawes-Davis and Lilburn).
>
> Vampire Weekend's latest CD shows a maturity that their previous release did not suggest was possible.

MLA Works Cited Entries

In MLA format, you provide readers with an end-of-paper list called Works Cited that contains all the sources used in your text. The reason sources are listed both in the text and at the end of the paper is to minimize the intrusion of citation in the text.

The Works Cited list provides complete bibliographic information for each source: where each source comes from, who wrote it, when it was published, and in what medium it was published (in print, on a CD, on the Web, etc.).

Your Works Cited list should include all the sources that you used in your paper; do not include any that you read but did not quote, paraphrase, or summarize. List sources alphabetically by the author's last name (or by the name of the organization if the organization is the author), or when there is no author, by the first word of the title (excluding the article a, an, or the). The first line of each entry begins at the left margin, and each subsequent line is indented. Below you will find examples and instruction on how to document the most common kinds of sources you are likely to use. See page 421 in Chapter 10: Research Reports for a complete Works Cited page in MLA format.

MLA Basic Format for Print Books

Give the full name of the author (middle initial is optional, but you should include it if it's given in the original). In the title of the book all major words are capitalized. Because it is a complete work, it is italicized: Do not underline. Provide the city of publication. Provide the publisher and the year of publication. And finally, provide the medium of publication (i.e., Print).

Lastname, Firstname. *Title of Book.* City of Publication: Publisher, Year of Publication. Print.

A Book with a Single Author

Casey, Edward S. *Getting Back into Place: Toward a Renewed Understanding of the Place-World.*
    Indianapolis: Indiana UP, 1993. Print.

Two or More Books by the Same Author

When listing more than one source from one author, order the sources alphabetically by the first word in the title. Format the first source as usual, but for all subsequent sources replace the author's name with three hyphens.

Showalter, Elaine. *The Female Malady: Women, Madness and English Culture 1830–1980.*
    New York: Penguin, 1985. Print.

---. Sexual Anarchy: *Gender and Culture at the Fin de Siècle.* New York: Viking Penguin, 1990. Print.

A Book with an Editor or Editors

Fox Keller, Evelyn, and Helen E. Longino, eds. *Feminism and Science.* Oxford: Oxford UP, 1996. Print.

An Introduction, Preface, Foreword, or Afterword of a Book

Because you are citing only part of the book, provide the page numbers.

Rankin, Ian. "Introduction: Exile on Princes Street." *Rebus: The Early Years.* Ed. Ian Rankin. London: Orion, 2002. vii–viii. Print.

A Work in Collections or Anthologies

List the author and title of the source within the collection or anthology that you are citing, and then provide the title of the collection, followed by the editor. Use the abbreviation "Ed." (for "edited by") and then provide the editor's name.

Rankin, Ian. "Knots & Crosses." *Rebus: The Early Years.* Ed. Ian Rankin. London: Orion, 2002. 1–183. Print.

A Work in Translation

The author's name comes first in a citation, followed by the work's title. Next, insert the abbreviation "Trans." (for "translated by") and provide the name of the translator. Note that the translator's name is not inverted.

Todorov, Tzvetan. *The Fantastic: A Structural Approach to a Literary Genre.* Trans. Richard Howard. Ithaca: Cornell UP, 1975. Print.

A Reference Work

Unless the reference work entry has a byline (an author), the title of the entry takes the first position in the citation. The citation also includes the editor of the reference work and applicable page number(s).

"Concoct." *A Dictionary of Word Origins.* Ed. John Ayto. New York: Arcade, 1990. 129. Print.

A Sacred Text

Provide the title of the work in italics, followed by the editor or translator (if applicable), publication information, the medium, and the name of the version (if applicable). Note the abbreviation of "Version" in this example.

Holy Bible. Nashville: Holman Bible Publishers, 1985. Print. New American Standard Vers.

Basic Format for Print Articles

Place the title of the article in quotation marks; the title of the periodical (journal, magazine, or newspaper) is italicized. Give both volume and issue numbers (if provided; sometimes only a volume is listed)), followed by the year and inclusive page numbers. Finally, give the medium of publication, "Print."

Lastname, Firstname. "Title of Article." *Title of Periodical* Volume.Issue (Year): pages. Print.

An Article or Essay from a Print Periodical

Provide the volume and issue number (when given) and the date of publication in parentheses.

Jaret, Peter. "How to Eat Your DNA." *Eating Well* 7.6 (Dec. 2008): 44–55. Print.

A Print Article with Two or Three Authors

List the lead author last name first, but list the first name first for all other authors.

Delchad, Lena, and Keshia Crosby. "Democratic Governance Opportunity—for Youth Involvement."

Nation's Cities Weekly 28.7 (14 Feb. 2005): 3. Print.

For works with more than three authors, you may replace all but the first author with the phrase "et al." or you can list all the authors following the guideline above for two or three authors.

A Print Article with an Unknown Author

When the author is unknown, list the source by its title.

"We, the Jury...." *Dissent* 55.1 (Winter 2008): 19–20. Print.

An Article from an Online Database

When using sources found through online databases (such as a library would subscribe to), after first providing the source's bibliographic details, provide the name of the database in italics, list the medium as Web, and give the date you accessed the database.

Butler, Kevin. "Tragic Lessons." *District Administration* 43.5 (May 2007): 56–60. *Academic Search*

Premier. Web. 13 Oct. 2007.

An Article Published on the Web

When no author is given, begin with the name of the Web page or article. List the owner or sponsor of the website after the website's name (if none is given, use "N.p." for "no publisher") and the date it was posted or last edited. Also provide your date of access.

A Magazine Article on the Web

Wiltz, Teresa. "Slumming It in Mumbai." *Theroot.com.* Washington Post/Newsweek Interactive, 14

Nov. 2008. Web. 15 Nov. 2008.

A Newspaper Article on the Web

French, Brett. "Advocates Hope to Keep *Older* Horses from Pryor Mountains Together at Saturday's

Adoption." *Billings Gazette.* Billings Gazette, 25 Sept. 2009. Web. 25 Sept. 2009.

A Scholarly Article on the Web

The format for scholarly articles found in online journals is the same as for those in print or found through a database. MLA requires page numbers for those journals that also publish a print edition. If no print edition is published, include "n. pag." in place of the page numbers.

> Kale, Radha D., and Natchimuthu Karmegam. "The Role of Earthworms in Tropics with Emphasis
>
> on Indian Ecosystems." *Applied and Environmental Soil Science* (2010): n. pag. Web. 20
>
> Mar. 2010.

An Editorial and Letter to the Editor on the Web

Signal the genre by writing "Editorial" after the title of the editorial or "Letter" after the letter writer's name. In addition to providing the name of the publication, you should also provide the sponsor or publisher of the website. If no sponsor is listed, write "N.p."

> "Health-care Compromise a Good 1st Step." Editorial. *Morning Sentinel.* Maine Today Media,
>
> 20 Sept. 2009. Web. 20 Sept. 2009.
>
> Hannibal, Bob. Letter. *Topeka Capital-Journal.* Topeka Capital-Journal, 17 Sept. 2009. Web.
>
> 20 Sept. 2009.

A Review on the Web

If the review has a title, provide it after the author. Write "Rev. of" and then the title of the work being reviewed and the author, director, or other creator.

> Ebert, Roger. Rev. of *Transformers: Revenge of the Fallen,* dir. Michael Bay. *Rogerebert.com.*
>
> Chicago Sun-Times, 23 June 2009. Web. 1 Sept. 2009.

An Online Book

Cite an online book as you would a print book, but after the original publication information, provide the name of the website where you accessed the book, the sponsor of the site (or "N.p." if none is given), date of publication or most recent update, medium, and date of access.

> Brisco, Norris A. *The Economics of Business.* New York, 1921. *Googlebooks.* Web. 4 Apr. 2010.

An Entire Website

> *The Purdue OWL Family of Sites.* The Writing Lab and OWL at Purdue and Purdue U, 2008. Web.
>
> 23 Apr. 2008.

A Weblog (Blog)

For weblogs, follow the format for entire websites: Provide the author, name of the weblog, the publisher or sponsor (if none is given, use "N.p."), and the date of the most recent update. Conclude with the medium and your date of access.
For an entire weblog:

> Armstrong, Heather B. *Dooce.com.* N.p., 9 Apr. 2010. Web. 10 Apr. 2010.

For an entry in a weblog, provide the author of the entry, followed by the title of the entry. If no title is given, write "Weblog entry." Follow this with the name of the weblog (italicized), the publisher or sponsor (if none is given, use "N.p."), the date it was posted, the medium, and your date of access.

> Armstrong, Heather B. "Marlo Crawls for the First Time." *Dooce.com.* N.p., 7 Apr. 2010. Web.
>
> 10 Apr. 2010.

A Podcast

Cite a podcast as you would an article from an online magazine. Provide the medium (e.g., Web, PDF, MP3, etc.) and date of access.

> Ashbrook, Tom. "Week in the News." *On Point.* Natl. Public Radio. WBUR, 9 Apr. 2010. MP3. 10
>
> Apr. 2010.

A Video from YouTube or Other Online Source

Citations of video clips from online sources such as YouTube should provide information on the author or producer, title of the video, version number or when it was produced, name of the site (italicized), the publication medium, and the date accessed.

> RockforEquality. "What Kind of Planet Are We On?" 2 Feb. 2010. *YouTube.* Web. 10 Apr. 2010.

An Entry in a Wiki

Provide the title of the entry, the name of the wiki (in italics), the sponsor or publisher of the wiki (use "N.p." if none is given), the date of last update (or "n.d." if none is given), the medium, and the date accessed.

> "Emacs History." *EmacsWiki.* N.p., n.d. Web. 8 Mar. 2010.

An Email Message

For email messages, provide the recipient of the message.

> Clar, Clare. "RE: Bono to Give Commencement Address." Message to Price Porter. 27 Aug. 2009. Email.

An Advertisement

Provide the name of the product or company being advertised and indicate that it is an advertisement. Provide the publication information appropriate to the source.

> RainhandleR by Savetime Corp. Advertisement. *Family Handyman* July/Aug. 2009: 69. Print.

> Amtrak. Advertisement. FOX News. 10 Sept. 2009. Television.

An Audio Recording

The basic format for an audio recording is to provide the author, the title of the work, the company or distributor, the date, and the medium. In the case of recordings found online, the medium should be the format of the file (e.g., MP3); if the specific file is not known, then list the medium as "Digital file."

U2. *The Unforgettable Fire*. Island, 1984. CD.

Martin, Steve. *Comedy Is Not Pretty*. Warner Bros., 1979. Digital file.

Giovanni, Nikki. *The Truth Is on Its Way*. Collectibles, 1993. CD.

A Television or Radio Program Broadcast

List the name of the episode, the series title in italics, and then both the network and the local station on which it aired.

"Company Picnic." *The Office*. NBC. KVOA, Tucson. 14 May 2009. Television.

A Television Program or Recording

Provide the name of the recording and give the production company.

"Stress Relief." *The Office—Season Five*. Universal, 2009. DVD.

A Recorded Film

Provide the title of the film, the director (signaled by the abbreviation "Dir."), the major performers (signaled by the abbreviation "Perf."), the distributor of the film, and the year it was released. Conclude with the format (DVD, Laser disc, Videocassette, etc.).

Hands on a Hard Body. Dir. S. R. Bindler. Perf. Benny Perkins, Russell Welch, and Sid Allen. Idea

Entertainment, 2000. DVD.

A Work of Visual Art

Provide the artist, title of the artwork (in italics), the date of composition, and the institution and city where the artwork is located. For art viewed in an online source, also provide the source name, medium, and date accessed. For art viewed in a text, also provide bibliographic information for the print source.

In this example of an online source, the photograph was viewed on the Museum of Modern Art's website, which is indicated by "Web" in the citation. Because this is an online source, the date the photograph was viewed is provided.

Talbot, William Henry Fox. *Loch Katrine*. 1844. Museum of Mod. Art, New York. *The Collection:*

Photography. Web. 14 Nov. 2008.

The following example is the citation for a work of art viewed in a text, so the text's bibliographic information is provided at the end.

Watkins, Carlton. *Nevada Falls*. 1861. Huntington Library, San Marino. *Representing Place:*

Landscape Painting and Maps. Ed. Edward Casey. Minneapolis: Minnesota UP, 2002. 22.

Print.

This example is for a work of art viewed in person. Note the composition (e.g. oil on canvas) of the artwork is provided.

> Lester, William. *Yucca and the Prickly Pear.* 1941. Lithograph. Dallas Museum of Art, Dallas.

A U.S. Government Document

List the branch or government office as the author. List the Government Printing Office (GPO) as the publisher.

> United States. Cong. Senate. Presidential Address before a Joint Session of Congress. 111th Cong.,
> 1st Sess. Washington: GPO, 2009. Print.

A Personal Interview

Provide the name of the interviewee, specify the kind of interview (Personal or Telephone), and give the date the interview was conducted.

> Jones, Sarah. Personal interview. 10 Oct. 2008.

A Published Interview

For published interviews, provide the interviewee's name, followed by the title of the interview (if applicable). If no title is given, write "Interview" after the name. Provide publication information for the source of the interview. If the interviewer is important, give his or her name after the interviewee ("Interview by . . ."). An interview found online follows a similar format.

> Gaiman, Neil. "Talking Manga with Neil Gaiman." *Publishers Weekly* 25 July 2005: 16. Print.

A Personal Letter

For a letter you have received, begin with the writer's name followed by "Letter to the author." For letters addressed to others, provide the name of the recipient. Include the date, and conclude with the medium: MS for a handwritten letter and TS for a typed letter.

> Smith, Linda. Letter to the author. 23 Jan. 2003. MS.

A Lecture or Live Address

Provide the speaker's name, the title of the address in quotation marks (if applicable), the sponsoring organization, the location, and date. Conclude with "Lecture" or "Address."

> Clift, Eleanor. Eastern Connecticut State University, Willimantic: 12 Feb. 2009. Lecture.

APA In-text Citations

The American Psychological Association publication style requires writers to give the *year* of publication immediately following the first mention of the author's name. The abbreviations "p." and "pp." are used with page numbers in parentheses.

In-text Citation for One Author

Here is Lenares' material (from page 570) formatted in APA style:

> For example, according to Butler (2007) in his article "Tragic Lessons," "a fifteen-year-old student walked into Weston School, armed with a shotgun and handgun. . . . The student used the handgun to shoot Principal Klang." According to the superintendent, "The guns came from the family's gun cabinet" (p. 58).

The year of publication in parentheses follows the author's last name. When the author's name appears in parentheses, it is separated from the date with a comma. While not required, inclusion of page numbers is encouraged by the APA. The page number preceded by the abbreviation "p." (or "pp." if the source spans pages) appears in parentheses at the end of the source being used. The parenthetical signals that the writer has finished quoting, paraphrasing, or summarizing the source. APA style allows writers to place the required information—author, year, and page number separated by commas—in the parenthetical citation at the end of the source. The choice of signal phrase can determine the way the source is cited.

> Studies show that these play an important role in school violence; the National School Boards Association, for instance, reported that changes in family situations is a primary cause of the increase in school violence (Kerr and Benny, 2004, p. 4).

In-text Citation for Sources with Two to Five Authors

For sources with two authors, provide the last names of both separated by "and."

> Delchad and Crosby (2005) explain the connection between youth volunteering and youth voting when they talk about a report by the Center for Information and Research on Civic Learning and Engagement saying that adolescents, volunteering is on the rise (p. 3).

For sources with three to five authors, list all last names separated by commas and use an ampersand ("&") before the last name listed.

In-text Citation for Six or More Authors

For sources with six or more authors, replace all but the first author's last name with "et al." ("and others").

> Sanchez et al. (2001) argue that "we no longer have the luxury of ignoring what has been an ugly part of our common culture and a painful part of growing up for most American children" (p. 158).

In-text Citation for Authors with the Same Last Name

When using sources by authors with same last name, provide the first initial of each author, or if they share the same initial, provide their full first names.

> When choosing running shoes, it is best to be professionally fitted at a store specializing in
> athletic shoes (K. Mitchell, 2007, p. 23); however, for the recreational runner, it is probably
> okay to "buy off the rack" (M. Mitchell, 2008, p. 12).

In-text Citation for Two Works by the Same Author in the Same Year

In cases where two or more works by the same author published in the same year are used, use a and b after the year to distinguish them.

> It is now commonly accepted that "students who are involved in campus activities are more likely to
> do well in their classes" (Husson, 1998a, p. 21). However, Husson (1998b) also claims that acceptance
> of this idea by faculty and administrators does not automatically translate into a "student body dedi-
> cated to participation in college activities as a means to self-improvement and career success" (p. 231).

In-text Citation for Sources with Unknown Author

When no author is listed, use the title of the work.

> It's a good start, but according to a study done by the *Advocate*, less than 25% of same-sex part-
> ners reside in a state that gives "marriage or marriage like rights" ("20%," 2007, p. 14).

In-text Citation for Sources with Group, Organization, Corporate, or Government as Author

Where there is no person named as author, use the name of the group as the author.

> Human Rights Watch (2009) claims that "human rights law protects students with disabilities
> from violence and cruel and inhuman treatment, and guarantees them non-discriminatory
> access to an inclusive education" (p. 2).

In-text Citation for Sources without a Date

Write "n.d." ("no date") in place of the date.

> Smith (n.d.) makes it clear that children whose parents are largely absent from their lives will
> carry that sense of abandonment well into adulthood (p. 55).

In-text Citation for Sources without Page Numbers

Indicate the lack of page numbers by writing "n.p."

> And gay couples are already "making families," to no ill effect: a study done by the Williams
> Institute of the University of California, Los Angeles found that "almost 2% of the nation's 3
> million same-sex households include adopted children" (Padgett, 2007, n.p.).

In-text Citation for Electronic Sources

Whenever possible, follow the same format for electronic sources as for print sources. Where paragraph numbers are given instead of page numbers, provide the paragraph number in place of the page number.

> Religion is an important factor in the opposition to gay marriage: "Overall, nearly six-in-ten Americans (59%) oppose gay marriage, up from 53% in July. But those with a high level of religious commitment now oppose gay marriage by more than six-to-one (80%–12%)" (Pew Forum, 2003, para. 3).

In-text Citation for Nonprint Sources

Whenever possible, provide the author, director, or producer, and the year.

In-text Citation for a Film

APA style requires that both the producer and the director be listed.

> In the documentary *This Is Nowhere,* the subculture of RV campers is explored, with particular attention being given to their tendency to spend their nights in Wal-Mart parking lots (Hawes-Davis & Lilburn, 2002).

In-text Citation for a Television Episode

For television episodes, list the writer of the episode as the author.

> The final episode of *Arrested Development,* where Michael learns who really controls the company, was perhaps the best episode of the series (Fortenberry, 2006).

In-text Citation for a Music Recording

> "Can't Stop Till You Get Enough" was arguably the best track on *Off the Wall* (Jackson, 1979, Track 1).

In-text Citation for Email Messages

Since APA does not include personal communications on the References page, writers should signal in the parenthetical that a personal message is being cited and provide the date.

> Hester Smith has stated that many first-year students find learning a citation system boring (personal communication, June 23, 2007).

In-text Citation for Indirect Quotations

Indirect sources are sources quoted in another source. When it is impossible to locate and cite the original source, introduce the indirect quotation by naming the author. In the parenthetical, use the words "as cited in" before the name of the source in which you found the quotation, along with the publication year and page number.

> Scott Beale, a regional director of Youth Venture, a nonprofit organization for adolescents start-
> ing their own businesses, has his own reason for why kids do not vote. He says, "The big reason
> young people don't vote is because they don't think their vote will make a difference" (as cited
> in Felchner, 2003, p. 8).

In-text Citation for an Entire Website

When citing an entire website, list the URL in parentheses after the quotation, summary, or paraphrase.

> The *Factcheck* website provides readers with critical analysis of how truthful our politicians and
> news commentators are (http://www.factcheck.org).

Note: APA does not list complete websites on the References page.

In-text Citation for the Bible

The title of the book of the Bible comes first (it can be abbreviated), followed by the chapter and verse. The version of the Bible concludes the citation and is italicized. If the same version is used throughout the text, it only needs to be given the first time it is cited. The Bible is not included on the APA References page.

> The book of Revelation in the Bible is full of passages that modern readers find hard to inter-
> pret; for instance, "In the center, around the throne, were four living creatures, and they were
> covered with eyes, in front and in back. The first living creature was like a lion, the second was
> like an ox, the third had a face like a man, the fourth was like a flying eagle" (Revelation 4.
> 7–8, *New International Version*).

APA References Entries

The list of sources at the end of an APA format paper is called References. The APA has standard rules for citations that apply to all references regardless of type: All authors are listed by last name, with the initials only of the first and middle names. The date of publication is always the second item in the citation and is in parentheses. Titles of books and articles are not in *title* case, but in *sentence* case (where only the first words of the title and subtitle are capitalized). For periodical titles use *title* case (where every major word is capitalized). Complete works such as books, CDs, films, and so on are italicized, whereas partial works, such as articles, individual songs, and so on, are not. Entries are listed alphabetically; the first line of each entry begins at the left margin, and each line thereafter is indented.

See page 29 in Chapter 1 for a complete References list in APA format.

APA Basic Format for Books

Lastname, I. S. (Year of publication). *Title of work*. Location: Publisher.

A Book by One Author

Casey, E. S. (1993). *Getting back into place: Toward a renewed understanding of the place-world.* Indianapolis: Indiana University Press.

Two or More Works by the Same Author

When listing two or more works by the same author, use the author's name for each entry, but arrange the titles by year in ascending order.

Wechsler, D. (1991). *Wechsler Intelligence Scale for Children* (3rd ed.). San Antonio, TX: Psychological Corporation.

Wechsler, D. (1997). *Wechsler Adult Intelligence Scale* (3rd ed.). San Antonio, TX: Psychological Corporation.

A Text with Multiple Authors

Separate authors with a comma and use an ampersand ("&") before the last author listed.

Stevens, A., Schwarz, J., Schwarz, B., Ruf, I., Kolter, T., & Czekalla, J. (2002). Implicit and explicit learning in schizophrenics treated with olanzapine and with classic neuroleptics. *Psychopharmacology, 160,* 299–306.

Note: For more than six authors, list the first six as above but without the ampersand, and then end the list with "et al." (which means "and others").

A Text with an Unknown Author

We, the jury . . . (2008, Winter). *Dissent, 55*(1), 19–20.

A Text with an Editor or Editors

Rankin, I. (Ed.). (2002). *Rebus: The early years.* London, England: Orion.

An Introduction, Preface, Foreword, Afterword

List the editor and the work from which the introduction, preface, foreword, or afterword is taken. Provide the page numbers.

Rankin, I. (2002). Introduction: Exile on Princes Street. In I. Rankin (Ed.), *Rebus: The early years* (pp. vii–viii). London, England: Orion.

An Edition Other Than the First

McCutcheon, M. (2000). *Descriptionary* (2nd ed.). New York, NY: Checkmark Books.

A Work in a Collection or in an Anthology

> Rankin, I. (2002). Knots & crosses. In I. Rankin (Ed.), *Rebus: The early years* (pp. 5–185). London, England: Orion.

An Organization/Government as Author

List the name or branch of the government as the author, and when the publisher is the same as the author, list "Author" after the place of publication.

> United States Department of Health and Human Services. (1993). *A guide to the United States Department of Health and Human Services.* Washington, DC: Author.

A Translation

List translations by the author of the original and provide both the publication date of the translation, listed after the author, and the date of the original publication in parenthesis at the end of the entry.

> Pacht, O. (2000). *The practice of art history: Reflections on method.* (D. Britt, Trans.). New York, NY: Harvey Miller. (Original work published 1977)

A Work Published in Several Volumes

> Wiener, P. (Ed.). (1973). *Dictionary of the history of ideas* (Vols. 1–4). New York, NY: Scribner's.

An Article in a Journal Paginated by Volume

Some journals paginate by volume, which means that each issue in a volume picks up where the previous one left off. Note that the volume number is italicized.

> Willingham, D. B., Salidis, J., & Gabrieli, J. D. E. (2002). Direct comparison of neural systems mediating conscious and unconscious skill learning. *Journal of Neurophysiology, 88,* 1451–1460.

An Article in a Journal or Magazine Paginated by Issue

Journals and magazines that paginate by issue start each issue with page one. Provide the issue number in parentheses after the volume.

> Jaret, P. (2008, December). How to eat our DNA. *Eating Well, 7*(6), 44–55.

A Newspaper Article

If the article appears on only one page, use "p."; if it continues on a later page or pages, use "pp."

> Braaten, O. (2009, September 18). Eight local schools fail to meet AYP. *Thompson Villager,* pp. A1, A12.

An Editorial or a Letter to the Editor

For editorials and letters to the editor include the type in brackets after the title or year.

Winfrey, C. (2009, October). Fevers [Editorial]. *Smithsonian,* 40(7), 3.

Haddad, F., & Lewerenze, H. (2006). [Letter to the editor]. *Crisis: The Journal of Crisis Intervention and Suicide Prevention, 27*(3), 149.

A Journal or Magazine Article (with DOI) from an Online Database

For articles found through a database, follow the format for print articles and provide the digital object identifier (DOI) as well.

Gabrieli, John. (2010, January 28). Deciphering the printed word. *Nature, 463,* 430–431. doi: 10.1038/463430a

A Journal or Magazine Article (no DOI) from an Online Database

For articles found through a database, follow the format for print articles. If there is no DOI, do not give the database name. Instead, find the journal's home page and provide its URL in a retrieval statement.

Butler, Kevin. (2007). Tragic lessons. *District Administration, 43*(5), 56–60. Retrieved from http://www.districtadministration.com

A Web Document

List the owner of the site as the author and provide the name of the page. Write "Retrieved from" and give the complete URL with no period at the end.

March of Dimes. (2008, November). Drinking alcohol during pregnancy. Retrieved from http://www.marchofdimes.com/professionals/14332_1170.asp

An Article from an Online Newspaper

Give the name of the newspaper and the URL for the main page.

Cooper, H., & Mazezetti, M. (2009, September 25). Cryptic Iranian note ignited an urgent nuclear strategy debate. *The New York Times.* Retrieved from http://www.nytimes.com

An Online Book

Provide the source of the online book. If the book must be purchased to be viewed, write "Available from" instead of "Retrieved from."

James, W. (1929). Varieties of religious experience. Retrieved from Google Books.

A Review

In brackets after the title of the review, write "Review of the" and state the medium (book, CD, etc.) and the title of the work being reviewed and its author.

> Lyall, Sarah. (2009, September 23). Recalling a home that really is a castle. [Review of the book *The Music Room*]. *The New York Times.* Retrieved from http://www.nytimes.com

A Photograph or Image Found Online

List the website where the image was viewed along with the name of the website.

> Ensing, J. (2008, October). In the early morning light, fishermen clean their nets by Erhai Lake. Retrieved from the *Smithsonian Magazine* website: http://www.smithsonianmag.com

A Film

List the director and/or the producer as the authors of a film, followed by their titles in parentheses. In brackets after the title provide the format (DVD, Motion picture, Videocassette, etc.). List the country where the film was made, followed by the studio that released the film.

> Bindler, S. R. (Director). (1998). *Hands on a hard body* [DVD]. United States: Idea Entertainment.

An Email Message

APA does not include email messages in the references list; instead, cite them in the text. See page 583.

A Weblog Post

When citing blogs, list the title of the posting and include "[Web log post]." The author's screen name is acceptable when an actual name is not available. Titles of posts are not italicized.

> Hansell, S. (2009, September 25). AT&T says Google Voice violates net neutrality principles [Web log post]. Retrieved from http://bits.blogs.nytimes.com

A Wiki Entry

APA advises caution when using material from a wiki because its collaborative nature makes content verification difficult. A retrieval date is necessary, as wiki entries change frequently.

> Pacific Ocean Fire. (n.d.). Retrieved October 1, 2009, from http://en.wikipedia.org

An Audio or Music Recording

> Auden, W. H. (Speaker). (2007). *The spoken word: W. H. Auden* [Audiobook]. London, England: The British Library.

> Timmins, M. (1993). Hunted [Recorded by Cowboy Junkies]. On *Pale sun crescent moon.* [CD]. New York, NY: RCA.

A Television or Radio Program

Single Episode

> Williams, C. (Writer), & McBride, J. (Director). (2001). Brotherhood [Television series episode]. In
>
> A. Ball (Producer), *Six feet under.* New York, NY: HBO.

Complete Series

> Ball, A. (Producer). (2001). *Six feet under* [Television series]. New York, NY: HBO.

A Personal Interview

In APA style, interviews are not listed on the References page; instead, cite them in the text.

MLA and APA Sample Papers

For a sample research paper that uses MLA documentation format and includes an MLA formatted Works Cited page, see Patrick Merrigan's "Civic Duties: Why It Is Not Just Your Parents' Problem Anymore" in Chapter 10: Research Reports, pages 416–421. For a sample report that uses sources and APA documentation format, including an APA formatted References page, see Gloria Ramos's "A Report on Same-Sex Marriage in America: A Human Right, a Family Right" in Chapter 1, pages 22–29.

Credits

Text Credits

Index

Abstracted articles, 566, 567
Academic genre
 civic genre vs, 9
 explanation of, 8
 rhetorical analysis as, 85–86
Academic Search Premier, 258
Academic Search Premier Database,
 518–520
Accuracy, of print sources, 535
Ad Council, 106
Adichie, Chimamanda Ngozi,
 265–267, 290–291
"Adolescent Sexual Health" (Sulak),
 449–452
Affective comments, 57
"The Aftermath of September 11:
 Rescuers and Citizens Not Our
 of Danger Yet" (Keane), 403
Amateurs, 160–161
American Psychological Association
 (APA), 568. *See also* APA
 format
American Rhetoric, 66
Analysis. *See also* Rhetorical
 analysis
 of arguments, 63–67
 of context of text, 45–48
 example of, 42–44
 explanation of, 41
 of parts of text, 48–54
 in reviews, 183–185
Analytic reviews, 160
"The Anatomist: A True Story of
 Gray's Anatomy" by Bill Hayes
 (Rutten), 164–166
Anecdotes
 in closings, 182
 in openings, 337
 research to provide, 543
Annotated bibliographies
 example of, 412–413
 function of, 538–539
Annotation

example of, 35–36
explanation of, 34
guidelines for, 36
APA format
 explanation of, 568, 569
 for in-text citations, 580–584
 for References list, 569, 584–589
Arguments
 analysis of, 63–67, 85–88
 assumptions of, 74–77
 claims of, 67–72
 creating convincing, 62–63
 evidence in, 72–74
 explanation of, 61
 identifying writer's, 50, 51
 repetition in, 85
 rhetorical appeals in, 77–81
 rhetorical devices in, 81–84
 ultimate terms in, 84–85
Assumptions, 74–75
Audience
 for essays, 237, 238, 241, 249
 expectations of, 5
 for memoirs, 285, 286, 294–295
 for profiles, 331–332, 343–344
 for proposals, 456–457, 470–471
 providing background
  information to, 542
 for public letters, 130, 133,
  136, 138
 for research reports, 398–399,
  402, 411–412
 for reviews, 176, 185, 187
Audio sources, 515

Background research, 508–509.
 See also Research
Balestracci, Tommy, 119–121
Banerji, Chitrita, 278–282
Banks, James A., 227–234
Beard, Jo Ann, 207–212, 243, 244
"Being Rosie the Riveter" (Miller),
 324–325

Berry, Mary Frances, 53–54
Bibliographic information
 for abstracted articles, 566, 567
 for articles, 567
 in books, 566
 explanation of, 565–566
 for Web pages, 567–568
"Big Brother Is on the Facebook"
 (Kuerschner), 69–71, 212–220,
 242, 244, 245
"Bingo!" (Parker), 326–328
"Black-White Conflict Isn't Society's
 Largest: The Public Assesses
 Social Divisions"
 (Morin), 371–378
Blogs, 113, 563
Books, 508, 566
Brainstorming, 508
Brochures
 example of, 359–360
 profiles as base for, 357–358

Captions, 93–95
Carafano, James Jay, 442–449
"CARandDRIVER.com: 2008
 Masrati GranTurismo - Road
 Test" (Phillips), 167–170
Cardona, Robert Andrew, 383–393
"Car Surfing: Case Studies
 of a Growing Dangerous
 Phenomenon" (Clark,
 Mangram, and Dunn), 379–382
Case studies
 explanation of, 488–489
 revision of, 490–493
Categorical questions, 531
Character, *ethos* as appeal to, 78–79
Characters, composite, 285
Charts
 critically reading, 99
 function of, 98–101
The Chicago Manual of Style,
 568–569

Chronological order, 288, 291. *See also* Organization
Civic genre. *See also* Open letters; Public letters
    academic genre vs., 9
    brochures as, 357
    explanation of, 9–10
    op-ed as, 35
    profiles as, 313, 357
Claims
    of differing views, 69, 462
    in essays, 241
    examination of, 51
    explanation of, 62, 67–68
    of fact, 68, 71, 72, 74
    function of, 69–71
    of policy, 69, 72, 74
    in proposals, 460–462
    in public letters, 132–134
    in research reports, 400–402
    in reviews, 180–182
    support for, 51, 72–75, 543
    of value, 68, 71, 72, 74
    in visual arguments, 104–106
Clark, Jenna, 494, 550, 551
Clark, Steven, 379–382
Closed-ended questions, 531
Closings
    analysis of, 48–50
    for essays, 244–245
    for memoirs, 289–290
    for profiles, 337
    for proposals, 464
    for public letters, 135–136
    for research reports, 404–405
    for reviews, 182
Coles, Michael, 259–261
Color, in visual arguments, 106, 107
Commentary
    development of, 245–247
    in essays, 205, 241–242
    writing effective, 57–58
Comments, peer review, 57–58
Common ground, 69, 462
"A Community Farm for Stanford" (Halweil), 438–441
Comparative reviews, 160
Composite characters, 285
Concession, 69, 462
Conclusions, about subjects, 205

Concrete details, 287, 288
Conover, Ted, 305–312
Context
    for images, 95–96
    for public letters, 136
    for text, 45–48
Correlation, 532
Counterarguments, 459
Cover letters. *See* Reflective letters
Creative Nonfiction, 237, 282
Credibility
    of print sources, 534
    of writer, 45–47
Critical analysis, 39. *See also* Analysis
Critical reading
    analysis as element of, 41–55
    of essays, 206–234
    explanation of, 31
    of memoirs, 264–282
    peer review and, 55–60
    of profiles, 314–329
    of proposals, 433–452
    of public letters, 114–127
    reasons for, 32
    of research reports, 364–393
    of reviews, 161–174
    of visual messages, 89–91
Critical reading strategies
    annotating as, 34–36
    outlining as, 36–37
    previewing as, 32–34
    responding as, 38–39
    summarizing as, 37–38
Critical reviews, 160

"Dan Marino" (Kellard), 86–88
Databases
    content of, 516
    methods for searching, 518–520
Davidson, Todd, 104
Day, Michael, 497
"Dearest Hip Hop" (Imarisha and Not4Prophet), 115–118
Deductive reasoning, 79–81
De Graff, Christian, 124–125
Demographic questions, 530
Descriptions
    in reviews, 183, 184
    sensory, 287, 288

Design elements
    function of, 97–98
    in visual arguments, 106–109
Details, concrete, 287, 288
Differing views
    explanation of, 69
    methods to address, 462
    presentation of, 465, 469–470
    responding to, 465
Digression, 288
Direct address, 182
Direct quotations
    explanation of, 544–545
    stringing together, 546–547
    use of, 545–546, 562
Disclaimers, 285
Discussions, 508
Documentary films, 198–204
Drafts
    of essays, 240–242, 249–252
    of memoirs, 287–288, 295–297
    of profiles, 334–338, 344–346
    of proposals, 460–465, 469–470
    of public letters, 132–136, 140–142
    of research reports, 400–405, 413–414
    of reviews, 179–183, 187–190
    use of research charts for, 560–561
Duke University Research Guide, 538
Dunn, Ernest, 379–382

Eat, Pray, Love: One Woman's Search for Everything Across Italy, India, and Indonesia (Gilbert), 305
Editorial comments, 58
Electronic portfolios (e-portfolios). *See also* Writing portfolios
    construction of, 496–497
    explanation of, 482, 496
    websites to find examples of, 497
Emails, documentation of, 563
Encyclopedias, for background information, 508
"End of the Line" (LeDuff), 318–323, 334

Essays
  audience, purpose, and situation
    for, 237–238, 249
  commentary in, 205, 241–242
  common pitfalls in, 236–237
  critically reading, 206–234
  drafts of, 240–242, 249–252
  explanation of, 205–206
  generating ideas for, 236–237,
    248
  genre analysis of, 207–212
  genre blurring in, 258–261
  openings for, 243–244
  organization of, 243–245
  purpose of, 206
  research for, 238–240
  revision of, 245–246, 252–256
Ethical issues, related to
    memoirs, 285
Ethos
  as appeal to character, 78–79
  as appeal to values, 77–78
  explanation of, 62, 77, 101
  in visual arguments, 102
  for writing portfolios, 482
Evaluation, in reviews, 178, 183–185
Evidence
  examination of, 51–52
  factual, 72–73
  opinion as, 73–74
  to support arguments, 62
  types of, 52, 72
  in visual arguments, 104–106
Exaggeration, 82
Examples
  as evidence, 52, 73
  research to provide, 543
Expert opinions, 52
Experts, 160

Fact
  claims of, 68, 71, 72, 74
  explanation of, 51
Factual evidence, 72–73
Field research. *See also* Research
  documentation of, 563
  function of, 523
  interviews as, 524–528
  observations as, 528–530
  for reviews, 179

subjectivity and, 523–524
  surveys as, 530–533
"Fighting Terrorism, Addressing
  Liability: A Global Proposal"
  (Carafano), 442–449
Fonts, 106–108
*FourthGenre: Explorations in
  Nonfiction,* 237, 282
French, Ray, 40–41
Frey, Kyle, 402

"Gay But Equal?" (Berry), 53–54
Geib, Gregory, 551–552
Genre
  academic, 8
  audience expectations and, 5
  characteristics of, 4, 161
  civic, 9–10, 35–36, 313
  examination of, 45, 161
  explanation of, 3
  functions of, 4–5
  research and, 505–507, 543
  rhetorical situation and, 6–8
  social settings of, 3–4
  writers and, 5–6
Genre analysis
  for essays, 207–212
  for memoirs, 264–267, 282
  for profiles, 314–318
  for proposals, 433–434
  for public letters, 115–127
  for research reports, 364–365
  for reviews, 161–164
Genre blurring
  in documentaries, 198–204
  explanation of, 10–11, 305
  in photographic essays, 258–261
  in travel memoirs, 11–17,
    305–311
Genre crossing
  explanation of, 18
  from profiles to brochures,
    357–360
  from public letters to research
    reports, 18–29, 149–158
  from reports to proposals,
    423–429
Gilbert, Elizabeth, 305
Google searches, 521–522
Graphs

critically reading, 99–101
  function of, 98

Halweil, Brian, 438–441
*Handbook for Writers of Research
  Papers* (Modern Language
  Association), 568. *See also*
  MLA format
Hiatt, Brian, 336
Hicks, Katie, 139–148
"Homeless People Shouldn't Make
  You Feel Sad Like That" (The
  Onion Staff), 83–84
Humor
  exaggeration as, 82
  irony as, 81–82
  sarcasm as, 82
  satire as, 82–84
  self-depreciation as, 82
Huxley, Aldous, 205

Idea generation
  for essays, 236–237, 248
  for memoirs, 284–286, 294
  for profiles, 330–331, 343
  for proposals, 454–456, 468–469
  for public letters, 127–129, 139
  for research reports, 395–397,
    410–411
  for reviews, 176
Images
  charts and graphs as, 98–101
  context for, 95–96
  design elements of, 97–98,
    106–108
  manipulation of, 108–109
  photographic, 96–97
  relationship between text and,
    93–95
  straightforward use of, 92–93
Imarisha, Walidah, 115–118
"An Immodest Proposal: Rewarding
  Women's Work to End
  Poverty" (Women's Committee
  of 100/Project 2002),
  434–437
Inductive reasoning, 79, 81
In media res opening, 289
Institute for Policy Studies Web site,
  537–538

"Inter-country Adoption and the Problems We Face" (Frey), 402

Internet. *See* Web searches; Web sources

Internet Movie Database, 176

Interview questions
design of, 525–527
for profiles, 332–333

Interviews
analyzing transcripts of, 527
function of, 525
method to conduct, 527–528
for profiles, 332–333
as research source, 524–525

In-text citations
APA format for, 580–584
explanation of, 569
MLA format for, 570–574

Introductory paragraphs, for portfolio items, 487–488

Issues
audience and, 456
explanation of, 455–456, 504
methods to emphasize, 462–463
purpose and, 456–457
for research, 504–505
research on, 542–543
situation and, 457

Journal articles, bibliographic information in, 567

"Just Another Beautiful Thunderstorm: A Travel Memoir" (Schneider), 12–17

"Just Chute Me!" brochure, 89–90

Keane, Colin, 248–257, 403

Kellard, Joseph, 86–88

King, Adam, 267–276

Kuerschner, Jim, 69–71, 212–220, 242, 244, 245

Kvetko, Pater, 170–173

Lamott, Anne, 122–123

Leading questions, 526

Leavitt, Mariah, 245, 246

LeDuff, Charlie, 318–323, 334

"Let It Snow" (Sedaris), 276–278

Letters. *See* Open letters; Public letters; Reflective letters

Lexicon, 84

LexisNexis, 46

Librarians, 513

Libraries
as research sources, 515, 516
searching archives of, 520–521

Library catalogs, methods for searching, 516–518

Likert scale questions, 531

Listing, 508

Logos
appeals to, 79–80
explanation of, 62, 79, 101
in visual arguments, 102–103

"Lucky?" (Poulos), 291, 294–304

Magazines, 508, 567

"Major College Football Needs Playoffs" (Stinebrink), 120

"Man Controlling Globe" (Davidson), 104–105

Mangram, Alicia, 379–382

Media sources, 509, 514–515

Meditative opening, 289

Meehan, Peter, 161–163

Memoirs
audience, purpose and situation for, 286, 294–295
common pitfalls in, 284
considerations for writing, 283
critically reading, 264–282
drafts of, 287–288, 295–297
ethical issues related to, 285
explanation of, 263
generating ideas for, 284–286, 294
organization of, 288–290
purpose of, 264
reflecting on process of, 293, 303–304
research for, 286–287
revision of, 290–292, 297–303
role of reflection in, 288, 290–291
sensory descriptions and concrete details for, 287–288
travel, 11–17, 305–311

Merrigan, Patrick, 187–197, 410–421, 424–429

Miller, Elaine, 324–325

MLA format
example of, 569–570
explanation of, 568, 569
for in-text citations, 570–574
for Works Cited entries, 574–580

Modern Language Association (MLA), 568. *See also* MLA format

Morello, Jamie, 457–458, 557–560

Morin, Rich, 371–378

Moses, Jennifer, 221–227, 240

Multiple choice questions, 531

Narration, 337, 338

Newspapers, 508

New York Times, Saturday Profiles, 330

"Noora: A Golden Voice; Wah Rangiya: Passionate Punjab; Bol Ni Chakkiye: The Singing Wheel of Life (Kvetko), 170–173

Not4Prophet, 115–118

Novices, 161

Numerical information, 548. *See also* Statistics

Numerical questions, 532

Obama, Barack, 63–65

O'Boyle, Shaun, 258

Observation
guidelines for, 529–530
for profiles, 333–334
as research source, 528–529

Online portfolios. *See* Electronic portfolios (e-portfolios)

"On the Trail of Poppa's Alaska" (Conover), 305–312

Op-eds, 35–36

Open-ended closing, 289

Open-ended questions, 526, 528, 531

Openings
analysis of, 48–50
for essays, 243–244
for memoirs, 289
for profiles, 336–337
for proposals, 463–464

Openings (*Continued*)
  for public letters, 134–135
  for research reports, 403–404
  for reviews, 182, 185
Open letters. *See also* Public letters
  as base for research reports,
    18–29
  example of, 19–21
  explanation of, 19
Opinion
  as evidence, 73–74
  personal, 68
Ordinal questions, 532
Organization
  chronological, 288, 291
  of essays, 243–245
  of memoirs, 288–290
  of portfolios, 493–494
  of profiles, 337–338
  of proposals, 462–464
  of public letters, 134–136
  of reviews, 182
  topical, 337, 338
  of visual arguments, 106, 107
Outlines, 36–37
Outlining comments, 57
"Out There" (Beard), 207–212,
  243–244

Paraphrases
  example of plagiarized, 564–565
  explanation of, 547, 549
  guidelines for using, 548, 563
Parenthetical citations. *See* In-text
  citations
Parker, Mary O., 326–328
"Part of the Carnival Show: The
  Man Behind the Masks"
  (Rohter), 315–318, 335
Pathos
  explanation of, 62, 79, 80, 101
  in visual arguments, 102–103
Patterns, in survey data, 532
Peer review
  benefits of, 55–56
  of case studies, 492–493
  of essays, 246
  explanation of, 55
  guidelines for, 56–57

of memoirs, 292
of profiles, 341
of proposals, 466–467
of public letters, 137
of research reports, 408
of reviews, 185
revision based on, 58–60,
  142–147
writing effective commentary as,
  57–58
Personal opinion, 68
Persuasion
  explanation of, 61
  proposals as, 431–432
Persuasive research reports, 394
Phillips, John, 167–170
Photographic essays, 258–261
Photographs
  captions to, 93–95
  manipulation of, 108–109
  as research source, 515
  to support text, 96–97
Place markers, 291, 292
Plagiarism
  explanation of, 543, 561
  methods to avoid, 561–563
  procrastination and intentional,
    563–565
Policy claims, 69, 72, 74
Policy research reports, 394
Portfolios, 481. *See also* Writing
  portfolios
Poulos, Eliza, 291, 294–304
Preliminary research, 507–508. *See
  also* Research
"President Obama: Healthcare; You
  Promised" (Lamott), 122–123
Previews
  example of, 34
  explanation of, 32–33
  guidelines for, 34
  reasons for, 33
Primary sources
  in archives, 521
  explanation of, 513
  interviews as, 524–528
  observations as, 528–530
  surveys as, 530–533
Print sources, 534–535
Privacy, 285

Product/service research
  reports, 394
Profiles
  angle in, 335–336, 338–339,
    344–349
  audience, purpose, and situation
    for, 331–332, 343–344
  to brochures, 357–360
  common pitfalls in, 330
  critically reading, 314–329
  drafts of, 334–338, 344–346
  explanation of, 313–314
  generating ideas for, 330–331, 343
  purpose of, 314
  reflecting on process of, 341,
    342, 356
  research for, 332–334
  revision of, 338–341, 346–355
  types of, 329
  visual rhetoric in, 340
Progress reports, 395
Project Muse database, 237, 258
Proposals
  audience, purpose and situation
    for, 456–459, 470–471
  as base for public service
    announcements, 478–480
  claims for, 468–469
  common pitfalls of, 454
  critically reading, 433–452
  drafts of, 460–465, 469–470
  explanation of, 432
  generating ideas for, 454–456,
    468–469
  purpose of, 432–433
  reflecting on process of, 467,
    476–477
  research for, 459–460
  research reports as base for,
    423–429
  revision of, 465–467, 470–476
  rhetorical situation of, 433,
    456–459, 461
  types of, 453
PsychINFO, 518
*Publication Manual of the American
  Psychological Association*
  (American Psychological
  Association), 568. *See also*
  APA format

Public letters. *See also* Open letters
  audience, purpose, and situation for, 130, 139–140
  as base for research reports, 18–29, 149–158
  critically reading, 114–127
  drafts of, 132–136, 140–142
  explanation of, 113–114
  generating ideas for, 127–129, 139
  open letters as, 19–21, 114
  organization of, 134–136
  purpose of, 114
  reflecting on choices for, 138, 148
  research for, 130–132
  revision of, 136–138, 142–147
  rhetorical situation of, 114
Public service announcements (PSAs)
  explanation of, 92, 478
  images in, 92–93
  proposals as base for, 478–480
  website for, 106

Questions
  categorical, 531
  closed-ended, 531
  interview, 332–333, 525–527
  leading, 526
  Likert scale, 531
  multiple choice, 531
  numerical, 532
  open-ended, 526, 528, 531
  in openings, 337
  ordinal, 532
  research, 502, 509–510, 512
  survey, 530–532
Quotations, direct, 544–547, 562

Reading. *See also* Critical reading
  for analysis, 41–55
  for comprehension, 32–39
"Real Food" (Adichie), 265–267, 290
Reasoning
  deductive, 79–81
  inductive, 79, 81
References (APA format), 569, 584–589
Reflection, 264

Reflective closings, 290
Reflective letters
  development of, 487
  example of, 484–486
  explanation of, 483
Reflective narratives, 483, 489
Refutation, 69, 80, 462
Relevance, source, 535, 536
Reliability, source, 534–536
"Remembering Brown: Silence, Loss, Rage, and Hope" (Banks), 228–234
Repetition
  of design elements, 97–98
  function of, 85
"A Report on Same-Sex Marriage in America: A Human Right, a Family Right (Ramos), 22–29
Reports. *See also* Research reports
  as base for proposals, 423–429
  explanation of, 363
Research
  assessing topic for, 504–505
  background, 508–509
  considering audience, purpose and genre for, 505–507, 543
  documentation of, 563
  for essays, 238–240
  field, 523–533
  function of, 501
  guidelines for, 503–504
  identifying gaps in, 406
  for information about writers, 46–47
  integration of, 406–407
  keyword search terms for, 510–511
  for memoirs, 286–287
  plagiarism and, 561–565
  preliminary, 507–508
  for profiles, 332–334
  for proposals, 459–460
  for public letters, 130, 131
  for research reports, 399–400, 412–413
  for reviews, 177–179, 185
  rhetorical situation and, 501–503, 505–507
  synthesis of, 402, 403

Research charts
  construction of, 560
  drafting from, 560–561
  example of, 558–559
  explanation of, 402, 403, 557
Research plans
  elements of, 511–513
  explanation of, 511
Research questions
  examples of, 502
  explanation of, 509–510, 512
Research reports
  audience, purpose and situation for, 398–399, 402, 411–412
  as base for proposals, 423–429
  common pitfalls in, 396
  critically reading, 364–393
  design and layout of, 407–408
  drafts of, 400–405, 413–414
  example of, 22–29
  explanation of, 363–364
  generating ideas for, 395–397, 410–411
  purpose of, 364
  reflecting on process for, 409, 421
  research for, 399–400, 412–413
  revision of, 405–408, 414–421
  topics for, 397–398
  types of, 394–395
Research source documentation
  APA format for, 568, 569, 580–589
  explanation of, 565
  finding bibliographic information for, 566–568
  formats for, 568–570
  MLA format for, 568–580
  reasons for, 565–566
Research sources
  annotated bibliographies of, 538–539
  archives as, 520–521
  for background information, 508–509
  databases as, 518–520
  direct quotations from, 544–547, 562
  evaluation of, 533–538
  as evidence, 52, 73

Research sources (*Continued*)
genre and, 505–507, 543
integration of, 550–552
introduction of, 552–555
library catalogs as, 516–518
media, 514–515
methods to locate, 515, 516
paraphrases from, 547–548
primary, 513, 514, 521, 523–533
reasons to use, 542–543
for rhetorical effects, 541–542
secondary, 513, 514
summaries from, 548–549
use of multiple, 555–557
World Wide Web as, 521–522,
536–538
Responses, 38–39
Revenge, 285
Reviews
audience for, 176, 177, 187
common pitfalls in, 175
criteria for evaluation of, 178
critically reading, 161–174
drafts of, 179–183, 187–190
example of writing process for,
187–197
explanation of, 159
generating ideas for, 176
integrating other reviews into
your, 184
purpose of, 159–160, 177, 187
research for, 177–179
revision of, 183–185, 190–197
rhetorical situation of, 160,
177, 187
types of, 160
writer's stance in, 160–161
Revision
based on peer feedback, 58–60,
142–147
of essays, 245–246, 252–256
of memoirs, 290–292, 297–303
of portfolio items, 490–493
of profiles, 338–341, 346–355
of proposals, 465–467, 470–476
of public letters, 136–138,
142–147
of research reports, 405–408,
414–421

of reviews, 183–185.190–197
Rhetoric, 62–63. *See also* Visual
rhetoric
Rhetorical analysis
as academic genre, 85
of documentary film, 198–204
explanation of, 65, 85
guidelines for, 86
of speech, 65–66
of visual messages, 89–91
Rhetorical appeals
ethos as, 62, 77–79, 101
explanation of, 77
logos as, 62, 79–81, 101–103
pathos as, 62, 79, 80, 101–103
in visual arguments, 101–103
Rhetorical situation
for argument, 63
for essays, 237–239, 241, 249
genre and, 6–8
for memoirs, 286, 294–295
for profiles, 332, 344
for proposals, 433, 456–459, 461
for public letters, 114, 130, 132,
133, 140
research and, 501–503, 505–507
for research reports, 398–399,
402, 411–412
for reviews, 160, 176, 177, 187
of writing portfolios, 482
"Rhode Island's Food Safety Net:
Ensuring Safe Food from
Production to Consumption"
(RI- PIRG), 365 –370, 404–405
Ritchie, Elspeth Cameron,
383–393
*River Teeth: A Journal of Nonfiction
Narrative,* 237
Rohter, Larry, 315–318, 335
Rutten, Tim, 164–166

"Same-Sex Marriage: An Open
Letter to Social Conservatives,"
19–21
San serif fonts, 107–108
Sarcasm, 82
Satire
example of, 83–84
explanation of, 82–83

Schirone, Christina, 468–477,
484–486, 492–493, 495
Scholarly research sources, 514
"School Supplies" (U.S. Department
of Agriculture), 92, 93
Schwartz, Briggita, 339
"Science in Defense" (De Graff),
124–125
"The Scientology Religion," 76–77
Scratch outlines, 36–37
Search engines
for background research, 508
use of, 521–522
Secondary sources, 513, 514
"The Second Coming of Pearl Jam"
(Hiatt), 336
Sedaris, David, 82, 276–278
Segmentation, 288–289
Self-depreciation, 82
"A Shared Plate" (Banerji), 278–282
Signal words, 291, 553
"Smash Palace - Model Four
Hundred" (Coles), 259–261
Source documentation. *See*
Research source
documentation
Sources. *See* Research sources
"Speech Against the Iraq War"
(Obama), 63–65
Speeches
example of, 63–65
repetition in, 85
"Sports Centered" (Weiner), 42–44,
544
Statistics
as evidence, 73
explanation of, 52
paraphrases of, 548
"Stepping Out" (Moses), 221–227,
240
Stinebrink, Michael, 119, 120
Strand, Kim Thomassen, 199–203
Subjects. *See* Topics
Substantive comments, 58
*Suburban Nation: The Rise of Sprawl
and the American Dream*
(Duany, Plater-Zyberk, and
Speck), 561–562
Sulak, Patricia, 449–452

Summaries
 example of, 38
 explanation of, 37
 guidelines for, 38
 of research sources, 548–549, 563
 in reviews, 183–185
Surveys
 analysis of data from, 532–533
 function of, 530
 questions for, 530–532
Synthesis, of research sources,
  555–557

Table of contents, writing portfolio,
  494–496
"Taking Back Out Tuition: Students
  Need to Push to Keep College
  Affordable" (French), 40–41
Testimony, 52, 80
Texts
 arguments in, 51
 evidence in, 51–52
 openings and closings of, 48–50
 relationship between images and,
  93–95
 straightforward use of, 92–93
 in visual messages, 92–95
 writer's position in, 50
"There Is Nothing Called Hope in
  My Future: A Rhetorical
  Analysis of Born Into Brothels"
  (Strand), 199–203
"These Stories" (King), 267–276
Thesis, 51, 85
Thesis statements, 179–180
"Think Before You Post" (AD
  Council), 106–107
Time markers, 291, 292
Tobler, Cory, 545–547, 553–556
Tone, 62, 286
Topical organization, 337, 338. See
  also Organization
Topics
 assessment of, 504–505
 for essays, 236, 239

 narrowing your, 455–456
 for profiles, 330
 for public letters, 128–129
 for research reports, 397–398
 for reviews, 175
Transition words, 291
Travel memoirs, 11–17, 305–311

Ultimate terms, 84–85
"U.S. Military Enlisted Accession
  Mental Health Screening:
  History and Current Practice"
  (Ritchie & Cardona), 383–393

Values
 claims of, 68, 71, 72, 74
 ethos as appeal to, 77–78
Viewpoints
 addressing differing, 69, 462, 465
 claims of, 69, 462
"A View to the Contrary"
  (Williston), 35
Visual rhetoric
 analysis of, 89–91
 appeals in, 101–104
 claims and evidence in, 104–106
 context of, 95–96
 design elements in, 106–109
 documentation of, 563
 elements of, 91, 92
 function of, 89
 images and graphics as, 96–101
 incorporation of, 554, 555
 method to construct, 109
 in photographic essays, 258–261
 in profiles, 340
 texts and images as, 92–95
Voice
 in profiles, 339–340
 of subject, 240
 of writers, 339–340

Warford, Lisa, 488, 490–492
Weaver, Richard, 84
Web searches

 for electronic portfolios, 497
 for information about writers, 46
 keyword terms for, 510–511
 for public service announcements, 106
 for survey and questionnaire
  data, 532
Web sources
 bibliographic information in,
  567–568
 evaluation of, 536–538
 research using, 516, 521–522
Weiner, Jay, 42–44, 544, 547
Williams, Brynna, 343–356, 358
Williston, Terry Starkey, 35
"Will Pigs' Feet Fly?" (Meehan),
  162–163
Word choice, in arguments, 62
Words
 signal or transition, 291, 553
 that resound, 84–85
Works Cited (MLA format), 569,
  574–580
Writers
 benefits of peer review for, 55
 determining credibility of, 45–47
 genre and, 5–6
 identifying argument of, 51
 identifying position of, 50, 51
 memoir, 283
 obtaining information about, 46
 voice of, 339–340
Writing portfolios
 case studies for, 488–493
 electronic, 482, 496–497
 explanation of, 481
 introductory paragraphs for items
  in, 487–488
 method to arrange, 493–494
 purpose of, 481–482
 reflective letters for, 483–487
 revision of items for, 490–493
 rhetorical situation of, 482
 table of contents for, 494–496

Choices Writers Make and the
WPA Outcomes Statement for First-Year Composition

WPA Outcomes	Choices Writers Make
Rhetorical Knowledge By the end of first-year composition, students should ■ Focus on a purpose ■ Respond to the needs of different audiences ■ Respond appropriately to different kinds of rhetorical situations ■ Use conventions of format and structure appropriate to the rhetorical situation ■ Adopt appropriate voice, tone, and level of formality ■ Understand how genres shape reading and writing ■ Write in several genres	Ch. 1 introduces genre and the rhetorical situation and provides tools for analyzing these concepts. Chs. 2–4 introduce strategies for critical reading, analysis, and argumentation and discuss how rhetorical strategies are used to affect audiences differently, depending on purpose and genre. Chs. 3–11 discuss characteristics of, and strategies for, writing rhetorically effective texts. "Transformations" in Chs. 5–11 demonstrates how genres can be adapted and transformed into new or "blurred" genres depending on rhetorical considerations.
Critical Thinking, Reading, and Writing By the end of first-year composition, students should ■ Use writing and reading for inquiry, learning, thinking, and communicating ■ Understand a writing assignment as a series of tasks, including finding, evaluating, analyzing, and synthesizing appropriate primary and secondary sources ■ Integrate their own ideas with those of others ■ Understand the relationships among language, knowledge, and power	Ch. 2 covers critical reading strategies such as previewing, annotating, and conducting background research to understand the social contexts of texts. Chs. 5–11 encourage students to think about genre as a means to a rhetorical end, to think critically about ways of altering genres to meet their needs, and to explore ideas through focused writing, collaborative brainstorming, and peer review. Ch. 12 emphasizes critical self-reflection through the development of a writing portfolio. Chs. 5–11 include sections that encourage research appropriate for that chapter's genre, whether fieldwork, library work, or online research. Chs. 13 and 14 help students locate, evaluate, integrate, and synthesize research with their own ideas, testing and supporting those ideas in the process.